Far from diminishing, Nansen's fame as one of the greatest explorers of modern times has only increased, perhaps because he was one of the few anti-heroes of the Age of Exploration. A brilliant scientist who intended to put his theories on the nature of the North Pole to a radical test, Nansen only gave in with great doubts to his thirst for adventure to reach the North Pole.

Farthest North — completed only two months after Nansen's return to safety — is the harrowing account of this extraordinary journey. Given up for dead, Nansen and his companion survived for fifteen months on a diet that included melted ice, walrus blubber and bear meat. A frank chronicle of his restless instincts and the irresistible attraction he felt, *Farthest North* is one of the great written monuments to the constantly changing ice-fields of the arctic and the haunting beauty of the aurora borealis unfurling across the polar night. A bestseller at the time — instantly translated in many languages — even Sigmund Freud enthused about the candour of the dreams Nansen reported.

This is the first edition of Nansen's entire journey for almost a century. It includes for the first time in that period a number of images from the original English edition. In addition, a number of images were included from the Norwegian edition which have not been published in an English publication before.

On the previous page: a photograph of Nansen (recto) and the composition for a meal that was copied by Scott and Shackleton (verso: Hansen, Johansen, Nansen, Pettersen, Nordahl, Amundsen, Bentzen, Juell, Henriksen, Mogstad, Jacobsen, Blessing and Sverdrup)..

Farthest North

The Voyage of Exploration of the *Fram* and the
Fifteen Month's Expedition by Fridtjof Nansen
and Hjalmar Johansen

Fridtjof Nansen

Foreword by Fergus Fleming

GIBSON SQUARE BOOKS

This first paperback edition of Nansens's journey first published in 2002.
Farthest North was first published in 1897 in two volumes by Constable with a
simultaneous colonial edition by Macmillan, followed in 1898 by an edition by
George Newnes and in 1904 by a new octavo edition by Constable.

Gibson Square Books Ltd
15 Gibson Square
London N1 0RD
tel: +44 (0)20 7689 4790
fax: +44 (0)20 7689 7395
publicity@gibsonsquare.com
www.gibsonsquare.com

UK Distribution and Sales by:
Turnaround Publishers Services
3 Olympia Trading Estate
Coburg Road
London UK N22 6TZ
tel: +44 (0)20 8829 3000
fax: +44 (0)20 8881 5088
oders@turnaround-uk.com
www.turnaround-uk.com

International sales and permissions please contact:
Gibson Square Books Ltd in London

ISBN 1-903933-09-9

Typesetting by Perseus
Printed by Bookwell Ltd

Contents

Foreword

Fergus Fleming

By 1890 governments in Europe and America were sick of the North Pole. They had been trying to reach it for so long; the race had cost so much in terms of money and lives; and, frankly, what was the point of it? Wild fantasies abounded as to what lay there — a continent, a sea, a hole leading to the centre of the globe — but if it was nothing save a sheet of empty ice, as an increasing number suspected was the case, then further expeditions were futile; science could be served equally profitably and far more safely by the ring of Arctic observatories that had been set up in the International Polar Year of 1882. Anyway, the question was hypothetical because the North Pole was unattainable. Certain individuals thought otherwise. Between 1894 and 1914 they launched repeated expeditions to the Arctic and Antarctic, raising funds where they could find them and utilising every new piece of technology as it became available. Their exploits, which climaxed with the conquest of the North Pole by Robert Peary in 1909 (so he said) and that of the South Pole by Roald Amundsen in 1911, were a triumph of private enterprise over public intervention. But they were also a triumph of sensationalism over sense — all too often the desire for fame resulted in death and disaster. It was a peculiarly driven era, marked by examples of courage and incompetence, failure and success, fierce individualism and hamfisted planning, wild dreams and sober assessments. Historians have dubbed it the Age of Heroes; and they credit Fridtjof Nansen as its inaugurator.

Nansen never particularly wanted to be a polar explorer. Born on 10 October 1861, he was by training a neuroscientist — rather a good one: certain nerves still bear his name — but he came to prominence in 1888 when, on a whim, and to prove that traditional man-hauled sledging methods were wrong, he used skis to make the first crossing of Greenland's ice cap. Thereafter he was infected by what 19th-century writers called "the Arctic virus." As he apologised to an inquirer in 1892, "It is rather more accidental circumstances that have forced me into this line... A great many plans and ideas how to explore the unknown Arctic regions have forced themselves upon my mind almost without my help and will, and now I think it my duty to try whether they are not right (as I feel convinced they are) though it is almost with pain that I think of my microscope and my histological work." On 24 June 1893, he sailed aboard the *Fram* from Christiania (modern Oslo) to put his plans to the test.

The voyage of the *Fram* was the most audacious and most successful polar experiment of Victorian times. From 1894 to 1896, its meander through the pack produced data on weather patterns, currents, and undersea topography; it demonstrated that a vessel need not sink when caught in the ice, that its daily energy requirements could be provided by windpower instead of steam, and that Europeans could actually survive for prolonged periods in the Arctic without succumbing to scurvy — though it demonstrated the latter by accident: Nansen's success lay in adopting a varied diet; but until the discovery in the 20th century of Vitamin C nobody could explain which element in his diet had kept the disease at bay. According to one expert, the *Fram*'s journey constituted, "almost as great an advance as has been accomplished by all other voyages in the nineteenth century put together."

The voyage also provided one of the great epics of polar exploration. In March 1895 Nansen left the *Fram* to its devices and, with crewmember Hjalmar Johanssen, skied towards the North Pole with dog-drawn sledges and kayaks. Their plan was to press north until their supplies began to run out and then, eating the dogs as they became redundant, retreat to Franz Josef Land where they would hitch a ride home on a whaling ship or, failing that, sail in their kayaks to Norway or Spitsbergen. The first part of the plan was sound; the second was hare-brained: there was no certainty of meeting a whaler, and their kayaks would have been swamped had they ever tried to cross the ocean. It was sheer luck that they were rescued by Frederick Jackson, a British explorer who happened to be on Franz-Josef Land in June 1896. As Jackson later said, "I can positively state that not a million to one chance of Nansen ever reaching Europe existed, and, but for our finding him on the ice, as we did, the world would never have heard of him again." Yet, despite his foolhardiness, Nansen had travelled farther north than any human being and had managed to survive fifteen months in the Arctic, almost five of which had been on the pack. When he returned to Norway he was hailed as "a Man in a Million.".

Farthest North is the book that describes his odyssey. It took just two months to write — an unbelievably swift time — and was illustrated by Nansen's own drawings and photographs. (For those interested in the history of polar images, it is worth recording that Nansen's composition for a meal aboard the *Fram* was later copied by both Shackleton and Scott.) The journal was an immediate best-seller both in Scandinavia and the rest of Europe. On its publication, Nansen became an international hero, fêted by geographical societies around the world. He had solved the great question: although he had not reached the Pole itself, he had ascertained that it was almost certainly ice and the "international steeple-chase," as one Austrian called it, could now cease.

Of, course, it did not cease. Nansen's example merely fired people to greater endeavour. He became a role model whose methods and equipment were widely copied. In both the Arctic and Antartcic, explorers used Nansen skis, Nansen sledges and Nansen kayaks. They used the Nansen method of travelling with a minimum of men, and adopted the Nansen principle of employing dogs both as beasts of burden and a source of food. They also benefited from Nansen's pioneering use of technology, such as the unsinkable *Fram* and the energy-efficient Primus stove. Popular too, in some circles, were his Jaeger woollens — albeit, furs were far better suited to polar conditions. That he set the standard for polar exploration was evident in the titles of subsequent journals: Peary's *Nearest the Pole*, for example, was an unsubtle piece of leg- cocking; even more blatant was the Duke of Abruzzi's *Farther North Than Nansen*. Later in life he would be described by the polar aeronaut Richard Evelyn Byrd as the "Great Dean of Arctic Exploration."

Nansen was certainly the first, and possibly the most outstanding, hero of the age. His achievement, although flawed, was rarely matched by his successors — his acolyte and fellow Norwegian, Roald Amundsen, being a notable exception. And it was not matched for this reason: he had set himself a goal, he had attained it, and, importantly, he had done so without the loss of a single life. Against his success, however, must be set his failings. Although a good planner he was an erratic leader. His charisma was powerful — "I have never met anyone who had such a magnetic personality, and such a profound confidence in himself," wrote one of Jackson's team in awe — but it was often too strong for comfort. His moods swung from introspection to exultation, marked at either extreme by references to the Nordic gods with whom he identified. He was domineering and at times intolerant. When he left the *Fram* most of the crew were only too happy to see him go. Hjalmar Johansen, who endured his company for some fifteen months, found him stiff and unapproachable: "He is too self-centred to be anybody's friend and one's patience is sorely tried," he wrote. "It is silent in the tent; no fun, never a joke. The fellow is unsociable and clumsy in the smallest things; egoistic in the highest degree." To give Nansen his due, Johansen seems to have been an equally miserable companion. (In 1911 he was given a place on Amundsen's South Pole expedition but was left at base camp because of his awkwardness. He later shot himself, in a fit of depression.) Nevertheless, such accusations could not have been levelled against contemporaries such as Peary, Scott or Shackleton.

Nansen made his name from the *Fram* expedition but, as his biographer Roland Huntford has shown, to view him solely in terms of exploration would be to categorise him unfairly. He toyed with the idea of returning to the ice — he wondered if the methods he had pioneered might be used to take the South Pole (Amundsen did it for him) or if he should fly to the North Pole (Amundsen, again, did it) — but, really, he was not that interested. Unlike his fellow heroes, who tended towards monomania, Nansen was a man of multifarious talents. He was a geologist and a ground-breaking oceanographer. He developed theories about tectonic shift and was one of the first to associate sun spots with climate change. His neurological research was drawn upon by the winners of the 1906 Nobel Prize for Science. He was a diplomat and international statesman: in 1922 he was awarded the Nobel Peace Prize for his work in repatriating the refugees of World War I. He could draw, he could paint and he enjoyed poetry — which he read in the several languages in which he was fluent.

When he died on 13 May 1930 from a heart attack, the thousands who attended his funeral remembered him only partly for his polar journey. It had been just one episode in an ever evolving career. As he wrote on his return from Franz Josef Land: "The ice and the long moonlit polar nights, with all their yearning, seemed like a far-off dream from another world, a dream that had come and passed away. But what would life be worth without its dreams?"

Fergus Fleming

TO

HER

who christened the ship

and

had the courage to stay behind.

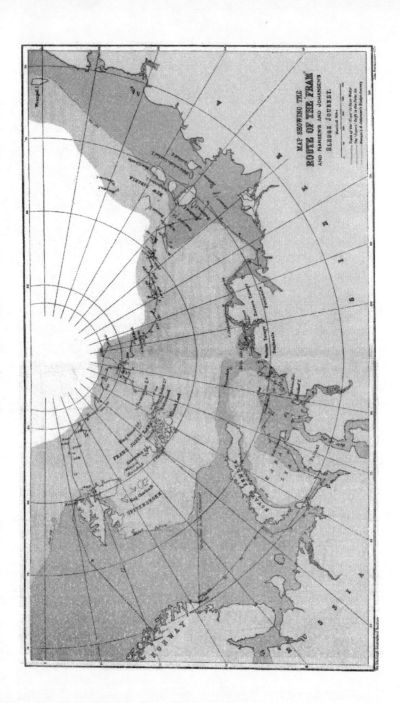

MAP SHOWING THE
ROUTE OF THE FRAM
AND NANSEN'S AND JOHANSEN'S
SLEDGE JOURNEY.

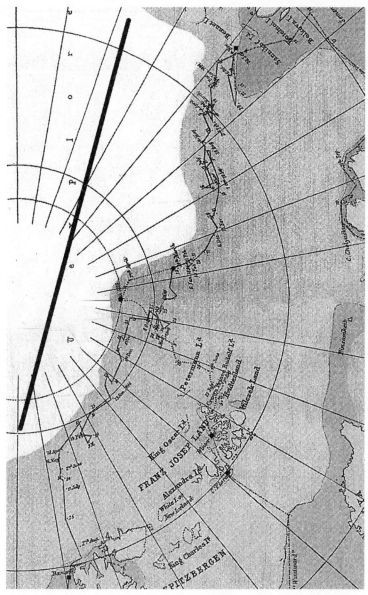

Close-up of the route of the *Fram's* drift on the arctic ice cap. The straight line indicates the route Nansen had calculated (taken from the Norwegian edition). Nansen and Johansen's fifteen-month route is highlighted by the dotted line. Unexplored territory is marked in white.

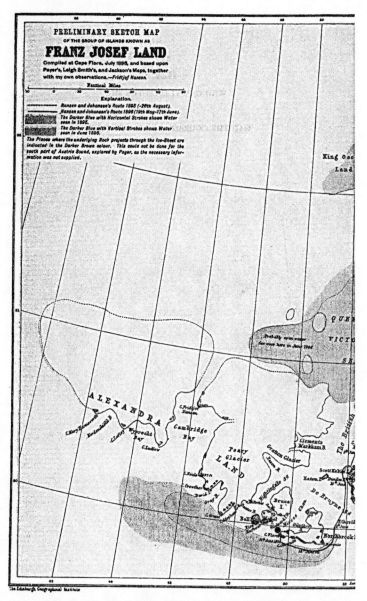

The map (both pages) Nansen sketched of Franz Josef Land in July 1896, based on the maps by Payer, Leigh Smith and Jackson and his own observations. The grey areas indicate water seen in 1895 and 1896 and the dark areas rocks projecting through the ice-sheet.

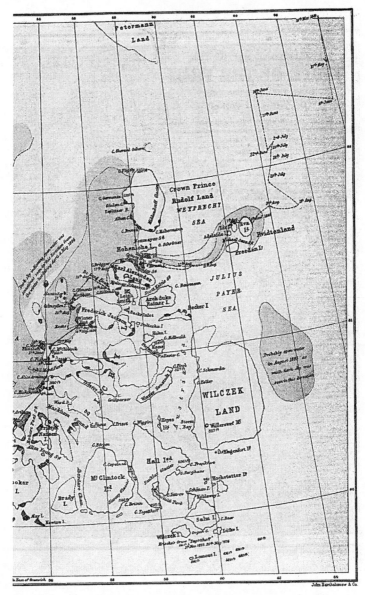

The dotted line starting in the top right hand corner represents Nansen's 1895 voyage — mostly by kayak — from 24 May and the straight line the 1896 journey from the Winter Hut ending at Cape Flora (on the facing page).

THE FRAM

"A time will come in later years when the Ocean will unloose the bands of things, when the unmeasurable earth will lie open, when seafarers will discover new countries and Thule will no longer be the extreme point among the lands." — SENECA.

Chapter 1

Introduction

Unseen and untrodden under their spotless mantle of ice the rigid polar regions slept the profound sleep of death from the earliest dawn of time. Wrapped in his white shroud, the mighty giant stretched his clammy ice-limbs abroad, and dreamed his age-long dreams.

Ages passed — deep was the silence.

Then, in the dawn of history, far away in the south, the awakening spirit of man reared its head on high and gazed over the earth. To the south it encountered warmth, to the north, cold; and behind the boundaries of the unknown, it placed in imagination the twin kingdoms of consuming heat and of deadly cold.

But the limits of the unknown had to recede step by step before the ever-increasing yearning after light and knowledge of the human mind, till they made a stand in the north at the threshold of Nature's great Ice Temple of the polar regions with their endless silence.

Up to this point no insuperable obstacles had opposed the progress of the advancing hosts, which confidently proceeded on their way. But here the ramparts of ice and the long darkness of winter brought them to bay. Host after host marched on towards the north, only to suffer defeat. Fresh ranks stood ever ready to advance over the bodies of their predecessors. Shrouded in fog lay the mythic land of Nivlheim, where the "Rimturser" (Frost Giants) carried on their wild gambols.

Why did we continually return to the attack? There in the darkness and cold stood Helheim, where the death-goddess held her sway; there lay Nåstrand, the shore of corpses. Thither, where no living being could draw breath, thither troop after troop made its way. To what end? Was it to bring home the dead, as did Hermod when he rode after Baldur? No! It was simply to satisfy man's thirst for knowledge. Nowhere, in truth, has knowledge been purchased at greater cost of privation and suffering. But the spirit of mankind will never rest till every spot of these regions has been trodden by the foot of man, till the very enigma has been solved.

Minute by minute, degree by degree, we have stolen forwards, with painful effort. Slowly the day has approached; even now we are but in its early dawn; darkness still broods over vast tracts around the Pole.

Our ancestors, the old Vikings, were the first Arctic voyagers. It has been said that their expeditions to the frozen sea were of no moment as they have left no enduring marks behind them. This, however, is scarcely correct. Just as surely as the whalers of our age, in their persistent struggles with ice and sea, form our outposts of investigation up in the north, so were the old Northmen, with Eric the Red, Leif and others at their head, the pioneers of the polar expeditions of future generations.

It should be borne in mind, that as they were the first ocean navigators, so also were they the first to combat with the ice. Long before other seafaring nations had ventured to do more than hug the coast lines, our ancestors had traversed the open seas in all directions, had discovered Iceland and Greenland, and had colonised them. At a later period they discovered America, and did not shrink from making a straight course over the Atlantic Ocean, from Greenland to Norway. Many and many a bout must they have had with the ice along the coasts of Greenland in their open barks, and many a life must have been lost.

And that which impelled them to undertake these expeditions was not the mere love of adventure, though that is, indeed, one of the essential traits of our national character. It was rather the necessity of discovering new countries for the many restless beings that could find no room in Norway. Furthermore, they were stimulated by a real interest for knowledge. Othar, who about 890 resided in England at Alfred's Court, set out on an errand of geographical investigation; or, as he says himself, "he felt an inspiration and a desire to learn, to know, and to demonstrate how far the land stretched towards the north, and if there were any regions inhabited by man northward beyond the desert waste." He lived in the northernmost part of Helgeland, probably at Bjarköi, and sailed round the North Cape and eastwards, even to the White Sea.

Adam of Bremen relates of Harald Hårdråde, "the experienced king of the Northmen," that he undertook a voyage out into the sea towards the north and "explored the expanse of the northern ocean with his ships, but darkness spread over the verge where the world falls away, and he put about barely in time to escape being swallowed in the vast abyss." This was Ginnungagap, the abyss at the world's end. How far he went, no one knows, but at all events he deserves recognition as one of the first of the polar navigators that were animated by pure love of knowledge. Naturally, these Northmen were not free from the superstitious ideas about the polar regions prevalent in their times. There, indeed, they placed their Ginnungagap, their Nivlheim, Helheim, and later on Trollebotn; but even these mythical and poetical ideas contained so large a kernel of observation, that our fathers may be said to have possessed a remarkably clear conception of the true nature of things. How soberly and correctly they observed, may best be seen a couple of hundred years later in Kongespeilet ("The Mirror of Kings"), the most scientific treatise of our ancient literature, where it is said that "as soon as one has traversed the greater part of the wild sea, one comes upon such a huge quantity of ice that nowhere in the whole world has the like been known. Some of the ice is so flat that it looks as if it were frozen on the sea itself; it is from 8 to 10 feet thick, and extends so far out into the sea that it would take a journey of four or more days to reach the land over it. But this ice lies more to the north-east or north, beyond the limits of the land, than to the south and south-west or West..."

"This ice is of a wonderful nature. It lies at times quite still, as one would expect, with openings or large fjords in it; but sometimes its movement is so strong and rapid as to equal that of a ship running before the wind, and it drifts against the wind as often as with it."

This is a conception all the more remarkable when viewed in the light of the crude ideas entertained by the rest of the world at that period with regard to foreign climes.

The strength of our people now dwindled away, and centuries elapsed before explorers once more sought the northern seas. Then it was other nations, especially the Dutch and the English, that led the van. The sober observations of the old Northmen were forgotten, and in their stead we meet with repeated instances of the attraction of mankind towards the most fantastic ideas; a tendency of thought that found ample scope in the regions of the north. When the cold proved not to be absolutely deadly, theories flew to the opposite extreme and marvellous were the erroneous ideas that sprang up, and have held their own down to the present day. Over and over again it has been the same — the most natural explanation of phenomena is the very one that men have most shunned; and, if no middle course was to be found, they have rushed to the wildest hypothesis. It is only thus that the belief in an open polar sea could have arisen and held its ground. Though everywhere ice was met with, people maintained that this open sea must lie behind the ice. Thus the belief in an ice-free north-east and north-west passage to the wealth of Cathay or of India, first propounded towards the close of the 15th century, cropped up again and again, only to be again and again refuted. Since the ice barred the southern regions, the way must lie further north; and finally a passage over the Pole itself was sought for. Wild as these theories were, they have worked for the benefit of mankind; for by their means our knowledge of the earth has been widely extended. Hence may see that no work done in the service of investigation is ever lost, not even when carried out under false assumptions. England has to thank these chimeras in no small degree for the fact that she has become the mightiest seafaring nation of the world.

By many paths and by many means mankind has endeavoured to penetrate this kingdom of death. At first the attempt was made exclusively by sea. Ships were then ill-adapted to combat the ice, and people were loth to make the venture. The clinker-built pine and fir barks of the old Northmen were no better fitted for the purpose than were the small clumsy carvels of the first English and Dutch Arctic explorers. Little by little they learnt to adapt their vessels to the conditions, and with ever-increasing daring they forced them in among the dreaded floes.

But the uncivilised polar tribes, both those that inhabit the Siberian tundras, and the Eskimo of North America, had discovered, long before polar expeditions had begun, another and a safer means of traversing these regions — to wit the sledge, usually drawn by dogs. It was in Siberia that this excellent method of locomotion was first applied to the service of polar exploration. Already in the 17th and 18th centuries the Russians undertook very extensive sledge journeys, and charted the whole of the Siberian coast from the borders of Europe to Bering Strait. And they did not merely travel along the coasts, but crossed the drift-ice itself to the New Siberian Islands, and even north of them. Nowhere, perhaps, have travellers gone through so many sufferings, or evinced so much endurance.

In America too the sledge was employed by Englishmen at an early date for the purpose of exploring the shores of the Arctic seas. Sometimes the toboggan or Indian sledge was used, sometimes that of the Eskimo. It was under the able leadership of M'Clintock that sledge journeys attained their highest development. While the Russians had generally travelled with a large number of dogs, and only a few men, the English employed many more men on their expeditions, and their sledges were entirely, or for the most part, drawn by the explorers themselves. Thus in the most energetic attempt ever made to reach high latitudes, Albert Markham's memorable march towards the north from the Alert's winter quarters, there were 33 men who had to draw the sledges, though there were plenty of dogs on board the ship. During his famous expedition in search of Franklin, M'Clintock used both men and dogs. The American traveller Peary has, however, adopted a totally different method of travelling on the inland ice of Greenland, employing as few men and as many dogs as possible. The great importance of dogs for sledge journeys was clear to me before I undertook my Greenland expedition, and the reason I did not use them then was simply that I was unable to procure any serviceable animals.[1]

A third method may yet be mentioned which has been employed in the Arctic regions namely boats and sledges combined. It is said of the old Northmen in the Sagas and in the Kongspeil, that for days on end they had to drag their boats over the ice in the Greenland sea, in order to reach land. The first in modern times to make use of this means of travelling was Parry, who, in his memorable attempt to reach the Pole in 1827, abandoned his ship and made his way over the drift-ice northwards, with boats which he dragged on sledges. He succeeded in attaining the highest latitude (82° 45') that had yet been reached; but here the current carried him to the south more rapidly than he could advance against it, and he was obliged to turn back.

Of later years this method of travelling has not been much employed in approaching the Pole. It may, however, be mentioned that Markham took boats with him also on his sledge expedition. Many expeditions have through sheer necessity accomplished long distances over the drift-ice in this way, in order to reach home after having abandoned or lost their ship. Special mention may be made of the Austro-Hungarian *Tegethoff* expedition to Franz Josef Land, and the ill-fated American *Jeannette* expedition.

It seems that but few have thought of following the example of the Eskimo — living as they do, and, instead of heavy boats, taking light kayaks, drawn by dogs. At all events, no attempts have been made in this direction.

The methods of advance have been tested on four main routes: the Smith Sound route, the sea route between Greenland and Spitzbergen, Franz Josef Land route, and the Bering Strait route.

In later times, the point from which the Pole has been most frequently assailed is Smith Sound, probably because American explorers had somewhat too hastily asserted that they had there descried the open Polar Sea, extending indefinitely towards the north. Every expedition was stopped, however, by immense masses of ice, which came drifting southwards, and piled themselves up against the coasts. The most important expedition by this route was the English one conducted by Nares in 1875-76, the equipment of which involved a vast expenditure. Markham, the next in command to Nares, reached the highest latitude till then attained, 83° 20', but at the cost of enormous exertion and loss; and Nares was of opinion that the impossibility of reaching the Pole by this route was fully demonstrated for all future ages.

During the stay of the Greely expedition from 1881 to 1884 in this same region, Lockwood attained a somewhat higher record, viz., 83° 24', the most northerly point on the globe that human feet had trodden previous to the expedition of which the present work treats.

By way of the sea between Greenland and Spitzbergen, several attempts have been made to penetrate the secrets of the domain of ice. In 1607 Henry Hudson endeavoured to reach the Pole along the east coast of Greenland, where he was in hopes of finding an open basin and a waterway to the Pacific. His progress was, however, stopped at 73° north latitude, at a point of the coast which he named "Hold with Hope." The German expedition under Koldewey (1869-70), which visited the same waters, reached by the aid of sledges as far north as 77° north latitude. Owing to the enormous masses of ice which the polar current sweeps southward along this coast, it is certainly one of the most unfavourable routes for a polar expedition. A better route is that by Spitzbergen, which was essayed by Hudson, when his progress was blocked off Greenland. Here he reached 80° 23' north latitude. Thanks to the warm current that runs by the west coast of Spitzbergen in a northerly direction, the sea is kept free from ice, and it is without comparison the route by which one can the most safely and easily reach high latitudes in ice-free waters. It was north of Spitzbergen that Edward Parry made his attempt in 1827, above alluded to.

Further eastwards, the ice-conditions are less favourable, and therefore few polar expeditions have directed their course through these regions. The original object of the Austro-Hungarian expedition under Weyprecht and Payer (1872-74) was to seek for the North-East Passage; but at its first meeting with the ice, it was set fast off the north point of Novaya Zemlya, drifted northwards, and discovered Franz Josef Land, whence Payer endeavoured to push forwards to the north with sledges, reaching 82° 5' north latitude on an island, which he named

Crown Prince Rudolf's Land. To the north of this he thought he could see an extensive tract of land, lying in about 83° north latitude, which he called Petermann's Land. Franz Josef Land was afterwards twice visited by the English traveller Leigh Smith, in 1880 and 1881-82; and it is here that the English Jackson-Harmsworth expedition is at present established.

The plan of the Danish Expedition under Hovgaard was to push forward to the North pole from Cape Chelyuskin along the east coast of an extensive tract of land which Hovgaard thought must lie to the east of Franz Josef Land. He got set fast in the ice, however, in the Kara Sea and remained the winter there, returning home the following year.

Only a few attempts have been made through Bering Strait. The first was Cook's in 1776; the last the *Jeannette* expedition 1879-81 under De Long, a Lieutenant in the American navy. Scarcely anywhere have polar travellers been so hopelessly blocked by ice in comparatively low latitudes. The last named expedition, however, had a most important bearing upon my own. As De Long himself says in a letter to Gordon Bennett, who supplied the funds for the expedition, he was of opinion that there were three routes to choose from, Smith Sound, the east coast of Greenland, or Bering Strait; but he put most faith in the last, and this was ultimately selected. His main reason for this choice was his belief in a Japanese current running north through Bering Strait and onwards along the east coast of Wrangel Land, which was believed to extend far to the north. It was urged that the warm water of this current would open a way along that coast, possibly up to the Pole. The experience of whalers showed that whenever their vessels were set fast in the ice here, they drifted northwards; hence it was concluded that the current generally set in that direction. "This will help explorers," says De Long, "to reach high latitudes; but at the same time will make it more difficult for them to come back." The truth of these words he himself was to learn by bitter experience.

The *Jeannette* stuck fast in the ice on September 6th, 1879, in 71° 35′ north latitude and 175° 6′ east longitude, south-east of Wrangel's Land — which, however, proved to be a small island — and drifted with the ice in a west-north-westerly direction for two years, when it foundered, June 12th, 1881, north of the New Siberian Islands, in 77° 15′ north latitude and 154° 59′ east longitude.

Everywhere, then, has the ice stopped the progress of mankind towards the north. In two cases only have ice-bound vessels drifted in a northerly direction — in the case of the *Tegethoff* and the *Jeannette* — while most of the others have been carried away from their goal by masses of ice drifting southwards.

On reading the history of Arctic explorations, it early occurred to me that it would be very difficult to wrest the secrets from these unknown regions of ice by adopting the routes and the methods hitherto employed. But where did the proper route lie?

It was in the autumn of 1884 that I happened to see an article by Professor Mohn in the Norwegian *Morgenblad,* in which it was stated that sundry articles which must have come from the *Jeannette* had been found on the south-west coast of Greenland. He conjectured that they must have drifted on a floe right across the Polar Sea. It immediately occurred to me that here lay the route ready to hand. If a floe could drift right across the unknown region, that drift might also be enlisted in the service of exploration — and my plan was laid. Some years, however, elapsed before, in February, 1890, after my return from my Greenland Expedition, I at last propounded the idea in an address before the Christiania Geographical Society. As this address plays an important part in the history of the expedition, I shall reproduce its principal features, as printed in the March number of *Naturen,* 1891.

After giving a brief sketch of the different polar expeditions of former years, I go on to say: "The results of these numerous attempts, as I have pointed out, seem somewhat discouraging. They appear to show plainly enough that it is impossible to sail to the Pole by any route whatever; for everywhere the ice has proved an impenetrable barrier, and has stayed the progress of invaders on the threshold of the unknown regions.

"To drag boats over the uneven drift-ice, which moreover is constantly moving under the influence of the current and wind, is an equally great difficulty. The ice lays such obstacles in the way that any one who has ever attempted to traverse it will not hesitate to declare it well-nigh impossible to advance in this manner with the equipment and provisions requisite for such an undertaking."

Had we been able to advance over land, I said, that would have been the most certain route; in that case the Pole could have been reached "in one summer by Norwegian snow-shoe runners." But there is every reason to doubt the existence of any such land. Greenland, I considered, did not extend further than the most northerly known point of its west coast. "It is not probable that Franz Josef Land reaches to the Pole; from all we can learn it forms a group of islands separated from each other by deep sounds, and it appears improbable that any large continuous track of land is to be found there.

"Some people are perhaps of opinion that one ought to defer the examination of regions like those around the Pole, beset, as they are, with so many difficulties, till new means of transport have been discovered. I have heard it intimated that one fine day we shall be able to reach the Pole by a balloon, and that it is only waste of time to seek to get there before that day comes. It need scarcely be shown that this line of reasoning is untenable. Even if one could really suppose that in the near or distant future this frequently mooted idea of travelling to the Pole in an air-ship would be realised, such an expedition, however interesting it might be in certain respects, would be far from yielding the scientific results of expeditions carried out in the manner here indicated. Scientific results of importance in all branches of research can be attained only by persistent observations during a lengthened sojourn in these regions; while those of a balloon expedition cannot but be of a transitory nature.

"We must, then, endeavour to ascertain if there are not other routes — and I believe there are. I believe that if we pay attention to the actually existent forces of nature, and seek to work with and not against them, we shall thus find the safest and easiest method of reaching the Pole. It is useless, as previous expeditions have done, to work against the current; we should see if there is not a current we can work with. The *Jeannette* Expedition is the only one, in my opinion, that started on the right track, though it may have been unwittingly and unwillingly.

"The *Jeannette* drifted for two years in the ice, from Wrangel Land to the New Siberian Islands. Three years after she foundered to the north of these islands, there was found frozen into the drift-ice in the neighbourhood of Julianehaab on the south-west coast of Greenland, a number of articles which appeared, from sundry indubitable marks, to proceed from the sunken vessel. These articles were first discovered by the Eskimo, and were afterwards collected by Mr. Lytzen, Colonial Manager at Julianehaab, who has given a list of them in the Danish Geographical Journal for 1885. Among them the following may especially be mentioned:

> 1. A list of provisions, signed by De Long the commander of the *Jeannette*.
> 2. An MS. list of the *Jeannette's* boats.
> 3. A pair of oilskin breeches marked 'Louis Noros,' the name of one of the *Jeannette's* crew, who was saved.
> 4. The peak of a cap on which, according to Lytzen's statement, was written F.C. Lindemann. The name of one of the crew of the *Jeannette*,

who was also saved, was F.C. Nindemann. This may either have been a clerical error on Lytzen's part or a misprint in the Danish journal.

"In America when it was reported that these articles had been found, people were very sceptical and doubts of their genuineness were expressed in the American newspapers. The facts, however, can scarcely be sheer Inventions; and it may therefore be safely assumed that an ice-floe bearing these articles from the *Jeannette* had drifted from the place where it sank to Julianehaab.

"By what route did this ice-floe reach the west coast of Greenland?

"Professor Mohn, in a lecture before the Scientific Society of Christiania in November, 1894, showed that it could have come by no other way than across the Pole.[2] "It cannot possibly have come through Smith Sound, as the current there passes along the western side of Baffin's Bay, and it would thus have been conveyed to Baffin's Land or Labrador, and not to the west coast of Greenland. The current flows along this coast in a northerly direction, and is a continuation of the Greenland polar current, which comes along the east coast of Greenland, takes a bend round Cape Farewell, and passes upwards along the west coast.

"It is by this current only that the floe could have come.

"But the question now arises what route did it take from the New Siberian Islands in order to reach the east coast of Greenland?

"It is conceivable that it might have drifted along the north coast of Siberia, south of Franz Josef Land, up through the sound between Franz Josef Land and Spitzbergen, or even to the south of Spitzbergen, and might after that have got into the polar current which flows along Greenland. If, however, we study the directions of the currents in these regions so far as they are at present ascertained, it will be found that this is extremely improbable, not to say impossible."

Having shown that this is evident from the *Tegethoff* drift and from many other circumstances, I proceeded: "The distance from the New Siberian Islands to the 80th degree of latitude on the east coast of Greenland is 1,360 miles, and the distance from the last-named place to Julianehaab 1,540 miles, making together a distance of 2,900 miles. This distance was traversed by the floe in 1,100 days, which gives a speed of 2.6 miles per day of 24 hours. The time during which the relics drifted after having reached the 80th degree of latitude, till they arrived at Julianehaab, can be calculated with tolerable precision, as the speed of the above-named current along the east coast of Greenland is well known. It may be assumed that it took at least 400 days to accomplish this distance; there remain, then, about 900 days as the longest time the drifting articles can have taken from the New Siberian Islands to the 80th degree of latitude. Supposing that they took the shortest route, i.e., across the Pole, this computation gives a speed of about 2 miles in 24 hours. On the other hand, supposing they went by the route south of Franz Josef Land, and south of Spitzbergen, they must have drifted at much higher speed. Two miles in the 24 hours, however, coincides most remarkably with the rate at which the *Jeannette* drifted during the last months of her voyage, from January 1st to June 12th, 1881. In this time she drifted at an average rate of a little over 2 miles in the 24 hours. If, however, the average speed of the whole of the *Jeannette's* drifting be taken, it will be found to be only 1 mile in the 24 hours.

"But are there no other evidences of a current flowing across the North Pole from Bering Sea on the one side to the Atlantic Ocean on the other?

"Yes, there are.

"Dr. Rink received from a Greenlander at Godthaab a remarkable piece of wood which had been found among the drift-timber on the coast. It is one of the 'throwing sticks' which the Eskimo use in hurling their bird-darts, but altogether unlike those used by the Eskimo on the west coast of Greenland. Dr. Rink conjectured that it possibly proceeded from the Eskimo on the east coast of Greenland.

"From later enquiries,[3] however, it appeared that it must have come from the coast of Alaska in the neighbourhood of Bering Strait, as that is the only place where 'throwing sticks' of a similar form are used. It was even ornamented with Chinese glass beads, exactly similar to those which the Alaskan Eskimo obtain by barter from Asiatic tribes, and use for the decoration of their 'throwing sticks.'

"We may, therefore, with confidence assert that this piece of wood was carried from the west coast of Alaska over to Greenland by a current the whole course of which we do not know, but which may be assumed to flow very near the North Pole, or at some place between it and Franz Josef Land.

"There are, moreover, still further proofs that such a current exists. As is well known, no trees grow in Greenland that can be used for making boats, sledges, or other appliances. The driftwood that is carried down by the polar current along the east coast of Greenland and up the west coast is, therefore, essential to the existence of the Greenland Eskimo But whence does this timber come?

"Here our enquiries again carry us to lands on the other side of the Pole.

I have myself had an opportunity of examining large quantities of driftwood both on the west coast and on the east coast of Greenland. I have, moreover, found pieces drifting in the sea off the east coast, and, like earlier travellers, have arrived at the conclusion that much the greater part of it can only have come from Siberia, while a smaller portion may possibly have come from America. For amongst it are to be found fir, Siberian larch, and other kinds of wood peculiar to the north, which could scarcely have come from any other quarter. Interesting in this respect are the discoveries that have been made on the east coast of Greenland by the second German Polar Expedition. Out of twenty-five pieces of driftwood, seventeen were Siberian larch, five Norwegian fir (probably *picea obovata*), two a kind of alder (*alnus incana?*), and one a poplar (*populus tremula?* the common aspen), all of which are trees found in Siberia.

"By way of supplement to these observations on the Greenland side, it may be mentioned that the *Jeannette* Expedition frequently found Siberian driftwood (fir and birch) between the floes in the strong northerly current to the northward of the New Siberian Islands.

"Fortunately for the Eskimo, such large quantities of this driftwood come every year to the coasts of Greenland, that in my opinion one cannot but assume that they are conveyed thither by a constantly-flowing current, especially as the wood never appears to have been very long in the sea, at all events not without having been frozen into the ice.

"That this driftwood passes south of Franz Josef Land and Spitzbergen is quite as unreasonable a theory as that the ice-floe with the relics from the *Jeannette* drifted by this route. In further disproof of this assumption it may be stated that Siberian driftwood is found north of Spitzbergen in the strong southerly current, against which Parry fought in vain.

"It appears, therefore, that on these grounds also we cannot but admit the existence of a current flowing across, or in close proximity to, the Pole.

"As an interesting fact in this connection, it may also be mentioned that the German botanist Grisebach has shown that the Greenland flora includes a series of Siberian vegetable forms that could scarcer have reached Greenland in any other way than by the help of such a current conveying the seeds.

"On the drift-ice in Denmark Strait (between Iceland and Greenland) I have made observations which tend to the conclusion that this ice too was of Siberian origin. For instance, I found quantities of mud on it, which seemed to be of Siberian origin, or might possibly have come from North American rivers. It is possible, however, to maintain that this mud originates in the glacier rivers that flow from under the ice in the north of Greenland, or in other unknown polar lands; so that this piece of evidence is of less importance than those already named.

"Putting all this together, we seem driven to the conclusion that a current flows at some point between the Pole and Franz Josef Land to the Siberian Arctic Sea to the east coast of Greenland.

"That such must be the case we may also infer in another way. If we regard, for instance, the polar current — that broad current which flows down from the unknown polar regions between Spitzbergen and Greenland — and consider what an enormous mass of water it carries along, it must seem self-evident that this cannot come from a circumscribed and small basin, but must needs be gathered from distant sources, the more so as the Polar Sea (so far as we know it) is remarkably shallow everywhere to the north of the European, Asiatic and American coasts. The polar current is no doubt fed by that branch of the Gulf Stream which makes its way up the west side of Spitzbergen; but this small stream is far from being sufficient, and the main body of its water must be derived from further northwards.

"It is probable that the polar current stretches its suckers, as it were, to the coast of Siberia and Bering Strait, and draws its supplies from these distant regions. The water it carries off is replaced partly through the warm current before mentioned which makes its way through Bering Strait, and partly by that branch of the ·Gulf Stream which, passing by the north of Norway, bends eastwards towards Novaya Zemlya, and of which a great portion unquestionably continues its course along the north coast of this island into the Siberian Arctic Sea. That a current coming from the south takes this direction, at all events in some measure, appears probable from the well-known fact that in the northern hemisphere the rotation of the earth tends to compel a northward-flowing current, whether of water or of air, to assume an easterly course. The earth's rotation may also cause a southward-flowing stream, like the polar current, to direct its course westward to the east coast of Greenland.

"But even if these currents flowing in the polar basin did not exist, I am still of opinion that in some other way a body of water must collect in it, sufficient to form a polar current. In the first place there are the North European, the Siberian and North American rivers debouching into the Arctic Sea, to supply this water. The fluvial basin of these rivers is very considerable, comprising a large portion of Northern Europe, almost the whole of Northern Asia or Siberia down to the Altai Mountains and Lake Baikal, together with the principal part of Alaska and British North America. All these added together form no unimportant portion of the earth, and the rainfall of these countries is enormous. It is not conceivable that the Arctic Sea of itself could contribute anything of importance to this rainfall; for, in the first place, it is for the most part covered with drift-ice, from which the evaporation is but trifling; and, in the next place, the comparatively low temperature: in these regions prevents any considerable evaporation taking place even from open surfaces of water. The moisture that produces this rainfall must consequently in a great measure come from elsewhere, principally from the Atlantic and Pacific Oceans, and the amount of water which thereby feeds the Arctic Sea, must be very considerable. If we possessed sufficient knowledge of the rainfall in the different localities it might be exactly calculated.[4]

"The importance of this augmentation appears even greater when we consider that the polar basin is comparatively small, and, as has been already remarked, very shallow; its greatest known depth being from 60 to 80 fathoms.

"But there is still another factor that must help to increase the quantity of water in the polar basin, and that is its own rainfall. Weyprecht has already pointed out the probability that the large influx of warm, moist atmosphere, from the south, attracted by the constant low atmospheric pressure in the polar regions, must engender so large a rainfall as to augment considerably the amount of water in the Polar Sea. Moreover, the fact that the polar basin receives large supplies of fresh water is proved by the small amount of salt in the water of the polar current.

"From all these considerations it appears unquestionable that the sea around the Pole is fed with considerable quantities of water, partly fresh, as we have just seen, partly salt, as we indicated further back, proceeding from the different ocean currents. It thus becomes inevitable, according to the law of equilibrium, that these masses of water should seek such an outlet as we find in the Greenland polar current.

"Let us now enquire whether further reasons can be found to show why this current flows exactly in the given direction.

"If we examine the ocean soundings, we at once find a conclusive reason 'Why the main outlet must lie between Spitzbergen and Greenland. The sea here, so far as we know it, is at all points very deep; there is, indeed, a channel of as much as 2,500 fathoms depth; while south of Spitzbergen and Franz Josef Land it is remarkably shallow, not more than 160 fathoms. As has been stated, a current passes northwards through Bering Strait; and Smith Sound, and the sounds between the islands north of America, though here, indeed, there is a southward current, are far too small and narrow to form adequate outlets for the mass of water of which we are speaking. There is, therefore, no other assumption left than that this mass of water must find its outlet by the route actually followed by the polar current. The channel discovered by the *Jeannette* Expedition between Wrangel Land and the New Siberian Islands may here be mentioned as a notable fact. It extended in a northerly direction, and was at some points more than 80 fathoms deep, while at the sides the soundings ran only to 40 or 50 fathoms. It is by no means impossible that this channel may be a continuation of the channel between Spitzbergen and Greenland,[5] in which case it would certainly influence, if not actually determine, the direction of the main current.

"If we examine the conditions of wind and atmospheric pressure over the Polar Sea, as far as they are known, it would appear that they must tend to produce a current across the Pole in the direction indicated. From the Atlantic to the south of Spitzbergen and Franz Josef Land a belt of low atmospheric pressure (minimum belt) extends into the Siberian Arctic Sea. In accordance with well-known laws, the wind must have a preponderating direction from west to east on the south side of this belt, and this would promote an eastward-flowing current along the north coast of Siberia, such as has been found to exist there.[6] The winds on the north side of the minimum belt must, however, blow mainly in a direction from east to west, and will consequently produce a westerly current, passing across the Pole towards the Greenland Sea, exactly as we have seen to be the case.

"It thus appears that, from whatever side we consider this question, even apart from the specially cogent evidences above cited, we cannot escape the conclusion that a current passes across or very near to the Pole into the sea between Greenland and Spitzbergen.

"This being so, it seems to me that the plain thing for us to do is to make our way into the current on that side of the Pole where it flows northward, and by its help to penetrate into those regions which all who have hitherto worked against it, have sought in vain to reach.

"My plan is, briefly, as follows: — I propose to have a ship built, as small and as strong as possible; just big enough to contain supplies of coals and provisions for twelve men for five years. A ship of about 170 tons (gross) will probably suffice. Its engine should be powerful enough to give a speed of 6 knots; but in addition it must also be fully rigged for sailing.

"The main point in this vessel is that it be built on such principles as to enable it to withstand the pressure of the ice. The sides must slope sufficiently to prevent the ice, when it presses together, from getting firm hold of the hull, as was the case with the *Jeannette* and other vessels. Instead of nipping the ship, the ice must raise it up out of the water. No very new departure in construction is likely to be needed, for the *Jeannette*, notwithstanding her preposterous build, was able to hold out against the ice pressure for about two years. That a vessel can easily be built on such lines as to fulfil these requirements no one will question, who has seen a ship nipped by the ice. For the same reason, too, the ship ought to be a small one; for besides being thus easier to manoeuvre in the ice, it will be more readily lifted by the pressure of the ice, not to mention that it will be easier to give it the requisite strength. It must, of course, be built of picked materials. A ship of the form and size here indicated will not be a good or comfortable sea-boat, but that is of minor importance in waters filled with ice such as we are here speaking of. It is true that it would have to travel a long distance over the open sea before it would get so far, but it would not be so bad a sea-boat as to be unable to get along, even though sea-sick passengers might have to offer sacrifices to the gods of the sea.

"With such a ship and a crew of ten, or at the most twelve, able-bodied and carefully picked men, with a full equipment for five years, in every respect as good as modern appliances permit of, I am of opinion that the undertaking would be well secured against risk. With this ship we should sail up through Bering Strait and westward along the north coast of Siberia towards the New Siberian Islands[7] as early in the summer as the ice would permit.

"Once at the New Siberian Islands, it will be advisable to employ the time to the best advantage in examining the conditions of currents and ice, and to wait for the most opportune moment to advance as far as possible in ice-free water, which, judging by the accounts of the ice conditions north of Bering Strait given by American whalers, will probably be in August or the beginning of September.

"When the right time has arrived, then we shall plough our way in amongst the ice as far as we can. We may venture to conclude from the experience of the *Jeannette* Expedition, that we should thus be able to reach a point north of the most northerly of the New Siberian Islands. De Long notes in his journal that while the expedition was drifting in the ice north of Rennet Island they saw all around them a dark 'water sky' — that is to say, a sky which gives a dark reflection of open water — indicating such a sea as would be, at all events, to some extent navigable by a strong ice-ship. Next, it must be borne in mind that the whole *Jeannette* Expedition travelled in boats, partly in open water, from Bennett Island to the Siberian coast, where, as we know, the majority of them met with a lamentable end. Nordenskiöld advanced no farther northwards than to the southernmost of the islands mentioned (at the end of August but here he found the water everywhere open).

"It is, therefore, probable that we may be able to push our way up past the New Siberian Islands, and that accomplished we shall be right in the current which carried the *Jeannette*. The thing will then be simply to force our way northwards till we are set fast.[8]

"Next we must choose a fitting place and moor the ship firmly, between suitable ice-floes, and then let the ice screw itself together as much as it likes — the more the better. The ship will simply be hoisted up and will ride safely and firmly. It is possible it may heel over to a certain extent under this pressure; but that will scarcely be of much importance... Henceforth the current will be our motive power, while our ship, no longer a means of transport, will become a barrack, and we shall have ample time for scientific observations.

"In this manner the expedition will, as above indicated, probably drift across the Pole, and onwards to the sea between Greenland and Spitzbergen. And when we get down to the 80th degree of latitude, or even sooner if it is summer, there is every likelihood of our getting the ship free, and being able to sail home. Should she, however, be lost before this — which is certainly possible, though as I think very unlikely if she is constructed in the way above described — the expedition will not, therefore, be a failure, for our homeward course must in any case follow the polar current on to the North Atlantic basin; there is plenty of ice to drift on, and of this means of locomotion we have already had experience. If the *Jeannette* Expedition had had sufficient provisions, and had remained on the ice-floe on which the relics were ultimately found, the result would doubtless have been very different from what it was. Our ship cannot possibly founder under the ice pressure so quickly but that there would be time enough to remove, with all our equipment and provisions, to a substantial ice-floe, which we should have selected beforehand in view of such a contingency. Here the tents which we should take with us to meet this contingency would be pitched. In order to preserve our provisions and other equipments we should not place them all together on one spot, but should distribute them over the ice, laying them on rafts of planks and beams which we should have built on it. This will obviate the possibility of any of our equipments sinking, even should the floe on which they are break up. The crew of the Hansa, who drifted for more than half a year along the east coast of Greenland, in this way lost a great quantity of their supplies.

"For the success of such an expedition two things only are required: viz., good clothing, and plenty of food, and these we can take care to have with us. We should thus be able to remain as safely on our ice-floe as in our ship, and should advance just as well towards the Greenland Sea. The only difference would be that on our arrival there, instead of proceeding by ship, we must take to our boats, which would convey us just as safely to the nearest harbour.

"Thus it seems to me there is an overwhelming probability that such an expedition would be successful. Many people, however, will certainly urge: — 'In all currents there are eddies and backwaters; suppose, then, you get into one of these, or perhaps stumble on an unknown land up by the Pole and remain lying fast there, how will you extricate yourselves?' To this I would merely reply, as concerns the backwater, that we must get out of it just as surely as we got into it, and that we shall have provisions for five years. And as regards the other possibility, we should hail such an occurrence with delight, for no spot on earth could well be found of greater scientific interest. On this newly discovered land we should make as many observations as possible. Should time wear on and find us still unable to get our ship into the set of the current again, there would be nothing for it but to abandon her, and with our boats and necessary stores to search for the nearest current in order to drift in the manner before mentioned.

"How long may we suppose such a voyage to occupy? As we have already seen, the relics of the *Jeannette* Expedition at most took two years to drift along the same course down to the 80th degree of latitude, where we may, with tolerable certainty, count upon getting loose. This would correspond to a rate of about two miles per day of twenty-four hours.

"We may therefore not unreasonably calculate on reaching this point in the course of two years; and it is also possible that the ship might be set free in a higher latitude than is here contemplated. Five years' provisions must therefore be regarded as ample.

"But is not the cold in winter in these regions so severe that life will be impossible? There is no probability of this. We can even say with tolerable certainty, that at the Pole itself it is not so cold in winter as it is (for example) in the north of Siberia, an inhabited region, or on the northern part of the west coast of Greenland, which is also inhabited. Meteorologists have calculated that the mean temperature at the Pole in January is about $-33°$ Fahr. $(-33°$ C.) while, for example, in Yakutsk it is −43° Fahr. (−42° C.), and in Verkhoyansk −54° Fahr. (−48° C.). We should remember that the Pole is probably covered with sea, radiation from which is considerably less than from large land surfaces, such as the plains of North Asia. The polar region has, therefore, in all probability a marine climate with comparatively mild winters, but, by way of a set-off, with cold summers.

"The cold in these regions cannot, then, be any direct obstacle. One difficulty, however, which many former expeditions have had to contend against, and which must not be overlooked here, is scurvy. During a sojourn of any long duration in so cold a climate, this malady will unquestionably show itself unless one is able to obtain fresh provisions. I think, however, it may be safely assumed that the very various and nutritious foods now available in the form of hermetically closed preparations of different kinds, together with the scientific knowledge we now possess of the food stuffs necessary for bodily health, will enable us to hold this danger at a distance. Nor do I think that there will be an entire absence of fresh provisions in the waters we shall travel through.

"Polar bears and seals we may safely calculate on finding far to the north, if not up to the very Pole. It may be mentioned also that the sea must certainly contain quantities of small animals that might serve as food in case of necessity.

"It will be seen that whatever difficulties may be suggested as possible, they are not so great but that they can be surmounted by means of a careful equipment, a fortunate selection of the members of the expedition, and judicious leadership; so that good results may be hoped for. We may reckon on getting out into the sea between Greenland and Spitzbergen as surely as we can reckon on getting into the *Jeannette* current off the New Siberian Islands.

"But if this *Jeannette* current does not pass right across the Pole? If, for instance, it passes between the Pole and Franz Josef Land, as above intimated? What will the expedition do in that case to reach the earth's axis? Yes, this may seem to be the Achilles' heel of the undertaking; for should the ship be carried past the Pole at more than one degree's distance, it may then appear extremely imprudent and unsafe to abandon it in mid-current and face such a long sledge-journey over uneven sea-ice, which itself is drifting. Even if one reached the Pole it would be very uncertain whether one could find the ship again on returning.

"I am, however, of opinion that this is of small import: — it is not to seek for the exact mathematical point that forms the northern extremity of the earth's axis that we set out, for to reach this point is intrinsically of small moment. Our object is to investigate the great unknown region that surrounds the Pole, and these investigations will be equally important from a scientific point of view whether the expedition passes over the polar point itself or at some distance from it."

In this lecture I had submitted the most important data on which my plan was founded; but in the following years I continued to study the conditions of the northern waters, and received ever fresh proofs that my surmise of a drift right across the Polar Sea was correct. In a lecture delivered before the Geographical Society in Christiania, on September 28th, 1892, I alluded to some of these enquiries.[9] I laid stress on the fact that on considering the thickness and extent of the drift-ice in the seas on both sides of the Pole, one cannot but be struck by the fact that while the ice on the Asiatic side, north of the Siberian coast, is comparatively thin (the ice in which the *Jeannette* drifted was as a rule not more than from 7 to 10 feet thick) that on the other side, which comes drifting from the north in the sea between Greenland and Spitzbergen, is remarkably massive, and this, notwithstanding that the sea north of Siberia is one of the coldest tracts of the earth. This, I suggested, could be explained only on the assumption that the ice is constantly drifting from the Siberian coast, and that, while passing through the unknown and cold sea there is time for it to attain its enormous thickness partly by freezing, partly by the constant packing that takes place as the floes screw themselves together.

I further mentioned in the same lecture that the mud found on this drift-ice seemed to point to a Siberian origin. I did not at the time attach great importance to this fact, but on a further examination of the deposits I had collected during my Greenland Expedition, it appeared that it could scarcely come from anywhere else but Siberia. On investigating its mineralogical composition, Dr. Törnebohm, of Stockholm, came to the conclusion that the greater part of it must be Siberian river mud. He found about twenty different minerals in it. "This quantity of dissimilar constituent mineral parts appears to me," he says, "to point to the fact that they take their origin from a very extensive tract of land, and one's thoughts naturally turn to Siberia." Moreover, more than half of this mud deposit consisted of humus or boggy soil. More interesting, however, than the actual mud deposit were the diatoms found in it, which were examined by Professor Cleve, of Upsala, who says: "These diatoms are decidedly marine (i.e., take their origin from salt water, with some few fresh-water forms which the wind has carried from land). The diatomous flora in this dust is quite peculiar and unlike what I have found in many thousands of other specimens, with one exception, with which it shows the most complete conformity, namely, a specimen which was collected by Kellman during the *Vega* Expedition on an ice-floe off Cape Wankarem, near Bering Strait. Species and varieties were perfectly identical in both specimens." Cleve was able to distinguish sixteen species of diatoms. All these appear also in the dust from Cape Wankarem, and twelve of them have been found at that place alone, and nowhere else in all the world. This was a notable coincidence between two such remote points, and Cleve is certainly right in saying: "It is, indeed, quite remarkable that the diatomous flora on the ice-floes off Bering Strait and on the east coast of Greenland should so completely resemble each other, and should be so utterly unlike all others: it points to an open connection between the seas east of Greenland and north of Asia." "Through this open connection," I continued in my address, "drift-ice is, therefore, yearly transported across the unknown Polar Sea. On this same drift-ice and by the same route, it must be no less possible to transport an expedition." When this plan was propounded it certainly met with approval in various quarters, especially here at home. Thus it was vigorously supported by Professor Mohn, who, indeed, by his explanation of the drift of the *Jeannette* relics, had given the original impulse to it. But, as might be expected, it met with opposition in the main, especially from abroad, while most of the polar travellers and Arctic authorities declared, more or less openly, that it was sheer madness. The year before we set out, in November, 1892, I laid it before the Geographical Society in London in a lecture at which the principal Arctic travellers of England were present. After the lecture a discussion took place,[10] which plainly showed how greatly I was at variance with the generally-accepted opinions as to the conditions in the interior of the polar Sea, the principles of ice navigation, and the methods that a polar expedition ought to pursue. The eminent Arctic traveller, Admiral Sir Leopold M'Clintock, opened the discussion with the remark: "I think I may say this is the most adventurous programme ever brought under the notice of the Royal Geographical Society." He allowed that the facts spoke in favour of the correctness of my theories, but was in a high degree doubtful whether my plan could be realised. He was especially of opinion that the danger of being crushed in the ice was too great. A ship could, no doubt, be built that would be strong enough to resist the ice pressure in summer; but should it be exposed to this pressure in the winter months, when the ice resembled a mountain frozen fast to the ship's side, he thought that the possibility of being forced up on the surface of the ice was very remote. He firmly believed, as did the majority of the others, that there was no probability of ever seeing the *Fram* again, when once she had given herself over to the pitiless polar ice, and concluded by saying, "I wish the doctor full and speedy success. But it will be a great relief to his many friends in England when he returns, and more particularly to those who have had experience of the dangers at all times inseparable from ice navigation, even in regions not quite so far north."

Admiral Sir George Nares said:

"The adopted Arctic axioms for successfully navigating an icy region are that it is absolutely necessary to keep close to a coast line, and that the farther we advance from civilization, the more desirable it is to insure a reasonably safe line of retreat. Totally disregarding these, the ruling principle of the voyage is that the vessel — on which, if the voyage is in any way successful, the sole future hope of the party will depend, is to be pushed deliberately into the pack-ice. Thus, her commander — in lieu of retaining any power over her future movements — will be forced to submit to be drifted helplessly about in agreement with the natural movements of the ice in which he is imprisoned. Supposing the sea currents are as stated, the time calculated as necessary to drift with the pack across the polar area is several years, during which time, unless new lands are met with, the ice near the vessel will certainly never be quiet, and the ship herself never free from the danger of being crushed by ice presses. To guard against this the vessel is said to be unusually strong, and of a special form to enable her to rise when the ice presses against her sides. This idea is no novelty whatever; but when once frozen into the polar pack the form of the vessel goes for nothing. She is hermetically sealed to and forms a part of the ice block surrounding her. The form of the ship is for all practical purposes the form of the block of ice in which she is frozen. This is a matter of the first importance, for there is no record of a vessel frozen into the polar pack having been disconnected from the ice, and so rendered capable of rising under pressure as a separate body detached from the ice block, even in the height of summer. In the event of the destruction of the vessel, the boats — necessarily fully stored, not only for the retreat, but for continuing the voyage — are to be available. This is well in theory, but extremely difficult to arrange for in practice. Preparation to abandon the vessel, is the one thing that gives us the most anxiety. To place boats, etc., on the ice packed ready for use involves the danger of being separated from them by a movement of the ice, or of losing them altogether, should a sudden opening occur. If we merely have everything handy for heaving over the side, the emergency may be so sudden that we have not time to save anything..."

As regards the assumed drift of the polar ice, Nares expressed himself on the whole at variance with me. He insisted that the drift was essentially determined by the prevailing winds:

"As to the probable direction of the drift, the *Fram*, starting from near the mouth of the Lena River, may expect to meet the main pack not farther north than about latitude 76° 30'. I doubt her getting farther north before she is beset, but taking an extreme case, and giving her 60 miles more, she will then only be in the same latitude as Cape Chelyuskin, 730 miles from the Pole, and about 600 miles from my supposed limit of the effective homeward carrying ocean current. After a close study of all the information we possess, I think the wind will be more likely to drift her towards the west than towards the east. With an ice-encumbered sea north of her, and more open water or newly-made ice to the southward, the chances are small for a northerly drift, at all events at first, and afterwards I know of no natural forces that will carry the vessel in any reasonable time much farther from the Siberian coast than the *Jeannette* was carried, and during the whole of this time, unless protected by newly discovered lands, she will be to all intents and purposes immovably sealed up in the pack, and exposed to its well-known dangers. There is no doubt that there is an ocean connection across the area proposed to be explored."

On one point, however, Nares was able to declare himself in agreement with me. It was the idea "that the principal aim of all such voyages is to explore the unknown polar regions, not to reach exactly that mathematical point in which the axis of our globe has its northern termination."[11]

Sir Allen Young says, among other things: "Dr. Nansen assumes the blank space around the axis of the earth to be a pool of water or ice: I think the great danger to contend with will be the land in nearly every direction near the pole. Most previous navigators seem to have continued seeing land again and again further and further north. These *Jeannette* relics may have drifted through narrow channels, and thus finally arrived at their destination, and, I think, it would be an extremely dangerous thing for the ship to drift through them, where she might impinge upon the land, and be kept for years."

With regard to the ship's form, Sir Allen Young says "I do not think the form of the ship is any great point, for, when a ship is fairly nipped, the question is if there is any swell or movement of the ice to lift the ship. If there is no swell the ice must go through her, whatever material she is made of."

One or two authorities, however, expressed themselves in favour of my plan. One was the Arctic traveller, Sir E. Inglefield, another Captain (now Admiral) Wharton, Director of the Hydrographic Department of England. In a letter to the Geographical Society, Admiral Sir George H. Richards says, on the occasion of my address: "I regret to have to speak discouragingly of this project, but I think that any one who can speak with authority ought to speak plainly where so much may be at stake."

With regard to the currents, he says: "I believe there is a constant outflow (I prefer this word to current) from the north, in consequence of the displacement of the water from the region of the Pole by the ice-cap which covers it, intensified in its density by the enormous weight of snow accumulated on its surface." This outflow takes place on all sides, he thinks, from the polar basin, but should be most pronounced in the tract between the western end of the Parry Islands and Spitzbergen; and with this outflow all previous expeditions have had to contend. He does not appear to make any exception as to the *Tegethoff* or *Jeannette*, and can find no reason "for believing that a current sets north over the Pole from the New Siberian Islands which Dr. Nansen hopes for and believes in."… "It is my opinion that when really within what may be called the inner circle, say about 78° of latitude, there is little current of any kind that would influence a ship in the close ice that must be expected; it is when we get outside this circle — round the corners, as it were — into the straight wide channels, where the ice is loose, that we are really affected by its influence, and here the ice gets naturally thinner, and more decayed in autumn, and less dangerous to a ship. Within the inner circle probably not much of the ice escapes; it becomes older and heavier every year, and in all probability completely blocks the navigation of ships entirely. This is the hind of ice which was brought to Nares' winter quarters at the head of Smith Sound in about 82° 30' north; and this is the ice which Markham struggled against in his sledge journey, and against which no human power could prevail."

He attached "no real importance" to the *Jeannette* relics. "If found in Greenland, they may well have drifted down on a floe from the neighbourhood of Smith Sound, from some of the American Expeditions which went to Greely's rescue." "It may also well be that some of De Long's printed or written documents in regard to his equipment, may have been taken out by these expeditions, and the same may apply to the other articles." He does not, however, expressly say whether there was any indication of such having been the case. In a similar letter to the Geographical Society the renowned botanist, Sir Joseph Hooker says: "Dr. Nansen's project is a wide departure from any hitherto put in practice for the purpose of polar discovery, and it demands the closest scrutiny both on this account, and because it is one involving the greatest peril…

"From my experience of three seasons in the Antarctic regions I do not think that a ship, of whatever build, could long, resist destruction if committed to the movements of the pack in the polar regions. One built as strongly as the *Fram* would no doubt resist great pressures in the open pack, but not any pressure or repeated pressures, and still less the thrust of the pack if driven with or by it against land. The lines of the *Fram* might be of service so long as she was on an even keel or in ice of no great height above the water-line; but amongst floes and bergs or when thrown on her beam-ends, they would avail her nothing."

If the *Fram* were to drift towards the Greenland coast or the American polar islands he is of opinion that, supposing a landing could be effected, there would be no probability at all of salvation. Assuming that a landing could be effected, it must be on an inhospitable and probably ice-bound coast, or on the mountainous ice of a palaeocrystic sea. With a certainly enfeebled, and probably reduced ship's company, there could, in such a case, be no prospect of reaching succour. Putting aside the possibility of scurvy (against which there is no certain prophylactic), have the depressing influence on the minds of the crew resulting from long confinement in very close quarters during many months of darkness, extreme cold, inaction, ennui, constant peril, and the haunting uncertainty as to the future, been sufficiently taken into account' Perfunctory duties and occupations do not avert the effects of these conditions; they hardly mitigate them, and have been known to aggravate them. I do not consider the attainment of Dr. Nansen's object by the means at his disposal to be impossible; but I do consider that the success of such an enterprise would not justify the exposure of valuable lives for its attainment."

In America, General Greely, the leader of the ill-fated expedition generally known by his name (1881-84), wrote an article in *The Forum* (August, 1891) in which he says among other things: "It strikes me as almost incredible that the plan here advanced by Dr. Nansen should receive encouragement or support. It seems to me to be based on fallacious ideas as to physical conditions within the polar regions, and to foreshadow, if attempted, barren results, apart from the suffering and death among its members. Dr. Nansen, so far as I know, has had no Arctic service; his crossing of Greenland, however difficult, is no more polar work than the scaling of Mount St. Elias. It is doubtful if any hydrographer would treat seriously his theory of polar currents, or if any Arctic traveller would indorse the whole scheme. There are perhaps a dozen men whose Arctic service has been such that the positive support of this plan by even a respectable minority would entitle it to consideration and confidence. These men are: — Admiral M'Clintock, Richards, Collinson and Nares, and Captain Markham of the Royal Navy, Sir Allen Young and Leigh-Smith of England, Koldewey of Germany, Payer of Austria, Nordenskiöld of Sweden, and Melville in our own country. I have no hesitation in asserting that no two of these believe in the possibility of Nansen's first proposition — to build a vessel capable of living or navigating in a heavy Arctic pack, into which it is proposed to put his ship. The second proposition is even more hazardous, involving as it does a drift of more than 2,000 miles in a straight line through an unknown region, during which the party in its voyage (lasting two or more years, we are told) would take only boats along, encamp on an iceberg, and live there while floating across."

After this General Greely proceeds to prove the falsity of all my assumptions. Respecting the objects from the *Jeannette*, he says plainly that he does not believe in them. "Probably some drift articles were found," he says, "and it would seem more reasonable to trace them to the *Porteus*, which was wrecked in Smith Sound about 1,000 miles north of Julianehaab."...

"It is further important to note that, if the articles were really from the *Jeannette*, the nearest route would have been, not across the North Pole along the east coast of Greenland, but down Kennedy Channel and by way of Smith Sound and Baffin Bay, as was suggested as to drift from the *Porteus*."

We could not possibly get near the Pole itself by a long distance, says Greely, as "we know almost as well as if we had seen it, that there is in the unknown regions an extensive land which is the birthplace of the flat-topped icebergs or the palaeocrystic ice." In this glacier-covered land, which he is of opinion must be over 300 miles in diameter, and which sends out icebergs to Greenland as well as to Franz Josef's Land,[12] the Pole itself must be situated.

"As to the indestructible ship," he says, "it is certainly a most desirable thing for Dr. Nansen." His meaning, however, is that it cannot be built. "Dr. Nansen appears to believe that the question of building on such lines as will give the ship the greatest power of resistance to the pressure of the ice-floe has not been thoroughly and satisfactorily solved, although hundreds of thousands of dollars have been spent for this end by the seal and whaling companies of Scotland and Newfoundland." As an authority he quotes Melville, and says "every Arctic navigator of experience agrees with Melville's dictum, that even if built solid a vessel could not withstand the ice-pressure of the heavy polar pack." To my assertion that the ice along the "Siberian coast is comparatively thin, 7 to 10 feet," he again quotes Melville, who speaks of ice "80 feet high, etc." (something we did not discover, by the way, during the whole of our voyage).

After giving still more conclusive proofs that the *Fram* must inevitably go to the bottom, as soon as it should be exposed to the pressure of the ice, he goes on to refer to the impossibility of drifting, in the ice with boats. And he concludes his article with the remark that "Arctic exploration is sufficiently credited with rashness and danger in its legitimate and sanctioned methods, without bearing the burden of Dr. Nansen's illogical scheme of self-destruction."

From an article Greely wrote after our return home, in Harper's Weekly for September 19th, 1896, he appears to have come to the conclusion that the *Jeannette* relics were genuine and that the assumption of their drift may have been correct, mentioning "Melville, Dall and others" as not believing, in them. He allows also that my scheme has been carried out in spite of what he had said. This time he concludes the article as follows: "In contrasting the expeditions of De Long and Nansen, it is necessary to allude to the single blemish that mars the otherwise magnificent career of Nansen, who deliberately quitted his comrades on the ice-beset ship hundreds of miles from any known land, with the intention of not returning, but, in his own reported words, 'to go to Spitzbergen where he felt certain to find a ship 600 miles away.' De Long and Ambler had such a sense of honour that they sacrificed their lives rather than separate themselves from a dying man whom their presence could not save. It passes comprehension how Nansen could have thus deviated from the most sacred duty devolving on the commander of a naval expedition. The safe return of brave Captain Sverdrup with the *Fram* does not excuse Nansen. Sverdrup's consistency, courage, and skill in holding fast to the *Fram* and bringing his comrades back to Norway, will win for him in the minds of many laurels even brighter than those of his able and accomplished chief."

One of the few who publicly gave to my plan the support of his scientific authority was Professor Supan, the well-known Editor of *Petermann's Mitteilungen*. In an article in this journal for 1891 (p. 191) he not only spoke warmly in its favour, but supported it with new suggestions. His view was that what he terms the Arctic "wind-shed" probably for the greater part of the year divides the unknown polar basin into two parts. In the eastern part the prevailing winds blow towards the Bering Sea, while those of the western part blow towards the Atlantic. He thought that, as a rule, this "wind-shed" must lie

Chapter 2

Preparations and Equipment

FOOLHARDY as the scheme appeared to some, it received powerful support from the Norwegian Government and the King of Norway. A Bill was laid before the Storthing for a grant of £11,250 (200,000 kroner) or two-thirds of the estimated cost. The remaining third I hoped to be able to raise from private sources, as I had already received promises of support from many quarters.

On June 30th, 1890, the amount demanded was voted by the Storthing; which thereby expressed its wish that the expedition should be a Norwegian one. In January, 1891, Mr. Thos. Fearnley, Consul Axel Heiberg, and Mr. Ellef Ringnes set to work to collect the further sum required, and in a few days the amount was subscribed.

Among foreign contributors may be mentioned the Royal Geographical Society of London, which showed its sympathy with the undertaking by subscribing £300 sterling. Baron Oscar Dickson provided at his own cost the electric installation (dynamo, accumulators, and conductors).

As the work of equipment proceeded, it appeared that the first estimate was not sufficient. This was especially due to the ship, which was estimated to cost £8,437 10s. (150,000 kroner) but which came to nearly double that sum. Where so much was at stake, I did not think it right to study the cost too much, if it seemed that a little extra outlay could ensure the successful result of the expedition. The three gentlemen who had taken the lead in the first collection, Mr. Thomas Fearnley, Consul Axel Heiberg, and Mr. Ellef Ringnes, undertook at my request to constitute themselves the Committee of the expedition and to take charge of its pecuniary affairs. In order to cover a portion of the deficiency, they, together with certain members of the Council of the Geographical Society, set on foot another private subscription all over the country; while the same society at a later period headed a national subscription. By these means about £956 5s. was collected in all. I had further to petition the Norwegian Storthing for an additional sum of £4,500, when our national assembly again gave proof of its sympathy with the undertaking by granting the amount named (June 9th, 1890).

Finally Consul Axel Heiberg and Mr. Dick subscribed an additional £337 10s. each, while I myself made up the deficiency that still remained on the eve of our departure.

It will be evident from the plan explained above, that the most important point in the equipment of our expedition was the building of the ship that was to carry us through the dreaded ice regions. The construction of this vessel was accordingly carried out with greater care, probably, than has been devoted to any ship that has hitherto ploughed the Arctic waters. I found in the well-known shipbuilder, Colin Archer, a man who thoroughly understood the task I set him, and who concentrated all his skill, foresight, and rare thoroughness upon the work. We must gratefully recognise that the success of the expedition was in no small degree due to this man.

If we turn our attention to the long list of former expeditions and to their equipment, it cannot but strike us that scarcely a single vessel had been built specially for the purpose in fact, the majority of explorers have not even provided themselves with vessels which were originally intended for ice navigation. This is the more surprising when we remember the sums of money that have been lavished on the equipment of some of these expeditions. The fact is, they have generally been in such a hurry to set out that there has been no time to devote to a more careful equipment. In many cases, indeed, preparations were not begun until a few months before the expedition sailed. The present expedition, however, could not be equipped in so short a time, and if the voyage itself took three years, the preparations took no less time, while the scheme was conceived thrice three years earlier.

Plan after plan did Archer make of the projected ship; one model after another was prepared and abandoned. Fresh improvements were constantly being suggested. The form we finally adhered to may seem to many people by no means beautiful; but that it is well adapted to the ends in view I think our expedition has fully proved. What was especially aimed at was, as mentioned above, to give the ship such sides that it could readily be hoisted up during ice pressure, without being crushed between the floes. Greely, Nares, etc., etc., are certainly right in saying that this is nothing new. I relied here simply on the sad experiences of earlier expeditions. What, however, may be said to be new is the fact that we not only realised that the ship ought to have such a form, but that we gave it that form, as well as the necessary strength for resisting great ice-pressure, and that this was the guiding idea in the whole work of construction. Colin Archer is quite right in what he says in an article in the Norsk *Tidsskrif for Sovaesen*, 1892: "When one bears in mind what is, so to speak, the fundamental idea of Dr. Nansen's plan in his North Pole Expedition...it will readily be seen that a ship which is to be built with exclusive regard to its suitability for this object must differ essentially from any other previously known vessel...

"In the construction of the ship two points must be especially studied, (1) that the shape of the hull be such as to offer as small a vulnerable target as possible to the attacks of the ice; and (2) that it be built so solidly as to be able to withstand the greatest possible pressure from without in any direction whatsoever."

And thus she was built, more attention being paid to making her a safe and warm stronghold while drifting in the ice, than to endowing her with speed or good sailing qualities.

As stated, our aim was to make the ship as small as possible. The reason of this was that a small ship is, of course, lighter than a large one, and can be made stronger in proportion to her weight. A small ship too is better adapted for navigation among the ice; it is easier to handle her in critical moments, and to find a safe berth for her between the packing ice-floes. I was of opinion that a vessel of 170 tons register would suffice, but the *Fram* is considerably

Colin Archer.

larger, 402 tons gross, and 307 tons net. It was also our aim to build a short vessel, which could thread her way easily among the floes, especially as great length would have been a source of weakness when ice-pressure set in. But in order that such a ship, which has, moreover, very sloping sides, shall possess the necessary carrying capacity, she must be broad; and her breadth is in fact about a third of her length. Another point of importance was to make the sides as smooth as possible, without projecting edges, while plane surfaces were as much as possible avoided in the neighbourhood of the most vulnerable points, and the hull assumed a plump and rounded form. Bow, stern, and keel — all were rounded off so that the ice should not be able to get a grip of her anywhere. For this reason, too, the keel was sunk in the planking so that barely three inches protruded and its edges were rounded. The object was that "the whole craft should be able to slip like an eel out of the embraces of the ice."

The hull was made pointed fore and aft, and somewhat resembles a pilot boat, minus the keel and the sharp garboard strakes. Both ends were made specially strong. The stem consists of three stout oak beams, one inside the other, forming an aggregate thickness of 4 feet (1.25 m.) of solid oak; inside the stem are fitted solid breasthooks of oak and iron to bind the ship's sides together, and from these breasthooks stays are placed against the pawl-hit. The bow is protected by an iron stem, and across it are fitted transverse bars which run some small distance backwards on either side as is usual in sealers.

The stern is of a special and somewhat peculiar construction. On either side of the rudder and propeller posts — which are sided 24 inches (65 cm.) — is fitted a stout oak counter-timber following the curvature of the stern right up to the upper deck, and forming, so to speak, a double stern post. The planking is carried outside these timbers, and the stern protected by heavy iron plates wrought outside the planking.

Between these two counter-timbers there is a well for the screw, and also one for the rudder, through which they can both be hoisted up on deck. It is usual in sealers to have the screw arranged in this way, so that it can easily be replaced by a spare screw should it be broken by the ice. But such an arrangement is not usual in the case of the rudder, and, while with our small crew, and with the help of the capstan, we could hoist the rudder on deck in a few minutes in case of any sudden ice pressure or the like, I have known it take sealers with a crew of over 60 men several hours, or even a whole day, to ship a fresh rudder.

The stern is, on the whole, the Achilles' heel of ships in the polar seas; here the ice can easily inflict great damage, for instance, by breaking the rudder. To guard against this danger, our rudder was placed so low down as not to be visible above water, so that if a floe should strike the vessel aft it would break its force against the strong stern-part, and could hardly touch the rudder itself. As a matter of fact, notwithstanding the violent pressures we met with, we never suffered any injury in this respect.

Everything was of course done to make the sides of the ship as strong as possible. The frame timbers were of choice Italian oak that had originally been intended for the Norwegian navy, and had lain under cover at Horten for 30 years. They were all grown to shape and 10-11 inches thick. The frames were built in two courses or tiers, closely wrought together, and connected by bolts, some of which were riveted. Over each joint flat iron bands were placed. The frames were about 21 inches (56 cm.) wide, and were placed close together, with only about an inch or an inch and a half between; and these interstices were filled with pitch and sawdust mixed, from the keel to a little distance above the waterline, in order to keep the ship moderately watertight, even should the outer skin be chafed through.

The outside planking consists of three layers. The inner one is of oak 3 inches thick, fastened with spikes and carefully caulked; outside this another oak sheathing 4 inches thick, fastened with through bolts and caulked; and outside these comes the ice-skin of greenheart, which like the other planking runs right down to the keel. At the water-line it is 6 inches thick, gradually diminishing towards the bottom to 3 inches. It is fastened with nails and jagged bolts, and not with through bolts, so that if the ice had stripped off the whole of the ice sheathing the hull of the ship would not have suffered any great damage. The lining inside the frame timbers is of pitch pine planks, some 4 some 8 inches thick; it was also carefully caulked once or twice.

The total thickness of the ship's sides is, therefore, from 24 to 28 inches of solid water-tight wood. It will readily be understood that such a ship's side, with its rounded form, would of itself offer a very good resistance to the ice; but to make it still stronger the inside was shored up in every possible way, so that the hold looks like a cobweb of balks, stanchions, and braces. In the first place, there are two rows of beams, the upper deck and between decks, principally of solid oak, partly also of pitch pine; and all of these are further connected with each other, as well as with the sides of the ship, by numerous supports. The accompanying diagrams will show how they are arranged. The diagonal stays are, of course, placed as nearly as possible at right angles to the sides of the ship, so as to strengthen them against external pressure and to distribute its force. The vertical stanchions between both tiers of beams and between the lower beams and keelson are admirably adapted for this latter object. All are connected together with strong knees and iron fastenings, so that the whole becomes as it were a single coherent mass. It should be borne in mind that, while in former expeditions it was thought sufficient to give a couple of beams amidships some extra strengthening, every single cross beam in the *Fram* was stayed in the manner described and depicted.

In the engine-room there was, of course, no space for supports in the middle, but in their place two stay ends were fixed on either side. The beams of the lower deck were placed a little under the water-line, where the ice-pressure would be severest. In the after-hold these beams had to be raised a little to give room for the engine. The upper deck aft, therefore, was somewhat higher than the main deck, and the ship had a poop or half-deck, under which were the cabins for all the members of the expedition, and also the cooking-galley. Strong iron riders were worked in for the whole length of the ship in the spaces between the beams, extending in one length from the clamp under the upper deck nearly to the keelson. The keelson was in two tiers and about 31 inches (80 cm.) high, saving in the engine-room where the height of the room only allows one tier. The keel consists of two heavy American elm logs 14 inches square; but, as has been mentioned, so built in that only 3 inches protrude below the outer planking. The sides of the hull are rounded downwards to the keel, so that a transverse section at the midship frame reminds one forcibly of half a cocoanut cut in two. The higher the ship is lifted out of the water, the heavier does she, of course, become, and the greater her pressure on the ice, but for the above reason the easier also does it become for the ice to lift. To obviate much heeling, in case the hull should be lifted very high, the bottom was made flat, and this proved to be an excellent idea. I endeavoured to determine experimentally the friction of ice against wood, and taking into account the strength of the ship, and the angle of her sides with the surface of the water, I came to the conclusion that her strength must be many times sufficient to withstand the pressure necessary to lift her. This calculation was amply borne out by experience.

The principal dimensions of the ship were as follows: Length of keel, 102 feet; length of water-line, 113 feet; length from stem to stern on deck, 128 feet; extreme breadth, 36 feet; breadth of water-line, exclusive of ice-skin, 34 feet; depth, 17 feet; draught of water with light cargo, 122 feet; displacement with light cargo, 530 tons; with heavy cargo, the draught is over 15 feet, and the

DESIGNS FOR THE FRAM

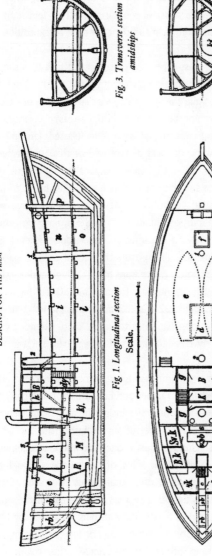

Fig. 1. Longitudinal section

Scale.

Fig. 2. Plan

Fig. 3. Transverse section amidships

Fig. 4. Transverse section at the engine-room

rb Rudder-well.
Bk Blessing's cabin.
M Engine.
dy Place for the dynamo
n Fore-hold.

sb Propeller-well.
4k Four-berth cabins.
kj Boiler.
d Main-hatch.
o Under fore-hold.

S Saloon.
Hk Scott-Hansen's cabin.
g Companions leading from saloon.
e Long boats.
p Pawl-bit.

s Sofas in saloon.
nk Nansen's cabin.
K Cook's galley.
i Main-hold.
1 Foremast.

b Table in saloon.
c Way down to engine-room.
B Chart-room.
1 Under-hold.
2 Mainmast.

Svk Sverdrup's cabin.
R Engine-room.
b Work-room.
f Fore-hatch.
3 Mizzenmast.

displacement is 800 tons; there is a freeboard of about 3 feet 6 inches. The hull with boilers filled was calculated to weigh about 420 tons, and with 800 tons displacement there should, therefore, be share carrying-power for coal and other cargo to the amount of 380 tons. Thus, in addition to the requisite provisions for dogs and men for more than five years, we could carry coal for four months steaming at full speed, which was more than sufficient for such an expedition as this.

As regards the rigging, the most important object was to have it as simple and as strong as possible, and at the same time so contrived as to offer the least possible resistance to the wind while the ship was under steam. With our small crew it was moreover of the last importance that it should be easy to work from deck. For this reason the *Fram* was rigged as a three-masted fore-and-aft schooner. Several of our old Arctic skippers disapproved of this arrangement. They had always been used to sail with square-rigged ships, and with the conservatism peculiar to their class were of opinion that what they had used was the only thing that could be used in the ice. However, the rig we chose was unquestionably the best for our purpose. In addition to the ordinary fore-and-aft sails we had two movable yards on the foremast for a square foresail and topsail. As the yards were attached to a sliding truss they could easily be hauled down when not in use. The ship's lower masts were tolerably high and massive. The mainmast was about 80 feet high, the main topmast was 50 feet high, and the crow's-nest on the top was about 102 feet (32 m.) above the water. It was important to have this as high as possible, so as to have a more extended view when it came to picking our way through the ice. The aggregate sail area was about 6,000 sq. feet.

The ship's engine, a triple expansion, was made with particular care. The work was done at the Akers Mechanical Factory, and Engineer Norbeck deserves especial credit for its construction. With his quick insight he foresaw the various possibilities that might occur, and took precautions against them. The triple expansion system was chosen as being the most economical in the consumption of coal; but as it might happen that one or other of the cylinders should get out of order, it was arranged, by means of separate pipes, that any of the cylinders could be cut off, and thus the other two, or, at a pinch, even one alone could be used. In this way the engine, by the mere turning of a cock or two, could be changed at will into a compound high-pressure or low-pressure engine. Although nothing ever went wrong with any of the cylinders, this arrangement was frequently used with advantage. By using the engine as a compound one, we could, for instance, give the *Fram* greater speed for a short time, and when occasion demanded we often took this means of forcing our way through the ice. The engine was of 220 indicated horse-power, and we could in calm weather with a light cargo attain a speed of 6 or 7 knots.

The propellers, of which we had two in reserve, were two-bladed, and made of cast-iron; but we never used either the spare propellers or a spare rudder which we had with us.

Our quarters lay, as before mentioned, abaft under the half-deck, and were arranged so that the saloon, which formed our dining-room and drawing-room, was in the middle, surrounded on all sides by the sleeping-cabins. These consisted of four state-rooms with one berth apiece and two with four berths. The object of this arrangement was to protect the saloon from external cold; but further, the ceiling, floors and walls were covered with several thick coatings of non-conducting material, the surface layer, in touch with the heat of the cabin, consisting of air-tight linoleum, to prevent the warm, damp air from penetrating to the other side and depositing moisture, which would soon turn to ice. The sides of the ship were lined with tarred felt, then came a space with cork padding, next a deal panelling, then a thick layer of felt, next air-tight linoleum, and last of all an inner panelling. The ceiling of the saloon and cabins consisted of many different layers: air, felt, deal panelling, reindeer hair stuffing, deal panelling, linoleum, air and deal panelling, which, with the 4-inch deck-planks, gave a total thickness of about 15 inches. To form the floor of the saloon, cork padding, 6 or 7 inches thick, was laid on the deck planks, on this a thick wooden floor, and above all linoleum. The skylight which was most exposed to the cold was protected by three panes of glass one within the other, and in various other ways. One of the greatest difficulties of life on board ship which former Arctic expeditions had had to contend with, was that moisture collecting on the cold outside walls either froze at once or ran down in streams into the berths and on to the floor. Thus it was not unusual to find the mattresses converted into more or less solid masses of ice. We, however, by these arrangements, entirely avoided such a wretched state of things, and when the fire was lighted in the saloon there, was not a trace of moisture on the walls even in the sleeping cabins. In front of the saloon lay the cook's galley, on either side of which was a companion leading to the deck.

As a protection against the cold, each of these companionways was fitted with four small solid doors consisting of several layers of wood with felt between, all of which had to be passed through on going out. And the more completely to exclude the cold air the thresholds of the doors were made more than ordinarily high. On the half-deck over the cook's galley, between the main-mast and the funnel, was a chart-room facing the bow, and a smaller work-room abaft.

In order to secure the safety of the ship in case of a leak, the hold was divided into three compartments by watertight bulkheads. Besides the usual pumps, we had a powerful centrifugal pump driven by the engine, which could be connected with each of the three compartments. It may be mentioned as an improvement on former expeditions that the *Fram* was furnished with an electric light installation. The dynamo was to be driven by the engine while we were under steam; while the intention was to drive it partly by means of the wind, partly by hand power, during our sojourn in the ice. For this purpose we took a windmill with us, and also a "horsemill" to be worked by ourselves. I had anticipated that this latter might have been useful in giving us exercise in the long polar night. We found, however, that there were plenty of other things to do, and we never used it; on the other hand, the windmill proved extremely serviceable. For illumination when we might not have enough power to produce electric light, we took with us about 16 tons of petroleum, which was also intended for cooking purposes and for warming the cabins. This petroleum, as well as 20 tons of common kerosene[13] intended to be used along with coal in the boiler, was stored in massive iron tanks, eight of which were in the hold, and one on deck. In all, the ship had eight boats, two of which were especially large, 29 feet long and 9 feet wide. These were intended for use in case the ship should, after all, be lost, the idea being that we should live in them while drifting in the ice. They were large enough to accommodate the whole ship's company with provisions for many months. Then there were four smaller boats of the form sealers generally use. They were exceedingly strong and lightly built, two of oak, and two of elm. The seventh boat was a small pram, and the eighth a launch with a petroleum engine, which, however, was not very serviceable, and caused us a great deal of trouble.

As I shall have frequent occasion later on to speak of other details of our equipment, I shall content myself here with mentioning a few of the most important.

Special attention was, of course, devoted to our commissariat with a view to obviating the danger of scurvy and other ailments. The principle on which I acted in the choice of provisions was to combine variety with wholesomeness. Every single article of food was chemically analysed before being adopted, and great care was taken that it should be properly packed. Such articles, even, as bread, dried vegetables, etc., etc., were soldered down in tins as a protection against damp.

A good library was of great importance to an expedition like ours, and thanks to publishers and friends both in our own and in other countries we were very well supplied in this respect.

The instruments for taking scientific observations of course formed an important part of our equipment and special care was bestowed upon them. In addition to the collection of instruments I had used on my Greenland expedition, a great many new ones were provided, and no pains were spared to get them as good and complete as possible. For meteorological observations, in addition to the ordinary thermometers, barometers, aneroids, psychrometers, hygrometers, anemometers, etc., etc., self-registering instruments were also taken. Of special importance were a self-registering aneroid barometer (barograph) and a pair of self-registering thermometers (thermographs). For astronomical observations we had a large theodolite and two smaller ones, intended for use on sledge expeditions, together with several sextants of different sizes. We had, moreover, four ship's chronometers and several pocket chronometers. For magnetic observations, for taking the declination, inclination and intensity (both horizontal and total intensity) we had a complete set of instruments. Among others may be mentioned a spectroscope especially adapted for the northern lights, an electroscope for determining the amount of electricity in the air, photographic apparatuses, of which we had seven, large and small, and a photographometer for making charts. I considered a pendulum apparatus with its adjuncts to be of special importance to enable us to make pendulum experiments in the far north. To do this, however, land was necessary, and, as we did not find any, this instrument unfortunately did not come into use. For hydrographic observations we took a full equipment of water-samplers, deep water thermometers, etc. To ascertain the saltness of the water, we had, in addition to the ordinary areometers, an electric apparatus specially constructed by Mr. Thornöe. Altogether, our scientific equipment was especially excellent, thanks in great measure to the obliging assistance rendered me by many men of science. I would take this opportunity of tendering my special thanks to Professor Mohn, who, besides seeing to the meteorological instruments, helped me in many other ways with his valuable advice; to Professor Geelmuyden, who undertook the supervision of the astronomical instruments; to Dr. Neumeyer, of Hamburg, who took charge of the magnetic equipment; and to Professor Otto

Petterson, of Stockholm, and Mr. Thornoe, of Christiania, both of whom superintended the hydrographic department. Of no less importance were the physiologico-medicinal preparations, to which Professor Torup devoted particular care.

As it might be of the utmost importance in several contingencies to have good sledge-dogs, I applied to my friend, Baron Edward von Toll, of St. Petersburg, and asked him whether it was possible to procure serviceable animals from Siberia.[14] With great courtesy Von Toll replied that he thought he himself could arrange this for me, as he was just on the point of undertaking his second scientific expedition to Siberia and the New Siberian Islands. He proposed to send the dogs to Khabarova, on Yugor Strait. On his journey through Tiumen in January, 1893, by the help of an English merchant named Wardroper, who resided there, he engaged Alexander Ivanovitch Trontheim to undertake the purchase of thirty Ostiak dogs, and their conveyance to Yuoor Strait. But Von Toll was not content with this. Mr. Nikolai Kelch having offered to bear the expense, my friend procured the East Siberian dogs, which are acknowledged to be better draught dogs than those of West Siberia (Ostiak dogs), and Johan Torgersen, a Norwegian, undertook to deliver them at the mouth of the Olenek, where it was arranged that we should touch.

Von Toll, moreover, thought it would be important to establish some depots of provisions on the New Siberian Islands, in case the *Fram* should meet with disaster and the expedition should be obliged to return home that way. On Von Toll's mentioning this, Kelch at once expressed himself willing to bear the costs, as he wished us in that event to meet with Siberian hospitality even on the New Siberian Islands. As it was difficult to find trustworthy agents to carry out a task involving so much responsibility, Von Toll determined to establish the depôts himself, and in May, 1893, he set out on an adventurous and highly interesting journey from the mainland over the ice to the New Siberian Islands, where, besides laying down three depots for us,[15] he made some very important geological researches.

Another important matter, I thought, was to have a cargo of coal sent out as far as possible on our route, so that when we broke off all connection with the rest of the world we should have on board the *Fram* as much coal as she could carry. I therefore joyfully accepted an offer from an Englishman, who was to accompany us with his steam yacht to Novaya Zemlya or the Kara Sea, and give us 100 tons of coal on parting company. As our departure was drawing nigh I learnt, however, that other arrangements had been made. It being now too late

Otto Sverdrup, Commander of the *Fram*.

to take any other measures, I chartered the sloop *Urania*, of Brönösund in Nordland, to bring a cargo of coals to Khabarova on the Yugor Strait.

No sooner did the plan of my expedition become known, than petitions poured in by the hundred from all quarters of the earth, from Europe, America, Australia, from persons who wished to take part in it, in spite of the many warning voices that had been raised. It was no easy thing to choose among all the brave men who applied. As a matter of course it was absolutely essential that every man should be strong and healthy, and not one was finally accepted till he had been carefully examined by Professor Hialmar Heiberg, of Christiania.

The following is a list of the members of the expedition:

Otto Neumann Sverdrup, Commander of the *Fram* was born in Bindal in Helgeland, 1855. At the age of seventeen he went to sea, passed his mate's examination in 1878, and for some years was captain of a ship. In 1888-89 he took part in the Greenland Expedition. As soon as he heard of the plan of the Polar Expedition he expressed his desire to accompany it, and I knew that I could not place the *Fram* in better hands. He is married and has one child.

Sigurd Scott-Hansen, First Lieutenant in the Navy, undertook the management of the meteorological, astronomical, and magnetic observations. He was born in Christiania in 1868. After passing through the Naval School at Horten, he became an officer in 1889, and First Lieutenant in 1892. He is a son of Andreas Hansen, parish priest in Christiania.

Henrik Greve Blessing, doctor and botanist to the expedition, was born in Drammen in 1866, where his father was at that time a clergyman. He became a student in 1885, and graduated in medicine in the spring of 1893.

Theodore Claudius Jacobsen, mate of the *Fram*, was born at Tromsö in 1855, where his father was a ship's captain, afterwards harbour master and head pilot. At the age of fifteen he went to sea, and passed his mate's examination four years later. He spent two years in New Zealand, and from 1886-90 he went on voyages to the Arctic Sea as skipper of a Tromsö sloop. He is married, and has one child.

Anton Amundsen, chief engineer of the *Fram*, was born at Horten in 1853. In 1884 he passed his technical examination, and soon afterwards his engineer's examination. For twenty-five years he has been in the Navy, where he attained the rank of chief engineer. He is married, and has six children.

Adolf Juell, steward and cook of the *Fram*, was born in the parish of Skatö, near Kragerö, in 1860. His father, Claus Nielsen, was a farmer and shipowner, In 1879 he passed his mate's examination, and has been captain of a ship many years. He is married, and has four children.

Lars Petterson, second engineer of the *Fram*, was born in 1860, at Borre, near Landskrona, in Sweden, of Norwegian parents. He is a fully qualified smith and machinist, in which capacity he has served in the Norwegian Navy for several years. Is married and has children.

Frederik Hjalmar Johansen, Lieutenant in the Reserve, was born at Skien in 1867, and matriculated at the University in 1886. In 1891-92 he went to the Military School and became a supernumerary officer. He was so eager to take part in the expedition that, as no other post could be found for him, he accepted that of stoker.

Peter Leonard Henriksen, harpooner, was born in Balsfjord, near Tromsö, in 1859. From childhood he has been a sailor, and from fourteen years old has gone voyages to the Arctic Sea as harpooner and skipper. In 1888 he was shipwrecked off Novaya Zemlya in the sloop *Enigheden*, from Christiansund. He is married and has four children.

Bernhard Nordahl was born in Christiania in 1862. At the age of fourteen he entered the Navy and advanced to be a gunner. Subsequently he has done a little of everything, and among other things has worked as an electrical engineer. He had charge of the dynamo and electric installation on board, acted, moreover, as stoker, and for a time assisted in the meteorological observations. He is married and has five children.

Ivar Otto Irgens Mogstad was born at Aure in Nordmöre in 1856. In 1877 passed his examination as first assistant, and from 1882 onwards was one of the head keepers at the Gaustad Lunatic Asylum.

Bernt Bentzen, born in 1860, went to sea for several years. In 1890 he passed his mate's examination, since which he has sailed as mate in several voyages to the Arctic Sea. We engaged him at Tromsö just as we were starting. It was 8.30 when he came on board to speak to me, and at 10 o'clock the *Fram* set sail.

Chapter 3

The Start

"So travel I north to the gloomy abode
That the sun never shines on —
There is no day."

IT WAS midsummer day. A dull, gloomy day; and with it came the inevitable leave-taking. The door closed behind me. For the last time I left my home, and went alone down the garden to the beach where the *Fram*'s little petroleum launch pitilessly awaited me. Behind me lay all I held dear in life. And what before me? How many years would pass ere I should see it all again? What would I not have given at that moment to be able to turn back; but up at the window little Liv was sitting clapping her hands. Happy child, little do you know what life is — how strangely mingled and how full of change. Like an arrow the little boat sped over Lysaker Bay, bearing me on the first stage of a journey on which life itself if not more, was staked.

At last everything was in readiness. The hour had arrived towards which the persevering labour of years had been incessantly bent, and with it the feeling that everything being provided and completed, responsibility might be thrown aside and the weary brain at last find rest. The *Fram* lies yonder at Pepperviken, impatiently panting and waiting for the signal, when the launch comes puffing past Dyna and runs alongside. The deck is closely packed with people come to bid a last farewell; and now all must leave the ship. Then the *Fram* weighs anchor, and, heavily laden and moving slowly, makes the tour of the little creek. The quays are black with crowds of people waving their hats and handkerchiefs. But silently and quietly the *Fram* heads towards the fjord, steers slowly past Bygdö and Dyna out on her unknown path, while little nimble craft, steamers, and pleasure-boats, swarm around her. Peaceful and snug lay the villas along, the shore behind their veils of foliage, just as they ever seemed of old. "Fair is the

Last farewells, Fridtjof Nansen second from the left.

child this last bit before leaving the ship. And then came the farewell hand-shake; but few words were spoken, and they got into the boat, he, my brothers, and a friend, while the *Fram* glided ahead with her heavy motion, and the bonds that united us were severed. It was sad and strange to see this last relic of home in that little skiff on the wide blue surface, Anker's cutter behind, and Laurvik further in the distance. I almost think a tear glittered on that fine old face as he stood erect in the boat and shouted a farewell to us and to the *Fram*. Do you think he does not love the vessel? That he believes in her I know well. So we gave him the first salute from the *Fram*'s guns — a worthier inauguration they could not well have had.

Full speed ahead, and in the calm, bright summer weather, while the setting sun shed his beams over the land, the *Fram* stood out towards the blue sea, to get its first roll in the long heaving swell. They stood up in the boat and watched us for long.

We bore along the coast in good weather, past Christiansund. The next evening, June 27th, we were off the Naze. I sat up and chatted with Scott-Hansen till late in the night. He acted as captain on the trip from Christiania to

Trondhjem, where Sverdrup was to join, after having accompanied his family to Steenkiaer. As we sat there in the chart-house and let the hours slip by while we pushed on in the ever increasing swell, all at once a sea burst open the door and poured in. We rushed out on deck. The ship rolled like a log, the seas broke in over the rails on both sides, and one by one up came all the crew. I feared most lest the slender davits which supported the long-boats should give way, and the boats themselves should go overboard, perhaps carrying away with them a lot of the rigging. Then twenty-five empty paraffin casks which were lashed on deck broke loose, washed backwards and forwards, and gradually tilled with water; so that the outlook was not altogether agreeable. But it was worst of all when the piles of reserve timber, spars, and planks, began the same dance, and threatened to break the props under the boats. It was an anxious hour. Sea-sick I stood on the bridge, occupying myself in alternately making libations to Neptune and trembling for the safety of the boats and the men, who were trying to make snug what they could forward on deck. I often saw only a hotch-potch of sea, drifting planks, arms, legs, and empty barrels. Now a green sea poured over us and knocked a man off his legs so that the water deluged him; now I saw the lads jumping over hurtling spars and barrels, so as not to get their feet crushed between them. There was not a dry thread on them. Juell, who lay asleep in the "Grand Hotel," as we called one of the long-boats, awoke to hear the sea roaring under him like a cataract. I met him at the cabin door as he came running down. It was no longer safe there, he thought; best to save one's rags — he had a bundle under his arm. Then he set off forward to secure his sea-chest, which was floating about on the fore-deck, and dragged it hurriedly aft, while one heavy sea after another swept over him. Once the *Fram* buried her bows and shipped a sea over the forecastle. There was one fellow clinging to the anchor-davits over the frothing water. It was poor Juell again. We were hard put to it to secure our goods and chattels. We had to throw all our good paraffin casks overboard, and one prime timber baulk after another went the same way, while I stood and watched them sadly as they floated off. The rest of the deck cargo was shifted aft on to the half-deck. I am afraid the shares in the expedition stood rather low at this moment. Then all at once, when things were about at their worst with us, we sighted a bark looming out of the fog ahead. There it lay with royals and all sails set, as snugly and peacefully as if nothing was the matter, rocking gently on the sea. It made one feel almost savage to look at it. Visions of the Flying Dutchman and other devilry fashed through my mind.

Terrible disaster in the cook's galley! Mogstad goes in and sees the whole

Sigurd Scott-Hansen

wall sprinkled over with dark red stains — rushes off to Nordahl, and says he believes Juell has shot himself through despair at the insufferable heat he complains so about. "Great revolver disaster on board the *Fram*!..." On close inspection, however, the stains appeared to proceed from a box of chocolate that had upset in the cupboard.

Owing to the fog we dared not go too near land, so kept out to sea, till at last, towards morning, the fog lifted somewhat, and the pilot found his bearings between Farsund and Hummerdus. We put into Lister Fjord, intending to anchor there and get into better sea trim; but as the weather improved we went on our way. It was not till the afternoon that we steered into Ekersund, owing to thick weather and a stiff breeze, and anchored in Hovland's Bay, where our pilot, Hovland,[16] lived. Next morning the boat davits, etc., were put in good working order. The *Fram*, however, was too heavily laden to be at all easy in a seaway; but this we could not alter. What we had we must keep, and if we only got everything on deck shipshape, and properly lashed, the sea could not do us much harm however rough it might be; for we knew well enough that ship and rigging would hold out.

It was late in the evening of the last day of June when we rounded Kvarven, and stood in for Bergen in the gloom of the sullen night. Next morning when I came on deck, Vågen lay clear and bright in the sun, all the ships being gaily decked out with bunting from topmast to deck. The sun was holding high festival in the sky — Ulriken, Flöiren and Lövstakken sparkled and glittered, and greeted me as of old. It is a marvellous place, that old Hanseatic town!

In the evening I was to give a lecture, but arrived half an hour too late. For just as I was dressing to go, a number of bills poured in, and if I was to leave the town as a solvent man I must needs pay them, and so the public perforce had to wait. But the worst of it was that the saloon was full of those everlastingly inquisitive tourists. I could hear a whole company of them besieging my cabin door while I was dressing, declaring "they must shake hands with the doctor!"[17] One of them actually peeped in through the ventilator at me, my secretary told me afterwards. A nice sight she must have seen, the lovely creature! Report says she drew her head back very quickly. Indeed, at every place where we put in we were looked on somewhat as wild animals in a menagerie. For they peeped unceremoniously at us in our berths as if we had been bears and lions in a den, and we could hear them loudly disputing among themselves as to who was who, and whether those nearest and dearest to us whose portraits hung on the walls could be called pretty or not. When I had finished my toilette I opened the door cautiously, made a rush through the gaping company. "There he is, there he is!"[18] they called to each other as they tumbled up the steps after me. It was no use, I was on the quay and in the carriage long before they had reached the deck.

At 8 o'clock there was a great banquet, many fine speeches, good fare and excellent wine, pretty ladies, music, and dancing till far into the night.

Next morning at 11 o'clock — it was Sunday — in bright sunshiny weather, we stood northwards over Bergen Fjord, many friends accompanying us. It was a lovely, never-to-be-forgotten summer day. In Herlö Fjord, right out by the skerries, they parted from us, amid wavings of hats and pocket-handkerchiefs;

The *Fram* leaving Bergen.

we could see the little harbour boat for a long while with its black cloud of smoke on the sparkling surface of the water. Outside, the sea rolled in the hazy sunlight; and within lay the flat Mangerland full of memories for me of zoological investigations in fair weather and foul, years and years ago. Here it was that one of Norway's most famous naturalists, a lonely pastor far removed from the outer world, made his great discoveries. Here I myself first groped my way along the narrow path of zoological research.

It was a wondrous evening. The lingering flush of vanished day suffused the northern sky, while the moon hung large and round over the mountains behind us. Ahead lay Alden and Kinn, like a fairyland rising up from the sea. Tired as I was, I could not seek my berth; I must drink in all this loveliness in deep refreshing draughts. It was like balm to the soul after all the turmoil and friction with crowds of strangers.

So we went on our way, mostly in fair weather, occasionally in fog and rain, through sounds and between islands, northwards along the coast of Norway. A glorious land — I wonder if another fairway like this is to be found the whole world over? Those never-to-be-forgotten mornings, when nature wakens to life, wreaths of mist glittering like silver over the mountains, their tops soaring above the mist like islands out of the sea! Then the day gleaming over the dazzling white snowpeaks! And the evenings, and the sunsets with the pale moon overhead, white mountains and islands lay hushed and dreamlike as a youthful longing! Here, and there past homely little havens with houses around them set in smiling green trees. — Ah! those snug homes in the lee of the skerries awake a longing for life and warmth in the breast. You may shrug your shoulders as much as you like at the beauties of nature, but it is a fine thing for a people to have a fair land, be it never so poor. Never did this seem clearer to me than now when I was leaving it.

Every now and then a hurrah from land — at one time from a troop of children, at another from grown-up people, but mostly from wondering peasants who gaze long at the strange-looking ship and muse over its enigmatic destination. And men and women on board sloops and ten-oared boats stand up in their red shirts that glow in the sunlight, and rest on their oars to look at us. Steamboats crowded with people came out from the towns we passed to greet us and bid us God-speed on our way with music, songs, and cannon salutes. The great tourist steamboats dipped flags to us and fired salutes, and the smaller craft did the same. It is embarrassing and oppressive to be the object of homage like this before anything has been accomplished. There is an old saying:

"At eve the day shall be praised,
The wife when she is burnt,
The sword when tried,
The woman when married,
The ice when passed over,
Ale when drunk."

Most touching was the interest and sympathy with which these poor fisher-folk and peasants greeted us. It often set me wondering. I felt they followed us with fervent eagerness. I remember one day — it was north in Helgeland — an old woman was standing waving and waving to us on a bare

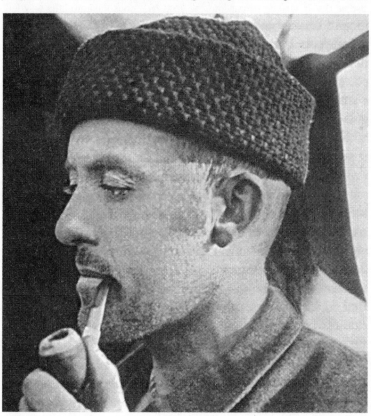

Ivar Mogstad.

crag. Her cottage lay some distance inland. "I wonder if it can really be us she is waving to," I said to the pilot, who was standing beside me. "You may be sure it is," was the answer. "But how can she know who we are?" "Oh! they know all about the *Fram* up here, in every cabin, and they will be on the look-out for you as you come back, I can tell you," he answered. Ay, truly, it is a responsible task we are undertaking, when the whole nation are with us like this. What if the thing should turn out a huge disappointment!

In the evening I would sit and look around — lonely huts lay scattered here and there on points and islets. Here the Norwegian people wear out their lives in the struggle with the rocks, in the struggle with the sea; and it is this people that is sending us out into the great hazardous unknown; the very folk who stand there in their fishing-boats and look wonderingly after the *Fram* as she slowly and heavily steams along on her northward course. Many of them wave their sou'-westers and shout "Hurrah!" Others have barely time to gape at us in wonderment. In on the point are a troop of women waving and shouting, outside a few boats with ladies in light summer dresses and gentlemen at the oars entertaining them with small-talk, as they wave their parasols and pocket-handkerchiefs. Yes, it is they who are sending us out. It is not a cheering thought. Not one of them, probably, knows what they are paying their money for. Maybe they have heard it is a glorious enterprise; but why? to what end? Are we not defrauding them? But their eyes are rivetted on the ship, and perhaps there dawns before their minds a momentary vision of a new and inconceivable world, with aspirations after a something of which they know naught... And here on board are men who are leaving wife and children behind them. How sad has been the separation — what longing, what yearning await them in the coming years! And it is not for profit they do it. For honour and glory then? These may be scant enough. It is the same thirst for achievement, the same craving to get beyond the limits of the known which inspired this people in the Saga times, that is stirring in them again to-day. In spite of all our toil for subsistence, in spite of all our "peasant politics," sheer utilitarianism is perhaps not so dominant among us after all.

As time was precious I did not, as originally intended, put in at Trondhjem, but stopped at Beian, where Sverdrup joined us. Here Professor Brögger also came on board, to accompany us as far as Tromsö.

Here, too, our doctor received three monstrous chests with the medicine supply, a gift from Apothecary Bruun of Trondhjem.

And so on towards the north along the lovely coast of Nordland. We

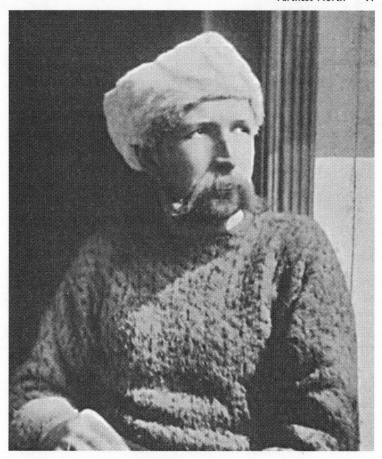

Adolf Juell, steward and cook.

stopped at one or two places to take dried fish on board as provision for the dogs. Past Torghatten, the Seven Sisters, and Hestemanden, past Lovunen — and Traenen, far out — yonder in the sea, past Lofoten and all the other lovely places — each bold gigantic form wilder and more beautiful than the last. It is unique — a fairyland — a land of dreams. We felt afraid to go on too fast — for fear of missing something.

On July 12th we arrived at Tromsö, where we were to take in coal and other things, such as reindeer cloaks "komager" (a sort of Lapp moccasin), Finn shoes, "senne" grass, dried reindeer flesh, etc., etc., all of which had been procured by that indefatigable friend of the expedition, Advocate Mack. Tromsö gave us a cold reception — a north-westerly gale, with driving snow and sleet. Mountains, plains, and house-roofs were all covered with snow down to the water's edge. It was the very bitterest July day I ever experienced. The people there said they could not remember such a July. Perhaps they were afraid the place would come into disrepute, for in a town where they hold snow-shoe races on Midsummer Day one may be prepared for anything in the way of weather.

In Tromsö the next day a new member of the expedition was engaged, Bernt Bentzen — a stout fellow to look at. He originally intended accompanying us only as far as Yugor Strait, but in the end he went the whole voyage with us, and proved a great acquisition, being not only a capital seaman, but a cheerful and amusing comrade.

After a stay of two days we again set out. On the night of the 16th, east of the North Cape or Magerö, we met with such a nasty sea, and shipped so much water on deck, that we put into Kjöllefjord to adjust our cargo better by shifting the coal and making a few other changes. We worked at this the whole of two days, and made everything clear for the voyage to Novaya Zemlya. I had at first thought of taking on board a fresh supply of coal at Vardö, but as we were already deeply laden, and the *Urania* was to meet us at Yugor Strait with coal, we thought it best to be contented with what we had already got on board, as we might expect bad weather in crossing the White Sea and Barents Sea. At ten o'clock in the evening we weighed anchor and reached Vardö next evening, where we met with a magnificent reception. There was a band of music on the pier, the fjord teemed with boats, flags waved on every hand, and salutes were fired. The people had been waiting for us ever since the previous evening, we were told — some of them, indeed, coming from Vadsö — and they had seized the opportunity to get up a subscription to provide a big drum for the town band, the "North Pole." And here we were entertained to a sumptuous banquet, with speeches and champagne flowing in streams, ere we bade Norway our last farewell.

The last thing that had now to be done for the *Fram* was to have her bottom cleaned of mussels and weeds, so that she might be able to make the best speed possible. This work was done by divers, who were readily placed at our service by the local inspector of the Government Harbour Department.

But our own bodies also claimed one last civilised feast of purification, before entering on a life of savagery. The bath-house of the town is a small timber building. The bath-room itself is low, and provided with shelves where you

Bernt Bentzen.

lie down and are parboiled with hot steam, which is constantly kept up by water being thrown on the glowing hot stones of an awful oven, worthy of hell itself; while all the time young Quaen (lasses) flog you with birch twigs. After that you are rubbed down, washed and dried delightfully — everything being well-managed, clean and comfortable. I wonder whether old father Mahomet has set up a bath like this in his paradise.

Chapter 4

Farewell to Norway

I FELT in a strange mood as I sat up the last night writing letters and telegrams. We had bidden farewell to our excellent pilot, Johan Hagensen, who had piloted us from Bergen, and now we were only the thirteen members of the expedition, together with my secretary, Christofersen, who had accompanied us so far, and was to go on with us as far as Yugor Strait. Everything was so calm and still, save for the scraping of the pen that was sending off a farewell to friends at home.

All the men were asleep below.

The last telegram was written, and I sent my secretary ashore with it. It was 3 o'clock in the morning when he returned, and I called Sverdrup up and one or two others. We weighed anchor, and stood out of the harbour in the silence of the morning. The town still lay wrapped in sleep, everything looked so peaceful and lovely all around, with the exception of a little stir of awakening toil on board one single steamer in the harbour. A sleepy fisherman stuck his head up out of the half-deck of his ten-oared boat, and stared at us as we steamed past the breakwater; and on the revenue cutter outside there was a man fishing in that early morning light.

This last impression of Norway was just the right one for us to carry away with us. Such beneficent peace and calm; such a rest for the thoughts; no hubbub and turmoil of people with their hurrahs and salutes. The masts in the harbour, the house roofs and chimneys stood out against the cool morning sky. Just then the sun broke through the mist, and smiled over the shore — rugged, bare, and weatherworn in the hazy morning, but still lovely-dotted here

First ice.

and there with tiny houses and boats, and all Norway lay behind it...

While the *Fram* was slowly and quietly working her way out to sea, towards our distant goal, I stood and watched the land gradually fading away on the horizon. I wonder what will happen to her and to us, before we again see Norway rising up over the sea?

But a fog soon came on, and obscured everything. And through fog, nothing but fog, we steamed away for four days without stopping, until, when I came on deck on the morning of the 25th of July, behold clear weather! The sun was shining in a cloudless sky, the bright blue sea was heaving with a gentle swell. Again it was good to be a living being, and to drink in the peacefulness of the sea in long draughts. Towards noon we sighted Goose Land on Novaya Zemlya, and stood in towards it. Guns and cartridges were got ready, and we looked forward with joyful anticipation to roast goose and other game; but we had gone but a short distance when the grey woolly fog from the south-east came up and enveloped us. Again we were shut off from the world around us. It was scarcely prudent to make for land, so we set our course eastwards towards Yugor Strait; but a head wind soon compelled us to beat up under steam and sail, which we went on doing for a couple of days, plunged in a world of fog. That endless, stubborn fog of the Arctic Sea! When it lowers its curtain, and shuts out the blue above and the blue below, and everything becomes a damp grey mist, day in and day out, then all the vigour and elasticity of the soul is needed to save one from being stifled in its clammy embrace. Fog, and nothing but fog, wherever we turn our eyes. It condenses on the rigging, and drips down on every tiniest spot on deck. It lodges on your clothes, and finally wets you through and through. — It settles down on the mind and spirits, and everything becomes one uniform grey.

On the evening of July 27th, while still fogbound, we quite unexpectedly met with ice; a mere strip, indeed, which we easily passed through, but it boded ill. In the night we met with more — a broader strip this time, which also we passed through. But next morning I was called up with the information that there was thick, old ice ahead. Well, if ice difficulties were to begin so soon, it would be a bad look out indeed. Such are the chill surprises that the arctic Sea has more than enough of. I dressed and was up in the crow's-nest in a twinkling. The ice lay extended everywhere, as far as the eye could reach through the fog, which had lifted a little. There was no small quantity of ice, but it was tolerably open, and there was nothing for it but to be true to our watch-word and "gå Fram" — push onwards. For a good while we picked our way. But now it began to lie closer with large floes every here and there, and at the same time the fog grew denser, and we could not see our way at all. To go ahead in difficult ice and in a fog is not very prudent, for it is impossible to tell just where you are going, and you are apt to be set fast before you know where you are. So we had to stop and wait. But still the fog grew ever denser, while the ice did the same. Our hopes meanwhile rose and fell, but mostly the latter I think. To encounter so much ice already in these waters, where at this time of year the sea is, as a rule, quite free from it, boded anything but good. Already at Tromsö and Vardö we had heard bad news; the White Sea, they said, had only been clear of ice a very short time, and a boat that had tried to reach Yugor Strait had had to turn back because of the ice. Neither were our anticipations of the Kara Sea altogether cheerful. What might we not expect there? For the *Urania* with our coal, too, this ice was a bad business; for it would be unable to make its way through unless it had found navigable water further south along the Russian coast.

Just as our prospects were at their darkest, and we were preparing to seek a way back out of the ice which kept getting ever denser, the joyful tidings came that the fog was lifting, and that clear water was visible ahead to the east on the other side of the ice. After forcing our way ahead for some hours between the heavy floes, we were once more in open water. This first bout with the ice, however, showed us plainly what an excellent ice-boat the *Fram* was. It was a royal pleasure to work her ahead through difficult ice. She twisted and turned "like a ball on a platter." No channel between the floes so winding and awkward but she could get through it. But it is hard work for the helmsman. "Hard a-starboard! Hard a-port Steady! Hard a-starboard again!" goes on incessantly without so much as a breathing-space. And he rattles the wheel round, the sweat pours off him, and round it goes again like a spinning-wheel. And the ship swings round, and wriggles her way forward among the floes without touching, if there is only just an opening wide enough for her to slip through; and where there is none she drives full tilt at the ice, with her heavy plunge, runs her sloping bows up on it, treads it under her and bursts the floes asunder. And how strong she is too! Even when she goes full speed at a floe, not a creak, not a sound is to be heard in her; if she gives a little shake it is all she does.

On Saturday, July 29th, we again headed eastwards towards Yugor Strait as fast as sails and steam could take us. We had open sea ahead, the weather was fine and the wind fair. Next morning we came under the south side of Dolgoi or Langoia, as the Norwegian whalers call it, where we had to stand to the northward. On reaching the north of the island we again bore eastwards. Here I descried from the crow's-nest, as far as I could make out, several islands which are not given on the charts. They lay a little to the east of Langoia.

It was now pretty clear that the *Urania* had not made her way through the ice. While we were sitting in the saloon in the forenoon talking about it, a cry was heard from deck that the sloop was in sight. It was joyful news, but the joy was of no long duration. The next moment we heard she had a crow's-nest on her mast, so she was doubtless a sealer. When she sighted us, she bore off to the south, probably fearing that we were a Russian war-ship or something equally bad. So, as we had no particular interest in her, we let her go on her way in peace.

Later in the day we neared Yugor Strait. We kept a sharp look-out for land ahead, but none could be seen. Hour after hour passed as we glided onwards at good speed, but still no land. Certainly it would not be high land, but nevertheless this was strange. Yes — there it lies like a low shadow over the horizon on the port bow. It is land — it is Vaigats Island. Soon we sight more of it — abaft the beam, then too the mainland on the south side of the strait.

More and more of it comes in sight — it increases rapidly. All low and level land, no heights, no variety, no apparent opening for the strait ahead. Thence it stretches away to the north and south in a soft low curve. This is the threshold of Asia's boundless plains, so different from all we have been used to.

We now glided into the strait with its low rocky shores on either side. The strata of the rocks lie endways, and are crumpled and broken, but on the surface everything is level and smooth. No one who travels over the flat green plains and tundras would have any idea of the mysteries and upheavals that lie hidden beneath the sward. Here once upon a time were mountains and valleys, now all worn away and washed out.

We looked out for Khabarova. On the north side of the sound there was a mark; a shipwrecked sloop lay on the shore, it was a Norwegian sealer. The wreck of a smaller vessel lay by its side. On the south side was a flag-staff, and on it a red flag; Khabarova must then lie behind it. At last one or two buildings or shanties appeared behind a promontory, and soon the whole place lay exposed to view, consisting of tents and a few houses. On a little jutting-out point close by us was a large red building, with white door frames, of a very homelike appearance. It was indeed a Norwegian warehouse which Sibiriakoff had imported from Finmarken. But here the water was shallow, and we had to proceed carefully for fear of running aground. We kept heaving the lead incessantly — we had 5 fathoms of water, and then 4, then not much more than we needed, and then it shelved to a little over 3 fathoms. This was rather too close work, so we stood out again a bit to wait till we got a little nearer the place before drawing in to the shore.

A boat was now seen slowly approaching from the land. A man of middle height, with an open kindly face and reddish beard, came on board. He might have been a Norwegian from his appearance. I went to meet him, and asked him in German if he was Trontheim. Yes, he was. After him there came a number of strange figures clad in heavy robes of reindeer skin, which nearly touched the deck. On their heads they wore peculiar "baschlik"-like caps of reincalf skin, beneath which strongly-marked bearded faces showed forth, such as might well have belonged to old Norwegian Vikings. The whole scene, indeed, called up in my mind a picture of the Viking Age, of expeditions to Gardarike and Bjarmeland. They were fine stalwart-looking fellows, these Russian traders, who barter with the natives, giving them brandy in exchange for bearskins, sealskins, and other valuables, and who, when once they have a hold on a man, keep him in such a state of dependence that he can scarcely call his soul his own. "Es ist

O. Chrstofersen and A. Trontheim.

eine alte Geschichte, doch wird sie immer neu." Soon, too, the Samoyedes came flocking on board, pleasant-featured people of the broad Asiatic type. Of course it was only the men who came.

The first question I asked Trontheim was about the ice. He replied that Yugor Strait had been open a long while, and that he had been expecting our arrival every day since then with ever-increasing anxiety. The natives and the Russians had begun to jeer at him as time went on, and no *Fram* was to be seen; but now he had his revenge and was all sunshine. He thought the state of the ice in the Kara Sea would be favourable; some Samoyedes had said so, who had been seal hunting near the eastern entrance of the Strait a day or two previously. This was not very much to build upon, certainly, but still sufficient to make us regret that we had not got there before. Then we spoke of the *Urania*, of which no one, of course, had seen anything. No ship had put in there for some time, except the sealing sloop we had passed in the morning. Next we enquired about the dogs and learned that everything was all right with them. To make sure, Trontheim had purchased forty dogs, though I had only asked for thirty. Five of these, from various mishaps, had died during their journey — one had been bitten to death, two had got hung fast and had been strangled while passing through a forest, etc., etc. One, moreover, had been taken ill a few days before, and was still on the sick list; but the remaining thirty-four were in good condition; we could hear them howling and barking. During this conversation we had come as near to Khabarova as we dared venture, and at seven in the evening cast anchor in about 3 fathoms of water.

Over the supper table Trontheim told us his adventures. On the way from Sopva and Ural to the Yechora he heard that there was a dog epidemic in that locality; consequently he did not think it advisable to go to the Yechora as he had intended, but laid his course instead direct from Ural to Yugor Strait. Towards the end of the journey the snow had disappeared, and, in company with a reindeer caravan, he drove on with his dogs over the bare plain, stocks and stones and all, using the sledges none the less. The Samoyedes and natives of Northern Siberia have no vehicles but sledges. The summer sledge is somewhat higher than the winter sledge, in order that it may not hang fast upon stones and stumps. As may be supposed, however, summer sledging is anything but smooth work.

After supper we went ashore, and were soon on the flat beach of Khabarova, the Russians and Samoyedes regarding us with the utmost curiosity. The first objects to attract our attention were the two churches — an old

The new and old church at Khabarova.

venerable-looking wooden shed of an oblong rectangular form, and an octagonal pavilion, not unlike many summer-houses or garden pavilions that I have seen at home. How far the divergence between the two forms of religion was indicated in the two mathematical figures I am unable to say. It might be that the simplicity of the old faith was expressed in the simple, four-sided building, while the rites and ceremonies of the other were typified in the octagonal form, with its double number of corners to stumble against. Then we must go and see the monastery — "Skit," as it was called — where the six monks had lived, or rather, died, from what people said was scurvy, probably helped out by alcohol. It lay over against the new church, and resembled an ordinary low Russian timber house. The priest and his assistants were living there now, and had asked Trontheim to take up his quarters with them. Trontheim, therefore, invited us in, and we soon found ourselves in a couple of comfortable log-built rooms with open fire-places like our Norwegian "peis."

After this we proceeded to the dog-camp, which was situated on a plain at some distance from the houses and tents. As we approached it the howling and barking kept getting worse and worse. When a short distance off, we were surprised to see a Norwegian flag on the top of a pole. Trontheim's face beamed with joy as our eyes fell on it. It was, he said, under the same flag as our expedition that his had been undertaken. There stood the dogs tied up, making a deafening clamour. Many of them appeared to be well-bred animals — long-haired, snow-white, with up-standing ears and pointed muzzles. With their gentle, good-natured looking faces they at once ingratiated themselves in our affections. Some of them more resembled a fox, and had shorter coats, while others were black or spotted. Evidently they were of different races, and some of them betrayed by their drooping ears a strong admixture of European blood. After having duly admired the ravenous way in which they swallowed raw fish (gwiniad), not without a good deal of snarling and wrangling we took a walk inland to a lake close by in search of game; but we only found an Arctic gull with its brood. A channel had been dug from this lake to convey drinking water to Khabarova. According to what Trontheim told us, this was the work of the monks — about the only work, probably, they had ever taken in hand. The soil here was a soft clay, and the channel was narrow and shallow, like a roadside ditch or gutter; the work could not have been very arduous. On the hill above the lake stood the flag-staff which we had noticed on our arrival. It had been erected by the excellent Trontheim to bid us welcome, and on the flag itself, as I afterwards discovered by chance, was the word "Vorwarts." Trontheim had been told that was the name of our ship, so he was not a little disappointed when he came on board to find it was *Fram* instead. I consoled him, however, by telling him they both meant the same thing, and that his welcome was just as well meant, whether written in German or Norwegian. Trontheim told me afterwards that he was by descent a Norwegian, his father having been a ship's captain from Trondhjem, and his mother, an Esthonian, settled at Riga. His father had been much at sea, and had died early, so the son had not learnt Norwegian. Naturally our first and foremost object was to learn all we could about the ice in the Arctic Sea. We had determined to push on as soon as possible; but we must have the boiler put in order first, while sundry pipes and valves in the engine wanted seeing to. As it would take several days to do this, Sverdrup, Peter Henriksen, and I set out next morning in our little petroleum launch to the eastern opening of the Yugor Strait, to see with our own eyes what might be the condition of the ice to the eastward. It was 28 miles thither. A quantity of ice was drifting through the strait from the east, and, as there was a northerly breeze, we at once turned our course northwards

Peter Henriksen.

to get under the lee of the north shore where the water was more open. I had the rather thankless task of acting as helmsman and engineer at one and the same time. The boat went on like a little hero and made about six knots. Everything looked bright. But alas! good fortune seldom lasts long, especially in the case of petroleum launches. A defect in the circulation pump soon stopped the engine, and we could only go for short distances at a time, till we reached the north shore, where, after two hours' hard work, I got the engines so far in order as to be able to continue our journey to the north-east through the sound between the drifting floes. We got on pretty well, except for an interruption every now and then when the engine took it into its head to come to a standstill. It caused a good deal of merriment when the stalwart Peter turned the crank to set her off again, and the engine gave a start, so as nearly to pull his arms out of joint, and upset him head over heels in the boat. Every now and then a flock of long-tailed duck (*harelda glacialis*) or other birds came whizzing by us, one or two of them invariably falling to our guns.

We had kept along the Vaigats shore, but now crossed over towards the south side of the strait. When about the middle of the channel I was startled by all at once seeing the bottom grow light under us, and had nearly run the boat on a shoal of which no one knew anything. There was scarcely more than 2 or 3 feet of water, and the current ran over it like a rapid river. Shoals and sunken rocks abound there on every hand, especially on the south side of the strait, and it required great care to navigate a vessel through it. Near the eastern mouth of the strait we put into a little creek, dragged the boat up on the beach, and then taking our guns made for some high-lying land we had noticed. We tramped along over the same undulating plain-land with low ridges as we had seen everywhere round the Yugor Strait. A brownish-green carpet of moss and grass spread over the plain, bestrewn with flowers of rare beauty. During the long, cold Siberian winter the snow lies in a thick mass over the tundra; but no sooner does the sun get the better of it than hosts of tiny northern flowers burst their way up through the last disappearing coating of snow, and open their modest calices, blushing in the radiant summer day that bathes the plain in its splendour. Saxifrages with large blooms, pale yellow mountain poppies (*papaver nudicaule*) stand in bright clusters, and here and there with bluish forget-me-nots and white cloud-berry flowers; in some boggy hollows the cotton-grass spreads its wavy down carpet, while in other spots small forests of blue-bells softly tingle in the wind on their upright stalks. These flowers are not at all brilliant specimens, being in most cases not more than a couple of inches high, but they are all the more exquisite on that account, and in such surroundings their beauty is singularly attractive. While the eye vainly seeks for a resting place over the boundless plain, these modest blooms smile at you, and take the fancy captive.

And over these mighty tundra-plains of Asia, stretching infinitely onwards from one sky-line to the other, the nomad wanders with his reindeer-herds, a glorious, free life! Where he wills he pitches his tent, his reindeer around him; and at his will again he goes on his way. I almost envied him. He has no goal to struggle towards, no anxieties to endure — he has merely to live. I well-nigh wished that I could live his peaceful life, with wife and child, on these boundless, open plains, unfettered, happy.

After we had proceeded a short distance, we became aware of a white object sitting on a stone heap beneath a little ridge, and soon noticed more in other directions. They looked quite ghostly as they sat there silent and motionless. With the help of my field-glass I discovered that they were snow-owls. We set out after them, but they took care to keep out of the range of a fowling-piece. Sverdrup, however, shot one or two with his rifle. There was a great number of them; I could count as many as eight or ten at once. They sat motionless on tussocks of grass or stones, watching, no doubt, for lemmings, of which, judging from their tracks, there must have been quantities. We did not see any, however.

From the tops of the ridges we could see over the Kara Sea to the north-east. Everywhere ice could be descried through the telescope, far on the horizon — ice, too, that seemed tolerably close and massive. But between it and the coast there was open water, stretching like a wide channel, as far as the eye could reach, to the south-east. This was all we could make out, but it was in reality all we wanted. There seemed to be no doubt that we could make our way forward, and, well satisfied, we returned to our boat. Here we lighted a fire of driftwood, and made some glorious coffee.

As the coffee-kettle was singing over a splendid fire, and we stretched ourselves at full length on the slope by its side and smoked a quiet pipe, Sverdrup made himself thoroughly comfortable, and told us one story after another. However gloomy a country might look, however desolate, if only there were plenty of driftwood on the beach, so that one could make a right good fire, the bigger the better, then his eyes would glisten with delight — that land was his El Dorado. So from that time forth he conceived a high opinion of the Siberian coast — a right good place for wintering, he called it.

On our way back we ran at full speed on to a sunken rock. After a bump or two, the boat slid over it; but just as she was slipping off on the other side, the propeller struck on the rock, so that the stern gave a bound into the air while the engine whizzed round at a tearing rate. It all happened in a second, before I had time to stop her. Unluckily one screw blade was broken off, but we drove ahead with the other as best we could. Our progress was certainly rather uneven, but for all that we managed to get on somehow.

Towards morning we drew near the *Fram*, passing two Samoyedes who had drawn their boat up on an ice-floe and were looking out for seals. I wonder what they thought when they saw our tiny boat shoot by them without steam, sails or oars. We, at all events, looked down on these "poor savages" with the self-satisfied compassion of Europeans, as, comfortably seated, we dashed past them.

But pride comes before a fall! We had not gone far when — whirr, whirr, whirr — a fearful racket! bits of broken steel springs whizzed past my ears, and the whole machine came to a dead stop. It was not to be moved either forwards or backwards. The vibration of the one-bladed propeller had brought the lead line little by little within the range of the flywheel, and all at once the whole line was drawn into the machinery, and got so dreadfully entangled in it that we had to take the whole thing to pieces to get it clear once more. So we had to endure the humiliation of rowing back to our proud ship, for whose fleshpots we had long been an-hungered.

The net result of the day was: tolerably good news about the Kara Sea; forty birds, principally geese and long-tailed ducks; one seal; and a disabled boat. Amundsen and I, however, soon put this in complete repair again — but in so doing I fear I forfeited for ever and a day the esteem of the Russians and Samoyedes in these parts. Some of them had been on board in the morning and seen me hard at work in the boat in my shirt sleeves, face and bare arms dirty with oil and other messes. They went on shore afterwards to Trontheim, and said that I could not possibly be a great person, slaving away like any other workman on board, and looking worse than a common rough. Trontheim, unfortunately, knew of nothing that could be said in my excuse; there is no fighting against facts.

In the evening some of us went on shore to try the dogs. Trontheim picked out ten of them, and harnessed them to a Samoyede sledge. No sooner were we ready and I had taken my seat, than the team caught sight of a wretched strange dog that had come near, and off dashed dogs, sledge, and my valuable person after the poor creature. There was a tremendous uproar; all the ten tumbled over each other like wild wolves, biting and tearing wherever they could catch hold; blood ran in streams, and the culprit howled pitiably, while Trontheim tore round like a madman, striking right and left with his long switch. Samoyedes and Russians came screaming from all sides. I sat passively on the sledge in the middle of it all, dumb with fright, and it was ever so long before it occurred to me that there was perhaps something for me too to do. With a horrible yell I flung myself on some of the worst fighters, got hold of

Anton Amundsen, first engineer.

them by the neck, and managed to give the culprit time to get away.

Our team had got badly mixed up during the battle, and it took some time to disentangle them. At last everything was once more ready for the start. Trontheim cracked his whip, and called, "Pr-r-r-r, pr-r-r-r," and off we went at a wild gallop, over grass, clay, and stones, until it seemed as if they were going to carry us right across the lagoon at the mouth of the river. I kicked and pulled in with all my might, but was dragged along, and it was all that Trontheim and I with our united strength could do to stop them just as they were going into the water, although we shouted "Sass, sass," so that it echoed over the whole of Khabarova. But at last we got our team turned in another direction, and off we set again merrily at such a pace that I had enough to do to hold on. It was an extraordinary summer ride; and it gave us a high opinion of the dogs' strength, seeing how easily they drew two men over this, to put it mildly, bad sledging ground. We went on board again well satisfied, also the richer, by a new experience; having learnt that dog-driving, at any rate to begin with, requires much patience.

Siberian dog-harness is remarkably primitive. A thick rope or a strap of sail-cloth passes round the animal's back and belly. This is held in its place above by a piece of cord attached to the collar. The single trace is fastened under the belly, goes back between the legs, and must often plague the animal. I was unpleasantly surprised when I noticed that, with four exceptions, all the dogs were castrated; and this surprise I did not conceal. But Trontheim on his side was at least equally astonished, and informed me that in Siberia castrated dogs are considered the best.[19] This was a disappointment to me, as I had reckoned on my canine family increasing on the way. For the present I should just have to trust to the four "whole" dogs and "Kvik," the bitch I had brought with me from home.

Next day, August 1st, there was a great religious festival in Khabarova, that of St. Elias. Samoyedes from far and near had come in with their reindeer teams to celebrate the day by going to church and then getting roaring drunk. We were in need of men in the morning to help with filling the boiler with fresh water and the tank with drinking-water, but on account of this festival it was difficult to get hold of any at all. At last, by dint of promising sufficient reward, Trontheim succeeded in collecting some poor fellows who had not money enough to drink themselves as drunk as the day required of them. I was on shore in the morning, partly to arrange about the provision of water, partly to collect fossils, in which the rock here abounds, especially one rock below Sibiriakoff's warehouse. I also took a walk up the hill to the west, to Trontheim's flagstaff, and looked out to sea in that direction after the *Urania*. But there was nothing to be seen except an unbroken sea-line. Loaded with my find I returned to Khabarova, where I, of course, took advantage of the opportunity to see something of the festival.

From early morning the women had been dressed in their finest clothes — brilliant colours, skirts with many tucks, and great coloured bows at the end of plaits of hair which hung far down their backs. Before service, an old

Samoyede and a comely young girl led out a lean reindeer which was to be offered to the church — to the old church, that is to say. Even up here, as already mentioned, religious differences have found their way. Nearly all the Samoyedes of these parts belong to the old faith and attend the old church. But they go occasionally to the new one too; as far as I could make out, so as not to offend the priest and Sibiriakoff — or perhaps to be surer of heaven? From what I got out of Trontheim on the subject, the chief difference between the two religions lies in the way they make the sign of the cross or something of that sort. To-day was high festival in both churches. All the Samoyedes first paid a short visit to the new church and then immediately streamed over into the old one. The old church was for the moment without a priest, but to-day they had clubbed together and offered the priest of the new church 2 roubles to hold a service in the old one too. After careful consideration, he agreed, and in all his priestly pomp crossed the old threshold. The air inside was so bad that I could not stand it for more than two minutes, so I now made my way on board again.

During the afternoon the howling and screaming began, and increased as time went on. We did not need to be told that the serious part of the festival had now begun. Some of the Samoyedes tore about over the plain with their reindeer teams like furious animals. They could not sit on their sledges, but lay on them or were dragged behind them, howling. Some of my comrades went on shore, and brought back anything but an edifying account of the state of things. Every single man and woman appeared to be drunk, reeling about the place. One Young Samoyede in particular had made an ineffaceable impression on them. He mounted a sledge, lashed at the reindeer, and drove "amuck in among the tents, over the tied-up dogs, foxes, and whatever came in his way; he himself fell off the sledge, was caught in the reins, and dragged behind, shrieking, through sand and clay. Good Saint Elias must be much flattered by such homage. Towards morning the howling gradually died away, and the whole town slept the loathsome sleep of the drunkard.

There was not a man to be got to help with our coal-shifting next day. Most of them slept all day after the orgie of the night. We had just to do without help; but we had not finished by evening, and I began to be impatient to get away. Precious time was passing; I had long ago given up the *Urania*. We did not really need more coal. The wind had been favourable for several days. It was a south wind, which was certainly blowing the ice to the northward in the Kara Sea. Sverdrup was now positive that we should be able to sail in open water all the way to the New Siberian Islands, so it was his opinion that there was no hurry for the present. But hope is a frail reed to lean on, and my expectations were not quite so bright; so I hurried things on, to bet away as soon as possible.

At the supper table this evening King Oscar's gold medal of merit was solemnly presented to Trontheim, in recognition of the great care with which he had executed his difficult commission, and the valuable assistance thereby rendered to the expedition. His honest face beamed at the sight of the beautiful medal and the bright ribbon.

Next day, August 3rd, we were at last ready for a start, and the 34 dogs were brought on board in the afternoon, with great noise and confusion. They were all tied up on the deck forward, and began by providing more musical entertainment than we desired. By evening the hour had come. We got up steam — everything was ready. But such a thick fog had set in that we could not see the land. Now came the moment when our last friend, Christofersen, was to leave the ship. We supplied him with the barest sufficiency of provisions and some Ringnes's ale. While this was being done, last lines were added in feverish eagerness to the letters home. Then came a last hand-clasp; Christofersen and Trontheim got into the boat, and had soon disappeared in the fog. With them went our last post; our last link with home was broken. We were alone in the mist on the sea. It was not likely that any message from us would reach the world before we ourselves brought the news of our success or defeat. How much anxiety were those at home to suffer between now and then? It is true we might possibly be able to send letters home from the mouth of the Olenek, where, according to the agreement with Baron Tell, we were to call in for another supply of dogs; but I did not consider this probable. It was far on in the summer, and I had an instinctive feeling that the state of the ice was not so favourable as I could have wished it to be.

On August 7th the *Urania* at last arrived. As I had supposed, she had been stopped by ice; but had at last got out of it uninjured. Christofersen and Trontheim were able to sail for home in her on the 11th, and reached Vardö on the 22nd, food having been very scarce during the last part of the time. The ship, which had left her home port, Brönö, in May, was not provided for so long a voyage, and these last days they lived chiefly on dry biscuits, water, and weevils.

Chapter 5

Voyage through the Kara Sea

IT was well into the night after Christofersen and Trontheim had left us, before we could get away. The channel was too dangerous for us to risk it in the thick fog. But it cleared a little, and the petroleum launch was got ready; I had determined to go on ahead with it and take soundings. We started about midnight. Hansen stood in the bow with the lead line. First we bore over towards the point of Vaigats to the northwest, as Palander directs, then on through the strait, keeping to the Vaigats side. The fog was often so thick that it was with difficulty we could catch a glimpse of the *Fram*, which followed close behind us, and on board the *Fram* they could not see our boat. But so long as we had enough water, and so long as we saw that they were keeping to the right course behind us, we went ahead. Soon the fog cleared again a little. But the depth was not quite satisfactory; we had been having steadily 4½ to 5 fathoms; then it dropped to 4 and then to 3½. This was too little. We turned and signalled to the *Fram* to stop. Then we held farther out from land and got into deeper water, so that the *Fram* could come on again at full speed.

From time to time our petroleum engine took to its old tricks and stopped. I had to pour in more oil to set it going again, and as I was standing doing this, the boat gave a lurch, so that a little oil was spilt, and took fire. The burning oil ran over the bottom of the boat, where a good deal had been spilt already. In an instant the whole stern was in a blaze, and my clothes, which were sprinkled with oil, caught fire. I had to rush to the bow, and for a moment the situation was a critical one, especially as a big pail that was standing full of oil also took fire. As soon as I had stopped the burning of my clothes, I rushed aft again, seized the pail, and poured the flaming oil into the sea, burning my fingers badly. At once the whole surface of the water round was in flames. Then I got hold of the baler, and baled water into the boat as hard as I could; and soon the worst was over. Things had looked anything but well from the *Fram*, however, and they were standing by with ropes and buoys to throw to us.

Soon we were out of Yugor Strait. There was now so little fog that the low land round us was visible, and we could also see a little way out to sea, and, in the distance, all drift-ice. At 4 o'clock in the morning (August 4th) we glided past Sokolii, or Hawk Island, out into the dreaded Kara Sea.

Now our fate was to be decided, I had always said that if we could get safely across the Kara Sea and past Cape Chelyuskin, the worst would be over. Our prospects were not bad — an open passage to the east, along the land, as far as we could see from the masthead.

An hour and a half later we were at the edge of the ice. It was so close that there was no use in attempting to go on through it. To the north-west it seemed much looser, and there was a good deal of blue in the atmosphere at the horizon there.[20] We kept south-east along the land through broken ice, but in the course of the day went further out to sea, the blueness of the atmosphere to the east and north-east promising more open water in that direction. However, about 3 p.m. the ice became so close, that I thought it best to get back into the open channel along the land. It was certainly possible that we might have forced our way through the ice in the sea here, but also possible that we might have stuck fast, and it was too early to run this risk.

Next morning (August 5th), being then off the coast near to the mouth of the River Kara, we steered across towards Yalmal. We soon had that low land in sight, but in the afternoon we got into fog and close ice. Next day it was no better, and we made fast to a great ice-block which was lying stranded off the Valmal coast.

In the evening some of us went on shore. The water was so shallow that our boat stuck fast a good way from the beach, and we had to wade. It was a perfectly flat, smooth sand beach, covered by the sea at full tide, and beyond that a steep sand bank, 30 to 40 feet, in some places probably 60 feet high.

We wandered about a little. Flat, bare country on every hand. Any driftwood we saw was buried in the sand, and soaking wet. Not a bird to be seen except one or two snipe. We came to a lake, and out of the fog in front of me I heard the cry of a loon, but saw no living creature. Our view was blocked by a wall of fog whichever way we turned. There were plenty of reindeer tracks, but of course they were only those of the Samoyedes' tame reindeer. This is the land of the Samoyedes — and oh! but it is desolate and mournful! The only one of us that bagged anything was the botanist. Beautiful flowers smiled to us here and there among the sand mounds — the one message from brighter world in this land of fogs. We went far in over the flats, but came only to sheets of water, with low spits running out into them, and ridges between. We often heard the cry of loons on the water, but could never catch sight of one. All these lakelets were of a remarkable, exactly circular conformation, with steep banks all round, just as if each had dug out a hole for itself in the sandy plain.

With the oars of our boat and a large tarpaulin we had made a sort of tent. We were lucky enough to find a little dry wood, and soon the tent was filled with the fragrant odour of hot coffee. When we had eaten and drunk and our pipes were lit, Johansen, in spite of fatigue and a full meal, surprised us by turning one somersault after another on the heavy, damp sand in front of the tent in his long military cloak and sea boots half full of water.

By 6.30 next morning we were on board again. The fog had cleared, but the ice, which lay drifting backwards and forwards according to the set of the tide, looked as close as ever towards the north. During the morning we had a visit from a boat with two stalwart Samoyedes, who were well received and treated to food and tobacco. They gave us to understand that they were living in a tent some distance inland and farther north. Presently they went off again, enriched with gifts. These were the last human beings we met.

Next day the ice was still close, and, as there was nothing else to be done, some of us went ashore again in the afternoon, partly to see more of this little-known coast; and partly, if possible, to find the Samoyedes' camp, and get hold of some skins and reindeer flesh.

It is a strange, flat country. Nothing but sand, sand everywhere. Still flatter, still more desolate than the country about Yugor Strait, with a still wider horizon. Over the plain lay a green carpet of grass and moss, here and there spoiled by the wind having torn it up and swept sand over it. But trudge as we might, and search as we might, we found no Samoyede camp. We saw three men in the far distance, but they went off as fast as they could the moment they caught sight of us. There was little game — just a few ptarmigan, golden plovers, and long-tailed ducks. Our chief gain was another collection of plants, and a few geological and geographical notes. Our observations showed that the land at this place was charted not less than half a degree or 36 to 38 minutes too far west.

It was not till next forenoon (August 9th) that we went on board again.

The ice to the north now seemed to be rather looser, and at 8 p.m. we at last began once more to make our way north. We found ice that was easy to get through, and held on our course until, three days later, we got into open water. On Sunday, August 13th, we stood out into the open Kara Sea, past the north point of Yalmal and Bieloi-Ostrov (White Island). There was no ice to be seen in any direction. During the days that followed we had constant strong east winds, often increasing to half a gale. We kept on tacking to make our way eastward, but the broad and keel-less *Fram* can hardly be called a good "beater;" we made too much lee-way, and our progress was correspondingly slow. In the journal there is a constantly-recurring entry of "Head wind, Head wind." The monotony was extreme, but as they may be of interest as relating to the navigation of this sea, I shall give the most important items of the journal, especially those regarding the state of the ice.

On Monday, August 14th, we beat with only sail against a strong wind. Single pieces of ice were seen during the middle watch, but after that there was none within sight.

Tuesday, August 15th. The wind slackened in the middle watch; we took in sail, and got up steam. At 5 in the morning we steamed away east over a sea perfectly clear of ice; but after mid-day the wind began to freshen again from E.N.E., and we had to beat with steam and sail. Single floes of ice were seen during the evening and night.

Wednesday, August 16th. As the Kara Sea seemed so extraordinarily free from ice, and as a heavy sea was running from the north-east, we decided to hold north as far as we could, even if it should be to the Einsamkeit (Lonely) Island. But about half-past three in the afternoon we had a strip of close ice ahead, so that we had to turn. Stiff breeze and sea. Kept on beating east along the edge of the ice. Almost lost the petroleum launch in the evening. The waves were constantly breaking into it and filling it, the gunwale was burst in at two places, and the heavy davits it hung on were twisted as if they had been copper wires. Only just in the nick of time, with the waves washing over us, some of us managed to get it lashed to the side of the ship. There seemed to be some fatality about this boat.

Thursday, August 17th. Still beating eastward under sail and steam through scattered ice, and along a margin of fixed ice. Still blowing hard, with a heavy sea as soon as we headed a little out from the ice.

Friday, August 18th. Continued storm. Stood south-east. At 4.30 a.m., Sverdrup, who had gone up into the crow's-nest to look out for bears and walrus

Hjalmar Johansen.

on the ice-floes, saw land to the south of us. At 10 a.m. I went up to look at it — we were then probably not more than 10 miles away from it. It was low land, seemingly of the same formation as Yalmal, with steep sandbanks and grass-grown above. The sea grew shallower as we neared it. Not far from us, small icebergs lay aground. The lead showed steadily less and less water; by 11.30 a.m., there were only some 8 fathoms, then to our surprise the bottom suddenly fell to 20 fathoms, and after that we found steadily increasing depth. Between the land and the blocks of stranded ice on our lee there appeared to be a channel with rather deeper water and not so much ice aground in it. It seemed difficult to conceive that there should be undiscovered land here, where both Nordenskiöld and Edward Johansen, and possibly several Russians, had passed without seeing anything. Our observations, however, were incontestable, and we immediately named the land Sverdrup's Island, after its discoverer.

As there was still a great deal of ice to windward, we continued our south-westerly course, keeping as close to the wind as possible. The weather was clear, and at 8 o'clock we sighted the mainland, with Dickson's Island ahead. It had been our intention to run in and anchor here, in order to put letters for home under a cairn, Captain Wiggins having promised to pick them up on his way to the Yenisei. But in the meantime the wind had fallen — it was a favourable chance, and time was precious. So gave up sending our post, and continued our course along the coast.

The country here was quite different from Yalmal. Though not very high, it was a hilly country, with patches and even large drifts of snow here and there, some of them lying close down by the shore. Next morning I sighted the southernmost of the Kamenni Islands. We took a tack in under it to see if there were animals of any kind, but could catch sight of none. The island rose evenly from the sea at all points, with steep shores. They consisted for the most part of rock, which was partly solid, partly broken up by the action of the weather into heaps of stones. It appeared to be stratified rock, with strongly marked oblique strata. The island was also covered with quantities of gravel, sometimes mixed with larger stones; the whole of the northern point seemed to be a sand heap, with steep sand-banks towards the shore. The most noticeable feature of the island was its marked shore lines. Near the top there was a specially pronounced one, which was like a sharp ledge on the west and north sides, and stretched across the island like a dark band. Nearer the beach were several other distinct ones. In form they all resembled the upper one with its steep ledges, and had evidently been formed in the same way, by the action of the sea, and more especially of the ice. Like the upper one, they also were most marked on the west and north sides of the island, which are those facing most to the open sea.

To the student of the history of the earth these marks of the former level of the sea are of great interest, showing as they do that the land has risen or the sea sunk since the time they were formed. Like Scandinavia, the whole of the north coast of Siberia has undergone these changes of level since the Great Ice Age.

It was strange that we saw none of the islands which, according to

Kamenni Islands.

Nordenskiöld's map, stretch in a line to the north-east from Kamenni Island. On the other hand, I took the bearings of one or two other islands lying almost due east, and next morning we passed a small island farther north.

We saw few birds in this neighbourhood — only a few flocks of geese, some Arctic gulls (*lestris parasitica* and *l. buffonii*), and a few sea-gulls and tern.

On Sunday, August 20th, we had, for us, uncommonly fine weather-blue sea, brilliant sunshine, and light wind, still from the north-east. In the afternoon we ran in to the Kjellman Islands. These we could recognise from their position on Nordenskiöld's map, but south of them we found many unknown ones. They all had smoothly rounded forms, these Kjellman Islands, like rocks that have been ground smooth by the glaciers of the Ice Age. The *Fram* anchored on the north side of the largest of them, and whilst the boiler was being refitted, some of us went ashore, in the evening, for some shooting. We had not left the ship when the mate, from the crow's-nest, caught sight of reindeer. At once we were all agog; everyone wanted to go ashore, and the mate was quite beside himself with the hunter's fever, his eyes as big as saucers, and his hands trembling as though he were drunk. Not until we were in the boat had we time to look seriously for the mate's reindeer. We looked in vain — not a living thing was to be seen in any direction. Yes — when we were close in shore, we at last descried a large flock of geese waddling upward from the beach. We were base enough to let a conjecture escape us, that these were the mate's reindeer — a suspicion which he at first rejected with contempt. Gradually, however, his confidence oozed away. But it is possible to do an injustice even to a mate. The first thing I saw when I sprang ashore was old reindeer tracks. The mate had now the laugh on his side, ran from track to track, and swore that it was reindeer he had seen.

When we got up on to the first height we saw several reindeer on flat ground to the south of us; but the wind being from the north, we had to go back and make our way south along the shore till we got to leeward of them. The only one who did not approve of this plan was the mate, who was in a state of feverish eagerness to rush straight at some reindeer he thought he had seen to the east, which, of course, was an absolutely certain way to clear the field of everyone of them. He asked and received permission to remain behind with Hansen, who was to take a magnetic observation; but had to promise not to move till he got the order.

On the way along the shore we passed one great flock of geese after another; they stretched their necks and waddled aside a little, until we were quite near, and only then took flight; but we had no time to waste on such small game. A little further on we caught sight of one or two reindeer we had not noticed before. We could easily have stalked them, but were afraid of getting to windward of the others, which were farther south. At last we got to leeward of these latter also, but they were grazing on flat ground, and it was anything but easy to stalk them — not a hillock, not a stone to hide behind. The only thing was to form a long line, advance as best we could, and, if possible, outflank them. In the meantime we had caught sight of another herd of reindeer farther to the north, but suddenly, to our astonishment, saw them tear off across the plain eastward, in all probability startled by the mate, who had not been able to keep quiet any longer.

A little to the north of the reindeer nearest us there was a hollow, opening from the shore, from which it seemed that it might be possible to get a shot at them. I went back to try this, whilst the others kept their places in the line. As I went down again towards the shore I had the sea before me, quiet and beautiful. The sun had gone down behind it not long before, and the sky was glowing, in the clear, light night. I had to stand still for a minute. In the midst of all this beauty, man was doing the work of a beast of prey! At this moment I saw to the north a dark speck move down the height where the mate and Hansen ought to be. It divided into two, and the one moved east, just to the windward of the animals I was to stalk. They would get the scent immediately, and be off. There was nothing for it but to hurry on, while I rained anything but good wishes on these fellows' heads. The gully was not so deep as I had expected. Its sides were just high enough to hide me when I crept on all fours. In the middle were large stones and clayey gravel, with a little runnel soaking through them. The reindeer were still grazing quietly, only now and then raising their heads to look round. My "cover" get lower and lower, and to the north I heard the mate. He would presently succeed in setting off my game. It was imperative to get on quickly, but there was no longer cover enough for me to advance on hands and knees. My only chance was to wriggle forward like a snake on my stomach. But in this soft clay in the bed of the stream? Yes — meat is too precious on board, and the beast of prey is too strong in a man. My clothes must be sacrificed; on I crept on my stomach through the mud. But soon there was hardly cover enough even for this. I squeezed myself flat among the stones and ploughed forward like a drain-cutting machine. And I did make way, if not quickly and comfortably, still surely.

All this time the sky was turning darker and darker red behind me, and it was getting more and more difficult to use the sights of my gun, not to mention the trouble I had in keeping the clay from them and from the muzzle. The reindeer still grazed quietly on. When they raised their heads to look round I had to lie as quiet as a mouse, feeling the water trickling gently under my stomach; when they began to nibble the moss main, off I went through the mud. Presently I made the disagreeable discovery that they were moving away from me about as fast as I could move forward, and I had to redouble my exertions. But the darkness was getting worse and worse, and I had the mate to the north of me, and presently he would start them off. The outlook was anything but bright either morally or physically. The hollow was getting shallower and shallower, so that I was hardly covered at all; I squeezed myself still deeper into the mud. A turn in the ground helped me forward to the next little height, and now they were right in front of me, within what I should have called easy range if it had been daylight. I tried to take aim, but could not see the bead on my gun.

Man's fate is sometimes hard to bear. My clothes were dripping with wet clay, and after what seemed to me most meritorious exertions, here I was at the goal, unable to take advantage of my position. But now the reindeer moved down into a small depression. I crept forward a little way further as quickly as I could. I was in a splendid position, so far as I could tell in the dark, but I could not see the bead any better than before. It was impossible to get nearer, for there was only a smooth slope between us. There was no sense in thinking of waiting for light to shoot by; it was now midnight, and I had that terrible mate to the north of me, besides the wind was not to be trusted. I held the rifle up against the sky to see the bead clearly, and then lowered it on the reindeer. I did this once, twice, thrice. The bead was still far from clear; but all the same I thought I might hit, and pulled the trigger. The two deer gave a sudden start, looked round in astonishment, and bolted off a little way south. There they stood still again, and at this moment were joined by a third deer, which had been standing rather farther north. I fired off all the cartridges in the magazine, and all to the same good purpose. The creatures started and moved off a little at each shot, and then trotted farther south. Presently they made another halt, to take a long careful look at me; and I dashed off westward, as hard as I could run, to turn them. Now they were off straight in the direction where some of my comrades ought to be. I expected every moment to hear shots and see one or two of the animals fall; but away they ambled southwards, quite unchecked. At last, far to the south, crack went a rifle. I could see by the smoke that it was at too long a range; so in high dudgeon I shouldered my rifle and lounged in the direction of the shot. It was pleasant to see such a good result for all one's trouble.

No one was to be seen anywhere. At length I met Sverdrup; it was he who had fired. Soon Blessing joined us, but all the others had long since left their posts. Whilst Blessing went back to the boat and his botanising box, Sverdrup and I went on to try our luck once more. A little farther south we came to a valley stretching right across the island. On the further side of it we saw a man standing on a hillock, and not far from him a herd of five or six reindeer. As it never occurred to us to doubt that the man was in the act of stalking these, we avoided going in that direction, and soon he and his reindeer disappeared to the west. I heard afterwards that he had never seen the deer. As it was evident that when the reindeer to the south of us were startled, they would have to come back across this valley, and as the island at this part was so narrow that we commanded the whole of it, we determined to take up our posts here and wait. We accordingly got in the lee of some great boulders, out of the wind. In front of Sverdrup was a large flock of geese, near the mouth of the stream, close down by the shore. They kept up an incessant gabble, and the temptation to have a shot at them was very great; but, considering the reindeer, we thought it best to leave them in peace. They gabbled and waddled away down through the mud, and soon took wing. The time seemed long. At first we listened with all our ears — the reindeer must come very soon — and our eyes wandered incessantly back and forwards along the slope on the other side of the valley. But no

Henrik Blessing, doctor and botanist.

reindeer came, and soon we were having a struggle to keep our eyes open and our heads up — we had not had much sleep the last few days. They *must* be coming! We shook ourselves awake, and gave another look along the bank, till again the eyes softly closed and the heads began to nod, while the chill wind blew through our wet clothes, and I shivered with cold. This sort of thing went on for an hour or two, until the sport began to pall on me, and I scrambled from my shelter along towards Sverdrup, who was enjoying it about as much as I was. We climbed the slope on the other side of the valley, and were hardly at the top before we saw the horns of six splendid reindeer on a height in front of us, They were restless, scenting westward, trotting round in a circle, and then sniffing again. They could not have noticed us as yet, as the wind was blowing at right angles to the line between them and us. We stood a long time watching their manoeuvres, and waiting their choice of a direction, but they had apparently great difficulty in making it. At last off they swung south and east, and off we went south-east as hard as we could go, to get across their course before they got scent of us. Sverdrup had got well ahead, and I saw him rushing across a flat piece of ground — presently he would be at the right place to meet them. I stopped, to be in readiness to cut them off on the other side if they should face about and make off northward again. There were six splendid animals, a big buck in front. They were heading straight for Sverdrup, who was now crouching down on the slope.

I expected every moment to see the foremost fall. A shot rang out! Round wheeled the whole flock like lightning, and back they came at a gallop. It was my turn now to run with all my might, and off I went over the stones, down towards the valley we had come from. I only stopped once or twice to take breath and to make sure that the animals were coming in the direction I had reckoned on — then off again. We were getting near each other now, they were coming on just where I had calculated, the thing now was to be in time for them. I made my long legs go their fastest over the boulders, and took leaps from stone to stone that would have surprised myself at a more sober moment. More than once my foot slipped and I went down head first among the boulders, gun and all. But the wild beast in me had the upper hand now. The passion of the chase vibrated through every fibre of my body.

We reached the slant of the valley almost at the same tune — a leap or two to get up on some big boulders, and the moment had come — I *must* shoot, though the shot was a long one. When the smoke cleared away I saw the big buck trailing a broken hind-leg. When their leader stopped, the whole flock turned and ran in a ring round the poor animal. They could not understand what was happening, and strayed about wildly with the balls whistling round them. Then off they went down the side of the valley again, leaving another of their number behind with a broken leg. I tore after them, across the valley and up the other side, in the hope of getting another shot, but gave that up and turned back to make sure of the two wounded ones. At the bottom of the valley stood one of the victims awaiting its fate. It looked imploringly at me, and then, just as I was going forward to shoot it, made off much quicker than I could have thought it possible for an animal on three legs to go. Sure of my shot, of course I missed; and now began a chase, which ended in the poor beast, blocked in every other direction, rushing down towards the sea and wading into a small lagoon on the shore, whence I feared it might get right out into the sea. At last it got its quietus there in the water. The other one was not far off, and a ball soon put an end to its sufferings also. As I was proceeding to rip it up, Henriksen and Johansen appeared; they had just shot a bear a little farther south.

After disembowelling the reindeer, we went towards the boat again meeting Sverdrup on the way. It was now well on in the morning, and as I considered that we had already spent too much time here, I was impatient to push northwards. Whilst Sverdrup and some of the others went on board to get ready for the start, the rest of us roved south to fetch our two reindeer and our bear. A strong breeze had begun to blow from the north-east, and as it would be hard work for us to row back against it, I had asked Sverdrup to come and meet us with the *Fram*, if the soundings permitted of his doing so. We saw quantities of seal and whitefish along the shore, but we had not time to go after them; all we wanted now was to get south, and in the first place to pick up the bear. When we came near the place where we expected to find it, we did see a large white heap resembling a bear lying on the ground, and I was sure it must be the dead one, but Henriksen maintained that it was not. We went ashore and approached it, as it lay motionless on a grassy bank. I still felt a strong suspicion that it had already had all the shot it wanted. We drew nearer and nearer, but it gave no sign of life. I looked into Henrikson's honest face, to make sure that they were not playing a trick on me; but he was staring fixedly at the bear. As I looked two shots went off, and to my astonishment the great creature bounded into the air, still dazed with sleep, poor beast! it was a harsh awakening. Another shot, and it fell lifeless.

We first tried to drag the bears down to the boat, but they were too heavy for us; and we now had a hard piece of work skinning and cutting them up, and carrying down all we wanted. But bad as it was, trudging through the soft clay with heavy quarters of bear on our backs, there was worse awaiting us on the beach. The tide had risen, and at the same time the waves had got larger and swamped the boat, and were now breaking over it. Guns and ammunition were soaking in the water; bits of bread, our only provision, floated round, and the butter dish lay at the bottom, with no butter in it. It required no small exertion to get the boat drawn up out of this heavy surf and emptied of water. Luckily, it had received no injury, as the beach was of a soft sand; but the sand had penetrated with the water everywhere, even into the most delicate parts of the locks of our rifles. But worst of all was the loss of our provisions, for now we were ravenously hungry. We had to make the best of a bad business, and eat pieces of bread soaked in sea water, and flavoured with several varieties of dirt. On this occasion, too, I lost my sketch-book, with some sketches that were of value to me.

It was no easy task to get our heavy game into the boat with these big waves breaking on the flat beach. We had to keep the boat outside the surf, and haul both skins and flesh on board with a line; a good deal of water came with them, but there was no help for it. And then we had to row north along the shore against the wind and sea as hard as we could. It was very tough work. The wind had increased, and it was all we could do to make headway against it. Seals were diving round us, white whales coming and going, but we had no eyes for them now. Suddenly Henriksen called out that there was a bear on the point in front. I turned round, and there stood a beautiful white fellow rummaging among the flotsam on the beach. As we had no time to shoot it, we rowed on, and it went slowly in front of us northwards along the shore. At last, with great exertions we reached the bay where we were to put in for the reindeer. The bear was there before us. It had not seen the boat hitherto; but now it got scent of us, and came nearer. It was a tempting shot. I had my finger on the trigger several times, but did not draw it. After all we had no use for the animal; it was quite as much as we could do to stow away what we had already. It made a beautiful target of itself by getting up on a stone to have a better scent and looked about, and after a careful survey it turned round and set off inland at an easy trot.

The surf was by this time still heavier. It was a flat, shallow shore, and the waves broke a good way out from land. We rowed in till the boat touched ground and the breakers began to wash over us. The only way of getting ashore was to jump into the sea and wade. But getting the reindeer on board was another matter. There was no better landing-place farther north, and hard as it was to give up the excellent meat after all our trouble, it seemed to me there was nothing else for it, and we rowed off towards our ship.

It was the hardest row I ever had a hand in. It went pretty well to begin with; we had the current with us, and got quickly out from land; but presently the wind rose, the current slackened, and wave after wave broke over us. After incredible toil, we had at last only a short way to go. I cheered up the good

The sleeping bear on Reindeer Island, 21 August 1893.

fellows as best I could, reminding them of the smoking hot tea that awaited them after a few more tough pulls, and picturing all the good things in store for them. We really were all pretty well done up now, but we still took a good grip of the oars, soaking wet as we were from the sea constantly breaking over us, for of course none of us had thought of such things as oilskins in yesterday's beautiful weather. But we soon saw that with all our pulling and toiling the boat was making no headway whatever. Apart from the wind and the sea we had the current dead against us here; all our exertions were of no avail. We pulled till our finger-tips felt as if they were bursting; but the most we could manage was to keep the boat where it was; if we slackened an instant it drifted back. I tried to encourage my comrades: "*Now* we made a little way! It was just strength that was needed!" But all to no purpose. The wind whistled round our ears, and the spray dashed over us. It was maddening to be so near the ship that it seemed as if we could almost reach out to her, and yet feel that it was impossible to get on any farther. We had to go in under the land again, where we had the current with us, and here we did succeed in making a little progress. We rowed hard till we were about abreast of the ship; then we once more tried to sheer across to her, but no sooner did we get into the current again than it mercilessly drove us back. Beaten again! And again we tried the same manoeuvre with the same result. Now we saw them lowering a buoy from the ship — if we could only reach it, we were saved; but we did not reach it. They were not exactly blessings that we poured on those on board. Why on earth could they not bear down to us, when they saw the straits we were in; or why, at any rate, could they not ease up the anchor, and let the ship drift a little in our direction? They saw how little was needed to enable us to reach them. Perhaps they had their reasons. We would make one last desperate attempt. We went at it with a will. Every muscle was strained to the utmost — it was only the buoy we had to reach this time. But to our rage we now saw the buoy being hauled up. We rowed a little way on, to the windward of the *Fram*, and then tried again to sheer over. This time we got nearer her than we had ever been before; but we were disappointed in still seeing no buoy, and none was thrown over; there was not even a man to be seen on deck. We roared like madmen for a buoy — we had no strength left for another attempt. It was not a pleasing prospect to have to drift back, and go ashore again in our wet clothes; — we *would* get on board! Once more we yelled like wild Indians, and now they came rushing aft and threw out the buoy in our direction. One more cry to my mates that we must put our last strength into the work. There were only a few boat lengths to cover, and we bent to our oars with a will. Now there were three boat lengths. Another desperate spurt. Now there were two-and-a-half boat lengths — presently two — then only one! A few more frantic pulls, and there was a little less. "Now boys, one or two more hard pulls and it's over! Hard! hard!! Keep to it! Now another! Don't give up! One more! *There we have it*!!!" And one joyful sigh of relief passed round the boat. "Keep the oars going or the rope will break. Row, boys!" And row we did, and soon they had hauled us alongside of the *Fram*. Not till we were lying there getting our bearskins and flesh hauled on board, did we really know what we had had to fight against. The current was running along the side of the ship like a rapid river. At last we were actually on board. It was evening by this time, and it was splendid to get some good hot food and then stretch one's limbs in a comfortable dry berth. There is a satisfaction in feeling that one has exerted one's self to some purpose. Here was the net result of four and twenty hours' hard toil — we had shot two reindeer, which we did not get, got two bears that we had no use for, and had totally ruined one suit of clothes. Two washings had not the smallest effect upon them, and they hung on deck to air for the rest of this trip.

I slept badly that night, for this is what I find in my diary: "Got on board after what I think was the hardest row I ever had. Slept well for a little, but am now lying tossing about in my berth, unable to sleep. Is it the coffee I drank after supper? or the cold tea I drank when I awoke with a burning thirst? I shut my eyes and try again time after time, but to no purpose. And now memory's airy visions steal softly over my soul. Gleam after gleam breaks through the mist. I see before me sunlit landscapes — smiling fields and meadows, green, leafy trees and woods, and blue mountain ridges. The singing of the steam in the boiler pipe turns to bell-ringing — church bells — ringing in Sabbath peace over Vestre-Aker on this beautiful summer morning. I am walking with father along the avenue of small birch-trees that mother planted, up towards the church which lies on the height before us, pointing up into the blue sky and sending its call far over the country-side. From up there you can see a long way. Naesodden looks quite close in the clear air, especially on an autumn morning. And we give a quiet Sunday greeting to the people that drive past us, all going our way. What a look of Sunday happiness dwells on their faces!

"I did not think it all so delightful then, and would much rather have run off to the woods with my bow and arrow after squirrels — but now — how fair, how wonderfully beautiful that sunlit picture seems to me! The feeling of peace and happiness that even then no doubt made its impression, though only a passing one, comes back now with redoubled strength, and all nature seems one mighty, thrilling song of praise! Is it because of the contrast with this poor, barren sunless land of mists — without a tree, without a bush — nothing but stones and clay? No peace in it either — nothing but an endless struggle to get north, always north, without a moment's delay. Oh, how one yearns for a little careless happiness!"

Next day we were again ready to sail, and I tried to force the *Fram* on under steam against wind and current. But the current ran strong as a river, and we had to be specially careful with the helm, if we gave her the least thing too much, she would take a sheer, and we knew there were shallows and rocks on all sides. We kept the lead going constantly. For a time all went well, and we made way slowly, but suddenly she took a sheer and refused to obey her helm. She went off to starboard. The lead indicated shallow water. The same moment came the order, "Let go the anchor!" And to the bottom it went with a rush and a clank. There we lay with 4 fathoms of water under the stern, and 9 fathoms in front at the anchor. We were not a moment too soon. We got the *Fram*'s head straight to the wind, and tried again time after time, but always with the same result. The attempt had to be given up. There was still the possibility of making our way out of the sound to leeward of the land, but the water got quickly shallow there, and we might come on rocks at any moment. We could have gone on in front with the boat and sounded, but I had already had more than enough of rowing in that current. For the present we must stay where we were and anoint ourselves with the ointment called Patience, a medicament of which every polar expedition ought to lay in a large supply. We hoped on for a change, but the current remained as it was, and the wind certainly did not decrease. I was in despair at having to lie here for nothing but this cursed current, with open sea outside, perhaps as far as Cape Chelyuskin, that eternal cape, whose name had been sounding in my ears for the last three weeks.

When I came on deck next morning (August 23rd) winter had come. There was white snow on the deck, and on every little projection of the rigging where it had found shelter from the wind; white snow on the land, and white snow floating through the air. Oh! how the snow refreshes one's soul, and drives away all the gloom and sadness from this sullen land of fogs! Look at it scattered so delicately, as if by a loving hand, over the stones and the grass flats on shore! But wind and current are much as they were, and during the day the wind blows up to a regular storm, howling and rattling in the *Fram*'s rigging.

The following day (August 24th) I had quite made up my mind that we must get out some way or other. When I came on deck in the morning the wind had gone down considerably, and the current was not so strong. A boat would almost be able to row against it; anyhow one could be eased away by a line from the stern, and keep on taking soundings there, while we "kedged" the *Fram* with her anchor just clear of the bottom. But before having recourse to this last expedient, I would make another attempt to go against the wind and the current. The engineers were ordered to put on as much pressure of steam as they dared, and the *Fram* was urged on at her top speed. Our surprise was not small when we saw that we were making way, and even at a tolerable rate. Soon we were out of the sound or "Knipa" (nipper) as we christened it, and could beat out to sea with steam and sail. Of course, we had, as usual, contrary wind, and thick weather. There is ample space between every little bit of sunshine in these quarters.

Next day we kept on beating northward between the edge of the ice and the land. The open channel was broad to begin with, but farther north it became so narrow that we could often see the coast when we put about at the edge of the ice. At this time we passed many unknown islands and groups of islands. There was evidently plenty of occupation here, for any one who could spare the time, in making a chart of the coast. Our voyage had another aim, and all that we could do was to make a few occasional measurements of the same nature as Nordenskiöld had made before us.

On August 25th, I noted in my diary that in the afternoon we had seven islands in sight. They were higher than those we had seen before, and consisted of precipitous hills. There were also small glaciers or snow-fields, and the rock formation showed clear traces of erosion by ice or snow, this being especially the case on the largest island, where there were even small valleys, partially filled with snow.

This is the record of August 26th: "Many new islands in various directions. There are here," the diary continues, "any number of unknown islands, so many that one's head gets confused in trying to keep account of them all. In the morning we passed a very rocky one, and beyond it I saw two others. After them land or islands farther to the north and still more to the north-east. We had to go out of our course in the afternoon, because we dared not pass between two large islands on account of possible shoals. The islands were round in form, like those we had seen farther back, but were of a good height. Now we held east again, with four biggish islands and two islets in the offing. On our other side we presently had a line of flat islands with steep shores. The channel was far from safe here. In the evening we suddenly noticed large stones standing up above the water among some ice-floes close on our port bow, and on our starboard beam was a shoal with stranded ice-floes. We sounded, but found over 21 fathoms of water."

I think this will suffice to give an idea of the nature of this coast. Its belt of skerries, though it certainly cannot be classed with the Norwegian one, is yet of the kind that it would be difficult to find except off glacier-formed coasts. This tends to strengthen the opinion I had formed of there having been a glacial period in the earlier history of this part of the world also. Of the coast itself, we unfortunately saw too little at any distance from which we could get an accurate idea of its formation and nature. We could not keep near land, partly because of the thick weather, and partly because of the number of islands. The little I did see was enough to give me the conviction that the actual coast line differs essentially from the one we know from maps; it is much more winding and indented than it is shown to be. I even, several times, thought that I saw the openings into deep fjords, and more than once the suspicion occurred to me that this was a typical fjord country we were sailing past, in spite of the hills being comparatively low and rounded. In this supposition I was to be confirmed by our experiences farther north.

Our record of August 27th reads as follows: "Steamed among a variety of small islands and islets. Thick fog in the morning. At 12 noon we saw a small island right ahead, and therefore changed our course and went north. We were soon close to the ice, and after 3 in the afternoon held north-east along its edge. Sighted land when the fog cleared a little, and were about a mile off it at 7 p.m."

It was the same striated, rounded land, covered with clay and large and small stones strewn over moss and grass flats. Before us we saw points and headlands, with islands outside, and sounds and fjords between; but it was all locked up in ice, and we could not see far for the fog. There was that strange Arctic hush and misty light over everything — that greyish-white light caused by the reflection from the ice being cast high into the air against masses of vapour, the dark land offering a wonderful contrast. We were not sure whether this was the land near Taimur Sound, or that by Cape Palander, but were agreed that in any case it would be best to hold a northerly course, so as to keep clear of Almquist's Islands, which Nordenskiöld marks on his map as lying off Taimur Island. If we shaped our course for one watch north, or north to west, we should be safe after that, and be able again to hold farther east. But we miscalculated after all.

At midnight we turned north-eastward, and at 4 a.m. (August 28th) land appeared out of the fog about half-a-mile off. It seemed to Sverdrup, who was on deck, the highest that we had seen since we left Norway. He consequently took it to be the mainland, and wished to keep well outside of it, but was obliged to turn from this course because of ice. We held to the W.S.W., and it was not till 9 a.m. that we rounded the western point of a lame island, and could steer north again. Fast of us were many islands or points with solid ice between them, and we followed the edge of the ice. All the morning we went north along the land against a strong current. There seemed to be no end to this land. Its discrepancy with every known map grew more and more remarkable, and I was in no slight dilemma. We had for long been far to the north of the most northern island indicated by Nordenskiöld.[21] My diary this day tells of great uncertainty. "This land (or these islands, or whatever it is) goes confoundedly far north. If it is a group of islands they are tolerably large ones. It has often the appearance of connected land, with fjords and points; but the weather is too thick for us to get a proper view... Can this that we are now coasting along be the Taimur Island of the Russian maps (or more precisely, Lapteff's map), and is it separated from the mainland by the broad strait indicated by him, whilst Nordenskiöld's Taimur Island is what Lapteff has mapped as a projecting tongue of land? This supposition would explain everything, and our observations would also fit in with it. Is it possible that Nordenskiöld found this strait, and took it for Taimur Strait, whilst in reality it was a new one; and that he saw Almquist's Islands, but had no suspicion that Taimur Island lay to the outside of them? The difficulty about this explanation is that the Russian maps mark no islands round Taimur Island. It is inconceivable that anyone should have travelled all about here in sledges without seeing all these small islands that lie scattered around.[22]

"In the afternoon, the water-gauge of the boiler got choked up; we had to stop to have it repaired, and therefore made fast to the edge of the ice. We spent the time in taking in drinking water. We found a pool on the ice, so small that we thought it would only do to begin with; but it evidently had a "subterranean" communication with other fresh water ponds on the floe. To our astonishment it proved inexhaustible, however much we scooped. In the evening we stood in to the head of an ice bay, which opened out opposite the most northern island we then had in sight. There was no passage beyond. The broken drift-ice lay packed so close in on the unbroken land-ice, that it was impossible to tell where the one ended and the other began. We could see islands still farther to the north-east. From the atmosphere it seemed as if there might also be open water in that direction. To the north it all looked very close, but to the west there was an open waterway as far as one could see from the masthead. I was in some doubt as to what should be done. There was an open channel for a short way up past the north point of the nearest island, but farther to the east the ice seemed to be close. It might be possible to force our way through there, but it was just as likely that we should be frozen in, so I thought it more judicious to go back and make another attempt between these islands and that mainland, which I had some difficulty in believing that Sverdrup had seen in the morning."

"Thursday, August 30th. Still foggy weather. New islands were observed on the way back. Sverdrup's high land did not come to much. It turned out to be an island, and that a low one. It is wonderful the way things loom up in the fog. This reminded me of the story of the pilot at home in the Dröbak Channel. He suddenly saw land right in front, and gave the order 'Full speed astern!' Then they approached carefully and found that it was half a baling-can floating in the water."

After passing a great number of new islands, we got into open water off Taimur Island, and steamed in still weather through the sound to the north-east. At five in the afternoon I saw from the crow's-nest thick ice ahead, which blocked further progress. It stretched from Taimur Island right across to the islands south of it. On the ice, bearded seals (*phoca barbata*) were to be seen in all directions, and we saw one walrus. We approached the ice to make fast to it, but the *Fram* had got into a dead-water, and made hardly any way, in spite of the engine going full pressure. It was such slow work that I thought I would row ahead to shoot seal. In the meantime the *Fram* advanced slowly to the edge of the ice with her machinery still going at full-speed.

For the moment we had simply to give up all thoughts of getting on. It was most likely, indeed, that only a few miles of solid ice lay between us and the probably open Taimur Sea; but to break through this ice was an impossibility. It was too thick, and there were no openings in it. Nordenskiöld had steamed through here earlier in the year (August 18th, 1878) without the slightest hindrance,[23] and here, perhaps, our hopes, for this year at any rate, were to be wrecked. It was not possible that the ice should melt before winter set in in earnest. The only thing to save us would be a proper storm from the south-west. Our other slight hope lay in the possibility that Nordenskiöld's Taimur Sound farther south might be open, and that we might manage to get the *Fram* through there, in spite of Nordenskiöld having said distinctly "that it is too shallow to allow of the passage of vessels of any size."

After having been out in the kayak and boat and shot some seals, we went on to anchor in a bay that lay rather farther south, where it seemed as if there would be a little shelter in case of a storm. We wanted now to have a thorough cleaning out of the boiler, a very necessary operation. It took us more than one watch to steam a distance we could have rowed in half an hour or less. We could hardly get on at all for the dead-water, and we swept the whole sea along with us.

It is a peculiar phenomenon, this dead-water. We had at present a better opportunity of studying it than we desired. It occurs where a surface layer of fresh water rests upon the salt water of the sea, and this fresh water is carried along with the ship, gliding on the heavier sea beneath as if on a fixed foundation. The difference between the two strata was in this case so great that while we had drinking water on the surface the water we got from the bottom

The *Fram*, fastened to the edge of the ice.

cock of the engine-room was far too salt to be used for the boiler. Dead-water manifests itself in the form of larger or smaller ripples or waves stretching across the wake, the one behind the other, arising sometimes as far forward as almost amidships. We made loops in our course, turned sometimes right round, tried all sorts of antics to get clear of it, but to very little purpose. The moment the engine stopped it seemed as if the ship were sucked back. In spite of the *Fram*'s weight, and the momentum she usually has, we could in the present instance go at full speed till within a fathom or two of the edge of the ice, and hardly feel a shock when she touched.

Just as we were approaching we saw a fox jumping backwards and forwards on the ice, taking the most wonderful leaps, and enjoying life. Sverdrup sent a ball from the forecastle which put an end to it on the spot.

About midday two bears were seen on land, but they disappeared before we got in to shoot them.

The number of seals to be seen in every direction was something extraordinary, and it seemed to me that this would be an uncommonly good hunting ground. The flocks I saw this first day on the ice reminded me of the crested-seal hunting grounds on the west coast of Greenland.

This experience of ours may appear to contrast stranger with that of the *Vega* Expedition. Nordenskiöld writes of this sea, comparing it with the sea to the north and east of Spitsbergen: "Another striking difference is the scarcity of warm-blooded animals in this region as yet unvisited by the hunter. We had not seen a single bird in the whole course of the day, a thing that had never before happened to me on a summer voyage in the Arctic regions; and we had hardly seen a seal." The fact that they had not seen a seal is simply enough explained by the absence of ice. From my impression of it, the region must, on the contrary, abound in seals. Nordenskiöld himself says that "numbers of seals, both *phoca barbata* and *phoca hispida* were to be seen" on the ice in Taimur Straits.

So this was all the progress we had made up to the end of August. On August 18th, 1878, Nordenskiöld had passed through this sound, and on the 19th and 20th passed Cape Chelyuskin, but here was an impenetrable mass of ice frozen on to the land lying in our way at the end of the month. The prospect was anything but cheering. Were the many prophets of evil — there is never any scarcity of than — to prove right even at this early stage of the undertaking? No! The Taimur Strait must be attempted, and should this attempt fail, another last one should be made outside all the islands again. Possibly the ice masses out there might in the meantime have drifted and left an open way. We could not stop here.

September came in with a still, melancholy snowfall; and this desolate land with its low, rounded heights, soon lay under a deep covering. It did not add to our cheerfulness to see winter thus gently and noiselessly ushered in after an all too short summer.

On September 2nd the boiler was ready at last, was filled with fresh water from the sea surface, and we prepared to start. While this preparation was going on, Sverdrup and I went ashore to have a look after reindeer. The snow was lying thick, and if it had not been so wet we could have used our snow-shoes. As it was, we tramped about in the heavy slush without them, and without seeing so much as the track of a beast of any kind. A forlorn land, indeed! Most of the birds of passage had already taken their way south; we had met small flocks of them at sea. They were collecting for the great flight to the sunshine, and we poor souls could not help wishing that it were possible to send news and greeting with them. A few solitary Arctic and ordinary gulls were our only company now. One day I found a belated straggler of a goose sitting on the edge of the ice.

We steamed south in the evening, but still followed by the dead water. According to Nordenskiöld's map, it was only about 20 miles to Talmur Strait, but we were the whole night doing this distance. Our speed was reduced to about a fifth part of what it would otherwise have been. At 6 a.m. (September 3rd) we got in among some thin ice that scraped the dead water off us. The change was noticeable at once. As the *Fram* cut into the ice crust she gave a sort of spring forward, and, after this, went on at her ordinary speed; and henceforth we had very little more trouble with dead water.

We found what, according, to the map, was Taimur Strait, entirely blocked with ice, and we held farther south, to see if we could not come upon some other strait or passage. It was not an easy matter, finding our way by the map. We had not seen Hovgaard's Islands, marked as lying north of the entrance to Taimur Strait; yet the weather was so beautifully clear, that it seemed unlikely they could have escaped us, if they lay where Nordenskiöld's sketch-map places them. On the other hand, we saw several islands in the offing. These, however, lay so far out that it is not probable that Nordenskiöld saw them, as the weather was thick when he was here; and, besides, it is impossible that islands lying many miles out at sea could have been mapped as close to land, with only a narrow sound separating them from it. Farther south we found a narrow open strait or fjord, which we steamed into, in order if possible to get some better idea of the lay of the land. I sat up in the crow's-nest, hoping for a general clearing up of matters; but the prospect of this seemed to recede farther and farther. What we now had to the north of us, and what I had taken to be a projection of the mainland, proved to be an island; but the fjord wound on farther inland. Now it got narrower — presently it widened out again. The mystery thickened. Could this be Taimur Strait after all? A dead calm on the sea. Fog everywhere over the land. It was well nigh impossible to distinguish the smooth surface of the water from the ice, and the ice from the snow-covered land. Everything is so strangely still and dead. The sea rises and falls with each twist of the fjord through the silent land of mists. Now we have open water ahead, now more ice, and it is impossible to make sure which it is. *Is* this Taimur Strait? Are we getting through? A whole year is at stake!... No! here we stop — nothing but ice ahead.

No! it is only smooth water with the snowy land reflected in it. This must be Taimur Strait.

But now we had several large ice-floes ahead, and it was difficult to get on; so we anchored at a point, in a good, safe harbour, to make a closer inspection. We now discovered that it was a strong tidal current that was carrying the ice-floes with it; and there could be no doubt that it was a strait we were lying in. I rowed out in the evening to shoot some seals, taking for the purpose my most precious weapon, a double-barrelled Express rifle, calibre .577. As we were in the act of taking a sealskin on board, the boat heeled over, I slipped and my rifle fell into the sea — a sad accident. Peter Henriksen and Bentzen, who were rowing me, took it so to heart that they could not speak for some time. They declared that it would never do to leave the valuable gun lying there in 5 fathoms of water. So we rowed to the *Fram* for the necessary apparatus, and dragged the spot for several hours, well on into the dark, gloomy night. While we were thus employed, a bearded seal circled round and round us, bobbing up its big startled face, now on one side of us, now on the other, and always coming nearer; it was evidently anxious to find out what our night work might be. Then it dived over and over again, probably to see how the dragging was getting on. Was it afraid of our finding the rifle?

At last it became too intrusive. I took Peter's rifle, and put a ball through its head; but it sank before we could reach it; and we gave up the whole business in despair. The loss of that rifle saved the life of many a seal; and, — alas! it had cost me £28.

We took the boat again next day and rowed eastward, to find out if there really was a passage for us through this strait. It had turned cold during the night, and snow had fallen, so the sea round the *Fram* was covered with tolerably thick snow ice, and it cost us a good deal of exertion to break through it into open water with the boat. I thought it possible that the land farther in on the north side of the strait might be that in the neighbourhood of Actinia Bay, where the *Vega* had lain; but I sought in vain for the cairn erected there by Nordenskiöld, and presently discovered to my astonishment that it was only a small island, and that this island lay on the south side of the principal entrance to Taimur Strait. The strait was very broad here, and I felt pretty certain that I saw where the real Actinia Bay cut into the land far to the north.

We were hungry now, and were preparing to take a meal before we rowed on from the island, when we discovered to our disappointment that the butter had been forgotten. We crammed down the dry biscuits as best we could, and worked our jaws till they were stiff on the pieces we managed to hack off a hard dried reindeer chine. When we were tired of eating, though anything but satisfied, we set off, giving this point the name of "Cape Butterless." We rowed far in through the strait, and it seemed to us to be a good passage for ships, 8 or 9 fathoms right up to the shore. However, we were stopped by ice in the evening, and as we ran the risk of being frozen in if we pushed on any farther, I thought it best to turn. We certainly ran no danger of starving, for we saw fresh tracks both of bears and reindeer everywhere, and there were plenty of seals in the water; but I was afraid of delaying the *Fram* in view of the possibility of progress in another direction. So we toiled back against a strong wind, not reaching the ship till next morning; and this was none too early, for presently we were in the midst of a storm.

On the subject of the navigability of Taimur Strait, Nordenskiöld writes that, "according to soundings made by Lieutenant Palander, it is obstructed by rocky shallows; and being also full of strong currents, it is hardly advisable to sail through it, at least until the direction of these currents has been carefully investigated." I have nothing particular to add to this, except that, as already mentioned, the channel was clear as far as we penetrated, and had the appearance of being practicable as far as I could see. I was, therefore, determined that we would, if necessary, try to force our way through with the *Fram*.

The 5th of September brought snow with a stiff breeze, which steadily grew stronger. When it was rattling in the rigging in the evening we congratulated each other on being safe on board — it would not have been an easy matter to row back to-day. But altogether I was dissatisfied. There was some chance, indeed, that this wind might loosen the ice farther north, and yesterday's experiences had given me the hope of being able, in case of necessity, to force a way through this strait; but now the wind was steadily driving larger masses of ice in past us; and this approach of winter was alarming — it might quite well be on us in earnest before any channel was opened. I tried to reconcile myself to the idea of wintering in our present surroundings. I had already laid all the plans for the way in which we were to occupy ourselves during the coming year. Besides an investigation of this coast, which offered problems enough to solve, we were to explore the unknown interior of the Taimur Peninsula right across to the mouth of the Chatanga. With our dogs and snow-shoes we should be able to go far and wide; so the year would not be a lost one as regarded geography and geology. But no! I could not reconcile myself to it! I could not! A year of one's life was a year; and our expedition promised to be a long one at best. What tormented me most was the reflection that if the ice stopped us now, we could have no assurance that it would not do the same at the same time next year. It has been observed so often that several bad ice-years come together, and this was evidently none of the best. Though I would hardly confess the feeling of depression even to myself, I must say that it was not on a bed of roses I lay these nights, until sleep came and carried me off into the land of forgetfulness.

Wednesday, the 6th of September, was the anniversary of my wedding-day. I was superstitious enough to feel when I awoke in the morning, that this day would bring a change, if one were coming at all. The storm had gone down a little, the sun peeped out, and life seemed brighter. The wind quieted down altogether in the course of the afternoon, the weather becoming calm and beautiful. The strait to the north of us, which was blocked before with solid ice, had been swept open by the storm; but the strait to the east, where we had been with the boat, was firmly blocked, and if we had not turned when we did that evening, we should have been there yet, and for no one knows how long. It seemed to us not improbable that the ice between Cape Lapteff and Almquist's Islands might be broken up. We, therefore, got up steam and set off north about 6.30 p.m. to try our fortune once more. I felt quite sure that the day would bring us luck. The weather was still beautiful, and we were thoroughly enjoying the sunshine. It was such an unusual thing that Nordahl, when he was working among the coals in the hold in the afternoon, mistook a sunbeam falling through the hatch on the coal dust for a plank, and leaned hard on it. He was not a little surprised when he fell right through it on to some iron lumber.

It became more and more difficult to make anything of the land, and our observation for latitude at noon did not help to clear up matters. It placed us at 76° 2' north latitude, or about 14 miles from what is marked as the mainland on Nordenskiöld's or Bove's nap. It was hardly to be expected that these should be correct, as the weather seems to have been foggy the whole time the explorers were here.

Nor were we successful in finding Hovgaard's Islands as we sailed north. When I supposed that we were off them, just on the north side of the entrance to Taimur Strait, I saw, to my surprise, a high mountain almost directly north of us, which seemed as if it must be on the mainland. What could be the explanation of this? I began to have a growing suspicion that this was a regular labyrinth of islands we had got into. We were hoping to investigate and clear up

Bernhard Nordahl.

the matter, when thick weather, with sleet and rain, most inconveniently came on, and we had to leave this problem for the future to solve.

The mist was thick, and soon the darkness of night was added to it, so that we could not see land at any great distance. It might seem rather risky to push ahead now, but it was an opportunity not to be lost. We slackened speed a little, and kept on along the coast all night, in readiness to turn as soon as land was observed ahead. Satisfied that things were in good hands, as it was Sverdrup's watch, I lay down in my berth with a lighter mind than I had had for long.

At 6 o'clock next morning (September 7th) Sverdrup roused me with the information that we had passed Taimur Island, or Cape Lapteff, at 3 a.m., and were now at Taimur Bay, but with close ice and an island ahead. It was possible that we might reach the island, as a channel had just opened through the ice in that direction; but we were at present in a tearing "whirlpool" current, and should be obliged to put back for the moment. After breakfast I went up into the crow's nest. It was brilliant sunshine. I found that Sverdrup's island must be mainland, which, however, stretched remarkably far west compared with that given on the maps. I could still see Taimur Island behind me, and the most easterly of Almquist's Islands lay gleaming in the sun to the north. It was a long sandy point that we had ahead, and I could follow the land in a southerly direction till it disappeared on the horizon at the head of the bay in the south. Then there was a small strip where no land, only open water, could be made out. After that the land emerged on the west side of the bay, stretching towards Taimur Island. With its heights and round knolls this land was essentially different from the low coast on the east side of the bay.

To the north of the point ahead of us I saw open water; there was some ice between us and it, but the *Fram* forced her way through. When we got out, right off the point, I was surprised to notice the sea suddenly covered with brown clayey water. It could not be a deep layer, for the track we left behind was quite clear. The clayey water seemed to be skimmed to either side by the passage of the ship. I ordered soundings to be taken, and found, as I expected, shallower water first 8 fathoms, then 6½, then 5½. I stopped now, and backed. Things looked very suspicious, and round us ice-floes lay stranded. There was also a very strong current running north-east. Constantly sounding, we again went slowly forwards. Fortunately the lead went on showing 5 fathoms. Presently we got into deeper water — 6 fathoms, then 6½ — and now we went on at full speed again. We were soon out into the clear, blue water on the other side. There was quite a sharp boundary line between the brown surface water and the clear blue. The muddy water evidently came from some river a little farther south.

From this point the land trended back in an easterly direction, and we held east and north-east in the open water between it and the ice. In the afternoon this channel grew very narrow, and we got right under the coast, where it again slopes north. We kept close along it in a very narrow cut, with a depth of 6 to 8 fathoms, but in the evening had to stop, as the ice lay packed close in to the shore ahead of us.

This land we had been coasting along bore a strong resemblance to Yalmal. The same low plains, rising very little above the sea, and not visible at any great

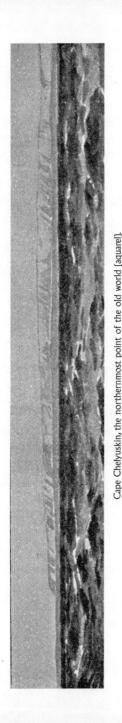

Cape Chelyuskin, the northernmost point of the old world [aquarel].

distance. It was perhaps rather more undulating. At one or two places I even saw some ridges of a certain elevation a little way inland. The shore the whole way seemed to be formed of strata of sand and clay, the margin sloping steeply to the sea.

Many reindeer herds were to be seen on the plains, and next morning (September 8th) I went on shore on a hunting expedition. Having shot one reindeer, I was on my way farther inland in search of more, when I made a surprising discovery, which attracted all my attention, and made me quite forget the errand I had come on. It was a large fjord cutting its way in through the land to the north of me. I went as far as possible to find out all I could about it, but did not manage to see the end of it. So far as I could see, it was a fine broad sheet of water, stretching eastwards to some blue mountains far, far inland, which, at the extreme limit of my vision, seemed to slope down to the water. Beyond them I could distinguish nothing. My imagination was fired, and for a moment it seemed to me as if this might almost be a strait, stretching right across the land here, and making an island of the Chelyuskin Peninsula. But probably it was only a river, which widened out near its mouth into a broad lake, as several of the Siberian rivers do. All about the clay plains I was tramping over, enormous erratic blocks, of various formations, lay scattered. They can only have been brought here by the great glaciers of the Ice Age. There was not much life to be seen. Besides reindeer there were just a few willow-grouse, snow-buntings, and snipe; and I saw tracks of foxes and lemmings. This farthest north part of Siberia is quite uninhabited, and has probably not been visited even by the wandering nomads. However, I saw a circular moss heap on a plain far inland, which looked as if it might be the work of man's hand. Perhaps, after all, some Samoyede had been here collecting moss for his reindeer; but it must have been long ago; for the moss looked quite black and rotten. The heap was quite possibly only one of Nature's freaks — she is often capricious.

What a constant alternation of light and shadow there is in this Arctic land. When I went up to the crow's-nest next morning (September 9th), I saw that the ice to the north had loosened from the land, and I could trace a channel which might lead us northwards into open water. I at once gave the order to get up steam. The barometer was certainly low — lower than we had ever had it yet; it was down to 733 mm. (28.8 inches); the wind was blowing in heavy squalls off the land, and in on the plains the gusts were whirling up clouds of sand and dust.

Sverdrup thought it would be safer to stay where we were; but it would be too annoying to miss this splendid opportunity: and the sunshine was so beautiful, and the sky so smiling and reassuring. I gave orders to set sail, and soon we were pushing on northwards through the ice, under steam, and with every stitch of canvas that we could crowd on. Cape Chelyuskin must be vanquished! Never had the *Fram* gone so fast; she made more than 8 knots by the log; it seemed as though she knew how much depended on her getting on. Soon we were through the ice, and had open water along the land as far as the eye could reach. We passed point after point, discovering new fjords and islands on the way, and soon I thought that I caught a glimpse through the large telescope of some mountains far away north; they must be in the neighbourhood of Cape Chelyuskin itself.

The land along which we to-day coasted to the northward was quite low, some of it like what I had seen on shore the previous day. At some distance from the low coast, fairly high mountains or mountain chains were to be seen. Some of them seemed to consist of horizontal sedimentary schist; they were flat-topped, with precipitous sides. Further inland the mountains were all white with snow. At one point it seemed as if the whole range were covered with a sheet of ice, or great snow field that spread itself down the sides. At the edge of this sheet I could see projecting masses of rock, but all the inner part was spotless white. It seemed almost too continuous and even to be new snow, and looked like a permanent snow mantle.

Nordenskiöld's map marks at this place, "high mountain chains inland"; and this agrees with our observations, though I cannot assert that the mountains are of any considerable height. But when, in agreement with earlier maps, he marks at the same place, "high rocky coast", his terms are open to objection. The coast is, as already mentioned, quite low, and consists, in great part at least, of layers of clay or loose earth. Nordenskiöld either took this last description from the earlier, unreliable maps, or possibly allowed himself to be misled by the fog which beset them during their voyage in these waters.

In the evening we were approaching the north end of the land, but the current, which we had had with us earlier in the day, was now against us, and it seemed as if we were never to get past an island that lay off the shore to the north of us. The mountain height which I had seen at an earlier hour through the telescope, lay here some way inland. It was flat on the top with precipitous sides, like those mountains last described. It seemed to be sandstone or basaltic rock; only the horizontal strata of the ledges on its sides were not visible. I calculated its height at 1,000 to 1,500 feet. Out at sea we saw several new islands, the nearest of them being of some size.

The moment seemed to be at hand, when we were at last to round that point which had haunted us for so long — the second of the greatest difficulties I expected to have to overcome on this expedition. I sat up in the crow's-nest in the evening, looking out to the north. The land was low and desolate. The sun had long since gone down behind the sea, and the dreamy evening sky was yellow and gold. It was lonely and still up here, high above the water. Only one star was to be seen. It stood straight above Cape Chelyuskin, shining clearly and sadly in the pale sky. As we sailed on and got the cape more to the east of us, the star went with it; it was always there, straight above. I could not help sitting watching it. It seemed to have some charm for me, and to bring such peace. Was it my star? Was it the spirit of home following and smiling to me now? Many a thought it brought to me, as the *Fram* toiled on through the melancholy night, past the northernmost point of the old world.

Towards morning we were off what we took to be actually the northern extremity. We stood in near land, and at the change of the watch, exactly at four o'clock, our flags were hoisted, and our three last cartridges sent a thundering salute over the sea. Almost at the same moment the sun rose. Then our poetic doctor burst forth into the following touching lines:

> "Up go the flags, off goes the gun;
> The clock strikes four — and lo, the sun!"

As the sun rose, the Chelyuskin troll, that had so long had us in his power, was banned. We had escaped the danger of a winter's imprisonment on this coast, and we saw the way clear to our goal, the drift ice to the north of the New Siberian Islands. In honour of the occasion, all hands were turned out, and punch, fruit, and cigars were served in the festively lighted saloon. Something special in the way of a toast was expected on such an occasion. I lifted my glass, and made the following speech: "Skoal, my lads, and be glad we've passed Chelyuskin!" Then there was some organ playing, during which I went up into the crow's-nest again, to have a last look at the land. I now saw that the height I had noticed in the evening, which has already been described, lies on the west side of the peninsula, while farther east a lower and more rounded height stretches southward. This last must be the one mentioned by Nordenskiöld, and, according to his description, the real north point must lie out beyond it; so that we were now off King Oscar's Bay; but I looked in vain through the telescope for Nordenskiöld's cairn. I had the greatest inclination to land, but did not think that we could spare the time. The bay, which was clear of ice at the time of the *Vega*'s visit, was now closed in with thick winter ice, frozen fast to the land.

We had an open channel before us; but we could see the edge of the drift-ice out at sea. A little farther west we passed a couple of small islands, lying a short way from the coast. We had to stop before noon at the north-western corner of Chelyuskin, on account of the drift-ice, which seemed to reach right into the land before us. To judge by the dark air, there was open water again on the other side of an island which lay ahead. We landed and made sure that some straits or fjords on the inside of this island to the south were quite closed with firm ice; and in the evening the *Fram* forced her way through the drift-ice on the outside of it. We steamed and sailed southwards along the coast all night, making splendid way; when the wind was blowing stiffest we went at the rate of 9 knots. We came upon ice every now and then, but got through it easily.

Towards morning (September 11th) we had high land ahead, and had to change our course to due east, keeping to this all day. When I came on deck before noon I saw a fine tract of hill country with high summits and valleys between. It was the first view of the sort since we had left Vardö, and after the monotonous low land we had been coasting along for months, it was refreshing to see such mountains again. They ended with a precipitous descent to the east, and eastward from that extended a perfectly flat plain. In the course of the day we quite lost sight of land, and strangely enough did not see it again; nor did

Skinning walruses, the *Fram* in the background (12 September 1893).

we see the Islands of St. Peter and St. Paul, though, according to the maps, our course lay close past them.

Thursday, September 12th. Henriksen awoke me this morning at six with the information that there were several walruses lying on a floe quite close to us. "By Jove!" Up I jumped and had my clothes on in a trice. It was a lovely morning — fine, still weather; the walruses' guffaw sounded over to us along the clear ice surface. They were lying crowded together on a floe a little to landward from us, blue mountains glittering behind them in the sun. At last the harpoons were sharpened, guns and cartridges ready, and Henriksen, Juell and I set off. There seemed to be a slight breeze from the south, so we rowed to the north side of the floe, to get to leeward of the animals. From time to time their sentry raised his head, but apparently did not see us. We advanced slowly, and soon were so near that we had to row very cautiously. Juell kept us going, while Henriksen was ready in the bow with a harpoon, and I behind him with a gun. The moment the sentry raised his head the oars stopped, and we stood motionless; when he sunk it again, a few more strokes brought us nearer.

Body to body they lay close-packed on a small floe, old and young ones mixed. Enormous masses of flesh they were! Now and again one of the ladies fanned herself by moving one of her flappers backwards and forwards over her body; then she lay quiet again on her back or side. "Good gracious! what a lot of meat!" said Juell, who was cook. More and more cautiously we drew near. Whilst I sat ready with the gun, Henriksen took a good grip of the harpoon shaft, and as the boat touched the floe he rose, and off flew the harpoon. But it struck too high, glanced off the tough hide, and skipped over the backs of the animals. Now there was a pretty to do! Ten or twelve great weird faces glared upon us at once; the colossal creatures twisted themselves round with incredible celerity, and came waddling with lifted heads and hollow bellowings to the edge of the ice where we lay. It was undeniably an imposing sight, but I laid my gun to my shoulder and fired at one of the biggest heads. The animal staggered, and then fell head foremost into the water. Now a ball into another head; this creature fell too, but was able to fling itself into the sea. And now the whole flock dashed in, and we as well as they were hidden in spray. It had all happened in a few seconds. But up they came again immediately round the boat, the one head bigger and uglier than the other — their young ones close beside them. They stood up in the water, bellowed and roared till the air trembled, threw themselves forward towards us, then rose up again, and new bellowings filled the air. Then they rolled over and disappeared with a splash, then bobbed up again. The water foamed and boiled for yards around — the ice-world that had been so still before seemed in a moment to have been transformed into a raging Bedlam. Any moment we might expect to have a walrus tusk or two through the boat, or to be heaved up and capsized. Something of this kind was the very least that could happen after such a terrible commotion. But the hurly-burly went on and nothing carne of it. I again picked out my victims. They went on bellowing and grunting like the others, but with blood streaming from their mouths and noses. Another ball, and one tumbled over and floated on the water; now a ball to the second, and it did the same. Henriksen was ready with the harpoons, and secured them both. One more was shot, but we had no more harpoons, and had to strike a seal-hook into it to hold it up. The hook slipped, however, and the animal sank before we could save it. Whilst we were towing our booty to an ice-floe, we were still, for part of the time at least, surrounded by walruses; but there was no use in shooting any more, for we had no means of carrying them off. The *Fram* presently came up and took our two on board, and we were soon going ahead along the coast. We saw many walruses in this part. We shot two others in the afternoon, and could have got many more if we had had time to spare. It was in this same neighbourhood that Nordenskiöld also saw one or two small herds.

We now continued our course, against a strong current, southwards along the coast, past the mouth of the Chatanga. This eastern part of the Talmur Peninsula is a comparatively high, mountainous region, but with a lower level stretch between the mountains and the sea — apparently the same kind of low land we had seen along the coast almost the whole way. As the sea seemed to be tolerably open and free from ice, we made several attempts to shorten our course by leaving the coast and striking across for the mouth of the Olenek; but every time thick ice drove us back to our channel by the land.

On September 14th we were off the land lying between the Chatanga and the Anabara. This also was fairly high mountainous country with a low strip by the sea. "In this respect," so I write in my diary, "this whole coast reminds one very much of Jaderen in Norway. But the mountains here are not so well separated and are considerably lower than those farther north. The sea is unpleasantly shallow; at one time during the night we had only 4 fathoms, and were obliged to put back some distance. We have ice outside, quite close; but yet there is a sufficient fairway to let us push on eastwards." The following day we got into good, open water, but shallow — never more than 6 to 7 fathoms. We heard the roaring of waves to the east, so there must certainly be open water in that direction, which indeed we had expected. It was plain that the Lena, with its masses of warm water, was beginning to assert its influence. The sea here was browner, and showed signs of some mixture of muddy river-water. It was also much less salt.

"It would be foolish," I write in my diary for this day (September 15th), "to go in to the Olenek now that we are so late. Even if there were no danger from shoals, it would cost us too much time — probably a year. Besides it is by no means sure that the *Fram* can get in there at all; it would be a very tiresome business if she went aground in these waters. No doubt we should be very much the better for a few more dogs, but to lose a year is too much; we shall rather head straight east for the New Siberian Islands, now that there is a good opportunity, and really bright prospects.

"The ice here puzzles me a good deal. How in the world is it not swept northwards by the current which, according to my calculations, ought to set north from this coast, and which indeed we ourselves have felt? And it is such hard, thick ice has the appearance of being several years old. Does it come from the eastward, or does it lie and grind round here in the sea between the 'north-going' current of the Lena and the Taimur Peninsula? I cannot tell yet, but anyhow it is different from the thin one-year-old ice we have seen until now in the Kara Sea and west of Cape Chelyuskin.

"Saturday, September 16th. We are keeping a north-westerly course (by compass through open water) and have got pretty well north, but see no ice, and the air is dark to the northward. Mild weather and water comparatively warm, as high as 35° Fahr. We have the current against us, and are always considerably west of our reckoning. Several flocks of eider-duck were seen in the course of the day. We ought to have land to the north of us; can it be that which is keeping back the ice?"

Next day we met ice, and had to hold a little to the south to keep clear of it; and I began to fear that we should not be able to get as far as I had hoped. But in my notes for the following day (Monday, September 18th) I read: "A splendid day. Shaped our course northwards, to the west of Bielkoff Island. Open sea; good wind from the west; good progress. Weather clear, and we had a little sunshine in the afternoon. Now the decisive moment approaches. At 12.15 shaped our course north to east (by compass). Now it is to be proved if my theory, on which the whole expedition is based, is correct if we are to find a little north from here a north-flowing current. So far everything is better than I had expected. We are in latitude 75½° N., and have still open water and dark sky to the north and west. In the evening there was ice-light ahead and on the starboard bow. About seven I thought that I could see ice, which, however, rose so regularly that it more resembled land, but it was too dark to see distinctly. It seemed as if it might be Bielkoff Island, and a big light spot farther to the east might even be the reflection from the snow-covered Kotelnoi. I should have liked to run in here, partly to see a little of this interesting island, and partly to inspect the stores which we knew had been deposited for us here by the friendly care of Baron von Toll; but time was precious, and to the north the sea seemed to lie open to us. Prospects were bright, and we sailed steadily northwards, wondering what the morrow would bring. Disappointment or hope? If all went well we should reach Sannikoff Land — that, as yet, untrodden ground.

"It was a strange feeling to be sailing away north in the dark night to unknown lands, over an open, rolling sea, where no ship, no boat had been before. We might have been hundreds of miles away in more southerly waters, the air was so mild for September in this latitude.

"Tuesday, September 19th. I have never had such a splendid sail. On to the north, steadily north, with a good wind, as fast as steam and sail can take us, and open sea mile after mile, watch after watch, through these unknown regions, always clearer and clearer of ice one might almost say! How long will this last? The eye always turns to the northward as one paces the bridge. It is gazing into the future. But there is always the same dark sky ahead, which means open sea. My plan was standing its test. It seemed as if luck had been on our side ever since the 6th of September. We see 'nothing but clean water,' as Henriksen answered from the crow's-nest when I called up to him. When he was standing at the wheel later in the morning, and I was on the bridge, he suddenly said: 'They little think at home in Norway just now that we are sailing straight for the Pole in clear water.' 'No, they don't believe we have got so far.' And I shouldn't have believed it myself if anyone had prophesied it to me a fortnight ago; but true it is. All my reflections and inferences on the subject had led me to expect open water for a good way farther north; but it is seldom that one's inspirations turn out to be so correct. No ice-light in any direction, not even now in the evening. We saw no land the whole day; but we had fog and thick weather all the morning and forenoon, so that we were still going at half speed, as we were afraid of coming suddenly on something. Now we are almost in 77° north latitude. How long is it to go on? I have said all along that I should be glad if we reached 78°; but Sverdrup is less easily satisfied; he says over 80° — perhaps 84°, 85°. He even talks seriously of the open Polar Sea, which he once read about; he always comes back upon it, in spite of my laughing at him.

"I have almost to ask myself if this is not a dream. One must have gone against the stream to know what it means to go with the stream. As it was on the Greenland Expedition, so it is here:

"'Dort ward der Traum zur Wirklichkeit,
Hier wird die wirklichkeit zum Traum!'

"Hardly any life visible here. Saw an auk or black guillemot to-day, and later a sea-gull in the distance. When I was hauling up a bucket of water in the evening to wash the deck, I noticed that it was sparkling with phosphorescence. One could almost have imagined one's self to be in the south.

"Wednesday, September 20th. I have had a rough awakening from my dream. As I was sitting at 11 a.m. looking at the map and thinking that my cup would soon be full — we had almost reached 78° — there was a sudden luff, and I rushed out. Ahead of us lay the edge of the ice, long and compact, shining through the fog. I had a strong inclination to go eastward, on the possibility of there being land in that direction; but it looked as if the ice extended farther south there, and there was the probability of being able to reach a higher latitude if we kept west; so we headed that way. The sun broke through for a moment just now, so we took an observation, which showed us to be in about 77° 44' north latitude."

We now held north-west along the edge of the ice. It seemed to me as if there might be land at no great distance, we saw such a remarkable number of birds of various kinds. A flock of snipe or wading birds met its, followed us for a time, and then took their way south. They were probably on their passage from some land to the north of us. We could see nothing as the fog lay persistently over the ice. Again, later, we saw flocks of small snipe, indicating the possible proximity of land. Next day the weather was clearer, but still there was no land in sight. We were now a good way north of the spot where Baron von Toll has mapped the south coast of Sannikoff Land, but in about the same longitude. So it is probably only a small island, and in any case cannot extend far north.

On September 21st we had thick fog again, and when we had sailed north to the head of a bay in the ice, and could get no farther, I decided to wait here for clear weather to see if progress farther north were possible. I calculated that we were now in about 78½° north latitude. We tried several tunes during the day to take soundings, but did not succeed in reaching the bottom with 215 fathoms of line.

"To-day made the disagreeable discovery that there are bugs on board. Must plan a campaign against them.

"Friday, September 22nd. Brilliant sunshine once again, and white dazzling ice ahead. First we lay still in the fog because we could not see which way to go; now it is clear and we know just as little about it. It looks as if we were at the northern boundary of the open water. To the west the ice appears to extend south again. To the north it is compact and white — only a small open rift or pool every here and there; and the sky is whitish-blue everywhere on the horizon. It is from the east we have just come, but there we could see very little; and for want of anything better to do, we shall make a short excursion in that direction, on the possibility of finding openings in the ice. If there were only time, what I should like would be to go east as far as Sannikoff Island, or, better still, all the way to Bennet Land, to see what condition things are in there; but it is too late now. The sea will soon be freezing, and we should run a great risk of being frozen in at a disadvantageous point."

Earlier Arctic explorers have considered it a necessity to keep near some coast. But this was exactly what I wanted to avoid. It was the drift of the ice that I wished to get into, and what I most feared was being blocked by land. It seemed as if we might do much worse than give ourselves up to the ice where we were, especially as our excursion to the east had proved that following the ice-edge in that direction would soon force us south again. So in the meantime we made fast to a great ice-block, and prepared to clean the boiler and shift coals. "We are lying in open water, with only a few large floes here and there; but I have a presentiment that this is our winter harbour.

"Great bug war today. We play the big steam hose on mattresses, sofa-cushions — everything that we think can possibly harbour the enemies. All clothes are put into a barrel, which is hermetically closed, except where the hose is introduced. Then full steam is set on. It whizzes and whistles inside, and a little forces its way through the joints, and we think that the animals must be having a fine hot time of it. But suddenly the barrel cracks, the steam rushes out, and the lid bursts off with a violent explosion, and is flung far along the deck. I still hope that there has been a great slaughter, for these are horrible enemies. Juell tried the old experiment of setting one on a piece of wood to see if it would creep north. It would not move at all, so he took a blubber hook and hit it to make it go; but it would do nothing but wriggle its head — the harder he hit the more it wriggled. 'Squash it, then,' said Bentzen. And squashed it was.

"Saturday, September 23rd. We are still at the same moorings, working at the coal. An enjoyable contrast — everything on board, men and dogs included, black and filthy, and everything around white and bright in beautiful sunshine. It looks as if more ice were driving in.

"Sunday, September 24th. Still coal shifting. Fog in the morning, which cleared off as the day went on, when we discovered that we were closely surrounded on all sides by tolerably thick ice. Between the floes lies slush-ice, which will soon be quite firm. There is an open pool to be seen to the north, but not a large one. From the crow's-nest, with the telescope, we can still descry the sea across the ice to the south.

It looks as if we were being shut in. Well, we must e'en bid the ice welcome. A dead region this; no life in any direction, except a single seal (*phoca foetida*) in the water; and on the floe beside us we can see a bear-track some days old. We again try to get soundings, but still find no bottom; it is remarkable that there should be such depth here."

Ugh! one can hardly imagine a dirtier, nastier job than a spell of coal-shifting on board. It is a pity that such a useful thing as coal should be so black! What we are doing now is only hoisting it from the hold, and filling the bunkers with it; but every man on board must help, and everything is in a mess. So many men must stand on the coal heap in the hold and fill the buckets, and so many hoist them. Jacobsen is specially good at this last job; his strong arms pull up bucket after bucket as if they were as many boxes of matches. The rest of us go backwards and forwards with the buckets between the main-hatch and the half-deck, pouring the coal into the bunkers; and down below stands Amundsen packing it, as black as he can be. Of course coal-dust is flying over the whole deck; the dogs creep into corners, black and tousled; and we ourselves — well, we don't wear our best clothes on such days. We got some amusement out of the remarkable appearance of our faces, with their dark complexions, black streaks at the most unlikely places, and eyes and white teeth shining through the dirt. Anyone happening to touch the white wall below with his hand leaves a black five-fingered blot; and the doors have a wealth of such mementoes. The seats of the sofas must have their wrong sides turned up, else they would bear lasting marks of another part of the body; and the tablecloth — well, we fortunately do not possess such a thing. In short, coal-shifting is as dirty and wretched an experience as one can well imagine in these bright and pure surroundings. One good thing is that there is plenty of fresh water to wash with; we can find it in every hollow on the floes, so there is some hope of our being clean again in time, and it is possible that this may be our last coal-shifting.

"Monday, September 25th. Frozen in faster and faster! Beautiful still weather; 13 degrees of frost last night. Winter is coming now. Had a visit from a bear, which was off again before anyone got a shot at it."

Chapter 6

Winter Night

IT really looked as if we were now frozen in for good and I did not expect to get the *Fram* out of the ice till we were on the other side of the Pole, nearing the Atlantic Ocean. Autumn was already well advanced; the sun stood lower in the heavens day by day; and the temperature sank steadily. The long night of winter was approaching — that dreaded night. There was nothing to be done except prepare ourselves for it, and by degrees we converted our ship, as well as we could, into comfortable winter quarters; while at the same time we took every precaution to assure her against the destructive influences of cold, drift-ice, and the other forces of nature to which it was prophesied that we must succumb. The rudder was hauled up, so that it might not be destroyed by the pressure of the ice. We had intended to do the same with the screw; but as it, with its iron case, would certainly help to strengthen the stern, and especially the rudder stock, we let it remain in its place. We had a good deal of work with the engine, too; each separate part was taken out, oiled, and laid away for the winter; slide-valves, pistons, shafts, were examined and thoroughly cleaned. All this was done with the very greatest care. Amundsen looked after that engine as if it had been his own child; late and early he was down tending it lovingly; and we used to tease him about it, to see the defiant look come into his eyes and hear him say: "It's all very well for you to talk, but there's not such another engine in the world, and it would be a sin and a shame not to take good care of it." Assuredly he left nothing undone. I do not suppose a day passed, winter or summer, all these three years, that he did not go down and caress it, and do something or other for it.

We cleared up in the hold to make room for a joiner's workshop down there; our mechanical workshop we had in the engine-room. The smithy was at first on deck, and afterwards on the ice; tinsmith's work was done chiefly in the chart room, shoemaker's and sailmaker's, and various odd sorts of work, in the saloon. And all these occupations were carried on with interest and activity during the rest of the expedition. There was nothing, from the most delicate instruments down to wooden shoes and axe-handles, that could not be made on board the *Fram*. When we were found to be short of sounding-line, a grand rope-walk was constructed on the ice. It proved to be a very profitable undertaking, and was well patronised.

Presently we began putting up the windmill which was to drive the dynamo and produce the electric light. While the ship was going, the dynamo was driven by the engine, but for a long time past we had had to be contented with petroleum lamps in our dark cabins. The windmill was erected on the port side of the fore-deck, between the main hatch and the rail. It took several weeks to get this important appliance into working order.

As mentioned before, we had also brought with us a "horse-mill" for driving the dynamo. I had thought that it might be of service in giving us exercise whenever there was no other physical work for us. But this time never came, and so the "horse-mill" was never used. There was always something to occupy us; and it was not difficult to find work for each man that gave him sufficient exercise, and so much distraction that the time did not seem to him unbearably long.

There was the care of the ship and rigging, the inspection of sails, ropes, etc., etc.; there were provisions of all kinds to be got out from the cases down in the hold, and handed over to the cook; there was ice — good, pure, fresh-water ice — to be found and carried to the galley to be melted for cooking, drinking and washing-water. Then, as already mentioned, there was always something doing in the various workshops. Now "Smith Lars" had to straighten the longboat davits which had been twisted by the waves in the Kara Sea; now it was a hook, a knife, a bear-trap, or something else to be forged. The tinsmith, again "Smith Lars," had to solder together a great tin pail for the ice melting in the galley. The mechanic, Amundsen, would have an order for some instrument or other — perhaps a new current-gauge. The watchmaker, Mogstad, would have a thermograph to examine and clean, or a new spring to put into a watch. The sail-maker might have an order for a quantity of dog harness. Then each man had to be his own shoemaker — make himself canvas boots with thick, warm,

The smithy on board. Henriksen, Pettersen, Sverdrup and Bentzen.

wooden soles, according to Sverdrup's newest pattern. Presently there would come an order to mechanician Amundsen for a supply of new zinc music-sheets for the organ — these being a brand-new invention of the leader of the expedition. The electrician would have to examine and clean the accumulator batteries, which were in danger of freezing. When at last the windmill was ready, it had to be attended to, turned according to the wind, etc. And when the wind was too strong, some one had to climb up and reef the mill sails, which was not a pleasant occupation in this winter cold, and involved much breathing on fingers and rubbing of the tip of the nose.

It happened now and then, too, that the ship required to be pumped. This became less and less necessary as the water froze round her and in the interstices in her sides. The pumps, therefore, were not touched from December, 1893, till July, 1895. The only noticeable leakage during that time was in the engine-room; but it was nothing of any consequence; just a few buckets of ice that had to be hewn away every month from the bottom of the ship and hoisted up.

To these varied employments was presently added, as the most important of all, the taking of scientific observations, which gave many of us constant occupation. Those that involved the greatest labour were, of course, the meteorological observations, which were taken every four hours day and night; indeed, for a considerable part of the time, every two hours. They kept one man, sometimes two, at work all day. It was Hansen who had the principal charge of this department, and his regular assistant until March, 1895, was Johansen, whose place was then taken by Nordahl. The night observations were taken by whoever was on watch. About every second day when the weather was clear, Hansen and his assistant took the astronomical observation which ascertained our position. This was certainly the work which was followed with most interest by all the members of the expedition; and it was not uncommon to see Hansen's cabin, while he was making his calculations, besieged with idle spectators, waiting to hear the result — whether we had drifted north or south since the last observation, and how far. The state of feeling on board very much depended on these results.

Hansen had also at stated periods to take observations to determine the magnetic constant in this unknown region. These were carried on at first in a tent, specially constructed for the purpose, which was soon erected on the ice; but later we built him a large snow hut, as being both more suitable and more comfortable.

For the ship's doctor there was less occupation. He looked long and vainly for patients, and at last had to give it up and in despair take to doctoring the dogs. Once a month he too had to make his scientific observations, which consisted in the weighing of each man, and the counting of blood corpuscles, and estimating the amount of blood pigment, in order to ascertain the number of red blood corpuscles and the quantity of red colouring matter (haemoglobin) in the blood of each. This was also work that was watched with anxious interest, as every man thought he could tell from the result obtained how long it would be before scurvy overtook him.

Among our scientific pursuits may also be mentioned the determining of the temperature of the water and of its degree of saltness at varying depths; the collection and examination of such animals as are to be found in these northern seas; the ascertaining of the amount of electricity in the air; the observation of the formation of the ice, its growth and thickness, and of the temperature of the different layers of ice; the investigation of the currents in the water under it, etc., etc. I had the main charge of this department. There remains to be

Dr Blessing in his cabin.

mentioned the regular observation of the aurora borealis, which we had a splendid opportunity of studying. After I had gone on with it for some time, Blessing undertook this part of my duties; and when I left the ship, I made over to him all the other observations that were under my charge. Not an inconsiderable item of our scientific work were the soundings and dredgings. At the greater depths, it was such an undertaking that everyone had to assist; and from the way we were obliged to do it later, one sounding sometimes gave occupation for several days.

One day differed very little from another on board, and the description of one is, in every particular of any importance, a description of all.

We all turned out at eight, and breakfasted on hard bread (both rye and wheat), cheese (Dutch clove cheese), Cheddar, Gruyere, and Mysost, or goat's-whey cheese, prepared from dry powder, corned beef or corned mutton, luncheon ham or Chicago tinned tongue or bacon, cod-caviar, anchovy roe; also oatmeal biscuits or English ship-biscuits with orange marmalade or Frame Food jelly. Three times a week we had fresh-baked bread as well, and often cake of some kind. As for our beverages we began by having coffee and chocolate day about; but afterwards had coffee only two days a week, tea two, and chocolate three.

After breakfast some men went to attend to the dogs — give them their food, which consisted of half a stock-fish or a couple of dog biscuits each; let them loose; or do whatever else there was to do for them. The others went all to their different tasks. Each took his turn of a week in the galley — helping the cook to wash up, lay the table, and wait. The cook himself had to arrange his bill of fare for dinner immediately after breakfast, and to set about his preparations at once. Some of us would take a turn on the floe to get some fresh air, and to examine the state of the ice, its pressure, etc. At one o'clock all were assembled for dinner, which generally consisted of three courses — soup, meat, and dessert; or, soup, fish, and meat; or fish, meat, and dessert; or sometimes only fish and meat. With the meat we always had potatoes and either green vegetables or maccaroni. I think we were all agreed that the fare was good; it would hardly have been better at home; for some of us it would perhaps have been worse. And we looked like fatted pigs; one or two even began to cultivate a double chin and a corporation. As a rule, stories and jokes circulated at table along with the bockbeer.

After dinner the smokers of our company would march off, well fed and contented, into the galley, which was smoking-room as well as kitchen, tobacco being tabooed in the cabins except on festive occasions. Out there they had a good smoke and chat; many a story was told, and not seldom some warm dispute arose. Afterwards came, for most of us, a short siesta. Then each went to his work again until we were summoned to supper at six o'clock, when the regulation day's work was done. Supper was almost the same as breakfast, except that tea was always the beverage. Afterwards there was again smoking in the galley, while the saloon was transformed into a silent reading-room. Good use was made of the valuable library presented to the expedition by generous publishers and other friends. If the kind donors could have seen us away up there, sitting round the table at night with heads buried in books or collections of illustrations, and could have understood how invaluable these companions were to us, they would have felt rewarded by the knowledge that they had conferred a real boon — that they had materially assisted in making the *Fram* the little oasis that it was in this vast ice desert. About half-past seven or eight cards or other games were brought out, and we played well on into the night,

View over the drift ice.

seated in groups round the saloon table. One or other of us might go to the organ, and with the assistance of the crank handle, perform some of our beautiful pieces, or Johansen would bring out the accordion and play many a fine tune. His crowning efforts were "Oh, Susanna!" and "Napoleon's March across the Alps in an Open Boat." About midnight we turned in, and then the night watch was set. Each man went on for an hour. Their most trying work on watch seems to have been writing their diaries and looking out, when the dogs barked, for any signs of bears at hand. Besides this, every two hours or four hours, the watch had to go aloft or on to the ice to take the meteorological observations.

I believe I may safely say that on the whole the time passed pleasantly and imperceptibly, and that we thrived in virtue of the regular habits imposed upon us.

My notes from day to day will give the best idea of our life, in all its monotony. They are not great events that are here recorded, but in their very bareness they give a true picture. Such, and no other, was our life. I shall give some quotations direct from my diary: —

"Tuesday, September 26th. Beautiful weather. The sun stands much lower now; it was 9° above the horizon at midday. Winter is rapidly approaching; there are 14½° of frost this evening, but we do not feel it cold. To-day's observations unfortunately show no particular drift northwards; according to them we are still in 78° 50' north latitude. I wandered about over the floe towards evening. Nothing more wonderfully beautiful can exist than the Arctic night. It is dreamland, painted in the imagination's most delicate tints; it is colour etherealised. One shade melts into the other, so that you cannot tell where one ends and the other begins, and yet they are all there. No forms — it is all faint, dreamy colour music, a far-away, long-drawn-out melody on muted strings. Is not all life's beauty high, and delicate, and pure like this night? Give it brighter colours, and it is no longer so beautiful. The sky is like an enormous cupola, blue at the zenith, shading down into green, and then into lilac and violet at the edges. Over the ice-fields there are cold violet-blue shadows, with lighter pink tints where a ridge here and there catches the last reflection of the vanished day. Up in the blue of the cupola shine the stars, speaking peace, as they always do, those unchanging friends. In the south stands a large red-yellow moon, encircled by a yellow ring and light golden clouds floating on the blue background. Presently the aurora borealis shakes over the vault of heaven its veil of glittering silver — changing now to yellow, now to green, now to red. It spreads, it contracts again, in restless change, next it breaks into waving, many-folded bands of shining silver, over which shoot billows of glittering rays; and then the glory vanishes. Presently it shimmers in tongues of flame over the very zenith; and then again it shoots a bright ray right up from the horizon, until the whole melts away in the moonlight, and it is as though one heard the sigh of a departing spirit. Here and there are left a few waving streamers of light, vague as a foreboding — they are the dust from the aurora's glittering cloak. But now it is growing again; new lightnings shoot up; and the endless game begins afresh. And all the time this utter stillness, impressive as the symphony of infinitude. I have never been able to grasp the fact that this earth will some day be spent and desolate and empty. To what end, in that case, all this beauty, with not a creature to rejoice in it? Now I begin to divine it. *This* is the coming earth — here are beauty and death. But to what purpose? Ah, what is the purpose of all these spheres? Read the answer if you can in the starry blue firmament.

"Wednesday, September 27th. Grey weather and strong wind from the south-south-west. Nordahl, who is cook to-day, had to haul up some salt meat which, rolled in a sack, had been steeping for two days in the sea. As soon as he got hold of it he called out, horrified, that it was crawling with animals. He let go the sack, and jumped away from it, the animals scattering round in every direction. They proved to be sand-hoppers, or *amphipodae* which had eaten their way into the meat. There were pints of them, both inside and outside of the sack. A pleasant discovery; there will be no need to starve when such food is to be had by hanging a sack in the water.

"Bentzen is the wag of the party; he is always playing some practical joke. Just now one of the men came rushing up and stood respectfully waiting for me to speak to him. It was Bentzen that had told him I wanted him. It won't be long before he has thought of some new trick.

"Thursday, September 28th. Snowfall with wind. To-day the dogs' hour of release has come. Until now their life on board has been really a melancholy one. They have been tied up ever since we left Khabarova. The stormy seas have broken over them, and they have been rolled here and there in the water on the deck; they have half hanged themselves in their leashes, howling miserably; they have had the hose played over them every time the deck was washed; they have been sea-sick; in bad as in good weather they have had to lie on the spot hard fate had chained them to, without more exercise than going backwards and forwards the length of their chains. It is thus you are treated, you splendid animals, who are to be our stay in the hour of need! When that time comes, you

16. Hemlandssång. 'A le misérable.'
17. Diamanten und Perlen.
18. Marsch de 'Det lustiga Kriget.'
19. Valse de 'Det lustige Kriget.'
20. Priere du Freischütz."

I hope my readers will admit that this was quite a fine entertainment to be given in latitude 79° north; but of such we had many on board the *Fram* at still higher latitudes.

"Coffee and sweets were served after dinner; and after a better supper than usual, came strawberry and lemon ice (*alias* granitta) and limejuice toddy, without alcohol. The health of the hero of the day was first proposed in a few well-chosen words; and then we drank a bumper to the seventy-ninth degree, which we were sure was only the first of many degrees to be conquered in the same way.

"Saturday, September 30th. I am not satisfied that the *Fram*'s present position is a good one for the winter. The great floe on the port side to which we are moored sends out an ugly projection about amidships, which might give her a bad squeeze in case of the ice packing. We therefore began to-day to warp her backwards into better ice. It is by no means quick work. The comparatively open channel around us is now covered with tolerably thick ice, which has to be hewn and broken in pieces with axes, ice-staves, and walrus-spears. Then the capstan is manned, and we heave her through the broken floe foot by foot. The temperature this evening is 9.4° Fahr. (−12.6? C.). A wonderful sunset."

"Sunday, October 1st. Wind from the W.S.W. and weather mild. We are taking a day of rest, which means eating, sleeping, smoking, and reading.

"Monday, October 2nd. Warped the ship farther astern, until we found a good berth for her out in the middle of the newly-frozen pool. On the port side we have our big floe, with the dogs' camp — thirty-five black dogs tied up on the white ice. This floe turns a low, and by no means threatening, edge towards us. We have good low ice on the starboard too; and between the ship and the floes we have on both sides the newly-frozen surface ice, which has, in the process of warping, also got packed in under the ship's bottom, so that she lies in a good bed.

"As Sverdrup, Juell, and I were sitting in the chartroom in the afternoon splicing rope for the sounding-line, Peter[24] rushed in shouting, 'A bear! a bear!' I snatched up my rifle, and tore out. 'Where is it?' 'There, near the tent, on the starboard side; it came right up to it, and had almost got hold of them.'

"And there it was, big and yellow, sniffing away at the tent gear. Hansen, Blessing, and Johansen were running at the top of their speed towards the ship. On to the ice I jumped, and off I went, broke through, stumbled, fell, and up again. The bear in the meantime had done sniffing, and had probably determined that an iron spade, an ice-staff, an axe, some tent-pegs, and a canvas tent were too indigestible food even for a bear's stomach. Anyhow it was following with mighty strides in the track of the fugitives, It caught sight of me, and stopped astonished, as if it were thinking, 'What sort of insect can that be?' I went on to within easy range; it stood still, looking hard at me. At last it turned its head a little, and I gave it a ball in the neck. Without moving a limb, it sank slowly to the ice. I now let loose some of the dogs, to accustom them to this sort of sport, but they showed a lamentable want of interest in it; and 'Kvik,' on whom all our hope in the matter of bear-hunting rested, bristled up and approached the dead animal very slowly and carefully, with her tail between her legs — a sorry spectacle.

"I must now give the story of the others who made the bear's acquaintance first. Hansen had to-day begun to set up his observatory tent a little ahead of the ship on the starboard bow. In the afternoon he got Blessing and Johansen to help him. While they were hard at work they caught sight of a bear not far from them, just off the bow of the *Fram*.

"'Hush! Keep quiet, in case we frighten him,' says Hansen.

"'Yes, yes!' And they crouch together and look at him.

"'I think I'd better try to slip on board and announce him,' says Blessing.

"'I think you should,' says Hansen.

"And off steals Blessing on tiptoe, so as not to frighten the bear. By this time Bruin has seen and scented them, and comes jogging along, following his nose, towards them.

"'Hansen now began to get over his fear of startling him. The bear caught sight of Blessing slinking off to the ship, and set after him. Blessing also was now much less concerned than he had been as to the bear's nerves. He stopped uncertain what to do; but a moment's reflection brought him to the conclusion that it was pleasanter to be three than one just then, and he went back to the others faster than he had gone from them. The bear followed at a good rate. Hansen did not like the look of things, and thought the time had come to try a dodge he had seen recommended in a book. He raised himself to his full height, flung his arms about, and yelled with all the power of his lungs, ably

Scott Hansen's tent for magnetic observations.

assisted by the others. But the bear came on quite undisturbed. The situation was becoming critical. Each snatched up his weapon — an ice-staff, Johansen an axe, and Blessing nothing. They screamed with all their strength, 'Bear! bear!' and set off for the ship as hard as they could tear. But the bear held on his steady course to the tent, and examined everything there before (as we have seen) he went after them.

"It was a lean he-bear. The only thing that was found in its stomach when it was opened was a piece of paper, with the names 'Lütken and Mohn.' This was the wrapping paper of a 'ski' light, and had been left by one of us somewhere on the ice. After this day some of the members of the expedition would hardly leave the ship without being armed to the teeth."

"Wednesday, October 4th. North-westerly wind yesterday and to-day. Yesterday we had −16° (3° F.), and to-day −14° C. (7° F.). I have worked all day at soundings and got to about 800 fathoms depth. The bottom samples consisted of a layer of grey clay 4 to 4¼ inches thick, and below that brown clay or mud. The temperature was, strangely enough, just above freezing point (+0.18° C.) at the bottom, and just below freezing point (−0.4° C.) 75 fathoms up. This rather disposes of the story of a shallow polar basin, and of the extreme coldness of the water of the Arctic Ocean.

"While we were hauling up the line in the afternoon, the ice cracked a little astern of the *Fram*, and the crack increased in breadth so quickly, that three of us, who had to go out to save the ice-anchors, were obliged to make a bridge over it with a long board to get back to the ship again. Later in the evening there was some packing in the ice, and several new passages opened out behind this first one.

"Thursday, October 5th. As I was dressing this morning, just before breakfast, the mate rushed down to tell me a bear was in sight. I was soon on deck and saw him coming from the south, to the lee of us. He was still a good way off, but stopped and looked about. Presently he lay down, and Henriksen and I started off across the ice, and were lucky enough to send a bullet into his breast at about 350 yards, just as he was moving off.

"We are making everything snug for the winter and for the ice pressure. This afternoon we took up the rudder. Beautiful weather, but cold, −18° C. (−0.4° F.) at 8 p.m. The result of the medical inspection to-day was the discovery that we still have bugs on board; and I do not know what we are to do. We have no steam now, and must fix our hopes on the cold.

"I must confess that this discovery made me feel quite ill. If bugs got into our winter furs the thing was hopeless. So the next day there was a regular feast of purification, according to the most rigid antiseptic prescriptions. Each man had to deliver up his old clothes, every stitch of them, wash himself, and dress in new ones from top to toe. All the old clothes, fur rugs, and such things, were carefully carried up on to the deck, and kept there the whole winter. This was more than even these animals could stand; −53° C. (−63° F.) of cold proved to be too much for them, and we saw no more of them. As the bug is made to say in the popular rhyme:

'Put me in the boiling pot, and shut me down tight;

But don't leave me out on a cold winter night!'

"Friday, October 6th. Cold, down to 11° below zero (Fahr.). To-day we have begun to rig up the windmill. The ice has been packing to the north of the *Fram's* stern. As the dogs will freeze if they are kept tied up and get no exercise, we let them loose this afternoon, and are going to try if we can leave them so. Of course they at once began to fight, and some poor creatures limped away from the battle-field scratched and torn. But otherwise great joy prevailed; they leaped, and ran, and rolled themselves in the snow. Brilliant aurora in the evening.

"Saturday, October 7th. Still cold, with the same northerly wind we have had all these last days. I am afraid we are drifting far south now. A few days ago we were, according to the observations, in 78° 47' north latitude. That was 16' south in less than a week. This is too much; but we must make it up again: we must get north. It means going away from home now, but soon it will mean going nearer home. What depth of beauty, with an undercurrent of endless sadness, there is in these dreamily glowing evenings! The vanished sun has left its track of melancholy flame. Nature's music, which fills all space, is instinct with sorrow that all this beauty should be spread out day after day, week after week, year after year, over a dead world. Why? Sunsets are always sad, at home too. This thought makes the sight seem doubly precious here and doubly sad. There is red burning blood in the west against the cold snow — and to think that this is the sea, stiffened in chains, in death, and that the sun will soon leave us, and we shall be in the dark, alone! 'And the earth was without form, and void'; is this the sea that is to come?

"Sunday, October 8th. Beautiful weather. Made a snow-shoe expedition westward, all the dogs following. The running was a little spoiled by the brine, which soaks up through the snow from the surface of the ice — flat, newly frozen ice, with older, uneven blocks breaking through it. I seated myself on a snow hummock far away out; the dogs crowded round to be patted. My eye wandered over the great snow plain, endless and solitary, nothing but snow, snow everywhere.

"The observations to-day gave us an unpleasant surprise; we are now down in 78° 35' north latitude; but there is a simple enough explanation of this, when one thinks of all the northerly and north-westerly wind we have had lately, with open water not far to the south of us. As soon as everything is frozen we must go north again: there can be no question of that; but none the less this state of matters is unpleasant. I find some comfort in the fact that we have also drifted a little east, so that at all events we have kept with the wind and are not drifting down westward.

"Monday, October 9th. I was feverish both during last night and to-day. Goodness knows what is the meaning of such nonsense. When I was taking water samples in the morning I discovered that the water-lifter suddenly stopped at the depth of a little less than 80 fathoms. It was really the bottom. So we have drifted south again to the shallow water. We let the weight lie at the bottom for a little, and saw by the line that for the moment we were drifting north. This was some small comfort anyhow.

"All at once in the afternoon, as we were sitting idly chatting, a deafening noise began, and the whole ship shook. This was the first ice-pressure. Every one rushed on deck to look. The *Fram* behaved beautifully, as I had expected she would. On pushed the ice with steady pressure, but down under us it had to go, and we were slowly lifted up. These 'squeezings' continued off and on all the afternoon, and were sometimes so strong that the *Fram* was lifted several feet; but then the ice could no longer bear her, and she broke it below her. Towards evening the whole slackened again, till we lay in a good-sized piece of open water, and had hurriedly to moor her to our old floe, or we should have drifted off. There seems to be a good deal of movement in the ice here. Peter has just been telling us that he hears the dull booming of strong pressures not far off.

"Tuesday, October 10th. The ice continues disturbed.

"Wednesday, October 11th The bad news was brought this afternoon that 'Job' is dead, torn in pieces by the other dogs. He was found a good way from the ship, 'Old Suggen' lying watching the corpse, so that no other dog could get to it. They are wretches, these dogs; no day passes without a fight. In the daytime one of us is generally at hand to stop it, but at night they seldom fail to tear and bite one of their comrades. Poor 'Barabbas' is almost frightened out of his wits. He stays on board now, and dares not venture on the ice, because he knows the other monsters would set on him. There is not a trace of chivalry about these curs. When there is a fight, the whole pack rush like wild beasts on the loser. But is it not, perhaps, the law of nature that the strong, and not the weak, should be protected? Have not we human beings, perhaps, been trying to turn nature topsy-turvy by protecting and doing our best to keep life in all the weak?

"The ice is restless, and has pressed a good deal to-day again. It begins with a gentle crack and moan along the side of the ship, which gradually sounds louder in every key. Now it is a high plaintive tone, now it is a grumble, now it is a snarl, and the ship gives a start up. The noise steadily grows till it is like all the pipes of an organ; the ship trembles and shakes, and rises by fits and starts, or is sometimes gently lifted. There is a pleasant, comfortable feeling in sitting listening to all this uproar and knowing the strength of our ship. Many a one would have been crushed long ago. But outside the ice is ground against our ship's sides, the piles of broken-up floe are forced under her heavy, invulnerable hull, and we lie as if in a bed. Soon the noise begins to die down; the ship sinks into its old position again, and presently all is silent as before. In several places round us the ice is piled up, at one spot to a considerable height. Towards evening there was a slackening, and we lay again in a large, open pool.

"Thursday, October 12th. In the morning we and our floe were drifting on blue water in the middle of a large, open lane, which stretched far to the north,

The dogs chained on the ice.

and in the north the atmosphere at the horizon was dark and blue. As far as we could see from the crow's-nest with the small field-glass, there was no end to the open water, with only single pieces of ice sticking up in it here and there. These are extraordinary changes. I wondered if we should prepare to go ahead. But they had long ago taken the machinery to pieces for the winter, so that it would be a matter of time to get it ready for use main. Perhaps it would be best to wait a little. Clear weather, with sunshine — a beautiful, inspiriting winter day — but the same northerly wind. Took soundings and found 50 fathoms of water (90 metres). We are drifting slowly southwards. "Towards evening the ice packed together again with much force; but the *Fram* can hold her own. In the afternoon I fished in a depth of about 27 fathoms (50 metres) with Murray's silk-net,[25] and had a good take, especially of small crustaceans (*kopepodae*, *ostrakodae*, *amphipodae*, etc.) and of a little Arctic worm (*spadella*) that swims about in the sea. It is horribly difficult to manage a little fishing here. No sooner have you found an opening to slip your tackle through, than it begins to close again, and you have to haul up as hard as you can, so as not to get the line nipped and lose everything. It is a pity, for there are interesting hauls to be made. One sees phosphorescence [26] in the water here whenever there is the smallest opening in the ice. There is by no means such a scarcity of animal life as one might expect.

"Friday, October 13th. Now we are in the very midst of what the prophets would have had us dread so much. The ice is pressing and packing round us with a noise like thunder. It is piling itself up into long walls, and heaps high enough to reach a good way up the *Fram*'s rigging; in fact, it is trying its very utmost to grind the *Fram* into powder. But here we sit quite tranquil, not even going up to look at all the hurly-burly, but just chatting and laughing, as usual. Last night there was tremendous pressure round our old dog-floe. The ice had towered up higher than the highest point of the floe, and hustled down upon it. It had quite spoilt a well, where we till now had found good drinking water, filling it with brine. Furthermore, it had cast itself over our stern ice-anchor and part of the steel cable which held it, burying them so effectively that we had afterwards to cut the cable. Then it covered our planks and sledges, which stood on the ice. Before long the dogs were in danger, and the watch had to turn out all hands to save them. At last the floe split in two. This morning the ice was one scene of melancholy confusion, gleaming in the most glorious sunshine. Piled up all round us were high, steep ice walls. Strangely enough, we had lain on the very verge of the worst confusion, and had escaped with the loss of an ice-anchor, a piece of steel cable, a few planks and other bits of wood, and half of a Samoyede sledge, all of which might have been saved if we had looked after them in time. But the men have grown so indifferent to the pressure now, that they do not even go up to look, let it thunder ever so hard. They feel that the ship can stand it, and so long as that is the case there is nothing to hurt except the ice itself.

"In the morning the pressure slackened again, and we were soon lying in a large piece of open water, as we did yesterday. To-day, again, this stretched far away towards the northern horizon, where the same dark atmosphere indicated some extent of open water. I now gave the order to put the engine together again; they told me it could be done in a day and a half or at most two days.

A channel opening up in front of the *Fram*.

We must go north and see what there is up there. I think it possible that it may be the boundary between the ice-drift the *Jeannette* was in and the pack we are now drifting south with — or can it be land?

"We had kept company quite long enough with the old, now broken-up floe, so worked ourselves a little way astern after dinner, as the ice was beginning to draw together. Towards evening the pressure began again in earnest, and was especially bad round the remains of our old floe, so that I believe we may congratulate ourselves on having left it. It is evident that the pressure here stands in connection with, is perhaps caused by, the tidal wave. It occurs with the greatest regularity. The ice slackens twice and packs twice in 24 hours. The pressure has happened about 4, 5, and 6 o'clock in the morning, and almost at exactly the same hour in the afternoon, and in between we have always lain for some part of the time in open water. The very great pressure just now is probably due to the spring tide; we had new moon on the 9th, which was the first day of the pressure. Then it was just after midday when we noticed it, but it has been later every day, and now it is at 8 p.m."

The theory of the ice-pressure being caused to a considerable extent by the tidal wave has been advanced repeatedly by Arctic explorers. During the *Fram*'s drifting we had better opportunity than most of them to study this phenomenon, and our experience seems to leave no doubt that over a wide region the tide produces movement and pressure of the ice. It occurs especially at the time of the spring, tides, and more at new moon than at full moon. During the intervening periods there was as a rule little or no trace of pressure. But these tidal pressures did not occur during the whole time of our drifting. We noticed them especially the first autumn, while we were in the neighbourhood of the open sea north of Siberia, and the last year, when the *Fram* was drawing near the open Atlantic Ocean; they were less noticeable while we were in the polar basin. Pressure occurs here more irregularly, and is mainly caused by the wind driving the ice. When one pictures to one's self these enormous ice-masses, drifting in a certain direction, suddenly meeting hindrances — for example, ice-masses drifting from the opposite direction, owing to a change of wind in some more or less distant quarter — it is easy to understand the tremendous pressure that must result.

Such an ice conflict is undeniably a stupendous spectacle. One feels one's self to be in the presence of Titanic forces, and it is easy to understand how timid souls may be overawed and feel as if nothing could stand before it. For when the packing begins in earnest, it seems as though there could be no spot

A pressure mound near the *Fram*.

on the earth's surface left unshaken. First you hear a sound like the thundering rumble of an earthquake far away on the great waste; then you hear it in several places, always coming nearer and nearer. The silent ice world re-echoes with thunders; nature's giants are awakening to the battle. The ice cracks on every side of you, and begins to pile itself up; and all of a sudden you too find yourself in the midst of the struggle. There are howlings and thunderings round you; you feel the ice trembling, and hear it rumbling under your feet; there is no peace anywhere. In the semi-darkness you can see it piling and tossing itself up into high ridges nearer and nearer you — floes 10, 12, 15 feet thick, broken, and flung on the top of each other as if they were featherweights. They are quite near you now, and you jump away to save your life. But the ice splits in front of you, a black gulf opens, and water streams up. You turn in another direction, but there through the dark you can just see a new ridge of moving ice-blocks coming towards you. You try another direction, but there it is the same. All round there is thundering and roaring, as of some enormous waterfall, with explosions like cannon salvoes. Still nearer you it comes. The floe you are standing on gets smaller and smaller; water pours over it; there can be no escape except by scrambling over the rolling ice-blocks to get to the other side of the pack. But now the disturbance begins to calm down. The noise passes on, and is lost by degrees in the distance.

This is what goes on away there in the north month after month and year after year. The ice is split and piled up into mounds which extend in every direction. If one could get a bird's-eye view of the ice-fields, they would seem to be cut up into squares or meshes by a network of these packed ridges, or pressure-dykes as we called them, because they reminded us so much of snow-covered stone dykes at home, such as, in many parts of the country, are used to enclose fields. At first sight these pressure-ridges appeared to be scattered about in all possible directions, but on closer inspection I was sure that I discovered certain directions which they tended to take, and especially that they were apt to run at right angles to the course of the pressure which produced them. In the accounts of Arctic expeditions one often reads descriptions of pressure-ridges or pressure-hummocks as high as 50 feet. These are fairy tales. The authors of such fantastic descriptions cannot have taken the trouble to measure. During the whole period of our drifting and of our travels over the ice-fields in the far north I only once saw a hummock of a greater height than 23 feet. Unfortunately I had not the opportunity of measuring this one, but I believe I may say with certainty that it was very nearly 30 feet high. All the highest blocks

I measured — and they were many — had a height of 18 to 23 feet; and I can maintain with certainty that the packing of sea ice to a height of over 25 feet is a very rare exception.[27]

"Saturday, October 14th. To-day we have got on the rudder; the engine is pretty well in order, and we are clear to start north when the ice opens to-morrow morning. It is still slackening and packing quite regularly twice a day, so that we can calculate on it beforehand. To-day we had the same open channel to the north, and beyond it open sea as far as our view extended. What can this mean? This evening the pressure has been pretty violent. The floes were packed up against the *Fram* on the port side, and were once or twice on the point of toppling over the rail. The ice, however, broke below; they tumbled back again, and had to go under us after all. It is not thick ice, and cannot do much damage, but the force is something enormous. On the masses come incessantly without a pause; they look irresistible; but slowly and surely they are crushed against the *Fram*'s sides. Now (8.30 p.m.) the pressure has at last stopped. Clear evening, sparkling stars, and flaming northern lights."

I had finished writing my diary, gone to bed, and was lying reading, in *The Origin of Species*, about the struggle for existence, when I heard the dogs out on the ice making more noise than usual. I called into the saloon that some one ought to go up and see if it was bears they were barking at. Hansen went, and came back immediately, saying that he believed he had seen some large animal out in the dark. "Go and shoot it, then." That he was quite ready to do, and went up again at once, accompanied by some of the others. A shot went off on deck above my head, then another; shot followed shot, nine in all. Johansen and Henriksen rushed down for more cartridges, and declared that the creature was shot, it was roaring so horribly; but so far they had only indistinctly seen a large greyish-white mass out there in the dark, moving about among the dogs. Now they were going on to the ice after it. Four of them set off, and not far away they really did find a dead bear, with marks of two shots. It was a young one. The old one must be at hand, and the dogs were still barking loudly. Now they all felt sure that they had seen two together, and that the other also must be badly wounded. Johansen and Henriksen heard it groaning in the distance when they were out on the ice again afterwards to fetch a knife they had left lying where the dead one had lain. The creature had been dragged on board and skinned at once, before it had time to stiffen in the cold.

"Sunday, October 15th. To our surprise, the ice did not slacken away much during last night, after the violent pressure; and what was worse, there was no indication of slackening in the morning, now that we were quite ready to go. Slight signs of it showed themselves a little later, upon which I gave orders to get up steam; and while this was being done, I took a stroll on the ice, to look for traces of yesterday evening. I found tracks not only of the bear that had been killed and of a larger one that might be the mother, but of a third, which must have been badly wounded, as it had sometimes dragged itself on its hindquarters, and had left a broad track of blood. After following the traces for a good way and discovering that I had no weapon to despatch the animal with but my own fists, I thought it would be as well to return to the ship to get a gun and companions who would help to drag the bear back. I had also some small hope that in the meantime the ice might have slackened, so that, in place of going after game, we might go north with the *Fram*. But no such luck! So I put on my snowshoes and set off after our bear, some of the dogs with me, and one or two men following. At some distance we came to the place where it had spent the night ? poor beast, a ghastly night! Here I also saw tracks of the mother. One shudders to think of her watching over her poor young one, which must have had its back shot through. Soon we came up to the cripple, dragging itself away from us over the ice as best it could. Seeing no other way of escape, it threw itself into a small water opening and dived time after time. While we were putting a noose on a rope, the dogs rushed round the hole as if they had gone mad, and it was difficult to keep them from jumping into the water after the bear. At last we were ready, and the next time the creature came up it got a noose round one paw and a ball in the head. Whilst the others drew it to the ship, I followed the mother's tracks for some way, but could not find her. I had soon to turn back to see if there was no prospect of moving the *Fram*; but I found that the ice had packed together again a little at the very time when we could generally calculate on its slackening. In the afternoon Hansen and I went off once more after the bear. We saw, as I expected, that she had come back, and had followed her daughter's funeral procession for some way, but then she had gone off east, and as it grew dark we lost her tracks in some newly packed ice. We have only one matter for regret in connection with this bear episode, and that is the disappearance of two dogs; 'Narrifas' and 'Fox.' Probably they went off in terror on the first appearance of the three bears. They may have been hurt, but I have seen nothing to suggest this. The ice is quiet this evening also, only a little pressure about 7 o'clock.

"Monday, October 16th. Ice quiet and close. Observations on the 12th placed us in 78° 5' north latitude. Steadily southwards. This is almost depressing.

The two runaways returned this morning.

"Tuesday, October 17th. Continuous movement in the ice. It slackened a little again during the night; some way off to starboard there was a large opening. Shortly after midnight there was strong pressure, and between 11 and 12 a.m. came a tremendous squeeze; since then it has slackened again a little."

"Wednesday, October 18th. When the meteorologist, Johansen, was on deck this morning reading the thermometers, he noticed that the dogs, which are now tied up on board, were barking loudly down at something on the ice. He bent over the rail astern, near the rudder, and saw the back of a bear below him, close in at the ship's side. Off he went for a gun, and the animal fell with a couple of shots. We saw afterwards by its tracks that it had inspected all the heaps of sweepings round the ship.

"A little later in the morning I went for a stroll on the ice. Hansen and Johansen were busy with some magnetic observations to the south of the ship. It was beautiful sunshiny weather. I was standing beside an open pool a little way ahead, examining the formation and growth of the new ice, when I heard a gun go off on board. I turned, and just caught a glimpse of a bear making off towards the hummocks. It was Henriksen, who had seen it from the deck coming marching towards the ship. When it was a few paces off it saw Hansen and Johansen, and made straight for them. By this time Henriksen had got his gun, but it missed fire several times. He has an unfortunate liking for smearing the lock so well with vaseline that the spring works as if it lay in soft soap. At last it went off, and the ball went through the bear's back and breast in a slanting direction. The animal stood up on its hindlegs, fought the air with its fore-paws, then flung itself forward and sprang off, to fall after about 30 steps; the ball had grazed the heart. It was not till the shot went off that Hansen saw the bear, and then he rushed up and put two revolver balls into its head. It was a large bear, the largest we had got yet."

"About mid-day I was in the crow's-nest. In spite of the clear weather I could not discover land on any side. The opening far to the north has quite disappeared; but during the night a large new one has formed quite close to us. It stretches both north and south, and has now a covering of ice. The pressure is chiefly confined to the edges of this opening, and can be traced in walls of packed ice as far as the horizon in both directions. To the east the ice is quite unbroken and flat. We have lain just in the worst pressure."

"Thursday, October 19th. The ice again slackened a little last night. In the morning I attempted a drive with six of the dogs. When I had managed to harness them to the Samoyede sledge, had seated myself on it, and called 'Pr-r-r-r, pr-r-r-r!' they went off in quite good style over the ice. But it was not long before we came to some high pack-ice and had to turn. This was hardly done before they were off back to the ship at lightning speed, and they were not to jobe got away from it again. Round and round it they went, from refuse-heap to refuse-heap. If I started at the gangway on the starboard side, and tried by thrashing them to drive them out over the ice, round the stern they flew to the gangway on the port side. I tugged, swore, and tried everything I could think of, but all to no purpose. I got out and tried to hold the sledge back, but was pulled off my feet, and dragged merrily over the ice in my smooth sealskin breeches, on back, stomach, side, just as it happened. When I managed to stop them at some pieces of pack-ice or a dust-heap, round they went again to the starboard gangway, with me dangling behind, swearing madly that I would break every bone in their bodies when I got at them. This game went on till they probably tired of it, and thought they might as well go my way for a change. So now they went off beautifully across the flat floe until I stopped for a moment's breathing space. But at the first movement I made in the sledge they were off again, tearing wildly back the way we had come. I held on convulsively, pulled, raged, and used the whip; but the more I lashed the faster they went on their own way. At last I got them stopped by sticking my legs down into the snow between the sledge-shafts, and driving a strong seal-hook into it as well. But while I was off my guard for a moment they gave a tug. I lay with my hinder-part where my legs had been, and we went on at lightning speed — that substantial part of my body leaving a deep track in the snow. This sort of thing went on time after time. I lost the board I should have sat on, then the whip, then my gloves, then my cap — these losses not improving my temper. Once or twice I ran round in front of the dogs, and tried to force them to turn by lashing at them with the whip. They jumped to both sides, and only tore on the faster; the reins got twisted round my ankles, and I was thrown flat on the sledge, and they went on more wildly than ever. This was my first experience in dog-driving on my own account, and I will not pretend that I was proud of it. I inwardly congratulated myself that my feats had been unobserved." "In the afternoon I examined the melted water of the newly-formed brownish-red ice, of which there is a good deal in the openings round us here. The microscope proved this colour to be produced by swarms of small organisms, chiefly plants — quantities of diatoms and some algae, a few of them very peculiar in form."

"Saturday, October 21st. I have stayed in to-day because of an affection of

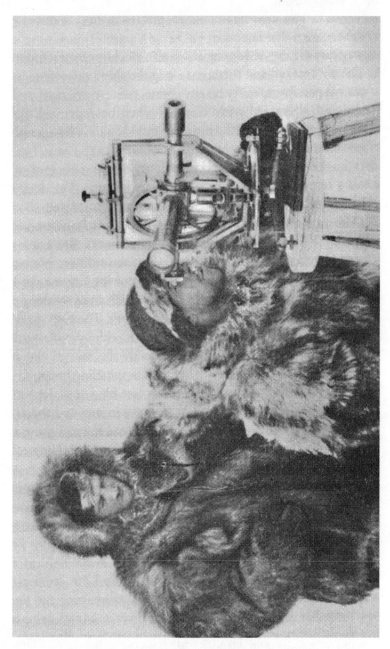

Chronometer observation with the theodolite, Johansen and Hansen.

the muscles or rheumatism, which I have had for some days on the right side of my body, and for which the doctor is 'massaging' me, thereby greatly adding to my sufferings. Have I really grown so old and palsied, or is the whole thing imagination? It is all I can do to limp about; but I just wonder if I could not get up and run with the best of them, if there happened to be any great occasion for it: I almost believe I could. A nice Arctic hero of 32, lying here in my berth! Have had a good time reading home letters, dreaming, myself at home, dreaming of the home-coming — in how many years? Successful or unsuccessful, what does that matter?

"I had a sounding taken; it showed over 73 fathoms (135 m.), so we are in deeper water again. The sounding-line indicated that we are drifting south-west. I do not understand this steady drift southwards. There has not been much wind either lately; there is certainly a little from the north to-day, but not strong. What can be the reason of it? With all my information, all my reasoning, all my putting of two and two together, I cannot account for any south-going current here — there ought to be a north-going one. If the current runs south here, how is that great open sea we steamed north across, to be explained? and the bay we ended in farthest north? These could only be produced by the north-going current which I pre-supposed. The only thing which puts me out a bit is that west-going current which we had against us during our whole voyage along the Siberian coast. We are never going to be carried away south by the New Siberian Islands, and then west along the coast of Siberia, and then north by Cape Chelyuskin, the very way we came! That would be rather too much of a good thing — to say nothing of its being dead against every calculation. "Well, who cares? Somewhere we must go; we can't stay here for ever. 'It will all come right in the end,' as the saying goes; but I wish we could get on a little faster wherever we are going. On our Greenland Expedition, too, we were carried south to begin with, and that ended well."

"Sunday, October 22nd. Henriksen took soundings this morning, and found 70 fathoms (129 m.) of water. 'If we are drifting at all,' said he, 'it is to the east; but there seems to be almost no movement.' No wind to-day. I am keeping in my den."

"Monday, October 23rd. Still in the den. To-day, 5 fathoms shallower than yesterday. The line points south-west, which means that we are drifting north-eastward. Hansen has calculated the observation for the 19th, and finds that we must have got 10 minutes farther north, and must be in 78° 15' N. lat. So at last, now that the wind has gone down, the north-going current is making itself felt.

Some channels have opened near us, one along the side of the ship, and one ahead, near the old channel. Only slight signs of pressure in the afternoon."

"Tuesday, October 24th. Between 4 and 5 a.m. there was strong pressure, and the *Fram* was lifted up a little. It looks as if the pressure were going to begin again; we have spring-tide with full-moon. The ice opened so much this morning that the *Fram* was afloat in her cutting; later on it closed again, and about 11 there was some strong pressure; then came a quiet time; but in the afternoon the pressure began once more, and was violent from 4 to 4.30. The *Fram* was shaken and lifted up; didn't mind a bit. Peter gave it as his opinion that the pressure was coming from the north-east, for he had heard the noise approaching from that direction. Johansen let down the silk net for me about 11 fathoms. It was all he could do to get it up again in time, but it brought up a good catch. Am still keeping in."

"Wednesday, October 25th. We had a horrible pressure last night. I awoke and felt the *Fram* being lifted, shaken, and tossed about, and heard the loud cracking of the ice breaking against her sides. After listening for a little while I fell asleep again, with a snug feeling that it was good to be on board the *Fram*; it would be confoundedly uncomfortable to have to be ready to turn out every time there was a little pressure, or to have to go off with our bundles on our backs like the '*Tegethoff*' people."

"It is quickly getting darker. The sun stands lower and lower every time we see it; soon it will disappear altogether, if it has not done so already. The long dark winter is upon us, and glad shall we be to see the spring; but nothing matters much if we could only begin to move north. There is now south-westerly wind, and the windmill, which has been ready for several days, has been tried at last and works splendidly. We have beautiful electric light to-day, though the wind has not been specially strong (5-8 m. (16-26 feet) per second). Electric lamps are a grand institution. What a strong influence light has on one's spirits! There was a noticeable brightening-up at the dinner table to-day; the light acted on our spirits like a draught of good wine. And how festive the saloon looks! We felt it quite a great occasion — drank to Oscar Dickson's health, and voted him the best of good fellows.

"Wonderful moonshine this evening, light as day; and along with it aurora borealis, yellow and strange in the white moonlight; a large ring round the moon — all this over the great stretch of white, shining ice, here and there in our neighbourhood piled up high by the pressure. And in the midst of this silent silvery ice-world the windmill sweeps round its dark wings against the deep blue sky and the aurora. A strange contrast civilization making a sudden incursion into this frozen ghostly world.

"To-morrow is the *Fram*'s birthday. How many memories it recalls of the launch day a year ago."

"Thursday, October 26th. 164 fathoms (300 m.) of water when the soundings were taken this morning. We are moving quickly north — due north — says Peter. It does look as if things were going better. Great celebration of the day, beginning with target-shooting. Then we had a splendid dinner of four courses, which put our digestive apparatus to a severe test. The *Fram*'s health was drunk amidst great and stormy applause. The proposer's words were echoed by all hearts when he said that she was such an excellent ship for our purpose, that we could not imagine a better (great applause), and we therefore wished her, and ourselves with her, long life (hear, hear). After supper came strawberry and lemon punch, and prizes were presented with much ceremony and a good deal of fun; all being 'taken off' in turn in suitable mottoes, for the most part composed by the ship's doctor. There was a prize for each man. The first prize-taker was awarded the wooden cross of the Order of the *Fram*, to wear suspended from his neck by a ribbon of white tape; the last received a mirror, in which to see his fallen greatness. Smoking in the saloon was allowed this evening, so now pipes, toddy, and an animated game of whist, ended a bright and successful holiday.

"Sitting here now alone, my thoughts involuntarily turn to the year that has gone since we stood up there on the platform, and she threw the champagne against the bow, saying: '*Fram* is your name!' and the strong, heavy hull began to glide so gently. I held her hand tight; the tears came into eyes and throat, and one could not get out a word. The sturdy hull dived into the glittering water; a sunny haze lay over the whole picture. Never shall I forget the moment we stood there together, looking out over the scene. And to think of all that has happened these four last months! Separated by sea and land and ice; coming years, too, lying between us — it is all just the continuation of what happened that day. But how long is it to last? I have such difficulty in feeling that I am not to see home again soon. When I begin to reflect, I know that it may be long, but I will not believe it.

"To-day, moreover, we took solemn farewell of the sun. Half of its disc showed at noon for the last time above the edge of the ice in the south, a flattened body, with a dull red glow, but no heat. Now we are entering the night of winter. What is it bringing us? Where shall we be when the sun returns? No

The *Fram* by moonlight.

one can tell. To console us for the loss of the sun, we have the most wonderful moonlight; the moon goes round the sky night and day. There is, strange to say, little pressure just now; only an occasional slight squeeze. But the ice often opens considerably; there are large pieces of water in several directions; to-day there were some good-sized ones to the south."

"Friday, October 27th. The soundings this morning showed 52 fathoms (95 m.) of water. According to observations taken yesterday afternoon, we are about 3' farther north, and a little farther west than on the 19th. It is disgusting the way we are muddling about here. We must have got into a hole where the ice grinds round and round, and can't get farther. And the time is passing all to no purpose; and goodness only knows how long this sort of thing may go on. If only a good south wind would come and drive us north, out of this hobble!

The boys have taken up the rudder again today. While they were working at this in the afternoon, it suddenly grew as bright as day. A strange fire-ball crossed the sky in the west — giving a bluish-white light, they said. Johansen ran down to the saloon to tell Hansen and me; he said they could still see the bright trails it had left in its train. When we got on deck we saw a bent bow of light in the 'Triangle,' near 'Deheb.' The meteor had disappeared in the neighbourhood of 'Epsilon Cygni' (constellation 'Swan'), but its light remained for a long time floating in the air like glowing dust. No one had seen the actual fire-ball, as they had all had their backs turned to it, and they could not say if it had burst. This is the second great meteor of exceptional splendour that has appeared to us in these regions. The ice has a curious inclination to slacken, without pressure having occurred, and every now and then we find the ship floating in open water. This is the case to-day."

"Saturday, October 28th. Nothing of any importance. Moonshine night and day. A glow in the south from the sun."

"Sunday, October 29th. Peter shot a white fox this morning close in to the ship. For some time lately we have been seeing fox tracks in the mornings, and one Sunday Mogstad saw the fox itself. It has, no doubt, been coming regularly to feed on the offal of the bears. Shortly after the first one was shot another was seen; it came and smelt its dead comrade, but soon set off again and disappeared. It is remarkable that there should be so many foxes on this drift-ice so far from land. But after all it is not much more surprising than my coming upon fox tracks out on the ice between Jan Mayen and Spitzbergen."

"Monday, October 30th. To-day the temperature has gone down 18° F. below zero (−27° C.). I took up the dredge I had put out yesterday. It brought up two pails of mud from the bottom, and I have been busy all day washing this out in the saloon in a large bath, to get the many animals contained in it. They were chiefly starfish, waving starfish, medusae (*astrophyton*), sea-slugs, coral insects (*alcyonariae*), worms, sponges, shell-fish, and crustaceans; and were, of course, all carefully preserved in spirits."

"Tuesday, October 31st. Forty-nine fathoms (90 m.) of water to-day, and the current driving us hard to the south-west. We have good wind for the mill now, and the electric lamps burn all day. The arc lamp under the skylight makes us quite forget the want of sun. Oh! light is a glorious thing, and life is fair in spite of all privations! This is Sverdrup's birthday, and we had revolver practice in the morning. Of course a magnificent dinner of five courses: chicken soup, boiled mackerel, reindeer ribs with baked cauliflower and potatoes, macaroni pudding, and stewed pears with milk — Ringnes ale to wash it down."

"Thursday, November 2nd. The temperature keeps at about 22° F. below zero (−30° C.) now; but it does not feel very cold, the air is so still. We can see the aurora borealis in the day-time too. I saw a very remarkable display of it about 3 this afternoon. On the south-western horizon lay the glow of the sun; in front of it light clouds were swept together — like a cloud of dust rising above a distant troop of riders. Then dark streamers of gauze seemed to stretch from the dust-cloud up over the sky, as if it came from the sun, or perhaps rather as if the sun were sucking it in to itself from the whole sky. It was only in the south-west that these streamers were dark; a little higher up, farther from the sun glow, they grew white and shining, like fine, glistening silver gauze. They spread over the vault of heaven above us, and right away towards the north. They certainly resembled aurora borealis; but perhaps they might be only light vapours hovering high up in the sky, and catching the sunlight? I stood long looking at them. They were singularly still, but they were northern lights, changing gradually in the south-west into dark cloud-streamers, and ending in the dust-cloud over the sun. Hansen saw them too, later, when it was dark. There was no doubt of their nature. His impression was that the aurora borealis spread from the sun over the whole vault of heaven like the stripes on the inner skin of an orange."

"Sunday, November 5th. A great race on the ice was advertised for to-day. The course was measured, marked off, and decorated with flags. The cook had prepared the prizes — cakes, numbered, and properly graduated in size. The expectation was great; but it turned out that, from excessive training during the few last days, the whole crew were so stiff in the legs that they were not able to move. We got our prizes all the same, One man was blind-folded, and he decided who was to have each cake as it was pointed at. This just arrangement met with general approbation, and we all thought it a pleasanter way of getting the prizes than running half-a-mile for them."

"So it is Sunday once more. How the days drag past. I work, read, think, and dream; strum a little on the organ; go for a walk on the ice in the dark. Low on the horizon in the south-west there is the flush of the sun — a dark fierce red, as if of blood aglow with all life's smouldering longings — low and far-off, like the dreamland of youth. Higher in the sky it melts into orange, and that into green and pale blue; and then comes deep blue, star sown, and then infinite space, where no dawn will ever break. In the north are quivering arches of faint aurora, trembling now like awakening longings, but presently, as if at the touch of a magic wand, to storm as streams of light through the dark blue of heaven — never at peace, restless as the very soul of man. I can sit and gaze and gaze, my eyes entranced by the dream-glow yonder in the west, where the moon's thin pale, silver-sickle is dipping its point into the blood; and my soul is borne beyond the glow, to the sun, so far off now — and to the home-coming! Our task accomplished, we are making our way up the fjord as fast as sail and steam can carry us. On both sides of us the homeland lies smiling in the sun; and then...the sufferings of a thousand days and hours melt into a moment's inexpressible joy. That was a bitter gust — I jump up and walk on. What am I dreaming about! so far yet from the goal — hundreds and hundreds of miles between us, ice and land and ice again. And we are drifting round and round in a ring, bewildered attaining nothing, only waiting, always waiting, for what?

> "I dreamt I lay on a grassy bank,
> And the sun shone warm and clear,
> I wakened on a desert isle,
> And the sky was black and drear."

"One more look at the star of home, the one that stood that evening over Cape Chelyuskin, and I creep on board, where the windmill is turning in the cold wind, and the electric light is streaming out from the skylight upon the icy desolation of the Arctic night."

"Wednesday, November 8th. The storm (which we had had the two previous days) has quite gone down not even enough breeze for the mill. We tried letting the dogs sleep on the ice last night, instead of bringing them on board in the evening, as we have been doing lately. The result was that another dog was torn to pieces during the night. It was 'Ulabrand,' the old brown, toothless fellow, that went this time. 'Job' and 'Moses' had gone the same way before. Yesterday evening's observations place us in 77° 43' N. lat. and 138° 8' E. long. This is farther south than we have yet been. No help for it; but it is a sorry state of matters; and that we are farther east than ever before is only a poor consolation. It is new moon again, and we may therefore expect pressure; the ice is, in fact, already moving; it began to split on Saturday, and has broken up more each day. The channels have been of a good size, and the movement becomes more and more perceptible. Yesterday there was slight pressure, and we noticed it again this morning about 5 o'clock. To-day the ice by the ship has opened, and we are almost afloat.

"Here I sit in the still winter night on the drifting ice-floe, and see only stars above me. Far off I see the threads of life twisting themselves into the intricate web which stretches unbroken from life's sweet morning dawn to the eternal death-stillness of the ice. Thought follows thought — you pick the whole to pieces, and it seems so small — but high above all towers one form... Why did you take this voyage?...Could I do otherwise? Can the river arrest its course and run up hill? My plan has come to nothing. That palace of theory, which I reared in pride and self-confidence, high above all silly objections, has fallen like a house of cards at the first breath of wind. Build up the most ingenious theories, and you may be sure of one thing — that fact will defy them all. Was I so very sure? Yes, at times; but that was self-deception, intoxication. A secret doubt lurked behind all the reasoning. It seemed as though the longer I defended my theory, the nearer I came to doubting it. But no, there is no getting over the evidence of that Siberian drift-wood.

"But if, after all, we are on the wrong track, what then? Only disappointed human hopes, nothing more. And even if we perish, what will it matter in the endless cycles of eternity?"

"Thursday, November 9th. I took temperatures and sea-water samples to-day every 10 yards from the surface to the bottom. The depth was 92 fathoms. An extraordinarily even temperature of 30° Fahr. (−1.5 C.) through all the layers. I have noticed the same thing before as far south as this. So it is only polar water here? There is not much pressure; an inclination to it this morning, and a little at 8 o'clock this evening, also a few squeezes later, when we were playing cards."

"Friday, November 10th. This morning made despairing examinations of yesterday's water samples with Thornöe's electric apparatus. There must be absolute stillness on board when this is going on. The men are all terrified, slip about on tiptoe, and talk in the lowest possible whispers. But presently one begins to hammer at something on deck, and another to file in the engine-room, when the chiefs commanding, voice is at once heard, ordering silence. These examinations are made by means of a telephone, through which a very faint noise is heard, which dies slowly away; the moment at which it stops must be exactly ascertained.

"I find remarkably little salt all the way to the bottom in the water here; it must be mixed with fresh water from the Siberian river.

"There was some pressure this morning, going on till nearly noon, and we heard the noise of it in several directions. In the afternoon the ice was quite slack, with a large opening alongside the port side of the ship. At half-past seven pretty strong pressure began, the ice crashing and grinding along the ship's side. About midnight the roar of packing was heard to the south.

"Saturday, November 11th. There has been some pressure in the course of the day. The newly-formed ice is about 15 inches thick. It is hard on the top, but looser and porous below. This particular piece of ice began to form upon a large opening in the night between the 27th and 28th October, so it has frozen 15 inches in 15 days. I observed that it froze 3 inches the first night, and 5 inches altogether during the three first nights; so that it has taken 12 days to the last 10 inches."

Even this small observation serves to show that the formation of ice goes on most easily where the crust is thin, becoming more and more difficult as the thickness increases, until at a certain thickness, as we observed later, it stops altogether. "It is curious that the pressure has gone on almost all day? no slackening such as we have usually observed."

"Sunday, November 19th. Our life has gone on in its usual monotonous routine since the 11th. The wind has been steadily from the south all the week, but today there is a little from N.N.W. have had pressure several times, and have heard sounds of it in the south-east. Except for this, the ice has been unusually quiet, and it is closed in tightly round the ship. Since the last strong pressure we have probably 10 to 20 feet of ice packed in below us.[28] Hansen to-day worked out an observation taken the day before yesterday, and surprised us with the welcome intelligence that we have travelled 44' north and a little east since the 8th. We are now in 78° 27' north latitude, 139° 23' east longitude. This is farther east than we have been yet. For any sake let us only keep on as we are going.

"The *Fram* is a comfortable abode. Whether the thermometer stands at 22° above zero or at 22° below it, we have no fire in the stove. The ventilation is excellent, especially since we rigged up the air sail, which sends a whole winter's cold in through the ventilator; yet in spite of this we sit here warm and comfortable, with only a lamp burning. I am thinking of having the stove removed altogether; it is only in the way. At least, as far as our protection from the winter cold is concerned, my calculations have turned out well. Neither do we suffer much from damp. It does collect and drop a little from the roof in one or two places, especially astern in the four-man cabins; but nothing in comparison with what is common in other ships; and if we lighted the stove it would disappear altogether. When I have burned a lamp for quite a short time in my cabin, every trace of damp is gone.[29] These are extraordinary fellows for standing the cold. With the thermometer at 22° F. below zero Bentzen goes up

Bernt Bentzen.

in his shirt and trousers to read the thermometer on deck."

"Monday, November 27th. The prevailing wind has been southerly, with sometimes a little east. The temperature still keeps between 13° and 22° below zero; in the hold it has fallen to 12°."

It has several times struck me that the streamers of the aurora borealis followed in the direction of the wind, from the wind's eye on the horizon. On Thursday morning, when we had very slight north-easterly wind, I even ventured to prophesy, from the direction of the streamers, that it would go round to the south-east, which it accordingly did. On the whole there has been much less of the aurora borealis lately than at the beginning of our drift. Still, though it may have been faint, there has been a little every day."To-night it is very strong again. These last days the moon has sometimes had rings round it, with mock-moons and axes — accompanied by rather strange phenomena. When the moon stands so low that the ring touches the horizon, a bright field of light is formed where the horizon cuts the ring. Similar expanses of light are also formed where the perpendicular axis from the moon intersects the horizon. Faint rainbows are often to be seen in these shining light-fields; yellow was generally the strongest tint nearest the horizon, passing over into red, and then into blue. Similar colours could also be distinguished in the mock-moons. Sometimes there are two large rings — the one outside the other — and then there may be four mock-moons. I have also seen part of a new ring above the usual one, meeting it at a tangent directly above the moon. As is well known, these various ring formations round the sun, as well as round the moon, are produced by the refraction of rays of light by minute ice crystals floating in the air.

"We looked for pressure with full moon and spring tide on 23rd of November; but then, and for several days afterwards, the ice was quite quiet. On the afternoon of Saturday, the 25th, however, its distant roar was heard from the south, and we have heard it from the same direction every day since. This morning it was very loud, and came gradually nearer. At nine o'clock it was quite close to us, and this evening we hear it near us main. It seems, however, as if we had now got out of the groove to which the pressure principally confines itself. We were regularly in it before. The ice round us is perfectly quiet. The probability is that the last severe pressure packed it very tight about us, and that the cold since has frozen it into such a thick strong mass that it offers great resistance, while the weaker ice in other places yields to the pressure. The depth of the sea is increasing steadily, and are drifting north. This evening Hansen has worked out the observations of the day before yesterday, and finds that we are in 79° 11' north latitude. That is good news, and the way we ought to get on. It is the most northern point we have reached yet, and to-day we are in all likelihood still farther north. We have made good way these last days, and the increasing depth seems to indicate a happy change in the direction of our drift. Have we, perhaps, really found the right road at last? We are drifting about 5' a day. The most satisfactory thing is that there has not been much wind lately, especially the two last days; yesterday it was only about 3 feet per second; today is perfectly still, and yet the depth has increased 21 fathoms (40 m.) in these two days. It seems as if there were a northerly current after all. No doubt many disappointments await us yet; but why not rejoice while fortune smiles?"

"Tuesday, November 28th. The disappointment lost no time in coming. There had been a mistake either in the observation or in Hansen's calculations. An altitude of Jupiter taken yesterday evening shows us to be in 78° 36' north latitude. The soundings to-day showed 74 fathoms (142 m.) of water, or about the same as yesterday, and the sounding-line indicated a south-westerly drift. However anxious one is to take things philosophically, one can't help feeling a little depressed. I try to find solace in a book; absorb myself in the learning of the Indians — their happy faith in transcendental powers, in the supernatural faculties of the soul, and in a future life. Oh, if one could only get hold of a little supernatural power now, and oblige the winds always to blow from the south!

"I went on deck this evening in rather a gloomy frame of mind, but was nailed to the spot the moment I got outside. There is the supernatural for you — the northern lights flashing in matchless power and beauty over the sky in all the colours of the rainbow! Seldom or never have I seen the colours so brilliant. The prevailing one at first was but that gradually flickered over into green, and then a sparkling ruby-red began to show at the bottom of the rays on the under side of the arch, soon spreading over the whole arch. And now from the far-away western horizon a fiery serpent writhed itself up over the sky, shining brighter and brighter as it came. It split into three, all brilliantly glittering. Then the colours changed. The serpent to the south turned almost ruby-red, with spots of yellow; the one in the middle, yellow; and the one to the north, greenish-white. Sheaves of rays swept along the sides of the serpents, driven through the ether-like waves before a storm-wind. They sway backwards and forwards, now strong, now fainter again. The serpents reached and passed the zenith. Though I was thinly dressed and shivering with cold, I could not tear myself away till the spectacle was over, and only a faintly-glowing fiery serpent near the western horizon showed where it had begun. When I came on deck later the masses of light had passed northwards, and spread themselves in incomplete arches over the northern sky. If one wants to read mystic meanings into the phenomena of nature, here, surely, is the opportunity.

"The observation this afternoon showed us to be in 78° 38' 42" N. lat. This is anything but rapid progress.

"Wednesday, November 29th. Another dog has been bitten to death to-day — 'Fox,' a handsome, powerful animal. He was found lying dead and stiff on the ice at our stern this evening when they went to bring the dogs in, 'Suggen' performing her usual duty of watching the body. They are wretches, these dogs. But now I have given orders that some one must always watch them when they are out on the ice."

"Thursday, November 30th. The lead showed a depth of exactly, fathoms (170 m.) to-day, and it seemed by the line as if we were drifting, north-west. We are almost certainly further north now; hopes are rising, and life is looking brighter again. My spirits are like a pendulum, if one could imagine such an instrument giving all sorts of irregular swings backwards and forwards. It is no good trying to take the thing, philosophically; I cannot deny that the question whether we are to return successful or unsuccessful affects me very deeply. It is quite easy to convince myself with the most incontrovertible reasoning that what really matters is to carry through the expedition, whether successfully or not, and get safe home again. I could not but undertake it; for my plan was one that I felt must succeed, and therefore it was my duty to try it. Well, if it does not succeed, is that my affair? I have done my duty, done all that could be done, and can return home with an easy conscience to the quiet happiness I have left behind. What can it matter whether chance, or whatever name you like to give it, does or does not allow the plan to succeed and make our names immortal? The worth of the plan is the same whether chance smiles or frowns upon it. And as to immortality, happiness is all we want, and that is not to be had here.

"I can say all this to myself a thousand times; I can bring myself to believe honestly that it is all a matter of indifference to me; but none the less my spirits change like the clouds of heaven according, as the wind blows from this direction or from that, or the soundings show the depth to be increasing, or not, or the observations indicate a northerly or southerly drift. When I think of the many that trust us, think of Norway, think of all the friends that gave us their time, their faith, and their money, the wish comes that they may not be disappointed, and I grow sombre when our progress is not what we expected it would be. And she that gave most — does she deserve that her sacrifice should have been made in vain? Ah, yes, we must and will succeed!"

"Sunday, December 3rd. Sunday main, with its feeling of peace, and its permission to indulge in the narcotic of happy day-dreams, and let the hours go idly by, without any prickings of conscience.

"To-day the bottom was not reached with over 135½ fathoms (250 m.) of line. There was a north-easterly drift. Yesterday's observation showed us to be in 78° 44 north latitude, that is 5' farther north than on Tuesday. It is horribly slow; but it is forward, and forward we must go, there can be no question of that."

'Suggen'.

"Tuesday, December 5th. — This is the coldest day we have had yet, with the thermometer 31° below zero (−35.7° C.) and a biting wind from the E.S.E. Observation in the afternoon shows 78° 50′ north latitude, that is 6′ farther north than on Saturday, or 2′ per day. In the afternoon we had magnificent aurora borealis — glittering arches across the whole vault of the sky from the east towards the west; but when I was on deck this evening the sky was overcast, only one star shone through the cloudy veil — the home star. How I love it! It is the first thing my eye seeks, and it is always there, shining on our path. I feel as if no ill could befall us as long as I see it there...

"Wednesday, December 6th. This afternoon the ice cracked abaft the starboard quarter; this evening I see that the crack has opened. We may expect pressure now, as it is new moon either to-day or to-morrow."

"Thursday, December 7th. The ice pressed at the stern at five o'clock this morning for about an hour. I lay in my berth and listened to it creaking and grinding and roaring. There was slight pressure again in the afternoon; nothing to speak of. No slackening in the forenoon."

"Friday, December 8th. Pressure from seven till eight this morning. As I was sitting drawing in the afternoon I was startled by a sudden report or crash. It seemed to be straight overhead, as if great masses of ice had fallen from the rigging on to the deck above my cabin. Every one starts up and throws on some extra garment; those that are taking an afternoon nap jump out of their berths right into the middle of the saloon, calling out to know what has happened. Pettersen rushes up the companion ladder in such wild haste that he bursts open the door in the face of the mate, who is standing in the passage holding back 'Kvik,' who has also started in fright from the bed in the chart-room, where she is expecting her confinement. On deck we could discover nothing, except that the ice was in motion, and seemed to be sinking slowly away from the ship. Great piles had been packed up under the stern this morning and yesterday. The explosion was probably caused by a violent pressure suddenly loosening all the ice along the ship's side, the ship at the same time taking a strong list to port. There was no cracking of wood to be heard, so that, whatever it was, the *Fram* cannot have been injured. But it was cold, and we crept down again.

"As we were sitting at supper, about six o'clock, pressure suddenly began. The ice creaked and roared so along the ship's sides close by us that it was not possible to carry on any connected conversation; we had to scream, and all agreed with Nordahl when he remarked that it would be much pleasanter if the pressure would confine its operations to the bow instead of coming bothering us here aft. Amidst the noise we caught every now and again from the organ: a note or two of Kjerulf's melody: 'I could not sleep for the nightingale's voice.' The hurly-burly outside lasted for about twenty minutes, and then all was still.

"Later in the evening Hansen came down to give notice of what really was a remarkable appearance of aurora borealis. The deck was brightly illuminated by it, and reflections of its light played all over the ice. The whole sky was ablaze with it, but it was brightest in the south; high up in that direction glowed waving masses of fire. Later still Hansen came again to say that now it was quite extraordinary. No words can depict the glory that met our eyes. The glowing fire-masses had divided into glistening, many-coloured bands, which were writhing and twisting across the sky both in the south and north. The rays sparkled with the purest, most crystalline rainbow colours, chiefly violet-red or carmine and the clearest green. Most frequently the rays of the arch were red at the ends, and changed higher up into sparkling green, which quite at the top turned darker, and went over into blue or violet before disappearing in the blue of the sky; or the rays in one and the same arch might change from clear red to clear green, coming and going as if driven by a storm. It was an endless phantasmagoria of sparking colour, surpassing anything that one can dream. Sometimes the spectacle reached such a climax that one's breath was taken away; one felt that now something extraordinary must happen — at the very least the sky must fall. But as one stands in breathless expectation, down the whole thing trips, as if in a few quick, light scale-runs, into bare nothingness. There is something most undramatic about such a *dénouement,* but it is all done with such confident assurance that one cannot take it amiss; one feels one's self in the presence of a master who has the complete command of his instrument. With a single stroke of the bow he descends lightly and elegantly from the height of passion into quiet, every-day strains, only with a few more strokes to work himself up into passion again. It seems as if he were trying to mock, to tease us. When we are on the point of going below, driven by 61 degrees of frost (−34.7 C.), such magnificent tones again vibrate over the strings that we stay, until noses and ears are frozen. For a finale, there is a wild display of fireworks in every tint of flame — such a conflagration that one expects every minute to have it down on the ice, because there is not room for it in the sky. But I can hold out no longer. Thinly dressed, without a proper cap, and without gloves, I have no feeling left in body or limbs, and I crawl away below."

"Sunday, December 10th. Another peaceful Sunday. The motto for the day in the English almanac is: 'He is happy whose circumstances suit his temper: but he is more excellent who can suit his temper to any circumstances' (Hume). Very true, and exactly the philosophy I am practising at this moment. I am lying on my berth in the light of the electric lamp, eating cake and drinking beer whilst I am writing my journal; presently I shall take a book and settle down to read and sleep. The arc lamp has shone like a sun to-day over a happy company. We have no difficulty now in distinguishing hearts from diamonds on our dirty cards. It is wonderful what an effect light has. I believe I am becoming a fire-worshipper. It is strange enough that fire-worship should not exist in the Arctic countries.

'For the sons of men

Fire is the best,
And the sight of the sun.'

"A newspaper appears on board now. *Framsjaa*[30] (news of, or outlook from, the *Fram*) is its name, and our doctor is its irresponsible editor. The first number was read aloud this evening, and gave occasion for much merriment. Amongst its contents are:

(Contribution to the Infant *Framsjaa*.)
'Winter in the Ice.'

Far in the ice there lies a ship, boys,
Mast and sail, ice to the very tip, boys;
But, perfectly clear,
If you listen you can hear,
There is life and fun on hoard that ship, boys.
What can it be?
Come along and see —
It is Nansen and his men that laugh, boys.
Nothing to be heard at night but glasses' clink, boys,
Fall of greasy cards and counters' chink, boys;
If he won't "declare,"
Nordahl he will swear
Bentzen is stupid as an owl, boys.
Bentzen cool, boys,
Is not a fool, boys;
"You're another!" quickly he replies, boys.
Among those sitting at the table, boys,
Is "Heika,"[31] with his body big and stable, boys;
He and Lars, so keen,
It would almost seem
They would stake their lives if they were able, boys.
Amundsen, again,
Looks at these two men,
Shakes his head and sadly goes to bed, boys.[32]

Sverdrup, Blessing, Hansen, and our Mohn,[33] boys,

Say of "marriage" "this game is our own," boys;
Soon for them, alas
The happy hour is past;
And Hansen he says, "Come away, old Mohn!" boys.
"It is getting late,
And the stars won't wait,
You and I must up and out alone," boys.

The doctor here on board has nought to do, boys;
Not a man to test his skill among the crew, boys;
Well may he look blue,
There's nought for him to do,
When every man is strong and hearty, too, boys.
"Now on the *Fram*," boys,
He says "I am," boys,
"Chief editor of newspaper for you." boys.

"WARNING

"I think it is my duty to warn the public that a travelling watchmaker has been making the round of this neighbourhood lately, getting watches to repair, and not returning them to their owners. How long is this to be allowed to go on under the eyes of the authorities?

"The watchmaker's appearance is as follows: Middle height, fair, grey eyes, brown full beard, round shoulders, and generally delicate-looking.

"A. JUELL.[34]

"The person above notified was in our office yesterday, asking for work, and we consider it right to add the following particulars as completing the description. He generally goes about with a pack of mongrel curs at his heels; he chews tobacco, and of this his beard shows traces. This is all we have to say, as we did not consider ourselves either entitled or called upon to put him under the microscope.

"Ed. *Framsjaa.*"

"Yesterday's observation placed us in 79° 0′ north latitude, 139° 14′ east longitude. At last, then, we have got as far north again as we were in the end of September, and now the northerly drift seems to be steady: 10′ in 4 days.

"Monday, December 11th. This morning I took a long excursion to westward. It is hard work struggling over the packed ice in the dark; something like scrambling about a moraine of big boulders at night. Once I took a step in the air, fell forward, and bruised my right knee. It is mild to-day, only 9½° F. below zero (−23° C.). This evening there was a strange appearance of aurora borealis — white, shining clouds, which I thought at first must be lit up by the moon, but there is no moon yet. They were light cumuli, or cirro-cumuli, shifting into a brightly shining mackerel sky. I stood and watched them as long as my thin clothing permitted, but there was no perceptible pulsation, no play of flame; they sailed quietly on. The light seeded to be strongest in the south-east, where there were also dark clouds to be seen. Hansen said that it moved over later into the northern sky; clouds came and went, and for a time there were many white shining ones — 'white as lambs,' he called them — but no aurora played behind them."

"In this day's meteorological journal I find noted for 4 p.m.: 'Faint aurora borealis in the north. Some distinct branchings or antlers (they are of ribbon crimped like blonde) in some diffused patches on the horizon in the N.N.F.' In his aurora borealis journal Hansen describes that of this evening as follows: 'About 8 p.m. an aurora borealis arch of light was observed, stretching from E.S.E. to N.W., through the zenith; diffused quiet intensity 3-4, most intense in N.W. The arch spread at the zenith by a wave to the south. At 10 o'clock there was a fainter aurora borealis in the southern sky; eight minutes later it extended to the zenith, and two minutes after this there was a shining broad arch across the zenith with intensity 6. Twelve seconds later flaming rays shot from the zenith in an easterly direction. During the next half-hour there was constant aurora, chiefly in bands across or near the zenith, or lower in the southern sky. The observation ended about 10.38. The intensity was then 2, the aurora diffused over the southern sky. There were cumulus clouds of varying closeness all the time. They came up in the south-east at the beginning of the observation, and disappeared towards the end of it; they were closest about 10 minutes past 10. At the time that the broad shining arch through the zenith was at its highest intensity, the cumulus clouds in the north-west shone quite white, though we were unable to detect any aurora borealis phenomena in this quarter. The reflection of light on the ice field was pretty strong at the same time. In the aurora borealis the cumulus clouds appeared of a darker colour, almost the grey of wool. The colours of the aurora were yellowish, bluish-white, milky blue-cold colouring.' According to the meteorological journal there was still aurora borealis in the southern sky at midnight."

"Tuesday, December 12th. Had a long walk south-east this morning. The ice is in much the same condition there as it is to the west, packed or pressed up into mounds, with flat floes between. This evening the dogs suddenly began to make a great commotion on deck. We were all deep in cards, some playing whist, others 'marriage.' I had no shoes on, so said that some one else must go up and see what was the matter. Mogstad went. The noise grew worse and worse. Presently Mogstad came down and said that all the dogs that could get at the rail were up on it, barking out into the dark towards the north. He was sure there must be an animal of some sort there, but perhaps it was only a fox, for he thought he had heard the mark of a fox far in the north; but he was not sure. Well, it must be a devil of a fox to excite the dogs like that. As the disturbance continued, I at last went up myself, followed by Johansen. From different positions we looked long and hard into the darkness in the direction in which the dogs were barking, but we could see nothing moving. That something must be there was quite certain; and I had no doubt that it was a bear, for the dogs were almost beside themselves. 'Pan' looked up into my face with an odd expression, as if he had something important to tell me, and then jumped up on the rail and barked away to the north. The dogs' excitement was quite remarkable; they had not been so keen when the bear was close in to the side of the ship. However, I contented myself with remarking that the thing to do would be to loose some dogs and go north with them over the ice. But these wretched dogs won't tackle a bear, and besides it is so dark that there is hardly a chance of finding anything. If it is a bear he will come again. At this season, when he is so hungry, he will hardly go right away from all the good food for him here on board. I struck about with my arms to get a little heat into me, then went below and to bed. The dogs went on barking, sometimes louder than before. Nordahl, whose watch it was, went up several times, but could discover no reason for it. As I was lying reading in my berth I heard a peculiar sound; it was like boxes being dragged about on deck, and there was also scraping, like a dog that wanted to get out, scratching violently at a door. I thought of 'Kvik,' who was shut up in the chart-room. I called into the saloon to Nordahl that he had better go up again and see what this new noise was. He did so, but came back saying that there was still nothing to be seen. It was difficult to sleep, and I lay long tossing about. Peter came on watch. I told him to go up and turn the air-sail to the wind, to make the ventilation better. He was a good time on deck doing this and other things, but he also could see no reason for the to-do the dogs were still making. He had to go forward, and then noticed that the three dogs nearest the starboard gang-way were missing. He came down and told me, and we agreed that possibly this might be what all the excitement was about; but never before had they taken it so to heart when some of their number had run away. At last I fell asleep, but heard them in my sleep for a long time."

"Wednesday, December 13th. Before I was rightly awake this morning I heard the dogs 'at it' still, and the noise went on all the time of breakfast, and had, I believe, gone on all night. After breakfast Mogstad and Peter went up to feed the wretched creatures and let them loose on the ice. Three were still missing. Peter came down to get a lantern; he thought he might as well look if there were any tracks of animals. Jacobsen called after him that he had better take a gun. No, he did not need one, he said. A little later, as I was sitting sorrowfully absorbed in the calculation of how much petroleum we have used, and how short a time our supply will last if we go on burning it at the same rate, I heard a scream at the top of the companion. 'Come with a gun.' In a moment I was in the saloon, and there was Peter tumbling in at the door, breathlessly shouting, 'A gun? a gun?' The bear had bitten him in the side. I was thankful that it was no worse, hearing him put on so much dialect[35] I had thought it was a matter of life and death. I seized one gun, he another, and up we rushed, the mate with his gun after us. There was not much difficulty in knowing in what direction to turn, for from the rail on the starboard side came confused shouts of human voices, and from the ice below the gangway the sound of a frightful uproar of dogs. I tore out the tow-plug at the muzzle of my rifle, then up with the lever and in with the cartridge; it was a case of hurry. But, hang it! there is a plug in at this end too. I poked and poked, but could not get a grip of it. Peter screamed: 'Shoot, shoot! mine won't go off!' He stood clicking and clicking, his lock full of frozen vaseline again, while the bear lay chewing at a dog just below us at the ship's side. Beside me stood the mate, groping after a tow-plug which he also had shoved down into his gun, but now he flung the gun angrily away and began to look round the deck for a walrus spear to stick the bear with. Our fourth man, Mogstad, was waving an empty rifle (he had shot away his cartridges), and shouting to some one to shoot the bear. Four men, and not one that could shoot, although we could have prodded the bear's back with our gun-barrels. Hansen, making a fifth, was lying in the passage to the chart-room, groping with his arm through a chink in the door for cartridges; he could not get the door to open because of 'Kvik's' kennel. At last Johansen appeared and sent a ball straight down into the bear's hide. That did some good. The monster

Jacobse, mate of the *Fram*.

let go the dog and gave a growl. Another shot flashed and hissed down on the same spot. One more, and we saw the white dog the bear had under him jump up and run off, while the other dogs stood round, barking. Another shot still, for the animal began to stir a little. At this moment my plug came out, and I gave him a last ball through the head to make sure. The dogs had crowded round barking as long as he moved, but now that he lay still in death they drew back terrified. They probably thought it was some new ruse of the enemy. It was a little thin, one-year-old bear that had caused all this terrible commotion.

"Whilst it was being flayed I went off in a north-westerly direction to look for the dogs that were still missing. I had not gone far when I noticed that the dogs that were following me had caught scent of something to the north, and wanted to go that way. Soon they got frightened, and I could not get them to go on; they kept close in to my side or slunk behind me. I held my gun ready, while I crawled on all fours over the pack-ice, which was anything but level. I kept a steady look-out ahead, but it was not far my eyes could pierce in that darkness. I could only just see the dogs, like black shadows; when they were a few steps away from me. I expected every moment to see a huge form rise among the hummocks ahead, or come rushing towards me. The dogs got more and more cautious, one or two of them sat down, but they probably felt that it would be a shame to let me go on alone, so followed slowly after. Terrible ice to force one's way over! Crawling along on hands and knees does not put one in a very convenient position to shoot from if the bear should make a sudden rush. But unless he did this, or attacked the dogs, I had no hope of getting him. We now came out on some flat ice. It was only too evident that there must be something quite near now. I went on, and presently saw a dark object on the ice in front of me. It was not unlike an animal. I bent down — it was poor 'Johansen's Friend,' the black dog with the white tip to his tail, in a sad state, and frozen stiff. Beside him was something else dark. I bent down again and found the second of the missing dogs, brother of the corpse-watcher, 'Suggen.' This one was almost whole, only eaten a little about the head, and it was not frozen quite stiff. There seemed to be blood all round on the ice. I looked about in every direction, but there was nothing more to be seen. The dogs stood at a respectful distance, staring and sniffing in the direction of their dead comrades. Some of us went not long after this to fetch the dogs' carcasses, taking a lantern to look for bear tracks, in case there had been some big fellows along with the little one. We scrambled on among the pack-ice. 'Come this way with the lantern, Bentzen; I think I see tracks here.' Bentzen came, and we turned the light on some indentations in the snow; they were bear-paw marks sure enough, but only the same little fellow's. 'Look! the brute has been dragging a dog after him here.' By the light of the lantern we traced the blood-marked path on among the hummocks. We found the dead dogs, but no footprints except small ones, which we all thought must be those of our little bear. 'Svarten,' alias 'Johansen's Friend,' looked bad in the lantern-light. Flesh and skin and entrails were gone; there was nothing to be seen but a bare breast and backbone, with some stumps of ribs. It was a pity that the fine strong dog should come to such an end. He had just one fault: he was rather bad-tempered. He had a special dislike for Johansen; barked and showed his teeth whenever he came on deck, or even opened a door,

Hjalmar Johansen.

and when he sat whistling in the top, or in the crow's-nest these dark winter days, the 'Friend' would answer with a howl of rage from far out on the ice. Johansen bent down with the lantern to look at the remains.

"'Are you glad, Johansen, that your enemy is done for?'

"'No, I am sorry.'

"'Why?'

"'Because we did not make it up before he died.' And we went on to look for more bear-tracks, but found none; so we took the dead dogs on our backs and turned homewards.

"On the way I asked Peter what had really happened with him and the bear. 'Well, you see,' said he, 'when I came along with the lantern we saw a few drops of blood by the gangway; but that might quite well have been a dog that had cut itself. On the ice below the gangway we saw some bear-tracks, and we started away west, the whole pack of dogs with us, running on far ahead. When we had got away a bit from the ship, there was suddenly an awful row in front, and it wasn't long before a great beast came rushing at us, with the whole troop of dogs around it. As soon as we saw what it was, we turned and ran our best for the ship. Mogstad, you see, he had moccasins (komager) on, and knew his way better and got there before me. I couldn't get along so fast with my great wooden shoes, and in my confusion I got right on to the big hummock to the west of the ship's bow, you know. I turned here and lighted back to see if the bear was behind me, but I saw nothing and pushed on again, and in a minute these slippery wooden shoes had me flat on my back among the hummocks. I was up again quick enough; but when I got down on to the flat ice close to the ship, I saw something coming straight for me on the right-hand side. First I thought it was a dog — it's not so easy to see in the dark, you know — I had no time for a second thought, for the beast jumped on me and bit me in the side. I had lifted my arm like this, you see, and so he caught me here, right on the hip. He growled and hissed as he bit.

"'What did you think then, Peter?'

"'What did I think? I thought it was all up with me. What was I to do? I had neither gun nor knife. But I took the lantern and gave him such a whack on the head with it that the thing broke, and went flying away over the ice. The moment he felt the blow he sat down and looked at me. I was just taking to my heels when he got up; I don't know whether it was to grip me again or what it was for, but anyhow at that minute he caught sight of a dog coming, and set off after it, and I got on board.'

"'Did you scream, Peter?'

"'Scream! I screamed with all my might.' And apparently this was true, for he was quite hoarse.

"'But where was Mogstad all this time?'

"'Well, you see, he had reached the ship long before me, but he never thought of running down and giving the alarm, but takes his gun from the round-house wall and thinks he'll manage all right alone, but his gun wouldn't go off, and the bear would have had time to eat me up under his nose.'

"We were now near the ship, and Mogstad, who had heard the last part of the story from the deck, corrected it in so far that he had just reached the gangway when Peter began to roar. He jumped up and fell back three times before he got on board, and had no time to do anything then but seize his gun and go to Peter's assistance.

"When the bear left Peter and rushed after the dogs, he soon had the whole pack about him again. Now he would make a spring and get one below him; but then all the rest would set upon him and jump on his back, so that he had to turn to defend himself. Then he would spring upon another dog, and the whole pack would be on him again. And so the dance went on; backwards and forwards over the ice, until they were once more close to the ship. A dog stood there, below the gangway, wanting to get on board; the bear made a spring on it, and it was there, by the ship's side, that the villain met his fate.

"An examination on board showed that the hook of 'Svarten's' leash was pulled out quite straight; 'Gammelen's' was broken through; but the third dog's was only wrenched a little: it hardly looked as if the bear had done it. I had a slight hope that this dog might still be in life, but, though we searched well, we could not find it.

"It was altogether a deplorable story. To think that we should have let a bear scramble on board like this, and should have lost three dogs at once! Our dogs are dwindling down; we have only 26 now. That was a wily demon of a bear, to be such a little one. He had crawled on board by the gangway, shoved away a box that was standing in front of it, taken the dog that stood nearest, and gone off with it. When he had satisfied the first pangs of his hunger, he had come back and fetched No. 2, and, if he had been allowed, he would have continued the performance until the deck was cleared of dogs. Then he would probably have come bumping downstairs 'and beckoned with cold hand' in at the galley door to Juell. It must have been a pleasant feeling for 'Svarten' to stand there in the dark and see the bear come creeping in upon him.

"When I went below after this bear affair, Juell said as I passed the galley door: 'You'll see that "Kvik" will have her pups to-day; for it's always the way here on board, that things happen together.' And, sure enough, when we were sitting in the saloon in the evening, Mogstad, who generally plays 'master of the hounds,' came and announced the arrival of the first. Soon there was another, and then one more. This news was a little balsam to our wounds. 'Kvik' has got a good warm box, lined with fur, up in the passage on the starboard; it is so warm there that she is lying sweating, and we hope that the young ones will live, in spite of 54 degrees of frost. It seems this evening as if every one had some hesitation in going out on the ice unarmed. Our bayonet-knives have been brought out, and I am providing myself with one. I must say that I felt quite certain that we should find no bears as far north as this in the middle of winter; and it never occurred to me, in making long excursions on the ice without so much as a penknife in my pocket, that I was liable to encounters with them. But, after Peter's experience, it seems as if it might be as well to have, at any rate, a lantern to hit them with. The long bayonet-knife shall accompany me henceforth.

"They often chaffed Peter afterwards about having screamed so horribly when the bear seized him. 'H'm! I wonder, said he, 'if there aren't others that would have screeched just as loud. I had to yell after the fellows that were so afraid of frightening the bear that when they ran they covered seven yards at each stride.'

"Thursday, December 14th. 'Well, Mogstad, how many pups have you now?' I asked at breakfast. 'There are five now.' But soon after he came down to tell me that there were at least twelve. Gracious! That is good value for what we have lost. But we were almost as pleased when Johansen came down and said that he heard the missing dog howling on the ice far away to the north-west. Several of us went up to listen, and we could all hear him quite well; but it sounded as if he were sitting still, howling in despair. Perhaps he was at an opening in the ice that he could not get across. Blessing had also heard him during his night-watch, but then the sound had come more from a south-westerly direction. When Peter went after breakfast to feed the dogs, there was the lost one, standing below the gangway wanting to get on board. Hungry he was — he dashed straight into the food — dish, but otherwise hale and hearty.

"This evening Peter came and said that he was certain he heard a bear moving about and pawing the ice; he and Pettersen had stood and listened to him scraping at the snow crust. I put on my 'pesk' (a fur blouse), got hold of my double-barrelled rifle, and went on deck. The whole crew were collected aft, gazing out into the night. We let loose 'Ulenka' and 'Pan,' and went in the direction where the bear was said to be. It was pitch-dark, but the dogs would find the tracks, if there was anything there. Hansen thought he had seen something moving about the hummock near the ship, but we found and heard nothing, and, as several of the others had by this time come out on the ice and could also discover nothing, we scrambled on board again. It is extraordinary, all the sounds that one can fancy one hears out on that great, still space, mysteriously lighted by the twinkling stars.

"Friday, December 15th. This morning Peter saw a fox on the ice astern, and he saw it again later, when he was out with the dogs. There is something remarkable about this appearance of bears and foxes now, after our seeing no life for so long. The last time we saw a fox we were far south of this, possibly near Sannikoff Land. Can we have come into the neighbourhood of land again?

"I inspected 'Kvik's' pups in the afternoon. There were thirteen, a curious coincidence — thirteen pups on December 13th, for thirteen men. Five were killed; 'Kvik' can manage eight, but more would be bad for her. Poor mother! she was very anxious about her young ones, wanted to jump up into the box beside them and take them from us. And you can see that she is very proud of them.

"Peter came this evening and said that there must be a ghost on the ice, for he heard exactly the same sounds of walking and pawing as yesterday evening. This seems to be a populous region, after all.

"According to an observation taken on Tuesday, we must be pretty nearly in 79° 8' north latitude. That was 8' drift in the three days from Saturday; we are getting on better and better.

"Why will it not snow? Christmas is near, and what is Christmas without snow, thickly falling snow? We have not had one snowfall all the time we have been drifting. The hard grains that come down now and again are nothing. Oh, the beautiful white snow, falling so gently and silently, softening every hard outline with its sheltering purity! There is nothing more deliciously restful, soft, and white. This snowless ice-plain is like a life without love — nothing to soften it. The marks of all the battles and pressures of the ice stand forth just as when they were made, rugged and difficult to move among. Love is life's snow. It falls deepest and softest into the gashes left by the fight — whiter and purer than snow itself. What is life without love? It is like this ice — a cold, bare, rugged mass, the wind driving it and rending it and then forcing it together again, nothing to cover over the open rifts, nothing to break the violence of the collisions, nothing to round away the sharp corners of the broken floes —

nothing, nothing but bare, rugged drift-ice.

"Saturday, December 16th. In the afternoon Peter came quietly into the saloon, and said that he heard all sorts of noises on the ice. There was a sound to the north exactly like that of ice packing against land, and then suddenly there was such a roar through the air that the dogs started up and barked. Poor Peter! They laugh at him when he comes down to give an account of his many observations; but there is not one among us as sharp as he is.

"Wednesday, December 20th. As I was sitting at breakfast, Peter came roaring that he believed he had seen a bear on the ice. 'And that "Pan" set off the moment he was let loose.' I rushed on to the ice with my gun. Several men were to be seen in the moonlight, but no bear. It was long before 'Pan' came back; he had followed him far to the north-west.

"Sverdrup and 'Smith Lars' in partnership have made a great bear-trap, which was put out on the ice to-day. As I was afraid of more dogs than bears being caught in it, it was hung from a gallows, too high for the dogs to jump up to the piece of blubber which hangs as bait right in the mouth of the trap. All the dogs spend the evening now sitting on the rail barking at this new man they see out there on the ice in the moonlight.

"Thursday, December 21st. It is extraordinary, after all, how the time passes. Here we are at the shortest day, though we have no day. But now we are moving on to light and summer again. We tried to sound to-day; had out 2,100 metres (over 1,100 fathoms) of line without reaching the bottom. We have no more line; what is to be done? Who could have guessed that we should find such deep water? There has been an arch of light in the sky all day, opposite the moon; so it is a lunar rainbow, but without colours, so far as I have been able to see.

"Friday, December 22nd. A bear was shot last night. Jacobsen saw it first, during his watch. He shot at it. It made off; and he then went down and told about it in the cabin. Mogstad and Peter came on deck; Sverdrup was called, too, and came up a little later. They saw the bear on his way towards the ship again; but he suddenly caught sight of the gallows with the trap on the ice to the west, and went off there. He looked well at the apparatus, then raised himself cautiously on his hind-legs, and laid his right paw on the cross-beam just beside the trap, stared for a little, hesitating, at the delicious morsel, but did not at all like the ugly jaws round it. Sverdrup was by this time out at the deck-house, watching in the sparkling moonshine. His heart was jumping — he expected every moment to hear the snap of his trap. But the bear shook his head suspiciously, lowered himself cautiously on to all-fours again, and snuffed

Sverdrup's bear trap.

carefully at the wire that the trap was fastened by, following it along to where it was made fast to a great block of ice. He went round this, and saw how cleverly it was all arranged, then slowly followed the wire back, raised himself up as before, with his paw on the beam of the gallows, had a long look at the trap, and shook his head again, probably saying to himself 'These wily fellows have planned this very cleverly for me.' Now he resumed his march to the ship. When he was within 60 paces of the bow Peter fired. The bear fell, but jumped up again and made off. Jacobsen, Sverdrup, and Mogstad all fired now, and he fell among some hummocks. He was flayed at once, and in the skin there was only the hole of one ball, which had gone through him from behind the shoulder-blade. Peter, Jacobsen, and Mogstad all claimed this ball. Sverdrup gave up his claim, as he had stood so far astern. Mogstad, seeing the bear fall directly after his shot, called out, 'I gave him that one;' Jacobsen swears that it was he that hit; and Bentzen, who was standing looking on, is prepared to take his oath any Where that it was Peter's ball that did the deed. The dispute upon this weighty point remained unsettled during the whole course of the expedition.

"Beautiful moonlight. Pressure in several directions. To-day we carried our supply of gun-cotton and cannon and rifle powder on deck. It is safer there than in the hold. In case of fire or other accident, an explosion in the hold might blow the ship's sides out and send us to the bottom before we had time to turn round. Some we put on the forecastle, some on the bridge. From these places it would be quickly thrown on to the ice.

"Saturday, December 23rd. What we call in Norway 'Little Christmas Eve.' I went a long way west this morning, coming home late. There was packed up ice everywhere, with flat floes between. I was turned by a newly formed opening in the ice, which I dared not cross on the thin layer of fresh ice. In the afternoon, as a first Christmas entertainment, we tried an ice-blasting with four prisms of gun-cotton. A hole was made with one of the large iron drills we had brought with us for this purpose, and the charge, with the end of the electric connecting wire, was sunk about a foot below the surface of the ice. Then all retired, the knob was touched, there was a dull crash, and water and pieces of ice were shot up into the air. Although it was 60 yards off, it gave the ship a good jerk that shook everything on board, and brought the hoar-frost down from the rigging. The explosion blew a hole through the four-feet-thick ice, but its only other effect was to make small cracks round this hole.

"Sunday, December 24th. Christmas Eve. 67° of cold (−37° C.). Glittering moonlight and the endless stillness of the Arctic night. I took a solitary stroll over the ice. The first Christmas Eve, and how far away! The observation shows us to be in 79° 11' north latitude. There is no drift; 2' farther south than six days ago."

There are no further particulars given of this day in the diary, but when I think of it, how clearly it all comes back to me! There was a peculiar elevation of mood on board that was not at all common among us. Every man's inmost thoughts were with those at home, but his comrades were not to know that, and so there was more joking and laughing than usual. All the lamps and lights we had on board were lit, and every corner of the saloon and cabins was brilliantly illuminated. The bill of fare for the day, of course, surpassed any previous one — food was the chief thing we had to hold festival with. The dinner was a very fine one indeed; so was the supper, and after it piles of Christmas cakes came on the table; Juell had been busy making them for several weeks. After that we enjoyed a glass of toddy and a cigar, smoking in the saloon being, of course, allowed. The culminating point of the festival came when two boxes with Christmas presents were produced. The one was from Hansen's mother, the other from his fiancée — Miss Fougner. It was touching to see the childlike pleasure with which each man received his gift — it might be a pipe or a knife or some little knack-knack — he felt that it was like a message from home. After this there were speeches; and then the *Framsjaa* appeared, with an illustrated supplement, selections from which are given. The drawings are the work of the famous Arctic draughtsman, Huttetu. Here are two verses from the poem for the day:

> When the ship's path is stopped by fathom-thick ice,
> And winter's white covering is spread,
> When we're quite given up to the power of the stream,
> Oh! 'tis then that so often of home we must dream.

> We wish them all joy at this sweet Christmas-tide,
> Health and happiness for the next year,
> Ourselves patience to wait; 'twill bring us to the Pole,
> And home the nest spring, never fear!

"There were many more poems, amongst others one giving some account of the principal events of the last weeks, in this style:

"Bears are seen, and dogs are born,
Cakes are baked, both small and large;
Henriksen, he does not fall,
Spite of bear's most violent charge;
Mogstad with his rifle clicks,
Jacobsen with long lance sticks,"

and so on. There was a long ditty on the subject of the

'Dog Rape on board the *Fram*'
Up and down on a night so cold,
Kvirre virre vip, bom, bom,
Walk harpooner and kennelman bold,
Kvirre virre vip, bom, bom;
Our kennelman swings, I need hardly tell,
Kvirre virre vip, bom, bom,
The long, long lash you know so well,
Kvirre virre vip, bom, bom;
Our harpooner, he is a man of light,
Kvirre virre vip, bom bom,
A burning lantern he grasps-tight,
Kvirre virre vip, bom, bom,
They as they walk the time beguile,
Kvirre virre vip, bom, bom,
With tales of bears and all their wile,
Kvirre virre vip, bom, bom.

Now suddenly a bear they see,
Kvirre virre vip, bom, bom,
Before whom all the dogs do flee,
Kvirre virre vip, bom, bom;
Kennelman, like a deer, runs fast,
Kvirre virre vip, bom, bom,
Harpooner slow comes in the last,
Kvirre virre vip, bom, bom,"

and so on.

Among the announcements are—

"Instruction in Fencing.

"In consequence of the indefinite postponement of our departure, a limited number of pupils can be received for instruction in both fencing and boxing.

"MAJAKOFT,

"Teacher of Boxing,

"Next door to the Doctor's."

Again—

"On account of want of storage room, a quantity of old clothes are at present for sale, by private arrangement, at No. 2, Pump Lane.[36] Repeated requests to remove them having been of no effect, I am obliged to dispose of them in this way. The clothes are quite fresh, having been in salt for a long time."

After the reading of the newspaper came instrumental music and singing, and it was far on in the night before we sought our berths.

"Monday, December 25th. Christmas Day. Thermometer at −36° F. (−38° C.) below zero. I took a walk south in the beautiful light of the full moon. At a newly made crack I went through the fresh ice with one leg and got soaked; but such an accident matters very little in this frost. The water immediately stiffens into ice; it does not make one very cold, and one feels dry again soon.

"They will be thinking much of us just now at home and giving many a pitying sigh over all the hardships we are enduring in this cold, cheerless, icy region. But I am afraid their compassion would cool if they could look in upon us, hear the merriment that goes on, and see all our comforts and good cheer. They can hardly be better off at home. I myself have certainly never lived a more sybaritic life, and have never had more reason to fear the consequences it brings in its train. Just listen to to-day's dinner menu:

1. Ox-tail soup;

2. Fish-pudding, with potatoes and melted butter;

3. Roast of reindeer, with peas, French beans, potatoes, and cranberry jam;

4. Cloudberries with cream

5. Cake and marzipan (a welcome present from the baker to the expedition; we blessed that man).

And along with all this that Ringnes bock-beer which is so famous in our part of the world. Was this the sort of dinner for men who are to be hardened against the horrors of the Arctic night?

Every one had eaten so much that supper had to be skipped altogether. Later in the evening coffee was served, with pine-apple preserve, gingerbread, vanilla cakes, cocoanut macaroons, and various other cakes, all the work of our excellent cook, Juell ; and we ended up with figs, almonds, and raisins.

"Now let us have the breakfast, just to complete the clay : coffee, freshly baked bread, beautiful Danish butter, Christmas cake, Cheddar cheese, clove-cheese, tongue, corned beef, and marmalade. And if any one thinks that this is a specially good breakfast because it is Christmas Day, he is wrong. It is just what we have always, with the addition of the cake, which is not part of the every-day diet.

"Add now to this good cheer our strongly built, safe house, our comfortable saloon, lighted up with the large petroleum lamp and several smaller ones (when we have no electric light, constant gaiety, card-playing, and books in any quantity, with or without illustrations, good and entertaining reading, and then a good sound sleep-what more could one wish.

"... But, O Arctic night, thou art like a woman, a marvellously lovely woman. Thine are the noble, pure outlines of antique beauty, with its marble coldness. On thy high, smooth brow, clear with the clearness of ether, is no trace of compassion for the little sufferings of despised humanity, on thy pale, beautiful cheek no blush of feeling. Among thy raven locks, waving out into space, the hoar-frost has sprinkled its glittering crystals. The proud lines of thy throat, thy shoulders' curves, are so noble, but, oh! unbendingly cold; thy bosom's white chastity is feelingless as the snowy ice. Chaste, beautiful, and proud, thou floatest through ether over the frozen sea, thy glittering garment, woven of aurora beams, covering the vault of heaven. But sometimes I divine a twitch of pain on thy lips, and endless sadness dreams in thy dark eye.

"Oh, how tired I am of thy cold beauty! I long to return to life. Let me get home again, as conqueror or as beggar; what does that matter? But let me get home to begin life anew. The years are passing here, and what do they bring ? Nothing but dust, dry dust, which the first wind blows away ; new dust comes in its place, and the next wind takes it too. Truth ? Why should we always make so much of truth? Life is more than cold truth, and we live but once.

Tuesday, December 26th. 36° F. below zero (−38° C.). This (the same as yesterday's) is the greatest cold we have had yet. I went a long way north to-

Moonlight on the dark waves.

day; found a big lane covered with newly frozen ice, with a quite open piece of water in the middle. The ice rocked up and down under my steps, sending waves out into the open pool. It was strange once more to see the moonlight playing on the coal-black waves, and awakened a remembrance of well-known scenes. I followed this lane far to the north, seemed to see the outlines of high land in the hazy light below the moon, and went on and on; but in the end it turned out to be a bank of clouds behind the moonlit vapour rising from the open water. I saw from a high hummock that this opening stretched north as far as the eye could reach.

"The same luxurious living as yesterday; a dinner of four courses. Shooting with darts at a target for cigarettes has been the great excitement of the day. Darts and target are Johansen's Christmas present from Miss Fougner."

"Wednesday, December 27th. Wind began to blow this afternoon, 19½ to 26 feet per second; the windmill is going again, and the arc-lamp once more brightens our lives. Johansen gave notice of 'a shooting match by electric light, with free concert,' for the evening. It was a pity for himself that he did, for he and several others were shot into bankruptcy and beggary, and had to retire one after the other, leaving their cigarettes behind them."

"Thursday. December 28th. A little forward of the *Fram* there is a broad, newly formed open lane, in which she could lie crossways. It was covered with last night's ice, in which slight pressure began to-day. It is strange how indifferent we are to this pressure, which was the cause of such great trouble to many earlier Arctic navigators. We have not so much as made the smallest preparation for possible accident, no provisions on deck, no tent, no clothing, in readiness. This may seem like recklessness, but in reality there is not the slightest prospect of the pressure harming us; we know now what the *Fram* can bear. Proud of our splendid, strong ship, we stand on her deck watching the ice come hurtling against her sides, being crushed and broken there and having to go down below her, while new ice-masses tumble upon her out of the dark, to meet the same fate. Here and there, amid deafening noise, some great mass rises up and launches itself threateningly upon the bulwarks, only to sink down suddenly, dragged the same way as the others. But at times when one hears the roaring of tremendous pressure in the night, as a rule so deathly still, one cannot but call to mind the disasters that this uncontrollable power has wrought.

"I am reading the story of Kane's expedition just now. Unfortunate man, his preparations were miserably inadequate; it seems to me to have been a reckless, unjustifiable proceeding to set out with such equipments. Almost all the dogs died of bad food; all the men had scurvy from the same cause, with snow-blindness, frost-bites, and all kinds of miseries. He learned a wholesome awe of the Arctic night, and one can hardly wonder at it. He writes on page 173: 'I feel that we are fighting the battle of life at disadvantage, and that an Arctic day and an Arctic night age a man more rapidly and harshly than a year anywhere else in this weary world. In another place he writes that it is impossible for civilised men not to suffer in such circumstances. These were sad, but by no means unique experiences. An English Arctic explorer, with whom I had some conversation, also expressed himself very discouragingly on the subject of life in the Polar regions, and combated my cheerful faith in the possibility of preventing scurvy. He was of opinion that it was inevitable, and that no expedition yet had escaped it, though some might have given it another name; rather a humiliating view to take of the matter, I think. But I am fortunately in a position to maintain that it is not justified; and I wonder if they would not both change their opinions if they were here. For my own part, I can say that the Arctic night has had no ageing, no weakening, influence of any kind upon me; I seem, on the contrary, to grow younger. This quiet, regular life suits me remarkably well, and I cannot remember a time when I was in better bodily health balance than I am at present. I differ from these other authorities to the extent of feeling inclined to recommend this region as an excellent sanatorium in cases of nervousness and general breakdown. This is in all sincerity.

"I am almost ashamed of the life we lead, with none of those darkly painted sufferings of the long winter night which are indispensable to a properly exciting Arctic expedition. We shall have nothing to write about when we get home. I may say the same of my comrades as I have said for myself: they all look healthy, fat, in good condition; none of the traditional pale, hollow faces, no low spirits — any one hearing the laughter that goes on in the saloon, 'the fall of greasy cards,' etc. (see Juell's poem), would be in no doubt about this. But how, indeed, should there be any illness? With the best of food of every kind, as much of it as we want, and constant variety, so that even the most fastidious cannot tire of it, good shelter, good clothing, good ventilation, exercise in the open air *ad libitum*, no over-exertion in the way of work, instructive and amusing books of every kind, relaxation in the shape of cards, chess, dominoes, halma, music, and story-telling — how should any one be ill? Every now and then I hear remarks expressive of perfect satisfaction with the life. Truly the whole secret lies in arranging things sensibly, and especially in being careful about the food. A thing that I believe has a good effect upon us is this living together in the one saloon,

Of your old father to be the double;
Your lineage, honour, and fight hard to merit
Our praise for the habits we trust you inherit.
On we must go if you want to please us;
To make us lie still is the way to tease us.
In the old year we sailed not so badly,
Be it so still, or you'll hear us groan sadly.
When the time comes you must break up the ice for us;
When the time comes you must win the great prize for us;
We fervently hope, having reached our great goal,
To eat next Christmas dinner beyond the North Pole."

During the evening we were regaled with pine-apple, figs, cakes, and other sweets, and about midnight Hansen brought in toddy, and Nordahl cigars and cigarettes. At the moment of the passing of the year all stood up, and I had to make an apology for a speech — to the effect that the old year had been after all a good one, and I hoped the new would not be worse; that I thanked them for good comradeship, and was sure that our life together this year would be as comfortable and pleasant as it had been during the last. Then they sang the songs that had been written for the farewell entertainment in our honour at Christiania and at Bergen:

"Our mother, weep not! it was thou
Gave them the wish to wander,
To leave our coasts and turn their prow
Towards night and perils yonder.
Thou pointed'st to the open sea,
The long cape was thy finger;
The white sail wings they got from thee;
Thou can'st not bid them linger!
"Yes, they are thine, O mother old!
And proud thou dost embrace them;
Thou hear'st of dangers manifold,
But know'st thy sons can face them.
And tears of joy thine eyes will rain,
The day the *Fram* comes steering
Up fjord again to music strain,

And the roar of thousands cheering.

"E.N.'

Then I read aloud our last greeting, a telegram we received at Tromsö from Moltke Moe:

"Luck on the way,
Sun on the sea,
Sun on your minds,
Help from the winds;
May the packed floes
Part and unclose
Where the ship goes. F
onward her progress be,
E'en though the silent sea
Then
After her freeze up again.

"Strength enough, meat enough,
Hope enough, beat enough;
The *Fram* will go sure enough then
To the Pole and so back to the dwellings of men.
Luck on the way
To thee and thy band.
And welcome back to the fatherland!"

After this we read some of Vinje's poems, and then sang songs from the *Framsjaa* and others.

It seems strange that we should have seen the New Year in already, and that it will not begin at home for eight hours yet. It is almost 4 a.m. now. I had thought of sitting up till it was New Year in Norway too; but no, I will rather go to bed and sleep, and dream that I am at home.

"Monday, January 1st, 1894. The year began well. I was awakened by Juell's cheerful voice wishing me a Happy New Year. He had come to give me a cup of coffee in bed — delicious Turkish coffee, his Christmas present from Miss Fougner. It is beautiful clear weather, with the thermometer at 36° below zero (−38° C.). It almost seems to me as if the twilight in the south were beginning surface, and this itself freezes into pretty salt flowers, resembling hoar-frost. The temperature is between 38° F. (−39° C.) and 40° F. (−40° C.) below zero, but when there is added to this a biting wind, with a velocity of from 9 to 16 feet per second, it must be allowed that it is rather 'cool in the shade.'"

"Sverdrup and I agreed to day that the Christmas holidays had better stop now, and the usual life begin again; too much idleness is not good for us. It cannot be called a full nor a complicated one, this life of ours, but it has one advantage, that we are all satisfied with it, such as it is."

"They are still working in the engine-room, but expect to finish what they are doing to the boiler in a few days, and then all is done there. Then the turning lathe is to be set up in the hold, and tools for it have to be forged. There is often a job for Smith Lars, and then the forge flames forward by the forecastle, and sends its red glow on to the rime-covered rigging, and farther up into the starry night, and out over the waste of ice. From far off you can hear the strokes on the anvil ringing through the silent night. When one is wandering alone out there, and the well known sound reaches one's ear, and one sees the red glow, memory recalls less solitary scenes. While one stands gazing, perhaps a light moves along the deck, and slowly up the rigging. It is Johansen, on his way up to the crow's-nest to read the temperature. Blessing is at present engaged in counting blood corpuscles again, and estimating amounts of haemoglobin. For this purpose he draws blood every month from every mother's son of us, the bloodthirsty dog, with supreme contempt for all the outcry against vivisection, Hansen and his assistant take observations. The meteorological ones, which are taken every four hours, are Johansen's special department. First he reads the thermometer, hygrometer, and thermograph on deck (they were afterwards kept on the ice); next the barometer, barograph, and thermometer in the saloon; and then the minimum and maximum thermometers in the crow's-nest (this to take the record of the temperature of a higher air stratum). Then he goes to read the thermometers that are kept on the ice to measure the radiations from its surface, and perhaps down to the hold, too, to see what the temperature is there. Every second day, as a rule, astronomical observations are taken, to decide our whereabouts, and keep us up to date in the crab's progress we are making. Taking these observations with the thermometer between 22 F. and 40° F. below zero (−30° C. to −40°) is a very mixed pleasure. Standing still on deck working with these fine instruments and screwing in metal screws with one's bare fingers is not altogether agreeable. It often happens that they must slap their arms about and tramp hard up and down the deck. They are received with shouts of laughter

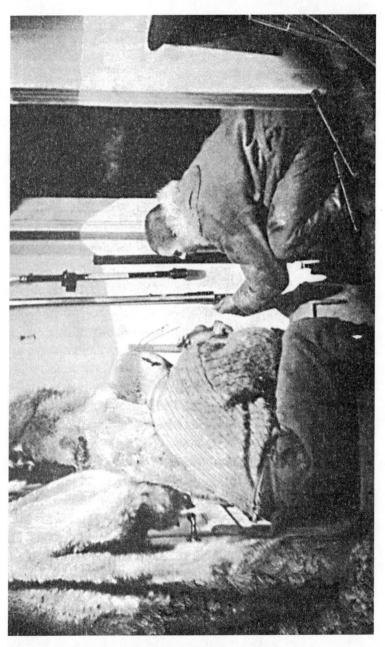

Hansen and Johanseninspecting the barometers.

when they reappear in the saloon after the performance of one of these thundering nigger break-downs above our heads, that has shaken the whole ship. We ask innocently if it was cold on deck? 'Not the very least,' says Hansen; 'just a pleasant temperature.' 'And your feet are not cold now?' 'No, I can't say that they are, but one's fingers get a little cold sometimes.' Two of his had just been frost-bitten; but he refused to wear one of the wolf-skin suits which I had given out for the meteorologists. 'It is too mild for that yet; and it does not do to pamper one's self,' he says.

"I believe it was when the thermometer stood at 40° below zero that Hansen rushed up on deck one morning in shirt and drawers to take an observation. He said he had not time to get on his clothes.

"At certain intervals they also take magnetic observations on the ice, these two. I watch them standing there with lanterns, bending over their instruments; and presently I see them tearing away over the floe, their arms swinging like the sails of the windmill when there is a wind pressure of 32 to 39 feet — but 'it is not at all cold.' I cannot help thinking of what I have read in the accounts of some of the earlier expeditions, namely that at such temperatures it was impossible to tale observations. It would take worse than this to make these fellows give in. In the intervals between their observations and calculations I hear a murmuring in Hansen's cabin, which means that the principal is at present occupied in inflicting a dose of astronomy or navigation upon his assistant.

"It is something dreadful, the amount of card-playing that goes on in the saloon in the evenings now; the gaming demon is abroad, far into the night; even our model Sverdrup is possessed by him. They have not yet played the shirts off their backs, but some of them have literally played the bread out of their mouths; two poor wretches have had to go without fresh bread for a whole month because they had forfeited their rations of it to their opponents. But all the same, this card-playing is a healthy, harmless recreation, giving, occasion for much laughter, fun, and pleasure.

"An Irish proverb says: 'Be happy; and if you cannot be happy, be careless; and if you cannot be careless, be as careless as you can.' This is good philosophy, which — no, what need of proverbs here, where life is happy! It was in all sincerity that Amundsen burst out yesterday with: 'Yes, isn't it just as I say, that we are the luckiest men on earth that can live up here where we have no cares, get everything given us without needing to trouble about it, and are well off in every possible way!' Hansen agreed that it certainly was a life without care. Juell said much the same a little ago; what seems to please him most is that there are

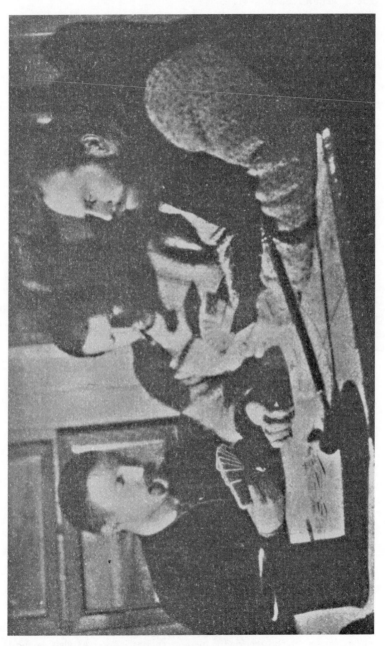

Blessing, Hansen and Sverdrup playing cards.

no summonses here, no creditors, no bills. And I? Yes, I am happy too. It is an easy life: nothing that weighs heavy on one, no letters, no newspapers, nothing disturbing; just that monastic, out-of-the-world existence that was my dream when I was younger and yearned for quietness in which to give myself up to my studies. Longing, even when it is strong and sad, is not unhappiness. A man has truly no right to be anything but happy when fate permits him to follow up his ideals, exempting him from the wearing strain of every-day cares, that he may with clearer vision strive towards a lofty goal.

"'Where there is work, success will follow,' said a poet of the land of work. I am working as hard as I can, so I suppose success will pay me a visit by-and-by. I am lying on the sofa, reading about Kane's misfortunes, drinking beer, smoking cigarettes — truth obliges the to confess that I have become addicted to the vice I condemn so strongly — but flesh is grass; so I blow the smoke clouds into the air and dream sweet dreams. It is hard work, but I must do the best I can."

"Thursday, January 4th. It seems as if the twilight were increasing quite perceptibly now, but this is very possibly only imagination. I am in good spirits in spite of the fact that we are drifting south again. After all, what does it matter? Perhaps the gain to science will be as great, and after all. I suppose this desire to reach the North Pole is only a piece of vanity. I have now a very good idea of what it must be like up there. ('I like that!' you say.) Our deep water here is connected with, is a part of, the deep water of the Atlantic Ocean — of this there can be no doubt. And have not I found that things go exactly as I calculated they would whenever we get a favourable wind? Have not many before us had to wait for wind? And as to vanity — that is a child's disease, got over long ago. All calculations, with but one exception, have proved correct. We made our way along the coast of Asia, which many prophesied we should have great difficulty in doing. We were able to sail farther north than I had dared to hope for in my boldest moments, and in just the longitude I wished. We are closed in by the ice, also as I wished. The *Fram* has borne the ice-pressure splendidly, and allows herself to be lifted by it without so much as creaking, in spite of being mon, heavily loaded with coal, and drawing more water than we reckoned on when we made our calculations; and this after her certain destruction and ours was prophesied by those most experienced in such matters. I have not found the ice higher nor heavier than I expected it to be; and the comfort, warmth, and good ventilation on board are far beyond my expectations. Nothing is wanting in our equipment, and the food is quite exceptionally good. As Blessing and I

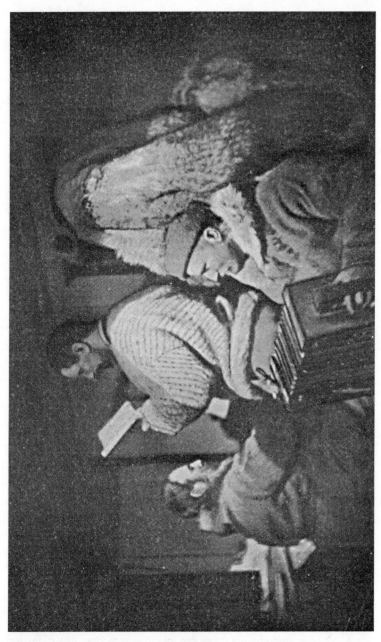

Nordahl playing the organ, Blessing singing and Johansen playing the accordeon in the saloon.

agreed a few days ago, it is as good as at home; there is not a thing we long for; not even the thought of a beefsteak à la Châteaubriand, or a pork cutlet with mushrooms, and a bottle of Burgundy, can make our mouths water; we simply don't care about such things. The preparations for the expedition cost me several years of precious life; but now I do not grudge them, my object is attained. On the drifting ice we live a winter life, not only in every respect better than that of previous expeditions, but actually as if we had brought a bit of Norway, of Europe, with us. We are as well off as if we were at home. All together in one saloon, with everything in common, we are a little part of the fatherland, and daily we draw closer and closer together. In one point only have my calculations proved incorrect, but unfortunately in one of the most important. I pre-supposed a shallow Polar Sea, the greatest depth known in these regions up till now being 80 fathoms, found by the *Jeannette*. I reasoned that all currents would have a strong influence in the shallow Polar Sea, and that on the Asiatic side the current of the Siberian rivers would be strong enough to drive the ice a good way north. But here I already find a depth which we cannot measure with all our line, a depth of certainly 1,000 fathoms, and possibly double that. This at once upsets all faith in the operation of a current; we find either none, or an extremely slight one; my only trust now is in the winds. Columbus discovered America by means of a mistaken calculation, and even that not his own; heaven only knows where my mistake will lead us. Only I repeat once more — the Siberian driftwood on the coast of Greenland cannot lie, and the way it went we must go.

"Monday, January 8th. Little Liv is a year old today; it will be a fête day at home. As I was lying on the sofa reading after dinner, Peter put his head in at the door and asked me to come up and look at a strange star which had just shown itself above the horizon, shining like a beacon flame. I got quite a start when I came on deck and saw a strong red light just above the edge of the ice in the south. It twinkled and changed colour; it looked just as if some one were coming carrying a lantern over the ice; I actually believe that for a moment I so far forgot our surroundings as to think that it really was some person approaching from the south. It was Venus, which we see to-day for the first time, as it has till now been beneath the horizon. It is beautiful with its red light. Curious that it should happen to come to-day. It must be Liv's star, as Jupiter is the home star. And Liv's birthday is a lucky day — we are on our way north again. According to observations we are certainly north of 79° N. lat. On the home day, September 6th, the favourable wind began to blow that carried us along the coast of Asia; perhaps Liv's day has brought us into a good current, and we are making the real start for the north under her star.

"Friday, January 12th. There was pressure about ten o'clock this morning in the opening forward, but I could see no movement when I was there a little later, I followed the opening some way to the north. It is pretty cold work walking with the thermometer at 40° F. below zero, and the wind blowing with a velocity of 16 feet per second straight in your face. But now we are certainly drifting fast to the north under Liv's star. After all it is not quite indifferent to me whether we are going north or south. When the drift is northwards new life seems to come into me, and hope, the ever-young, springs fresh and green from under the winter snow. I see the way open before me, and I see the home-coming in the distance — too great happiness to believe in."

Sunday, January 14th. Sunday again. The time is passing almost quickly, and there is more light every day. There was great excitement to-day when yesterday evening's observations were being calculated. All guessed that we had come a long way north again. Several thought to 79° 18' or 20'. Others, I believe, insisted on 80°. The calculation places us in 79° N. lat.; 137° 31' E. long. A good step onwards. Yesterday the ice was quiet, but this morning there was considerable pressure in several places. Goodness knows what is causing it just now; it is a whole week after new-moon. I took a long walk to the south-west, and got right in among it. Packing began where I stood, with roars and thunders below me and on every side. I jumped, and ran like a hare, as if I had never heard such a thing before; it came so unexpectedly. The ice was curiously flat there to the south; the farther I went the flatter it grew, with excellent sledging surface. Over such ice one could drive many miles a day."

"Monday, January 15th. There was pressure forward both this morning and towards noon, but we heard the loudest sounds from the north. Sverdrup, Mogstad, and Peter went in that direction and were stopped by a large open channel. Peter and I afterwards walked a long distance N.N.E., past a large opening that I had skirted before Christmas. It was shining, flat ice, splendid for sledging on, always better the farther north we went. The longer I wander about and see this sort of ice in all directions, the more strongly does a plan take hold of me that I have long had in my mind. It would be possible to get with dogs and sledges over this ice to the Pole, if one left the ship for good and made one's way back in the direction of Franz Josef Land, Spitzbergen, or the west coast of Greenland. It might almost be called an easy expedition for two men.

"But it would be too hasty to go off in spring. We must first see what kind of drift the summer brings. And as I think over it, I feel doubtful if it would be right to go off and leave the others. Imagine if I came home and they did not! Yet it was to explore the unknown Polar regions that I came; it was for that the Norwegian people gave their money; and surely my first duty is to do that if I can. I must give the drift plan a longer trial yet, but if it takes us in a wrong direction, then there is nothing for it but to try the other, come what may.

"Tuesday, January 16th. The ice is quiet today. Does longing stupefy one, or does it wear itself out and turn at last into stolidity? Oh, that burning longing night and day was happiness! but now its fire has turned to icy. Why does home seem so far away.' It is one's all-life, without it is so empty, so empty — nothing but dead emptiness. Is it the restlessness of spring that is beginning to come over one, the desire for action, for something different from this indolent, enervating life? Is the soul of man nothing but a succession of moods and feelings, shifting as incalculably as the changing winds? Perhaps my brain is over-tired; day and night my thoughts have turned on the one point, the possibility of reaching the Pole and getting home. Perhaps it is rest I need, to sleep, sleep! Am I afraid of venturing my life? No, it cannot be that. But what else then can be keeping me back? Perhaps a secret doubt of the practicability of the plan? My mind is confused; the whole thing has got into a tangle; I am a riddle to myself. I am worn out, and yet I do not feel any special tiredness. Is it perhaps because I sat up reading last night? Everything around is emptiness, and my brain is a blank. I look at the home pictures and ana moved by them in a curious, dull way; I look into the future, and feel as if it does not much matter to me whether I get home in the autumn of this year or next. So long as I get home in the end, a year or two seem almost nothing. I have never thought this before. I have no inclination to read, nor to draw, nor to do anything else whatever. Folly! Shall I try a few pages of Schopenhauer? No, I will go to bed, though I am not sleepy. Perhaps, if the truth were known, I am longing now more than ever. The only thing that helps me is writing, trying to express myself on these pages, and then looking at myself as it were from the outside. Yes, man's life is nothing but a succession of moods, half memory and half hope."

"Thursday, January 18th. The wind that began yesterday has gone on blowing all to-day with a velocity of 16 to 19 feet per second, from S.S.E., S.E., and E.S.E. It has no doubt helped us on a good way north; but it seems to be going down; now, about midnight, it has sunk to 13 feet; and the barometer, which has been rising all the time, has suddenly begun to fall; let us hope that it is not a cyclone passing over us, bringing northerly wind. It is curious that

Juell, Amundsen, Johansen and Pettersen reading in the saloon.

there is almost always a rise of the thermometer with these stronger winds; to-day it rose to 13° F. below zero (−25° C.). A south wind of less velocity generally lowers the temperature, and a moderate north wind raises it. Payer's explanation of this raising of the temperature by strong winds is that the wind is warmed by passing over large; openings in the ice. This can hardly be correct, at any rate in our case, for we have few or no openings. I am rather inclined to believe that the rise is produced by air from higher strata being brought down to the surface of the earth. It is certain that the higher air is warmer than the lower, which comes into contact with snow and ice surfaces cooled by radiation. Our observations go to prove that such is the case. Add to this that the air in its fall is heated by the rising pressure. A strong wind, even if it does not come from the higher strata of the atmosphere, must necessarily make some confusion in the mutual position of the various strata, mixing the higher with those below them and vice versâ.

"I had a strange dream last night. I had got home. I can still feel something of the trembling joy, mixed with fear, with which I neared land and the first telegraph station. I had carried out my plan; we had reached the North Pole on sledges, and then got down to Franz Josef Land. I had seen nothing but drift-ice; and when people asked what it was like up there, and how we knew we had been to the Pole, I had no answer to give; I had forgotten to take accurate observations, and now began to feel that this had been stupid of me. It is very curious that I had an exactly similar dream when we were drifting on the ice-floes along the east coast of Greenland, and thought that we were being carried farther and farther from our destination. Then I dreamed that I had reached home after crossing Greenland on the ice; but that I was ashamed because I could give no account of what I had seen on the way — I had forgotten everything. Is there not a lucky omen in the resemblance between these two dreams? I attained my aim the first time, bad as things looked — shall I not do so this time, too? If I were superstitious I should feel surer of it; but even though I am not at all superstitious, I have a firm conviction that our enterprise must be successful. This belief is not merely the result of the two last days' south wind; something within me says that we shall succeed; I laugh now: at myself for having been weak enough to doubt it. I can spend hours staring into the light, dreaming of how, when we land, I shall grope my way to the first telegraph station, trembling with emotion and suspense. I write out telegram after telegram; I ask the clerk if he can mc, any news from home."

"Friday, January 19th. Splendid wind with velocity of 13 to 29 feet per second; we arc going north at a grand rate. The red, glowing twilight is now so bright about midday, that, if we were in more southern latitudes, we should expect to see the sun rise bright and glorious above the horizon in a few minutes, but we shall have to wait a month yet for that."

"Saturday, January 20th. I had about 600 lbs. of pemmican and 200 lbs. of bread brought up from the hold to-day, and stowed on the forecastle. It is wrong not to have some provisions on deck against any sudden emergency, such as fire.

"Sunday, January 21st. We took a long excursion to the north-west; the ice in that direction, too, was tolerably Nat. Sverdrup and I got on the top of a high pressure mound at some distance from here. It was in the centre of what had been very violent packing, but all the same the wall at its highest was not over 17 feet, and this was one of the highest and biggest altogether that I have seen yet. An altitude of the moon taken this evening showed us to be in 79° 35′ N. lat. — exactly what I had thought. We are so accustomed now to calculating our drift by the wind, that we are able to tell pretty nearly where we are. This is a good step northwards, if we could take many more such. In honour of the King's birthday we have a treat of figs, raisins, and almonds.

"Tuesday, January 23rd. When I came on deck this morning 'Caiaphas' was sitting out on the ice on the port quarter, barking incessantly to the east. I knew there must be something there, and went off with a revolver, Sverdrup following with one also. When I got near the dog he came to meet me, always wriggling his head round to the east and barking; then he ran on before us in that direction; it was plain that there was some animal there, and of course it could only be a bear. The full moon stood low and red in the north, and sent its feeble light obliquely across the broken ice-surface. I looked out sharply in all directions over the hummocks, which cast long, many-shaped shadows; but I could distinguish nothing in this confusion. We went on, 'Caiaphas' first, growling and barking and pricking his ears, and I after him, expecting every moment to see a bear loom up in front of us. Our course was eastwards along the opening. The dog presently began to go more cautiously and straighter forward; then he stopped making any noise except a low growl — we were evidently drawing near. I mounted a hummock to look about, and caught sight among the blocks of ice of something dark, which seemed to be coming towards us. 'There comes a black dog,' I called. 'No, it is a bear,' said Sverdrup, who was more to the side of it and could see better. I saw now, too, that it was a large animal, and that it had only been its head that I had taken for a dog. It was not unlike a bear in its movements, but it seemed to me remarkably dark in colour. I pulled the revolver out of the holster and rushed forward to empty all its barrels into the creature's head. When I was just a few paces from it, and preparing to shoot, it raised its head and I saw that it was a walrus, and that same moment it threw itself sideways into the water. There we stood. To shoot at such a fellow with a revolver would be of as much use as squirting water at a goose. The great black head showed again immediately in a strip of moonlight on the dark water. The animal took a long look at us, disappeared for a little, appeared again nearer, bobbed up and down, blew, lay with its head under water, shoved itself over towards us, raised its head again. It was enough to drive one mad if we had only had a harpoon I could easily have stuck it into its back. Yes, if we had had — and back to the *Fram* we ran as fast as our legs would carry us, to get harpoon and rifle. But the harpoon and line were stored away, and were not to be had at once; who could have guessed that they would be needed here? The harpoon point had to be sharpened, and all this took time. And for all our searching afterwards east and west along the opening, no walrus was to be found. Goodness knows where it had gone, as there are hardly any openings in the ice for a long distance round. Sverdrup and I vainly fret over not having known at once what kind of animal it was, for if we had only guessed we should have him now. But who expects to meet a walrus on close ice in the middle of a wild sea of a thousand fathoms depth, and that in the heart of winter? None of us ever heard of such a thing before; it is a perfect mystery. As I thought we might have come upon shoals or into the neighbourhood of land, I had soundings taken in the afternoon with 130 fathoms (240 metres) of line, but no bottom was found.

"By yesterday's observations we are in 79° 41' N. lat., and 135° 29' E. long. That is good progress north, and it does not much matter that we have been taken a little west. The clouds are driving this evening More a strong south wind, so we shall likely be going before it soon too; in the meantime there is a breeze, from the south, so slight that you hardly feel it.

"The opening on our stern lies almost east and west. We could see no end to it westwards when we went after the walrus; and Mogstad and Peter had gone three miles east, and it was as broad as ever there.

"Wednesday, January 24th. At supper this evening Peter told some of his remarkable Spitzbergen stories about his comrade Andreas Bek. 'Well, you see, it was up about Dutchman's Island, or Amsterdam Island, that Andreas Bek and I were on shore and got in among all the graves. We thought we'd like to see what was in them, so we broke up some of the coffins, and there they lay. Some of them had still flesh on their jaws and noses, and some of them still had their caps on their heads. Andreas, he was a devil of a fellow, you see, and he broke up the coffins and got hold of the skulls, and rolled them about here and there. Some of them he set up for targets and shot at. Then he wanted to see if there was marrow left in their bones, so he took and broke a thigh-bone, and, sure enough, there was marrow; he took and picked it out with a wooden pin.'

"'How could he do a thing like that?'

"'Oh, it was only a Dutchman, you know. But he had a bad dream that night, had Andreas. All the dead men came to fetch him, and he ran from them and got right out on the bowsprit, and there he sat and yelled, while the dead men stood on the forecastle. And the one with his broken thigh-bone in his hand was foremost, and he came crawling out, and wanted Andreas to put it together again. But just then he wakened. We were lying in the same berth, you see, Andreas and me, and I sat up in the berth and laughed, listening to him yelling. I wouldn't waken him, not I. I thought it was fun to hear him getting paid out a little.'

"'It was bad of you, Peter, to have any part in that horrid plundering of dead bodies.'

Johansen and Hansen playing Halma.

"'Oh, I never did anything to them, you know. Just once I broke up a coffin to get wood to make a fire for our coffee; but when we opened it the body just fell to pieces. But it was juicy wood, that, better to burn than the best fir-roots — such a fire as it made!'

"One of the others now remarked, 'Wasn't it the devil that used a skull for his coffee-cup?'

"'Well, he hadn't anything else, you see, and he just happened to find one. There was no harm in that, was there?'

"Then Jacobsen began to hold forth: 'It's not at all such an uncommon thing to use skulls for shooting at, either because people fancy them for targets, or because of some other reason; they shoot in through the eyeholes,' etc., etc.

"I asked Peter about 'Tobiesen's' coffin — if it had ever been dug up to find out if it was true that his men had killed him and his son.'

"'No, that one has never been dug up.'

"'I sailed past there last year,' begins Jacobsen, again; 'I didn't go ashore, but it seems to me that I heard that it had been dug up.'

"'That's just rubbish; it has never been dug up.'

"'Well,' said I, 'it seems to me that I've heard something about it too; I believe it was here on board, and I am very much mistaken if it was not yourself that said it, Peter.'

"'No, I never said that. All I said was that a man once struck a walrus spear through the coffin, and it's sticking there yet.'

"'What did he do that for?'

"'Oh! just because he wanted to know if there was anything in the coffin; and yet he didn't want to open it, you know. But let him lie in peace now.'

"Friday, January 26th. Peter and I went eastwards along the opening this morning for about seven miles, and we saw where it ends, in some old pressure ridges; its whole length is over seven miles. Movement in the ice began on our way home; indeed, there was pretty strong pressure all the time. As we were walking on the new ice in the opening, it rose in furrows or cracked under our feet. Then it raised itself up into two high walls, between which we walked as if along a street, amidst unceasing noises, sometimes howling and whining like a dog complaining of the cold, sometimes a roar like the thunder of a great waterfall. We were often obliged to take refuge on the old ice, either because we came to open water with a confusion of floating blocks, or because the line of the packing had gone straight across the opening, and there was a wall in front of us like a high frozen wave. It seemed as if the ice on the south side of the opening where the *Fram* is lying, were moving east, or else that on the north side was moving west; for the floes on the two sides slanted in towards each other in these directions. We saw tracks of a little bear which had trotted along the opening the day before. Unfortunately it had gone off south-west, and we had small hope, with this steady south wind, of its getting scent of the ship and coming to fetch a little of the flesh on board.

"Saturday, January 27th. The days are turning distinctly lighter now. We can just see to read *Verdens Gang*[37] about midday. At that time to-day Sverdrup thought he saw land far astern; it was dark and irregular, in some places high; he fancied that it might be only an appearance of clouds. When I returned from a walk, about one o'clock, I went up to look, but saw only piled-up ice. Perhaps this was the same as he saw, or possibly I was too late. (It turned out next day to be only an optical illusion.) Severe pressure has been going on this evening. It began at 7.30 astern in the opening, and went on steadily for two hours. It sounded as if a roaring waterfall were rushing down upon us with a force that nothing could resist. One heard the big floes crashing and breaking against each other. They were flung and pressed up into high walls, which must now stretch along the whole opening east and west, for one hears the roar the whole way. It is coming nearer just now; the ship is getting violent shocks; it is like waves in the ice. They come on us from behind, and move forward. We stare out into the night, but can see nothing, for it is pitch-dark. Now I hear cracking and shifting in the hummock on the starboard quarter; it gets louder and stronger, and extends steadily. At last the waterfall roar abates a little. It becomes more unequal; there is a longer interval between each shock. I am so cold that I creep below.

"But no sooner have I seated myself to write, than the ship begins to heave and tremble again, and I hear through her sides the roar of the packing. As the bear-trap may be in danger, three men go off to see to it, but they find that there is a distance of 50 paces between the new pressure-ridge and the wire by which the trap is secured, so they leave it as it is. The pressure-ridge was an ugly sight, they say, but they could distinguish nothing well in the dark.

"Most violent pressure is beginning again. I must go on deck and look at it. The loud roar meets one as one opens the door. It is coming from the bow now, as well as from the stern. It is clear that pressure-ridges are being thrown up in both openings, so if they reach us we shall be taken by both ends and lifted lightly and gently out of the water. There is pressure near us on all sides. Creaking has begun in the old hummock on the port quarter; it is getting louder, and, so far as I can see, the hummock is slowly rising. A lane has opened right across the large floe on the port side; you can see the water, dark as it is. Now both pressure and noise get worse and worse; the ship shakes, and I feel as if I myself were being gently lifted with the stern-rail, where I stand gazing out at the welter of ice-masses, that resemble giant snakes writhing and twisting their great bodies out there under the quiet, starry sky, whose peace is only broken by one aurora serpent waving and flickering restlessly in the north-east. I once more think what a comfort it is to be safe on board the *Fram*, and look out with a certain contempt at the horrible hurly-burly nature is raising to no purpose whatever; it will not crush us in a hurry, nor even frighten us. Suddenly I remember that my fine thermometer is in a hole on a floe to port on the other side of the opening, and must certainly be in danger. I jump on to the ice, find a place where I can leap across the opening, and grope about in the dark until I find the piece of ice covering the hole; I get hold of the string, and the thermometer is saved. I hurry on board again well pleased, and down into my comfortable cabin to smoke a pipe of peace — alas! this vice grows upon me more and more — and to listen with glee to the roar of the pressure outside and feel its shakings, like so many earthquakes, as I sit and write my diary. Safe and comfortable, I cannot but think with deep pity of the many who have had to stand by on deck in readiness to leave their frail vessels on the occurrence of any such pressure. The poor *Tegethoff* fellows — they had a bad time of it, and yet theirs was a good ship in comparison with many of the others. It is now 11.30, and the noise outside seems to be subsiding.

"It is remarkable that we should have this strong pressure just now, with the moon in its last quarter and neap tide. This does not agree with our previous experiences; no more does the fact that the pressure the day before yesterday was from 12 a.m. to about 2 p.m., and then again at 2 a.m., and now we have had it from 7.30 to 10.30 p.m. Can land have something to do with it here after all? The temperature to-day is 42° F. below zero (−41.4° C.), but there is no wind, and we have not had such pleasant weather for walking for a long time; it feels almost mild here when the air is still.

"No, that was not the end of the pressure. When I was on deck at a quarter to twelve, roaring and trembling began again in the ice forward on the port quarter; then suddenly came one loud boom after another, sounding out in the distance, and the ship gave a start; there was again a little pressure, and after that quietness. Faint aurora borealis.

"Sunday, January 28th. Strange to say, there has been no pressure since 12 o'clock last night; the ice seems perfectly quiet. The pressure-ridge astern showed what violent packing yesterday's was; in one place its height was 18 or 19 feet above the surface of the water floe-ice 8 feet thick was broken, pressed up in square blocks, and crushed to pieces. At one point a huge monolith of such floe-ice rose high into the air. Beyond this pressure-wall there was no great disturbance to be detected. There had been a little packing here and there, and the floe to port had four or five large cracks across it, which no doubt accounted for the explosions I heard last night. The ice to starboard was also cracked in several places. The pressure had evidently come from the north or N.N.E. The ridge behind us is one of the highest I have seen yet. I believe that if the *Fram* had been lying there she would have been lifted right out of the water. I walked for some distance in a north-easterly direction, but saw no signs of pressure there.

"Another Sunday. It is wonderful that the time can pass so quickly as it does. For one thing, we are in better spirits, knowing that we are drifting steadily north. A rough estimate of to-day's observation gives 79° 50′ N. lat. That is not much since Monday; but then yesterday and to-day there has been almost no wind at all, and the other days it has been very light, only once or twice with as much as 9 feet velocity, the rest of the time 3 and 6.

"A remarkable event happened yesterday afternoon I got Munthe's picture of the 'Three Princesses' fastened firmly on the wall. It is a thing that we have been going to do ever since we left Christiania, but we have never been able to summon up energy for such a heavy undertaking — it meant knocking in four nails — and the picture has amused itself by constantly falling and guillotining whoever happened to be sitting on the sofa below it.

"Tuesday, January 30th. 79° 49′ N. lat., 134° 57′ E. long., is the tale told by this afternoon's observations, while by Sunday afternoon's we were in 79° 50′ N. lat., and 133° 23′ E. long. This fall-off to the south-east again was not more than I had expected, as it has been almost calm since Sunday. I explain the thing to myself thus: When the ice has been set adrift in a certain direction by the wind blowing that way for some time, it gradually in process of drifting becomes more compressed, and when that wind dies away, a reaction in the opposite direction takes place. Such a reaction must, I believe, have been the cause of Saturday's pressure, which stopped entirely as suddenly as it began. Since then there has not been the slightest appearance of movement in the ice. Probably the pressure indicates the time when the drift turned. A light breeze has sprung up this afternoon from S.E. and E.S.E., increasing gradually to almost 'mill wind.' We are going north again; surely we shall get the better of the 80th degree this time.

"Wednesday, January 31st. The wind is whistling among the hummocks; the snow flies rustling through the air; ice and sky are melted into one. It is dark; our skins are smarting with the cold; but we are going north at full speed, and are in the wildest of gay spirits." Thursday, February 1st. The same sort of weather as yesterday, except that it has turned quite mild — 7½° F. below zero (−22° C.). The snow is falling exactly as it does in winter weather at home. The wind is more southerly, S.S.E. now, and rather lighter. It may be taken for granted that we have passed the 80th degree, and we had a small preliminary fête this evening — figs, raisins, and almonds — and dart-shooting, which last resulted for me in a timely replenishment of my cigarette case.

"Friday, February 2nd. High festival to-day in honour of the 80th degree, beginning with fresh rye bread and cake for breakfast. Took a long walk to get up an appetite for dinner. According to this morning's observation, we are in 80° 10′ N. lat. and 132° 10′ E. long. Hurrah! Well sailed! I had offered to bet heavily that we had passed 80°, but no one would take the bet. Dinner menu: Ox-tail soup, fish pudding, potatoes; rissoles, green peas, haricot beans, cloudberries with milk, and a whole bottle of beer to each man. Coffee and a cigarette after dinner. Could one wish for more? In the evening we had tinned pears and peaches, gingerbread, dried bananas, figs, raisins, and almonds. Complete holiday all day. We read aloud the discussions of this expedition published before we left, and had some good laughs at the many objections raised. But our people at home, perhaps, will not laugh if they read them now.

"Monday, February 5th. Last time we shall have Ringnes beer at dinner. Day of mourning.

"Tuesday, February 6th. Calm, clear weather. A strong sun-glow above the horizon in the south; yellow, green, and light blue above that; all the rest of the sky deep ultramarine. I stood looking at it, trying to remember if the Italian sky was ever bluer; I do not think so. It is curious that this deep colour should always occur along with cold. Is it perhaps that a current from more northerly, clear regions produces drier and more transparent air in the upper strata? The colour was so remarkable to-day that one could not help noticing it. Striking contrasts to it were formed by the *Fram*'s red deck-house and the white snow on roof and rigging. Ice and hummocks were quite violet wherever they were turned from the, day-light. This colour was specially strong over the fields of snow upon the floes. The temperature has been 52° F. and 54° F. below zero (−47° and −48° C.). There is a sudden change of 125° F. when one comes up from the saloon, where the thermometer is at 72° F. (+22° C.); but, although thinly clad and bareheaded, one does not feel cold, and can even with impunity take hold of the brass door-handle or the steel cable of the rigging. The cold is visible, however; one's breath is like cannon smoke before it is out of one's mouth; and when a man spits there is quite a little cloud of steam round the fallen moisture. The *Fram* always gives off a mist, which is carried along by the wind, and a man or a dog can be detected far off among the hummocks or pressure-ridges by the pillar of vapour that follows his progress.

"Wednesday, February 7th. It is extraordinary what a frail thing hope, or rather the mind of man, is. There was a little breeze this morning from the N.N.E., only 6 feet per second, thermometer at 57° F. below zero (−49.6° C.), and immediately one's brow is clouded over, and it becomes a matter of indifference how we get home, so long as we only get home soon. I immediately assume land to the northward from which come these cold winds, with clear atmosphere and frost and bright blue skies, and conclude that this extensive tract of land must form a pole of cold with a constant maximum of air pressure, which will force us south with north-east winds. About midday the air began to grow more hazy, and my mood less gloomy. No doubt there is a south wind coming, but the temperature is still too low for it. Then the temperature, too, rises, and now we can rely on the wind. And this evening it came, sure enough, from S.S.W., and now, 12 p.m., its velocity is 11 feet, and the temperature has risen to 43° F. below zero (−42° C.). This promises well. We should soon reach 81°. The land to the northward has now vanished from my mind's eye.

"We had lime-juice with sugar at dinner to-day instead of beer, and it seemed to be approved of. We call it wine, and we agreed that it was better than cider. Weighing has gone on this evening, and the increase in certain cases is still disquieting. Some have gained as much as 4 pounds in the last month, for instance, Sverdrup, Blessing, and Juell, who beats the record on board with 13 stone. 'I never weighed so much as I do now,' says Blessing, and it is much the same story with us all. Yes, this is a fatiguing expedition, but our menus are always in due proportion to our labours. To-day's dinner: Knorr's bean soup, toad-in-the-hole, potatoes, rice, and milk with cranberry jam. Yesterday's dinner: Fiskegratin (hashed fish with potatoes), curried rabbit with potatoes and French beans, stewed bilberries, and cranberries with milk. At breakfast yesterday we had freshly baked wheat-bread, at breakfast to-day freshly baked rye-bread. These are specimens of our ordinary bills of fare. It is as I expected: I hear the wind roaring in the rigging now; it is going to be a regular storm, according to our ideas of one here.

"Saturday, February 10th. Though that wind the other day did not come to much after all, we still hoped that we had made good way north, and it was consequently an unwelcome surprise when yesterday's observation showed our latitude to be 79° 57' N., 13' farther south instead of farther north. It is extraordinary how little inured one gets to disappointments; the longing begins again; and again attainment seems so far off, so doubtful. And this though I dream at nights just now of getting out of the ice west of Iceland. Hope is a rickety craft to trust oneself to. I had a long, successful drive with the dogs to-day.

"Sunday, February 11th. To-day we drove out with two teams of dogs. Things went well; the sledges got on much better over this ice than I thought they would, They do not sink much in the snow. On flat ice four dogs can draw two men.

"Tuesday, February 13th. A long drive south-west yesterday with white dogs. To-day still farther in the same direction on snow-shoes. It is good healthy exercise, with a temperature of 43° F. to 47° F. below zero (−42 and −44° C.) and a biting north wind. Nature is so fair and pure, the ice is so spotless, and the lights and shadows of the growing day so beautiful on the new-fallen snow. The *Fram*'s hoax-frost-covered rigging rises straight and white with rime towards the sparkling blue sky. One's thoughts turn to the snow-shoeing days at home.

"Thursday, February 15th. I went yesterday on snow-shoes farther north-east than I have ever been before, but I could still see the ship's rigging above the edge of the ice. I was able to go fast, because the ice was flat in that direction. To-day I went the same way with dogs. I am examining the 'lie of the land' all round, and thinking of plans for the future.

"What exaggerated reports of the Arctic cold are in circulation! It was cold in Greenland, and it is not milder here; the general day temperature just now is about 40° F. and 43° F. below zero. I was clothed yesterday as usual as regards the legs-drawers, knickerbockers, stockings, frieze leggings, snow-socks, and moccasins; my body covering consisted of an ordinary shirt, a wolf-skin cape, and a sealskin jacket, and I sweated like a horse. To-day I sat still, driving with only thin ducks above my ordinary leg wear, and on my body woollen shirt, vest, Iceland woollen jersey, a frieze coat, and a sealskin one. I found the temperature quite pleasant, and even perspired a little to-day, too. Both yesterday and to-day I had a red flannel mask on my face, but it made me too warm, and I had to take it off, though there was a bitter breeze from the north. That north wind is still persistent, sometimes with a velocity of 9 or even 13 feet, but yet we do not seem to be drifting south; we lie in 80° N. lat., or even a few minutes farther north. What can be the reason of this? There is a little pressure every day just now. Curious that it should again occur at the moon's change of quarter. The moon stands high in the sky, and there is daylight now, too. Soon the sun will be making his appearance, and when he does we shall hold high festival.

"Friday, February 16th. Hurrah! A meridian observation today shows 80° 1' N. lat., so that we have come a few minutes north since last Friday, and that in spite of constant northerly winds since Monday. There is something very singular about this. Is it, as I have thought all along from the appearance of the clouds and the haziness of the air, that there has been south wind in the south, preventing the drift of the ice that way, or have we at last come under the influence of a current? That shove we got to the south lately in the face of southerly winds was a remarkable thing, and so is our remaining where we are now in spite of the northerly ones. It would seem that new powers of some kind must be at work.

"To-day another noteworthy thing happened, which was that about midday we saw the sun, or, to be more correct, an image of the sun, for it was only a mirage. A peculiar impression was produced by the sight of that glowing fire lit just above the outermost edge of the ice. According to the enthusiastic descriptions given by many Arctic travellers of the first appearance of this god of life after the long winter night, the impression ought to be one of jubilant excitement; but it was not so in my case. We had not expected to see it for some days yet, so that my feeling was rather one of pain, of disappointment, that we must have drifted farther south than we thought. So it was with pleasure I soon discovered that it could not be the sun itself. The mirage was at first like a flattened-out glowing red streak of fire on the horizon; later there were two streaks, the one above the other, with a dark space between; and from the main top I could see four, or even five such horizontal lines directly over one another, and all of equal length; as if one could only imagine a square dull-red sun with horizontal dark streaks across it. An astronomical observation we took in the afternoon showed that the sun must in reality have been 2° 22' below the horizon at noon; we cannot expect to see its disc above the ice before Tuesday at the earliest: it depends on the refraction, which is verv strong in this cold air. All the same, we had a small sun-festival this evening, on the occasion of the appearance of its image — a treat of figs, bananas, raisins, almonds, and gingerbread.

"Sunday, February 18th. I went eastwards yesterday on snow-shoes, and found a good snow-shoeing and driving road out to the flats that lie in that direction. There is a pretty bad bit first, with hummocks and pressure-ridges, and then you come out on these great wide plains, which seem to extend for miles and miles to the north, east, and south-east. To-day I drove out there with eight dogs; the driving goes capitally now; some of the others followed on snow-shoes. Still northerly wind. This is slow work; but anyhow we are having clear, bright weather. Yes, it is all very well — we snow-shoe, sledge, read both for instruction and amusement, write, take observations, play cards, chat, smoke, play chess, eat and drink; but all the same it is an execrable life in the long run, this — at least, so it seems to me at times. When I look at the picture of our beautiful home in the evening light, with my wife standing in the garden, I feel as if it were impossible that this could go on much longer. But only the merciless fates know when we shall stand there together again, feeling all life's sweetness as we look out over the smiling fjord, and… Taking everything into calculation, if I am to be perfectly honest, I think this is a wretched state of matters. We are now in about 80° N. lat., in September we were in 79°; that is, let us say, one degree for five months. If we go on at this rate we shall be at the Pole in forty-five, or say fifty, months, and in ninety or one hundred months at 80° N. lat. on the other side of it, with probably some prospect of getting out of the ice and home in a month or two more. At best, if things go on as they are doing now, we shall be home in eight years. I remember Brogger writing before I left, when I was planting small bushes and trees in the garden for future generations, that no one knew what length of shadow these trees would cast by the time I came back. Well, they are lying under the winter snow now, but in spring they will shoot and grow again — how often? At times this inactivity crushes one's very soul; one's life seems as dark as the winter night outside; there is sunlight upon no part of it except the past and the far, far distant future. I feel as if I *must* break through this deadness, this inertia, and find some outlet for my energies. Can't something happen? Could not a hurricane come and tear up this ice, and set it rolling in high waves like the open sea? Welcome danger, if it only brings us the chance of fighting for our lives — only lets us move onwards! The miserable thing is to be inactive onlookers, not to be able to lift a hand to help ourselves forwards. It wants ten times more strength of mind to sit still and trust in your theories and let nature work them out without your being able so much as to lay one stick across another to help, than it does to trust in working them out by your own energy — that is nothing when you have a pair of strong arms. Here I sit, whining like an old woman. Did I not know all this before I started? Things have not gone worse than I expected, but on the contrary, rather better. Where is now the serene hopefulness that spread itself in the daylight and the sun? Where are these proud imaginings now that mounted like young eagles towards the brightness of the future? Like broken-winged, wet crows they leave the sun-lit sea, and hide themselves in the misty marshes of despondency. Perhaps it will all come back again with the south wind; but no, I must go and rummage up one of the old philosophers again.

"There is a little pressure this evening, and an observation just taken seems to indicate a drift of 3' south.

"11 p.m. Pressure in the opening astern. The ice is cracking and squeezing against the ship, making it shake.

"Monday, February 19th. Once more it may be said that the night is darkest just before the dawn. Wind began to blow from the south to-day, and has reached a velocity of 13 feet per second. We did some ice-boring this morning, and found that the ice to port is 5 feet 11 5/8 inches (1.875 metres) thick, with a layer of about 1½ inches of snow over it. The ice forward was 6 feet 7½ inches (2.08 metres) thick, but a couple of inches of this was snow. This cannot be called much growth for quite a month, when one thinks that the temperature has been down to 58° F. below zero.

"Both to-day and yesterday we have seen the mirage of the sun again; to-day it was high above the horizon, and almost seemed to assume a round, disc-like form. Some of the others maintain that they have seen the upper edge of the sun itself; Peter and Bentzen that they have seen at least half of the disc and Juell and Hansen declare that the whole of it was above the horizon. I am afraid it is so long since they saw it that they have forgotten what it is like.

"Tuesday, February 10th. Great sun festival to-day without any sun. We felt certain we should see it, but there were clouds on the horizon. However we were not going to be cheated out of our festival; we can hold another on the occasion of really seeing it for the first time. We began with a grand rifle practice in the morning; then there was a dinner of three or four courses and '*Fram* wine,' otherwise lime-juice, coffee afterwards with '*Fram* cake.' In the evening pine-apple, cake, figs, bananas, and sweets. We go off to bed feeling that we have over-eaten ourselves, while half a gale from the S.E. is blowing us northwards. The mill has been going to-day, and though the real sun did not come to the festival, our saloon sun lighted up our table both at dinner and supper. Great face-washing in honour of the day. The way we are laying on flesh is getting serious. Several of us are like prize pigs, and the bulge of cook Juell's cheeks, not to mention another part of his body, is quite alarming. I saw him in profile to-day, and wondered how he would ever manage to carry such a corporation over the ice if we should have to turn out one of these fine days. Must begin to think of a course of short rations now.

"Wednesday, February 21st. The south wind continues. Took up the bag-nets to-day which were put out the day before yesterday. In the upper one, which hung near the surface, there were chiefly amphipodae; in Murray's net, which hung at about 50 fathoms depth, there was a variety of small crustacea and other small animals shining with such a strong phosphorescence that the contents of the net looked like glowing embers as I emptied them out in the cook's galley by lamplight. To my astonishment the net-line pointed north-west, though from the wind there ought to be a good northerly drift. To clear this matter up I let the net down in the afternoon, and as soon as it got a little way under the ice the line pointed north-west again, and continued to do so the whole afternoon. How is this phenomenon to be explained? Can we after all be in a current moving north-west? Let us hope that the future will prove such to be the case. We can reckon on two points of variation in the compass, and in that case the current would make due N.N.W. There seems to be strong movement in the ice. It has opened and formed channels in several places."

"Thursday, February 22nd. The net-line has pointed west all day till now, afternoon, when it is pointing straight up and down, and we are presumably lying still. The wind slackened to-day till it was quite calm in the afternoon. Then there came a faint breeze from the south-west and from the west, and this evening the long-dreaded north-wester has come at last. At 9 p.m. it is blowing pretty hard from N.N.W. An observation of Capella taken in the afternoon would seem to show that we are in any case not farther north than 80° 11′, and this after almost four days' south wind. Whatever can be the meaning of this? Is there dead-water under the ice keeping it from going either forwards or backwards The ice to starboard cracked yesterday, away beyond the bear trap. The thickness of the solid floe was 11½ feet (3.45 metres), but beside this other ice was packed on to it below. Where it was broken across, the floe showed a marked stratified formation, recalling the stratification of a glacier. Even the darker and dirtier strata were there, the colour in this case produced by the brownish-red organisms that inhabit the water, specimens of which I found at an earlier date. In several places the strata were bent and broken, exactly in the same manner as the geological strata forming the earth's crust. This was evidently the result of the horizontal pressure in the ice at the time of packing. It was especially noticeable at one place, near a huge mound formed during the last pressure. Here the strata looked very much as they are represented in annexed drawing.[38]

It was extraordinary too to see how this floe of over three yards in thickness was bent into great waves without breaking. This was clearly done by pressure and was specially noticeable near the pressure-ridges, which had forced the floe down so that its upper surface lay even with the water-line, whilst at other places it was a good half-yard above it, in these last cases thrust up by ice pressed in below. It all shows how extremely plastic these floes are, in spite of the cold; the temperature of the ice near the surface must have been from 4° F. to 22° F. below zero (−20° to −30° C.) at the time of these pressures. In many places the bending had been too violent, and the floe had cracked. The cracks were often covered with loose ice, so that one could easily enough fall into them, just as in crossing a dangerous glacier.

"Saturday, February 24th. Observations today show us to be in 79° 54 N.

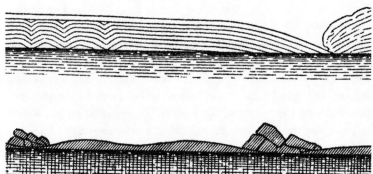

Ice stratification.

lat., 132° 57' E. long. Strange that we should have come so far south when the north or north-west wind only blew for twenty-four hours.

"Sunday, February 25th. It looks as if the ice were drifting eastwards now. Oh! I see pictures of summer and green trees and rippling streams. I am reading of valley and mountain life, and I grow sick at heart and enervated. Why dwell on such things just now? It will be many a long day before we can see all that again. We are going at the miserable pace of a snail, but not so surely as it goes. We carry our house with us; but what we do one day is undone the next.

"Monday, February 26th. We are drifting north-east. A tremendous snowstorm is going on. The wind has at times a velocity of over 35 feet per second; it is howling in the rigging, whistling over the ice, and the snow is drifting so badly that a man might be lost in it quite near at hand. We are sitting here listening to the howling in the chimney, and in the ventilators, just as if we were sitting in a house at home in Norway. The wings of the windmill have been going round at such a rate that you could hardly distinguish them; but we have had to stop the mill this evening because the accumulators are full, and we fastened up the wings, so that the wind might not destroy them. We have had electric light for almost a week now.

"This is the strongest wind we have had the whole winter. If anything can shake up the ice and drive us north, this must do it. But the barometer is falling too fast; there will be north wind again presently. Hope has been disappointed too often; it is no longer elastic; and the gale makes no great impression on me. I look forward to spring and summer, in suspense as to what change they will bring. But the Arctic night, the dreaded Arctic night, is over, and we have daylight once again. I must say that I see no appearance of the sunken, wasted faces which this night ought to have produced; in the clearest daylight and the brightest sunshine, I can only discover plump, comfortable-looking ones. It is curious enough though about the light. We used to think it was like real day down here when the incandescent lamps were burning, but now, coming down from the daylight, though they may be all lit, it is like coming into a cellar. When the arc lamp has been burning all day, as it has to-day, and is then put out and its place supplied by the incandescent ones, the effect is much the same."

"Tuesday, February 27th. Drifting E.S.E. My pessimism is justified. A strong west wind has blown almost all day; the barometer is low, but has begun to rise unsteadily. The temperature is 'the highest we have had all winter; to-day's maximum is 15° F. above zero (−9.7° C.). At 8 p.m. the thermometer stood at 7° F. below zero (−22° C.). The temperature rises and falls almost exactly conversely with the barometer. This afternoon's observation places us in about 80° 10′ N. lat."

"Wednesday, February 28th. Beautiful weather to-day, almost still, and temperature only about 15° F. to 22° F. below zero (−26° to −30.5° C.). There were clouds in the south, so that not much was to be seen of the sun; but it is light wonderfully long already. Sverdrup and I went snow-shoeing after dinner — the first time this year that we have been able to do anything of the kind in the afternoon. We made attempts to pump yesterday and to-day; there ought to be a little water, but the pump would not suck, though we tried both warm water and salt. Possibly there is water frozen round it, and possibly there is no water at all. In the engine-room there has been no appearance of water for more than a month, and none comes into the forehold, especially now that the bow is raised up by the pack-ice; so if there is any it can only be a little in the hold. This tightening may be attributed chiefly to the frost.

"The wind has begun to blow again from the S.S.W. this evening, and the barometer is falling, which ought to mean good wind coming; but the barometer of hope does not rise above its normal height. I had a bath this evening in a tin tub in the galley; trimmed and clean, one feels more of a human being."

"Thursday, March 1st. We are lying almost still. Beautiful mild weather, only 2½° F. below zero (−19° C.), sky overcast; light fall of snow, and light wind. We made attempts to sound to-day, having lengthened our hemp line with a single strand of steel. This broke off with the lead. We put on a new lead and the whole line ran out, about 2,000 fathoms, without touching bottom, so far as we could make out. In process of hauling in, the steel line broke again. So the results are: no bottom, and two sounding leads, each of 100 lbs. weight, making their way down. Goodness knows if they have reached the bottom yet. I declare I feel inclined to believe that Bentzen is right, and that it is the hole at the earth's axis we are trying to sound."

"Friday, March 2nd. The pups have lived until now in the chart-room, and have done all the mischief there that they could, gnawing the cases of Hansen's instruments, the log-books, etc. They were taken out on deck yesterday for the first time, and to-day they have been there all the morning. They are of an enquiring turn of mind, and examine everything, being specially interested in the interiors of all the kennels in this new large town."

"Sunday, March 4th. The drift is still strong south. There is north-westerly wind to-day again, but not quite so much of it. I expected we had come a long way south, but yesterday's observation still 'shows 79° 54' N. lat. We must have drifted a good way north during the last days before this wind came. The weather yesterday and to-day has been bitter, 35° F. and 36½° F. below zero (−37° and −38° C.), with sometimes as much as 35 feet of wind per second must be called cool. It is curious that now the northerly winds bring cold, and the southerly warmth. Earlier in the winter it was just the opposite.

"Monday, March 5th. Sverdrup and I have been a long way north-east on snow-shoes. The ice was in good condition for it; the wind has tossed about the snow finely, covering over the pressure-ridge, as far as the scanty supply of material has permitted.

"Tuesday, March 6th. No drift at all. It has been a bitter day to-day, 47° F. to 50° F. below zero (−44° to −46° C.), and wind up to 19 feet. This has been a good occasion for getting hands and face frost-bitten, and one or two have taken advantage of it. Steady north-west wind. I am beginning to get indifferent and stolid as far as the wind is concerned. I photographed Johansen to-day at the anemometer, and during the process his nose was frost-bitten.

"There has been a general weighing this evening again. These weighings are considered very interesting performances, and we stand watching in suspense to see whether each man has gained or lost. Most of them have lost a little this time. Can it be because we have stopped drinking beer, and begun lime-juice? But Juell goes on indefatigably — he has gained nearly a pound this time. Our doctor generally does very well in this line too, but to-day it is only 10 oz. In other ways he is badly off on board, poor fellow — not a soul will turn ill. In despair he set up a headache yesterday himself, but he could not make it last over the night. Of late he has taken to studying the diseases of dogs; perhaps he may find a more profitable practice in this department.

"Thursday, March 8th. Drifting south. Sverdrup and I had a good snow-shoeing trip to-day, to the north and west. The snow was in splendid condition after the winds; you fly along like thistledown before a breeze, and can get about everywhere, even over the worst pressure-mounds. The weather was beautiful, temperature only 38° F. below zero (–39° C.); but this evening it is quite bitter again, 55° F. (–48.5° C.) and from 16 to 26 feet of wind. It is by no means pleasant work standing up on the windmill, reefing or taking in the sails; it means aching nails, and sometimes frost-bitten cheeks; but it has to be done, and it is done. There is plenty of 'mill-wind' in the daytime now — this is the third week we have had electric light — but it is wretched that it should be always this north and north-west wind; goodness only knows when it is going to stop. *Can* there be land north of us? We are drifting badly south. It is hard to keep one's faith alive. There is nothing for it but to wait and see what time will do.

"After a long rest the ship got a shake this afternoon. I went on deck. Pressure was going on in an opening just in front of the bow. We might almost have expected it just now, as it is new moon; only we have got out of the way of thinking at all about the spring tides, as they have had so little effect lately. They should of course be specially strong just now, as the equinox is approaching.

"Friday, March 9th. The net line pointed slightly south-west this morning; but the line attached to a cheese which was only hanging a few fathoms below the ice to thaw faster, seemed to point in the opposite direction. Had we got a southerly current together with the wind now? In that case something must come of it. Or was it, perhaps, only the tide setting that way?

"Still the same northerly wind; we are steadily bearing south. This, then, is the change I hoped the March equinox would bring! We have been having northerly winds for more than a fortnight. I cannot conceal from myself any longer that I am beginning to despond. Quietly and slowly, but mercilessly, one hope after the other is being crushed and… have I not a right to be a little despondent? I long unutterably after home, perhaps I am drifting away farther

Johansen checking the anemometer (wind meter).

from it, perhaps nearer; but anyhow it is not cheering to see the realisation of one's plans again and again delayed, if not annihilated altogether, in this tedious and monotonously killing way. Nature goes her age-old round impassively; summer changes into winter; spring vanishes away, autumn comes, and finds us still a mere chaotic whirl of daring projects and shattered hopes. As the wheel revolves, now the one and now the other comes to the top — but memory between whiles lightly touches her ringing silver chords — now loud like a roaring waterfall, now low and soft like far off sweet music. I stand and look out over this desolate expanse of ice with its plains and heights and valleys, formed by the pressure arising from the shifting tidal currents of winter. The sun is now shining over them with his cheering beams. In the middle lies the *Fram*, hemmed in immovably. When, my proud ship, will you float free in the open water again?

> "Ich schau dich an, und Wehmuth,
>   Schleicht mir in's Herz hinein."

Over these masses of ice, drifting by paths unknown, a human being pondered and brooded so long that he put a whole people in motion to enable him to force his way in among them — a people who had plenty of other claims upon their energies. For what purpose all this to do? If only the calculations were correct, these ice-floes would be glorious, nay irresistible auxiliaries. But if there has been an error in the calculation — well, in that case they are not so pleasant to deal with. And how often does a calculation come out correct? But were I now free? Why, I should do it all over again, from the same starting-point. One must persevere till one learns to calculate correctly.

"I laugh at the scurvy; no sanatorium better than ours.

"I laugh at the ice; we are living as it were in an impregnable castle.

"I laugh at the cold; it is nothing.

"But I do not laugh at the winds; they are everything; they bend to no man's will.

"But why always worry about the future? Why distress yourself as to whether you are drifting forwards or backwards? Why not carelessly let the days glide by like a peacefully flowing river? every now and then there will come a rapid that will quicken the lazy flow. Ah! what a wondrous contrivance is life — one eternal hurrying forwards, ever forwards — to what end? And then comes death and cuts all short before the goal is reached.

"I went a long snow-shoe tour to-day. A little way to the north there were a good many newly-formed lanes and pressure-ridges which were hard to cross, but patience overcomes everything, and I soon reached a level plain where it was delightful going. It was, however, rather cold, about 54 F. below zero (−48° C.) and 16 feet of wind from N.N.E., but I did not feel it much. It is wholesome and enjoyable to be out in such weather. I wore only ordinary clothes such as I might wear at home with a sealskin jacket and linen outside breeches, and a half-mask to protect the forehead, nose, and cheeks.

"There has been a good deal of ice-pressure in different directions to-day. Oddly enough, a meridian altitude of the sun gave 79° 45'. We have therefore drifted only 8' southwards during the four days since March 4th. This slow drift is remarkable in spite of the high winds. If there should be land to the north? I begin more and more to speculate on this possibility. Land to the north would explain at once our not progressing northwards, and the slowness of our southward drift. But it may also possibly arise from the fact of the ice being so closely packed together, and frozen so thick and massive. It seems strange to me that there is so much north-west wind, and hardly any from the north-east, though the latter is what the rotation of the earth would lead one to expect. As a matter of fact, the wind merely shifts between north-west and south-east, instead of between south-west and north-east, as it ought to do. Unless there is land I am at a loss to find a satisfactory explanation, at all events, of this north-west direction. Does Franz Josef Land jut out eastwards or northwards, or does a continuous line of islands extend from Franz Josef Land in one or other of those directions? It is by no means impossible. Directly the Austrians got far enough to the north they met with prevailing winds from the north-east, while we get north-westerly winds. Does the central point of these masses of land lie to the north, midway between our meridian and theirs? I can hardly believe that these remarkably cold winds from the north are engendered by merely passing over an ice-covered sea. If, indeed, there is land, and we get hold of it, then all our troubles would be over. But no one can tell what the future may bring forth, and it is better, perhaps, not to know.

"Saturday, March 10. The line shows a drift north-wards; now, too, in the afternoon, a slight southerly breeze has sprung up. As usual it has done me good to put my despondency on paper and get rid of it. To-day I am in good spirits again, and can indulge in happy dreams of a large and high land in the north, with mountains and valleys, where we can sit under the mountain wall, roast ourselves in the sun, and see the spring come. And over its inland ice we can make our way to the very Pole.

"Sunday, March 11th. A snow-shoe run north-wards. Temperature, −50° C. (58° F. below zero), and 10 feet wind from N.N.E. We did not feel the cold very much, though it was rather bad for the stomach and thighs, as none of us had our wind trousers[39] on. We wore our usual dress of a pair of ordinary trousers and woollen pants, a shirt, and wolf's skin cloak, or a common woollen suit with a light sealskin jacket over it. For the first time in my life I felt my thighs frozen, especially just over the knee, and on the kneecap; my companions also suffered in the same way. This was after going a long while against the wind. We rubbed our legs a little, and they soon got warm again, but had we kept on much longer without noticing it, we should probably have been severely frost-bitten. In other respects we did not suffer the least inconvenience from the cold, on the contrary found the temperature agreeable; and I am convinced that 10°, 20°, or even 30°, lower would not have been unendurable. It is strange how one's sensations alter. When at home, I find it unpleasant if I only go out of doors when there are some 20 degrees of cold, even in calm weather. But here I don't find it any colder when I turn out in 50 degrees of cold with a wind into the bargain. Sitting in a warm room at home one gets exaggerated ideas about the terribleness of the cold. It is really not in the least terrible: we all of us find ourselves very well in it, though sometimes one or another of us does not take quite so long a walk as usual when a strong wind is blowing, and will even turn back for the cold; but that is when he is only lightly clad and has no wind clothes on. This evening it is 51.2° F. below zero, and 14½ feet N.N.E. wind. Brilliant northern lights in the south. Already there is a very marked twilight even at midnight.

"Monday, March 12th. Slowly drifting southwards. Took a long snow-shoe run alone, towards the north; today had on my wind-breeches, but found them almost too warm. This morning it was 51.6° F. below zero, and about 13 feet N. wind; at noon it was some degrees warmer. Ugh! this north wind is freshening; the barometer has risen again, and I had thought the wind would have changed, but it is and remains the same.

"This is what March brings us — the month on which my hopes relied. Now I must wait for the summer. Soon the half-year will be past, it will leave us about in the same place as when it began. I am weary — so weary — let me sleep, sleep! Come sleep! noiselessly close the door of the soul, stay the flowing stream of thought! Come dreams, and I let the sun beam over the snowless strand of Godthaab!

"Wednesday, March 14th. In the evening the dogs all at once began to bark, as we supposed on account of bears. Sverdrup and I took our guns, let 'Ulenka' and Pan' loose, and set off. There was twilight still, and the moon moreover began to shine. No sooner were the dogs on the ice than off they started westward like a couple of rockets, we after them as quickly as we could. As I was jumping over a lane I thrust one leg through the ice up to the knee. Oddly enough, I did not get wet through to the skin, though I only had Finn shoes and frieze gaiters on; but in this temperature, 8° F. below zero (−39° C.), the water freezes on the cold cloth before it can penetrate it. I felt nothing of it afterwards; it became, as it were, a plate of ice armour that almost helped to keep me warm. At a channel some distance off we at last discovered that it was not a bear the dogs had winded, but either a walrus or a seal. We saw holes in several places on the fresh-formed ice where it had stuck its head through. What a wonderfully keen nose those dogs must have: it was quite two-thirds of a mile from the ship, and the creature had only had just a little bit of its snout above the ice. We returned to the ship to get a harpoon, but saw no more of the animal, though we went several times up and down the channel. Meanwhile 'Pan,' in his zeal, got too near the edge of the lane and fell into the water. The ice was so high that he could not get up on it again without help, and if I had not been there to haul him up I am afraid he would have been drowned. He is now lying in the saloon, and making himself comfortable and drying himself; but he, too, did not get wet through to the skin, though he was a good time in the water: the inner hair of his close, coarse coat is quite dry and warm. The dogs look on it as a high treat to come in here, for they are not often allowed to do so. They go round all the cabins and look out for a snug corner to lie down in.

"Lovely weather, almost calm, sparklingly bright, and moonshine: in the north the faint flush of evening, and the aurora over the southern sky, now like a row of flaming spears, then changing into a silvery veil, undulating in wavy folds with the wind, every here and there interspersed with red sprays. These wonderful night effects are ever new, and never fail to captivate the soul.

"Thursday, March 15th. This morning 41.7° and at 8 o'clock p.m. 40.7° F. below zero, while the daytime was rather warmer. At noon it was 40.5° and at 4 p.m. 39 F. below zero. It would almost seem as if the sun began to have power.

"The dogs are strange creatures. This evening they are probably sweltering in their kennels again, for four or five of them are lying outside or on the roof. When there is 50° of cold most of them huddle together inside, and lie as close to one another as possible. Then, too, they are very loth to go out for a walk, they prefer to lie in the sun under the lee of the ship. But now they find it so mild and such pleasant walking that to-day it was not difficult to get them to follow.

"Friday, March 16th. Sverdrup has of late been occupied in making sails for the ship's boats. To-day there was a light south-westerly breeze, so we tried one of the sails on two hand-sledges lashed together. It is first-rate sailing, and does not require much wind to make them glide along. This would be a great assistance if we had to go home over the ice.

"Wednesday, March 21st. At length a re-action has set in: the wind is S.E. and there is a strong drift northwards again. The equinox is past, and we are not one degree further north since the last equinox. I wonder where the next will find us. Should it be more to the south, then victory is uncertain; if more to the north the battle is won, though it may last long. I am looking forward to the summer; it must bring a change with it. The open water we sailed in up here cannot possibly be produced by the melting of the ice alone; it must be also due to the winds and current. And if the ice in which we are now, drifts so far to the north as to make room for all this open water, we shall have covered a good bit on our way. It would seem, indeed, as if summer must bring northerly winds, with the cold Arctic Sea in the north and warm Siberia in the south. This makes me somewhat dubious — but, on the other hand, we have warm seas in the west; they may be stronger; and the *Jeannette* moreover drifted north-west.

"It is strange, that notwithstanding these westerly winds we do not drift eastwards. The last longitude was only 135° E. long.

"Maundy Thursday, March 22nd. A strong south-easterly wind still, and a good drift northwards. Our spirits are rising. The wind whistles through the rigging overhead, and sounds like the sough of victory through the air. In the forenoon one of the puppies had a severe attack of convulsions; it foamed at the mouth, and bit furiously at everything round it. It ended with tetanus and we carried it out and laid it down on the ice. It hopped about like a toad, its legs stiff and extended, neck and head pointing upwards, while its back was curved like a saddle. I was afraid it might be hydrophobia or some other infectious sickness and shot it on the spot. Perhaps I was rather too hasty, we can scarcely have any infection among us now. But what could it have been? Was it an epileptic attack? The other day one of the other puppies alarmed me by running round and round in the chart-house as if it were mad, hiding itself after a time between a chest and the wall. Some of the others, too, had seen it do the same thing; but after a while it got all right again, and for the last few days there has been nothing amiss with it.

"Good Friday, March 23rd. Noonday observation gives 80° N. lat. In four days and nights we have drifted as far north as we drifted southwards in three weeks. It is a comfort, at all events, to know that!

"It is remarkable how quickly the nights have grown light. Even stars of the first magnitude can now barely manage to twinkle in the pale sky at midnight.

"Saturday, March 24th. Easter Eve. To-day a notable event has occurred. We have allowed the light of spring to enter the saloon. During the whole of the winter the skylight was covered with snow to keep the cold out, and the dogs' kennels, moreover, had been placed round it. Now we have thrown out all the

Johansen in front of the *Fram*, 24 March 1894.

snow upon the ice, and the panes of glass in the skylight have been duly cleared and cleaned.

"Monday, March 26th. We are lying motionless — no drift. How long will this last? Last equinox how proud and triumphant I was; the whole world looked bright; but now I am proud no longer.

"The sun mounts up and bathes the ice-plain with its radiance. Spring is coming, but brings no joys with it. Here it is as lonely and cold as ever. One's soul freezes. Seven more years of such life — or say only four — how will the soul appear then? And she...? If I dared to let my longings loose — to let my soul thaw. I long more than I dare confess.

"I have not courage to think of the future... And how will it be at home, when year after year rolls by and no one comes?

"I know this is all a morbid mood; but still this inactive, lifeless monotony, without any change, wrings one's very soul. No struggle, no possibility of struggle! All is so still and dead, so stiff and shrunken under the mantle of ice... the very soul freezes. What would I not give for a single day of struggle — for even a moment of danger!

"Still I must wait, and watch the drift; but, should it take a wrong direction, then I will break all the bridges behind me, and stake everything on a northward march over the ice. I know nothing better to do. It will be a hazardous journey, a matter, may be, of life or death. But have I any other choice?

"It is unworthy of a man to set himself a task and then give in when the brunt of the battle is upon him. There is but one way, and that is *Fram* — forwards.

"Tuesday, March 27th. We are again drifting southwards, and the wind is northerly. The midday observation showed 80° 4' N. lat. But why so dispirited? I am staring myself blind at one single point — am thinking solely of reaching the Pole and forcing our way through to the Atlantic Ocean. And all the time our real task is to explore the unknown polar regions. Are we doing nothing in the service of science? It will be a goodly collection of observations that we shall take home with us from this region, with which we are now rather too well acquainted. The rest is, and remains, a mere matter of vanity. 'Love truth more, and victory less.'

"I look at Eilif Peterssen's picture, a Norwegian pine forest, and I am there in spirit. How marvellously lovely it is there now, in the spring, in the dim, melancholy stillness that reigns among the stately stems. I can feel the damp moss in which my foot sinks softly and noiselessly; the brook released from the winter bondage is murmuring through the clefts and among the rocks, with its brownish-yellow water; the air is full of the scent of moss and pine needles, while overhead against the light blue sky, the dark pine tops rock to and fro in the spring breeze., ever uttering their murmuring wail, and beneath their shelter the soul fearlessly expands its wings and cools itself in the forest dew.

"Oh, solemn pine forest, the only confidant of my childhood, it was from you I learned nature's deepest tones, its wildness, its melancholy. You coloured my soul for life.

"Alone — far in the forest — beside the glowing embers of my fire on the shore of the silent, murky woodland tarn, with the gloom of night overhead, how happy I used to be in the enjoyment of Nature's harmony.

"Thursday, March 29th. It is wonderful what a change it makes to have daylight once more in the saloon. On turning out for breakfast and seeing the light gleaming in, one feels that it really is morning.

"We are busy on board. Sails are being made for the boats and hand-sledges. The windmill, too, is to have fresh sails, so that it can go in any kind of weather. If we could but give the *Fram* wings as well. Knives are being forged, bear spears which we never have any use for, bear-traps in which we never catch a bear, axes and many other things of like usefulness. For the moment there is a great manufacture of wooden shoes going on, and a newly started nail-making industry. The only shareholders in this company are Sverdrup and Smith Lars, called 'Storm King,' because he always comes upon us like hard weather. The output is excellent and is in active demand, as all our small nails for the hand-sledge fittings have been used. Moreover, we are very busy putting German-silver plates under the runners of the hand sledges, and providing appliances for lashing sledges together. There is, moreover, a workshop for snow-shoe fastenings, and a tinsmith's shop busied for the moment with repairs to the lamps. Our doctor too for lack of patients has set up a bookbinding establishment which is greatly patronised by the *Fram*'s library, whereof several books that are in constant circulation, such as *Gjest Baardsens Liv og Levnes*, etc., etc., are in a very bad state. We have also a saddlers' and sailmakers' workshop, a photographic studio, etc., etc. The manufacture of diaries, however, is the most extensive — every man on board works at that. In fine, there is no thing between heaven and earth that we cannot turn out — excepting constant fair winds.

"Our workshops can be highly recommended; they turn out good solid work. We have lately had a notable addition to our industries, the firm 'Nansen and Amundsen' having established a music factory. The cardboard plates of the organ had suffered greatly from wear and damp, so that we had been deplorably short of music during the winter. But, yesterday, I set to work in earnest to manufacture a plate of zinc. It answers admirably, and now we shall go ahead with music sacred and profane, especially valses, and these halls shall once more resound with the pealing tones of the organ, to our great comfort and edification. When a valse is struck up it breathes fresh life into many of the inmates of the *Fram*.

"I complain of the wearing monotony of our surroundings; but in reality I am unjust. The last few days dazzling sunshine over the snowhills; to-day, snowstorm and wind, the *Fram* enveloped in a whirl of foaming white snow. Soon the sun appears again, and the waste around gleams as before.

"Here, too, there is sentiment in Nature. How often when least thinking of it, do I find myself pause, spell-bound by the marvellous hues which evening wears. The ice-hills steeped in bluish-violet shadows, against the orange-tinted sky, illumined by the glow of the setting sun, form as it were a strange colour-poem, imprinting an ineffaceable picture on the soul. And these bright dream-like nights, how many associations they have for us Northmen! One pictures to oneself those mornings in spring when one went out into the forest after blackcock, under the dim stars, and with the pale crescent moon peering over the treetops. Dawn, with its glowing hues up, here in the north, is the breaking of a spring day over the forest wilds at home; the hazy blue vapour beneath the morning glow, turns to the fresh early mist over the marshes; the dark low clouds on a background of dim red, seem like distant ranges of hills.

"Daylight here with its rigid, lifeless whiteness has no attractions; but the evening and night thaw the heart of this world of ice; it dreams mournful dreams, and you seem to hear in the hues of the evening, sounds of its smothered wail. Soon these will cease, and the Sun will circle round the everlasting light blue expanse of heaven,' imparting one uniform colour to day and night alike;

"Friday, April 6th. A remarkable event was to take place to-day, which naturally we all looked forward to with lively interest. It was an eclipse of the sun. During the night Hansen had made a calculation that the eclipse would begin at 12.56 o'clock. It was important for us to be able to get a good observation, as we should thus be able to regulate our chronometers to a nicety. In order to make everything sure, we set up our instruments a couple of hours beforehand, and commenced to observe. We used the large telescope, and our

Workshop on deck.

large theodolite. Hansen, Johansen, and myself took it by turns to sit for five minutes each at the instruments, watching the rim of the sun, as we expected a shadow would become visible on its lower western edge, while another stood by with the watch. We remained thus full two hours without anything occurring. The exciting moment was now at hand, when, according to calculation, the shadow should first be apparent. Hansen was sitting by the large telescope, when he thought he could discern a quivering in the sun's rim; 33 seconds afterwards he cried out, 'Now!' as did Johansen simultaneously. The watch was then at 12 hrs. 56 m. 15 s. A dark body advanced over the border of the sun 7½ seconds later than we had calculated on. It was an immense satisfaction for us all, especially for Hansen, for it proved our chronometers to be in excellent order. Little by little the sunlight sensibly faded away, while we went below to dinner. At 2 o'clock the eclipse was at its height, and we could notice even down in the saloon how the daylight had diminished. After dinner we observed the moment when the eclipse ended, and the moon's dark disc cleared the rim of the sun.

"Sunday, April 8th. I was lying awake yesterday morning thinking about getting up, when all at once I heard the hurried footsteps of some one running over the half-deck above me, and then another followed. There was something in those footsteps that involuntarily made me think of bears, and I had a hazy sort of an idea that I ought to jump up out of bed, but I lay still listening for the report of a gun. I heard nothing, however, and soon fell a-dreaming again. Presently Johansen came tearing down into the saloon, crying out that a couple of bears were lying half or quite dead on the large ice hummock astern of the ship. He and Mogstad had shot at them, but they had no more cartridges left. Several of the men seized hold of their guns and hurried up. I threw on my clothes and came up a little after, when I gathered that the bears had taken to flight, as I could see the other fellows following them over the ice. As I was putting on my snow-shoes they returned, and said that the bears had made off. However, I started after them as fast as my snow-shoes would take me across the floes and the pressure-ridges. I soon got on their tracks, which at first were a little bloodstained. It was a she-bear, with her cub, and, as I believed, hard hit — the she-bear had fallen down several times after Johansen's first bullet. I thought, therefore, it would be no difficult matter to overtake them. Several of the dogs were on ahead of me on their tracks. They had taken a north-westerly course, and I toiled on, perspiring profusely in the sun, while the ship sank deeper and deeper down below the horizon. The surface of the snow, sparkling with its eternal whiteness all around me, tried my eyes severely, and I seemed to get no nearer the bears. My prospects of coming up with them were ruined by the dogs, who were keen enough to frighten the bears, but not so keen as to press on and bring them to bay. I would not, however, give up. Presently a fog came on, and hid everything from view except the bear-tracks, which steadily pointed forward; then it lifted, and the sun shone out again clear and bright as before. The *Fram*'s masts had long since disappeared over the edge of the ice, but still I kept on. Presently, however, I began to feel faint and hungry, for in my hurry I had not even had my breakfast, and at last had to bite the sour apple and turn back without any bears.

"On my way I came across a remarkable hummock. It was over 20 feet in height (I could not manage to measure it quite to the top); the middle part had fallen in, probably from pressure of the ice, while the remaining part formed a magnificent triumphal arch of the whitest marble, on which the sun glittered

Johansen, Nansen and Hansen, observing the solar eclipse of 6 April 1894.

with all its brilliancy. Was it erected to celebrate my defeat? I got up on it to look out for the *Fram*, but had to go some distance yet before I could see her rigging over the horizon. It was not till half-past five in the afternoon that I found myself on board again, worn out and famished from this sudden and unexpected excursion. After a day's fasting, I heartily relished a good meal. During my absence some of the others had started after me with a sledge to draw home the dead bears that I had shot; but they had barely reached the spot where the encounter had taken place, when Johansen and Blessing, who were in advance of the others, saw two fresh bears spring up from behind a hummock a little way off. But before they could get their guns in readiness the bears were out of range; so a new hunt began. Johansen tore after them in his snow-shoes, but several of the dogs got in front of him and kept the bears going, so that he could not get within range, and his chase ended as fruitlessly as mine.

"Has good luck abandoned us? I had plumed myself on our never having shot at a single bear without bagging it, but to-day...! Odd that we should get a visit from four bears on one day, after having seen nothing of them for three months! Does it signify something? Have we got near the land in the north-west which I have so long expected? There seems to be change in the air. An observation the day before yesterday gave 80° 15' N. lat., the most northerly we have had yet.

"Sunday, April 15th. So we are in the middle of April! What a ring of joy in that word, a wellspring of happiness! Visions of spring rise up in the soul at its very mention — a time when doors and windows are thrown wide open to the spring air and sun, and the dust of winter is blown away; a time when one can no longer sit still, but must perforce go out of doors to inhale the perfume of wood and field and fresh-dug earth, and behold the fjord, free from ice, sparkling in the sunlight. What an inexhaustible fund of the awakening joys of nature does that word April contain. But here — here that is not to be found. True, the sun shines long and bright, but its beams fall not on forest or mountain or meadow, but only on the dazzling whiteness of the fresh-fallen snow. Scarcely does it entice one out from one's winter retreat. This is not the time of revolutions here. If they come at all, they will come much later. The days roll on uniformly and monotonously; here I sit, and feel no touch of the restless longings of the spring, and shut myself up in the snail-shell of my studies. Day after day I dive down into the world of the microscope, forgetful of time and surroundings. Now and then, indeed, I may make a little excursion from darkness to light — the daylight beams around me, and my soul opens a tiny loophole for light and courage to enter in — and then down, down into the darkness, and to work once more. Before turning in for the night I must go on deck. A little while ago the daylight would by this time have vanished, a few solitary stars would have been faintly twinkling, while the pale moon shone over the ice. But now even this has come to an end. The sun no longer sinks beneath the icy horizon; it is continual day. I gaze into the far distance, far over the barren plain of snow, a boundless, silent, and lifeless mass of ice in imperceptible motion. No sound can be heard save the faint murmur of the air through the rigging, or perhaps far away the low rumble of packing ice. In the midst of this empty waste of white there is but one little dark spot, and that is the *Fram*.

"But beneath this crust, hundreds of fathoms down, there teems a world of chequered life in all its changing forms, a world of the same composition as ours, with the same instincts, the same sorrows, and also, no doubt, the same joys; everywhere the same struggle for existence. So it ever is. If we penetrate within even the hardest shell, we come upon the pulsations of life, however thick the crust may be.

"I seem to be sitting here in solitude listening to the music of one of nature's mighty harp-strings. Her grand symphonies peal forth through the endless ages of the universe, now in the tumultuous whirl of busy life, now in the stiffening coldness of death, as in Chopin's Funeral March; and we — we are the minute, invisible vibrations of the strings in this mighty music of the universe, ever changing yet ever the same. Its notes are worlds; one vibrates for a longer, another for a shorter period, and all in turn give way to new ones...

"The world that shall be!...Again and again this thought comes back to my mind. I gaze far on through the ages...

"Slowly and imperceptibly the heat of the sun declines, and the temperature of the earth sinks by equally slow degrees. Thousands, hundreds of thousands, millions of years pass away, glacial epochs come and go; but the heat still grows ever less; little by little these drifting masses of ice extend far and wide, ever towards more southern shores; and no one notices it, but at last all the seas of earth become one unbroken mass of ice. Life has vanished from its surface, and is to be found in the ocean depths alone.

"But the temperature continues to fall, the ice grows thicker and ever thicker; life's domain vanishes. Millions of years roll on, and the ice reaches the bottom. The last trace of life has disappeared; the earth is covered with snow. All that we lived for is no longer; the fruit of all our toil and sufferings has been blotted out millions and millions of years ago, buried beneath a pall of snow. A stiffened, lifeless mass of ice this earth rolls on in her path through eternity. Like a faintly glowing disc, the sun crosses the sky; the moon shines no more, and is scarcely visible. Yet still, perhaps, the northern lights flicker over the desert, icy plain, and still the stars twinkle in silence, peacefully as of yore. Some have burnt out, but new ones usurp their place; and round them revolve new spheres, teeming with new life, new sufferings without any aim. Such is the infinite cycle of eternity; such are nature's everlasting rhythms.

"Monday, April 30th. Drifting northwards. Yesterday observations gave 80° 42', and to-day 80° 44½'. The wind steady from the south and south-east.

"It is lovely spring weather. One feels that springtime must have come, though the thermometer denies it. 'Spring cleaning' has begun on board; the snow and ice along the *Fram*'s sides are cleared away, and she stands out like the crags from their winter covering decked with the flowers of spring. The snow lying on the deck is little by little shovelled overboard; her rigging rises up against the clear sky clean and dark, and the gilt trucks at her mastheads sparkle in the sun. We go and bathe ourselves in the broiling sun along her warm sides, where the thermometer is actually above freezing point, smoke a peaceful pipe, gazing at the white spring clouds that lightly fleet across the blue expanse. Some of us perhaps think of spring-time yonder at home, when the birch trees are bursting into leaf."

Chapter 7

The Spring and Summer of 1894

SO CAME the season which we at home call spring, the season of joy and budding life, when nature awakens after her long winter sleep. But there, it brought no change; day after day we had to gaze over the same white lifeless mass, the same white boundless ice-plains. Still we wavered between despondency, idle longing, and eager energy, shifting with the winds as we drift forwards to our goal or are driven back from it. As before, I continued to brood upon the possibilities of the future and of our drift. One day I would think that everything was going on as we hoped and anticipated. Thus on April 17th I was convinced that there must be a current through the unknown polar basin, as we were unmistakably drifting northwards. The midday observation gave 80° 20′ N.E., that is 9′ since the day before yesterday. Strange. A north wind of four whole days took us to the south, while twenty-four hours of this scanty wind drifts us 9′ northwards. This is remarkable; it looks as if we were done with drifting southwards. And when, in addition to this, I take into consideration the striking warmth of the water deep down, it seems to me that things are really looking brighter. The reasoning runs as follows: The temperature of the water in the East Greenland current, even on the surface, is nowhere over zero (the mean temperature for the year), and appears generally to be −1° C. (30.2° F.), even in 70° N. lat. In this latitude the temperature steadily falls as you get below the surface: nowhere at a greater depth than 100 fathoms is it above −1° C., and generally from −1.5° (29.30° F.) to −1.7° C. (28.94° F.) right to the bottom. Moreover, the bottom temperature of the whole sea north of the Goth degree of latitude is under −1° C., a strip along the Norwegian coast and between Norway and Spitzbergen alone excepted, but here the temperature is over −1°

C., from 86 fathoms (160 metres) downward, and 135 fathoms (250 metres) the temperature is already +0.55° C. (32.99° F.), and that, too, be it remarked, north of the 80th degree of latitude, and in a sea surrounding the pole of maximum cold.

This warm water can hardly come from the Arctic Sea itself, while the current issuing thence towards the south has a general temperature of about −1.5° C. It can hardly be anything other than the Gulf Stream that finds its way hither, and replaces the water which in its upper layers flows towards the north, forming the sources of the East Greenland polar current. All this seems to chime in with my previous assumptions, and supports the theory on which this expedition was planned. And when, in addition to this, one bears in mind that the winds seem, as anticipated, to be as a rule south-easterly, as was, moreover, the case at the international station at Sagastyr (by the Lena mouth), our prospects do not appear to be unfavourable.

Frequently, moreover. I thought I could detect unmistakable symptoms of a steadily flowing north-westerly current under the ice, and then, of course, my spirits rose; but at other times, when the drift main bore southwards — and that was often — my doubts would return, and it seemed as if there was no prospect of getting through within any reasonable time. Truly such drifting in the ice is extremely trying to the mind; but there is one virtue it fosters, and that is patience; the whole expedition was in reality one long course of training in this useful virtue.

Our progress as the spring advanced grew somewhat better than it had been during the winter, but on the whole it was always the same sort of crablike locomotion; for each time we made a long stretch to the north, a longer period of reaction was sure to follow. It was, in the opinion of one of our number, who was somewhat of a politician, a constant struggle between the Left and Right, between Progressionists and Recessionists. After a period of Left wind and a glorious drift northwards, as a matter of course the "Radical Right" took the helm, and we remained lying in dead water or drifted backwards, thereby putting Amundsen into a very bad temper. It was a remarkable fact that during the whole time, the *Fram*'s bow turned towards the south, generally S. ¼ W., and shifted but very little during the whole drift. As I say on May 14th: "She went backwards towards her goal in the north, with her nose ever turned to the south. It is as though she shrank from increasing her distance from the world; as though she were longing for southern shores, while some invisible power is drawing her on towards the unknown. Can it be an ill omen, this backward

Taking a sounding of 2,058 fathoms, 30 April 1894.

advance towards the interior of the Polar Sea? I cannot think it; even the crab ultimately reaches its goal."

A statement of our latitude and longitude on different days will best indicate the general course of our drift May 1st, 80° 46' N. lat.; May 4th, 80° 50'; May 6th, 80° 49'; May 8th, 80° 55' N. lat., 129° 58' E. long.; May 12th, 80° 52' N. lat.; May 15th, 129° 20' E. long.; May 21st, 81° 20' N. lat., 125° 45' E. long.; May 23rd, 81° 26' N. lat.; May 27th, 81° 31'; June 2nd, 81° 31' N. lat., 121° 47' E. long.; June 13th, 81° 46'; June 18th, 81° 52'. Up to this we had made fairly satisfactory progress towards the north, but now came the reaction: June 24th, 81° 42'; July 1st, 81° 33': July 10th, 81° 20; July 14th, 81° 32'; July 18th, 81° 26'; July 31st, 81° 2' N. lat., 126° 5' 5" E. long.; August 8th, 81° 8'; August 14th, 81° 5' N. lat., 127° 38' E. long.; August 26th, 81° 1'; September 5th, 81° 14' N. lat., 123° 36' E. long.

After this we began once more to drift northwards, but not very fast.

As before, we were constantly on the look-out for land, and were inclined first from one thing, then from another, to think we saw sins of its proximity; but they always turned out to be imaginary, and the great depth of the sea, moreover, showed that at all events land could not be near.

Later on — on August 7th — when I had found over 2,085 fathoms (3,850 metres) depth, I say in my diary "I do not think we shall talk any more about the shallow Polar Sea, where land may be expected anywhere. We may very possibly drift out into the Atlantic Ocean without having seen a single mountain-top. An eventful series of years to look forward to!"

The plan already alluded to of travelling over the ice with dogs and sledges occupied me a good deal, and during my daily expeditions partly on snow-shoes, partly with dogs, my attention was constantly given to the condition of the ice and our prospects of being able to make our way over it. During April it was specially well adapted for using dogs. The surface was good, as the sun's power had made it smoother than the heavy drift-snow earlier in the winter; besides, the wind had covered the pressure-ridges pretty evenly, and there were not many crevasses or channels in the ice, so that one could proceed for miles without much trouble from them. In May, however, a change set in. As early as May 8th the wind had broken up the ice a good deal, and now there were lanes in all directions, which proved a great obstacle when I went out driving with the dogs. The temperature, however, was still so low that the channels were quickly frozen over again and became passable; but later on in the month the temperature rose, so that ice was no longer so readily formed On the water, and the channels became ever more and more numerous.

On May 20th I write: "Went out on snow — shoes in the forenoon. The ice has been very much broken up in various directions, owing to the continual winds during the last week. The lanes are difficult to cross over, as they are full of small pieces of ice, that lie dispersed about, and are partly covered with drift-snow. This is very deceptive, for one may seem to have firm ice under one at places where, on sticking one's staff in, it goes right down without any sign of ice. On many occasions I nearly got into trouble in crossing over snow like this on snow-shoes. I would suddenly find that the snow was giving way under me, and would manage with no little difficulty to get safely back on to the firm ice.

On June 5th the ice and the snow surface were about as before. I write: "Have just been out on a snow-shoe excursion with Sverdrup in a southerly direction, the first for a long while. The condition of the ice has altered, but not for the better; the surface, indeed, is hard and good, butt the pressure-ridges are very awkward, and there are crevasses and hummocks in all directions. A sledge expedition would make poor enough progress on such ice as this."

Hitherto, however, progress had always been possible, but now the snow began to melt, and placed almost insuperable difficulties in the way. On June 13th I write: "The ice gets softer and softer every day, and large pools of water are formed on the floes all around us. In short, the surface is abominable. The snowshoes break through into the water everywhere. Truly one would not be able to get far in a day now should one be obliged to set off towards the south or west. It is as if every outlet were blocked, and here we stick — we stick. Sometimes it strikes me as rather remarkable that none of our fellows have become alarmed, even when we are bearing farther and farther northwards, farther and farther into the unknown; but there is no sign of fear in any one of them. All look gloomy when we are bearing south or too much to the west, and all are beaming with joy when we are drifting to the northward, the farther the better. Yet none of them can be blind to the fact that it is a matter of life and death, if anything of what nearly every one prophesied should now occur. Should the ship be crushed in this ice and go to the bottom, like the *Jeannette*, without our being able to save sufficient supplies to continue our drift on the ice, we should have to turn our course to the south, and then there would be little doubt as to our fate. The *Jeannette* people fared badly enough, but their ship went down in 77° N. lat., while the nearest land to us is many times more than double the distance it was in their case, to say nothing of the nearest inhabited land. We are now more than 70 miles from Cape Chelyuskin, while from there to any inhabited region we are a long way farther. But the *Fram* will not be crushed, and nobody believes in the possibility of such an event. We are like the kayak-rower, who knows well enough that one faulty stroke of his paddle is enough to capsize him and send him into eternity; but none the less, he goes, on his way serenely, for he knows that he will not make a faulty stroke. This is absolutely the most comfortable way of undertaking a polar expedition; what possible journey, indeed, could be more comfortable? Not even a railway journey, for then you have the bother of changing carriages. Still a change now and then would be no bad thing."

Later on — in July — the surface was even worse. The floes were everywhere covered with slush, with water underneath, and on the pressure-ridges and between the hummocks where the snow-drifts were deep one would often sink in up to the middle, not even the snow-shoes bearing one up in this soft snow. Later on in July matters improved, the snow having gradually melted away, so that there was a firmer surface of ice to go on.

But large pools of water now formed on the ice-floes. Already on the 8th and 9th of June such a pool had begun to appear round the ship, so that she lay in a little lake of fresh water, and we were obliged to make use of a bridge in order to reach a dry spot on the ice. Some of these fresh-water pools were of respectable dimensions and depth. There was one of these on the starboard side of the ship, so large that in the middle of July we could row and sail on it with the boats.

This was a favourite evening amusement with some of us, and the boat was fully officered with captain, mate, and second mate, but had no common sailors. They thought it an excellent opportunity of practising sailing with a square sail; while the rest of our fellows standing on the icy shore, found it still more diverting to bombard the navigators with snowballs and lumps of ice. It was in this same pool that we tried one day if one of our boats could carry all thirteen of us at once. When the dogs saw us all leave the ship to go to the pool they followed us in utter bewilderment as to what this unusual movement could mean; but when we got into the boat they, all of them, set to work and howled in wild despair; thinking, probably, that they would never see us again. Some of them swam after us, while two cunning ones, "Pan" and "Kvik," conceived the brilliant idea of galloping round the pool to the opposite side to meet us. A few days afterwards I was dismayed to find the pool dried up; a hole had been worn

Sailing in the life boat, 12 July 1894.

through the ice at the bottom, and all the fresh water had drained out into the sea. So that amusement came to an end.

In the summer when we wanted to snake an excursion over the ice, in addition to such pools we met with lanes in the ice in all directions, but as a rule could easily cross them by jumping from one loose floe to another, or leaping right across at narrow places.

These lanes never attained any great width, and there was consequently no question of getting the *Fram* afloat in any of them; and even could we have done so, it would have been of very little avail, as none of them was large enough to have taken her more than a few cable-lengths further north. Sometimes there were indications in the sky that there must be large stretches of open water in our vicinity, and we could now and then see from the crow's-nest large spaces of clear water in the horizon; but they could not have been large enough to be of much use when it came to a question of pushing, forward with a ship.

Sanguine folk on board, however, attached more importance to such open stretches. June 15th I wrote in my diary:"There are several lanes visible in different directions, but none of them is wide or of any great extent. The mate, however, is always insisting that we shall certainly get open water before autumn, and be able to creep along northwards, while, with the rest, Sverdrup excepted, it seems to be a generally accepted belief. Where they are to get their open water from I do not know. For the rest, this is the first ice-bound expedition that has not spent the summer spying after open water, and sighing and longing for the ice to disperse. I only wish it may keep together, and hurry up and drift northwards. Everything in this life depends on what one has made up one's mind to. One person sets forth to sail in open water, perhaps to the very Pole, but gets stuck in the ice and laments; another is prepared to get stuck in the ice, but will not grumble even should he find open water. It is ever the safest plan to expect the least of life, for then one often gets the most."

The open spaces, the lanes, and the rifts in the ice are, of course, produced, like the pressure and packing, by the shifting winds and the tidal currents that set the ice drifting first in one direction, then in another. And they best prove, perhaps, how the surface of the Polar Sea must be considered as one continuous mass of ice-floes in constant motion, now frozen together, now torn apart, or crushed against each other.

During the whole of our drift I paid great attention to this ice, not only with respect to its motion, but to its formation and growth as well. In the Introduction of this book I have pointed out that, even if the ice should pass year after year in the cold Polar Sea, it could not by mere freezing attain more than a certain thickness. From measurements that were constantly being made, it appeared that the ice which was formed during the autumn in October or November continued to increase in size during the whole of the winter and out into the spring, but more slowly the thicker it became. On April 10th it was about 2.31 metres; April 21st, 2.41 metres; May 5th, 2.45 metres; May 31, 2.52 metres; June 9th, 2.58 metres. It was thus continually increasing in bulk, notwithstanding that the snow now melted quickly on the surface, and large pools of fresh water were formed on the floes. On June 10th the thickness was the same, although the melting on the surface had now increased considerably. On July 4th the thickness was 2.57 metres. On July 10th I was amazed to find that the ice had increased to 2.76 metres, notwithstanding that it would now diminish several centimetres daily from surface melting. I bored in many places, but found it everywhere the same — a thin, somewhat loose, ice mass lay under the old floe. I first thought it was a thin ice-floe that had got pushed under, but subsequently discovered that it was actually a new formation of fresh-water ice on the lower side of the old ice, due to the layer of fresh water of about 9 feet 9 inches (3 metres) in depth, formed by the melting of the snow on the ice. Owing to its lightness this warm fresh water floated on the salt sea water, which was at a temperature of about (−1.5° C.) on its surface. Thus by contact with the colder sea water the fresh water became cooler, and so a thick crust of ice was formed on the fresh water, where it came in contact with the salt water lying underneath it. It was this ice crust then that augmented the thickness of the ice on its under side. Later on in the summer, however, the ice diminished somewhat, owing to melting on the surface. On July 23rd, the old ice was only 2.33 metres, and with the newly-formed layer 2.49 metres. On August 10th the thickness of the old ice had decreased to 1.94 metres, and together the aggregate thickness to 3.17 metres. On August 22nd the old ice was 1.86 metres, and the aggregate thickness 3.06 metres. On September 3rd the aggregate thickness was 2.02 metres, and on September 30th 1.98 metres. On October 3rd it was the same; the thickness of the old ice was then 1.75 metres. On October 12th the aggregate thickness was 2.08 metres, while the old ice was 1.8 metres. On November 10th it was still about the same, with only a slight tendency to increase. Further on in November and in December it increased quite slowly. On December 11th the aggregate thickness reached 2.11 metres. On January 3rd, 1895, 2.32 metres; January 10th. 2.48 metres; February 6th, 2.59 metres. Hence it will be seen that the ice does not attain any enormous thickness by direct freezing. The packing caused by pressure can, however, produce blocks and floes of a very different size. It often happens that the floes get shoved in under each other in several layers, and are frozen together so as to appear like one originally continuous mass of ice. Thus the *Fram* had got a good bed under her.

Juell and Peter had often disputed together during the winter as to the thickness of ice the *Fram* had under her. Peter, who had seen a good deal of the ice before, maintained that it must at least be 20 feet thick, while Juell would not believe it, and betted 20 kroner that it was not as thick as that. On April 19th this dispute again broke out, and I say of it in my diary: "Juell has undertaken to make a bore, but unfortunately our borer reaches no farther than 16 feet down. Peter, however, has undertaken to cut away the 4 feet that are

A pressure ridge on the port quarter of the *Fram*, 1 July 1894.

lacking. There has been a lot of talk about this wager during the whole winter, but they could never agree about it. Peter says that Juell should begin to bore, while Juell maintains that Peter ought to cut the 4 feet first. This evening it ended in Juell incautiously offering 10 kroner to anyone who would bore. Bentzen took him at his word, and immediately set to work at it with Amundsen; he thought one did not always have the chance of earning 10 kroner so easily. Amundsen offered him a kroner an hour, or else payment per foot; and time payment was finally agreed to. They worked till late on into the night, and when they had got down 12 feet, the borer slipped a little way, and water rose in the hole, but this did not come to much, and presently the borer struck on ice again. They went on for some time, but now the borer would reach no further, and Peter had to be called up to cut his four feet. He and Amundsen worked away at cutting till they were dripping with perspiration. Amundsen, as usual, was very eager and vowed he would not give in till he had got through it, even if it were 30 feet thick. Meanwhile Bentzen had turned in, but a message was

A view of the pools on the ice, 1 July 1894. Pettersen standing in the foreground.

sent to him to say that the hole was cut, and that boring could now begin again. When it was only an inch or an inch-and-a-half short of 20 feet, the borer slipped through, and the water spurted up and filled the hole. They now sank a lead line down it, and at 30 feet it again brought up against ice. Now they were obliged to give it up. A fine lump of ice we are lying on! Not taking into account a large, loose ice floe that is lying packed up on the ice, it is 16 inches above the water; and adding to this the 2 feet which the *Fram* is raised up above the ice, there is no small distance between her and the water.

The temperature on the ice in summer is about thawing point, but gradually as the winter cold comes on, it, of course, falls rapidly on the surface, whence the cold slowly penetrates deeper and deeper down towards the lower surface, where it naturally keeps at an even temperature with the underlying water. Observations of the temperature of the ice in its different layers were constantly taken in order to ascertain how quickly this cooling-down process of the ice took place during the winter, and also how the temperature rose again towards spring. The lowest temperature of the ice occurred in March and the beginning of April, when at 1.2 metres it was about 3.2° F. (−16° C.), and at 0.8 metre about 22° F. below zero (−30° C.). After the beginning of April it began to rise slowly.

At these low temperatures the ice became very hard and brittle, and was readily cracked or broken up by a blow or by packing. In the summer, on the other hand, when its temperature was near melting-point, the ice became tough and plastic, and was not so readily broken up under packing. This difference between the condition of the ice in summer and winter was apparent also to the ear, as the ice-packing in winter was always accompanied by the frequently mentioned loud noises, while the hacking of the tough summer ice was almost noiseless, so that the most violent convulsions might tale place close to us without our noticing them.

In the immediate vicinity of the *Fram* the ice remained perfectly at rest the whole year through, and she was not at this time exposed to any great amount of pressure; she lay safe and secure on the ice-floe to which she was firmly frozen; and gradually as the surface of the ice thawed under the summer sun she rose up higher and higher. In the autumn she again began to sink a little, either because the ice gave way under her weight, or because it melted somewhat on the under surface, so that it no longer had so much buoyancy as before.

Meanwhile, life on board went on in its usual way. Now that we had daylight there was of course more work of various descriptions on the ice than had been the case during the winter. I have already alluded more than once to our unsuccessful endeavours to reach the bottom by sounding. Unfortunately we were not prepared for such great depths, and had not brought any deep-sea sounding apparatus with us. We had, therefore, to do the best we could under the circumstances; and that was to sacrifice one of the ship's steel cables in order to make a lead-line. It was not difficult to find sufficient space on the ice for a rope walk, and although a temperature of from 22° F. below zero (−30° C.) to 40° F. below zero (−40° C.) is not the most comfortable in which to manipulate such things as steel-wire, yet for all that the work went on well. The cable was unlaid into its separate strands, and a fresh, pliant lead-line manufactured by twisting two of these strands together. In this way we made a line of between 4,000 to 5,000 metres (2,150 to 2,700 fathoms) long, and could now at last reach the bottom. The depth proved to range between 3,300 and 3,900 metres (1,800 to 2,100 fathoms).

Nansen measuring deep water temperatures with the water fetcher, 7 July 1894.

Depths.		Temperature.	
	- Fathoms.	Degrees Centigrade.	Fahrenheit.
Surface ...	...	+ 1·02	= 33·83
2 metres =	1	− 1·32	29·62
20 ,,	10	− 1·33	29·61
40 ,,	21	− 1·50	29·3
60 ,,	32	− 1·50	29·3
80 ,,	43	− 1·50	29·3
100 ,,	54	− 1·40	29·48
120 ,,	65	− 1·24	29·77
140 ,,	76	− 0·97	30·254
160 ,,	87	− 0·58	30·96
180 ,,	98	− 0·31	31·44
200 ,,	109	− 0·03	31·95
220 ,,	120	+ 0·19	32·34
240 ,,	131	+ 0·20	32·36
260 ,,	142	+ 0·34	32·61
280 ,,	153	+ 0·42	32·76
300 ,,	164	+ 0·34	32·61
350 ,,	191	+ 0·44	32·79
400 ,,	218	+ 0·35	32·63
450 ,,	246	+ 0·36	32·66
500 ,,	273	+ 0·34	32·61
600 ,,	328	+ 0·26	32·47
700 ,,	382	+ 0·14	32·25
800 ,,	437	+ 0·07	32·126
900 ,,	492	− 0·04	31·928
1,000 ,,	546	− 0·10	31·82
1,200 ,,	656	− 0·28	31·496
1,400 ,,	765	− 0·34	31·39
1,600 ,,	874	− 0·46	31·17
1,800 ,,	984	− 0·60	30·92
2,000 ,,	1,093	− 0·66	30·81
2,600 .,	1,421	− 0·74	30·67
2,900 ,,	1,585	− 0·76	30·63
3,000 ..	1,640	− 0·73	30·69
3,400 ..	1,859	− 0·69	30·76
3,700 ..	2,023	− 0·65	30·83
3,800 ,,	2,077	− 0·64	30·85
325 ,,	177	+ 0·49	32·88

This was a remarkable discovery, for, as I have frequently mentioned, the unknown polar basin has always been supposed to be shallow, with numerous unknown lands and islands. I, too, had assumed it to be shallow when I sketched out my plan, and had thought it was traversed by a deep channel which might possibly be a continuation of the deep channel in the North Atlantic (see the Introduction).

From this assumption of a shallow Polar Sea it was concluded that the regions about the Pole had formerly been covered with an extensive tract of land, of which the existing islands are simply the remains. This extensive tract of polar land was furthermore assumed to have been the nursery of many of our animal and plant forms, whence they had found their way to lower latitudes. These conjectures now appear to rest on a somewhat infirm basis.

This great depth indicates that here, at all events, there has not been land in any very recent geological period; and this depth is, no doubt, as old as the depth of the Atlantic Ocean, of which it is almost certainly a part.

Another task to which I attached great importance and to which I have frequently alluded, was the observation of the temperature of the sea at different depths, from the surface down to the bottom. These observations we took as often as time permitted, and, as already mentioned, they gave some surprising results, showing the existence of warmer water below the cold surface stratum. This is not the place to give the results of the different measurements, but as they are all very similar I will instance one of them in order that an idea may be formed how the temperature is distributed.

This series of temperatures, of which an extract is given here, was taken from the 13th to the 17th of August.

These temperatures of the water are in many respects remarkable. In the first place the temperature falls, as will be seen, from the surface downwards to a depth of 80 metres, after which it rises to 280 metres, falls again at 300 metres, then rises again at 326 metres, where it was +0.49°; then falls to rise again at 450 metres, then falls steadily down to 2,000 metres, to rise once more slowly at the bottom. Similar risings and fallings were to be found in almost all the series of temperatures taken, and the variations from one month to another were so small that at the respective depths they often merely amounted to the two-hundredth part of a degree. Occasionally the temperature of the warm strata mounted even higher than mentioned here. Thus on October 17th at 300 metres it was +0.85°, at 350 metres +0.76°, at 400 metres +0.78, and at 500 metres +0.62°, after which it sank evenly until, towards the bottom, it again rose as before.

We had not expected to meet with much bird life in these desolate regions. Our surprise, therefore, was not small when on Whit Sunday, May 13th, a gull paid us a visit. After that date we regularly saw birds of different kinds in our vicinity, till at last it became a daily occurrence, to which we did not pay any particular attention. For the most part they were ice *mews* (*larus eburneus*), kittiwakes (*rissa tridactyla*), fulmars (*procellaria glacialis*), and now and then a blue gull (*l. glaucus*), a herring gull (*l. argentatus?*), or a black guillemot (*uria grylle*), once or twice we also saw a skua (probably *lestris parasitica*), (for instance, on July 14th). On July 21st we had a visit from a snow bunting.

On August 3rd a remarkable occurrence took place, we were visited by the Arctic rose gull (*rhodostethia rosea*). I wrote as follows about it in my diary:"Today my longing has at last been satisfied. I have shot Ross's gull,"[40] three specimens in one day. This rare and mysterious inhabitant of the unknown north, which is only occasionally seen, and of which no one knows whence it cometh or whither it goeth, which belongs exclusively to the world to which the imagination aspires, is what, from the first moment I saw these tracts, I had always hoped to discover, as my eyes roamed over the lonely plains of ice. And now it came when I was least thinking of it. I was out for a little walk on the ice by the ship, and as I was sitting down by a hummock my eyes wandered northwards and lit on a bird hovering over the great pressure-mound away to the north-west. At first I took it to be a kittiwake, but soon discovered it rather resembled the skua by its swift flight, sharp wings, and pointed tail. When I had got my gun, there were two of them together flying round and round the ship. I now got a closer view of them and discovered that they were too light coloured to be skuas. They were by no means shy, but continued flying about close to the ship. On going after them on the ice I soon shot one of them, and was not a little surprised on picking it up to find it was a little bird about the size of a snipe; the mottled back, too, reminded me also of that bird. Soon after this I shot the other. Later in the day there came another which was also shot. On picking this one up I found it was not quite dead, and it vomited up a couple of large shrimps, which it must have caught in some channel or other. All three were young birds, about 12 inches in length, with dark mottled grey plumage on the back and wings; the breast and under-side white, with a scarcely perceptible tinge of orange-red, and round the neck a dark ring sprinkled with grey." At a somewhat later age this mottled plumage disappears; they then become blue on

the back, with a black ring round the neck, while the breast assumes a delicate pink hue. Some few days afterwards (August 6th and 8th) some more of these birds were shot, making eight specimens in all.

While time was passing on, the plan I had been revolving in my mind during the winter was ever upper-most in my thoughts — the plan, that is to say, of exploring the unknown sea apart from the track in which the *Fram* was drifting. I kept an anxious eye upon the dogs, for fear anything should happen to them, and also to see that they continued in good condition, for all my hopes centered in them. Several of them, indeed, had been bitten to death, and two had been killed by bears; but there were still twenty-six remaining, and as a set-off against our losses we had the puppies, eight of which had been permitted to live. As spring advanced, they were allowed to roam the deck, but on May 5th their world was considerably extended. I wrote thus: "In the afternoon we let the puppies loose on the ice, and 'Kvik' at once took long expeditions with them to familiarise them with their surroundings. First she introduced them to our meteorological apparatus, then to the bear-trap, and after that to different pressure-mounds. They were very cautious at first, staring timidly all around, and venturing out very slowly, a step at a time from the ship's side; but soon they began to run riot in their newly-discovered world.

"'Kvik' was very prowl to conduct her litter out into the world, and roamed about in the highest of spirits, though she had only just returned from a long driving expedition, in which, as usual, she had done good work in harness. In the afternoon, one of the black and white puppies had an attack of madness. It ran round the ship, barking furiously; the others set on it, and it bit at everything that came in its way. At last we got it shut in on the deck forward, where it was furious for a while, then quieted down, and now seems to be all right again. This makes the fourth that has had a similar attack. What can it possibly be? It cannot be hydrophobia, or it would have appeared among the grown-up dogs. Can it be toothache, or hereditary epilepsy, or some other infernal thing?" Unfortunately, several of them died from these strange attacks. The puppies were such fine, nice animals, that we were all very sorry when a thing like this occurred.

On June 3rd I write: "Another of the puppies died in the forenoon from one of those mysterious attacks, and I cannot conceal from myself that I take it greatly to heart, and feel low-spirited about it. I have been so used to these small polar creatures living their sorrowless life on deck, romping and playing around us from morning to evening and a little of the night as well. I can watch them with pleasure by the hour together, or play with them as with little children — have a game at hide and seek with them round the skylight, the while they are beside themselves with glee. It is the largest and strongest of the lot that has just died, a handsome dog; I called him 'Lova' (Lion). He was such a confiding, gentle animal, and so affectionate. Only yesterday he was jumping and playing about and rubbing himself against me, and to-day he is dead. Our ranks are thinning, and the worst of it is we try in vain to make out what it is that ails them. This one was apparently quite in his normal condition and as cheerful as ever until his breakfast was given him; then he began to cry and tear round yelping and barking as if distracted, just as the others had done. After this convulsions set in, and the froth poured from his mouth. One of these convulsions no doubt carried him off. Blessing and I held a post mortem upon him in the afternoon, but we could discover no signs of anything unusual. It does not seem to be an infectious ailment I cannot understand it.

"'Ulenka,' too, the handsomest dog in the whole pack, our consolation and our hope, suddenly became ill the other day. It was the morning of May 24th that we found it paralyzed and quite helpless, lying in its cask on deck. It kept trying to get up but couldn't, and immediately fell down again — just like a man

who has had a stroke and has lost all power over his limbs. It was at once put to bed in a box and nursed most carefully; except for being unable to walk, it is apparently quite well." It must have been a kind of apoplectic seizure that attacked the spinal cord in some spot or other, and paralysed one side of the body. The dog recovered slowly, but never got the complete use of its legs again. It accompanied us, however, on our subsequent sledge expedition.

The dogs did not seem to like the summer, it was so wet on the ice, and so warm. On June IIth I write: "To-day the pools on the ice all round us have increased wonderfully in size, and it is by no means agreeable to go off the ship with shoes that are not water-tight; it is wetter and wetter for the dogs in the daytime, and they sweat more and more from the heat, though it as yet only rarely rises above zero (C.) A few days ago they were shifted on to the ice, where two long kennels were set up for them."[41] They were made out of boxes, and really consist of only a wall and a roof. Here they spend the greater part of the twenty-four hours, and we are now rid of all uncleanliness on board, except for the four puppies which still remain, and lead a glorious life of it up there between sleep and play. "Ulenka" is still on deck, and is slowly recovering.

There is the same daily routine for the dogs as in the winter. We let them loose in the morning about half past eight, and as the time for their release draws near they begin to get very impatient. Every time any one shows himself on deck a wild chorus of howls issues from twenty-six throats, clamouring for food and freedom. After being let loose they get their breakfast, consisting of half a dried fish, or three biscuits a-piece. The rest of the forenoon is spent in rooting round among all the refuse heaps they can find; and they gnaw and lick all the empty tin cases which they have ransacked hundreds of times before. If the cook sends a fresh tin dancing along the ice a battle immediately rages around the prize. It often happens that one or another of them trying to get at a tempting piece of fat at the bottom of a deep, narrow tin, sticks his head so far down into it that the tin sits fast, and he cannot release himself again; so with this extinguisher on his head he sprawls about blindly over the ice, indulging in the most wonderful antics in the effort to get rid of it, to the great amusement of us, the spectators. When tired of their work at the rubbish heaps they stretch out their round, sausage-like bodies, panting in the sun, if there is any, and if it is too warm they get into the shade. They are tied up again before dinner; but "Pan," and others like-minded, sneak away a little before that time, and hide up behind a hummock, so that one can only see a head or an ear sticking up here and there. Should anyone go to fetch him in he will probably growl, show his teeth, or even snap; after which he will lie flat down, and allow himself to be dragged off to prison. The remainder of the twenty-four hours they spend sleeping, puffing and panting in the excessive heat, which, by the way, is two degrees of cold. Every now and then they set up a chorus of howls that certainly must be heard in Siberia, and quarrel amongst themselves till the fur flies in all directions. This removal of the dogs on to the ice has imposed upon the watch the arduous duty of remaining on deck at nights, which was not the practice before. But a bear having once been on board and taken off two of our precious animals, we don't want any more such visitors.

"On July 31st 'Kvik' again increased our population by bringing eleven puppies into the world, one of which was deformed, and was at once killed; two

The 17th March procession celebrating Norwegian independence.

others died later, but most of them grew up and became fine handsome animals. They are still living.

"Few or no incidents occurred during this time, except, naturally, the different red-letter days were celebrated with great ceremony."

May 17th we observed with special pomp; [42] the following description of which I find in my journal:

"Friday, May 18th. May 17th was celebrated yesterday with all possible festivity. In the morning we were awakened with organ music — the enlivening strains of the 'College Hornpipe.' After this a splendid breakfast off smoked salmon, ox tongues, etc., etc. The whole ship's company wore bows of ribbon in honour of the day-even old 'Suggen' had one round his tail. The wind whistled, and the Norwegian flag floated on high, fluttering bravely at the masthead. About 11 o'clock the company assembled with their banners on the ice on the port side of the ship, and the procession arranged itself in order. First of all came the leader of the expedition with the 'pure' Norwegian flag; after him Sverdrup with the *Fram*'s pennant, which, with its 'FRAM' on a red ground, 3 fathoms long, looked splendid. Next came a dog-sledge, with the band (Johansen with the accordion), and Mogstad, as coachman; after them came the mate, with rifles and harpoons, Henriksen carrying a long harpoon; then Amundsen and Nordahl, with a red banner. The doctor followed, with a demonstration flag in favour of a normal working day. It consisted of a woollen jersey, with the letters 'N.A.'[43] embroidered on the breast, and at the top of a very long pole it looked most impressive. After him followed our chef Juell, with 'peik's'[44] saucepan on his back; and then came the meteorologists, with a curious apparatus, consisting of a large tin escutcheon, across which was fastened a red band, with the letters 'Al. St., signifying 'almindelig stemmeret,' or 'universal suffrage.'"[45]

"At last the procession began to move on. The dogs marched demurely, as if they had never done anything else in all their lives than walk in procession, and the band played a magnificent festive march, not composed for the occasion. The stately cortege marched twice round the *Fram* after which with great solemnity it moved off in the direction of the large hummock, and was photographed on the way by the photographer of the expedition. At the hummock a hearty cheer was given for the *Fram*, which had brought us hither so well, and which would, doubtless, take us equally well home again. After this the procession turned back, cutting across the *Fram*'s bow. At the port gangway a halt was called, and the photographer, mounting the bridge, made a speech in honour of the day. This was succeeded by a thundering salute, consisting of six shots, the result of which was that five or six of the dogs rushed off over hummocks and pressure-ridges, and hid themselves for several hours. Meanwhile we went down into the comfortable cabin, decorated with flags for the occasion in a right festive manner, where we partook of a splendid dinner, preluded by a lovely valse. The *menu* was as follows: Minced fish with curried lobster, melted butter and potatoes; music, pork cutlets, with green peas, potatoes, mango chutney, and Worcester sauce; music; apricots and custard, with cream ; much music. After this a siesta; then coffee, currants, figs, cakes ; and the photographer stood cigars. Great enthusiasm, then more siesta. After supper the violinist, Mogstad, gave a recital, when refreshments were served in the shape of figs, sweetmeats, apricots, and gingerbread (honey cakes). On the whole a charming and very successful Seventeenth of May, especially considering that we had passed the 81st degree of latitude.

"Monday, May 28th. I am tired of these endless, white plains-cannot even be bothered snow-shoeing over them, not to mention that the lanes stop one on every hand. Day and night I pace up and down the deck, along the ice by the ship's sides, revolving the most elaborate scientific problems. For the past few days it is especially the shifting of the Pole that has fascinated me. I am beset by the idea that the tidal wave, along with the unequal distribution of land and

A rest on the afterdeck, Hansen, Blessing, Sverdrup, Juell, Johansen, Pettersen, 16 June 1894.

sea, must have a disturbing effect on the situation of the earth's axis. When such an idea gets into one's head, it is no easy matter to get it out again. After pondering over it for several days, I have finally discovered that the influence of the moon on the sea must be sufficient to cause a shifting of the Pole to the extent of one minute in 800,000 years. In order to account for the European Glacial Age, which was my main object, I must shift the Pole at least ten or twenty degrees. This leaves an uncomfortably wide interval of time since that period, and shows that the human race must have attained a respectable age. Of course, it is all nonsense. But while I am indefatigably tramping the deck in a brown study, imagining myself no end of a great thinker, I suddenly discover that my thoughts are at home, where all is summer and loveliness, and those I have left are busy building castles in the air for the day when I shall return. Yes, yes. I spend rather too much time on this sort of thing ; but the drift goes as slowly as ever, and the wind, the all-powerful wind, is still the same. The first thing my eyes look for when I set foot on deck in the morning is the weathercock on the mizentop, to see how the wind lies; thither they are for ever straying during the whole day, and there again they rest. the last thing before I turn in. But it ever points in the same direction, west and south-west, and we drift now quicker, now more slowly westwards, and only a little to the north. I have no doubt now about the success of the expedition, and my miscalculation was not so great after all; but I scarcely think we shall drift higher than 85°, even if we do that. It will depend on how far Franz Josef Land extends to the north. In that case it will be hard to give up reaching the Pole; it is in reality a mere matter of vanity, merely child's play, in comparison with what we are doing; and hoping to do; and yet I must confess that I am foolish enough to want to take in the Pole while I am about it, and shall probably have a try at it if we get into its neighbourhood within any reasonable time.

"This is a mild May; the temperature has been about zero several times of late, and one can walk up and down and almost imagine one's self at home. There is seldom more than a few degrees of cold; but the summer fogs are beginning with occasional hoar frost. As a rule, however, the sky with its light, fleeting clouds is almost like a spring sky in the south.

"We notice, too, that it has become milder on board; we no longer need to light a fire in the stove to make ourselves warm and comfortable; though, indeed, we have never indulged in much luxury in this respect. In the store-room, the rime frost and ice that had settled on the ceiling and walls are beginning to melt; and in the compartments astern of the saloon, and in the hold, we have been obliged to set about a grand cleaning-up, scraping off and sweeping away the ice and rime, to save our provisions from taking harm, through the damp penetrating the wrappings, and rusting holes in the tin cases. We have, moreover, for a long time kept the hatchways in the hold open, so that there has been a thorough draught through it, and a good deal of the rime has evaporated. It is remarkable how little damp we have on board. No doubt this is due to the *Fram*'s solid construction, and to the deck over the hold being panelled on the underside. I am getting fonder and fonder of this ship."

"Saturday, June 9th. Our politician, Amundsen, is celebrating the day with a white shirt and collar.[46] To-day I have moved with my work up into the deck-house again, where I can sit and look out of the window in the day-time, and feel that I am living in the world and not in a cavern, where one must have lamplight night and day. I intend remaining here as long as possible out into the winter: it is so cosy and quiet, and the monotonous surroundings are not constantly forcing themselves in upon me.

I really have the feeling that summer has come. I can pace up and down the deck by the hour together with the sun, or stand still and roast myself in it, while I smoke a pipe, and my eyes glide over the confused masses of snow and ice. The snow is everywhere wet now, and pools are beginning to form every here and there. The ice too is getting more and more permeated with salt water; if one bores ever so small a hole in it, it is at once filled with water. The reason, of course, is that owing to the rise in the temperature, the particles of salt contained in the ice begin to melt their surroundings, and more and more water is formed with a good admixture of salt in it, so that its freezing point is lower than the temperature of the ice around it. This, too, had risen materially; at about 4 feet depth it is only 25.2° F. (−3.8° C.), at 5 feet it is somewhat warmer again, 26.5° F. (−3.1° C.).

"Sunday, June 10th. Oddly enough we have had no cases of snow-blindness on board, with the exception of the doctor, who, a couple of days ago, after we had been playing at ball, got a touch of it in the evening. The tears poured from his eyes for some time, but he soon recovered. Rather a humiliating trick of fate that he should be the first to suffer from this ailment." Subsequently we had a few isolated cases of slight snow-blindness, so that one or two of our men had to go about with dark spectacles; but it was of little importance and was due to their not thinking it worth while to take the necessary precautions.

"Monday, June 11th. To-day I made a joyful discovery. I thought I had begun my last bundle of cigars and calculated that by smoking one a day they would last a month, but found quite unexpectedly a whole box in my locker. Great rejoicing! it will help to while away a few more months, and where shall we be then? Poor fellow, you are really at a low ebb! 'To while away time'— that is an idea that has scarcely ever entered your head before. It has always been your great trouble that time flew away so fast, and now it cannot go fast enough to please you. And then so addicted to tobacco — you wrap yourself in clouds of smoke to indulge in your everlasting day dreams. Hark to the south wind, how it whistles in the rigging; it is quite inspiriting to listen to it. On Midsummer Eve we ought, of course, to have had a bonfire as usual, but from my diary it does not seem to have been the sort of weather for it.

> 'Mid the shady vales, and the leafy trees,
> How sweet the approach of the summer breeze;
> When the mountain slopes in the sunlight gleam,
> And the eve of St. John comes in like a dream.

The north wind continues with sleet. Gloomy weather. Drifting south. 81° 43′ N. lat., that is 9′ southward since Monday.

"I have seen many midsummer eve's under different shies, but never such a one as this. So far, far from all that one associates with this evening. I think of the merriment round the bonfires at home, hear the scraping of the fiddle, the peals of laughter, and the salvoes of the guns, with the echoes answering froth the purple tinted heights. And then I look out over this boundless, white expanse into the fog and sleet, and the driving wind. Here is truly no trace of midsummer merriment. It is a gloomy look-out altogether! Midsummer is past — and now the days are shortening again, and the long night of winter approaching, which, maybe, will find us as far advanced as it left us.

"I was busily engaged with my examination of the salinity of the sea water this afternoon, when Mogstad stuck his head in at the door, and said that a bear must be prowling about in the neighbourhood. On returning after dinner to their work at the great hummock, where they were busy making an ice-cellar for fresh meat,[47] the men found bear tracks which were not there before. I put on my snow-shoes and went after it. But what terrible going it had been the last few days! Soft slush, in which the snow-shoes sink helplessly. The bear had come from the west right up to the *Fram*, had stopped and inspected the work that was going on, had then retreated a little, made a considerable detour, and set off eastwards at its easy, shambling gait, without deigning pay any further attention

Nansen sitting in front of the stern of the *Fram*.

to such a trifle as a ship. It had rummaged about in every hole and corner where there seemed to be any chance of finding food, and had rooted in the snow after anything the dogs had left, or whatever else it might be. It had then gone to the lanes in the ice, and skirted them carefully, no doubt in the hope of finding a seal or two, and after that it had gone off between the hummocks and over floes, with a surface of nothing but slush and water. Had the surface been good I should no doubt have overtaken Master Bruin, but he had too long a start in the slushy snow.

"A dismal, dispiriting landscape — nothing but white and grey. No shadows — merely half obliterated forms melting into the fog and slush. Everything is in a state of disintegration, and one's foothold gives way at every step. It is hard work for the poor snow-shoer who stamps along through the slush and fog after bear tracks that wind in and out among the hummocks, or over them. The snow-shoes sink deep in, and the water often reaches up to the ankles, so that it is hard work to get them up or to force them forward; but without them one would be still worse off.

"Every here and there this monotonous greyish-whiteness is broken by the coal-black water, which winds, in narrower or broader lanes, in between the high hummocks. White, snow-laden floes and lumps of ice float on the dark surface, looking like white marble on a black ground. Occasionally there is a larger dark-coloured pool, where the wind gets a hold of the water and forms small waves that ripple and plash against the edge of the ice, the only signs of life in this desert tract. It is like an old friend the sound of these playful wave-lets! And here, too, they eat away the floes and hollow out their edges. One could almost imagine one's self in more southern latitudes. But all around is wreathed with ice, towering aloft in its ever-varying fantastic forms, in striking contrast to the dark water on which a moment before the eye had rested. Everlastingly is this shifting ice modelling, as it were, in pure, grey marble, and, with nature's lavish prodigality strewing around the most glorious statuary which perishes, without any eye having seen it. Wherefore? To what end all this shifting pageant of loveliness? It is governed by the mere caprices of nature, following out those everlasting laws, that pay no heed to what we regard as aims and objects.

"In front of me towers one pressure-ridge after another, with lane after lane between. It was in June the *Jeannette* was crushed and sank; what if the *Fram* were to meet her fate here! No, the ice will not get the better of her. Yet, if it should in spite of everything! As I stood gazing around me I remembered it was Midsummer Eve. Far away yonder, her masts pointed aloft, half lost to view in the snowy haze. They must, indeed, have stout hearts those fellows on board that craft. Stout hearts, or else blind faith in a man's word.

"It is all very well that he who has hatched a plan, be it never so wild, should go with it to carry it out; he naturally does his best for the child to which his thoughts have given birth. But they — they had no child to tend, and could, without feeling any yearning baulked, have refrained from taking part in an expedition like this. Why should any human being renounce life to be wiped out here?"

"Sunday, June 24th. The anniversary of our departure from home. Northerly wind; still drifting south. Observations to-day gave 81° 41′ 7″ N. lat., so we are not going at a breakneck speed.

"It has been a long year — a great deal has been gone through in it — though we are quite as far advanced as I had anticipated. I am sitting, and look out of the window at the snow, whirling round in eddies as it is swept along by the north wind. A strange Midsummer Day. One might think we had had enough of snow and ice; I am not, however, exactly pining after green fields — at all events, not always. On the contrary, I find myself sitting by the hour laying plans for other voyages into the ice after our return from this one... Yes, I know what I have attained, and, more or less, what awaits me. It is all very well for me to sketch plans for the future. But those at home... No, I am not in a humour for writing this evening; I will turn in."

"Wednesday, July 11th. Lat. 81° 18′ 8″. At last the southerly wind has returned, so there is an end of drifting south for the present.

"Now I am almost longing for the polar night, for the everlasting wonderland of the stars with the spectral northern lights, and the moon sailing through the profound silence. It is like a dream, like a glimpse into the realms of fantasy. There are no forms, no cumbrous reality — only a vision woven of silver and violet ether, rising up from earth and floating out into infinity... But this eternal day, with its oppressive actuality, interests me no longer — does not entice me out of my lair. Life is one incessant hurrying from one task to another, everything must be done and nothing neglected, day after day, week after week; and the working day is long, seldom ending till far over midnight. But through it all runs the same sensation of longing and emptiness, which must not be noted. But at times there is no holding it aloof, and the hands sink down without will or strength — so weary, so unutterably weary.

"Life's peace is said to be found by holy men in the desert. Here, indeed, there is desert enough; but peace — of that I know nothing. I suppose it is the holiness that is lacking.

"Wednesday, July 18th. Went on excursion with Blessing in the forenoon to collect specimens of the brown snow and ice, and gather seaweed and diatoms in the water. The upper surface of the floes is nearly everywhere of a dirty brown colour, or, at least, this sort of ice preponderates, while pure white floes, without any traces of a dirty brown on their surface, are rare. I imagined this brown colour must be due to the organisms I found in the newly-frozen, brownish-red ice last autumn (October); but the specimens I took to-day consist for the most part of mineral dust mingled with diatoms and other ingredients of organic origin.[48]

"Blessing collected several specimens on the upper surface of the ice earlier in the summer, and came to the same conclusions. I must look farther into this, in order to see whether all this brown dust is of a mineral nature, and consequently originates from the land.[49] We found in the lanes quantities of algae like what we had often found previously. There were large accumulations of them in nearly every little channel. We could also see that a brown surface layer spread itself on the sides of the floes far down into the water. This is due to an alga that grows on the ice. There were also floating in the water a number of small viscid lumps, some white, some of a yellowish-red colour; and of these I collected several. Under the microscope they all appeared to consist of accumulations of diatoms, among which, moreover, were a number of larger cellular organisms of a very characteristic appearance.[50] All of these diatomous accumulations kept at a certain depth, about a yard below the surface of the water; in some of the small lanes they appeared in large masses. At the same depth the above-named alga seemed especially to flourish, while parts of it rose up to the surface. It was evident that these accumulations of diatoms and alba remained floating exactly at the depth where the upper stratum of fresh water rests On the sea water. The water on the surface was entirely fresh, and the masses of diatoms sank in it, but floated on reaching the salt water below.

'Thursday, July 19th. It is as I expected. I am beginning to know the ways of the wind up here pretty well now. After having blown a 'windmill breeze' today it falls calm in the evening, and to-morrow we shall probably have wind from the west or north-west.

"Yesterday evening the last cigar out of the old box. And now I have smoked the first out of the last box I have got. We were to have got so far by the time that box was finished; but are scarcely any further advanced than when

Johansen and 'Sultan', 16 June 1894.

I began it, and goodness knows if we shall be that when this, too, has disappeared. But enough of that. Smoke away."

"Sunday, July 22nd. The north-west wind did not quite come up in time; on Friday we had north-east instead, and during the night it gradually went round to N.N.E., and yesterday forenoon it blew due north. To-day it has ended in the west, the old well known quarter, of which we have had more than enough. This evening the line[51] shows about N.W. to N., and it is strong, so we are moving south again.

"I pass the day at the microscope. I am now busied with the diatoms and algae of all kinds that grow on the ice in the uppermost fresh stratum of the sea. These are undeniably most interesting things, a whole new world of organisms that are carried off by the ice from known shores across the unknown Polar Sea, there to awaken every summer, and develop into life and bloom. Yes, it is very interesting work, but yet there is not that same burning interest as of old, although the scent of oil of cloves, Canada balsam, and wood-oil, awakens many dear reminiscences of that quiet laboratory at home, and every morning as I come in here the microscope and glasses and colours on the table invite me to work. But though I work indefatigably day after day till late in the night, it is mostly duty work, and I am not sorry when it is finished, to go and lie for some few hours in my berth reading a novel and smoking a cigar. With what exultation would I not throw the whole aside, spring up, and lay hold of real life, fighting my way over ice and sea with sledges, boats, or kayaks. It is more than true that it is 'easy to live a life of battle'; but here there is neither storm nor battle, and I thirst after them. I long to enlist titanic forces and fight my way forward — that would be living! But what pleasure is there in strength when there is nothing for it to do? Here we drift forward, and here we drift back, and now we have been two months on the same spot.

"Everything, however, is being got ready for a possible expedition, or for the contingency of its becoming necessary to abandon the ship. All the hand-sledges are lashed together, and the iron fittings carefully seen to. Six dog-sledges are also being made, and to-morrow we shall begin building 'kayaks' ready for the men. They are easy to draw on hand-sledges in case of a retreat over the ice without the ship. For a beginning we are making 'kayaks' to hold two men each. I intend to have them about 12 feet long, 3 feet wide, and 18 inches in depth. Six of these are to be made. They are to be covered with sealskin or sailcloth, and to be decked all over, except for two holes — one for each man.

"I feel that we have, or rather shall have, everything needful for a brilliant retreat. Sometimes I seem almost to be longing for a defeat — a decisive one — so that we might have a chance of showing what is in us, and putting an end to this irksome inactivity.

"Monday, July 30th. Westerly, wind, with north-westerly by way of a pleasant variety; such is our daily hare week after week On coming up in the morning, I no longer care to look at the weather-cock on the masthead, or at the line in the water; for I know beforehand that the former points east or south-east, and the line in the contrary direction, and that we are ever bearing to the south-east. Yesterday it was 81° 7′ N. lat., the day before 81° 11′, and last Monday, July 25th, 81° 26′.

"But it occupies my thoughts no longer. I know well enough there will be a change some time or other, and the way to the stars leads through adversity. I have found a new world; and that is the world of animal and plant life that exists in almost every fresh-water pool on the ice-floes. From morning till evening and till late in the night I am absorbed with the microscope, and see nothing around me; I live with these tiny beings in their separate universe, where they are born and die, generation after generation, where they pursue each other in the struggle for life, and carry on their love affairs with the same feelings, the same sufferings, and the same joys that permeate every living being, from these microscopic animalcules up to man — self-preservation and propagation, that is the whole story. Fiercely, as we human being, struggle to push our way on through the labyrinth of life, their struggles are assuredly no less fierce than ours — one incessant, restless hurrying to and fro, pushing all others aside, to burrow out for themselves what is needful to them. And as to love, only mark with what passion they seek each other out. With all our brain-cells we do not feel more strongly than they, never live so entirely for a sensation. But what is life? What matters the individual's suffering so long as the struggle goes on.

"And these are small, one-celled lumps of viscous matter, teeming in thousands and millions, on nearly every single floe over the whole of this boundless sea, which we are apt to regard as the realm of death. Mother Nature has a remarkable power of producing, life everywhere — even this ice is a fruitful soil for her.

"In the evening a little variety occurred in our uneventful existence, Johansen having discovered a bear to the south-east of the ship, but out of range. It had, no doubt, been prowling about for some time while we were below at supper, and had been quite near us; but being, alarmed by some sound or other, had gone off eastwards. Sverdrup and I set out after it, but to no purpose; the lanes hindered us too much, and moreover a fog came on, so that we had to return after having gone a good distance."

The world of organisms I above alluded to was the subject of special research through the short summer, and in many respects was quite remarkable. When the sun's rays had gained power on the surface of the ice, and melted the show, so that pools were formed, there was soon to be seen at the bottom of these pools small yellowish-brown spots, so small that at first one hardly noticed them. Day by day they increased in size, and absorbing, like all dark substances, the heat of the sun's rays, they gradually melted the underlying ice and formed round cavities, often several inches deep. These brown spots were the above mentioned algae and diatoms. They developed speedily in the summer light, and would fill the bottoms of the cavities with a thick layer. But there were not plants only, the water also teemed with swarms of animalcules, mostly infusoria and flagellata, which subsisted on the plants. I actually found bacteria — even these regions are not free from them!

But I could not always remain chained by the microscope. Sometimes when the fine weather tempted me irresistibly, I had to go out and bake myself in the sun, and imagine myself in Norway.

"Saturday, August 4th. Lovely weather yesterday and to-day. Light, fleecy clouds sailing high aloft through the sparkling, azure sky — filling one's soul with longings to soar as high and as free as they. I have just been out on deck this evening; one could almost imagine oneself at home by the fjord. Saturday evening's peace seemed to rest on the scene and on one's soul.

"Our sailmakers, Sverdrup and Amundsen, have to-day finished covering the first double kayak with sail-cloth. Fully equipped, it weighs 30.5 kilos. (60 lbs.). I think it will prove a first rate contrivance. Sverdrup and I tried it on a pool. It carried us splendidly, and was so stiff that even sitting on the deck we could handle it quite comfortably. It will easily carry two men with full equipment for 100 days. A handier or more practical craft for regions like this I cannot well imagine."

"Sunday, August 5th. 81° 7.3" N. lat.

"I can't forget the sparkling fjord
When the church boat rows in the morning."

"Brilliant summer weather. I bathe in the sun and dream I am at home

Blessing collecting samples of algae, 21 July 1894.

either on the high mountains or — heaven knows why — on the fjords of the west coast. The same white fleecy clouds in the clear blue summer sky; heaven arches itself overhead like a perfect dome, there is nothing to bar one's way, and the soul rises up unfettered beneath it. What matters it that the world below is different, the ice no longer single glittering glaciers, but spread out on every hand? Is it not these same fleecy clouds far away in the blue expanse that the eye looks for at home on a bright summer day? Sailing on these, fancy steers its course to the land of wistful longing. And it is just at these glittering glaciers in the distance that we direct our longing gaze. Why should not a summer day be as lovely here? It is lovely, pure as a dream, without desire, without sin, a poem of clear white sunbeams refracted in the cool crystal blue of the ice. How unutterably delightful does not this world appear to us on some stifling summer day at home?

"Have rested and 'kept Sunday.' I could not remain in the whole day, so took a long trip over the ice. Progress is easy except for the lanes.

"Hansen practised kayak-paddling this afternoon on the pool around the ship, from which several channels diverge over the ice, but he was not content with paddling round in them, but must, of course, make an experiment in capsizing and recovering himself as the Eskimos do. It ended by his not coming up again, losing his paddle, remaining head downwards in the water, and beating about with his hands till the 'kayak' filled, and he got a cold bath from top to toe. Nordahl who was standing by on the ice to help him, at last found it necessary to go in after him and raise him up on an even keel again, to the great amusement of us others.

"One can notice that it is summer. This evening a game of cards is being played on deck, with 'Peik's'[52] big pot for a card-table. One might almost think it was an August evening at home; only the toddy is wanting, but the pipes and cigars we have."

Sunday, August 12th. "We had a shooting competition in the forenoon.

"A glorious evening. I took a stroll over the ice among the lanes and hummocks. It was so wonderfully calm and still. Not a sound to be heard but the drip, drip of water from a block of ice, and the dull sound of a snow-slip from some hummock in the distance. The sun is low down in the north, and overhead is the pale blue dome of heaven, with gold-edged clouds. The profound peace of the Arctic solitude. My thoughts fly free and far. If one could only give utterance to all that stirs one's soul on such an evening as this! What an incomprehensible power one's surroundings have over one.

"Why is it that at times I complain of the loneliness? With Nature around one, with one's books and studies, one can never be quite alone."

"Thursday, August 16th. Yesterday evening, as I was lying in my berth reading, and all except the watch had turned in, I heard the report of a gun on deck over my head. Thinking it was a bear, I hurriedly put on my sea boots and sprang on deck. There I saw Johansen bare-headed, rifle in hand. 'Was it you that fired the shot?' 'Yes. I shot at the big hummock yonder — I thought something was stirring there, and I wanted to see what it was, but it seems to have been nothing.' I went to the railings, and looked out. 'I fancied it was a bear that was after our meat — but it was nothing.' As we stood there one of the dogs came jogging along from the big hummock. 'Then you see what you have shot at,' I said, laughing. 'I'm bothered if it wasn't a dog!' he replied. 'Ice-bear' it was, true enough, for so we called this dog. It had seemed so large in the fog, scratching at the meat-hummock. 'Did you aim at the dog and miss' That was a lucky chance!' 'No! I simply fired at random in that direction, for I wanted to see what it was.' I went below and turned in again. At breakfast to-day he had, of course, to run the gauntlet of some sarcastic questions about his 'harmless thunder-bolt,' but he parried them adroitly enough.

"Tuesday, August 21. North latitude, 81° 4.2'. Strange how little alteration there is — we drift a little to the north, then a little to the south, and keep almost to the same spot. But I believe, as I have believed all along, since before we even set out, that we should be away three years, or rather three winters and four summers, neither more nor less, and that in about two years' time from this present autumn we shall reach home.[53] The approaching winter will drift us further, however slowly, and it begins already to announce itself, for there were four degrees of cold last night."

"Sunday, August 26th, It seems almost as if winter had come, the cold has kept on an average between 24.8° F. (−4° C.) and 21.2° F. (−6° C.) since Thursday. There are only slight variations in the temperature up here, so we may expect it to fall regularly from this time forth, though it is rather early for winter to set in. All the pools and lanes are covered with ice, thick enough to bear a man, even without snow-shoes.

"I went out on my snow-shoes both morning and afternoon. The surface was beautiful everywhere. Some of the lanes had opened out, or been compressed a little, so that the new ice was thin, and bent unpleasantly under the snow-shoes; but it bore me, though two of the dogs fell through. A good deal of snow had fallen, so there was fine, soft new snow to travel over. If it keeps on as it is now, there will be excellent snow-shoeing in the winter; for it is fresh water that now freezes on the surface, so that there is no salt that the wind can carry from the new ice to spoil the snow all around, as was the case last winter. Such snow with salt in it makes as heavy a surface as sand.

"Monday, August 27th. Just as Blessing was going below after his watch to-night, and was standing by the rail looking out, he saw a white form that lay rolling in the snow a little way off to the south-east. Afterwards it remained for a while lying, quite still. Johansen, who was to relieve Blessing, now joined him, and they both stood watching the animal intently. Presently it got up, so there was no longer any doubt as to what it was. Each got hold of a rifle and crept stealthily towards the forecastle, where they waited quietly while the bear cautiously approached the ship, making long tacks against the wind A fresh breeze was blowing, and the windmill going round at full speed; but this did not alarm him at all; very likely it was this very thing he wanted to examine. At last he reached the lane in front, when they both fired and he fell down dead on the spot. It was nice to get fresh meat again. This was the first bear we had shot this year, and of course we had roast bear for dinner to-day. Regular winter with snowstorms."

"Wednesday, August 29th. A fresh wind; it rattles and pipes in the rigging aloft. An enlivening change and no mistake. The snow drifts as if it were mid-winter. Fine August weather! But we are bearing north again, and we have need to. Yesterday our latitude was 80° 53' 5". This evening I was standing in the hold at work on my new bamboo kayak, which will be the very acme of lightness. Pettersen happened to come down and gave me a hand with some lashings that I was busy with. We chatted a little about things in general; and he was of opinion 'that we had a good crib of it on board the *Fram*, because here we had everything we wanted, and she was a devil of a ship — and any other ship would have been crushed flat long ago.' But for all that he would not be afraid, he said, to leave her, when he saw all the contrivances, such as these new kayaks, we had been getting ready. He was sure no former expedition had ever had such contrivances, or been so equipped against all possible emergencies as we. But, after all, he would prefer to return home on the *Fram*." Then we talked about what we should do when we did get home.

"'Oh, for your part, no doubt you'll be off to the South Pole,' he said.

"'And you?' I replied. 'Will you tuck up your sleeves and begin again at the old work?'

"'Oh, very likely! but on my word I ought to have a week's holiday first.

Nansen going for a walk with his camera.

After such a trip I should want it, before buckling to at the sledge hammer again.'"

Chapter 8

Second Autumn in the Ice

So summer was over, and our second autumn and winter were beginning. But we were now more inured to the trials of patience attendant on this life, and time passed quickly. Besides, I myself was now taken up with new plans and preparations. Allusion has several times been made to the fact that we had, during the course of the summer, got everything into readiness for the possibility of having to make our way home across the ice. Six double kayaks had been built, the hand sledges were in good order, and careful calculation had been made of the amount of food, clothing, fuel, etc., that it would be necessary to carry. But I had also quietly begun to make preparations for my own meditated expedition north. In August, as already mentioned, I had begun to work at a single kayak, the framework made of bamboo. I had said nothing about my plan yet, except a few words to Sverdrup; it was impossible to tell how far north the drift would take us, and so many things might happen before spring.

In the meantime life on board went on as usual. There were the regular observations and all sorts of occupations, and I myself was not so absorbed in my plans that I did not find time for other things too. Thus I see from my diary that in the end of August and in September I must have been very proud of a new invention that I made for the galley. All last year we had cooked on a particular kind of copper range, heated by petroleum lamps. It was quite satisfactory, except that it burned several quarts of petroleum a day. I could not help fearing sometimes that our lighting supply might run short, if the expedition lasted longer than was expected, and always wondered if it would not be possible to construct an apparatus that would burn coal-oil 'black-oil,' as we call it on board — of which we had 20 tons, originally intended for the engine.

And I succeeded in making such an apparatus. On August 30th I write: "Have tried my newly-invented coal-oil apparatus for heating the range, and it is beyond expectation successful. It is splendid that we shall be able to burn coal-oil in the galley. Now there is no fear of our having to cry ourselves blind for lack of light bye-and-bye. This adds more than 4,000 gallons to our stock of oil; and we can keep all our fine petroleum now for lighting purposes, and have lamps for many a year, even if we are a little extravagant. The 20 tons of coal-oil ought to keep the range going for 4 years, I think.

"The contrivance is as simple as possible. From a reservoir of oil a pipe leads down and in to the fireplace; the oil drips down from the end of this pipe into an iron bowl, and is here sucked up by a sheet of asbestos, or by coal ashes. The flow of oil from the pipe is regulated by a fine valve cock. To ensure a good draught, I bring a ventilating pipe from outside right by the range door. Air is pressed through this by a large wind-sail on deck, and blows straight on to the iron bowl, where the oil burns briskly with a clear, white flame. Whoever lights the fire in the morning has only to go on deck and see that the wind-sail is set to the wind, to open the ventilator, to turn the cock so that the oil runs properly, and then set it burning with a scrap of paper. It looks after itself, and the water is boiling in twenty minutes or half-an-hour. One could not have anything much easier than this, it seems to me. But of course in our as in other communities, it is difficult to introduce reforms; everything new is looked upon with suspicion."

Somewhat later I write of the same apparatus: "We are now using the galley again, with the coal-oil fire; the moving down took place the day before yesterday,[54] and the fire was used yesterday. It works capitally; a 3-foot wind is enough to give a splendid draught. The day before yesterday, when I was sitting with some of the others in the saloon in the afternoon, I heard a dull report out in the galley, and said at once that it sounded like an explosion. Presently Pettersen[55] stuck a head in at the door as black as a sweep's, great lumps of soot all over it, and said that the stove had exploded right into his face; he was only going to look if it was burning rightly, and the whole fiendish thing flew out at him. A stream of words not unmingled with oaths flowed like peas out of a sack, while the rest of us yelled with laughter. In the galley it was easy to see that something had happened; the walls were covered with soot in lumps and stripes pointing towards the fire-place. The explanation of the accident was simple enough. The draught had been insufficient, and a quantity of gas had formed

Henriksen looking at the *Fram*.

which bad not been able to burn until air was let in by Pettersen opening the door.

"This is a good beginning. I told Pettersen in the evening that I would do the cooking myself next day, when the real trial was to be made. But he would not hear of such a thing; he said 'I was not to think that he minded a trifle like that; I might trust to its being all right' — and it was all right. From that day I heard nothing but praise of the new apparatus, and it was used until the *Fram* was out in the open sea again.

"Thursday, September 6th. 81° 13.7' N. lat. Have I been married five years to-day? Last year this was a day of victory — when the ice-fetters burst at Taimur Island — but there is no thought of victory now; we are not so far north as I had expected; the north-west wind has come again, and we are drifting south. And yet the future does not seem to me so long and so dark as it sometimes has done. Next September 6th,…can it be possible that then every fetter will have burst, and we shall be sitting together talking of this time in the far north and of all the longing, as of something that once was and that will never be again. The long, long night is past; the morning is just breaking, and a glorious new day lies before us. And what is there against this happening next year? Why should not this winter carry the *Fram* west to some place north of Franz Josef Land?... and then my time has come, and off I go with dogs and sledges — to the north. My heart beats with joy at the very thought of it. The winter shall be spent in making every preparation for that expedition, and it will pass quickly.

"I have already spent much time on these preparations. I think of everything that must be taken, and how it is to be arranged, and the more I look at the thing from all points of view, the more firmly convinced do I become that the attempt will be successful, if only the *Fram* can get north in reasonable time, not too late in the spring. If she could just reach 84° or 85°, then I should be off in the end of February or the first days of March, as soon as the daylight comes, after the long winter night, and the whole would go like a dance. Only four or five months, and the time for action will have come again. What joy! When I look out over the ice now, it is as if my muscles quivered with longing to be striding off over it in real earnest-fatigue and privation will then be a delight. It may seem foolish that I should be determined to go off on this expedition, when, perhaps, I might do more important work quietly here on board. But the daily observations will be carried on exactly the same.

"I have celebrated the day by arranging my work-room for the winter. I have put in a petroleum stove, and expect that this will make it warm enough even in the coldest weather, with the snow walls that I intend to build round the outside of it, and a good roof-covering of snow. At least, double the amount of work will be done if this cabin can be used in winter, and I can sit up here instead of in the midst of the racket below. I have such comfortable times of it now, in peace and quietness, letting my thoughts take their way unchecked.

"Sunday, September 9th. 81° 4' N. lat. The midnight sun disappeared some days ago, and already the sun sets in the north-west; it is gone by 10 o'clock in the evening, and there is once more a glow over the eternal white. Winter is coming fast.

"Another peaceful Sunday, with rest from work, and a little reading. Out snow-shoeing to-day I crossed several frozen-over lanes, and very slight packing has begun here and there. I was stopped at last by a broad open lane lying pretty nearly north and south; at places it was 400 to 500 yards across, and I saw no end to it either north or south. The surface was good; one got along quickly, with no exertion at all when it was in the direction of the wind.

"This is undeniably a monotonous life. Sometimes it feels to me like a long dark night, my life's Ragnarok ["Twilight of the Gods"], dividing it into two... 'The sun is darkened, the summers with it, all weather is weighty with woe'; snow covers the earth, the wind whistles over the endless plains, and for three years this winter lasts, till comes the time for the great battle, and 'men tramp Hell's way.' There is a hard struggle between life and death; but after that comes the reign of peace. The earth rises from the sea again, and decks itself anew with verdure. Torrents roar, eagles hover over them watching for fish among the rocks,' and then 'Valhalla,' fairer than the sun and long length of happy days.

"Pettersen, who is cook this week, came in here this evening, as usual, to get the bill of fare for next day. When his business was done, he stood for a minute, and then said that he had had such a strange dream last night; he had wanted to be taken as cook with a new expedition, but Dr. Nansen wouldn't have him.

"'And why not?'

"'Well, this was how it was. I dreamed that Dr. Nansen was going off across the ice to the Pole with four men, and I asked to be taken, but you said that you didn't need a cook on this expedition, and I thought that was queer enough, for you would surely want food on this trip as well. It seemed to me that you had ordered the ship to meet you at some other place; anyhow you were not coming back here, but to some other land. It's strange that one can lie and rake up such a lot of nonsense in one's sleep.'

"'That was perhaps not such very great nonsense, Pettersen; it is quite possible that we might have to make such an expedition, but if we did, we should certainly not come back to the *Fram.*'

"'Well, if that happened, I would ask to go, sure enough; for it's just what I should like. I'm no great snow-shoer, but I would manage to keep up somehow.'

"'That's all very well; but there's a great deal of weary hard work on a journey like that; you needn't think it's all pleasure.'

"'No, no one would expect that; but it would be all right if I might only go.'

"'But there might be worse than hardships, Pettersen. It would more than likely mean risking your life.'

"'I don't care for that either. A man has got to die some time.

"'Yes, but you don't want to shorten your life?'

"'Oh, I would take my chance of that. You can lose your life at home, too, though, perhaps, not quite so easily as here. But if a man was always to be thinking about that he would never do anything.'

"'That's true. Anyhow he would not need to come on an expedition like this. But remember that a journey northward over the ice would be no child's play.'

"'No, I know that well enough, but if it was with you I shouldn't be afraid. It would never do if we had to manage alone. We'd be sure to go wrong; but it's quite a different thing, you see, when there is one to lead that you know has been through it all before.'

"It is extraordinary the blind faith such men have in their leader! I believe they would set off without a moment's reflection if they were asked to join in an expedition to the Pole now, with black winter at the door. It is grand as long as the faith lasts, but God be merciful to him on the day that it fails!"

"Saturday, September 15th. This evening we have seen the moon again for the first time — beautiful full moon, and a few stars were also visible in the night sky, which is still quite light.

"Notices were posted in several places to-day. They ran as follows:

"As fire here on board might be followed by the most terrible consequences, too great precaution cannot be taken. For this reason every man is requested to observe the following rules most conscientiously:

1. No one is to carry matches.

2. The only places where matches may be kept are:

(1) The galley, where the cook for the time being is responsible for them.

(2) The four single cabins, where the inmate of each is responsible for his box.

(3) The work-cabin, when work is going on.

(4) On the mast in the saloon, from which neither box nor single matches must be taken away under any circumstances.

3. Matches must not be struck anywhere except in the places above named.

4. The one exception to the above rules is made when the forge has to be lighted.

5. All the ship's holds are to be inspected every evening at 8 o'clock by the fire-inspector, who will give in his report to the undersigned. After that time no one may, without special permission, take a light into the holds or into the engine-room.

Dog kennels being built alongside the *Fram*, 17 September 1894.

6. Smoking is only allowed in the living-rooms and on deck. Lighted pipes or cigars must on no account be seen elsewhere.

FRIDTJOF NANSEN. *Fram*, September 15th, 1894

"Some of these regulations may seem to infringe on the principle of equality which I have been so anxious to maintain; but these seem to me the best arrangements I can make to ensure the good of all — and that must come before everything else."

"Friday, September 21st. We have had tremendously strong wind from the north-west and north for some days, with a velocity at times of 39 and 42 feet. During this time we must have drifted a good way south. 'The Radical Right' had got hold of the helm, said Amundsen; but their time in power was short; for it fell calm yesterday, and now we are going north again, and it looks as if the 'Left' were to have a spell at the helm, to repair the wrongs done by the 'Right.'

"Kennels for the dogs have been built this week — a row of splendid ice-houses along the port side of the ship; four dogs in each house; good warm winter quarters. In the meantime our eight little pups are thriving on board; they have a grand world to wander round — the whole fore-deck, with an awning over it. You can hear their little barks and yelps as they rush about among shavings, hand-sledges, the steam-winch, mill axle, and other odds and ends. They play a little, and they fight a little, and forward under the forecastle they have their bed among the shavings, a very comfortable corner, where 'Kvik' lies stretched out like a lioness in all her majesty. There they tumble over each other in a heap round her, sleep, yawn, eat, and pull each other's tails. It is a picture of home and peace here near the Pole, which one could watch by the hour.

"Life goes its regular, even, uneventful way, quiet as the ice itself; and yet it is wonderful how quickly the time passes. The equinox has come, the nights are beginning to turn dark, and at noon the sun is only 9 degrees above the horizon. I pass the day busily here in the work cabin, and often feel as if I were sitting in my study at home, with all the comforts of civilisation round me. If it were not for the separation, one could be as well off here as there. Sometimes I forget where I am. Not infrequently in the evening, when I have been sitting absorbed in work, I have jumped up to listen when the dogs barked, thinking to myself: who can be coming? Then I remember that I am not at home, but drifting out in the middle of the frozen Polar Sea, at the commencement of the second long Arctic night.

"The temperature has been down to 1.4° F. below zero (−17° C.) to-day; winter is coming on fast. There is little drift just now, and yet we are in good spirits. It was the same last autumn equinox; but how many disappointments we have had since then! How terrible it was in the later autumn when every calculation seemed to fail, as we drifted farther and farther south! Not one bright spot on our horizon! But such a time will never come again. There may still be great relapses; there may be slow progress for a time; but there is no doubt as to the future; we see it dawning bright in the west, beyond the Arctic night."

"Sunday, September 23rd. It was a year yesterday since we made fast for the first time to the great hummock in the ice. Hansen improved the occasion by making a chart of our drift for the year. It does not look so very bad, though the distance is not great, the direction is almost exactly what I had expected. But more of this to-morrow; it is so late that I cannot write about it now. The nights are turning darker and darker; winter is settling down upon us."

"Tuesday, September 25th. I have been looking more carefully at the calculation of our last year's drift. If we reckon from the place where we were shut in on the 22nd of September last year, to our position on the 22nd of September this year, the distance we have drifted is 189 miles, equal to 3' 9' lat. Reckoning from the same place, but to the farthest north point we reached in summer (July 16th), makes the drift 225 miles, or 3° 46'. But if we reckon from our most southern point in the autumn of last year (November 7th), to our most northern point this summer, then the drift is 305 miles, or 5° 5'. We got fully 4° north, from 77° 43' to 81° 53'. To give the course of the drift is a difficult task in these latitudes, as there is a perceptible deviation of the compass with every degree of longitude as one passes east or west; the change, of course, given in degrees will be almost exactly the same as the number of degrees of longitude that have been passed. Our average course will be about N. 36° W. The direction of our drift is consequently a much more northerly one than the *Jeannette's* was, and this is just what we expected; ours cuts hers at an angle of 59°. The line of this year's drift continued will cut the north-east island of Spitzbergen, and take us as far north as 84° 7', in 75° E. long., somewhere N.N.E. of Franz Josef Land. The distance by this course to the North East Island is 827 miles. Should we continue to progress only at the rate of 189 miles a year, it would take us 4.4 years to do this distance. But assuming our progress to be at the rate of 305 miles a year, we shall do it in 2.7 years. That we should drift at least as quickly as this seems probable, because we can hardly now be driven back as we were in October last year, when we had the open water to the south, and the great mass of ice to the north of us.

The past summer seems to me to have proved that while the ice is very unwilling to go back south, it is most ready to go north-west as soon as there is ever so little easterly, not to mention southerly wind. I therefore believe, as I always have believed, that the drift will become faster as we get farther north-west, and the probability is that the *Fram* will reach Norway in two years, the expedition having lasted its full three years, as I somehow had a feeling that it would. As our drift is 59° more northerly than the *Jeannette's*, and as Franz Josef Land must force the ice north (taking for granted that all that comes from this great basin goes round to the north of Franz Josef Land), it is probable that our course will become more northerly the farther on we go, until we are past Franz Josef Land, and that we shall consequently reach a higher latitude than our drift so far would indicate. I hope 85° at least. Everything has come right so far; the direction of our drift is exactly parallel with the course which I conjectured to have been taken by the floe with the *Jeannette* relics, and which I pricked out on the chart prepared for my London Address.[56] This course touched about 87½° N. lat. I have no right to expect a more northerly drift than parallel to this, and have no right to be anything but happy if I get as far. Our aim, as I have so often tried to make clear, is not so much to reach the point 'in which the earth's axis terminates,' as to traverse and explore the unknown Polar Sea; and yet I should like to get to the Pole, too, and hope that it will be possible to do so, if only we can reach 84° or 85° by March — and why should we not?"

"Thursday, September 27th. Have determined that, beginning from to-morrow, every man is to go out snow-shoeing two hours daily, from 11 to 13 so long as the daylight lasts. It is necessary. If anything happened that obliged us to make our way home over the ice, I am afraid some of the company would be a terrible hindrance to us, unpractised as they are now. Several of them are first-rate snow-shoers, but five or six of them would soon be feeling the pleasures of learning; if they had to go out on a long course, and without snow-shoes, it would be all over with us.

"After this we used to go out regularly in a body. Besides being good exercise, it was also a great pleasure; every one seemed to thrive on it, and they all became accustomed to the use of the shoes on this ground, even though they often got them broken 'in the unevennesses of the pressure-ridges; we just patched and riveted them together to break them again."

"Monday, October 1st. We tried a hand-sledge to-day with a load of 250 lbs. It went along easily, and yet was hard to draw, because the snow-shoes were apt to slip to the side on the sort of surface we had. I almost believe that Indian snow-shoes would be better on this ground, where there are so many knobs and smooth hillocks to draw the sledges over. When Amundsen first began to pull the sledge, he thought it was nothing at all; but when he had gone on for a time he fell into a fit of deep and evidently sad thought, and went silently home. When he got on board, he confided to the others that if a man had to draw a load like that, he might just as well lie down at once — it would come to the same thing in the end. That is how practice is apt to go. In the afternoon I yoked three dogs to the same little sledge with the 250 lbs. load, and they drew it along as if it were nothing at all."

"Tuesday, October 2nd. Beautiful weather, but coldish; 49° F. of frost (−27° C.) during the night, which is a good deal for October, surely. It will be a cold winter if it goes on at the same rate. But what do we care whether there are 90° of frost or 120°? A good snow-shoeing excursion to-day. They are all becoming most expert now; but darkness will be on us presently, and then there will be no

A skiing trip, Amundsen, Henriksen, Mogstad, Blessing and Sverdrup.

more of it. It is a pity; this exercise is so good for us — we must think of something to take its place.

"I have a feeling now as if this were to be my last winter on board. Will it really come to my going off north in spring? The experiment in drawing a loaded hand-sledge over this ice was certainly anything but promising; and if the dogs should not hold out, or should be of less use than we expect; and if we should come to worse ice instead of better — well, we should only have ourselves to trust to. But if we can just get so far on with the *Fram* that the distance left to be covered is at all a reasonable one, I believe that it is my duty to make the venture, and I cannot imagine any difficulty that will not be overcome when our choice lies between death — and onward and home!"

"Thursday, October 4th. The ice is rather impassable in places, but there are particular lanes or tracts; taking it altogether, it is in good condition for sledging and snow-shoeing, though the surface is rather soft, so that the dogs sink in a little. This is probably chiefly owing to there having been no strong winds of late, so that the snow has not been well packed together.

"Life goes on in the regular routine; there is always some little piece of work turning up to be done. Yesterday the breaking in of the young dogs began.[57] It was just the three 'Barbara,' 'Freia,' and 'Surine.' 'Gulabrand' is such a miserable, thin wretch, that he is escaping for the present. They were unmanageable at first, and rushed about in all directions; but in a little while they drew like old dogs, and were altogether better than we expected. 'Kvik,' of course, set them a noble example. It fell to Mogstad's lot to begin the training, as it was his week for looking after the dogs. This duty is taken in turns now, each man has his week of attending to them both morning and afternoon.

"It seems to me that a very satisfactory state of feeling prevails on board at present, when we are just entering on our second Arctic night, which we hope is to be a longer, and probably also a colder one, than any people before us have experienced. There is appreciably less light every day; soon there will be none; but the good spirits do not wane with the light. It seems to me that we are more uniformly cheerful than we have ever been. What the reason of this is I cannot tell; perhaps just custom. But certainly, too, we are well off — in clover, as the saying is. We are drifting gently, but it is to be hoped surely, on through the dark unknown Nivlheim, where terrified fancy has pictured all possible horrors. Yet we are living a life of luxury and plenty, surrounded by all the comforts of civilisation. I think we shall be better off this winter than last.

"The firing apparatus in the galley is working splendidly, and the cook

Skiing contest on a hill.

himself is now of opinion that it is an invention which approaches perfection. So we shall burn nothing but coal-oil there now; it warms the place well, and a good deal of the heat comes up here into the work-room, where I sometimes sit and perspire until I have to take off one garment after another, although the window is open and there are 30 odd degrees of cold outside. I have calculated that the petroleum which this enables us to keep for lighting purposes only, will last at least 10 years, though we burn it freely 300 days in the year. At present we are not using petroleum lamps at the rate assumed in my calculation, because we frequently have electric light; and then even here summer comes once a year, or, at any rate, something which we must call summer. Even allowing for accidents, such as the possibility of a tank springing a leak and the oil running out, there is still no reason whatever for being sparing of light, and every man can have as much as he wants. What this meas can best be appreciated by one who, for a whole year, has felt the stings of conscience every time he went to work or read alone in his cabin, and burned a lamp that was not absolutely necessary, because he could have used the general one in the saloon.

"As yet the coals are not being touched, except for the stove in the saloon, where they are to be allowed to burn as much as they like this winter. The quantity thus consumed will be a trifle in comparison with our store of about 100 tons, for which we cannot well have any other use until the *Fram* once more forces her way out of the ice on the other side. Another thing that is of no little help in keeping us warm and comfortable, is the awning that is now stretched over the ship.[58] The only part I have left open is the stern, abaft the bridge, so as to be able to see round over the ice from there.

"Personally, I must say that things are going well with me; much better than I could have expected. Time is a good teacher: that devouring longing does not gnaw so hard as it did. Is it apathy beginning Shall I feel nothing at all by the time ten years have passed? Oh! sometimes it comes on with all its old strength — as if it would tear me in pieces! But this is a splendid school of patience. Much good it does to sit wondering whether they are alive or dead at home; it only almost drives one mad.

"All the same, I never grow quite reconciled to this life. It is really neither life nor death, but a state between the two. It means never being at rest about anything or in any place — a constant waiting for what is coming; a waiting in which, perhaps, the best years of one's manhood will pass. It is like what a young boy sometimes feels when he goes on his first voyage. The life on board is hateful to him; he suffers cruelly from all the torments of sea-sickness; and being shut in within the narrow walls of the ship is worse than prison; but it is something that has to be gone through. Beyond it all lies the south, the land of his youthful dreams, tempting with its sunny smile. In time he arises, half dead. Does he find his south? How often it is but a barren desert he is cast ashore on!"

"Sunday, October 7th. It has cleared up this evening, and there is a starry sky and aurora borealis. It is a little change from the constant cloudy weather, with frequent snow-showers, which we have had these last days.

"Thoughts come and thoughts go. I cannot forget, and I cannot sleep. Everything is still; all are asleep. I only hear the quiet step of the watch on deck; the wind rustling in the rigging and the canvas, and the clock gently hacking the time in pieces there on the wall. If I go on deck there is black night, stars sparkling high overhead, and faint aurora flickering across the gloomy vault, and out in the darkness I can see the glimmer of the great monotonous plain of the ice, it is all so inexpressibly forlorn, so far, far removed from the noise and unrest of men and all their striving. What is life thus isolated? A strange, aimless process; and man a machine which eats, sleeps, awakes: eats and sleeps again, dreams dreams, but never lives. Or is life really nothing else? And is it just one more phase of the eternal martyrdom, a new mistake of the erring human soul, this banishing of one's self to the hopeless wilderness, only to long there for what one has left behind? Am I a coward? Am I afraid of death? Oh, no! but in these nights such longing can come over one for all beauty, for that which is

Skiing trip with a dogsled.

contained in a single word, and the soul flees from this interminable and rigid world of ice. When one thinks how short life is, and that one came away from it all of one's own free will, and remembers, too, that another is suffering the pain of constant anxiety, 'true, true till death.' 'Oh, mankind, thy ways are passing strange! We are but as flakes of foam, helplessly driven over the tossing sea.'

"Wednesday, October 10th. Exactly 33 years old, then. There is nothing to be said to that, except that life is moving on, and will never turn back. They have all been touchingly nice to me to-day, and we have held fête. They surprised me in the morning by having the saloon ornamented with flags. They had hung the 'Union' above Sverdrup's place. We accused Amundsen of having done this, but he would not confess to it. Above my door and over Hansen's they had the pennant with *Fram* in big letters. It looked most festive when I came into the saloon, and they all stood up and wished me 'Many happy returns.' When I went on deck the flag was waving from the mizzen mast-head.

"We took a snow-shoeing excursion south in the morning. It was windy, bitter weather; I have not felt so cold for long. The thermometer is down to 24° F. below zero (−31° C.) this evening; this is certainly the coldest birthday I have had yet. A sumptuous dinner: 1. Fish-pudding. 2. Sausages and tongue, with potatoes, haricot beans, and peas. 3. Preserved strawberries, with rice and cream. Crown extract of malt. Then, to everyone's surprise, our doctor began to take out of the pocket of the overcoat he always wears, remarkable-looking little glasses — medicine glasses, measuring glasses, test glasses — one for each man, and lastly a whole bottle of Lysholmer liqueur, real native Lysholmer, which awakened general enthusiasm. Two drams of that per man was not so bad, besides a quarter of a bottle of extract of malt. Coffee after dinner, with a surprise in the shape of apple cake, baked by our excellent cook, Pettersen, formerly smith and engineer. Then I had to produce my cigars, which were also much enjoyed; and of course we kept holiday all the afternoon. At supper there was another surprise, a large birthday cake, from the same baker, with the inscription: 'T.L.M.D.' (Til lykke med dagen, the Norwegian equivalent for: Wishing you a happy birthday) '10.10.94.' In the evening came pineapples, figs, and sweets. Many a worse birthday might be spent in lower latitudes than 81°. The evening is passing with all kinds of merriment, every one is in good spirits; the saloon resounds with laughter — how many a merry meeting it has seen!

"But when one has said good-night and sits here alone, sadness comes; and if one goes on deck, there are the stars high overhead in the clear sky. In the south is a smouldering aurora arch, which from time to time sends up streamers; a constant restless flickering.

"We have been talking a little about this expedition, Sverdrup and I. When we were out on the ice in the afternoon he suddenly said: 'Yes, next October you will, perhaps, not be on board the *Fram*.' To which I had to answer that, unless the winter turned out badly, I probably should not. But still I cannot believe in this rightly myself.

"Every night I am at home in my dreams, but when the morning breaks I must again, like Helge, gallop back on the pale horse by the way of the reddening dawn, not to the joys of Valhalla, but to the realm of eternal ice:

> "For thee alone Sigrun,
> Of the Saeva Mountain,
> Must Helge swim
> In the dew of sorrow."

"Friday, October 12th. A regular storm has been blowing from the E.S.E. since yesterday evening. Last night the mill went to bits; the teeth broke off one of the toothed wheels, which has been considerably worn by a year's use. The velocity of the wind was over 40 feet this morning, and it is long since I have heard it blow as it is doing this evening. We must be making good progress north just now. Perhaps October is not to be such a bad month as I expected from our experiences of last year. Was out snow-shoeing before dinner. The snow

Sverdrup in his cabin.

was whistling about my ears. I had not much trouble in getting back; the wind saw to that. A tremendous snow squall is blowing just now. The moon stands low in the southern sky, sending a dull glow through the driving masses. One has to hold on to one's cap. This is a real dismal polar night, such as one imagines it to oneself sitting at home far away in the south. But it makes me cheerful to come on deck, for I feel that we are moving onward.

"Saturday, October 13th. Same wind to-day; velocity up to 39 feet and higher, but Hansen has taken an observation this evening in spite of it. He is, as always, a fine, indefatigable fellow. We are going north-west (81° 32' 8" N. lat., 118° 28' E. long.).

"Sunday, October 14th. Still the same storm going on. I am reading of the continual sufferings which the earlier Arctic explorers had to contend with for every degree, even for every minute, of their northward course. It gives me almost a feeling of contempt for us, lying here on sofas, warm and comfortable, passing the time reading, and writing, and smoking, and dreaming, while the storm is tugging and tearing at the rigging above us, and the whole sea is one mass of driving snow, through which we are carried degree by degree northwards to the goal our predecessors struggled towards, spending their strength in vain. And yet...

'Now sinks the sun, now comes the night.'

"Monday, October 15th. Went snow-shoeing east-wards this morning, still against the same wind and the same snowfall. You have to pay careful attention to your course these days, as the ship is not visible any great distance, and, if you did not find your way back, well — . But the tracks remain pretty distinct, as the snow-crust is blown bare in most places, and the drifting snow does not fasten upon it. We are moving northwards, and meanwhile the Arctic night is making its slow and majestic entrance. The sun was low to-day; I did not see it because of banks of cloud in the south, but it still sent its light up over the pale sky. There the full moon is now reigning, bathing the great ice plain and the drifting snow in its bright light. How a night such as this raises one's thoughts! It does not matter if one has seen the like a thousand dines before: it makes the same solemn impression when it comes again; one cannot free one's mind from its power. It is like entering a still, holy temple, where the spirit of nature hovers through the place on glittering silver beams, and the soul must fall down and adore — adore the infinity of the universe.

"Wednesday, October 17th. We are employed in taking deep-water temperatures. It is a doubtful pleasure at this time of year. Sometimes the water-lifter gets coated with ice, so that it will not close down below in the water, and has therefore to hang for ever so long each time; and sometimes it freezes tight during the observation after it is brought up, so that the water will not run out of it into the sample bottles, not to mention all the bother there is getting the apparatus ready to lower. We are lucky if we do not require to take the whole thing into the galley every time to thaw it. It is slow work, the temperatures have sometimes to be read by lantern light. The water samples are not so reliable, because they freeze in the lifter. But the thing can be done, and we must just go on doing it. The same easterly wind is blowing, and we are drifting onwards. Our latitude this evening is about 81° 47′ N.

"Thursday, October 18th. I continue taking the temperatures of the water, rather a cool amusement with the thermometer down to −29° C. (20.2° F. below zero) and a wind blowing. Your fingers are apt to get a little stiff and numb when you have to manipulate the wet or ice-covered metal screws with bare hands and have to read off the thermometer with a magnifying-glass in order to ensure accuracy to the hundredth part of a degree, and then to bottle the samples of water, which you have to keep close against your breast, to prevent the water from freezing. It is a nice business!

"There was a lovely aurora borealis at 8 o'clock this evening. It wound itself like a fiery serpent in a double coil across the sky. The tail was about 10° above the horizon in the north. Thence it turned off with many windings in an easterly direction, then round again, and westwards in the form of an arch from 30° to 40° above the horizon, sinking down again to the west and rolling itself up into a ball, from which several branches spread out over the sky. The arches were in active motion, while pencils of streamers shot out swiftly from the west towards the east, and the whole serpent kept incessantly undulating into fresh curves. Gradually it mounted up over the sky nearly to the zenith, while at the same time the uppermost bend or arch separated into several fainter undulations, the ball in the north-east glowed intensely, and brilliant streamers shot upwards to the zenith from several places in the arches, especially from the ball and from the bend farthest away in the north-east. The illumination was now at its highest, the colour being principally a strong yellow, though at some spots it verged towards a yellowish-red, while at other places it was a greenish-white. When the upper wave reached the zenith, the phenomenon lost something of its brilliancy, dispersing little by little, leaving merely a faint indication of an aurora in the southern sky. On coming up again on deck later in the evening, I found nearly the whole of the aurora collected in the southern half of the sky. A low arch, 5° in height, could be seen far down in the south over the dark segment of the horizon. Between this and the zenith were four other vague, wavy arches, the topmost of which passed right across it; here and there vivid streamers shot flaming upwards, especially from the undermost arch in the south. 'No arch was to be seen in the northern part of the sky, only streamers every here and there. To-night, as usual, there are traces of aurora to be seen over the whole sky; light mists or streamers are often plainly visible, and the sky seems to be constantly covered with a luminous veil,[59] in which every here and there are dark holes.

There is scarcely any night, or rather I may safely say there is no night, on which no trace of aurora can be discerned as soon as the sky becomes clear, or even when there is simply, a rift in the clouds large enough for it to be seen; and as a rule we have strong light phenomena dancing in ceaseless unrest over the firmament. They mainly appear, however, in the southern part of the sky.

"Friday, October 19th. A fresh breeze from E.S.E. Drifting northwards at a good pace. Soon we shall probably have passed the long-looked-for 82° and that will not be far from 82° 27' when the *Fram* will be the vessel that will have penetrated farthest to the north on this globe. But the barometer is falling; the wind probably will not remain in that quarter long, but will shift round to the west. I only hope for this once the barometer may prove a false prophet. I have become rather sanguine; things have been going pretty well for so long; and October, a month which last year's experience had made me dread, has been a month of marked advance, if only it doesn't end badly.

"The wind to-day, however, was to cost a life. The mill, which had been repaired after the mishap to the cog-wheel the other day, was set going again. In the afternoon a couple of the puppies began fighting over a bone, when one of them fell underneath one of the cogwheels on the axle of the mill, and was dragged in between it and the deck. Its poor little body nearly made the whole thing come to a standstill; and, unfortunately, no one was on the spot to stop it in time. I heard the noise, and rushed on deck; the puppy had just been drawn out nearly dead; the whole of its stomach was torn open. It gave a faint whine, and was at once put out of its misery. Poor little frolicsome creature! Only a little while ago you were gambolling around, enjoying an innocent romp with your brothers and sisters; then came the thigh-bone of a bear trundling along the deck from the galley; you and the others made a headlong rush for it, and now there you lie, cruelly lacerated and dead as a herring. Fate is inexorable!

Nansen.

"Sunday, October 3lst. N. lat. 82° 0.2'; E. long. 114° 9'. It is late in the evening, and my head is bewildered, as if I had been indulging in a regular debauch, but it was a debauch of a very innocent nature.

"A grand banquet to-day to celebrate the eighty-second degree of latitude. The observation gave 82° 0.2' last night, and we have now certainly drifted a little farther north. Honey-cakes (gingerbread) were baked for the occasion, first-class honey-cakes, too, you may take my word for it; and then, after a refreshing snow-shoe run, came a festal banquet. Notices were stuck up in the saloon requesting the guests to be punctual at dinner-time, for the cook had exerted himself to the utmost of his power. The following deeply felt lines by an anonymous poet also appeared on a placard:

'When dinner is punctually served at the time,
No fear that the milk soup will surely be prime;
But the viands are spoilt if you come to it late,
The fish-pudding will lie on your chest a dead weight;
What's preserved in tin cases, there can be no doubt,
If you wait long enough will force its way out,
Even meat of the ox, of the sheep, or of swine,
Very different in this from the juice of the vine!
Ramornie, and Armour, and Thorne, and Herr Thüs,
Good meats have preserved, and they taste not amiss;
So I'll just add a word, friends, of warning to you
If you want a good dinner, come at one, not at two.'

The lyrical melancholy which here finds utterance must have been the outcome of many bitter disappointments, and furnishes a valuable internal evidence as to the anonymous author's profession. Meanwhile the guests assembled with tolerable punctuality, the only exception being your humble servant, who was obliged to take some photographs in the rapidly waning daylight. The menu was splendid: (1) ox-tail soup; (2) fish-pudding with melted butter and potatoes; (3) turtle with marrowfat, peas, etc., etc.; (4) rice with multer (cloudberries) and cream. Crown malt extract. After dinner, coffee and honey-cakes. After supper, which also was excellent, there was a call for music, which was liberally supplied throughout the whole evening by various accomplished performers on the organ, among whom Bentzen specially distinguished himself, his late experiences on the ice with the crank-handle[60] having put him in first-rate training. Every now and then the music dragged a bit, as though it were being hauled up from an abyss some 1,000 or 1,500 fathoms deep; then it would quicken and get more lively, as it came nearer to the surface. At last the excitement rose to such a pitch, that Pettersen and I had to get up and have a dance, a waltz, and a polka or two; and we really executed some very tasteful *pas de deux* on the limited floor of the saloon. Then Amundsen also was swept into the mazes of the dance, while the others played cards. Meanwhile refreshments were served in the form of preserved peaches, dried bananas, figs, honey-cakes, etc., etc. In short, we made a jovial evening of it, and why should we not? We are progressing merrily towards our goal, we are already half-way between the New Siberian Islands and Franz Josef Land, and there is not a soul on board who doubts that we shall accomplish what we came out to do; so long live merriment.

"But the endless stillness of the polar night holds its sway aloft; the moon, half full, shines over the ice, and the stars sparkle brilliantly overhead; there are no restless northern lights, and the south wind sighs mournfully through the rigging. A deep, peaceful stillness prevails everywhere. It is the infinite loveliness of death — Nirvana."

"Monday, October 22nd. It is beginning to be cold now ; the thermometer was −34.6° C. (30.2° F. below zero) last night, and this evening; it is −36° C. (32.8° F. below zero).

"A lovely aurora this evening (11.30). A brilliant corona encircled the zenith with a wreath of streamers in several layers, one outside the other; then larger and smaller sheaves of streamers spread over the sky. especially low down towards S.W. and E.S.E. All of them, however, tended upwards towards the corona which shone like a halo. I stood watching it a long while. Every now and then I could discern a dark patch in its middle, at the point where all the rays converged. It lay a little south of the Pole Star. and approached Cassiopeia in the position it then occupied. But the halo kept smouldering and shifting just as if a gale in the upper strata of the atmosphere were playing the bellows to it. Presently fresh streamers shot out of the darkness outside the inner halo, followed by other bright shafts of light in a still wider circle, and meanwhile the dark space in the middle was clearly visible; at other times it was entirely covered with masses of light. Then it appeared as if the storm abated, and the whole turned pale, and glowed with a faint whitish hue for a little while, only to shoot wildly up once more and to begin the same dance over again. Then the entire mass of light around the corona began to rock to and fro in large waves over the zenith and the dark central point, whereupon the gale seemed to increase and whirl the streamers into an inextricable tangle, till they merged into a luminous vapour, that enveloped the corona and drowned it in a deluge of light, so that neither it, nor the streamers, nor the dark centre could be seen — nothing, in fact, but a chaos of shining mist. Again it became paler. and I went below. At midnight there was hardly anything of the aurora to be seen.

"Friday. October 26th. Yesterday evening we were in 82° 3' N. lat. To-day the *Fram* is two years old. The sky has been overcast during the last two days, and it has been so dark at midday that I thought we should soon have to stop our snow-shoe expeditions. But this morning brought us clear, still weather, and I went out on a delightful trip to the westward, where there had been a good deal of fresh packing, but nothing of any importance. In honour of the occasion we had a particularly good dinner, with fried halibut, turtle, pork chops with haricot beans and green peas, plum-pudding (real burning plum-pudding for the first time) with custard sauce, and wound up with strawberries. As usual, the beverages consisted of wine (that is to say, lime-juice, with water and sugar) and Crown malt extract. I fear there was a general overtaxing of the digestive apparatus. After dinner, coffee and honey-cakes, with which Nordahl stood cigarettes. General holiday.

"This evening it has begun to blow from the north, but probably this does not mean much; I must hope so, at all events, and trust that we shall soon get a south wind again. But it is not the mild zephyr we yearn for, not the breath of the blushing dawn. No, a cold, biting south wind, roaring with all the force of the Polar Sea, so that the *Fram*, the two-year-old *Fram*, may be buried in the snowstorm, and all around her be but a reeking frost — it is this we are waiting for, this that will drift us onwards to our goal. To-day, then, *Fram*, thou art two years old. I said at the dinner-table that if a year ago we were unanimous in believing that the *Fram* was a good ship, we had much better grounds for that belief to-day, for safely and surely she is carrying us onwards, even if the speed be not excessive; and so we drank the *Fram's* good health and good progress. I did not say too much. Had I said all that was in my heart, my words would not have been so measured; for, to say the truth, we all of us dearly love the ship, as much as it is possible to love any impersonal thing. And why should we not love her? No mother can give her young more warmth and safety under her wings than she affords to us. She is indeed like a home to us. We all rejoice to return to her from out on the icy plains, and when I have been far away and have seen her masts rising over the everlasting mantle of snow, how often has my heart glowed with warmth towards her. To the builder of this home grateful

Nansen in his cabin.

thoughts often travel during the still nights. He, I feel certain, sits yonder at home often thinking of us; but he knows not where his thought can seek the *Fram* in the great white tract around the Pole. But he knows his child; and though all else lose faith in her, he will believe that she will hold out. Yes, Colin Archer, could you see us now, you would know that your faith in her is not misplaced.

"I am sitting alone in my berth, and my thoughts glide back over the two years that have passed. What demon is it that weaves the threads of our lives, that makes us deceive ourselves, and ever sends us forth on paths we have not ourselves laid out, paths on which we have no desire to walk? Was it a mere feeling of duty that impelled me? I was simply a child yearning for a great adventure out in the unknown, who had dreamed of it so long that at last I believed it really awaited me; and it has, indeed, fallen to my lot, the great adventure of the ice, deep and pure as infinity, the silent, starlit polar night, nature itself in its profundity, the mystery of life, the ceaseless circling of the universe, the feast of death, without suffering, without regret, eternal in itself. Here in the great night thou standest in all thy naked pettiness, face to face with nature; and thou sittest devoutly at the feet of eternity, intently listening; and thou knowest God the all-ruling, the centre of the universe. All the riddles of life seem to grow clear to thee, and thou laughest at thyself that thou couldst be consumed by brooding, it is all so little, so unutterably little...'Whoso sees Jehovah dies.'

"Sunday, November 4th. At noon I had gone out on a snow-shoe expedition, and had taken some of the dogs with me. Presently I noticed that those that had been left behind at the ship began to bark. Those with me pricked up their ears, and several of them started off back, with 'Ulenka' at their head. Most of them soon stopped, listening and looking behind them to see if I were following. I wondered for a little while whether it could be a bear, and then continued on my way; but at length I could stand it no longer, and set off homewards, with the dogs dashing wildly on in front. On approaching the ship I saw some of the men setting off with guns; they were Sverdrup, Johansen, Mogstad, and Henriksen. They had got a good start of me in the direction in which the dogs were barking before I, too, got hold of a gun and set off after them. All at once I saw through the darkness the flash of a volley from those in front, followed by another shot, then several more, until at last it sounded like regular platoon firing. What the deuce could it be? They were standing on the same spot, and kept firing incessantly. Why on earth did they not advance nearer? I hurried on, thinking it was high time I came up with my snow-shoes to follow the game, which must evidently be in full flight. Meanwhile they advanced a little, and then there was another flash to be seen through the darkness, and so they went on two or three times. One of the number at last dashed forward over the ice and fired straight down in front of him, while another knelt down and fired towards the east. Were they trying their guns? But surely it was a strange time for doing so, and there were so many shots. Meanwhile the dogs tore around over the ice, and gathered in clumps, barking furiously. At length I overtook them, and saw three bears scattered over the ice, a she-bear and two cubs, while the dogs lay over them, worrying them like mad and tearing away at paws, throat, and tail. Ulenka especially was beside herself. She had gripped one of the cubs by the throat, and worried it like a mad thing, so that it was difficult to get her away. The bears had gone very leisurely away from the dogs, which dared not come to sufficiently close quarters to use their teeth till the old she-bear had been wounded and had fallen down. The bears, indeed, had acted in a very suspicious manner. It seemed just as if the she-bear had some deep design, some evil intent, in her mind, if she could only have lured the dogs near enough to her. Suddenly she halted, let the cubs go on in front, sniffed a little, and then came back to meet the dogs, who at the same time, as if at a word of command, all turned tail, and set off towards the west It was then that the first shot was fired, and the old bear tottered and fell headlong, when immediately some of the dogs set to and tackled her. One of the cubs then got its quietus, while the other one was fired at and made off over the ice, with three dogs after it. They soon overtook it and pulled it down, so that when Mogstad came up he was obliged first of all to get the dogs off before he could venture to shoot. It was a glorious slaughter, and by no means unwelcome, for we had that very day eaten the last remains of our last bear in the shape of meat cakes for dinner. The two cubs made lovely Christmas pork.

"In all probability these were the same bears whose tracks we had seen before. Sverdrup and I had followed on the tracks of three such animals on the last day of October, and had lost them to N.N.W. of the ship. Apparently they had come from that quarter now.

"When they wanted to shoot, Peter's gun, as usual, would not go off; it had again been drenched with vaseline, and he kept calling out: 'Shoot! shoot! Mine won't go off.' Afterwards, on examining the gun I had taken with me to the fray, I found there were no cartridges in it. A nice account I should have given of myself had I come on the bears alone with that weapon.

"Monday, November 5th. As I was sitting at work last night I heard a dog on the deck howling fearfully. I sprang up and found it was one of the puppies, that had touched an iron bolt with its tongue and was frozen fast to it. There the poor beast was, straining to get free, with its tongue stretched out so far that it looked like a thin rope proceeding out of its throat; and it was howling piteously. Bentzen, whose watch it was, had come up, but scarcely knew what to do. He took hold of it, however, by the neck, and held it close to the bolt, so that its tongue was less extended. After having warmed the bolt somewhat with his hand, he managed to get the tongue free. The poor little puppy seemed overjoyed at its release, and, to show its gratitude, licked Bentzen's hand with its bloody tongue, and seemed as if it could not be grateful enough to its deliverer. It is to be hoped that it will be some time before this puppy, at any rate, gets fast again in this way; but such things happen every now and then.

"Sunday, November 11th. I am pursuing my studies as usual day after day; and they lure me, too, deeper and deeper into the insoluble mystery that lies behind all these inquiries. Nay! why keep revolving in this fruitless circle of thought? Better go out into the winter night. The moon is up, great and yellow and placid; the stars are twinkling overhead through the drifting snow-dust... Why not rock yourself into a winter night's dream, filled with memories of summer?

"The wind is howling too shrilly øver the barren ice-plains, there are 33 degrees of cold, and surruner, with its flowers, is far, far away. I would give a year of my life to hold them in my embrace; they loom far away in the distance, as if I should never come back to them.

"But the northern lights, with their eternally shifting loveliness, flame over the heavens each day and each night. Look at them; drink oblivion and drink hope from them: they are even as the aspiring soul of man, Restless as it, they will wreathe the whole vault of heaven with their glittering, fleeting light, surpassing all else in their wild loveliness, fairer than even the blush of dawn; but, whirling idly through empty space, they bear no message of a coming day. The sailor steers his course by a star. Could you but concentrate yourselves, you, too, oh, northern lights, might lend your aid to guide the wildered wanderer. But dance on, and let me enjoy you; stretch a bridge across the gulf between the present and the time to come, and let me dream far, far ahead into the future.

"Oh, thou mysterious radiance, what art thou, and whence comest thou? Yet why ask? Is it not enough to admire thy beauty and pause there? Can we at best get beyond the outward show of things? What would it profit even if we could say that it is an electric discharge or currents of electricity through the upper regions of the air, and were able to describe in minutest detail how it all came to be? It would be mere words. We know no more what an electric current really is, than what the aurora borealis is. Happy is the child...We, With all our views and theories, are not in the last analysis a hair's-breadth nearer the truth than it.

"Tuesday, November 13th. Thermometer −38° C. (−36.° F.). The ice is packing in several quarters during the day, and the roar is pretty loud, now that the ice has become colder. It can be heard from afar — a strange roar, which would sound uncanny to any one who did not know what it was.

"A delightful snow-shoe run in the light of the full moon. Is life a vale of tears? Is it such a deplorable fate to dash off like the wind, with all the dogs skipping around one, over the boundless expanse of ice through a night like this in the fresh, crackling frost, while the snow-shoes glide over the smooth surface, so that you scarcely know you are touching the earth, and the stars hang high in the blue vault above? This is more, indeed, than one has any right to expect of life; it is a fury-tale from another world, from a life to come.

"And then to return home to one's snug study-cabin, kindle the stove, light the lamp, fill a pipe, stretch oneself on the sofa, and send dreams out into the world with the curling clouds of smoke — is that a dire infliction? Thus I catch myself sitting staring at the fire for hours together, dreaming myself away — a useful way of employing the time. But at least it makes it slip unnoticed by, until the dreams are swept away in an ice-blast of reality, and I sit here in the midst of desolation, and nervously set to work again.

"Wednesday, November 14th. How marvellous are these snow-shoe runs through this silent nature The ice-fields stretch all around bathed in the silver moonlight; here and there dark, cold shadows project from the hummocks, whose sides faintly reflect the twilight. Far, far out a dark line marks the horizon, formed by the packed-up ice, over it a shimmer of silvery vapour and above all the boundless deep blue, starry sky, where the full moon sails through the ether. But in the south is a faint glimmer of day low down of a dark, glowing red hue, and higher up a clear yellow and pale green arch, that loses itself in the, blue above. The whole melts into a pure harmony, one and indescribable. At times one longs to be able to translate such scenes into music. What mighty chords, one require to interpret them!

"Silent, oh, so silent! You can hear the vibrations of your own nerves. I seem as if I were gliding over and over these plains into infinite space. Is this not an image of what is to come? Eternity and peace are here. Nirvana must be cold and bright as such an eternal star-night. What are all our research and understanding in the midst of this infinity?

"Friday, November 16th. In the forenoon I went out with Sverdrup on snow-shoes in the moonlight, and we talked seriously of the prospects of our drift and of the proposed expedition northwards over the ice in the string. In the evening we went into the matter more thoroughly in his cabin. I stated my views, in which he entirely coincided. I have of late been meditating a great deal on what is the proper course to pursue, supposing the drift does not take us far north by the month of March as I had anticipated.

But the more I think of it, the more firmly am I persuaded that it is the thing to do. For if it be right to set out at 85°, it must be no less right to set out at 82° or 83°. In either case we should penetrate into more Northerly regions than we should otherwise reach, and this becomes all the more desirable if the *Fram* herself does not get so far north as we had hoped. If we cannot actually reach the Pole, why, we must turn back before reaching it. The main consideration, as I must constantly repeat, is not to reach that exact mathematical point, but to explore the unknown parts of the Polar Sea, whether these be near to or more remote from the Pole. I said this before setting out, and I must keep it continually in mind. Certainly there are many important observations to be made on board during the further drift of the: ship, many which I would dearly like to carry on myself; but all the more important of these will be made equally well here, even though two of our number leave the ship; and there can scarcely be any doubt that the observations we shall make farther north will not many times outweigh in value those I could have made during the remainder of the time on board. So far, then, *it is absolutely desirable that we set off.*

"Then comes the question: What is the best time to start? That the spring, March at the latest, is the only season for such a venture, there can he no doubt at all. But shall it be next spring? Suppose, at the worst we have not advanced farther than to 83° N. lat. and 110° E. long.; then something might be said for waiting till the spring of 1896; but I cannot but think that we should thus in all probability let slip the propitious moment. The drifting could not be so wearingly slow but that after another year had elapsed we should be far beyond the point from which the sledge expedition ought to set out. If I measure the distance we have drifted from November of last year with the compasses and mark off the same distance ahead, by next November we should be north of Franz Josef Land, and a little beyond it. It is conceivable, of course, that we were no farther advanced in February, 1896, either; but it is more likely from all I can make out, that the drift will increase rather than diminish as we work westwards, and consequently in February, 1896, we should have got too far; while, even if one could imagine a better starting-point than that which the *Fram* will probably offer us by March 1st, 1895, it will, at all events, be a possible one. It must consequently be the safest plan not to wait for another spring.

"Such then are the prospects before us of pushing through. The distance from this proposed starting-point to Cape Fligely, which is the nearest known land, I set down at about 370 miles,[61] consequently not much more than the distance we covered in Greenland, and that would be easy work enough over this ice, even if it did become somewhat bad towards land. If once a coast is reached, any reasonable being can surely manage to subsist by hunting, whether large or small game, whether bears or sandhoppers. Thus we can always make for Cape Fligely or Petermann's Land, which lies north of it, if our situation becomes untenable. The distance will, of course, be increased the farther we advance northwards, but at no point whatever between here and the Pole is it greater than we can and will manage, with the help of our dogs. 'A line of retreat' is therefore secured, though there are those doubtless who hold that a barren coast, where you must first scrape your food together before you can eat it, is a poor retreat for hungry men; but that is really an advantage, for such a retreat would not be too alluring. A wretched invention, forsooth, for people who wish to push on, is a 'line of retreat,' an everlasting inducement to look behind, when they should have enough to do in looking ahead.

"But now for the expedition itself. It will consist of 28 dogs, two men, and 2,100 lbs. of provisions and equipments. The distance to the Pole from 83° is 483 miles. Is it too much to calculate that we may be able to accomplish that distance in 50 days? I do not of course know what the staying powers of the dogs may be; but that, with two men to help, they should be able to do 9½ miles a day with 75 lbs. each for the first few days, sounds sufficiently reasonable, even if they are not very good ones. This, then, can scarcely be called a wild calculation, always, of course, supposing the ice to be as it is here, and there is no reason why it should not be. It indeed, steadily improves the farther north we get; and it also improves with the approach of spring. In 50 days, then, we should reach the Pole: in 65 days we went 345 miles over the inland ice of Greenland at an elevation of more than 8,000 feet without dogs and with defective provisions, and could certainly have gone considerably farther. In 50 days we shall have consumed a pound of pemmican a day for each dog,[62] that is 1,400 lbs. altogether; and 2 lbs. of provisions for each man daily is 200 lbs. As some fuel will also be consumed during this time, the freight on the sledges will diminish to less than 500 lbs., but a burden like this is nothing for 28 dogs to draw, so that they ought to go ahead like a gale of wind during the latter part of the time, and thus do it in less than the 50 days. However, let us suppose that it takes this time. If all has gone well, we shall now direct our course for the Seven islands, north of Spitzbergen. That is 9°, or 620 miles. But if are not in first-rate condition, it will be safer to make for Cape Fligely or the land to the north of it. Let us suppose we decide on this route. We set out from the *Fram* on March 1st (if circumstances are favourable, we should start sooner), and therefore arrive at the Pole April 30th. We shall have about 500 lbs. of our provisions left, enough for another 50 days; but we can share none for the dogs. We must, therefore, begin killing some of them, either for food for the others or for ourselves, giving our provisions to them. Even if my figures are somewhat too low, I may assume that by the time twenty-three dogs have been killed we shall have travelled 41 days, and still have five dogs left. How far south shall we have advanced in this time? The weight of baggage was, to begin with, less than 500 lbs., that is to say less than 18 lbs. for each dog to draw. After 41 days this will at least have been reduced to 280 lbs. (by the consumption of provisions and fuel and by dispensing with sundry articles of our equipment, such as sleeping-bags, tent, etc., etc., which will have become superfluous). There remain, then, 56 lbs. for each of the five dogs, if we draw nothing ourselves; and should it be desirable, our equipment might be still further diminished. With a burden of from 18 to 56 lbs. apiece (the latter would only be towards the end), the dogs would on an average be able to do 13 4/5 miles a day, even if the snow-surface should become somewhat more difficult. That is to say, we shall have gone 565 miles to the south, or we shall' be 18½ miles past Cape Fligely, on June 1st, with five dogs and nine days' provisions left. But it is probable, in the first place, that we shall long before this have reached land; and, secondly, so early as the first half of April the Austrians found open water by Cape Fligely and abundance of birds. Consequently in May and June we should have no difficulty as regards food, not to mention that it would be strange indeed if we had not before that time met with a bear, or a seal, or some stray birds.

"That we should now be pretty safe I consider as certain, and we can choose whichever route we please either along the north-west coast of Franz Josef Land by Gillis Land towards North-East Island and Spitzbergen, and should circumstances prove favourable, this would decidedly be my choice, or we can go south, through Austria Sound towards the south coast of Franz Josef Land, and thence to Novaya Zemlya or Spitzbergen, the latter by preference. We may, of course, find Englishmen on Franz Josef Land, but that we must not reckon on.

"Such, then, is my calculation. Have I made it recklessly? No, I think not. The only difficulty would be if during the latter part of the journey, in May, we should find the surface like that we had here last spring, at the end of May, and should be considerably delayed by it. But this would only be towards the very end of our time, and at worst it could not be entirely impassable.

Besides, it would be strange if we could not manage to average 11 ½ miles a-day during the whole of the journey, with an average load for each dog of from 30 to 40 lbs. — it would not be more. However, if our calculations should prove faulty, we can always, as afore-said, turn back at any moment.

"What unforeseen obstacles may confront us?

"1. The ice may be more impracticable than was supposed.

"2. We may meet with land.

"3. The dogs may fail us, may sicken, or freeze to death.

"4. We ourselves may suffer from scurvy.

"1 and 2. That the ice may be more impracticable further north is certainly possible, but hardly probable. I can see no reason why it should be, unless we have unknown lands to the north. But should this be so — very well, we must take what chance we find. The ice can scarcely be altogether impassable. Even Markham was able to advance with his scurvy-smitten people. And the coasts of this land may possibly be advantageous for an advance; it simply depends on their direction and extent. It is difficult to say anything beforehand, except that I think the depth of water we have here, and the drift of the ice render it improbable that we can have land of any extent at all close at hand. In any case there must, somewhere or other, be a passage for the ice, and at the worst we can follow that passage.

"3. There is always a possibility that the dogs may fail us, but, as may be seen, I have not laid out any scheme of excessive work for them. And, even if one or two of them should prove failures, that could not be the case with all. With the food they have hitherto had they have got through the winter and the cold without mishap, and they food they will get on the journey will be better. In my calculations, moreover, I have taken no account of what we shall draw ourselves. And, even supposing all the dogs to fail us, we could manage to get along by ourselves pretty well.

"4. The worst event would undeniably be that we ourselves should be attacked by scurvy; and, notwithstanding our excellent health, such a contingency is quite conceivable, when it is borne in mind how in the English North Pole Expedition all the men, with the exception of the officers, suffered from scurvy when the spring and the sledge journeys began, although as long as they were on board ship they had not the remotest suspicion that anything of the kind was lying in wait for them. As far, however, as we are concerned, I consider this contingency very remote. In the first place, the English Expedition was remarkably unfortunate, and hardly any others can show a similar experience, although they may have undertaken sledge journeys of equal length — for example, M'Clintock's. During the retreat of the *Jeannette* party, so far as is known, no one was attacked with scurvy. Peary and Astrup did not suffer from scurvy either. Moreover our supply of provisions has been more carefully selected, and offers greater variety than has been the case in former expeditions, not one of which has enjoyed such perfect health as ours. I scarcely think, therefore, that we should take with us from the *Fram* any germs of scurvy, and as regards the provisions for the sledge journey itself, I have taken otre that they shall consist of good all-round, nutritious articles of food, so that I can scarcely believe that they would be the means of developing an attack of this disease. Of course, one must run some risk; but in my opinion all possible precautions have been taken, and, when that is done, it is one's duty to go ahead.

"There is yet another question that must be taken into consideration. Have I the right to deprive the ship and those who remain behind of the resources such an expedition entails? The fact that there will be two men less is of little importance, for the *Fram* can be handled quite as well with eleven men. A more important point is that we shall have to take with us all the dogs except the seven puppies; but they are amply supplied with sledge provisions and first-class sledge equipments on board, and it is inconceivable that in case anything happened to the *Fram* they should be unable to reach Franz Josef Land or Spitzbergen. It is scarcely likely that in case they had to abandon her, it would be further north than 85°; probably not even so far north. But suppose they were obliged to abandon her at 85°, it would probably be about north of Franz Josef Land, when they would be 207 miles from Cape Fligely; or if further to the east it would be some 276 miles from the Seven Islands; and it is hard to believe that they could not manage a distance like that with our equipment. Now, as before, I am of opinion that the *Fram* will in all probability drift right across the polar basin and out on the other side without being stopped, and without being destroyed; but even if any accident should occur, I do not see why the crew should not be able to make their way home in safety, provided due measures of precaution are observed. Consequently, I think there is no reason why a sledge expedition should not leave the *Fram*, and I feel that as it promises such good results it ought certainly to be attempted."

THE SLEDGE JOURNEY

Chapter 9

We Prepare for the Sledge Expedition.

Who are to be the two members of the expedition? Sverdrup and I have tested each other before at this sort of work, and we could manage very well; but we cannot both leave the *Fram*; that is perfectly clear without further argument. One of us must remain behind to take on himself the responsibility of bringing the others home in safety; but it is equally clear that one of us two must conduct the sledge expedition, as it is we who have the necessary experience. Sverdrup has a great desire to go but I cannot think otherwise than that there is more risk in leaving the *Fram* than in remaining on board her. Consequently, if I were to let him go, I should be transferring to him the more dangerous task, while keeping the easier one to myself. If he perished, should I ever be able to forgive myself for letting him go, even if it was at his own desire? He is nine years older than I am; I should certainly feel it to be a very uncomfortable responsibility. And, as regards our comrades, which of us would it be most to their interest to keep on board? I think they have confidence in both of us, and I think either of us would be able to take them home in safety, whether with or without the *Fram*. But the ship is his special charge, while on me rests the conduct of the whole, and especially of the scientific investigations; so that I ought to undertake the task in which important discoveries are to be made. Those who remain with the ship will be able, as aforesaid, to carry on the observations which are to be made on board. It is my duty, therefore, to go, and his to remain behind. He, too, thinks this reasonable.

I have chosen Johansen to be my companion, and he is in all respects well qualified for that work. He is an accomplished snow-shoer, and few can equal his powers of endurance — a fine fellow, physically and mentally. I have not yet asked him, but think of doing so soon, in order that he may be prepared betimes. Blessing and Hansen also would certainly be all eagerness to accompany me; but Hansen must remain behind to take charge of the observations, and Blessing cannot desert his post as doctor. Several of the others, too, would do quite well, and would, I doubt not, be willing enough. This expedition to the north, then, is provisionally decided on. I shall see what the winter will bring us. Light permitting, I should prefer to start in February.

"Sunday, November 18th. It seems as if I could not properly realise the idea that I am really to set out, and that in three months' time. Sometimes I delude myself with charming dreams of my return home after toil and victory, and then all is clear and bright. Then these are succeeded by thoughts of the uncertainty and deceptiveness of the future and what may be lurking in it, and my dreams fade away like the northern lights, pale and colourless.

"'Ihr naht euch wieder, schwankende Gestalten.'

"These everlasting cold fits of doubt! Before every decisive resolution the dice of death must be thrown. Is there too much to venture, and too little to gain? There is more to be gained, at all events, than there is here. Then is it not my duty? Besides, there is only one to whom I am responsible, and she…? I shall come back, I know it. I have strength enough for the task. 'Be thou faithful unto death, and thou shalt inherit the crown of life.'

"We are oddly constructed machines. At one moment all resolution, at the next all doubt. To-day our intellect, our science, all our 'Leben and Treiben' seem but a pitiful Philistinism, not worth a pipe of tobacco; to-morrow we throw ourselves heart and soul into these very researches, consumed with a burning thirst to absorb everything into ourselves, longing to spy out fresh paths, and fretting impatiently at our inability to solve the problem fully and completely. Then down we sink again in disgust at the worthlessness of it all.

"'As a grain of dust in the balance is the whole world; as a drop of morning dew that falls on the ground.' If man has two souls, which then is the right one?

"It is nothing new to suffer from the fact that our knowledge can be but fragmentary, that we can never fathom what lies behind. But suppose, now, that we could reckon it out, that the inmost secret of it all lay as clear and plain to us as a rule-of-three sum, should we be any the happier? Possibly just the reverse. Is it not in the struggle to attain knowledge that happiness consists? I am very ignorant, consequently the conditions of happiness are mine.

Hansen and Henriksen on deck.

"Let me fill a soothing pipe and be happy.

"No, the pipe is not a success. Twist tobacco is not delicate enough for airy dreams. Let me get a cigar. Oh! if one had a real Havanna!

"As if dissatisfaction, longing, suffering, were not the very basis of life. Without privation there would be no struggle, and without struggle no life — that is as certain as that two and two make four. And now the struggle is to begin, it is looming yonder in the north. Oh! to drink delight of battle, in long, deep draughts. Battle means life, and behind it victory beckons us on.

"I close my eyes. I hear a voice singing to me

"'In amongst the fragrant birch,
In amongst the flowers' perfume,
Deep into the pinewood's church.'"

"Monday, November 19th. Confounded affectation all this Weltschmerz; you have no right to be anything but a happy man. And if you feel out of spirits, it ought to cheer you up simply to go on deck and look at these seven puppies that come frisking and springing about you, and are ready to tear you to pieces in sheer enjoyment of life. Life is sunshine to them, though the sun has long since gone, and they live on deck beneath a tent, so that they cannot even see the stars. There is 'Kvik,' the mother of the family, among them, looking so plump and contented as she wags her tail. Have you not as much reason to be happy as they? Yet they too have their misfortunes. The afternoon of the day before yesterday, as I was sitting at work, I heard the mill going round and round, and Peter taking food to the puppies, which as usual had a bit of a fight over the meat pan; and it struck me that the axle of the mill, whirling unguarded on the deck, was an extremely dangerous affair for them. Ten minutes later I heard a dog howling, a more long-drawn, uncomfortable kind of howl than was usual when they were fighting; and at the same moment the mill slowed down. I rushed out. There I saw a puppy right in the axle, whirling round with it and howling piteously, so that it cut one to the soul. Bentzen was hanging on to the brake rope, hauling at it with all his might and main; but still the mill went round. My first idea was to seize an axe that was lying there to put the dog out of its misery, its cries were so heartrending; but on second thoughts I hurried on to help Bentzen, and we got the mill stopped. At the same moment Mogstad also came up, and while we held the mill he managed to set the puppy free. Apparently there was still some life in it, and he set to work to rub it gently and coax it. The hair of its coat had somehow or other got frozen on to the smooth steel axle, and the poor beast had been swung round and bumped on the deck at every revolution of the wheel. At last it actually raised its head, and looked round in a dazed way. It had made a good many revolutions, so that it is no wonder if it found some difficulty in getting its bearings at first. Then it raised itself on its fore-paws, and I took it aft to the half-deck and stroked and patted it. Soon it got on all four legs again, and began shambling about, without knowing where it was going.

"'It is a good thing it was caught by the hair,' said Bentzen, 'I thought it was hanging fast by its tongue, as the other one did.' Only think of being fixed by the tongue to a revolving axle — the mere notion makes one shudder! I took the poor thing down into the saloon and did all I could for it. It soon got all right again, and began playing with its companions as before. A strange life, to rummage about on deck in the dark and cold; but whenever one goes up with a lantern they come tearing round, stare at the light, and begin bounding and dancing and gambolling with each other round it, like children round a Christmas tree. This goes on day after day, and they have never seen anything

Hjalmar Johansen.

else but this deck with a tarpaulin over it, not even the clear blue sky; and we men have never seen anything other than this earth!

"The last step over the bridge of resolution has now been taken. In the forenoon I explained the whole matter to Johansen in pretty much the same terms as I have used above; and then I detailed the difficulties that might occur, and laid strong emphasis on the dangers one must be prepared to encounter. It was a serious matter — a matter of life or death — this one must not conceal from oneself. He must think the thing well over before determining whether he would accompany me or not. If he was willing to come I should be glad to have him with me; but I would rather, I said, he should take a day or two to think it well over before he gave me his answer. He did not need any time for reflection, he said; he was quite willing to go. Sverdrup had long ago mentioned the possibility of such an expedition, and he had thought it well over, and made up his mind that if my choice should fall on him he would take it as a great favour to be permitted to accompany me. 'I don't know whether you'll be satisfied with this answer, or whether you would like me still to think it over; but I should certainly never change my mind.' 'No, if you have already thought seriously about it — thought what risks you expose yourself to — the chance, for instance, that neither of us may ever see the face of man again — and if you have reflected that even if we get through safe and sound we must necessarily face a great deal of hardship on an expedition like this — if you have made up your mind to all this, I don't insist on your reflecting any longer about it.' 'Yes, that I have.' 'Well, then, that is settled. To-morrow we shall begin our preparations for the trip. Hansen must see about appointing another meteorological assistant.'"

"Tuesday, November 20th. This evening I delivered an address to the whole ship's company, in which I announced the determination that had been arrived at, and explained to them the projected expedition. First of all I briefly went through the whole theory of our undertaking, and its history from the beginning, laying stress on the idea on which my plans had been built up, namely that a vessel which got frozen in north of Siberia must drift across the Polar Sea and out into the Atlantic, and must pass somewhere or other north of Franz Josef Land, and between it and the Pole. The object of the expedition was to accomplish this drift across the unknown sea, and to pursue investigations there. I pointed out to them that these investigations would be of equal importance whether the expedition actually passed across the Pole itself or at some distance from it. Judging from our experiences hitherto, we could not entertain any doubt that the expedition would solve the problem it had set before it; everything had up to the present gone according to our anticipations, and it was to be hoped and expected that this would continue to be the case for the remainder of the voyage. We had, therefore, every prospect of accomplishing the principal part of our task; but then the question arose whether more could not be accomplished; and thereupon I proceeded to explain, in much the same terms as I have used above, how this might be effected by an expedition northwards.

"I had the impression that everyone was deeply interested in the projected expedition, and that they all thought it most desirable that it should be attempted. The greatest objection, I think, they would have urged against it, had they been asked, would have been that they themselves could not take part in it. I impressed on them, however, that while it was unquestionably a fine thing to push on as far as possible towards the north, it was no whit less honourable an undertaking to bring the *Fram* safe and sound right through the Polar Sea, and out on the other side — or if not the *Fram*, at all events themselves, without any loss of life. This done, we might say, without fear of contradiction, that it was well done. I think they all saw the force of this and were satisfied. So now the die is cast, and I must believe that this expedition will really take place."

So we set about our preparations for it in downright earnest. I have already mentioned that at the end of the summer I had begun to make a kayak for a single man, the frame of which was of bamboo carefully lashed together. It was rather slow work, and took several weeks, but it turned out both light and strong. When completed the frame-work weighed 16 lbs. It was afterwards covered with sail-cloth by Sverdrup and Blessing, when the whole boat weighed 30 lbs. After finishing this, I had entrusted Mogstad with the task of building a similar one. Johansen and I now set to work to make a cover for it. These kayaks were 3.70 metres (12 feet) long, about 0.7 metre (28 inches) wide in the middle, and one was 30 centims. (12 inches) and the other 38 centims. (15 inches) deep. This is considerably shorter and wider than an ordinary Eskimo kayak, and consequently these boats were not so light to propel through the water. But as they were chiefly intended for crossing over channels and open spaces in the ice, and coasting along possible land, speed was not of much importance. The great thing was that the boats should be strong and light, and should be able to carry, in addition to ourselves, provisions and equipments for a considerable time. If we had made them longer and narrower, besides being heavier they would have been more exposed to injury in the course of transport over the uneven ice. As they were built, they proved admirably adapted for our purpose. When we loaded them with care, we could stow away in them provisions and equipment for three months at least for ourselves, besides a good deal of food for the dogs; and we could, moreover, carry a dog or two on the deck. In other respects they were essentially like the Eskimo-kayaks, full decked, save for an aperture in the middle for a man to sit in. This aperture was encircled by a wooden ring, after the Eskimo fashion, over which we could slip the lower part of our sealskin jackets, specially adjusted for this purpose, so that the junction between boat and cape was watertight. When these jackets were drawn tight round the wrists and face the sea might sweep right over us without a drop of water coming into the kayak. We had to provide ourselves with such boats, in case of having to cross open stretches of sea on our way to Spitzbergen, or, if we chose the other route, between Franz Josef Land and Novaya Zemlya. Besides this aperture in the middle, there were small trap-doors fore and aft in the deck, to enable us to put our hands in and stow the provisions, and also get things out more readily, without having to take out all the freight through the middle aperture, in case what we wanted lay at either extremity. These trap-doors, however, could be closed so as to be quite watertight. To make the canvas quite impervious to water the best plan would have been to have sized it, and then painted it externally with ordinary oil paint; but on the one hand it was very difficult to do this work in the extreme cold (in the hold the temperature was −20° C. (−4° F.)), and on the other hand I was afraid the paint might render the canvas too hard and brittle, and apt to have holes knocked in it during transport over the ice. Therefore I preferred to steep it in a mixture of paraffin and tallow, which added somewhat to the weight of the kayaks, so that altogether they came to weigh about 36 lbs. apiece.

I had, moreover, some hand sledges made especially for this expedition; they were supple and strong, designed to withstand the severe tests to which an expedition with dogs and heavy freights over the uneven drift-ice would necessarily expose them. Two of these sledges were about the same length as the kayaks, that is, 12 feet. I also made several experiments with respect to the clothes we should wear, and was especially anxious to ascertain whether it would do to go in our thick wolf-skin garments, but always came to the conclusion that they were too warm. Thus, on November 29th, I write "Took another walk northwards in my wolf-skin dress; but it is still too mild, −35.2° F. (−37.6° C.). I sweated like a horse, though I went fasting, and quite gently. It is rather heavy going now in the dark, when one cannot use snow-shoes. I wonder when it will be cold enough to use this dress."

On December 9th again, we went out on snow-shoes. It was −41° C. (−41.8° F.). Went in wolf-skin dress, but the perspiration poured down our backs, enough to turn a mill. Too warm yet; goodness knows if it ever will be cold enough."

Of course, we made some experiments with the tent and with the cooking apparatus. On December 7th I write:"I pitched the silk tent we are going to take, and used our cooking apparatus in it. From repeated trials it appeared that from ice of −35° C. (−31° F.) we boiled 3 litres of water (5¼ pints), and at the same time melted 5 litres (8¾ pints), in an hour and a half, with a consumption of about 120 grammes of snowflake petroleum. Next day we boiled 2½ litres of water (over 4 pints), and melted 2½ litres, in one hour, with 100 grammes of snowflake petroleum. Yesterday we made about 2 litres of excellent oatmeal porridge, and at the same time got some half melted ice and a little water in little over half-an-hour, with 50 grammes of snowflake petroleum. Thus there will be no very great consumption of fuel in the day."

Then I made all kinds of calculations and computations in order to find out what would be the most advantageous kind of provisions for our expedition, it being of the greatest moment that the food both for dogs and men should be nutritious, and yet should not weigh more than was absolutely necessary. Later on, in the list of our equipments, I shall give the final result of my deliberations on this matter. Besides all this, we had of course to consider and test the instruments to be taken with us, and to go into many other matters, which, though perhaps trifles in themselves, were yet absolutely necessary. It is on the felicitous combination of all these trifles, that ultimate success depends.

We two passed the greater portion of our time in these preparations, which also kept many of the others pretty busy during the winter. Mogstad, for instance, found steady employment in making sledges and fitting them with runners, etc. Sverdrup busied himself in making sleeping-bags and many other things. Juell was appointed dog-tailor, and when he was not busy in the galley, his time was devoted to taking the measurements of the dogs, making harness for them and testing it. Blessing too, fitted up for us a small, light medicine chest, containing selected drugs, bandages and such other things as might be of use. One man was constantly employed in copying out all our journals and scientific observations, etc., etc., on thin paper, in a contracted form, as I wanted, by way of making doubly sure of their preservation, to take a copy of them along with me. Hansen was occupied in preparing tabular forms necessary for our observations, curves of the movement of our chronometers, and other such things. Besides this, he was to make a complete chart of our voyage and drifting up to the present time.

I could not, however, make too great a claim on his valuable time, as it was necessary that he should continue his scientific observations without interruption. During this autumn he had greatly increased the comfort of his work, by building, along with Johansen, an observation-hut of snow, not unlike an Eskimo cabin. He found himself very much at his ease in it, with a petroleum lamp hanging from the roof, the light of which, being reflected by the white snow walls made quite a brilliant show. Here he could manipulate his instruments quietly and comfortably, undisturbed by the biting wind outside. He thought it quite warm there, too, when he could get the temperature up to something like 20° below freezing-point, so that he was able without much inconvenience to adjust his instruments with bare hands. Here he worked away indefatigably at his observations day after day, watching the often mysterious movements of the magnetic needle, which would sometimes give him no end of trouble. One day — it was November 24th — he came in to supper a little after 6 o'clock, quite alarmed, and said, "There has just been a singular inclination of the needle to 24°, and, remarkably enough, its northern extremity pointed to the east. I cannot remember ever having heard of such an inclination." He also had several others of about 15°. At the same time, through the opening into his observatory, he noticed that it was unusually light out of doors, and that not only the ship but the ice in the distance was as plainly visible as if it had been full moonlight. No aurora, however, could be discerned through the thick clouds that covered the sky. It would appear, then, that this unusual inclination was in some way connected with the northern lights, though it was to the east and not to the west as usual. There could be no question of any movement of the floe on which we were lying; for everything had been perfectly still and quiet, and it is inconceivable that a disturbance which could cause such a remarkable oscillation of two points and back again in so short a space of time should not have been noticed and heard on board. This theory, therefore, is entirely excluded, and the whole matter seems to me, for the present, to be incomprehensible. Blessing and I at once went on deck to look at the sky. Certainly it was so light that we could see the lanes in the ice astern quite plainly; but there was nothing remarkable in that, it happened often enough.

"Friday, November 30th. I found a bear's track on the ice in front of our bow. The bear had come from the east, trotting very gently along the lane, on the newly frozen ice, but he must have been scared by something or other ahead of the vessel, as he had gone off again with long strides in the direction from which he had come. Strange that living creatures should be roaming about in this desert. What can they have to do here? If only one had such a stomach, one could at least stand a journey to the Pole and back without a meal. We shall probably have him back again soon, that is if I understand his nature aright, and then perhaps he will come a little closer so that we may have a good look at him.[63]

"I paced the lane in front of the port bow. It was 348 paces across and maintained the same width for a considerable distance eastward, nor can it be much narrower for a great distance to the west. Now, when one bears in mind

Scott Hansen's Observatory.

that the lane behind us is also of considerable width, it is rather consoling, after all, to think that the ice does permit of such large openings There must be room enough to drift, if we only get wind — wind which will never come. On the whole, November has been an uncommonly wretched month. Driven back instead of forward — and yet this month was so good last year. But one can never rely on the seasons in this dreadful sea; taking all in all, perhaps, the winter will not be a bit better than the summer. Yet, it surely must improve — I cannot believe otherwise.

"The skies are clouded with a thick veil, through which the stars barely glisten. It is darker than usual; and in this eternal night we drift about, lonely and forsaken.'For the whole world was filled with a shining light and undisturbed activity. Above those men alone brooded nought but depressing night — an image of that gloom which was soon to swallow them up.'

"This dark, deep, silent void is like the mysterious unfathomable well, into which you look for that something which you think must be there, only to meet the reflection of your own eyes. The worn-out thoughts you can never get rid of, become in the end very wearisome company. Is there no means of fleeing from oneself, to grasp one single thought, only a single one, which lies outside oneself — is there no way except death? But death is certain; one day it will come, silent and majestic, it will open Nirvana's mighty portal, and we shall be swept away into the sea of eternity."

"Sunday, December 2nd. Sverdrup has now been ill for some days; during the last day or two he has been laid up in his berth, and is still there. I trust it is nothing serious; he himself thinks nothing of it, nevertheless it is very disquieting. Poor fellow, he lives entirely on oatmeal gruel. It is an intestinal catarrh, which he probably contracted through catching cold on the ice. I am afraid he has been rather careless in this respect. However, he is now improving, so that probably it will soon pass off; but it is a warning not to be over-confident. I went for a long walk this morning along the lane; it is quite a large one, extending a good way to the east, and being of considerable breadth at some points. It is only after walking for a while on the newly frozen ice, where walking is as easy and comfortable as on a well-trodden path, and then coming up to the snow-covered surface of the old ice again, that one thoroughly appreciates for the first time what it means to go without snow-shoes; the difference is something marvellous. Even if I have not felt warm before, I break out into a perspiration after going a short distance over the rough ice. But what can one do? One cannot use snow-shoes; it is so dark that it is difficult enough to grope one's way about with ordinary boots, and even then one stumbles about, or slips down between great blocks of ice.

"I am now reading the various English stories of the polar expeditions during the Franklin period, and the search for him, and I must admit I am filled with admiration for these men and the amount of labour they expended. The English nation, truly, has cause to be proud of them. I remember reading these stories as a lad, and all my boyish fancies were strangely thrilled with longing for the scenery and the scenes which were displayed before me. I am reading them now as a man, after having had a little experience myself, and now, when my mind is uninfluenced by romance, I bow in admiration. There was grit in men like Parry, Franklin, James Ross, Richardson, and last, but not least, in M'Clintock — and, indeed, in all the rest. How well was their equipment thought out and arranged, with the means they had at their disposal. Truly, there is nothing new under the sun. Most of what I prided myself upon, and what I thought to be new, I find they had anticipated. M'Clintock used the same thing forty years ago. It was not their fault that they were born in a country where the use of snow-shoes is unknown, and where snow is scarcely to be found throughout the whole winter. Nevertheless, despite the fact that they had to gain their experience of snow and snow travel during their sojourn up here — despite the fact that they were without snow-shoes and had to toil on as best they could with sledges with narrow runners over uneven snow-covered drift-ice — what distances did they not cover, what fatigues and trials did they not endure No one has surpassed, and scarcely anyone approached them, unless, perhaps, the Russians on the Siberian coast; but then they have the great advantage of being natives of a country where snow is not uncommon."

"Friday, December 14th. Yesterday we held a great festivity in honour of the *Fram* as being the vessel which has attained the highest latitude (the day before yesterday we reached 82° 30′ N. lat.).

"The bill of fare at dinner was boiled mackerel, with parsley-butter sauce; pork cutlets and French peas; Norwegian wild strawberries, with rice and milk; crown malt extract; afterwards coffee. For supper: — New bread and currant cake, etc., etc. Later in the evening, a grand concert. Sweets and preserved pears were handed round. The culminating point of the entertainment was reached when a steaming hot and fragrant bowl of cherry-punch was carried in and served round among general hilarity. Our spirits were already very high, but this gave colour to the whole proceedings. The greatest puzzle to most of them was where the ingredients for the punch, and more particularly the alcohol, had come from.[64]

"Then followed the toasts. First, a long and festive one to 'The *Fram*,' which had now shown what she was capable of. It ran somewhat to this effect: 'There were many wise men who shook their heads when we started, and sent us ominous farewell greetings. But their head-shakings would have been less vigorous, and their evil forebodings milder, if they could have seen us at this moment, drifting quietly and at our ease across the most northerly latitudes ever attained by any vessel, and still further northward. And the *Fram* is now not only the most northerly vessel on the globe, but has already passed over a large expanse of hitherto unknown regions, many degrees further north than have ever been reached in this ocean on this side of the Pole. But we hope she will not stop here; concealed behind the mist of the future there are many triumphs in store for us, triumphs which will dawn upon us one by one when their time has come. But we will not speak of this now, we will be content with what has actually been achieved; and I believe that the promise implied in Björnson's greeting to us and to the *Fram* when she was launched, has already been fulfilled, and with him we can exclaim:

> "Hurrah for the ship and her voyage dread!
> Where never before a keel has sped,
> Where never before a name was spoken,
> By Norway's name is the silence broken."

"'We could not help a peculiar feeling, almost akin to shame, when comparing the toil and privation, and frequently incredible sufferings, undergone by our predecessors in earlier expeditions, with the easy manner in which we are drifting across unknown expanses of our globe, larger than it has been the lot of most, if not all, of the former polar explorers to travel over at a stretch. Yes, truly, I think we have every reason to be satisfied with our voyage so far, and with the *Fram*, and I trust we shall be able to bring something back to Norway in return for the trust, the sympathy and the money which she has expended on us. But let us not on this account forget our predecessors; let us admire them for the way in which they struggled and endured, let us remember that it is only through their labours and achievements that the way has been prepared for the present voyage. It is thanks to their collective experience, that mankind has now got so far as to be able to cope, to some extent, with what has hitherto been

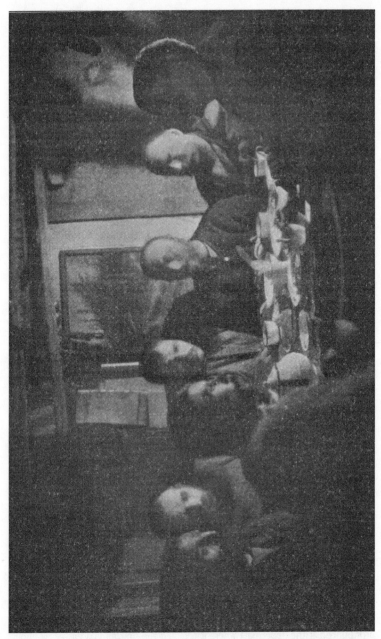

Lower end of the supper table: Bentzen, Juell, Amundsen, Henriksen, Mogstad, Nordahl, Pettersen.

his most dangerous and obstinate enemy in the Arctic regions, viz., the drift-ice, and to do so by the very simple expedient of going with it, and not against it, and allowing oneself to be hemmed in by it, not involuntarily but intentionally, and preparing for it beforehand. On board this vessel we try to cull the fruits of all our predecessors' experiences; it has taken years to collect them; but I felt that with these I should be enabled to face any vicissitude of fate in unknown waters. I think we have been fortunate. I think we are all of the opinion that there is no imaginable difficulty or obstacle before us that we ought not to be able to overcome with the means and resources we possess on board, and be thus enabled to return at last to Norway safe and sound, with a rich harvest. Therefore let us drink a bumper to the *Fram!*'

"Next there followed some musical items and a performance by Lars the smith, who danced a *pas seul* to the great amusement of the company. Lars assured us that if he ever reached home again and were present at a gathering similar to those held at Christiania and Bergen on our departure, his legs should be taxed to their uttermost. This was followed by a toast to those at home who were waiting for us year after year, not knowing where to picture us in thought, who were vainly yearning for tidings of us, but whose faith in us and our voyage was still firm — to those who consented to our departure and who may well be said to have made the greatest sacrifice.

"The festivity continued with music and merriment throughout the evening, and our good humour was certainly not spoilt when our excellent doctor came forward with cigars, a commodity which is getting highly valued up here, as unfortunately it is becoming very scarce. The only cloud in our existence is that Sverdrup has not yet quite recovered from his catarrh. He must keep strict diet, and this does not at all suit him, poor fellow; he is only allowed wheaten bread, milk, raw bear's flesh, and oatmeal porridge, whereas if he had his own way he would eat everything, including cake, preserves, and fruit. But he has returned to duty now, and has already been out for a turn on the ice.

"It was late at night when I retired to my cabin, but I was not yet in a fit mood to go to sleep. I felt I must go out and saunter in the wonderful moonlight. Around the moon there was, as usual, a large ring, and above it there was an arc which just touched it at the upper edge, but the two ends of which curved downwards instead of upwards. It looked as if it were part of a circle whose centre was situated far below the moon. At the lower edge of the ring there was a large mock moon, or rather a large luminous patch, which was most pronounced at the upper part where it touched the ring, and had a yellow upper

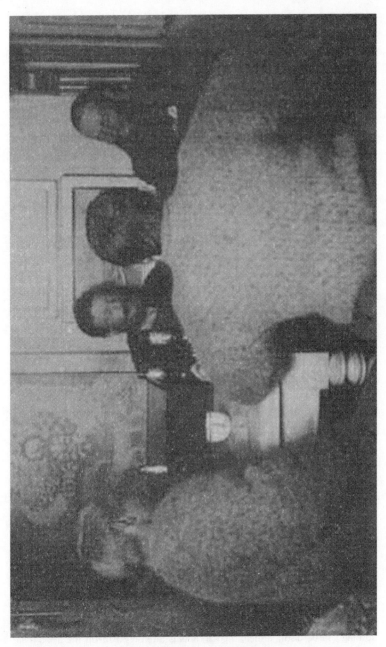

Johansen, Blessing, Hansen and Sverdrup.

edge from which it spread downwards in the form of a triangle. It looked as if it might be an arc of a circle on the lower side of, and in contact with the ring. Right across the moon there were drifting several luminous cirrhus streaks. The whole produced a fantastic effect."

"Saturday, December 22nd. The same south-easterly wind has turned into a regular storm, howling and rattling cheerily through the rigging, and we are doubtless drifting northwards at a good rate. If I go outside the tent on deck, the wind whistles round my ears, and the snow beats into my face, and I am soon covered with it. From the snow-hut observatory, or even at a lesser distance, the *Fram* is invisible, and it is almost impossible to keep one's eyes open, owing to the blinding snow. I wonder whether we have not passed 83°? But I am afraid this joy will not be a lasting one, the barometer has fallen alarmingly, and the wind has generally been up to 13 or 14 metres (44 or 50 feet) per second. About half-past twelve last night the vessel suddenly received a strong pressure, rattling everything on board. I could feel the vibration under me for a long time afterwards while lying in my berth. Finally, I could hear the roaring and grating caused by the ice pressure. I told the watch to listen carefully, and ascertain where the pressure was, and to notice whether the floe on which we were lying was likely to crack, and whether any part of our equipment was in danger. He thought he could hear the noise of ice pressure both forward and aft, but it was not easy to distinguish it from the roar of the tempest in the rigging. To-day about 12.30 at noon the *Fram* received another violent shock, even stronger than that we had experienced during the night. There was another shake a little later; I suppose there has been a pressure aft, but could hear nothing for the storm. It is odd about this pressure; one would think that the wind was the primary cause; but it recurs pretty regularly, notwithstanding the fact that the spring-tide has not yet set in; indeed, when it commenced a few days ago it was almost a neap-tide. In addition to the pressure of yesterday and last night, we had pressure on Thursday morning at half-past nine, and again at half-past eleven. It was so strong that Peter, who was at the sounding-hole, jumped up repeatedly, thinking that the ice would burst underneath him. It is very singular, we have been quiet for so long now that we feel almost nervous when the *Fram* receives these shocks; everything seems to tremble as if in a violent earthquake."

"Sunday, December 23rd. Wind still unchanged, and blowing equally fresh, up to 13 or 14 metres (44 or 47 feet). The snow is drifting and sweeping so that nothing can be distinguished; the darkness is intense. Abaft on the deck, there are deep mounds of snow lying round the wheel and the rails, so that when we go up on deck we get a genuine sample of an Arctic winter. The outlook is enough to make you shudder, and feel grateful that instead of having to turn out in such weather, you may dive back again into the tent, and down the companionway into your warm bunk; but soon, no doubt, Johansen and I will have to face it out, day and night, even in such weather as this, whether we like it or not. This morning, Pettersen, who has had charge of the dogs this week, came down to the saloon and asked whether someone would come out with him on the ice with a rifle, as he was sure there was a bear. Peter and I went, but we could not find anything. The dogs left off barking when we arrived on the scene, and commenced to play with each other. But Pettersen was right in saying that it was 'horrid weather,' it was almost enough to take away one's breath to face the wind, and the drifting snow forced its way into the mouth and nostrils. The vessel could not be distinguished beyond a few paces, so that it was not advisable to go any distance away from her, and it was very difficult to walk, for what with snow-drifts and ice-mounds at one moment you stumbled against the frozen edge of a snow-drift, at another you tumbled into a hole. It was pitch dark all round. The barometer had been falling steadily and rapidly, but at last it has commenced to rise slightly. It now registers about 726 mm. (28.6 inches). The thermometer, as usual, is describing the inverse curve. In the afternoon it rose steadily until it registered −21.3° C. (−6° F.). Now it appears to be falling again a little, but the wind still keeps exactly in the same quarter. It has surely shifted us by now a good way to the north, well beyond the 83rd degree. It is quite pleasant to hear the wind whistling and rattling in the rigging overhead. Alas! we know that all terrestrial bliss is short-lived.

"About midnight the mate, who has the watch, comes down and reports that the ice has cracked just beyond the thermometer house, between it and the sounding hole. This is the same crack that we had in the summer, and it has now burst open again, and probably the whole floe in which we are lying is split from the lane ahead to the lane astern of us. The thermograph and other instruments are being brought on board, so that we may run no risk of losing them in the event of pressure of ice. But otherwise there is scarcely anything that could be endangered. The sounding apparatus is at some distance from the open channel, on the other side. The only thing left there is the shears with the iron block standing over the hole."

"Thursday, December 27th. Christmas has come round again, and we are still so far from home. How dismal it all is! Nevertheless I am not melancholy. I might rather say I am glad; I feel as if awaiting something great which lies hidden in the future. After long hours of uncertainty I can now discern the end of this dark night; I have no doubt all will turn out successfully, that the voyage is not in vain and the time not wasted, and that our hopes will be realised. An explorer's lot is, perhaps, hard and his life full of disappointments, as they all say; but it is also full of beautiful moments, moments when he beholds the triumphs of human faith and human will, when he catches sight of the haven of success and peace.

"I am in a singular frame of mind just now, in a state of sheer unrest. I have not felt inclined for writing during the last few days; thoughts come and go, and carry me irresistibly ahead. I can scarcely make myself out; but who can fathom the depths of the human mind? The brain is a puzzling piece of mechanism: 'We are such stuff as dreams are made of.' Is it so? I almost believe it — a microcosm of eternity's infinite 'stuff that dreams are made of.'

"This is the second Christmas spent far away in the solitude of night, in the realm of death, farther north and deeper into the midst of it than any one has been before. There is something strange in the feeling; and then this, too, is our last Christmas on board the *Fram*. It makes one almost sad to think of it. The vessel is like a second home, and has become dear to us. Perhaps our comrades may spend another Christmas here, possibly several, without us who will go forth from them into the midst of the solitude. This Christmas passed off quietly and pleasantly, and everyone seems to be well content. By no means the least circumstance that added to our enjoyment was that the wind brought us the 83rd degree as a Christmas box. Our luck was, this time, more lasting than I had anticipated; the wind continued fresh on Monday and Tuesday, but little by little it lulled down and veered round to the north and north-east. Yesterday and to-day it has been in the north-west. Well, we must put up with it; one cannot help having a little contrary wind at times, and probably it will not last long.

"Christmas Eve was, of course, celebrated with great feasting. The table presented a truly imposing array of Christmas confectionery: 'Poor man's' pastry, 'Staghorn' pastry, honey-cakes, macaroons, 'Sister' cake, and what not, besides sweets, and the like, many may have fared worse. Moreover, Blessing and I had worked during the day in the sweat of our brow and produced a 'Polar Champagne 83rd Degree,' which made a sensation, and which we two, at least, believed we had every reason to be proud of, being a product derived from the noble grape of the polar regions, viz., the cloudberry [*multer*]. The others seemed to enjoy it too, and, of course, many toasts were drunk in this noble beverage. Quantities of illustrated books were then brought forth; there was music, and stories, and songs, and general merriment.

"On Christmas Day, of course, we had a special dinner. After dinner, coffee and curaçao made here on board, and Nordahl then came forward with Russian cigarettes. At night a bowl of cloudberry punch was served out, which did not seem by any means unwelcome. Mogstad played the violin, and Pettersen was electrified thereby to such a degree that he sang and danced to us. He really exhibits considerable talent as a comedian, and has a decided bent towards the ballet. It is astonishing what versatility he displays: engineer, blacksmith, tinsmith, cook, master of ceremonies, comedian, dancer, and, last of all, he has come out in the capacity of a first-class barber and hairdresser. There was a grand 'ball' at night; Mogstad had to play till the perspiration poured from him; Hansen and I had to figure as ladies. Pettersen was indefatigable. He faithfully and solemnly vowed that if he has a pair of boots to his feet when he gets home he will dance as long as the soles hold together.

"Day after day, as we progressed with a rattling wind, first from S.E., and later on E.S.E. and E., we felt more anxious to know how far we had got, but there had always been a snowstorm or a cloudy sky, so that we could not make any observations. We were all confident that we must have got a long way up north, but how far beyond the 83rd degree no one could tell. Suddenly Hansen was called on deck this afternoon by the news that the stars were visible overhead. All were on the tip-toe of expectation. But when he came down he had only observed one star, which, however, was so near the meridian that he could calculate that, at any rate, we were north of 83° 20' N. lat., and this communication was received with shouts of joy. If we were not yet in the most northerly latitude ever reached by man, we were, at all events, not far from it. This was more than we had expected, and we were in high spirits. Yesterday, being 'the Second Christmas Day,' of course, both on this account and because it was Juell's birthday, we had a special dinner, with oxtail soup, pork cutlets, red whortleberry preserve, cauliflower, fricandeau, potatoes, preserved currants, also pastry and a wonderful iced almond cake, with the words 'Glaedelig Jul' [A Merry Christmas] on it, from Hansen, baker, Christiania, and then malt-extract. We cannot complain that we are faring badly here. About 4 o'clock this morning the vessel received a violent shock which made everything tremble, but no noise of ice-packing was to be heard. At about half-past five I heard, at intervals, the crackling and crunching of the pack-ice which was surging in the land ahead. At night similar noises were also heard; otherwise the ice was quiet, and the crack on the portside has closed up tight again."

"Friday, December 28th. I went out in the morning to have a look at the crack on the port-side, which has now widened out so as to form an open lane. Of course, all the dogs followed me, and I had not got far when I saw a dark form disappear. This was 'Pan,' who rolled down the high steep edge of the ice and fell into the water. In vain he struggled to get out again; all around him there was nothing but snow slush which afforded no foot-hold. I could scarcely hear a sound of him, only just a faint whining now and then. I leant down over the edge in order to get near him, but it was too high, and I very nearly went after him head-first; all that I could get hold of was loose fragments of ice and lumps of snow. I called for a seal-hook, but before it was brought to me 'Pan' had scrambled out himself, and was leaping to and fro on the floe with all his might to keep himself warm, followed by the other dogs who loudly barked and gambolled about with him, as though they wished to demonstrate their joy at his rescue. When he fell in they all rushed forward, looking at me and whining; they evidently felt sorry for him and wished me to help him. They said nothing, but just ran up and down along the edge until he got out. At another moment, perhaps, they may all unite in tearing him to pieces; such is canine and human nature. 'Pan' was allowed to dry himself in the saloon all the afternoon.

"A little before half-past nine to-night the vessel received a tremendous shock. I went out, but no noise of ice-packing could be heard. However, the wind howled so in the rigging that it was not easy to distinguish any other sound. At half-past ten another shock followed; later on, from time to time, vibrations were felt in the vessel, and towards half-past eleven the shocks became stronger. It was clear that the ice was packing at some place or other about us, and I was just on the point of going out when Mogstad came to announce that there was a very ugly pressure-ridge ahead. We went out with lanterns. Fifty-six paces from the bow there extended a perpendicular ridge stretching along the course of the lane, and there was a terrible pressure going on at the moment. It roared and crunched and crackled all along; then it abated a little and recurred at intervals, as though in a regular rhythm; finally it passed over into a continuous roar. It seemed to be mostly newly-frozen ice from the channels which had formed this ridge; but there were also some ponderous blocks of ice to be seen among it. It pressed slowly but surely forward towards the vessel; the ice had given way before it to a considerable distance and was still being borne down little by little. The floe around us has cracked, so that the block of ice in which the vessel is embedded is smaller than it was. I should not like to have that pressure-ridge come in right under the nose of the *Fram*, as it might soon do some damage. Although there is hardly any prospect of its getting so far, nevertheless I have given orders to the watch to keep a sharp look out, and if it comes very near, or if the ice should crack under us, he is to call me. Probably the pressure will soon abate, as it has now kept up for several hours. At this moment (12.45 a.m.) there have just been some violent shocks, and above the howling of the wind in the rigging I can hear the roar of the ice-pressure as I lie in my berth."

Chapter 10

The New Year, 1895

"WEDNESDAY, January 2nd, 1895. Never before have I had such strange feelings at the commencement of the New Year. It cannot fail to bring some momentous events, and will possibly become one of the most remarkable years in my life, whether it leads me to success or to destruction. Years come and go unnoticed in this world of ice, and we have no more knowledge here of what these years have brought to humanity, than we know of what the future ones have in store. In this silent nature no events ever happen; all is shrouded in darkness; there is nothing in view save the twinkling stars, immeasurably far away in the freezing night, and the flickering sheen of the aurora borealis. I can just discern close by the vague outline of the *Fram*, dimly standing out in the desolate gloom, with her rigging showing dark against the host of stars. Like an infinitesimal speck, the vessel seems lost amidst the boundless expanse of this realm of death. Nevertheless under her deck there is a snug and cherished home for thirteen men, undaunted by the majesty of this realm. In there, life is freely pulsating, while far away outside in the night there is nothing save death and silence, only broken now and then, at long intervals, by the violent pressure of the ice as it surges along in gigantic masses. It sounds most ominous in the great stillness, and one cannot help an uncanny feeling as if supernatural powers were at hand, the Jotuns and Rimturser (frost-giants) of the Arctic regions, with whom we may have to engage in deadly combat at any moment; but we are not afraid of them.

"I often think of Shakespeare's Viola who sat 'like patience on a monument.' Could we not pass as representatives of this marble patience, imprisoned here on the ice while the years roll by, awaiting our time? I should like to design such a monument. It should be a lonely man in shaggy wolf-skin clothing, all covered with hoar-frost, sitting on a mound of ice, and gazing out into the darkness across these boundless, ponderous masses of ice, awaiting the return of daylight and spring.

"The ice-pressure was not noticeable after 1 o'clock on Friday night, until it suddenly recommenced last night. First I heard a rumbling outside, and some snow fell down from the rigging upon the tent roof as I sat reading; I thought it sounded like packing in the ice, and just then the *Fram* received a violent shock such as she had not received since last winter. I was rocked backwards and forwards on the chest on which I was sitting. Finding that the trembling and rumbling continued, I went out. There was a loud roar of ice packing to the west and north-west, which continued uniformly for a couple of hours or so. Is this the New Year's greeting from the ice?

"We spent New Year's Eve comfortably, with a cloudberry punch bowl, pipes, and cigarettes; needless to say, there was an abundance of cakes and the like, and we spoke of the Old and the New Year, and days to come. Some selections were played on the organ and violin. Thus midnight arrived. Blessing produced from his apparently inexhaustible store a bottle of genuine 'linje akkevit' (Line eau de vie) and in this Norwegian liquor we drank the Old Year out and the New Year in. Of course there was many a thought that would obtrude itself, at the change of the year, being the second which we had seen on board the *Fram*, and also, in all probability, the last that we should all spend together. Naturally enough, one thanked one's comrades individually and collectively for all kindness and goodfellowship. Hardly one of us had thought, perhaps, that the time would pass so well up here. Sverdrup expressed the wish that the journey which Johansen and I were about to make in the coming year might be fortunate and bring success in all respects. And then we drank to the health and well-being in the coming year of those who were to remain behind on board the *Fram*. It so happened that just now at the turn of the year we stood on the verge of an entirely new world. The wind which whistled up in the rigging overhead was not only wafting us on to unknown regions, but also up into higher latitudes than any human foot had ever trod. We felt that this year, which was just commencing, would bring the culminating point of the expedition, when it would bear its richest fruits. Would that this year might prove a good year for those on board the *Fram*, that the *Fram* might go ahead, fulfilling her task as she has hitherto done, and in that case none of us could doubt that those on board would also prove equal to the work entrusted to them.

"New Year's day was ushered in with the same wind, the same stars and the same darkness as before. Even at noon one cannot see the slightest glimmer of twilight in the south. Yesterday I thought I could trace something of the kind; it extended like a faint gleam of light over the sky, but it was yellowish-white, and stretched too high up, hence I am rather inclined to think that it was an aurora borealis. Again to-day the sky looks lighter near the edge, but this can scarcely be anything except the gleam of the aurora borealis, which extends all round the sky, a little above the fog-banks on the horizon, and which is strongest at the edge. Exactly similar lights may be observed, at other times, in other parts of the horizon. The air was particularly clear yesterday, but the horizon is always somewhat foggy or hazy. During the night we had an uncommonly strong aurora borealis; wavy streamers were darting in rapid twists over the southern sky, their rays reaching to the zenith, and beyond it there was to be seen for a time a band in the form of a gorgeous corona, casting a reflection like moonshine across the ice. The sky had lit up its torch in honour of the New Year — a fairy dance of darting streamers in the depth of night. I cannot help often thinking that this contrast might be taken as typical of the Northman's character and destiny. In the midst of this gloomy, silent nature, with all its numbing cold, we have all these shooting, glittering, quivering rays of light. Do they not typify our impetuous 'spring-dances,' our wild mountain melodies, the auroral gleams in our souls, the rushing, surging, spiritual forces behind the mantle of ice? There is dawning life in the slumbering night, if it could only reach beyond the icy desert, out over the world.

"Thus 1895 comes in

> "Turn, Fortune, turn thy wheel and lower the proud;
> Turn thy wild wheel thro' sunshine, storm, and cloud;
> Thy wheel and thee we neither love nor hate.
> Smile and we smile, the lords of many lands;
> Frown and we smile, the lords of our own hands;
> For man is man and master of his fate."

"Thursday, January 3rd. A day of unrest, a changeful life notwithstanding all its monotony. But yesterday we were full of plans for the future, and to-day how easily might we have been left on the ice without a roof over our heads! At half-past four in the morning a fresh rush of ice set in in the lane aft, and at 5 it commenced in the lane on our port side. About 8 o'clock I awoke, and heard the crunching and crackling of the ice, as if ice-pressure were setting in. A slight trembling was felt throughout the *Fram*, and I heard the roar outside. When I came out I was not a little surprised to find a large pressure-ridge all along the channel on the port side, scarcely thirty paces from the *Fram*; the cracks on this side extended to quite eighteen paces from us. All loose articles that were lying on the ice on this side were stowed away on board; the boards and planks, which during the summer had supported the meteorological hut and the screen for the same, were chopped up, as we could not afford to lose any materials, but the line, which had been left out in the sounding hole with the bag-net attached to it, was caught in the pressure. Just after I had come on board again shortly before noon, the ice suddenly began to press on again. I went out to have a look; it was again in the lane on the port side; there was a strong pressure, and the ridge was gradually approaching. A little later on Sverdrup went up on deck, but soon after came below and told us that the ridge was quickly bearing down on us, and a few hands were required to come up and help to load the sledge with the sounding apparatus, and bring it round to the starboard side of the *Fram*, as the ice had cracked close by it. The ridge began to come alarmingly near, and, should it be upon us before the *Fram* had broken loose from the ice, matters might become very unpleasant. The vessel had now a greater list to the port side than ever.

"During the afternoon various preparations were made to leave the ship if the worst should happen. All the sledges were placed ready on deck, and the kayaks were also made clear; 25 cases of dog-biscuits were deposited on the ice on the starboard side, and 19 cases of bread were brought up and placed forward; also four drums holding altogether 22 gallons of petroleum were put on deck. Ten smaller-sized tins had previously been filled with 100 litres of snowflake oil, and various vessels containing gasoline were also standing on deck. As we were sitting at supper we again heard the same crunching and crackling noise in the ice as usual, coming nearer and nearer, and finally we heard a crash proceeding from right underneath where we sat. I rushed up. There was a pressure of ice in the lane a little way off, almost on our starboard beam. I went down again, and continued my meal. Peter, who had gone out on the ice, soon after came down and said, laughing as usual, that it was no wonder we heard some crackling, for the ice had cracked not a sledge-length away from the dog-biscuit cases, and the crack was extending abaft of the *Fram*. I went out and found the crack was a very considerable one. The dog-biscuit cases were now shifted a little more forward for greater safety. We also found several minor cracks in the ice around the vessel. I then went down and had a pipe and a pleasant chat with Sverdrup in his cabin. After we had been sitting a good while the ice again began to crack and jam. I did not think that the noise was greater than usual, nevertheless I asked those in the saloon, who sat playing halma, whether there was anyone on deck; if not, would one of them be kind enough to go and see where the ice was packing. I heard hurried steps above; Nordahl came down and reported that it was on the port side, and that it would be best for us to be on deck. Peter and I jumped up and several followed. As I went down the ladder Peter called out to me from above: 'We must get the dogs out; see, there is water on the ice!' It was high time that we came; the water was rushing in and already stood high in the kennel. Peter waded into the water up to his knees and pushed the door open; most of the dogs rushed out and jumped about splashing in the water, but some, being frightened, had crept back into the innermost corner and had to be dragged out, although they stood in water reaching high up their legs. Poor brutes, it must have been miserable enough in all conscience to be shut up in such a place while the water was steadily rising about them, yet they are not more noisy than usual.

"The dogs having been put in safety, I walked round the *Fram* to see what else had happened. The ice had cracked along her, to the fore, near the star-board bow; from this crack the water had poured aft along the port side, which was weighed down by the weight of the ridge steadily pressing on towards us. The crack has just passed under the middle of the portable forge, which was thus endangered, and it was therefore put on a sledge and removed to the great hummock on the starboard quarter. The pemmican, altogether eleven cases, the cases of dog-biscuits, and nineteen cases of bread, were conveyed to the same place. Thus we have now a complete depot lying over there, and, I trust, in entire safety, the ice being so thick that it is not likely to give way. This has brought life into the lads; they have all turned out. We took out four more tin cans of petroleum to the hummock, and then proceeded to bring up from the hold and place on deck ready for removal, twenty-one cases of bread, and a supply of pemmican, chocolate, butter, 'vril-food,' soup, etc., calculated to last us 200 days. Also tents, cooking apparatus, and the like were got ready, so that now all is clear up there, and we may sleep securely; but it was past midnight before we had done. I still trust that it is all a false alarm, and that we shall have no occasion for these supplies now at any rate; nevertheless it is our duty to keep everything ready in case the unthinkable should happen. Moreover the watch has been enjoined to mind the dogs on the ice and to keep a sharp look-out in case the ice should crack underneath our cases or the ice-pressure should recommence; if anything should happen we are to be called out at once, too early rather than too late. While I sit here and write I hear the crunching and crackling beginning again outside, so that there must still be a steady pressure on the ice. All are in the best spirits; it almost appears as if they looked upon this as a pleasant break in the monotony of our existence. Well, it is half-past one; I had better turn into my bunk; I am tired, and goodness knows how soon I may be called up.

"Friday, January 4th. The ice kept quiet during the night, but all day with some intervals it has been crackling and settling; and this evening there have been several fits of pressure, from 9 o'clock onwards. For a time it came on, sometimes rather lightly, at regular intervals, sometimes with a rush and a regular roar, then it subsided somewhat, and then it roared anew. Meanwhile the pressure-ridge towers higher and higher and bears right down upon us slowly, while the pressure comes on at intervals only, and more quickly when the onset continues for a time. One can actually see it creeping nearer and nearer, and now at one o'clock at night it is not many feet — scarcely five — away from the edge of the snowdrift on the port side near the gangway, and thence to the vessel is scarcely more than 10 feet, so that it will not be long now before it is upon us. Meanwhile the ice continues to split, and the solid mass in which we are embedded grows less and less both to port and starboard. Several fissures extend right up to the *Fram*. As the ice sinks down under the weight of the ridge on the port side and the *Fram* lists more that way, more water rushes up over the new ice which has frozen on the water that rose yesterday. This is like dying by inches. Slowly but surely the baleful ridge advances, and it looks as if it meant going right over the rail; but if the *Fram* will only oblige by getting free of the ice, she will, I feel confident, extricate herself yet, even though matters look rather awkward at present. We shall probably have a hard time of it, however, before she can break loose, if she does not do so at once. I have been out and had a look at the ridge, and seen how surely it is advancing; I have looked at the fissures in the ice, and noted how they are forming and expanding round the vessel; I have listened to the ice crackling and crunching under foot; and I do not feel much disposed to turn into my berth before I see the *Fram* quite released. As I sit here now I hear the ice making a fresh assault, and roaring and packing outside, and I can tell that the ridge is coming nearer. This is an ice-pressure with a vengeance, and it seems as if it would never cease. I do not think there is anything more that we can do now. All is in readiness for leaving the vessel, if need be. To-day the clothing, etc., was taken out and placed ready for removal, in separate bags for each man.

"It is very strange; there is certainly a possibility that all our plans may be crossed by unforeseen events, although it is not very probable that this will happen. As yet, I feel no anxiety in that direction, only I should like to know whether we are really to take everything on to the ice or not. However, it is past 1 o'clock, and I think the most sensible thing to do would be to turn in and sleep. The watch has orders to call me when the hummock reaches the *Fram*. It is lucky it is moonlight now, so that we are able to see something of all this abomination.

"The day before yesterday we saw the moon for the first time just above the horizon, yesterday it was shining a little, and now we have it both day and night. A most favourable state of things. But it is nearly 2 o'clock, and I must go to sleep now. The pressure of the ice, I can hear, is stronger again."

"Saturday, January 5th. To-night everybody sleeps fully dressed, and with the most indispensable necessaries either by his side or secured to his body, ready to jump on the ice at the first warning. All other requisites such as provisions, clothing, sleeping-bags, etc., etc., have been brought out on the ice. We have been at work at this all day, and have got everything into perfect order, and are now quite ready to leave if necessary, which, however, I do not believe will be the case, though the ice-pressure has been as bad as it could be.

"I slept soundly, woke up only once and listened to the crunching and jamming and grinding till I fell asleep again. I was called at 5.30 in the morning by Sverdrup, who told me that the hummock had now reached the *Fram*, and was bearing down on us violently, reaching as high as the rail; I was not left in doubt very long, as, hardly had I opened my eyes, when I heard a thundering and crashing outside in the ice, as if Doomsday had come. I jumped up. There was nothing left for it but to call all hands, to put all the remaining provisions on the ice, and then put all our furs and other equipment on deck, so that they could be thrown overboard at a moment's notice if necessary. Thus the day passed, but the ice kept quiet. Last of all, the petroleum launch, which was hanging in the davits on the port-side, was lowered, and was dragged towards the great hummock. At about 8 o'clock in the evening, when we thought the ice-pressure had subsided, it started thundering and crashing again worse than ever. I hurried up. Masses of snow and ice rushed on us, high above the rail amidships and over the tent. Peter, who also came up, seized a spade and rushed forward outside the awning as far as the forepart of the half-deck, and stood in the midst of the ice, digging away, and I followed to see how matters stood. I saw more than I cared to see; it was hopeless to fight that enemy with a spade. I called out to Peter to come back, and said 'We had better see to getting everything out on to the ice.' Hardly had I spoken, when it pressed on again with renewed strength, and thundered and crashed, and, as Peter said, laughing till he shook again 'Nearly sent both me and the spade to the deuce.' I rushed back to the main-deck; on the way I met Mogstad, who hurried up, spade in hand, and sent him back. Running forward under the tent towards the ladder, I saw that the tent-roof was bent down under the weight of the masses of ice, which were rushing over it and crashing in over the rail and bulwarks to such an extent that I expected every moment to see the ice force its way through and block up the passage. When I got below, I called all hands on deck; but told them when going up not to go out through the door on the port-side, but through the chart-room and out on the starboard side. In the first place, all the bags were to be brought up from the saloon, and then we were to take those lying on deck. I was afraid that if the door on the port-side were not kept closed, the ice might, if it suddenly burst through the bulwarks and tent, rush over the deck, and in through the door, fill the passage, and rush down the ladder, and thus imprison us like mice in a trap. True, the passage up from the engine-room had been cleared for this emergency, but this was a very narrow hole to get through with heavy bags, and no one could tell how long this hole would keep open, when the ice once attacked us in earnest. I ran up again to set free the dogs, which were shut up in 'Castle-garden' — an enclosure on the deck along the port bulwark. They whined and howled most dolefully under the tent, as the snow masses threatened at any moment to crush it and bury them alive. I cut away the fastening with a knife, pulled the door open, and out rushed most of them by the starboard gangway at full speed.[65]

"Meantime the hands started bringing up the bags. It was quite unnecessary to ask them to hurry up — the ice did that, thundering against the ship's sides in a way that seemed irresistible. It was a fearful hurly-burly in the darkness; for, to cap all, the mate had, in the hurry, let the lanterns go out. I had to go down again to get something on my feet; my Finland shoes were hanging up to dry in the galley. When I got there the ice was at its worst, and the half-deck beams were creaking overhead, so that I really thought they were all coming down.

"The saloon and the berths were soon cleared of bags and the deck as well, and we started taking them along the ice. The ice roared and crashed against the ship's side, so that we could hardly hear ourselves speak; but all went quickly and well, and before long everything was in safety.

"While we were dragging the bags along, the pressure and jamming of the ice had at last stopped, and all was quiet again as before.

"But, what a sight! The *Fram's* port-side was quite buried under the snow; all that could be seen was the top of the tent sticking out. Had the petroleum launch been hanging in the davits, as it was a few hours previously, it would hardly have escaped destruction. The davits were quite buried in ice and snow. It is curious that both fire and water have been powerless against that boat, and it has now come unscathed from the ice, and lies there bottom upwards on the floe. She has had a stormy existence and continual mishaps; I wonder what is next in store for her?

"It was, I must admit, a most exciting scene, when it was at its worst, and we thought it was imperative to get the bags up from the saloon with all possible speed. Sverdrup now tells me that he was just about to have a bath, and was as naked as when he was born, when he heard me call all hands on deck. As this had not happened before, he understood there was something serious the matter, and he jumped into his clothes anyhow. Amundsen, apparently, also realised that something was amiss. He says he was the first who came up with his bag; he had not understood, or had forgotten in the confusion, the order about going out through the starboard door; he groped his way out on the port-side and fell in the dark over the edge of the half-deck. 'Well, that did not matter,' he said, he was quite used to that kind of thing; but having pulled himself together after the fall, and as he was lying there on his back, he dared not move, for it seemed to him as if tent and all were coming down on him, and it thundered and crashed against the gunwale and the hull as if the last hour had come. It finally dawned on him why he ought to have gone out on the starboard and not on the port side.

"All that could possibly be thought to be of any use was taken out. The mate was seen dragging along a big bag of clothes, with a heavy bundle of cups fastened outside it. Later, he was stalking about with all sorts of things such as mittens, knives, cups, etc., fastened to his clothes and dangling about him, so that the rattling noise could be heard afar off. He is himself to the last." In the evening the men all started eating their stock of cakes, sweetmeats, and such-like, smoked tobacco, and enjoyed themselves in the most animated fashion. They evidently thought it was uncertain when they should next have such a time on board the *Fram*, and therefore they thought it was best to avail themselves of the opportunity. We are now living in marching order on an empty ship.

"By way of precaution we have now burst open again the passage on the starboard side which was used as a library and had therefore been closed; and all doors are now kept always open, so that we can be sure of getting out, even if anything should give way. We do not want the ice-pressure to close the doors against us, by jamming the doorposts together. But she certainly is a strong ship. It is a mighty ridge that we have in our port side, and the masses of ice are tremendous. The ship is listing more than ever, nearly 7°; but since the last pressure she has righted herself a little again, so that she must surely have broken away from the ice, and begun to rise, and all danger is doubtless over. So, after all, it has been a case of 'Much ado about nothing.'"

"Sunday, January 6th. A quiet day; no jamming since last night. Most of the fellows slept well on into the morning. This afternoon all have been very busy digging the *Fram* out of the ice again, and we have now got the rail clear right aft to the half-deck; but a tremendous mass had fallen over the tent. It was above the second ratline in the fore-shrouds, and fully 6 feet over the rail. It is a marvel that the tent stood it; but it was a very good thing that it did do so, for otherwise it is hard to say what might have become of many of the dogs. This afternoon Hansen took a meridian observation, which gave 83° 34' N. lat. Hurrah! We are getting on well, northward; thirteen minutes since Monday, and the most northern latitude is now reached. It goes without saying that the occasion was duly celebrated with a bowl of punch, preserved fruits, cakes, and the doctor's cigars.

"Last night we were running with the bags for our lives; to-night we are drinking punch and feasting; such are, indeed, the vicissitudes of fate. All this roaring and crashing for the last few days has been, perhaps, a cannonade to celebrate our reaching such a high latitude. If that be so it must be admitted that the ice has done full honour to the occasion. Well, never mind, let it crash on so long as we only get northward. The *Fram* will, no doubt, stand it now; she has lifted fully one foot forward and fully six inches aft; and she has slipped a little a-stern. Moreover, we cannot find so much as a single stancheon in the bulwarks that has started; yet to-night every man will sleep fully prepared to make for the ice."

"Monday, January 7th. There was a little jamming of the ice occasionally during the day, but only of slight duration; then all was quiet again. Evidently the ice has not yet settled, and we have perhaps more to expect from our friend to port, whom I would willingly exchange for a better neighbour.

It seems, however, as if the ice pressure had altered its direction since the wind has changed to S.E. It is now confined to the ridges fore and aft, athwart the wind; while our friend to port, lying almost in the line of the wind, has kept somewhat quieter.

"Everything has an end, as the boy said when he was in for a birching. Perhaps the growth of this ridge has come to an end now, perhaps not; the one thing is just as likely as the other.

"To-day the work of extricating the *Fram* is proceeding; we will at all events get the rails clear of the ice. It presents a most imposing sight by the light of the moon, and however conscious of one's own strength, one cannot help respecting an antagonist who commands such powers, and who, in a few moments, is capable of putting mighty machinery into action. It is rather an awkward battering-ram to face. The *Fram* is equal to it, but no other ship could have resisted such an onslaught. In less than an hour this ice can build up a wall alongside us and over us, which it might take us a month to get out of, and possibly longer than that. There is something gigantic about it; it is like a struggle between dwarfs and an ogre, in which the pigmies have to resort to cunning and trickery to get out of the clutches of one who seldom relaxes his grip. The *Fram* is the ship which the pigmies have built with all their cunning in order to fight the ogre, and on board this ship they work as busily as ants, while the ogre only thinks it worth while to roll over and twist his body about now and then, but every time he turns over it seems as though the nutshell would be smashed and buried, and would disappear; but the pigmies have built their nutshell so cleverly that it always keeps afloat, and wriggles itself free from the deadly embrace. The old traditions and legends about giants, about Thor's battles in the Jotunheim, when rocks were split and crags were hurled about, and the valleys were filled with falling boulders, all come back to me, when I look at these mighty ridges of ice winding their way far off in the moonlight; and when I see the men standing on the ice heap, cutting and digging to remove a fraction of it, then they seem to me smaller than pigmies, smaller than ants. But although each ant carries only a single fir-needle, yet in course of time the ants build an anthill, where they can live comfortably, sheltered from storm and winter.

"Had this attack on the *Fram* been planned by the aid of all the wickedness in the world, it could not have been a worse one. The floe, 7 feet thick, has borne down on us on the port side, forcing itself up on the ice in which we are lying,

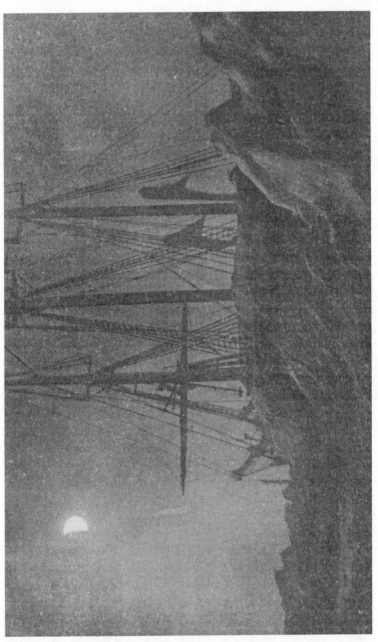

The Fram bathed in moonlight next to the pressure ridge, 14 January 1895.

and crushing it down. Thus the *Fram* was forced down with the ice, while the other floe, packed up on the ice beneath, bore down on her, and took her amidship while she was still frozen fast. As far as I can judge, she could hardly have had a tighter squeeze; it was no wonder that she groaned under it; but she withstood it, broke loose, and eased. Who shall say after this that a vessel's shape is of little consequence? Had the *Fram* not been designed as she was, we should not have been sitting here now. Not a drop of water is to be found in her anywhere. Strangely enough, the ice has not given us another such squeeze since then; perhaps it was its expiring grip we felt on Saturday?

"It is hard to tell, but it was terrific enough. This morning Sverdrup and I went for a walk on the ice, but when we got a little way from the ship, we found no sign of any new packing, the ice was smooth and unbroken as before. The packing has been limited to a certain stretch from east to west, and the *Fram* has been lying at the very worst point of it.

This afternoon Hansen has worked out yesterday's observation, the result being 83° 34′ 2″ N. lat. and 102° 51′ E. long. We have therefore drifted north and westward; 15 miles west, indeed, and only 13.5 north, since New Year's Eve, while the wind has been mostly from the south-west. It seems as if the ice has taken a more decided course towards the north-west than ever, and therefore it is not to be wondered at that there is some pressure when the wind blows athwart the course of the ice. However, I hardly think we need any particular explanation of the pressure, as we have evidently again got into a packing-centre with cracks, lanes, and ridges, where the pressure is maintained for some time, such as we were in during the first winter. We have constantly met with several similar stretches on the surrounding ice, even when it has been most quiet.

"This evening there was a most remarkable brightness right under the moon. It was like an immense luminous haycock, which rose from the horizon, and touched the great ring round the moon. At the upper side of this ring there was a segment of the usual inverted arc of light."

The next day, January 8th, the ice began grinding occasionally, and while Mogstad and I stood in the hold working on hand-sledges we heard creakings in the ship both above and below us. This was repeated several times; but in the intervals it was quiet. I was often on the ice listening to the grinding and watching how it went on, but it did not go beyond crackling and creaking beneath our feet and in the ridge at our side. Perhaps it is to warn us not to be too confident! I am not so sure that it is not necessary. It is in reality like living on a smoking volcano. The eruption that will seal our fate may occur at any moment. It will either force the ship up or swallow her down. And what are the stakes? Either the *Fram* will get home and the expedition be fully successful, or we shall lose her and have to be content with what we have done, and possibly on our way home we may explore parts of Franz Josef Land. That is all; but most of us feel that it would be hard to lose the ship, and it would be a very sad sight to see her disappear.

"Some of the hands under Sverdrup are working, trying to cut away the hummock-ice on the port side, and they have already made good headway. Mogstad and I are busy getting the sledges in order, and preparing them for use as I want them, whether we go north or south.

"Liv is two years old to-day.

"She is a big girl now. I wonder if I should be able to recognise her; I suppose I should hardly find a single familiar feature. They are sure to celebrate the day, and she will get all kinds of presents. Many a thought will be sent northwards; but they know not where to look for us; are not aware that we are drifting here embedded in the ice in the highest northern latitudes ever reached, in the deepest polar-night ever penetrated."

During the following days the ice became steadily quieter. In the course of the night of the 9th of January the ice was still slightly cracking and grinding; then it quite subsided, and on the 10th of January the report is "ice perfectly quiet, and if it were not for the ridge on the port side, one would never have thought there had ever been any breach in the eternal stillness, so calm and peaceful is it." Some men went on cutting away the ice, and little by little we could see it is getting less. Mogstad and I were busily engaged in the hold with the new sledges, and during this time I also made an attempt to photograph the *Fram* by moonlight from different points. The results surpassed my expectations; but as the top of the pressure-ridge had now been cut away, these photos do not give an exact impression of the pack-ice, and of how it came hurtling down upon the *Fram*. We then put in order our depôt on the great hummock on the starboard quarter, and all sleeping bags, Lapland boots, Finn-shoes, wolf-skin clothing, etc., were wrapped in the foresail and placed to the extreme west, the provisions were collected into six different heaps, and the rifles and guns were distributed among three of the heaps and wrapped up in boat-sails. Next, Hansen's instrument-case and my own, together with a bucket-full of rifle-cartridges, were placed under a boat-sail. Then the forge and the smith's tools were arranged separately; and up on the top of the great hummock we laid a heap of sledges and snow-shoes. All the kayaks were laid side by side bottom upwards, the cooking apparatus and lamps, etc., being placed under them. They were spread out in this way, so that in the improbable event of thick floe splitting suddenly, our loss would not be so great. We knew where to find everything, and it might blow and drift to its heart's content, without our losing anything.

On the evening of January 14th, I wrote in my diary "Two sharp reports were heard in the ship, like shots from a cannon, and then followed a noise, as of something splitting — presumably this must be the cracking of the ice, on account of the frost. It appeared to me that the list on the ship increased at that moment, but perhaps it was only imagination."

As time passed on we all gradually got busy again preparing for the sledge-expedition. On Tuesday, January 15th, I say: "This evening the doctor gave a lesson to Johansen and myself in bandaging and repairing broken limbs. I lay on the table and had a plaster of Paris bandage put round the calf of my leg, while all the crew were looking on. The very sight of this operation cannot fail to suggest unpleasant thoughts. An accident of this nature out in the Polar night with 40° to 50° of cold, would be anything but pleasant, to say nothing of how easily it might mean death to both of us. But who knows? — we might manage somehow. However, such things must not be allowed to happen, and what is more they *shall not*."

As January went on, we could by noon just see the faint dawn of day — that day at whose sunrise we were to start. On January 18th, I say: "By 9 o'clock in the morning I could already distinguish the first indications of dawn, and by noon, it seemed to be getting bright; but it seems hardly credible that in a month's time there will be light enough to travel by, Yet it must be so. True, February is a month which all 'experienced' people consider far too early and much too cold for travelling; hardly anyone would do so in the month of March. But it cannot be helped, we have no time to waste in waiting for additional comfort, if we are to make any progress before the summer, when travelling will be impossible. I am not afraid of the cold, we can always protect ourselves against that.

"Meantime all preparations are proceeding, and I am now getting everything in order connected with copying of diaries, observation books, photographs, etc., that we are to take with us. Mogstad is working in the hold, making maple guard-runners to put under the sledges. Jacobsen has commenced to put a new sledge together. Pettersen is in the engine-room, making nails for the sledge-fittings, which Mogstad is to put on. In the meantime some of the

Removing the snow of an Ice Pressure.

others have built a large forge out on the ice with blocks of ice and snow, and to-morrow Sverdrup and I will heat and bend the runners in tar and stearine at such a heat as we can produce in the forge. We trust we shall be able to get a sufficient temperature to do this important work thoroughly, in spite of the 40 degrees of frost. Amundsen is now repairing the mill, as there is something wrong with it again, the cog-wheels being worn. He thinks he will be able to get it all right again. Rather chilly work to be lying up there in the wind on the top of the mill, boring in the hard steel and cast-iron by lantern light, and at such a temperature as we are having now. I stood and watched the lantern-light up there to-day, and I soon heard the drill working; one could tell the steel was hard; then I could hear clapping of hands. 'Ah,' thought I, 'you may well clap your hands together, it is not a particularly warm job to be lying up there in the wind.' The worst of it is one cannot wear mittens for such work, but has to use the bare hands if one is to make any progress, and it would not take long to freeze them off; but it has to be done, he says, and he will not give in. He is a splendid fellow in all he undertakes, and I console him by saying that there are not many before him who have worked on the top of a mill in such frost north of 83°. On many expeditions they have avoided out-of-door work when the temperature got so low. 'Indeed,' he says, 'I thought that other expeditions were in advance of us in that respect. I imagined we had kept indoors too much.' I had no hesitation in enlightening him on this point; I know he will do his best in any case.

"This is, indeed, a strange time for me; I feel as if I were preparing for a summer trip, and the spring was already here; yet it is still mid-winter, and the conditions of the summer trip may be somewhat ambiguous. The ice keeps quiet, the cracking in it and in the *Fram* is due only to the cold. I have during the last few days again read Payer's account of his sledge expedition northwards through Austria Sound. It is not very encouraging. The very land he describes as the realm of Death, where he thinks he and his companions would inevitably have perished had they not recovered the vessel, is the place to which we look for salvation; that is the region we hope to reach when our provisions have come to an end. It may seem reckless, but nevertheless I cannot imagine that it is so. I cannot help believing that a land, which even in April teems with bears, auks, and black guillemots, and where seals are basking on the ice, must be a 'Canaan, flowing with milk and honey,' for two men who have good rifles and good eyes; it must surely yield food enough not only for the needs of the moment, but also provisions for the journey onwards to Spitzbergen. Sometimes, however, the thought will present itself that it may be very difficult to get the food when it is most sorely needed; but these are only passing moments. We must remember Carlyle's words: 'A man shall and must be valiant, he must march forward, and quit himself like a man — trusting imperturbably in the appointment and choice of the Upper Powers.' I have not, it is true, any 'Upper Powers'; it would probably be well to have them in such a case; but we nevertheless are starting, and the time approaches rapidly. Four weeks or a little more soon pass by, and then farewell to this snug nest, which has been our home for eighteen months, and we go out into the darkness and cold, out into the still more unknown

> "Out yonder 'tis dark,
> But onward we must,
> Over the dewy wet mountains,
> Ride through the land of the ice-troll;
> We shall both be saved,
> Or the ice-troll's hand
> Shall clutch us both."

On January 23rd I write: "The dawn has grown so much that there was a visible light from it on the ice, and for the first time this year I saw the crimson glow of the sun low down in the dawn." We now took soundings with the lead, before I was to leave the vessel; we found 1,876 fathoms (3,450 metres). I then made some snowshoes down in the hold; it was important to have them smooth, tough and light, on which one could make good headway; "they shall be well rubbed with tar, stearine, and tallow, and there shall be speed in them; then it is only a question of using one's legs, and I have no doubt that can be managed."

Tuesday, January 29th. Latitude yesterday 83° 30'. Some days ago we had been so far north as 83° 40', but had again drifted southwards. The light keeps on steadily increasing, and by noon it almost seems to be broad daylight. I believe I could read the title of a book out in the open if the print were large and clear. I take a stroll every morning, greeting the dawning day, before I go down into the hold to my work at the snow-shoes and equipment. My mind is filled with a peculiar sensation, which I cannot clearly define; there is certainly an exulting feeling of triumph deep in the soul, a feeling that all one's dreams are about to be realised with the rising sun, which steers northwards across the icebound waters. But while I am busy in these familiar surroundings, a wave of sadness sometimes comes over me; it is like bidding farewell to a dear friend and

The Fram after the Ice Pressure of 10 January 1895.

The *Fram*, seen from the stern after the Ice Pressure of 10 January 1895.

to a home, which has long afforded me a sheltering roof; at one blow all this and my dear comrades are to be left behind for ever; never again shall I tread this snow-clad deck, never again creep under this tent, never hear the laughter ring in this familiar saloon, never again sit in this friendly circle.

"And then I remember that when the *Fram* at last bursts from her bonds of ice, and turns her prow towards Norway, I shall not be with her. A farewell imparts to everything in life its own tinge of sadness, like the crimson rays of the sun, when the day, good or bad, sinks in tears below the horizon.

"Hundreds of times my eye wanders to the map hanging there on the wall, and each time a chill creeps over me. The distance before us seems so long, and the obstacles in our path may be many; but then again the feeling comes, that we are bound to pull through; it cannot be otherwise; everything is too carefully prepared to fail now; and meanwhile the south-east wind is whistling above us and we are continually drifting northwards nearer our goal. When I go up on deck and step out into the night, with its glittering starry vault and the flaring aurora borealis, then all these thoughts recede and I must as ever pause on the threshold of this sanctuary, this dark, deep, silent space, this infinite temple of nature, in which the soul seeks to find its origin. Toiling ant, what matters it, whether you reach your goal with your fir-needle or not! Everything disappears none the less in the ocean of eternity, in the great Nirvana. 'And as time rolls on our names are forgotten, our deeds pass into oblivion and our lives flit by like the traces of a cloud and vanish like the mist, dispelled by the warm rays of the sun. Our time is but a fleeting shadow, hurrying us on to the end, so it is ordained; and having reached that end none ever retraced his steps.'

"Two of us will soon be journeying further through this immense waste, into greater solitude and deeper stillness."

"Wednesday, January 30th. To-day the great event has happened, that the windmill is again at work for the first time after its long rest. In spite of the cold and the darkness, Amundsen had got the cogwheels into order, and now it is running as smoothly and steadily as "guttapercha."

We have now constant north-east winds, and we again bore northwards. On Sunday, February 3rd, we were at 83° 43'. The time for our departure approached, and the preparations were carried on with great activity. The sledges were completed, and I tried them under various conditions. I have alluded to the fact that we made maple guards to put under the fixed nickel-plated runners. The idea of this was to strengthen both the sledges and the runners, so that they would at the beginning of the journey, when the loads were heavy, be less liable to breakage from the jolting to which they would probably be exposed. Later on, when the load got lighter, we might, if we thought fit, easily remove them. These guards were also to serve another purpose. I had an idea that, in view of the low temperature we had during the winter, and on the dry drift-snow, which then covered the ice-floes, metal would glide less easily than smooth wood, especially if the latter were well rubbed with rich tar and stearine. By February 8th one of the sledges with wooden guardrunners was finished, so that we could make experiments in this direction, and we then found that it was considerably easier to haul than a similar sledge running on the nickel-plate, though the load on each was exactly the same. The difference was so great that we found that it was at least half as hard again to draw a sledge on the nickel runners as on the tarred maple runners.

Our new ash sledges were now nearly finished and weighed 30 lbs. without the guard-runners. "Everybody is hard at work. Sverdrup is sewing bags or bolsters to put on the sledges as beds for the kayaks to rest on. To this end the bags are to be made up to fit the bottoms of the boats. Johansen and one or two other men are stuffing the bags with pemmican, which has to be warmed, beaten, and kneaded in order to give it the right form for making a good bed for our precious boats. When these square, flat bags are carried out into the cold they freeze as hard as stone, and keep their form well. Blessing is sitting up in the work-room, copying the photographs of which I have no prints. Hansen is working out a map of our route so far, and copying out his observations for us, etc., etc. In short, there is hardly a man on board who does not feel that the moment for departure approaches; perhaps the galley is the only place where everything goes on in the usual way under the management of Lars. Our position yesterday was 83° 32.1′ N. lat., and 102° 28′ E. long., so we are southwards again; but never mind, what do a dozen miles more or less matter to us?"

"Sunday, February 10th. To-day there was so much daylight that at 1 o'clock I could fairly well read the *Verdens Gang*, when I held the paper up towards the light; but when I held it towards the moon, which was low in the north, it was no go. Before dinner I went for a short drive with 'Gulen' and 'Susine' (two of the young dogs) and 'Kaifas.' 'Gulen' had never been in harness before, but yet she went quite well; she was certainly a little awkward at first, but that soon disappeared, and I think she will make a good dog when she is well trained. 'Susine,' who was driven a little last autumn, conducted herself quite like an old sledge-dog. The surface is hard, and easy for the dogs to haul on. They get a good foothold, and the snow is not particularly sharp for their feet; however, it is not over smooth; this drift-snow makes heavy going. The ice is smooth, and easy to run on, and I trust we shall be able to make good day-journeys; after all, we shall reach our destination sooner than we had expected. I cannot deny that it is a long journey, and scarcely anyone has ever more effectually burnt his boats behind him. If we wished to turn back we have absolutely nothing to return to, not even a bare coast. It will be impossible to find the ship, and before us lies the great unknown. But there is only one road, and that lies straight ahead, right through, be it land or sea, be it smooth or rough, be it mere ice or ice and water. And I cannot but believe that we must get through, even if we should meet with the worst, viz., land and pack-ice.

"Wednesday, February 13th. The pemmican bolsters and dried liver pie are now ready; the kayaks will get an excellent bedding, and I venture to say that such meat bolsters are an absolute novelty. Under each kayak there are three of them, they are made to fit the sledge, and as already stated, are moulded to the shape of the kayak. They weigh 100 to 120 lbs. each. The empty sacks weigh 2 or 3 lbs. each, so that altogether the meat (pemmican and liver pie) in these three bags will weigh about 320 lbs. We each had our light sleeping-bags of reindeer's-skin, and we tried to sleep out in them last night, but both Johansen and I found it rather cold, although it was only 37° F. of frost. We were, perhaps, too lightly clad under the wolf's-skin clothing; we are doing another experiment with a little more on to-night."

"Saturday, February 16th. The outfitting is still progressing; but there are various small things yet to do which take time, and I do not know whether we shall be ready to start on Wednesday, February 20th, as I originally intended. The day is now so light that as far as that is concerned we might quite well start then, but, perhaps, we had better wait a day or two longer. Three sledge-sails (for single sledges) are now finished; they are made of very light calico, and are about 7 feet 2 inches broad by 4 feet 4 inches long; they are made so that two of them may be laced together and used as one sail for a double sledge, and I believe they will act well; they weigh a little over 1 lb. each. Moreover, we have now most of the provisions ready stowed away in bags."

Chapter 11

We Make a Start

"TUESDAY, February 26th. At last the day has arrived, the great day, when the journey is to commence. The week has passed in untiring work to get everything ready. We should have started on the 20th, but it has been postponed from day to day; there was always something still to do. My head has been full night and day, with all that was to be done and that must not be forgotten. Oh, this unceasing mental strain, which does not allow a minute's respite in which to throw off the responsibility, to give loose rein to the thoughts and let the dreams have full sway; the nerves are in a state of tension from the moment of awaking in the morning till the eyes close late at night. Ah! how well I know this state, which I have experienced each time I have been about to set out, and retreat was to be cut off — never, I believe, more effectively than now. The last few nights I did not get to bed before half-past three or half-past four o'clock in the morning. It is not only what we ought to take with us that has to be taken care of, but we have to leave the vessel; its command and responsibility have to be placed in other hands, and care must be taken that nothing is forgotten in the way of instructions to the men who remain; for the scientific observations will have to be continued on the same lines as they have been carried on hitherto, and other observations of all kinds will have to be made, etc., etc."

The last night we were to spend on board the *Fram* eventually arrived, and we had a farewell party. In a strange, sad way, reminiscences were revived of all that had befallen us here on board, mingled with hope and trust in what the future would bring. I remained up till far into the night; letters and remembrances had to be sent to those at home, in case the unforeseen should happen. Amongst the last thing I wrote were the following instructions to Sverdrup, in which I handed over to him the command of the expedition:

"CAPTAIN OTTO SVERDRUP.

"Commander of the *Fram*.

"As I am now leaving the *Fram*, accompanied by Johansen, to undertake a journey northwards — if possible to the Pole — and from there to Spitzbergen, most likely *via* Franz Josef Land, I make over to you the command of the remaining part of the expedition. From the day I leave the *Fram*, all the authority which hitherto was vested in me shall devolve upon you to an equal extent, and the others will have to render absolute obedience to you, or to whomsoever you may depute as their leader. I consider it superfluous to give any orders about what is to be done under various contingencies, even if it were possible to give any. I am certain you will know best yourself, what ought to be done in any emergency, and I therefore consider that I may with confidence leave the *Fram*.

"The chief aim of the expedition is to push through the unknown Polar Sea from the region around the New Siberian Islands, north of Franz Josef Land, and onward to the Atlantic Ocean near Spitzbergen or Greenland. The most essential part of this task, I consider, we have already accomplished; the remainder will be achieved as the expedition gets farther west. In order to make the expedition still more fruitful of results, I am making an attempt to push further up north with the dogs. Your task will then be to convey home, in the safest manner possible, the human lives now confided to your care, and not to expose them to any unnecessary danger, either out of regard for the ship or cargo, or for the scientific outcome of the expedition. No one can tell how long it may take before the *Fram* drifts out into open water. You have provisions for several years to come; if for any unknown reason it should take too long, or if the crew should begin to suffer in health, or if from other reasons you should think it best to abandon the vessel, it should unquestionably be done. As to the time of the year when this should be done, and the route to be chosen, you yourself will be best able to judge. If it should be necessary, I consider Franz Josef Land and Spitzbergen favourable lands to make for. If search is made for the expedition after the arrival home of Johansen and myself, it will be made there first. Wherever you come to land, you should, as often as you can, erect conspicuous beacons on promontories and projecting headlands, and place within the beacons a short report of what has occurred, and whither you are going. In order to distinguish these beacons from others, a small beacon should be erected 13 feet from the larger one in the direction of the magnetic North Pole. The question as to what outfit would be most advantageous, in case the *Fram* should have to be abandoned, is one which we have so frequently discussed that I consider it superfluous to dwell on it here. I know that you will take care that the requisite number of kayaks for all the men, sledges, snow-shoes, 'truger,' and other articles of outfit are put in complete order as soon as possible, and kept in readiness, so that such a journey home over the ice could be undertaken with the greatest possible ease. Elsewhere I give you directions as to the provisions which I consider most suitable for such a journey, and the quantity necessary for each man.

"I also know that you will hold everything in readiness to abandon the *Fram* in the shortest possible time in the event of her suffering sudden damage, whether through fire or ice-pressure. If the ice permits it, I consider it advisable that a depôt, with sufficient provisions, etc., should be established at a safe place on the ice, such as we have lately had. All necessaries which cannot be kept on the ice ought to be so placed on board that they are easy to get at under any circumstances. As you are aware, all the provisions now in the depôt are concentrated foods for sledging journeys only; but as it may happen that you will have to remain inactive for a time before going further, it would be highly desirable to save as much tinned meat, fish, and vegetables as possible; should troubled times come then, I should consider it advisable to have a supply of these articles ready on the ice.

"Should the *Fram* while drifting be carried far to the north of Spitzbergen, and get over into the current under the east coast of Greenland, many possibilities may be imagined which it is not easy to form an opinion on now; but should you be obliged to abandon the *Fram* and make for the land, it would be best for you to erect beacons there as stated above (with particulars as to whither you are going, etc.), as search might possibly be made there for the expedition. Whether in that case you ought to make for Iceland (which is the nearest land), and where you should be able to get in the early part of summer, if following the edge of the ice, or for the Danish colonies west of Cape Farewell, you will be best able to judge on considering all the circumstances.

"As regards what you ought to take with you in the event of abandoning the *Fram*, besides the necessary provisions, I may mention weapons, ammunition, and equipment, *all scientific and other journals and observations, all scientific collections that are not too heavy*, or if too heavy small samples thereof;

photographs, preferably the original plates (or films), or should these prove too heavy, then prints taken from them; also the 'Aderman' aerometer, with which most of the observations on the specific gravity of sea-water are taken; as well as, of course, all journals and memoranda which are of any interest. I leave behind some diaries and letters, which I would request you to take special care of, and deliver to Eva, if I should not return home, or if, contrary to all expectation, you should return home before us.

"Hansen and Blessing will, as you know, attend to the various scientific expeditions and to the collecting of specimens. You yourself will attend to the soundings, and see that they are taken as frequently as possible and as the condition of the line permits. I should consider at least once in every 60 miles covered to be *extremely desirable*; if it can be done oftener so much the better. Should the depth become less than now and more variable, it goes without saying that soundings should be taken more frequently.

"As the crew was small before, and will now be still further reduced by two men, more work will probably fall to each man's lot; but I know that, whenever you can, you will spare men to assist in the scientific observations, and make them as complete as possible. Please also see that every tenth day (the first, tenth, and twentieth of every month) the ice is bored through, and the thickness measured, in the same way as has been done hitherto. Henriksen has for the most part made these borings, and is a trustworthy man for this work.

"In conclusion, I wish all possible success to you, and to those for whom you are now responsible, and may we meet again in Norway, whether it be on board of this vessel, or without her.

"Yours affectionately,

"FRIDTJOF NANSEN.

"On board the *Fram*, February 25, 1895."

"Now at last the brain was to get some rest, and the work for the legs and arms was to commence. Everything was got ready for the start this morning. Five of our comrades, Sverdrup, Hansen, Blessing, Henriksen, and Mogstad were to see us off on our way, bringing a sledge and a tent with them. The four sledges were got ready, the dogs harnessed to them, lunch with a bottle of malt extract per man, was taken just before starting, and then we bade the last hearty farewell to those left behind. We were off into the drifting snow. I myself took the lead with 'Kvik' as leading dog, in the first sledge, and then sledge after sledge followed amid cheers, accompanied by the cracking of whips and the barking of dogs. At

Crew photograph: Mogstad, Blessing, Hansen, Amundsen, Bentzen, Sverdrup, Jacobsen, Juell, Nordahl, Pettersen, Henriksen.

the same time a salute was fired from the quarter-deck, shot after shot, into the whirling drift. The sledges moved heavily forward; it was slow travelling uphill, and they came to a dead stop where the ascent was too steep, and we all had to help them along, one man alone could not do it; but over level ground we flew along like a whirlwind, and those on snow-shoes found it difficult enough to keep pace with the sledges. I had to strike out as best I could when they came up to me to avoid getting my legs entangled in the line. A man is beckoning with his staff far in the rear. It is Mogstad, who comes tearing along and shouting that three 'flöitstokker'[66] (cross-bars) had been torn off a sledge in driving. The sledge, with its heavy load, had lurched forward over an upright piece of ice, which struck the cross-bars, breaking all three of them, one after the other; one or two of the perpendicular supports of the runners were also smashed. There was nothing for it but to return to the ship to get it repaired and have the sledges made stronger. Such a thing ought not to happen again. During the return one of the sledges lurched up against another, and a cane in the bow snapped. The bows would, therefore, also have to be made stronger.[67]

"The sledges have again been unloaded and brought on board, in order that this may be done, and here we are again to-night. I am glad, however, that this happened when it did; it would have been worse to have had such an experience a few days later. I will now take six sledges instead of four, so that the load on each may be less, and so that it will be easier to lift them over the irregularities of the ground. I shall also have a broad board fitted lengthwise to the sledge, underneath the cross-bars, so as to protect them against projecting pieces of ice. As a great deal of time is saved in the end by doing such things thoroughly before starting, we shall not be ready to start before the day after to-morrow. It seemed strange to be on board again after having said good-bye, as I thought, for ever, to these surroundings. When I carne up on the after-deck, I found the guns lying there in the snow, one of them turned over on its back, the other had recoiled a long way aft, when saluting us; from the mizzen-top the red and black flag was still waving.

"I am in wonderfully high spirits, and feel confident of success; the sledges seemed to glide so easily, although carrying 200 lbs. more than was originally intended (about 2,200 lbs. altogether), and everything looks very promising. We shall have to wait a couple of days, but as we are having a south-easterly wind all day long, we are no doubt getting on towards the north, all the same. Yesterday we were 83° 41', today I suppose we are at least 83° 50'."

At last, on Thursday, February 28th, we started again with our six sledges. Sverdrup, Hansen, Blessing, Henriksen, and Mogstad saw us off. When we started most of the others also accompanied us some distance. We soon found that the dogs did not draw as well as I had expected, and I came to the conclusion that with this load we should get on too slowly. We had not proceeded far from the ship before I decided to leave behind some of the sacks with provisions for the dogs, and these were later on taken back on board by the others.

At 4 o'clock in the afternoon, when we stopped, our odometer[68] showed that we had gone about 4 miles from the *Fram*. We had a pleasant evening in the tent together with our friends who were going back the next day. To my surprise a punch-bowl was prepared, and toasts were proposed for those who were starting and those who remained behind. It was not until 11 o'clock that we crept into our sleeping-bags.

There were illuminations in our honour that night on board the *Fram*. The electric arc lamp was hoisted on the main-top, and the electric light for the first time shone forth over the ice masses of the Polar Sea. Torches had also been lit, and bonfires of oakum-ends and other combustibles were burning on several floes around the *Fram* and making a brilliant show. Sverdrup had, by the way,

Last farewell from our comerades.

given orders that the electric light or a lantern should be hoisted on the main-top every night until he and the others had returned, for fear they might lose their way if the tracks should be obliterated by bad weather. It would then be very difficult to find the ship; but such a light can be seen a long distance over these plains, where by merely standing on a hummock one can easily get a view for many miles round.

I was afraid that the dogs, if they got loose, would go back to the *Fram*, and I therefore got two steel-lines made to which short leashes were fastened, a little distance apart, so that the dogs could be secured to these lines between two sticks or sledges. In spite of this several of the dogs got loose, but strange to say, they did not leave us, but remained with their comrades and us. There was of course a doleful howling round the tents the first night, and they disturbed our sleep to some extent.

The next morning (Friday, March 1st) it took one of our comrades three hours to make the coffee, being unaccustomed to the apparatus. We had then a very nice breakfast together. Not before 11.30 a.m. did we get underway. Our five comrades accompanied us for an hour or two and then turned to get back to the *Fram* the same evening. "It was certainly a most cheerful good-bye," says the diary, "but it is always hard to part even at 84°, and may be there was a tearful eye or two." The last thing Sverdrup asked me when sitting on his sledge, just as we were about to part, was, if I thought I should go to the South Pole when I got home, for if so he hoped I would wait till he arrived; and then he asked me to give his love to his wife and child.

And so we proceeded, Johansen and I, but it was slow work for us alone with six sledges, which were impeded on their way by all sorts of obstacles and inequalities. Besides this, the ice became rougher, and it was difficult to get on during the afternoon on account of the darkness, the days being still very short, for the sun was not yet above the horizon. We therefore camped rather early.

"Wednesday, March 6th. We are again on board the *Fram* to make a fresh start for the third time, and then, I suppose, it will be in earnest. On Saturday, March 2nd, we proceeded with the six sledges after I had been a trip to the northward, and found it passable. Progress was slow, and we had to do nearly six turns each, as the sledges stopped everywhere and had to be helped along. I saw now too clearly that we should never get on in this manner; a change would have to be made, and I decided to camp in order to have a look at the ice northward and consider the matter. Having tied up the dogs, I set out, while Johansen was to feed the dogs and put up the tent. They were fed once in every 24 hours, at night, when the day's march was done.

"I had not gone far when I came upon excellent spacious plains, good progress could be made, and so far everything was all right; but the load had to be diminished and the number of sledges reduced. Undoubtedly, therefore, it would be best to return to the *Fram* to make the necessary alterations on board, and get the sledges we were to take with us further strengthened, so as to have perfect confidence in their durability.

"We might, of course, have dragged along, somehow, towards the north for a while, and the load would gradually have decreased; but it would have been slow work, and before the load would be sufficiently lightened the dogs would perhaps be worn out. It was cold for them at night; we heard many of them howling most of the night. If, however, we diminished the load, and consequently allowed a shorter time for the journey, it would be preferable to wait, and not start till a little later in the month, when we could make more out of the time, as the days would be lighter and not so cold, and the snowsurface better. Having spent another night in the tent — into which it was a hard job to get dressed in a fur that was stiff with frost, and then into a bag that was also hard frozen

Campsite of 1 March 1895.

— I decided next morning (Sunday, March 3rd) to return to the *Fram*. I harnessed a double team of dogs to one of the sledges, and off they went over pressure-ridges and all other obstacles so rapidly that I could hardly keep up with them. In a few hours I covered the same distance which had taken us three days when we started out. The advantage of a lighter load was only too apparent.

"As I approached the *Fram* I saw to my surprise the upper edge of the sun above the ice in the south. It was the first time this year, but I had not expected it as yet. It was the refraction caused by the low temperature which made it visible so soon. The first news I heard from those who came to meet me was that Hansen had the previous afternoon taken an observation, which gave 84° 4' N. lat.

"It was undoubtedly very pleasant once more to stretch my limbs on the sofa in the *Fram's* saloon, to quench my thirst in delicious lime juice with sugar, and again to dine in a civilised manner. In the afternoon Hansen and Nordahl went back to Johansen with my team of dogs, to keep him company over-night. When I left him it was understood that he was to start on the return journey as best he could, until I came with others to help him. The dogs lost no time and the two men reached Johansen's tent in an hour and twenty minutes. At night both they and we had rejoicings in honour of the sun and the 84th degree.

"The next morning three of us went off and fetched the sledges back. Now, when we made for the ship, the dogs dragged much better, and in a short time we should have been on board had it not been for a long lane in the ice which we could see no end to, and which stopped us. Finally we left the sledges and together with the dogs managed to cross over on some loose pieces of ice and got on board. Yesterday we twice tried to fetch the sledges, but there had evidently been some movement in the lane, and the new ice was still so thin that we dared not trust it. We have, however, to-day got the sledges on board, and we will now for the last time, it is to be hoped, prepare ourselves for the journey. I will now plan out the journey so as to take the shortest possible time, using light sledges and tearing along as fast as legs and snow-shoes will carry us. We shall be none the worse for this delay, provided we do not meet too much pack-ice or too many openings in the ice.

"I have weighed all the dogs, and have come to the conclusion that we can feed them on each other and keep going for about fifty days; having, in addition to this, dog provisions for about thirty days, we ought to be able to travel with dogs for eighty days, and in that time it seems to me we should have arrived somewhere. And besides we have provisions for ourselves for one hundred days. This will be about 440 lbs. on each sledge if we take three, and with nine dogs per sledge we ought to manage it."

So here we were again, busy with preparations and improvements. In the meantime the ice moved a little, broke up, and lanes were formed in various directions. On March 8th I say: The crack in the large floe to starboard, formed while we were away, opened yesterday into a broad lane, which we can see stretching with newly-frozen ice towards the horizon both north and south. It is odd how that petroleum launch is always in 'hot water' wherever it is. This crack formed underneath it, so it was hanging with the stern over the water, when they found it in the morning. We have now decided to cut it up and use the elm-boards for the sledge runners. That will be the end of it."

"Wednesday, March 13th. 84° N. lat., 101° 55′ E. long. The days have passed, working again at the equipment. Everything is now in order. Three sledges are standing ready out on the ice, properly strengthened in every way, with iron fastenings between uprights and cross-bars. These last-mentioned are securely strengthened with extra top-pieces of ash, and protected underneath by boards.

The *Fram* in the ice.

This afternoon we tried the dogs with sledges loaded, and they went as easily as could be, and to-morrow we start again for the last time full of courage and confidence, and with the sun up, in the assurance that we are going towards ever brighter days.

"To-night there has been a great farewell feast, with many hearty speeches, and early to-morrow we depart as early as possible, provided our dissipation has not delayed us. I have to-night added the following postscript to Sverdrup's instructions:

"P.S. In the foregoing instructions, which I wrote rather hurriedly on the night of February 25th, I omitted to mention things that should have been alluded to. I will restrict myself here to stating further that should you sight unknown land, everything ought, of course, to be done in order to ascertain and examine it, as far as circumstances will permit. Should the *Fram* drift so near that you think it can be reached without great risk, everything that can be done to explore the land would be of the greatest interest. Every stone, every blade of grass, lichen, or moss, every animal, from the largest to the smallest, would be of great importance; photographs, and an exact description should not be neglected, at the same time it should be traversed to the greatest possible extent, in order to ascertain its coast-line, size, etc. All such things should, however, only be done, provided they can be accomplished without danger. If the *Fram* is adrift in the ice, it is clear that only short excursions should be made from her, as the members of such expeditions might encounter great difficulties in reaching the vessel again. Should the *Fram* remain stationary for any time, such expeditions should still be undertaken only with great discretion, and not be extended over any great length of time, as no one can foresee when she may commence to drift again, and it would be very undesirable for all concerned if the crew of the *Fram* were to be still further reduced.

"We have so often spoken together about the scientific researches, that I do not consider it necessary to give any further suggestions here. I am certain that you will do everything in your power to make them as perfect as possible, so that the expedition may return with as good results as the circumstances will permit. And now once again, my wishes for all possible success, and may we meet again before long.

"Your affectionate,
"FRIDTJOF NANSEN.
"The *Fram*, March 13th, 1895."

Before leaving the *Fram* for good, I ought, perhaps, to give a short account of the equipment we finally decided on as the most likely to suit our purposes.

I have already mentioned the two kayaks that had been made during the course of the winter, and that we required to have with us in order to cross possible channels and pools, and also for use when we should come to open sea. Instead of these kayaks, I had at first thought of taking ready-made canvas boat-covers, and of using the sledges as frames to stretch them over. By this means a craft perfectly capable of carrying us over lanes and short bits of open sea could have been rigged up in a very short space of time. I subsequently gave up this idea, however, and decided on the kayak, a craft with which I was familiar, and which I could rely on to render valuable assistance in several respects. Even if we had been able to contrive a cover for the sledges in such a manner that a boat could have been got ready in a short space of time, it would not have been such quick work as simply launching a ready-made kayak. Added to this the craft would, necessarily, have been heavy to row, and, when it was a question of long distances in open water, such as along the coasts of Franz Josef Land, or across thence to Spitzbergen, much time would have been lost. One consideration indeed, and that of some moment, was the saving in weight if the sledges were made use of; but even this was not of so much importance as it seemed, as the covers of both kinds of craft would have weighed about the same, and what would have been saved in the weight of the frames was not much, if one remembers that a whole kayak-frame only weighs about 16 lbs. Moreover, if kayaks were used, some weight would be saved by being able to carry our provisions and other *impedimenta* in bags of thin material, which could be stowed away in the kayaks, and the latter lashed to the sledges. Our provisions would thus be protected against all risk of attack by dogs, or of being cut by sharp pieces of ice. The other alternative — the canvas cover — which would have required fitting on and folding up again after being in the water, would necessarily, in the low temperatures we had to expect, have become spoiled and leaky. Last, but not least, the kayak with its tightly-covered deck, is a most efficient sea-boat, in which one can get along in any kind of weather, and is also an admirable craft for shooting and fishing purposes. The boat which one could have contrived by the other expedient, could with difficulty have been made at all satisfactory in this respect.

I have also mentioned the sledges which I had made for this expedition. They were of the same pattern as those built for the Greenland one; somewhat resembling in shape the Norwegian "skikjelke,"[69] which is a low, hand-sledge on broad runners, similar to our ordinary snow-shoes. But instead of the broad, flat runners we used in Greenland, I had the runners made in this case about the same in width (3 1/6 inches), but somewhat convex underneath, as those to be found on the "skikjelke" of Osterdalen and elsewhere. These convex runners proved to move very easily on the kind of country which we had to travel over, and they enabled the long sledges to be turned with ease, which was particularly convenient in the drift-ice, where the many irregularities often necessitated a very zig-zag route. The runners were covered with a thin plate of German silver, which, as it always keeps bright and smooth, and does not rust, answered its purpose well. As I mentioned before, there were thin, loose, well tarred, guard-runners of a kind of maple (*acor platonides*) underneath the German silver ones. The sledges were also prepared in various other ways which have been treated of before, for the heavy loads they were to carry at the beginning. The result of this was that they were somewhat heavier than I had intended at first; but in return I had the satisfaction of their being fit for use during the whole journey, and not once were we stopped or delayed by their breaking down. This has hardly been the case with former sledge journeys.

I have referred several times to our *clothes*, and our trial-trips in them. Although we had come to the conclusion that our wolf-skin garments were too warm for travelling in, we took them with us all the same on our first trip, and wore them too, to a certain extent; but we soon discovered that they were always too warm, and caused undue perspiration. By absorbing all the moisture of the body they became so heavy that they made an appreciable difference in the weight of our loads, and on our return from our three days' absence from the vessel, were so wet that they had to be hung for a long time over the saloon stove to dry. To this was added the experience that when we took them off in the cold, after having worn them for a time, they froze so stiff that it was difficult to get them on again. The result of all this was that I was not very favourably disposed towards them, and eventually made up my mind to keep to my woollen clothes, which I thought would give free outlet to the perspiration. Johansen followed my example. Our clothes then came to consist of about the following on the upper part of the body: two woollen shirts (Jaeger's); outside these I had a camel's-hair coat, and last of all a thick rough jersey. Instead of the jersey, Johansen wore what is called on board ship an "anorak," of thick homespun, provided with a hood, which he could pull forward in front of his face, and made after an Eskimo pattern. On our legs we had, next our skin, woollen drawers, and over these knicker-bockers and loose gaiters of close

Norwegian homespun. To protect us from wind and fine-driven snow, which, being of the nature of dust, forces itself into every pore of a woollen fabric, we wore a suit which has been mentioned before, made of a thin, close kind of cotton canvas, and consisting of an upper garment to pull over the head, provided with a hood in Eskimo fashion, and a lower one in the shape of a pair of wide overalls.

An important item in an outfit is the *foot-gear*. Instead of wearing long stockings, I preferred to use loose stocking-legs and socks, as these are easy to dry on one's chest when asleep at night. On a journey of this kind, where one is continually travelling over snow and in a low temperature, whether it be on snowshoes or not, my experience is that Finn-shoes are, without doubt, the most satisfactory covering for the feet in every way, but they must be made of the skin of the hind-legs of the reindeer buck. They are warm and strong, are always flexible, and very easy to put on and take off. They require careful management, however, if they are not to be spoiled at the outset, and one must try as well as one can to dry them when asleep at night. If it be sunny and good drying weather outside, the best plan is to hang them on a couple of snowshoe staffs, or something of the kind, in the wind outside the tent, preferably turned inside out, so that the skin itself can dry quickly. If one does not take this precaution the hair will soon begin to fall out. In severe cold, such as we had on the first part of the journey, it was impossible to dry them in this way, and our only resource was then to dry them on the feet at night, after having carefully brushed and scraped them free from snow and moisture. Then the next process is to turn them inside out, fill them with "sennegraes" or sedge, if one have it, thrust one's feet in, and creep into the sleeping bag with them on.[70] For milder weather later on, we had provided ourselves with leather boots, of the "komager" type, such as the Lapps use in summer. In this case they were made of under-tanned ox-hide, with soles of the skin of the blue seal (*phoca barbara*); well rubbed in with a composition of tar and tallow they make a wonderfully strong and watertight boot, especially for use in wet weather. Inside the Finn shoes we used, at the beginning of our journey, this "sennegraes" (*cairex oesicaria*), of which we had taken a supply. This is most effective in keeping the feet dry and warm, and if used Lapp-wise, i.e., with bare feet, it draws all moisture to itself. At night the wet "sennegraes" must be removed from the boots, well pulled out with the fingers so that it does not cling together, and then dried during the night by being worn inside the coat or trouser-leg. In the morning it will be about dry, and can be pressed into the boots again. Little by little, however, it becomes used up, and if it is to last out a long journey a good supply must be taken.

We also had with us socks made of sheep's wool and human hair, which were both warm and durable. Then, too, we took squares of "vadmel" or Norwegian homespun, such as are used in our army, which we wore (particularly myself) inside our "komager" on the latter part of the journey, when the snow was wet. They are comfortable to wear and easy to dry, as one can spread them out under one's coat or trousers at night.

On our *hands* we wore large gloves of wolf-skin, in addition to ordinary woollen mittens underneath, neither of them having separate divisions for the fingers. Exactly the same drying process had to be gone through with the gloves as with the foot-gear. Altogether the warmth of one's unfortunate body, which is the only source of heat one has for this sort of work, is chiefly expended in the effort to dry one's various garments; and we spent our nights in wet compresses, in order that the morrow might pass in a little more comfort.

On our *heads* we wore felt hats, which shaded the eyes from the dazzling light, and were less pervious to the wind than an ordinary woollen cap. Outside the hat we generally had one or two hoods of cloth. By this means we could regulate the warmth of our heads to a certain extent, and this is no unimportant thing.

It had been my original intention to use light one-man *sleeping-bags*, made of the skin of the reindeer calf. As these, however, proved to be insufficiently warm, I had to resort to the same principle we went on in Greenland, i.e., a double bag of adult reindeer skin; a considerable increase of warmth is thus attained by the fact that the occupants warm each other. Furthermore, a bag for two men is not a little lighter than two single bags. An objection has been raised to joint bags on the score that one's night's rest is apt to be disturbed, but this I have not found to be the case.

Something which in my opinion ought not to be omitted from a sledge journey is a *tent*. Even if thin and frail, it affords the members of an expedition so much protection and comfort that the inconsiderable increase in weight to the equipment is more than compensated for. The tents which I had had made for the expedition were of strong undressed silk and very light. They were square at the base and pointed at the top, and were pitched by means only of a tent pole in the middle, on the same principle as the four-man tents used in our army. Most of them had canvas floors attached. On our first start we took with us a tent of this kind, intended to hold four men and weighing a little over 7 lbs.

The floor is a certain advantage, as it makes the whole tent compact and quick to put up, besides being more impervious to wind. The whole tent is sewn in one piece, walls and floor together, and the only opening is a little slit through which to crawl. One drawback, however, to it is, that it is almost impossible not to carry in with one a certain amount of snow on the feet. This melts during the night from the heat of one's body lying on it and the floor absorbs the moisture, thereby causing the tent to be always a good deal heavier than the figures given here.

I accordingly relinquished all idea of a tent of this kind, and took with me one of about the same dimensions, and of the same silk material as the other, but without a floor. It took a little longer to put up, but the difference was not great. The walls were kept down by pegs, and when all was finished we would bank it carefully round with snow to exclude wind and draughts. Then came the actual pitching of the tent, which was accomplished by crawling in through the entrance and poking it up with a snowshoe-staff, which also served as tent-pole. It weighed a fraction over 3 lbs., including sixteen pegs, lasted the whole journey through — that is to say, until the autumn — and was always a cherished place of refuge.

The *cooking apparatus* we took with us had the advantage of utilising to the utmost the fuel consumed. With it we were able, in a very short space of time, to cook food and simultaneously to melt an abundance of drinking water, so that both in the morning and in the evening we were able to drink as much as we wished, and even a surplus remained. The apparatus consisted of two boilers and a vessel for melting snow or ice in, and was constructed in the following manner: Inside a ring-shaped vessel was placed the boiler, while underneath this again was the lamp. The entire combustion output was thus forced to mount into the space between the boiler and the ring-shaped vessel. Over this was a tight-fitting lid with a hole in the middle, through which the hot air was obliged to pass before it could penetrate farther and reach the bottom of a flat snow-melter, which was placed above it. Then, after having delivered some part of its heat, the air was forced down again on the outside of the ring-shaped vessel by the help of a mantle, or cap, which surrounded the whole. Here it parted with its last remaining warmth to the outerside of the ring-vessel, and finally escaped, almost entirely cooled, from the lower edge of the mantle.

For the heating was used a Swedish gas-petroleum lamp, known as "the Primus," in which the heat turns the petroleum into gas before it is consumed.

By this means it renders the combustion unusually complete. Numerous experiments made by Professor Torup at his laboratory proved that the cooker in ordinary circumstances yielded 90 to 93 per cent. of the heat which the petroleum consumed should, by combustion, theoretically evolve. A more satisfactory result, I think, it would be difficult to obtain. The vessels in this cooker were made of German silver, while the lid, outside cap, etc., were of aluminium. Together with two tin mugs, two tin spoons, and a tin ladle, it weighed exactly 8 lbs. 13 ozs., while the lamp, the "Primus," weighed 4½ ozs.

As *fuel*, my choice this time fell on petroleum ("snow-flake"). Alcohol, which has generally been used before on Arctic expeditions, has several advantages, and, in particular, is easy to burn. One decided drawback to it, however, is the fact that it does not by any means generate as much heat in comparison with its weight as petroleum when the latter is entirely consumed, as was the case with the lamp used by us. As I was afraid that petroleum might freeze, I had a notion of employing gas-oil, but gave up the idea, as it escapes so easily that it is difficult to preserve, and is, moreover, very explosive. We had no difficulties with our "snowflake" petroleum on account of the cold. We took with us rather more than 4 gallons, and this quantity lasted us 120 days enabling us to cook two hot meals a day and melt an abundance of water.

Of *snowshoes* we took several pairs, as we had to be prepared for breakages in the uneven drift-ice; besides this they would probably get considerably worn in the summer-time when the snow became wet and granular. Those we took with us were particularly tough, and slid readily. They were, for the most part, of the same kind of maple as the sledges, and of birch and hickory. They had all been well rubbed in with a concoction of tar, stearine, and tallow.

As we calculated to subsist, in a measure, on what we could shoot ourselves, it was necessary for us to have *fire-arms*. The most important gun for this kind of work is, naturally, the rifle; but as, in all likelihood, we should have to go across large expanses of snow, where, probably, there would be little big game, and whereas, on the other hand, birds might very likely come flying over our heads, I thought shot-guns would be the most serviceable to us. Therefore we decided on the same equipment in this respect as we had in Greenland. We took with us two double-barrelled guns (Büchsflints); each of them having a shot-barrel of 20-bore and a barrel for ball (Express) of about .360 calibre. Our supply of ammunition consisted of about 180 rifle cartridges and 150 shot cartridges.

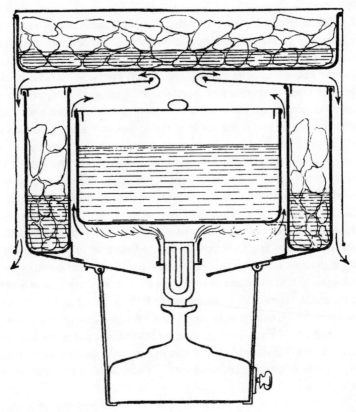

The cooking apparatus

Our *instruments* for determining our position and for working sights were: a small light theodolite, specially constructed for the purpose, which, with its case (this I had also had made to act as a stand) only weighed a little over two pounds. We had, furthermore, a pocket sextant and an artificial glass horizon, a light azimuth compass of aluminium, and a couple of other compasses. For the meteorological observations we had a couple of aneroid barometers, two minimum spirit-thermometers, and three quicksilver sling-thermometers. In addition to these we had a good aluminium telescope, and also a photographic camera.

The most difficult, but also, perhaps, the most important, point in the equipment of a sledge-expedition is thoroughly good and adequate *victualling*. I have already mentioned, in the Introduction to this book, that the first and foremost object is to protect oneself against scurvy and other maladies by the choice of foods, which, through careful preparation and sterilisation, are assured against decomposition. On a sledge expedition of this kind, where so much attention must be paid to the weight of the equipment, it is hardly possible to take any kinds of provisions except those whose weight has been reduced as much as possible by careful and complete drying. As, however, meat and fish are not so easily digested when dried, it is no unimportant thing to have them in a pulverised form. The dried food is, in this manner, so finely distributed that it can, with equal facility, be digested and received into the organism. This preparation of meat and fish was, therefore, the only kind we took with us. The meat was muscular beef, taken from the ox, and freed from all fat, gristle, etc.; it was then dried as quickly as possible, in a completely fresh condition, and thereupon ground and mixed with the same proportion of beef suet as is used in the ordinary preparation of pemmican. This form of food, which has been used for a considerable time on sledge expeditions, has gained for itself much esteem, and rightly; if well prepared, as ours was, it is undeniably a nourishing and easily digested food.[71] One ought not, however, to trust to its always being harmless, for, if carelessly prepared, i.e., slowly or imperfectly dried, it may also be very injurious to the health.

Another item of our provisions, by which we set great store, was Våge's fish flour. It is well prepared and has admirable keeping qualities; if boiled in water and mixed with flour and butter or dried potatoes, it furnishes a very appetising dish. Another point which should be attended to is that the food be of such a kind that it can be eaten without cooking. Fuel is part of the equipment, no doubt, but if for some reason or other this be lost or used up, one would be in a bad case indeed, had one not provided against such a contingency by taking food which could be eaten in spite of that. In order to save fuel, too, it is important that the food should not require cooking, but merely warming. The flour that we took with us had therefore been steamed and could, if necessary, have been eaten as it was, without further preparation. Merely brought to a boil it made a good hot dish. We also took dried boiled potatoes, pea-soup, chocolate vril-food, etc. Our bread was partly carefully-dried wheaten biscuits, and partly aleuronate bread, which I had caused to be made of wheat-flour mixed with about 30 per cent. of aleuronate flour (vegetable albumen).

We also took with us a considerable quantity of butter (86 lbs.) which had been well worked on board in order to get out all superfluous water. By this means not only was considerable weight saved, but the butter did not become so hard in the cold. On the whole it must be said that our menus included considerable variety, and we were never subjected to that sameness of food which former sledge expeditions have complained so much of. Finally we always had ravenous appetites, and always thought our meals as delicious as they could be.

Our *medicine-chest* consisted, on this occasion, of a little bag, containing, naturally, only the most absolutely necessary drugs, etc. Some splints and some ligatures, and plaster of Paris bandages, for possible broken legs and arms; aperient pills and laudanum for derangements of the stomach, which were never required; chloroform in case of an amputation, for example, from frost-bite; a couple of small glasses of cocaine in solution for snow-blindness (also unused); drops for toothache, carbolic acid, iodoform gauze, a couple of curved needles, and some silk for sewing up wounds; a scalpel, two artery tweezers (also for amputations), and a few other sundries. Happily our medicines were hardly ever required, except that the ligatures and bandages came in very handily the following winter as wicks for our train-oil lamps. Still better for this purpose, however, is Nicolaysen's plaster, of which we had taken a supply for possible broken collar-bones. The layer of wax we scraped carefully off, and found it most satisfactory for caulking our leaky kayaks.

Chapter 12

We Say Good-bye to the *Fram*

AT LAST by mid-day, on March 14th, we finally left the *Fram*, to the noise of a thundering salute. For the third time farewells and mutual good wishes were exchanged. Some of our comrades came a little way with us, but Sverdrup soon turned back in order to be on board for dinner at 1 o'clock. It was on the top of a hummock that we two said good-bye to each other; the *Fram* was lying behind us, and I can remember how I stood watching him as he strode easily homewards on his snow-shoes. I half wished I could turn back with him and find myself again in the warm saloon; I knew only too well that a life of toil lay before us, and that it would be many a long day before we should again sleep and eat under a comfortable roof; but that that time was going to be so long as it really proved to be, none of us then had any idea. We all thought that either the expedition would succeed, and that we should return home that same year, or that it would not succeed.

A little while after Sverdrup had left us, Mogstad also found it necessary to turn back. He had thought of going with us till the next day, but his heavy wolf-skin trousers were, as he un-euphemistically expressed it, "almost full of sweat, and he must go back to the fire on board to get dry." Hansen, Henriksen, and Pettersen were then the only ones left, and they laboured along each with his load on his back. It was difficult for them to keep up with us on the flat ice, so quickly did we go; but when we came to pressure-ridges we were brought to a standstill and the sledges had to be helped over. At one place the ridge was so bad that we had to carry the sledges a long way. When, after considerable trouble, we had managed to get over it, Peter shook his head reflectively, and said to Johansen that we should meet plenty more of the same kind, and have

Group photograph on 14 March 1895: Sverdrup, Nansen, Henriksen, Pettersen, Mogstad, Amundsen, Johansen, Jacobsen, Hansen, Juell.

enough hard work before we had eaten sufficient of the loads to make the sledges run lightly. Just here we came upon a long stretch of bad ice, and Peter became more and more concerned for our future; but towards evening matters improved, and we advanced more rapidly. When we stopped at 6 o'clock the odometer registered a good 7 miles, which was not so bad for a first day's work. We had a cheerful evening in our tent, which was just about big enough to hold all five. Pettersen, who had exerted himself and become overheated on the way, shivered and groaned while the dogs were being tied up and fed, and the tent pitched. He, however, found existence considerably brighter when he sat inside it, in his warm wolf-skin clothes, with a pot of smoking chocolate before him, a big lump of butter in one hand and a biscuit in the other, and exclaimed, "Now I am living like a prince." He thereafter discoursed at length on the exalting thought that he was sitting in a tent in the middle of the Polar Sea. Poor fellow, he had begged and prayed to be allowed to come with us on this expedition; he would cook for us and make himself generally useful, both as a tin and blacksmith; and then, he said, three would be company. I regretted that I could not take more than one companion, and he had been in the depths of woe for several days but now found comfort in the fact that he had, at any rate, come part of the way with us, and was out on this great desert sea, for, as he said, "not many people have done that."

The others had no sleeping-bag with them, so they made themselves a snug little hut of snow, into which they crawled in their wolf-skin garments, and had a tolerably good night. I was awake early the next morning; but when I crept out of the tent I found that somebody else was on his legs before me, and this was Pettersen, who, awakened by the cold, was now walking up and down to warm his stiffened limbs. He had tried it now, he said; he never should have thought it possible to sleep in the snow, but it had not been half bad. He would not quite admit that he had been cold, and that that was the reason why he had turned out so early. Then we had our last pleasant breakfast together, got the sledges ready, harnessed the dogs, shook hands with our companions, and, without many words being uttered on either side, started out into solitude. Peter shook his head sorrowfully as we went off. I turned round when we had gone some little way, and saw his figure on the top of the hummock; he was still looking after us. His thoughts were probably sad; perhaps he believed that he had spoken to us for the last time.

We found large expanses of flat ice, and covered the ground quickly, farther and farther away from our comrades, into the unknown, where we two alone

Last hours with the crew.

and the dogs were to wander for months. The *Fram*'s rigging had disappeared long ago behind the margin of the ice. We often came on piled-up ridges and uneven ice, where the sledges had to be helped and sometimes carried over. It often happened, too, that they capsized altogether, and it was only by dint of strenuous hauling that we righted them again. Somewhat exhausted by all this hard work, we stopped finally at 6 o'clock in the evening, and had then gone about 9 miles during the day. They were not quite the marches I had reckoned on, but we hoped that by degrees the sledges would become lighter, and the ice better to travel over. The latter, too, seems to have been the case at first. On Sunday, March 17th, I say in my diary: "The ice appears to be more even the farther north we get; came across a lane, however, yesterday which necessitated a long detour.[72] At half-past six we had done about 9 miles. As we had just reached a good camping ground, and the dogs were tired, we stopped. Lowest temperature last night, −45° Fahr. (−42.8° C.)."

The ice continued to become more even during the following days, and our marches often amounted to 14 miles or more in the day. Now and then a misfortune might happen which detained us, as, for instance, one day a sharp spike of ice which was standing up cut a hole in a sack of fish-flour, and all the delicious food ran out. It took us more than an hour to collect it all again, and repair the damage. Then the odometer got broken through being jammed in some uneven ice, and it took some hours to mend it by a process of lashing. But on we went northwards, often over great, wide ice-plains which seemed as if they must stretch right to the Pole. Sometimes it happened that we passed through places where the ice was "unusually massive, with high hummocks, so that it looked like undulating country covered with snow." This was undoubtedly very old ice, which had drifted in the Polar Sea for a long time on its way from the Siberian Sea to the east coast of Greenland, and must have been subjected year after year to severe pressure. High hummocks and mounds are thus formed, which summer after summer are partially melted by the rays of the sun, and again in the winters covered with great drifts of snow, so that they assume forms which resemble ice-hills, rather than piles of sea-ice resulting from upheaval.

Wednesday, March 20th, my diary says: "Beautiful weather for travelling in, with fine sunsets; but somewhat cold, particularly in the bag, at nights (it was −41.8° and −43.6° Fahr., or −41° and −42° C.). The ice appears to be getting more even the farther we advance, and in some places it is like travelling over inland-ice. If this goes on the whole thing will be done in no time." That day we lost our odometer, and as we did not find it out till some time afterwards, and I did not know how far we might have to go back, I thought it was not worth while to return and look for. It was the cause, however, of our only being able subsequently to guess approximately at the distance we had gone during the day. We had another mishap, too, that day. This was that one of the dogs (it was 'Livjaegeren') had become so ill that he could not be driven any longer, and we had to let; him go loose. It was late in the day before we discovered that he was not with us; he had stopped behind at our camping-ground when we broke up in the morning, and I had to go back after him on snow-shoes, which caused a long delay.

"Thursday, March 21st. Nine in the morning −43.6° Fahr., or −42° C. (Minimum in the night, −47.2° Fahr., or −44° C.) Clear, as it has been every day. Beautiful, bright weather; glorious for travelling in, but somewhat cold at nights, with the quicksilver continually frozen. Patching Finn-shoes in this temperature inside the tent, with one's nose slowly freezing away, is not all pure enjoyment."

"Friday, March 22nd. Splendid ice for getting over; things go better and better. Wide expanses, with a few pressure-ridges now and then, but passable everywhere. Kept at it yesterday from about half-past eleven in the morning to half-past eight at night, did a good 21 miles, I hope. We should be in about latitude 85°. The only disagreeable thing to face now is the cold. Our clothes are transformed more and more into a cuirass of ice during the day, and wet bandages at night. The blankets likewise. The sleeping bag gets heavier and heavier from the moisture which freezes on the hair inside. The same clear settled weather every day. We are both longing now for a change; a few clouds and a little more mildness would be welcome." The temperature in the night, —44.8° Fahr. (—42.7° C.). By an observation which I took later in the forenoon, our latitude that day proved to be 85° 9′ N.

"Saturday, March 23rd. On account of observation, lashing the loads on the sledges, patching bags, and other occupations of a like kind, which are no joke in this low temperature, we did not manage to get off yesterday before 3 o'clock in the afternoon. We stuck to it till nine in the evening, when we stopped in some of the worst ice we have seen lately. Our day's march, however, had lain across several large tracts of level ice, so I think that we made 14 miles or so all the same. We have the same brilliant sunshine; but yesterday afternoon the wind from the north-east, which we have had for the last few days, increased, and made it rather raw.

"We passed over a large frozen pool yesterday evening; it looked almost like a large lake." It could not have been long since this was formed, as the ice on it was still quite thin. It is wonderful that these pools can form up there at that time of the year.

From this time forward there was an end of the flat ice, which it had been simple enjoyment to travel over; and now we had often great difficulties to cope with. On Sunday, March 24th, I write: "The ice not so good; yesterday was a hard day, but we made a few miles, not more, though, than seven, I am afraid. This continual lifting of the heavily-loaded sledges is calculated to break one's back; but better times are coming, perhaps. The cold is also appreciable, always the same; but yesterday it was increased by the admixture of considerable wind from the north-east. We halted about half-past nine in the evening. It is perceptible how the days lengthen, and how much later the sun sets; in a few days' time we shall have the midnight sun.

"We killed 'Livjaegeren' yesterday evening, and hard work it was skinning him." This was the first dog which had to be killed; but many came afterwards, and it was some of the most disagreeable work we had on the journey, particularly now at the beginning when it was so cold. When this first dog was dismembered and given to the others, many of them went supperless the whole night in preference to touching the meat. But as the days went by and they became more worn-out, they learned to appreciate dog's-flesh, and later on we were not even so considerate as to skin the butchered animal, but served it hair and all.

The following day the ice was occasionally somewhat better; but as a rule it was bad, and we became more and more worn-out with the never-ending work of helping the dogs, righting the sledges every time they capsized, and hauling, or carrying them bodily over hummocks and inequalities of the ground. Sometimes we were so sleepy in the evenings that our eyes shut and we fell asleep as we went along. My head would drop, and I would be awakened by suddenly falling forward on my snow-shoes. Then we would stop, after having found a camping-ground behind a hummock or ridge of ice, where there was some shelter from the wind. While Johansen looked after the dogs, it generally fell to my lot to pitch the tent, fill the cooker with ice, light the burner and start the supper as quickly as possible. This generally consisted of "lobscouse" one day, made of pemmican and dried potatoes; another day of a sort of fish rissole substance known as "fiskegratin" in Norway and in this case composed of fish-meal, flour, and butter. A third day it would be pea, bean, or lentil soup, with bread and pemmican. Johansen preferred the "lobscouse," while I had a weakness for the "fiskegratin." As time went by, however, he came over to my way of thinking, and the "fiskegratin" took precedence of everything else.

As soon as Johansen had finished with the dogs, and the different receptacles containing the ingredients and eatables for breakfast and supper were brought in, as well as our bags with private necessities; the sleeping-bags were spread out, the tent-door carefully shut, and we crept into the bag to thaw our clothes. This was not very agreeable work. During the course of the day the damp exhalations of the body had little by little become condensed in our outer garments, which were now a mass of ice and transformed into complete suits of ice-armour. They were so hard and stiff that if we had only been able to get them off they could have stood by themselves and they crackled audibly every time we moved. These clothes were so stiff that the sleeve of my coat actually rubbed deep sores in my wrists during our marches; one of these sores — the one on the right hand — got frost-bitten, the wound grew deeper and deeper, and nearly reached the bone. I tried to protect it with bandages, but not until late in the summer did it heal, and I shall probably have the scar for life. When we got into our sleeping-bags in the evening, our clothes began to thaw slowly, and on this process a considerable amount of physical heat was expended. We packed ourselves tight into the bag, and lay with our teeth chattering for an hour, or an hour and a half, before we became aware of a little of the warmth in our bodies which we so sorely needed. At last our clothes became wet and pliant only to freeze again a few minutes after we had turned out of the bag in the morning. There was no question of getting these clothes dried on the journey so long as the cold lasted, as more and more moisture from the body collected in them.

How cold we were as we lay there shivering in the bag, waiting for the supper to be ready! I, who was cook, was obliged to keep myself more or less awake to see to the culinary operations, and sometimes I succeeded. At last the supper was ready, was portioned out and, as always, tasted delicious. These occasions were the supreme moments of our existence, moments to which we looked forward the whole day long. But sometimes we were so weary that our eyes closed, and we fell asleep with the food on its way to our mouths. Our hands would fall back inanimate with the spoons in them and the food fly out on the bag. After supper we generally permitted ourselves the luxury of a little extra drink, consisting of water, as hot as we could swallow it, in which whey-powder had been dissolved. It tasted something like boiled milk, and we thought it wonderfully comforting; it seemed to warm us to the very ends of our toes. Then we would creep down into the bag again, buckle the flap carefully over our heads, lie close together, and soon sleep the sleep of the just. But even in our dreams we went on ceaselessly, grinding at the sledges and driving the dogs, always northwards, and I was often awakened by hearing Johansen calling in his sleep to 'Pan,' or 'Barrabas,' or 'Klapperslangen' "Get on, you devil, you! Go on, you brutes! Sass, sass![73] Now the whole thing is going over!" and execrations less fit for reproduction, until I went to sleep again.

In the morning, as cook, I was obliged to turn out to prepare the breakfast, which took an hour's time. As a rule, it consisted one morning of chocolate, bread, butter, and pemmican; another of oatmeal porridge, or a compound of flour, water, and butter, in imitation of our "butter-porridge" at home. This was washed down with milk, made of whey-powder and water. The breakfast ready, Johansen was roused; we sat up in the sleeping-bag, one of the blankets was spread out as a table-cloth, and we fell to work. We had a comfortable breakfast, wrote up our diaries, and then had to think about starting. But how tired we sometimes were, and how often would I not have given anything to be able to creep to the bottom of the bag again and sleep the clock round. It seemed to me as if this must be the greatest pleasure in life but our business was to fight our way northwards, always northwards. We performed our toilets, and then came the going out into the cold to get the sledges ready, disentangle the dogs' traces, harness the animals, and get off as quickly as possible. I went first to find the way through the uneven ice; then came the sledge with my kayak. The dogs soon learned to follow, but at every unevenness of the ground they stopped, and if one could not get them all to start again at the same time by a shout, and so pull the sledge over the difficulty, one had to go back to beat or help them, according as circumstances necessitated. Then came Johansen with the two other sledges, always shouting to the dogs to pull harder, always beating them, and himself hauling to get the sledges over the terrible ridges of ice. It was undeniable cruelty to the poor animals from first to last, and one must often look back on it with horror. It makes me shudder even now when I think of how we beat them mercilessly with thick ash sticks when, hardly able to move, they stopped from sheer exhaustion. It made one's heart bleed to see them, but we turned our eyes away and hardened ourselves. It was necessary; forward we must go, and to this end everything else must give place. It is the sad part of expeditions of this kind that one systematically kills all better feelings, until only hard-hearted egoism remains. When I think of all those splendid animals, toiling for us without a murmur, as long as they could strain a muscle, never getting any thanks or even so much as a kind word, daily writhing under the lash until the time came when they could do no more and death freed them from their pangs — when I think of how they were left behind, one by one, up there on those desolate ice-fields, which had been witness to their faithfulness and devotion, I have moments of bitter self-reproach.

It took us two alone such a long time to pitch the tent, feed the dogs, cook, etc., in the evening, and then break up again and get ready in the morning, that the days never seemed long enough if we were to do proper day's marches, and, besides, get the sleep we required at night. But when the nights became so light, it was not so necessary to keep regular hours any longer, and we started when we pleased, whether it was night or day. We stopped, too, when it suited us, and took the sleep which might be necessary for ourselves and the dogs. I tried to make it a rule that our marches were to be of nine or ten hours' duration. In the middle of the day we generally had a rest and something to eat; as a rule bread and butter with a little pemmican or liver pâté. These dinners were a harsh trial. We used to try and find a good sheltered place, and sometimes even rolled ourselves up in our blankets, but all the same the wind cut right through us as we sat on the sledges eating our meal. Sometimes, again, we spread the sleeping-bag out on the ice, took our food with us, and crept well in, but even then did not succeed in thawing either it or our clothes. When this was too much for us we walked up and down to keep ourselves warm and ate our food as we walked. Then came the no less bitter task of disentangling the dogs' traces and we were glad when we could get off again. In the afternoon, as a rule, we each had a piece of meat-chocolate.

Most Arctic travellers who have gone sledge journeys have complained of the so-called Arctic thirst and it has been considered an almost unavoidable evil in connection with a long journey across wastes of snow. It is often increased, too, by the eating of snow. I had prepared myself for this thirst, from which we had also suffered severely when crossing Greenland, and had taken with me a couple of india-rubber flasks, which we filled with water every morning from the cooker, and by carrying in the breast were able to protect from the cold. To my great astonishment, however, I soon discovered that the whole day would often pass by without my as much as tasting the water in my flask. As time went by, the less need did I feel to drink during the day, and at last I gave up taking water with me altogether. If a passing feeling of thirst made itself felt, a piece of fresh ice, of which, as a rule, there was always some to be found, was sufficient to dispel it.[74] The reason why we were spared this suffering which has been one of the greatest hardships of many sledge expeditions, must be attributed in a great measure to our admirable cooking apparatus. By the help of this we were able, with the consumption of a minimum of fuel, to melt and boil so much water every morning that we could drink all we wished. There was even some left over, as a rule, which had to be thrown away. The same thing was generally the case in the evening.

"Friday, March 29. We are grinding on, but very slowly. The ice is only tolerable, and not what I expected from the beginning. There are often great ridges of piled up ice of dismal aspect, which take up a great deal of time, as one must go on ahead to find a way, and, as a rule, make a greater or less detour to get over them. In addition, the dogs are growing rather slow and slack, and it is almost impossible to get them on. And then this endless disentangling of the hauling-ropes, with their infernal twists and knots which get worse and worse to undo! The dogs jump over, and in between one another incessantly, and no sooner has one carefully cleared the hauling-ropes, than they are twisted into a veritable skein again. Then one of the sledges is stopped by a block of ice. The dogs howl impatiently to follow their companions in front; then one bites through a trace and starts off on his own account, perhaps followed by one or two others, and these must be caught, and the traces knotted; there is no time to splice them properly, nor would it be a very congenial task in this cold. So we go on when the ice is uneven, and every hour and a half at least, have to stop and disentangle the traces.

"We started yesterday about half-past eight in the morning, and stopped about five in the afternoon. After dinner the north-easterly wind, which we have had the whole time, suddenly became stronger, and the sky overcast. We welcomed it with joy, for we saw in it the sign of a probable change of weather and an end to this perpetual cold and brightness. I do not think we deceived ourselves either. Yesterday evening the temperature had risen to −29.2° Fahr. (−34° C.), and we had the best night in the bag we have had for a long time. Just now, as I am getting the breakfast ready, I see that it is clear again, and the sun is shining through the tent wall.

"The ice we are now travelling over seems, on the whole, to be old; but sometimes we come across tract, of considerable width, of uneven new ice, which must have been pressed up a considerable time. I cannot account for it in any other way than by supposing it to be ice from great open pools which must have formed here at one time. We have traversed pools of this description, with level ice on them, several times." That day I took a meridian observation, which, however, did not make us farther north than 85° 30' — I could not understand this; thought that we must be in latitude 86°, and, therefore, supposed there must be something wrong with the observation.

"Saturday, March 30th. Yesterday was Tycho Brahe's day. At first we found much uneven ice and had to strike a devious route to get through it, so that our day's march did not amount to much, although we kept at it a long time. At the end of it, however, and after considerable toil, we found ourselves on splendid flat ice, more level than it had been for a long time. At last, then, we had come on some more of the good old kind, and could not complain of some rubble and snow-drifts here and there; but then we were stopped by some ugly pressure-ridges, of the worst kind, formed by the packing of enormous blocks. The last ride was the worst of all, and before it yawned a crack in the thick ice, about 12 feet deep. When the first sledge was going over all the dogs fell in and had to be hauled up again. One of them, 'Klapperslangen', slipped his harness and ran away. As the next sledge was going over it fell in bodily, but happily was not smashed to atoms, as it might have been. We had to unload it entirely in order to get it up again, and then reload, all of which took up a great deal of time. Then, too, the dogs had to be thrown down and dragged up on the other side. With the third sledge we managed better, and after we had gone a little way farther the runaway dog came back. At last we reached a camping-ground, pitched our tent, and found that the thermometer showed −45.4 Fahr. (−43° C.). Disentangling dog-traces in this temperature, with one's bare, frost-bitten, almost skinless hands is desperate work. But finally we were in our dear bag, with the 'Primus' singing cosily, when, to crown our misfortunes, I discovered that it would not burn. I examined it everywhere, but could find nothing wrong. Johansen had to turn out and go and fetch the tools and a reserve burner, while I studied the cooker. At last I discovered that some ice had got in under the lid, and this had caused a leakage. Finally we got it to light, and at 5 o'clock in the morning the pea-soup was ready, and very good it was. At three in the afternoon I was up again cooking. Thank Heaven, it is warm and comfortable in the bag, or this sort of life would be intolerable.

"Sunday, March 31st. Yesterday, at last, came the long-wished-for change of weather, with southerly wind and rising temperature. Early this morning the thermometer showed −22° Fahr. (−30° C.), regular summer weather, in fact. It was, therefore, with lightened hearts that we set off over good ice, and with the wind at our backs. On we went at a very fair pace, and everything was going well, when a lane suddenly opened just in front of the first sledge. We managed to get this over by the skin of our teeth; but just as we were going to cross the lane again after the other sledges a large piece of ice broke under Johansen, and he fell in, wetting both legs — a deplorable incident. While the lane was gradually opening more and more, I went up and down it to find a way over, but without success. Here we were, with one man and a sledge on one side, two sledges and a wet man on the other, with an ever-widening lane between. The kayaks could not be launched, as, through the frequent capsizing of the sledges, they had got holes in them, and for the time being were useless. This was a cheerful prospect for the night; I on one side with the tent, Johansen, probably frozen stiff, on the other. At last, after a long detour, I found a wayover; and the sledges were conveyed across. It was out of the question, however, to attempt to go on, as Johansen's nether extremities were a mass of ice and his overalls so torn that extensive repairs were necessary."

Chapter 13

A Hard Struggle

"TUESDAY, April 2nd. There are many different kinds of difficulty to overcome on this journey, but the worst of all, perhaps, is getting all the trifles done and starting off. In spite of my being up by 7 o'clock on Monday evening to do the cooking, it was nearly two this morning before we got clear of our camping-ground. The load on Johansen's sledge had to be relashed, as the contents of one grip had been eaten up, and we had to put a sack of bread in its place. Another grip had to be sewn together, as it was leaking pemmican. Then the sledge from which the bread-sack had been taken had to be lashed secure again, and while we had the ropes undone it was just as well to get out a supply of potatoes.[75] During this operation we discovered that there was a hole in the fish-flour sack, which we tied up, but no sooner had we done so, than we found another large one which required sewing. When we came to pack the potato-sack this too had a hole in it, which we tied up, and so on. Then the dogs' traces had to be disentangled; the whole thing was in an inextricable muddle, and the knots and twists in the icy, frozen rope got worse and worse to deal with. Johansen made haste and patched his trousers before breakfast. The south wind had become what on board the *Fram* we should have called a 'mill breeze' (i.e., 19 to 23 feet in the second); and, with this at our back, we started off in driving snow. Everything went splendidly at first, but then came one pressure-ridge after another, and each one was worse than the last. We had a long halt for dinner at eight or nine in the morning, after having chosen ourselves a sheltered place in the lee of a ridge. We spread out the sleeping-bag, crept down into it with our food, and so tired was I that I went to sleep with it in my hand. I dreamed I was in Norway, and on a visit to some people I had only seen once in my life before. It was Christmas Day, and I was shown into a great empty room, where we were intended to dine. The room was very cold, and I shivered, but there were already some hot dishes steaming on the table, and a beautiful fat goose. How unspeakably did I look forward to that goose. Then some other visitors began to arrive; I could see them through the window, and was just going out to meet them, when I stumbled into deep snow. How it all happened, in the middle of the dining-room floor, I know not. The host laughed in an amused way, and I woke up and found myself shivering in a sleeping-bag on the drift-ice in the far north. Oh, how miserable I felt! We got up, packed our things silently together, and started off. Not until 4 o'clock that afternoon did we stop, but everything was dull and cheerless, and it was long before I got over my disappointment. What would I not have given for that dinner, or for one hour in the room, cold as it was.

"The ridges and the lanes which had frozen together again, with rubble on either side, became worse and worse. Making one's way through these new ridges is desperate work. One cannot use snowshoes, as there is too little snow between the piled-up blocks of ice, and one must wade along without them. It is also impossible to see anything in this thick weather — everything is white — irregularities and holes; and the spaces between the blocks are covered with a thin, deceptive layer of snow, which lets one crashing through into cracks and pitfalls, so that one is lucky to get off, without a broken leg. It is necessary to go long distances on ahead in order to find a way; sometimes one must search in one direction, sometimes in another, and then back again to fetch the sledges, with the result that the same ground is gone over many times. Yesterday, when we stopped, I really was done. The worst of it all, though, was that when we finally came to a standstill we had been on the move so long that it was too late to wind up our watches. Johansen's had stopped altogether; mine was ticking, and happily still going when I wound it up, so I hope that it is all right. Twelve mid-day, −24.6° Fahr. (−31.5° C.). Clear weather, south-easterly wind (13 feet in the second).

"The ice seems to be getting worse and worse, and I am beginning to have doubts as to the wisdom of keeping northwards too long.

"Wednesday, April 3rd. Got under way yesterday about three in the afternoon. The snow was in first-rate condition after the south-east wind, which continued blowing till late in the day. The ice was tolerably passable, and everything looked more promising; the weather was fine, and we made good progress. But after several level tracts with old humpy ice, came some very uneven ones, intersected by lanes and pressure-ridges as usual. Matters did not grow any better as time went on, and at midnight or soon after we were stopped by some bad ice and a newly frozen lane which would not bear. As we should have had to make a long detour, we encamped, and 'Russen' was killed (this was the second dog to go). The meat was divided into 26 portions, but eight dogs refused it, and had to be given pemmican. The ice ahead does not look inviting. These ridges are enough to make one despair, and there seems to be no prospect of things bettering. I turned out at midday and took a meridian observation, which makes us in 85° 59′ N. It is astonishing that we have not got farther; we seem to toil all we can, but without much progress. Beginning to doubt seriously of the advisability of continuing northwards much longer. It is three times as far to Franz Josef Land as the distance we have now come. How may the ice be in that direction? We can hardly count on its being better than here, or our progress quicker. Then, too, the shape and extent of Franz Josef Land are unknown; and may cause us considerable delay, and perhaps we shall not be able to find any game just at once. I have long seen that it is impossible to reach the Pole itself or its immediate vicinity over such ice as this and with these dogs. If only we had more of them! What would I not give now to have the Olenek dogs? We must turn sooner or later. But as it is only a question of time, could we not turn it to better account in Franz Josef Land than by travelling over this drift-ice, which we have now had a good opportunity of learning to know? In all probability it will be exactly the same right to the Pole. We cannot hope to reach any considerable distance higher before time compels us to turn. We certainly ought not to wait much longer. Twelve midday, −20.8° Fahr. (−29.40° C.), clear weather, 3 feet wind from east; twelve midnight, −29.2° Fahr. (−34° C.) clear and still."

It became more and more of a riddle to me that we did not make greater progress northwards. I kept on calculating and adding up our marches as we went along, but always with the same result; that is to say, provided only the ice were still, we must be far above the eighty-sixth parallel. It was becoming only too clear to me, however, that the ice was moving south-wards, and that in its capricious drift, at the mercy of wind and current, we had our worst enemy to combat.

"Friday, April 5th. Began our march at three yesterday morning. The ice, however, was bad, with lanes and ridges, so that our progress was but little. These lanes, with rubble thrown up on each side, are our despair. It is like driving over a tract of rocks, and delays us terribly. First I must go on ahead to find a way, and then get my sledge through; then, perhaps, by way of a change, one falls into the water: yesterday I fell through twice. If I work hard in finding a way and guiding my sledge over rough places, Johansen is no better off, with his two sledges to look after. It is a tough job to get even one of them over the rubble, to say nothing of the ridges; but he is a plucky fellow, and no mistake, and never gives in. Yesterday he fell into the water again in crossing a lane, and got wet up to his knees. I had gone over on my snowshoes shortly before, and did not notice that the ice was weak. He came afterwards without snowshoes walking beside one of the sledges, when suddenly the ice gave, and he fell through. Happily he managed to catch hold of the sledge, and the dogs, which did not stop, pulled him up again. These baths are not an unmixed pleasure now that there is no possibility of drying or changing one's clothes, and one must wear a chain mail of ice until they thaw and dry on the body, which takes some time in this temperature. I took an observation for longitude and a magnetic observation yesterday morning, and have spent the whole forenoon to-day in calculations (inside the bag) to find out our exact position. I find our latitude yesterday was 86° 2.8' N. This is very little, but what can we do when the ice is what it is? And these dogs cannot work harder than they do, poor things. I sigh for the sledge-dogs from the Olenek daily now. The longitude for yesterday was 98° 47' 15", variation 44.4?.

"I begin to think more and more that we ought to turn back before the time we originally fixed.[76] It is probably 350 miles or so to Petermann's Land (in point of fact it was about 450 miles to Cape Fligely); but it will probably take us all we know to get over them. The question resolves itself into this: Ought we not, at any rate, to reach 87° N.? But I doubt whether we can manage it, if the ice does not improve.

"Saturday, April 6th. Two a.m., −11.4° Fahr. (−24.2° C.). The ice grew worse and worse. Yesterday it brought me to the verge of despair, and when we stopped this morning I had almost decided to turn back. I will go on one day longer, however, to see if the ice is really as bad farther northwards as it appears to be from the ridge, 30 feet in height, where we are encamped. We hardly made 4 miles yesterday. Lanes, ridges, and endless rough ice, it looks like an endless moraine of ice-blocks; and this continual lifting of the sledges over every irregularity is enough to tire out giants. Curious this rubble-ice. For the most part it is not so very massive, and seems as if it had been forced up somewhat recently, for it is incompletely covered with thin, loose snow, through which one falls suddenly up to one's middle. And thus it extends mile after mile north-wards, while every now and then there are old floes, with mounds that have been rounded off by the action of the sun in the summer — often very massive ice.

"I am rapidly coming to the conclusion that we are not doing any good here. We shall not be able to get much farther north, and it will be slow work indeed if there be much more of this sort of ice towards Franz Josef Land. On the other hand, we should be able to make much better use of our time there, if we should have any over. 8.30 p.m., −29.2° Fahr. (−34° C.).

"Monday, April 8th. No, the ice grew worse and worse, and we got no way. Ridge after ridge, and nothing but rubble to travel over. We made a start at two o'clock or so this morning, and kept at it as long as we could, lifting the sledges all the time; but it grew too bad at last. I went on a good way ahead on snowshoes, but saw no reasonable prospect of advance, and from the highest hummocks only the same kind of ice was to be seen. It was a veritable chaos of ice-blocks, stretching as far as the horizon. There is not much sense in keeping on longer; we are sacrificing valuable time and doing little. If there be much more such ice between here and Franz Josef Land, we shall, indeed, want all the time we have.

"I therefore determined to stop, and shape our course for Cape Fligely.

"On this northernmost camping-ground we indulged in a banquet, consisting of lobscouse, bread-and-butter, dry chocolate, stewed 'tytlebaer,' or red whortleberries, and our hot whey drink, and then, with a delightful and unfamiliar feeling of repletion, crept into the dear bag, our best friend. I took a meridian observation yesterday, by which I see that we should be in latitude 86° 10′ N., or thereabouts.[77] This morning I took an observation for longitude. At 8.30 a.m., –25.6° Fahr. (–32 C.).

"Tuesday, April 9th. Yesterday's was our first march homewards. We expected the same impracticable ice, but, to our amazement, had not gone far before we came on tolerably good ground, which improved steadily, and, with only a few stoppages, we kept at it till this morning. We came upon ridges, to be sure, but they always allowed themselves to be negotiated pretty easily, and we did well. Started yesterday about two in the afternoon, and kept going till one this morning."

"Thursday, April IIth. Better and better. Found nothing but beautiful level tracts of ice yesterday, with a few ridges, which were easy to get over, and some lanes, with young ice on, which gave us rather more trouble. They ran, however, about in our direction (our course is now the magnetic S. 22° W., or about the true W.S.W.), and we could go alongside them. At last, however, we had to make a crossing, and accomplished it successfully, although the ice bent under us and our sledges more than was desirable. Late in the afternoon we came across a channel, which we proposed to cross in the same way. We reached the other side with the first sledge safely enough, but not so with the other. Hardly had the leaders of the team got out to the dangerous place where the ice was thinnest, and where some water was on the surface, when they stopped and warily dipped their paws in the water. Then through went one of them, splashing and struggling to get out. The ice began to sink under the weight of the other dogs and the sledge, and the water came flowing up. I dragged dogs and sledge back as quickly as possible, and succeeded in driving them all on to the firm ice again in safety. We tried once again at another place, I running over first on snowshoes and calling to the dogs, and Johansen pushing behind, but the result was no better than the first time, as 'Suggen' fell in, and we had to go back. Only after a long detour, and very much fagged, did we finally succeed in getting the two last sledges over. We were lucky in finding a good camping-place, and had the warmest night and the most comfortable (I might almost say cosy) morning — spent, be it said, in repairs — that we have had on the trip. I think we did the longest day's march yesterday that we have yet achieved about 15 miles. Two in the afternoon, –17.6° Fahr. (–27.6° C.).

"Saturday, April 13th. We have traversed nothing but good ice for three days. If this goes on, the return journey will be quicker than I thought. I do not understand this sudden change in the nature of the ice. Can it be that we are travelling in the same direction with the trend of the ridges and irregularities, so that now we go along between them instead of having to make our way over them? The lanes we have come across seem all to point to this; they follow our course pretty closely. We had the misfortune yesterday to let our watches run down; the time between our getting into the bag on the previous night and encamping yesterday was too long. Of course we wound them up again, but the only thing I can now do to find Greenwich mean time is to take a time-observation and an observation for latitude, and then estimate the approximate distance from our turning-point on April 8th, when I took the last observation for longitude. By this means the error will hardly be great.

"I conclude that we have not gone less than 14 miles a day on an average the last three days, and have consequently advanced 40 or more miles in a direction S. 22° W. (magnetic). When we stopped here yesterday 'Barbara' was killed. These slaughterings are not very attractive episodes. Clear weather; at 6.30 this morning –22° Fahr. (–30° C.); wind south (6 to 9 feet).

"April 14th. Easter Day. We were unfortunate with lanes yesterday, and they forced us considerably out of our course. We were stopped at last by a particularly awkward one, and after I had gone alongside it to find a crossing for some distance without success, I thought we had better, in the circumstances, pitch our tent and have a festive Easter Eve. In addition, I wished to reckon out our latitude, longitude, our observation for time, and our variation; it was a question of getting the right time again as quickly as possible. The tent up, and Johansen attending to the dogs, I crept into the bag; but lying thawing in this frozen receptacle, with frozen clothes and shoes, and simultaneously working out an observation and looking up logarithms, with tender, frost-bitten fingers, is not pleasurable, even if the temperature be only −22° Fahr. It is slow work, and Easter Day has had to be devoted to the rest of the calculation, so that we shall not get off before this evening. Meanwhile we had a festive Easter Eve and regaled ourselves with the following delicacies: Hot whey and water, fish au gratin, stewed red whortleberries, and lime juice grog (i.e., lime-juice tablets and a little sugar dissolved in hot water). Simply a splendid dinner, and having feasted our fill, we at last, at 2 o'clock, crept in under the cover.

"I have calculated our previous latitudes and longitudes over again to see if I can discover any mistake in them. I find that we should yesterday have come farther south than 86° 5.3' N.; but, according to our reckoning, assuming that we covered 50 miles during the three days, we should have come down to 85 degrees and 50 odd minutes. I cannot explain it in any other manner than by the surmise that we have been drifting rapidly northwards, which is very good for the *Fram*, but less so for us. The wind has been southerly the last few days. I assume that we are now in longitude 86° E., and have reckoned the present reading of our watches accordingly.[78] The variation here I find to be 42.5°. Yesterday we steered S. 10° W. (magnetic); to-day I will keep S. 5° W., and to-morrow due south. By way of a change to-day, the sky has been overcast; but this evening, when we partook of our second breakfast, the sun was shining cheerily in through the tent-wall. Johansen has patched clothes to-day, while I have made calculations and pricked out the courses. So mild and balmy it has not been before. 10 p.m., −14° Fahr. (−25.6° C.).

"Tuesday, April 16th. As we were about to start off at 1 o'clock yesterday morning, 'Baro' sneaked away before we could harness him; he had seen a couple of the other dogs being put to, and knew what was coming. As I did not wish to lose the dog — he was the best I had in my team — this caused some delay. I called and called, and went peering round the hummocks in search of him, but saw nothing, only the ice-pack, ridge upon ridge disappearing towards the horizon, and farthest north the midnight sun shining over all. The world of ice was dreaming in the bright, cool morning light. We had to leave without the dog, but, to my great delight, I soon caught sight of him far behind us in our wake; I thought I had seen his good face for the last time. He was evidently ashamed of himself, and came and stood quite still, looking up at me imploringly when I took him and harnessed him. I had meant to whip the dog, but his eyes disarmed me.

"We found good passable ice, if not always quite flat, and made satisfactory progress. Some ridges, however, forced us west of our course. Later on in the morning I discovered that I had left my compass behind at some place or other where I had had it out to take our bearings. It could not be dispensed with, so I had

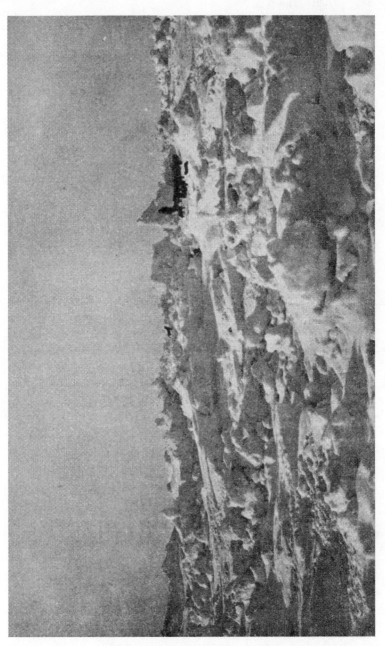

Baro, the runaway dog.

to return and look for it. I found it, too, but it was a hard pull-back, and on the way I was inconvenienced for the first time by the heat; the sun scorched quite unpleasantly. When I at last got back to the sledges, I felt rather slack; Johansen was sitting on the kayak fast asleep, basking in the sun. Then on again, but the light and warmth made us drowsy and slack, and, try as we would, we seemed to lag; so at ten in the forenoon we decided to camp, and I was not a little surprised, when I took the meteorological observation, to find that the swing-thermometer showed −15.2° Fahr. (−26.2° C.). The tent was accordingly pitched in the broiling sun, and nice and warm it soon was inside. We had a comfortable Easter dinner, which did service for both Easter Day and Easter Monday. I reckon the distances we covered on Easter Eve and yesterday at about 15 miles, and we should thus be altogether 60 miles on our way home.

"Wednesday, April 17th. −18.4° Fahr. (−28° C.) Yesterday, without doubt, we did our longest day's march. We began at half-past seven in the morning, and ended at about nine at night, with a couple of hours' rest in the bag at dinner-time. The ice was what I should previously have called anything but good; it was throughout extremely uneven, with pressed-up, rather new ice and older, rounded-off ridges. There were ridges here and there, but progress was possible everywhere, and by lanes, happily, we were not hindered. The snow was rather loose between all the irregularities of the ice; but the dogs hauled alone everywhere, and there is no cause to complain of them. The ice we are now stopping in seems to me to be something like that we had around the *Fram*. We have about got down to the region where she is drifting. I am certain we did 20 miles yesterday, and the distance homewards should now be altogether 368 miles.

"The weather is glorious nowadays, not so cold as to inconvenience one, and continual clear sunshine without any wind to signify. There is remarkable equableness and stagnancy in the atmosphere up here, I think. We have travelled over this ice for upwards of a month now, and not once have we been stopped on account of bad weather — the same bright sunshine the whole time, with the exception of a couple of days and even then the sun came out. Existence becomes more and more enjoyable; the cold is gone, and we are pressing forward towards land and summer. It is no trial now to turn out in the mornings, with a good day's march before one, and cook, and lie snug and warm in the bag and dream of the happy future when we get home. Home...?

"Have been engaged on an extensive sartorial undertaking to-day; my trousers were getting the worse for wear. It seems quite mild now to sit and sew in −18° Fahr, in comparison with −40° Fahr. Then certainly it was not enjoyable to ply one's needle.

"Friday, April 19th. We now have provender for the dogs for two or three days more, but I think of saving it a little longer and having the worst dogs eaten first. Yesterday 'Perpetuum' was killed. This killing of the animals, especially the actual slaughtering, is a horrible affair. We have hitherto stuck them with a knife but this was not very satisfactory. Yesterday, however, we determined to try a new method: strangulation. According to our usual custom, we led the dog away behind a hummock, so that the others should not know what was going on. Then we put a rope round the animal's neck, and each pulled with all his might, but without effect, and at last we could do no more. Our hands were losing all sense of feeling in the cold, and there was nothing for it but to use the knife. Oh, it was horrible! Naturally, to shoot them would be the most convenient and merciful way, but we are loath to expend our precious ammunition on them; the time may come when we shall need it sorely.

"The observations yesterday show that we have got down to 85° 37.8' N., and the longitude should be 79° 26' E. This tallies well with our reckoning. We have gone 50 miles or so since the last observation (April 13th), just what I had assumed beforehand.

"Still the same brilliant sunshine, day and night. Yesterday the wind from the north freshened, and is still blowing to-day, but does not trouble us much, as it is behind us. The temperature, which now keeps from about 4° to 22° below zero (Fahr.), can only be described as agreeable. This is undoubtedly fortunate for us; if it were warmer, the lanes would keep open a longer time. My greatest desire now is to get near land before the lanes become too bad. What we shall do then must be decided by circumstances.

"Sunday, April 21st. At 4 o'clock yesterday we got under way. During the night we stopped to have something to eat. These halts for dinner, when we take our food and crawl well down to the bottom of the bag, where it is warm and comfortable, are unusually cosy. After a good nap we set off again, but were soon stopped by the ugliest lane we have yet come across. I set off along it to find a passage, but only found myself going through bad rubble. The lane was everywhere equally broad and uncompromising, equally full of aggregated blocks and brash, testifying clearly to the manner in which, during a long period, the ice here has been in motion and been crushed and disintegrated by continual pressure. This was apparent, too, in numerous new ridges of rubble and hummocky ice, and the cracks running in all directions. I finally found a crossing, but when, after a long circuit, I had conveyed the caravan there, it had changed in the interval, and I did not think it advisable to make the attempt. But though I went 'farther than far,' as we say, I only found the same abominable lane, full of lumps of ice, grinning at one, and high pressure-ridges on each side. Things were becoming worse and worse. In several cases these lumps of ice were, I noticed, intermixed with earthy matter. In one place, the whole floe, from which blocks had been pressed up into a ridge, was entirely dark brown in colour, but whether this was from mud or from organic matter I did not get near enough to determine. The ridges were fairly high in some places, and reached a height of 25 feet or so. I had a good opportunity here of observing how they assume forms like ice-mountains with high, straight sides, caused by the splitting of old ridges transversely in several directions. I have often on this journey seen massive high hummocks with similar square sides, and of great circumference, sometimes quite resembling snow-covered islands. They are of 'palaeocrystic ice,' as good as any one can wish.[79]

"I was constrained at last to return with my mission unaccomplished. Nearly the most annoying thing about it was that on the other side of the lane I could see fine flat ice stretching southwards — and now to be obliged to camp here and wait! I had, however, already possessed my soul in patience, when, on coming back to our original stopping-place, I found a tolerably good crossing close by it. We eventually got the other side, with the ice grinding under our feet the while, and by that time it was 6 o'clock in the morning. We kept at it a little while longer over beautiful flat ice, but the dogs were tired, and it was nearly 48 hours since they had been fed. As we were hastening along we suddenly came across an immense piece of timber sticking up obliquely from the surface of the ice. It was Siberian larch as far as I could make out, and probably raised in this manner through pressure long ago. Many a good meal could we have cooked with it had we been able to drag it with us, but it was too heavy. We marked it 'F.N., H.J., 85° 30' N.,' and went on our way.

"Plains of ice still before us. I am looking forward to getting under way. Gliding over this flat surface on one's snowshoes almost reaches the ideal; land and home are nigher, and as one goes along one's thoughts fly southwards to everything that is beautiful. Six in the morning, −22° Fahr. (−30° C.)

"Monday, April 22nd. If we have made good progress the previous days, yesterday simply outdid itself. I think I may reckon our day's march at 25 miles, but, for the sake of certainty, lump the two last days together, and put them down at 40 miles. The dogs, though, are beginning to get tired; it is approaching the time for us to camp. They are impatient for food, and, grown more and more greedy for fresh dog's flesh, throw themselves on it like wolves as soon as a smoking piece, with hair and all on is thrown to them. 'Kvik' and 'Barnet' only still keep back as long as the flesh is warm, but let it become frozen, and they eat it voraciously. Twelve midnight, −27.8° Fahr. (−33.3° C.)

"Friday, April 26th. −24.7° Fahr. (−31.5° C.). Minimum temperature, −32° Fahr. (−35.7° C.). I was not a little surprised yesterday morning when I suddenly saw the track of an animal in the snow. It was that of a fox, came about W.S.W. true, and went in an easterly direction. The trail was quite fresh. What in the world was that fox doing up here? There were also unequivocal signs that it had not been entirely without food. Were we in the vicinity of land? Involuntarily I looked round for it, but the weather was thick all day yesterday, and we might have been near it without seeing it. It is just as probable, however, that this fox was following up some bear. In any case, a warm-blooded mammal in the eighty-fifth parallel! We had not gone far when we came across another fox-track; it went in about the same direction as the other, and followed the trend of the lane which had stopped us, and by which we had been obliged to camp. It is incomprehensible what these animals live on up here, but presumably they are able to snap up some crustacean in the open waterways. But why do they leave the coasts? That is what puzzles me most. Can they have gone astray? There seems little probability of that. I am eager to see if we may not come across the trail of a bear to-day. It would be quite a pleasure, and it would seem as if we were getting nearer inhabited regions again. I have just pricked out our course on the chart according to our bearings, calculating that we have gone 75 miles in the four days since our last observation, and I do not think this can be excessive. According to this, it should not be much more than 150 miles to Petermann's Land, provided it lie about where Payer determined it. I should have taken an observation yesterday, but it was misty.

"At the end of our day, yesterday, we went across many lanes and piled-up ridges; in one of the latter, which appeared to be quite new, immense pieces of fresh-water ice had been pressed up. They were closely intermixed with day and gravel, the result of infiltration, so that at a distance the blocks looked dark brown, and might easily be taken for stone; in fact, I really thought they were stone. I can only imagine that this ice is river-ice, probably from Siberia. I often saw huge pieces of fresh-water ice of this kind farther north, and even in latitude 86° there was clay on the ice.

"Sunday, April 28th. We made good way yesterday, presumably 20 miles. We began our march about half-past three in the afternoon the day before yesterday, and kept at it till yesterday morning. Land is drawing nigh, and the exciting time beginning, when we may expect to see something on the horizon. Oh, how I am longing for land, for something under one's feet that is not ice and snow; not to speak of something to rest one's eyes on. Another fox-track yesterday; it went in about the same direction as the previous ones. Later in the day 'Gulen' gave in; it seemed to be a case of complete exhaustion, he could hardly stand on his legs, reeled over, and when we placed him on one of the loads he lay quite still without moving. We had already decided to kill him that day. Poor beast, faithfully he worked for us, good tempered and willing to the end, and then for thanks, when he could do no more, to be killed for provender! He was born on the *Fram* on December 13th, 1893, and, true child of the polar night, never saw aught but ice and snow.

"Monday, April 29. −4° Fahr. (−20° C.). We had not gone far yesterday when we were stopped by open water — a broad pool or lane which lay almost straight across our course. We worked westwards alongside it for some distance, until it suddenly began to close violently together at a place where it was comparatively narrow. In a few minutes the ice was towering above us, and we got over by means of the noisy pressure-ridge, which was thundering and crashing under our feet. It was a case of bestirring ourselves and driving dogs and sledges quickly over if we did not wish to get jammed between the rolling blocks of ice. This ridge nearly swallowed up Johansen's snowshoes, which had been left behind for a minute while we got the last sledge over. When at last we got to the other side of the lane the day was far spent, and such work naturally deserved reward in the shape of an extra ration of meat-chocolate.

"Annoying as it is to be stopped in the midst of beautiful flat ice by a lane, when one is longing to get on, still, undeniably, it is a wonderful feeling to see open water spread out in front of one, and the sun playing on the light ripples caused by the wind. Fancy open water again, and glittering waves, after such a long time. One's thoughts fly back to home and summer. I scanned in vain to see if a seal's head were not visible above the surface, or a bear along the side. The dogs are beginning now to be very much reduced in strength and are difficult to urge on. 'Barnet' was quite done — he was killed this evening, and several of the others are very jaded. Even 'Baro,' my best dog, is beginning to cool in his zeal, to say nothing of 'Kvik'; perhaps I ought to cater a little more generously for them. The wind which was about south-east in the morning subsequently went over to an easterly direction, and I expect, to use Pettersen's customary expression on board for a good south-easter which drove us northwards to some purpose, 'a regular devil of a hiding.' I am only surprised the temperature still seems low. I had noticed a thick bank of clouds for a long time along the horizon in the south and south-west, and thought that this must mean land. It now began to grow higher and come nearer us in a suspicious manner. When, after having had dinner we crept out of the bag, we saw that the sky was entirely clouded over; and that the 'devil of a hiding' had come we felt when we went on.

"I saw another fox-track yesterday; it was almost effaced by the snow, but went in about the same direction as the others. This is the fourth we have come across, and seeing so many of them make me begin to believe seriously in the proximity of land. Yes, I expect to see it every minute; perhaps, though, it will be some days yet.[80]

"Tuesday, April 30th. −6.7° Fahr. (−21.4° C.). Yesterday, in spite of everything, was a bad day. It began well, with brilliant sunshine; was warm (4° below zero Fahr.), and there, bathed in the slumbering sunlight and alluring us on, were stretches of beautiful flat ice. Everything tended to predict a good day's work; but, alas, who could see the ugly dark cracks which ran right across our course, and which were destined to make life a burden to us. The wind had packed the snow well together, and made the surface firm and good, so that we made rapid progress; but we had not gone far before we were stopped by a lane of entirely open water which stretched right across our course. After following it some little distance we eventually found a way across.[81] Not long afterwards we met with another lane running in about the same direction. After a fairly long detour we got safely over this too, with the minor misfortune that three dogs fell into the water. A third lane we also got over, but the fourth was too much for us altogether. It was broad, and we followed it a long way in a westerly direction, but without finding a suitable crossing. Then I continued some three or four miles alone to scan the country, but as I could see no chance of getting over, I returned to Johansen and the sledges. It is a fruitless task this following a lane running at right angles to one's course. Better to camp and make one's self some good pemmican soup, à la julienne (it was highly delectable), and then give one's self up to sleep, in the hope of better things in the future. Either the lanes will close together again, or they will freeze now that it is tolerably cold. The weather is quiet, so it is to be hoped new ones will not form.[82] If it keep like this during the days we require to reach land, it will be a good thing; when once we are on land as many lanes may form as they like. Should matters become too bad before that time, there is nothing for us to do but to mend and patch our kayaks. As they are now they will not float. The continual capsizing of the sledges has cut holes in many places, and they would fill the instant they were put on the water."

I ought perhaps to explain here that I had deferred mending the kayaks as long as possible. This was partly because the work would take a long time, and the days were precious, now that it was a question of gaining land before the ice became impracticable; partly, too, because, in the temperature we now had, it would have been difficult to do the work properly; and also because the chances were that they would soon get holes in them again from being upset. In addition to this I was undesirous of crossing lanes at present; they were still covered with young ice which it would have been difficult to break through, even had it been possible to protect the bows of the kayaks from being cut, by means of a plate of German silver and some extra canvas. As I have mentioned before, not the least drawback was the fact that any water entering the kayaks would immediately have frozen and have been impossible to remove, thus increasing the weight of our loads at each crossing. It was undoubtedly a better plan to go round, even if the way was long, than to incur the hindrances and casualties that the other alternative would, most probably, have occasioned.

To continue quoting from my diary for the same day I write: "The dogs were at one of our precious pemmican grips last night; they have torn off a corner of the bag and eaten some of its contents, but happily not much. We have been fortunate inasmuch as they have let the provisions alone hitherto; but now hunger is becoming too much for them and nature is stronger than discipline."

"Wednesday, May 1st. −12.6° Fahr. (−24.8° C.). I 'half-soled' my Finn shoes to-day with sail-cloth, so I hope they will last a while; I feel as if I could hold my own again now. I have two pairs of Finn shoes, so that for once one pair can be dried in the sun. They have been wet the whole way and it has made them the worse for wear."

The ice was now growing very bad again and our marches shorter. On Friday, May 3rd, I write in my diary: "We did not do so good a day's work yesterday as we expected, although we made some progress. The ice was flat and the going good at one time, and we kept steadily at it for four hours or so; but then came several reaches with lanes and rubble-ice, which, however, we managed to pull through, though the ice was often packing under our feet. By degrees the wind from the south-east increased, and while we were having dinner it veered round to an easterly direction and became rather strong. The ice, too, grew worse, with channels and rubble, and when the wind reached a velocity of 29 to 33 feet in the second, and a driving snowstorm set in, completely obliterating everything around us, stumbling along through it all became anything but attractive. After being delayed several times by newly-formed rubble, I saw that the only sensible thing to be done was to camp, if we could find a sheltered spot. This was easier said than done, as the weather was so thick we could hardly see anything, but at last we found a suitable place, and well content to be under shelter, ate our 'fiskegratin,' and crept into the bag, while the wind rattled the tent-walls and made drifts round us outside. We had been

Pushing the sledges up, May 1895.

constrained to pitch our tent close beside a new ridge, which was hardly desirable, as packing might take place, but we had no choice; it was the only lee to be found. Before I went to sleep the ice under us began to creak, and soon the pressure-ridge behind us was packing with the well known jerks. I lay listening and wondering whether it would be better for us to turn out before the ice-blocks came tumbling upon us, but as I lay listening I went fast asleep and dreamed about an earth-quake. When I woke up again, some hours afterwards, everything was quiet except the wind, which howled and rattled at the tent walls, lashing the snow up against them.

"Yesterday evening 'Potifar' was killed. We have now sixteen dogs left; the numbers are diminishing horribly, and it is still so far to land. If only we were there!"

"Saturday, May 4. Did fourteen miles yesterday; but the lanes become worse and worse. When we got under way in the afternoon — after having re-loaded my sledge and kayak, and re-adjusted the dunnage under Johansen's kayak — the wind had fallen, and it was snowing quietly and silently, with big flakes, just as it does on a winter day at home. It was bad in one way, however, as in such a light it is difficult to see if the lie of the ground is against or with us; but the going was fairly good, and we made progress. It was heavenly to work in this mild weather, +11.8° Fahr. (−11.3° C.), and be able to use one's frost-bitten hands bare, without suffering torture untold every time they came in contact with anything.

"Our life, however, was soon embittered by open water-ways. By means of a circuitous route, and the expenditure of much valuable time, we at last succeeded in getting over them. Then came long stretches of good ice, and we went cheerfully on our way; bye-and-bye, too, the sun peeped out. It is wonderful what such encouragement does for one. A little while ago, when I was ploughing alongside a horrible lane, through rubble and over ridges, without a sign of any means of getting on, I was ready to sink from exhaustion at every step; no pleasure then could compare with that of being able to crawl into the bag; and now, when luck again sheds her smiles on one and progress is before one, all weariness is suddenly dissipated.

"During the night the ice began to be bad in earnest, lane after lane, the one worse than the other, and they were only overcome by deviations and intricate by-ways. It was terrible work, and when the wind increased to a good 'mill-breeze' matters became desperate. This is indeed toil without ceasing; what would I not give to have land, to have a certain way before me, to be able to reckon on a certain day's march and be free from this never-ending anxiety and uncertainty about the lanes. Nobody can tell how much trouble they may yet cause us, and what adversities we may have to go through before we reach land; and meanwhile the dogs are diminishing steadily. They haul all they can, poor things, but what good does it do? I am so tired that I stagger on my snowshoes, and when I fall down, only wish to lie there to save myself the trouble of getting up again. But everything changes, and we shall get to land in time.

"At five this morning we came to a broad lane, and as it was almost impossible to get the dogs on any further, we camped. Once well down in the bag with a pot of savoury-smelling lobscouse in front of one, a feeling of well-being is the result, which neither lanes nor anything else can disturb.

"The ice we have gone through has, on the whole, been flat, with the exception of the newly formed lanes and rubble. These appear, however, for the most part in limited stretches, with extensive flat ice between, as yesterday. All the channels seem in the main to go in the same direction, about straight across our course with a little deflection towards the south-west. They run about north-east to west-south-west (by compass). This morning the temperature had again sunk to +0.1° Fahr. (−17.8 C.), after having been up at +12.2° Fahr. (−11° C.), and therefore I am still in hopes that the water may freeze within a reasonable time. Perhaps it is wrong of us to curse this wind, for on board the *Fram* they are rejoicing that a south-easter has at last sprung up. However, in spite of our maledictions, I am really glad for their sake, although I could wish it deferred till we reach land."

"Wednesday, May 8th. The lanes still appear regularly in certain places, as a rule where the ice is very uneven, and where there are old and new ridges alternately; between these places there are long flat stretches of ice without lanes. These are often perfectly even, almost like 'inland ice.' The direction of the lanes is, as before, very often athwart our course, or a little more south-westerly. Others, again, seem to go in about the same direction as we do. This ice is extraordinary, it seems to become more and more even as we approach land, instead of the contrary as we expected. If it would only keep so! It is considerably flatter than it was about the *Fram* it seems to me. There are no really impracticable places, and the irregularities there are seem to be of small dimensions — rubble-ice and so forth — no huge mounds and ridges as we had farther north. Some of the lanes here are narrow and so far new that the water was only covered with brash. This can be deceptive enough; it appears to be even ice, but thrust your staff in, and it goes right through and into the water."

"This morning I made out our latitude and longitude. The former was (Sunday, May 5th) 84° 31' N., and the latter 66° 15' E. We were not so far south as I expected, but considerably farther west. It is the drift which has put us back and westwards. I shall, therefore, for the future, steer a more southerly course than before, about due south (true), as we are still drifting westwards, and, above everything, I am afraid of getting too far in that direction. It is to be hoped that we shall soon have land in sight, and we shall then know where to steer. We undoubtedly ought to be there now."

"No dog was killed yesterday, as there were two-thirds left of 'Ulenka' from the previous day, which provided an abundant repast. I now only intend to slaughter one every other day, and perhaps we shall soon come across a bear."

"Tuesday, May 9th. +9° F. (−13.3° C.). Yesterday was a fairly good day. The ice was certainly not first-rate, rather rubbly, and the going heavy, but all the same we are making steady way forwards. There were long, flat stretches every now and then. The weather had become quite fine when we got under way, about 3 o'clock this morning. The sun was shining through light cumulus clouds. It was hard work, however, making head against the ice, and soon the fog came down with the wind, which still blew from the same direction (N.N.E.).

"The work of hauling becomes heavier and heavier for the dogs, in proportion as their numbers diminish. The wooden runners, too (the under-runners), do not seem to ride well. I have long thought of taking them off, and to-day really decided to try the sledges without them. In spite of everything the dogs keep a very even pace, with only a halt now and then. Yesterday there were only four dogs for my sledge. One of them, 'Flint,' slipped his harness and ran away, and we did not get hold of him again before the evening, when he was killed by way of punishment. The ice was all along more uneven than it has been the last few days. In the afternoon the weather thickened, and the wind increased till, at about o'clock, a regular snowstorm was raging. No way was to be seen, only whiteness everywhere, except in places where the pointed blue ice from the ridges stuck up through the snow-drifts. After a while the ice grew worse, and I went headlong on to ridges and irregularities without even seeing them. I hoped this was only rough ice which we should pass through, but matters did not improve, and we thought there was no sense in going on. Luckily we had just then dropped on a good sheltered camping-ground; otherwise it would have been difficult enough to find one in such weather, where nothing could be discerned. Meanwhile we are getting southwards, and are more and more surprised at not seeing signs of land. We reckon now to have left the eighty-fourth parallel behind us.

"Friday, May 10th. +16.2° Fahr. (−8.8° C.). Our life has many difficulties to combat. Yesterday promised to be a good day, but thick weather hindered our advance. When we crept out of the tent yesterday forenoon it was fine, the sun was shining, the going was unusually good, and the ice appeared to be unusually even. We had managed in the snowstorm of the previous evening to get into a belt of foul ice, which was merely local. Before we started we thought of taking the removable wooden runners off the sledges, but on trying mine beforehand, found that it ran well as it was. I decided, therefore, to wait a little longer, as I was afraid that removing the wooden runners might weaken the sledge. Johansen, meanwhile, had taken them off the middle sledge, but as we then discovered that one of the birch runners had split right across under one of the uprights, there was nothing for it but to put it on again. It was a pity, though; as the sledge would have run much better on the newly-tarred runners than on the scratched underrunners. We made fairly good progress, in spite of there only being thirteen dogs left ? four to my sledge, four to the birch sledge, and five to Johansen's. But later in the afternoon the weather thickened rapidly and snow began to fall which prevented our seeing anything before us. The ice, however, was fairly even, and we kept going. We came across a lane, but this we crossed by means of a detour. Not long afterwards again we got among a number of abominable pressure-ridges, and ran right into high mounds and over steep brinks without seeing them. Wherever one turned there were sudden drops and pitfalls, although everything looked so fair and even under its covering of still-falling snow. As there seemed to be little good in continuing, we decided to camp, have our dinner of savoury hot lobscouse, make out our longitude, and then pass the time until it should clear again; and if this did not take place soon, then have a good sleep and be ready to get under way as soon as the weather should permit. After having slept for a couple of hours (it was 1 o'clock in the morning), I turned out of the tent and was confronted with the same thick, overcast weather, with only a strip of clear blue sky down by the horizon in the south-west, so I let Johansen sleep on and calculated our longitude, which proved to be 64° 20′ E. We have drifted considerably westwards since I last made it out, if my calculations be right. While I was thus occupied I heard a suspicious gnawing noise outside in the direction of the kayaks. I listened, and — quite right — it was the dogs up in Johansen's kayak. I ran out, caught 'Haren,' who was just lying gnawing at the portions of fresh dogs'-flesh destined for to-morrow's consumption, and gave him a good thrashing for his pains. The casing over the opening in the kayak was then properly secured and snowshoes and sticks piled on.

"The weather is still the same, overcast and thick; but the wind has veered round to a more southerly direction and the clear strip of blue sky in the south-west has risen a little higher from the ice-margin — can there be a west wind in prospect? Welcome, indeed, would it be, and longing were the glances I directed towards that blue strip — there lay sunshine and progress; perhaps, even, land was beneath it. I could see the cumulus clouds sailing through the blue atmosphere, and thought if only we were there, only had land under us, then all our troubles would sink into oblivion. But material needs must not be forgotten, and, perhaps, it would be better to get into the bag and have a good sleep while waiting. Many times in the morning did I peep out of the tent, but always saw the same cloudy sky and the same white prospect wherever the eye turned. Down in the west and south-west was always the same strip of clear blue sky, only that now it was lower again. When we, at last, turned out in the forenoon, the weather was just the same, and the azure strip on the horizon in the south-west was still there. I think it must have something to do with land, and it gives me hope that this may not be so far off. It is a tougher job than we thought, this gaining land, but we have had many enemies to make headway against — not only foul ice and bad going, but also wind, water, and thick weather — all of them equally obdurate adversaries to overcome."

"Sunday, May 12th. +0.6° Fahr. (−17.5° C.). Yesterday we had a better time than we expected. Overcast and thick it was the whole time, and we felt our way rather than saw it. The ice was not particularly good either, but we pressed onwards, and had the satisfaction now and then of travelling over several long stretches of flat ice.

A couple of channels which had partly opened, hindered us somewhat. Curiously enough the strip of clear sky was still there in the S.S.W. (true), and as we went along, rose higher in the heavens. We kept expecting it to spread, and that the weather would clear; we needed it sorely to find our way; but the strip never rose any higher, and yet remained there equally clear. Then it sank again, and only a small rim was left visible on the margin of the sky. Then this also disappeared. I cannot help thinking that this strip must have had something to do with land. At 7 o'clock this morning we carne to a belt of ice as bad, almost, as I have ever seen it, and as I thought it unadvisable to make an onslaught in such thick weather, we encamped. I hope we did our 14 miles, and can reckon on only 90 more to land, if it lie in 83° latitude. The ice is undoubtedly of a different character from what it was previously: it is less even, and old lanes and new ones, with ridges and rubble, are more frequent, all seeming, to point to the vicinity of land.

"Meanwhile time is going, and the number of dogs diminishing. We have now twelve left; yesterday 'Katta' was killed. And our provisions are also gradually on the decrease, though, thank Heaven, we have a good deal remaining. The first tin of petroleum (2½ gallons) came to an end three days ago, and we shall soon have finished our second sack of bread. We do nothing but scan the horizon longingly for land, but see nothing, even when I climb up on to the highest hummocks with the telescope.

"Monday, May 13th. +8.6° Fahr. (–13° C.); minimum +6.6° Fahr. (–14.2° C.) This is, indeed, a toilsome existence. The number of the dogs and likewise their hauling powers, diminish by degrees, and they are inert and difficult to urge on. The ice grows worse and worse as we approach land, and is, besides, covered with much deeper and looser snow than before. It is particularly difficult to get on in the broken-up ice, where the snow, although it covers up many irregularities, at the same time lets one sink through almost up to one's thighs between the pieces of ice, as soon as one takes one's snowshoes off to help the sledge. It is extremely tiring and shaky on this sort of surface to use one's snowshoes not firmly secured to the feet, but one cannot have them properly fastened on when one has to help the dogs at any moment, or pull and tug at these eternal sledges. I think in snow such as this Indian snow-shoes would be preferable, and I only wish I had some. Meanwhile, however, we covered some ground yesterday, and if I reckon 20 miles for yesterday and today together I do not think I shall be very far out. We should thus have only about 50 miles to the 83rd parallel and the land which Payer determined. We are keeping a somewhat southerly course, about due south (true), as this continual east wind is certainly driving us westwards, and I do not like the idea of drifting west past land. It is beginning to be tolerably warm inside the bag at night now, and last night I could hardly sleep for heat."

"Tuesday, May 14th. +6.8° Fahr. (−14° C.). Yesterday was a comfortable day of rest. Just as we were about to get under way after breakfast it clouded over, and a dense snow-storm set in, so that to start out in such weather, in the uneven ice we have now before us, would not have been worth while. I therefore made up my mind to halt for the time being and get some trifles done, and in particular the shifting of the load from the birch-sledge on to the two others, and so at last get rid of this third sledge, for which we can no longer spare any dogs. This took some time, and as it was absolutely necessary to do it, we lost nothing by stopping for a day.

"We had now so much wood from the sledge, together with broken snowshoe staves and the results of other casualties, that I thought we should be able to use it as fuel for some time to come, and so save the petroleum. We accordingly made a fire of it to cook the supper with, contrived a cooking-pot out of the empty petroleum tin, and hung it over in the approved fashion. At the first start-off we lighted the fire just outside the tent-door but soon gave that up, as, for the first thing, we nearly burned up the tent, and, secondly, the smoke came in till we could hardly see out of our eyes. But it warmed well and looked wonderfully cheerful. Then we moved it farther off, where it could neither burn up the tent, nor smoke us out; but therewith all the joy of it was departed. When we had about burned up the whole sledge and succeeded in getting a pot of boiling water, with the further result of having nearly melted through the floe on which we were living, I gave up the idea of cooking with sledges and went back to our trusty friend the 'Primus,' and a sociable and entertaining friend, too, which one can have by one's side as one lies in the bag. We have as much petroleum, I should imagine, as we shall require for the journey before us, and why bother about anything else? If the petroleum should come to an end too soon, why, then we can get as much train-oil from bear and seal and walrus as we shall require. I am very anxious to see the result of our reloading. Our two kayak sledges have undoubtedly become somewhat heavier, but then we shall have six dogs to each as long as they last. Our patience has been rewarded at last with the most brilliant sunshine and sparkling sky. It is so warm in the tent that I am lying basking in the heat. One might almost think one's self under an awning on a summer's day at home. Last night it was almost too warm to sleep."

The ice kept practicable to a certain extent during these days, though the lanes provided us with many an obstacle to overcome. Then, in addition to this, the dogs' strength was failing, they were ready to stop at the slightest unevenness, and we did not make much way. On Thursday, May 16th, I write in my diary: "Several of the dogs seem to be much exhausted. 'Baro' (the leader of my team) gave in yesterday. He could hardly move at last, and was slaughtered for supper. Poor animal. He hauled faithfully to the end.

"It was Johansen's birthday yesterday; he completed his twenty-eighth year, and of course a feast was held in honour of the occasion. It consisted of lobscouse, his favourite dish, followed by some good hot lime-juice grog. The midday sun made it warm and comfortable in the tent. Six a.m. +3.6° Fahr. (−15.8° C.).

"Have to-day calculated our latitude and longitude for yesterday, and find it was 83° 36' N. and 59° 55' E. Our latitude agrees exactly with what I supposed according to the dead reckoning, but our longitude is almost alarmingly westerly, in spite of the fact that our course has been the whole time somewhat southerly. There appears to be a strong drift in the ice here, and it will be better for us to keep east of the south, in order not to drift past land. To be quite certain, I have again calculated our observations of April 7th and 8th, but find no error, and cannot think otherwise than that we are about right. Still it seems remarkable that we have not yet seen any signs of land. Ten p.m., +1.4° Fahr. (−17° C.)."

"Friday, May 17th. +12.4° Fahr. (−10.9° C.); minimum −19° C. To-day is the 'Seventeenth of May'-Constitution Day. I felt quite certain that by to-day, at any rate, we should have been on land somewhere or other, but fate wills otherwise; we have not even seen a sign of it yet. Alas! here I lie in the bag, dreaming day-dreams and thinking of all the rejoicings at home, of the children's processions and the undulating mass of people at this moment in the streets. How welcome a sight to see the flags, with their red bunting, waving in the blue spring atmosphere, and the sun shining through the delicate young green of the leaves. And here we are in drifting ice, not knowing exactly where we are, uncertain as to our distance from an unknown land, where we hope to find means of sustaining life and thence carve our way on towards home; with two teams of dogs whose numbers and strength diminish day by day, and between us and our goal ice and water which may cause us untold trouble, with sledges which now, at any rate, are too heavy for our own powers. We press laboriously onwards mile by mile; and meanwhile, perhaps, the drift of the ice is carrying us westwards out to sea, beyond the land we are striving for. A toilsome life, undeniably, but there will be an end to it some time; some time we shall reach it, and meanwhile our flag for the 'Seventeenth of May' shall wave above the eighty-third parallel, and if fate send us the first sight of land to-day our joy will be twofold.

"Yesterday was a hard day. The weather was fine, even brilliant, the going splendid, and the ice good, so that one had a right to expect progress were it not

Pool stretching away to the horizon, May 1895.

for the dogs. They pull up at everything, and for the man ahead it is a continual going over the same ground three times: first to find a way and make a track, and then back again to drive on the dogs; it is slow work indeed. Across quite flat ice the dogs keep up to the mark pretty well, but at the first difficulty they stop. I tried harnessing myself in front of them yesterday, and it answered pretty well; but when it came to finding the way in foul ice it had to be abandoned.

"In spite of everything, we are pushing forward, and eventually shall have our reward; but for the time being this would be ample could we only reach land and land-ice without these execrable lanes. Yesterday we had four of them. The first that stopped us did not cause immoderate trouble; then we went over a short bit of middling ice, though with lane after lane and ridges. Then came another bad lane, necessitating a circuit. After this we traversed some fairly good ice, this time considerably more of it than previously, but soon came to a lane, or rather a pool, of greater size than we had ever seen before, exactly what the Russians would call a 'polynja.' It was covered with young ice too weak to bear. We started confidently alongside it in a south-westerly direction (true), in the belief that we should soon find way across; but 'soon' did not come. Just where we expected to find a crossing, an overwhelming sight presented itself to our gaze: the pool stretched away in a south-westerly direction to the very horizon, and we could see no end to it! In the mirage on the horizon, a couple of detached blocks of ice rose above the level of the pool; they appeared to be floating in open water, changed constantly in shape, and disappeared and reappeared. Everything seemed to indicate that the pool debouched right into the sea in the west. From the top of a high hummock I could, however, with the glass see ice on the other side, heightened by the looming. But it was anything but certain that it really was situated at the western end of the pool; more probably, it indicated a curve in the direction of the latter. What was to be alone here? To get over seemed for the moment an impossibility. The ice was too thin to bear and too thick to set the kayaks through, even if we should mend them. How long it might take at this time of year for the ice to become strong enough to bear, I did not know, but one day would scarcely do it. To settle down and wait, therefore, seemed too much. How far the pool extended and how long we might have to travel along it before we found a crossing and could again keep to our course no one could tell; but the probability was a long time, perhaps days. On the other hand, to retreat in the direction whence we came seemed an unattractive alternative: it would lead us away from our goal, and also perhaps necessitate a long journey in an opposite direction before we could find a crossing. The pool extended true S. 50° W. To follow it would undoubtedly take us out of our course, which ought now properly to be east of south: but on the whole this direction was nearest the line of our advance, and consequently we decided to try it. After a short time we came to a new lane running in a transverse direction to the pool. Here the ice was strong enough to bear, and on examining the ice on the pool itself beyond the confluence of this lane I found a belt where the young ice had through pressure been jammed up in several layers. This happily was strong enough to bear and we got safely over the pool, the trend of which we had been prepared to follow for days. Then on we went again, though in toil and tribulation, until at half-past eight in the evening we again found ourselves confronted by a pool, or lane, of exactly the same description as the former one, with the exception only that this time the view to the 'sea' opened towards the north-east, while in the south-west the sky-line was closed in by ice. The lane also was covered with young, ice, which in the middle was obviously of the same age as that on the last pool. Near the edge there was some thicker and older ice, which would bear, and over which I went on snowshoes to look for a crossing, but found none as far as I went. The strip of ice along the middle, sometimes broad and sometimes narrow, was everywhere too thin to risk taking the sledges over. We consequently decided to camp and wait till to-day, when it is to be hoped the ice will be strong enough to bear. And here we are still, with the same lane in front of us. Heaven only knows what surprises the day will bring.

"Sunday, May 19th. The surprise which the Seventeenth brought us was nothing less than that we found the lanes about here full of narwhals. When we had just got under way, and were about to cross over the lane we had been stopped by the previous day, I became aware of a breathing noise, just like the blowing of whales. I thought at first it must be from the dogs, but then I heard for certain that the sound came from the lane. I listened. Johansen had heard the noise the whole morning, he said, but thought it was only ice jamming in the distance. No, that sound I knew well enough, I thought, and looked over towards an opening in the ice whence I thought it proceeded. Suddenly I saw a movement which could hardly be falling ice, and quite right-up came the head of a whale; then came the body: it executed the well-known curve, and disappeared. Then up came another, accompanied by the same sound. There was a whole school of them. I shouted that they were whales, and running to the sledge, had my gun out in a second. Then came the adjusting of a harpoon, and after a little work this was accomplished, and I was ready to start in pursuit. Meanwhile the animals had disappeared from the opening in the ice where I had first seen them, though I heard their breathing from some openings farther east. I followed the lane in that direction, but did not come within range, although I got rather near them once or twice. They came up in comparatively small openings in the ice, which were to be found along the whole length of the lane. There was every prospect of being able to get a shot at them if we stopped for a day to watch the holes; but we had no time to spare, and could not have taken much with us had we got one, as the sledges were heavy enough already. We soon found a passage over, and continued our journey with the flags hoisted on the sledges in honour of the day. As we were going so slowly now that it was hardly possible for things to be worse, I determined at our dinner-hour that I really would take off the under-runners from my sledge. The change was unmistakable: it was not like the same sledge. Henceforth we got on well, and after a while the under-runners from Johansen's sledge were also removed. As we furthermore came on some good ice later in the day, our progress was quite unexpectedly good, and when we stopped at half-past eleven yesterday morning, I should think we had gone 10 miles during our day's march. This brings us down to latitude 83° 20' or so.

"At last then we have come down to latitudes which have been reached by human beings before us, and it cannot possibly be far to land. A little while before we halted yesterday, we crossed a lane, or pool, exactly like the two previous ones, only broader still. Here, too, I heard the blowing of whales, but although I was not far from the hole whence the noise presumably came, and although the opening there was quite small, I could perceive nothing. Johansen, who came afterwards with the dogs, said that as soon as they reached the frozen lane the dogs got scent of something and wanted to go against the wind. Curious that there should be so many narwhals in the lanes here.

"The ice we are now travelling over is surprisingly bad. There are few or no new ridges, only small older irregularities, with now and then deep snow in between, and then these curious broad, endless lanes, which resemble each other, and run exactly parallel, and are all unlike those we have met before. They are remarkable from the fact that, while formerly I always observed the ice on the north side of the lane to drift westwards in comparison with that which lay on the south side, the reverse was here the case. It was the ice on the south side which drifted westwards.

"As I am afraid that we are continually drifting rapidly westwards, I have kept a somewhat easterly course — S.S.E. or east of that, according as the drift necessitates. We kept the seventeenth of May — on the 18th admittedly — by a feast of unsurpassed magnificence, consisting of lobscouse, stewed red whortleberries, mixed with vril-food, and stamina lime juice mead (i.e., a concoction of lime-juice tablets and Frame Food stamina tablets dissolved in water), and then, having eaten our fill, crawled into our bag."

As we gradually made our way southwards, the ice became more impracticable and difficult to travel over. We still came across occasional good flat plains, but they were often broken up by broad belts of jammed-up ice and in a measure by channels which hindered our advance. On May 19th I write: "I climbed to the top of the highest hummock I have yet been up. I measured it roughly, and made it out to be about 24 feet above the ice whence I had climbed up; but as this latter was considerably above the surface of the water, the height was probably 30 feet or so. It formed the crest of quite a short and crooked pressure-ridge, consisting of only small pieces of ice."

That day we came across the first tracks of bears which we had seen on our journey over the ice. The certainty that we had got down to regions where these animals are to be found, and the prospect of a ham, made us very joyous. On May 20th there was a tremendous snow-storm, through which it was impossible to see our way on the uneven ice.

"Consequently there is nothing for it but to creep under the cover again and sleep as long as one can. Hunger at last, though, is too much for us, and I turn out to make a stew of delicious liver 'paté.' Then a cup of whey drink, and into the bag again, to write or slumber as we list. Here we are, with nothing to do but to wait till the weather changes and we can go on.

"We can hardly be far from 83° 10' N., and should have gained Petermann's Land if it be where Payer supposed. Either we must be unconscionably out of our bearings, or the country very small. Meanwhile, I suppose, this east wind is driving us westward, out to sea, in the direction of Spitzbergen. Heaven alone knows what the velocity of the drift may be here. Oh well, I am not in the least down-hearted. We still have ten dogs, and should we drift past Cape Fligely, there is land enough west of us, and that we can hardly mistake. Starve we scarcely can; and if the worst should come to the worst, and we have to make up our minds to winter up here, we can face that too — if only there were nobody waiting at home. But we shall get back before the winter. The barometer is falling steadily, so that it will be a case of patience long drawn out, but we shall manage all right."

On the afternoon of the following day (May 21st) we were at last able to get off, though the weather was still thick and snowy, and we often staggered along like blind men. "As the wind was strong and right at our back, and as the ice was fairly even, I at last put a sail to my sledge. It almost went by itself, but did not in the least change the dogs' pace; they kept the same slow time as before. Poor beasts, they become more and more tired, and the going is heavy and loose. We passed over many newly frozen pools that day, and some time previously there must have been a remarkable quantity of open water.

"I do not think I exceed when I put down our day's march at 14 miles, and we ought to have latitude 83° behind us, but as yet no sign of land. This is becoming rather exciting.

"Friday, May 24th. +18.8° Fahr. (−7.4° C.). Minimum −11.4° C. Yesterday was the worst day we have yet had. The lane we had before us when we stopped the previous day proved to be worse than any of the others had been. After breakfast at 1 a.m., and while Johansen was engaged in patching the tent, I trudged off to look for a passage across, but was away for three hours without finding any. There was nothing for it but to follow the bend of the lane eastwards and trust to getting over eventually; but it turned out to be a longer job than we had anticipated. When we came to the place where it appeared to end, the surrounding ice-mass was broken up in all directions, and the floes were grinding against each other as they tore along. There was no safe passage across to be found anywhere. Where at one moment, perhaps, I might have crossed over, at the next, when I had brought the sledges up, there was only open water. Meanwhile we executed some intricate manoeuvring from floe to floe, always farther east, in order to get round. The ice jammed under and around us, and it was often a difficult matter to get through. Often did we think we were well across, when still worse lanes and cracks in front of us met our disappointed gaze. It was enough sometimes to make one despair.

"There seemed to be no end to it; wherever one turned were yawning channels.

On the overcast sky the dark, threatening reflection of water was to be seen in all directions. It really seemed as if the ice was entirely broken up. Hungry and almost tired to death we were, but determined, if possible, to have our troubles behind us before we stopped for dinner. But at last matters came to a hopeless pitch, and at 1 o'clock, after nine hours' work, we decided to have a meal. It is a remarkable fact that, let things be as bad as they may, once in the bag, and with food in prospect, all one's troubles sink into oblivion. The human being becomes a happy animal, which eats as long as it can keep its eyes open, and goes to sleep with the food in its mouth. Oh, blissful state of heedlessness! But at 4 o'clock we had to turn to again at the apparently hopeless task of threading the maze of lanes. As a last drop in our cup of misery, the weather became so thick and shadowless that one literally could not see if one were walking up against a wall of ice or plunging into a pit. Alas, we have only too much of this mist! How many lanes and cracks we went across, how many huge ridges we clambered over, dragging the heavy sledges after us, I cannot say, but very many. They twisted and turned in all directions, and water and slush met us everywhere.

"But everything comes to an end, and so did this. After another two-and-a-half hours' severe exertion we had put the last lane behind us, and before us lay a lovely plain. Altogether we had now been at this sort of work for nearly twelve hours, and I had, in addition, followed the lane for three hours in the morning, which made fifteen altogether. We were thoroughly done, and wet too. How many times we had gone through the deceptive crust of snow which hides the water between the pieces of ice, it is impossible to say. Once during the morning I had had a narrow escape. I was going confidently along on snowshoes over what I supposed to be solid ice, when suddenly the ground began to sink beneath me. Happily there were some pieces of ice not far off on which I succeeded in throwing myself, while the water washed over the snow I had just been standing on. I might have had a long swim for it through the slush, which would have been anything but pleasant, particularly seeing that I was alone.

"At last we had level ice before us; but, alas, our happiness was destined to be short-lived. From the dark belt of clouds on the sky we saw that a new channel was in prospect, and at eight in the evening we had reached it. I was too tired to follow the trend of the lane (it was not short) in order to find a crossing, particularly as another channel was visible behind it. It was also impossible to see the ice around one in the heavily falling snow. It was only a question, therefore, of finding a camping-place; but this was easier said than done. A strong north wind was blowing, and no shelter was to be found from it on the level ice we had just got on to. Every mound and irregularity was examined as we passed by it in the snowstorm, but all were too small. We had to content ourselves at last with a little pressed-up hummock, which we could just get under the lee of. Then, again, there was too little snow, and only after considerable work did we succeed in pitching the tent. At last, however, the 'Primus' was singing cheerily inside it, the 'fiskegratin' diffusing its savoury odour, and two happy beings were ensconced comfortably inside the bag, enjoying existence, and satisfied, if not, indeed, at having done a good day's march, yet in the knowledge of having overcome a difficulty.

"While we were having breakfast to-day, I went out and took a meridian altitude, which, to our delight, made us 82° 52' N.

"Sunday, May 26th. When the ice is as uneven as it is now, the difficulty of making headway is incredible. The snow is loose, and if one takes one's snowshoes off for a moment one sinks in above one's knees. It is impossible to fasten them on securely, as every minute one must help the dogs with the sledges. Added to this, if the weather be thick, as yesterday, one is apt to run into the largest ridges or snow-drifts without seeing them; everything is equally white under its covering of new snow, and the light comes from all directions, so that it throws no shadows. Then one plunges in headlong, and with difficulty can get up and on to one's snowshoes again. This takes place continually, and the longer it lasts the worse it gets. At last one literally staggers on one's snowshoes from fatigue, just as if one were drunk. But we are gaining ground, and that is the chief thing, be one's shins ever so bruised and tender. This manner of progress is particularly injurious to the ankles, on account of the constant unsteadiness and swerving of the snowshoes, and many a day have mine been much swollen. The dogs, too, are becoming exhausted, which is worse.

"I have to-day calculated through the observations made yesterday, and find, to our joy, that the longitude is 61° 27' E., so that we have not drifted westwards, but have come about south according to our course. My constant fear of drifting past land is thus unfounded, and we should be able to reckon on reaching it before very long. We may possibly be farther east than we suppose, but hardly farther west, so that if we now go due south for a while, and then south-west, we must meet with land, and this within not many days. I reckon that we did 20 miles southwards yesterday, and should thus be now in latitude 82° 40' N. A couple more days, and our latitude will be very satisfactory.

"The ice we have before us looks practicable, but, to judge by the sky, we have a number of waterways a little farther on; we must manage somehow to fight our way across them. I should be very reluctant to mend the kayaks just now, before we have reached land and firm land ice. They require a thorough overhauling, both as to frames and covers. My one thought now is to get on while we still have some dogs, and thus use them up.

"A comfortable Sunday morning in the tent today. These observations put me in good spirits; life seems to look bright before us. Soon we must be able to start homewards at good speed and across open water. Oh what a pleasure it will be to handle paddle and gun again, instead of this continual toil with the sledges! Then, too, the shouting to the dogs to go on — it seems to wear and tear one's ears and every nerve in one's body.

"Monday, May 27th. Ever since yesterday morning we have seen the looming of water on the sky; it is the same looming that we saw on the previous day, and I set our course direct for the place where, to judge by it, there should be the greatest accumulation of ice, and where, consequently, a crossing should be easiest. During the course of the afternoon we came on one lane after the other, just as the water-sky had denoted, and towards evening the dark heavens before us augured open water of a worse kind. The reflection was particularly dark and threatening, both in the west and in the east. By 7 o'clock I could see a broad lane before us, stretching away west and east as far as the eye could reach from the highest hummock. It was broad, and appeared to be more impracticable than any of the previous ones. As the dogs were tired, our day's march had been a good one, and we had a splendid camping-place ready to hand, we decided to pitch the tent. Well satisfied and certain that we were now in latitude 82½°, and that land must inevitably be near, we disappeared into the bag.

"During breakfast this morning I went out and took a meridian altitude. It proves that we have not deceived ourselves. We are in latitude 82° 30′ N., perhaps even a minute or two farther south. But it is growing more and more remarkable that we see no sign of land. I cannot explain it in any other way than that we are some degrees farther east than we suppose.[83] That we should be so much farther west as to enable us to pass entirely clear of Petermann's Land and Oscar's Land, and not so much as get a glimpse of them, I consider an impossibility. I have again looked at our former observations; have again gone through our dead reckoning, the velocity and directions of the wind, and all the possibilities of drift during the days which passed between our last certain observation for longitude (April 8th) and the day when, according to the dead reckoning, we assumed ourselves to be in longitude 86° E. (April 13th). That there should be any great mistake is inconceivable. The ice can hardly have had such a considerable drift during those particular days, seeing that our dead reckoning in other respects tallied so well with the observations.

"Yesterday evening 'Kvik' was slaughtered. Poor thing, she was quite worn out, and did little or nothing in the hauling line. I was sorry to part with her, but what was to be done? Even if we should get fresh meat, it would have taken some time to feed her up again, and then, perhaps, we should have had no use for her and should only have had to kill her after all. But a fine big animal she was, and provided food for three days for our remaining eight dogs.

"I am in a continual state of wonderment at the ice we are now travelling over. It is flat and good, with only smallish pieces of broken-up ice lying about, and a large mound or small ridge here and there, but all of it is ice which can hardly be winter-old, or at any rate has been formed since last summer. It is quite a rarity to come across a small tract of older ice, or even a single old floe which has lain the summer through so rare, in fact, that at our last camping-place it was impossible to find any ice which had been exposed to the summer sun and consequently freed from salt. We were obliged to be content with snow for our drinking-water.[84] Certain is that where these great expanses of flat ice come from there was open water last summer or autumn, and that of no little extent, because we passed over many miles of this compact ice the whole day yesterday and a good part of the previous day, besides which there were formerly a considerable number of such tracts in between older, summer-old ice. There is little probability that this should have been formed in the vicinity hereabouts. More probably it has come from farther east or south-east, and was formed in open water on the east side of Wilczek's Land. I believe, consequently, that this must indicate that there cannot be a little open water along the east or north-east coast of Wilczek's Land in the summer or autumn months.[85]

"Now followed a time when the lanes grew worse than ever, and we began to toil in grim earnest. Lanes and cracks went crosswise in every direction. The ice was sometimes uneven, and the surface loose and heavy between the irregularities.

"If one could get a bird's-eye view of this ice, the lanes would form a veritable network of irregular meshes. Woe to him who lets himself get entangled in it.

"Wednesday, May 29th. Yesterday I inaugurated a great change, and began with 'komager.' It was an agreeable transition. One's feet keep nice and dry now, and one is furthermore saved the trouble of attending to the Finn shoes[86] night and morning. They were beginning in this mild temperature to assume a texture like our native 'lefser,' a kind of tough rye-cake. Then, too, one need no longer sleep with wet rags on one's chest and legs to dry them."

That day we saw our first bird: a fulmar (*procellaria glacialis*).

"Thursday, May 30th. At 5 o'clock yesterday morning we set forth with the buoyancy born of the belief that now at last the whole network of lanes was behind us; but we had not gone far before the reflection of new channels appeared in front.

I climbed up on to a hummock as quickly as possible, but the sight which met my eyes was anything but enlivening — lane after lane, crossing and recrossing, in front of us and on each side, as far as the eye could reach. It looked as if it mattered little what direction we chose it would be of no avail in getting out of the maze. I made a long excursion on ahead to see if there might not be a way of slipping through and over on the consecutive flat sheets as we had done before; but the ice appeared to be broken up, and so it probably is all the way to land. It was no longer with the compact, massive polar ice that we had to deal, but with thin, broken-up pack-ice, at the mercy of every wind of heaven, and we had to reconcile ourselves to the idea of scrambling from floe to floe as best we might. What would I not have given at this moment for it to be March, with all its cold and sufferings, instead of the end of May, and the thermometer almost above 32° F.? It was just this end of May I had feared all along, the time at which I considered it of the greatest importance to have gained land. Unhappily my fears proved to be well founded. I almost began to wish that it was a month or more later; the ice would then perhaps be slacker here, with more open pools and lanes, so that in a measure one could make one's way in a kayak. Well, who could tell? This miserable thin young ice appeared to be utterly treacherous, and there was a water-sky in every direction, but mostly far, far ahead. If only we were there! if only we were near land! Perhaps if the worst should come to the worst, we may be reduced to waiting till over the time when the mild weather and break-up of the ice come in earnest. But have we provisions enough to wait till that time? This was, indeed, more than doubtful... As I stood sunk in these gloomy reflections on the high hummock, and looking southwards over the ice, seeing ridge after ridge, and lane after lane before me, I suddenly heard the well-known sound of a whale blowing from a lane close behind. It was the solution of my troubles. Starve we should not; there are animals here, and we have guns, thank Heaven, and harpoons as well, and we know how to use them. There was a whole school of narwhals in the lane breathing and blowing ceaselessly. As some high ice hid them from view for a great part, I could only see their grey backs, now and then, as they arched themselves over the black surface of the water. I stood a long while looking at them, and had I had my gun and harpoon, it would have been an easy matter to get one. After all, the prospect was not so bad at present; and meanwhile what we had to do was not to mind lanes, but to keep on our course S.W. or S.W. to S. over them, and push on the best we could. And with that resolution I returned to the sledges. Neither of us, however, had a very firm belief that we should get much farther, and therefore all the more elated did we become as our advance proved by degrees to be tolerably easy, in spite of our exhausted dogs.

"While we were making our way during the morning between some lanes, I suddenly saw a black object come rushing through the air; it was a black guillemot (*uria grylle*), and it circled round us several times. Not long afterwards I heard a curious noise in a south-westerly direction; something like the sound made by a goat's horn when blown on; I heard it many times, and Johansen also remarked it, but I could not make out what it was. An animal, at all events, it must be, as human beings are hardly likely to be near us here.[87] A little while later a fulmar came sailing towards us and flew round and round just over our heads. I got out my gun, but before I had a cartridge in, the bird had gone again. It is beginning to grow lively here; it is cheering to see so much life, and gives one the feeling that one is approaching land and kindlier regions. Later on I saw a seal on the ice; it was a little ringed seal, which it would have been a satisfaction to capture, but before I had quite made out which it was, it had disappeared into the water.

"At ten o'clock we had dinner, which we shall no longer eat in the bag, in order to save time. We have also decided to shorten our marches to eight hours or so in the day on account of the dogs. At 11 o'clock, after dinner, we started off again, and at three stopped and camped. I should imagine we went seven miles yesterday, or let me say between twelve and fifteen during the last two days; the direction being about south-west; every little counts.

"In front of us on the horizon we have a water-sky, or at any rate a reflection which is so sharply defined and remains so immovable that it must either be over open water or dark land; our course just bears on it. It is a good way off, and the water it is over can hardly be of small extent; I cannot help thinking that it must be under land. May it be so! But between us, to judge by the sky, there seem to be plenty of lanes.

"The ice is still the same nowadays, barely of the previous winter's formation, where it is impossible to find any suitable for cooking. It seems to me that it is here, if possible, thinner than ever, with a thickness of from 2 to 3 feet. The reason of this I am still at a loss to explain.

"Friday, May 31st. It is wonderful; the last day of May this month, gone too without our reaching land; without even seeing it. June cannot surely pass in the same manner — it is impossible that we can have far to go now. I think everything seems to indicate this. The ice becomes thinner and thinner, we see more and more life around us, and in front is the same reflection of water or land, whichever it may be. Yesterday I saw two ringed seals (*phoca foetida*) in two small lanes; a bird, probably a fulmar, flew over a lane here yesterday evening, and at midday yesterday we came on the fresh tracks of a bear and two small cubs, which had followed the side of a lane. There seem to be prospects of fresh food in such surroundings, though, curiously enough, neither of us has any particular craving for it; we are quite satisfied with the food we have; but for the dogs it would be of great importance. We had to kill again last night; this time it was 'Pan,' our best dog. It could not be helped, he was quite worn out and could not do much more. The seven dogs we have left can now live three days on the food he provided.

"This is quite unexpected, the ice is very much broken up here, mere pack-ice, were it not for some large floes or flat spaces in between. If this ice had time to slacken it would be easy enough to row between the floes. Sometimes when we were stopped by lanes yesterday, and I went up on to some high hummock to look ahead, my heart sank within me, and I thought we should be constrained to give up the hope of getting farther; it was looking out over a very chaos of lumps of ice and brash mixed together in open water. To jump from piece to piece in such waters, with dogs, and two heavy sledges following one, is not exactly easy; but by means of investigation and experiment we managed eventually to get over this lane too, and after going through rubble for a while came upon flat ice again; and thus it kept on with new lanes repeatedly.

"The ice we are now travelling over is almost entirely new ice with occasional older floes in between. It continues to grow thinner; here it is for the greater part not more than 3 feet in thickness, and the floes are as flat as when they were frozen. Yesterday evening, however, we got on to a stretch of old ice on which we are stationed now, but how far it extends it is difficult to say. We camped yesterday at half-past six in the evening and found fresh ice again for the cooker, which was distinctly a pleasant change for the cook. We have not had it since May 25th.[88] A disagreeable wind from the south, it is true, has sprung up this evening, and it will be hard work going against it; we have a great deal of bad weather here, it is overcast nearly every day, with wind; south wind, which above everything is least desirable just now. But what are we to do? To settle down we have hardly provender enough; there is nothing for it, I suppose, but to grind on.

"Took a meridian altitude to-day, and we should be in 82° 21' N., and still no glimpse of land; this is becoming more and more of an enigma. What would I not give to set my foot on dry land now; but patience, always patience.

Chapter 14

By Sledge and Kayak

"SATURDAY, June 1st. So this is June. What has it in store for us? Will not this month either bring us the land we are longing for? Must hope and believe so, though the time is drawing out. Luck, for the matter of that, is a wonderful thing. I expected this morning as little of the day as was well possible; the weather was thick and snowy, and we had a strong contrary wind. It was no better when we came on a lane directly after we started, which appeared to be nearly impassable; everything was dark and dull. However, the day turned out to be better than we expected. By means of a detour to the north-east, I found a passage across the lane and we got on to long flat plains which we went over until quite midday. And from five this afternoon we had another hour and a half of good ice, but that was the end of it; a lane which ran in several directions cut off every means of advance, and although I spent more than an hour and a half in looking for a crossing, none was to be found. There was nothing for it but to camp, and hope that the morrow would bring an improvement. Now the morrow has come, but whether the improvement has come likewise, and the lane has closed more together, I do not yet know. We camped about nine yesterday evening. As usual latterly, after nearly a whole day of dismal snow, it suddenly cleared up as soon as we began to pitch the tent. The wind also went down, and the weather became beautiful, with blue sky and light white clouds, so that one might almost dream oneself far away to summer at home. The horizon in the west and south-west was clear enough, but nothing to be seen except the same water-sky, which we have been steering for, and, happily, it is obviously higher, so we are getting under it. If only we had reached it. Yonder, there must be a change, that I have no doubt of. How I long for that change!

"Curious how different things are. If we only reach land before our provisions give out we shall think ourselves well out of danger; while to Payer it stood for certain starvation if he should have to remain there and not find *Tegethoff* again. But then he had not been roaming about in the drift-ice between 83° and 86° for two months-and-a-half, without seeing a living creature. Just as were going to break up camp yesterday morning, we suddenly heard the angry cry of an ivory gull; there, above us, beautiful and white, were two of them sailing right over our heads. I thought of shooting them, but it seemed, on the whole, hardly worth while to expend cartridge apiece on such birds; they disappeared again, too, directly. A little while afterwards we heard them again. As we were lying in the bag to-day, and waiting for breakfast, we suddenly heard a hoarse scream over the tent, something like the croaking of a crow. I should imagine it must have been a gull (*larus argentatus?*).

"Is it not curious? The whole night long, whenever I was awake, did the sun smile in to us through our silken walls, and it was so warm and light that I lay and dreamed dreams of summer far from lanes and drudgery and endless toil. How fair life seems at such moments, and how bright the future! But no sooner do I turn out at half-past nine to cook, than the sun veils his countenance and snow begins to fall. This happens nearly every day now. Is it because he will have us settle down here and wait for the summer and the slackening of the ice and open water, will spare us the toil of finding a way over this hopeless maze of lanes? I am loath, indeed, that this should come to pass. Even if we could manage, as far as provisions are concerned, by killing and eating the dogs, and with a chance of game in prospect, our arrival in Spitzbergen would be late, and we might not improbably have to pass the winter there, and then those at home would have another year to wait."

"Sunday, June 2nd. So it is on Whit Sunday that this book[89] finishes. I could hardly have imagined that we should still be in the drift-ice without seeing land; but fate wills otherwise and she knows no mercy.

"The lane which stopped us yesterday did not close but opened wider until there was a big sea to the west of us, and we were living on a floe in the midst of it without a passage across anywhere. So, at last, what we have so often been threatened with has come to pass; we must set to work and make our kayaks seaworthy. But first of all we moved the tent into a sheltered nook of the hummock, where we are lying to, so that the wind does not reach us, and we can imagine it is quite still outside, instead of a regular 'mill-breeze' blowing from the south-west. To rip off the cover of my kayak and get it into the tent to patch it was the work of a very short time, and then we spent a comfortable, quiet Whit Sunday evening in the tent. The cooker was soon going, and we had some smoking hot lobscouse for dinner, and I hardly think either of us regretted he was not on the move; it is undeniably good to make a halt sometimes. The cover was soon patched and ready; then I had to go out and brace up the frame of my kayak where most of the lashings are slack, and must be lashed over again; this will be no inconsiderable piece of work; there are at least forty of them. However, only a couple of the ribs are split, so the framework can easily be made just as good as before. Johansen also took the cover off his kayak, and to-day it is going to be patched.

"When both the frames are put in order and the covers on, we shall be ready to start afresh, and to meet every difficulty, be it lanes, pools, or open sea. It will, indeed, be with a feeling of security that we shall set forth, and there will be an end to this continual anxiety lest we should meet with impassable lanes. I cannot conceive that anything now can prevent us from soon reaching land. It can hardly be long now before we meet with lanes and open water in which we can row. There will be a difficulty with the remaining dogs, however, and it will be a case of parting with them. The dogs' rations were portioned out yesterday evening, and we still have part of 'Pan' for supper; but 'Klapperslangen' must go too. We shall then have six dogs, which, I suppose, we can keep four days, and still get on a good way with them.

"Whitsuntide — there is something so lovely and summer-like in the word. It is hard to think how beautiful everything is now at home, and then to lie here still, in mist and wind and ice. How homesick one grows; but what good does it do? Little Liv will go to dinner with her grandmother to-day; perhaps they are dressing her in a new frock at this very moment! Well, well, the time will come when I can go with her — but when? I must set to work on the lashings, and it will be all right!"

We worked with ardour during the following days to get our kayaks ready, and even grudged the time for eating. Twelve hours sometimes went by between each meal, and our working-day often lasted for twenty four hours. But all the same it took time to make these kayaks fully seaworthy again. The worst of it was that we had to be so careful with our materials, as the opportunities of acquiring more were not immoderately abundant. When, for instance, a rib had to be re-lashed, we could not rip up the old lashing, but had to unwind it carefully in order not to destroy the line; and when there are many scores of such places to be re-lashed, this takes time. Then, too, several of the bamboo ribs which run along the side of the framework (particularly in Johansen's kayak) were split, and these had wholly or partly to be taken out and new ones substituted, or to be strengthened by lashings and side splints. When the covers were properly patched, and the frames after several days' work again in order, the covers were put on and carefully stretched. All this, of course, had to be done with care, and was not quick work; but then we had the satisfaction of knowing that the kayaks were fully seaworthy, and capable, if need be, of weathering a storm on the way over to Spitzbergen.

Meanwhile the time flew by, our precious time; but then we hoped that our kayaks would render us important assistance, and that we should get on all the quicker in them. Thus, on Tuesday, June 4th, I wrote in my diary: "It seems to me that it cannot be long before we come to open water or slack ice. The latter is, hereabouts, so thin and broken up, and the weather so summer-like. Yesterday the thermometer was a little below freezing-point, and the snow which fell was more like sleet than anything else; it melted on the tent, and it was difficult to keep things from getting wet inside; the walls dripped if we even went near them. We had abominable weather the whole day yesterday, with falling snow, but for the matter of that we are used to it; we have had nothing else lately. To-day, however, it is brilliant, clear blue sky, and the sun has just come over the top of our hummock and down into the tent. It will be a glorious day to sit out and work in; not like yesterday, when all one's tackle got wet; it is worst of all when one is lashing, for then one cannot keep the line taut. This sun is a welcome friend; I thought I was almost tired of it before when it was always there; but how glad we are to see it now, and how it cheers one. I can hardly get it out of my head that it is a glorious fresh June morning home by the bay. Only let us soon have water so that we can use our kayaks, and it will not be long before we are home.

"To-day,[90] for the first time on the whole of this journey, we have dealt out rations for breakfast, both of butter, 1 2/3 ozs., and aleuronate bread, 6 2/3 ozs. We must keep to weights in order to be certain the provisions will last out, and I shall take stock properly of what we have left before we go farther.

"Happiness is, indeed, short-lived. The sun has gone again, the sky is overcast, and snowflakes are beginning to fall.

"Wednesday, June 5th. Still at the same spot, but it is to be hoped it will not be long before we are able to get off. The weather was fine yesterday after all, and it was summer-like to sit out and work and bask in the sun; and then to look out over the water and the ice, with the glittering waves and snow.

"Yesterday we shot our first game. It was an ivory gull (*larus eberneus*), which went flying over the tent. There were other gulls here, yesterday, too, and we saw as many as four at once; but they kept at a distance. I went after them once and missed my mark. One cartridge wasted; this must not be repeated. If we had taken the trouble we could easily have got more gulls; but they are too small game, and it is also too early to use up our ammunition. In the pool here I saw a seal, and Johansen saw one too. We have both seen and heard narwhals. There is life enough here, and if the kayaks were in order, and we could row out on the water, I have no doubt we could get something. However, it is not necessary yet. We have provisions enough at present, and it is better to employ the time in getting on, on account of the dogs, though it would be well if we could get some big game, and not kill any more of them until our ice journey is over, and we take to the kayaks for good. Yesterday we had to kill 'Klapperslangen.' He gave twenty-five rations, which will last the six remaining dogs four days. The slaughtering was now entirely Johansen's business; he had achieved such dexterity that with a single thrust of my long Lapp knife he made an end of the animal, so that it had no time to utter a sound, and after a few minutes, with the help of the knife and our little axe, he had divided the animal into suitable doles. As I mentioned before, we left the skin and hair on; the former was carefully eaten up, and the only thing left after the dogs' meal was, as a rule, a tuft of hair here and there on the ice, some claws, and, perhaps, a well-gnawed cranium, the hard skull being too much for them.

"They are beginning to be pretty well starved now. Yesterday 'Lilleraeven' ate up the toe-strap (the reindeer-skin which is placed under the foot to prevent the snow from balling), and a little of the wood of Johansen's snowshoes which the dog had pulled down on to the ice. The late 'Kvik' ate up her sail-cloth harness, and I am not so sure these others do not indulge in a fragment of canvas now and then.

"I have just calculated our longitude according to an observation taken with the theodolite yesterday, and make it to be 61° 16.5′ E.; our latitude was 82° 17.8′ N. I cannot understand why we do not see land. The only possible explanation must be that we are farther east than we think, and that the land stretches southwards in that direction, but we cannot have much farther to go now. Just at this moment a bird flew over us which Johansen, who is standing just outside the tent, took to be a kind of sandpiper.

"Thursday. June 6th. Still on the same spot. I am longing to get off, see what things look like, and have a final solution of this riddle which is constantly before me. It will be a real pleasure to be under way again with whole tackle, and I cannot help thinking that we shall soon be able to use our kayaks in open water. Life would be another thing then! Fancy, to get clear for good of this ice and these lanes, this toil with the sledges, and endless trouble with the dogs, only oneself in a light craft dancing over the waves at play! It is almost too much to think of. Perhaps we have still many a hard turn before we reach it, many a dark hour; but some time it must come, and then — then life will be life again!

"Yesterday at last we finished mending the frame-work of both kayaks. We rigged up some plaited bamboo at the bottom of each to place the provisions on, in order to prevent them from getting wet in case the kayaks should leak. To-day we have only to go over them again, test the lashings, and brace (support) those that may require it, and finally put the covers on. Tomorrow evening I hope we shall get off. This repairing has taken it out of the cord; of our three balls we have rather less than one left. This I am very anxious to keep, as we may require it for fishing and so forth.

"Our various provisions are beginning to dwindle. Weighed the butter yesterday, and found that we only had 5 lbs. 1 1/3 oz. If we reckon our daily ration at 1 ozs. per man, it will last another 23 days, and by that time we shall have gone a little farther. To-day, for the first time, I could note down a temperature above freezing point, i.e., +35.6° Fahr. this morning. The snow outside was soft all through, and the hummocks are dripping. It will not be long now before we find water on the floes. Last night, too, it absolutely rained. It was only a short shower; first of all it drizzled, then came large, heavy drops, and we took shelter inside the tent in order not to get wet — but it was rain, rain! It was quite a summer feeling to sit in here and listen to the drops plashing on the tent-wall. As regards the going, this thaw will probably be a good thing if we should have frost again; but if the snow is to continue as it is now it will be a fine mess to get through among all these ridges and hummocks. Instead of such a contingency, it would be better to have as much rain as possible, to melt and wash the ice clear of snow. Well, well, it must do as it likes. It cannot be long now before it takes a turn for the better — land or open water, whichever it may be.

"Saturday, June 8th. Finished and tried the kayaks yesterday at last, but only by dint of sticking to our work from the evening of the day before yesterday to the evening of yesterday. It is remarkable that we are able to continue working so long at a stretch. If we were at home we should be very tired and hungry, with so many working hours between meals; but here it does not seem more than it should be, although our appetites, certainly, are first-rate, and our sleeping powers good. It does not seem as if we were growing weak or sickening for scurvy just yet. As a matter of fact, so far as I know, we are unusually strong and healthy just now and in full elasticity.

"When we tried the kayaks in a little lane just here, we found them considerably leaky in the seams and also in the canvas owing to their rough usage on the way, but it is to be hoped no more so than will be remedied when a little soaking makes the canvas swell out. It will not be agreeable to ferry over lanes and

Closing lanses, June 1895.

have to put our kayaks dry and leaky on the water. Our provisions may not improbably be reduced to a pulp; but we shall have to put up with that, too, like everything else.

"And so we really mean to get off to-day, after a week's stay on the same spot. Yesterday the south-east wind set in; it has increased to-day, and become rather strong, to judge by the whistling round the hummocks outside. I lay here this morning fancying I heard the sound of breakers a little way off. All the lanes about here closed yesterday, and there was little open water to be seen. It is owing to this wind, I suppose, and if it is going to close lanes for us, then let it blow on. The snow is covered with a crust of ice, the going is as good as possible, and the ice, it is to be hoped, is more or less flat, so we shall be all right.

"Johansen shot another ivory gull yesterday, and we had it and another one for dinner. It was our first taste of fresh food, and was, it cannot be denied, very good; but all the same not so delightful as one would expect, seeing that we have not had fresh meat for so many months. It is a proof, no doubt, that the food we have is also good.

"Weighed the bread yesterday; found we had 26 lbs. 4 ozs. of wheaten bread and 17 lbs. 1 oz. of aleuronate bread, so, for that matter, we can manage for another thirty-five or forty days, and how far we shall then have got the gods alone know, but some part of the way it must be.

"Sunday, June 9th. We got away from our camping-ground at last yesterday, and we were more than pleased. In spite of the weather, which was as bad as it could be, with a raging snow-storm from the east, we were both glad to begin our wanderings again. It took some time to fix grips under the kayaks, consisting of sack, sleeping-bag, and blankets, and so load the sledges; but eventually we made a start. We got well off the floe we had lived on so long, and did not even have to use the kayaks which we had spent a week in patching for that purpose. The wind had carefully closed the lanes. We found flat ice country, and made good way in spite of the most villainous going, with newly fallen snow, which stuck to one's snowshoes mercilessly, and in which the sledges stood as if fixed to the spot as soon as they stopped. The weather was such that one could not see many hundred feet in front of one, and the snow which accumulated on one's clothes, on the weather-side, wetted one to the skin; but still it was glorious to see ourselves making progress, progress towards our stubborn goal. We came across a number of lanes, and they were difficult to cross, with their complicated network of cracks and ridges in all directions. Some of them were broad and full of brash, which rendered it impossible to use the kayaks. In some places, however, the brash was pressed so tightly together that we could walk on it. But many journeys to and fro are nearly always necessary before any reasonable opportunity of advance is to be found. This time is often long to the one who remains behind with the dogs, being blown through or wetted through meanwhile, as the case may be. Often, when it seemed as if I was never coming back, did Johansen think, I had fallen through some lane and was gone for good. As one sits there on the kayak waiting and waiting and gazing in front of one into solitude, many strange thoughts pass through one's brain. Several times he climbed the highest hummock near at hand to scan the ice anxiously; and then, when at last he discovered a little black speck moving about on the white flat surface far, far away, his mind would be relieved. As Johansen was waiting in this way yesterday, he remarked that the sides of the floe in front of him were slowly moving up and down,[91] as they might if rocked by a slight swell. Can open water be near? Can it be that the great breakers from the sea have penetrated in here? How willingly would we believe it! But, perhaps, it was only the wind which set the thin ice we are travelling over now in wave-like motion. Or have we really open water to the south-east? It is remarkable that this wind welds the ice together, while the south-west wind here a little while ago slackened it. When all is said, is it possible that we are not far from the sea? I cannot help thinking of the water-reflections we have seen on the sky before us. Johansen has just left the tent, and says that he can

Packed ice, a coign of vantage.

see the same reflection in the south; it is higher now, and the weather tolerably clear. What can it be? Only let us go on and get there.

"We came across the track of a bear again yesterday. How old it was could not easily be determined in this snow, which obliterates everything in a few minutes, but it was probably from yesterday, for 'Haren' directly afterwards got scent of something and started off against the wind, so that Johansen thought the bear must be somewhere near. Well, well, old or new, a bear was there while we were a little farther north, stitching at the kayaks, and one day it will come our way, too, no doubt. The gull which Johansen shot brought up a large piece of blubber when it fell, and this tends to confirm us in the belief that bears are at hand, as the bird hardly could have done so, had it not been in company.

"The weather was wet and wretched, and, to make things worse, there was a thick mist, and the going was as heavy as it could be. To go on did not seem very attractive; but, on the other hand, a halt for dinner in this slush was still less so. We therefore continued a little while longer, and stopped at 10 o'clock for good. What a welcome change it was to be under the tent again! And the 'fiskegratin' was delicious. It gives one such a sense of satisfaction to feel that, in spite of everything, one is making a little way. The temperature is beginning to be bad now; the snow is quite wet, and some water has entered my kayak, which I suppose melted on the deck and ran down through the open side where the lacing is, which we have not yet sewn fast. We are waiting for good weather in order to get the covers thoroughly dry first, and then stretch them well.

"Monday, June 10th. In spite of the most impenetrable mist and the most detestable going on soppy snow, which has not yet been sufficiently exposed to frost to become granular, and where the sledges rode their very heaviest, we still managed to make good even progress the whole day yesterday. There were innumerable lanes, of course, to deal with, and many crossings on loose pieces of ice which we accomplished at a pinch. But the ice is flat here everywhere, and every little counts. It is the same thin winter ice of about 3 feet in thickness. I only saw a couple of old floes yesterday — they were in the neighbourhood of our camping-ground, which was also on an old floe — otherwise the ice is new, and in places very new. We went over some large expanses yesterday of ice one foot or less in thickness. The last of these tracts in particular was very remarkable, and must at one time have been an immense pool; the ice on it was so thin that it cannot be long before it melts altogether. There was water on all this ice, and it was like walking through gruel. As a matter of fact, the ice about here is nothing else but pure broken-up sea-ice, consisting of large and small floes, not infrequently very small floes closely aggregated; but when they have the chance of slackening they will spread over the whole sea hereabouts, and we shall have water enough to row in any direction we please.

"The weather seems to-day to be of the same kind as yesterday, with a south-west wind, which is tearing and rattling at the tent-walls. A thaw and wet snow. I do not know if we shall get any more frost, but it would make the snow in splendid condition for our snowshoes. I am afraid however, that the contrary will rather be the case, and that we shall soon be in for the worst break-up of the winter. The lanes otherwise are beginning to improve: they are no longer so full of brash and slush; it is melting away, and bridges and such-like have a better chance of forming in the clearer water.

"We scan the horizon unremittingly for land, every time there is a clear interval; but nothing, never anything, to be seen. Meanwhile we constantly see signs of the proximity of land or open water. The gulls increase conspicuously in number, and yesterday we saw a little auk (*mergulus alle*) in a lane. The atmosphere in the south and south-west is always apt to be dark, but the weather has been such that we can really see nothing. Yet I feel that the solution is approaching. But then how long have I not thought so? There is nothing for it but the noble virtue of patience.

"What beautiful ice this would have been to travel over in April, before all these lanes were formed — endless flat plains! For the lanes, as far as we know, are all newly formed ones, with some ridges here and there, which are also new.

"Tuesday, July 11th. A monotonous life this on the whole, as monotonous as one can well imagine it — to turn out day after day, week after week, month after month, to the same toil over ice which is sometimes a little better, sometimes a little worse — it now seems to be steadily getting worse ? always hoping to see an end to it, but always hoping in vain, ever the same monotonous range of vision over ice, and again ice. No sign of land in any direction and no open water, and now we should be in the same latitude as Cape Fligely, or at most a couple of minutes farther north. We do not know where we are, and we do not know when this will end. Meanwhile our provisions are dwindling day by day, and the number of our dogs is growing seriously less. Shall we reach land while we yet have food, or shall we, when all is said, ever reach it? It will soon be impossible to make any way against this ice and snow: the latter is only slush, the dogs sink through at every step; and we ourselves splash through it up above our knees when we have to help the dogs or take a turn at the heavy sledges, which happens frequently. It is hard to go on hoping in such circumstances, but still we do so; though sometimes, perhaps, our hearts fail us when we see the ice lying before us like an impenetrable maze of ridges, lanes, brash, and huge blocks thrown together pell-mell, and one might imagine one's self looking at suddenly congealed breakers. There are moments when it seems impossible that any creature not possessed of wings can get farther, and one longingly follows the flight of a passing gull, and thinks how far away one would soon be could one borrow its wings. But then, in spite of everything, one finds a way, and hope springs eternal. Let the sun peep out a moment from the bank of clouds, and the ice-plains glitter in all their whiteness; let the sunbeams play on the water, and life seems beautiful in spite of all, and worthy a struggle.

"It is wonderful how little it takes to give one fresh courage. Yesterday I found dead in a lane a little polar cod (*gadus polaris*), and my eyes, I am sure, must have shone with pleasure when I saw it. It was real treasure-trove. Where there is fish in the water one can hardly starve, and before I crept into the tent this morning I set a line in the lane beside us. But what a number of these little fish it would require to feed one, many more in one day than one could catch in a week, or perhaps in a month! Yet one is hopeful and lies counting the chances of there being larger fish in the water here, and of being able to fish to one's heart's content.

"Advance yesterday was more difficult than on the previous days, the ice more uneven and massive, and in some places with occasional old floes in between. We were stopped by many bad lanes, too, so did not make much I am afraid not more than 3 or 4 miles. I think we may now reckon on being in latitude 82° 8' or 9' N. if this continual south-east wind has not sent us northwards again. The going is getting worse and worse. The snow is water-soaked to the bottom, and will not bear the dogs any longer, though it has become a little more granular lately, and the sledges run well on it when they do not cut through, which happens continually, and then they are almost immovable. It is heavy for the dogs, and would be so even if they were not so wretchedly worn out as they are; they stop at the slightest thing, and have to be helped or driven forward with the whip. Poor animals, they have a bad time of it! 'Lilleraeven,' the last of my original team, will soon be unable to go farther — and such a good animal to haul! We have five dogs left ('Lilleraeven,' 'Storraeven,' and 'Kaifas' to my sledge, 'Suggen' and 'Heren' to Johansen's). We still have enough food for them for three days, from 'Isbjön,' who was killed yesterday morning; and before that time Johansen thinks the riddle will be solved. Vain hope, I am afraid, although the water-sky in the south-east or south-south-east (magnetic) seems always to keep in the same position and has risen much higher.

"We began our march at half-past six yesterday afternoon, and stopped before a lane at a quarter-past three this morning. I saw fresh-water pools on the ice under some hummocks yesterday for the first time. Where we stopped, however, there were none to be found, so we had to melt water again this morning; but it will not often be necessary hereafter, I hope, and we can save our oil, which, by the way, is becoming alarmingly reduced. Outside the weather and snow are the same; no pleasure in turning out to the toils of the day. I lie here thinking of our June at home, how the sun is shining over forest and fjord and wooded hills, and there is — But some time we shall get back to life, and then it will be fairer than it has ever been before.

"Wednesday, June 12th. This is getting worse and worse. Yesterday we did nothing, hardly advanced more than a mile. Wretched snow, uneven ice, lanes, and villainous weather stopped us. There was certainly a crust on the snow, on which the sledges ran well when they were on it; but when they broke through — and they did it constantly — they stood immovable. This crust, too, was bad for the dogs, poor things! They sank through it into the deep snow between the irregularities, and it was like swimming through slush for them. But all the same we made way. Lanes stopped us, it is true, but we cleared them somehow. Over one of them, the last, which looked nasty, we got by making a bridge of small floes, which we guided to the narrowest place. But then a shameless storm of wet snow, or more correctly sleet, with immense flakes, set in, and the wind increased. We could not see our way in this labyrinth of lanes and hummocks, and were as soaked as ducked crows, as we say. The going was impossible, and the sledges as good as immovable in the wet snow, which was soon deep enough to cling to our snowshoes underneath in great lumps, and prevent them from running. There was hardly any choice but to find a camping-ground as soon as possible, for to force one's way along in such weather, and on such snow, and make no progress, was of little use. We found a good camping-ground and pitched our tent after only four hours' march, and went without our dinner to make up.

"Here we are, then, hardly knowing what to do next. What the going is like outside I do not know yet, but probably not much better than yesterday, and whether we ought to push on the little we can, or go out and try to capture a seal, I cannot decide. The worst of it is that there do not seem to be many seals in the ice where we now are. We have seen none the last few days. Perhaps it is too thick and compact for them (?). The ice here is strikingly different in character from that we have been travelling over of late. It is considerably more uneven, for one thing, with mounds and somewhat old ridges, among them some very large ones. Nor does it look so very old in general, I should say, of last winter's formation, though there are occasional old floes in between. They appear to have been near land, as day and earthy matter are frequently to be seen, particularly in the newly formed ridges.

"Johansen, who has gone out, says the same water-sky is to be seen in the south. Why is it we cannot reach it? But there it is all the same, an alluring goal for us to make for, even if we do not reach it very soon. We see it again and again, looking so blue and beautiful; for us it is the colour of hope."

"Friday, June 14th. It is three months to-day since we left the *Fram*. A quarter of a year have we been wandering in this desert of ice, and here we are still. When we shall see the end of it I can no longer form any idea; I only hope whatever may be in store for us is not very far off, open water or land — Wilczek Land, Zichy Land, Spitzbergen, or some other country.

"Yesterday was not quite so bad a day as I expected. We really did advance, though not very far — hardly more than a couple of miles — but we must be content with that at this time of year. The dogs could not manage to draw the sledges alone; if there was nobody beside them, they stopped at every other step. The only thing to be done was to make a journey to and fro, and thus go over the ground three times. While I went on ahead to explore, Johansen drove the sledges as far as he could; first mine, and then back again after his own. By that time I had returned and drove my own sledge as far as I had found a way; and then this performance was repeated all over again. It was not rapid progress, but progress it was of a kind, and that was something. The ice we are going over is anything but even; it is still rather massive and old, with hummocks and irregularities in every direction, and no real flat tracts. When, added to this, after going a short distance, we came to a place where the ice was broken up into small floes, with high ridges and broad lanes filled with slush and brash, so that the whole thing looked like a single mass of *débris*, where there was hardly standing-room, to say nothing of any prospect of advance, it was only human to lose courage and give up, for the time being, trying to get on. Wherever I turned the way was closed, and it looked as if advance was denied us for good. To launch the kayaks would be of no avail, for we could hardly expect to propel them through this accumulation of fragments, and I was on the point of making up my mind to wait and try our luck with the net and line, and see if we could not manage to find a seal somewhere in these lanes.

"These are moments full of anxiety, when from some hummock one looks doubtingly over the ice, one's thoughts continually reverting to the same question: have we provisions enough to wait for the time when the snow will have melted, and the ice have become slacker, and more intersected with lanes, so that one can row between the floes? Or is there any probability of our being able to obtain sufficient food, if that which we have should fall short? These are great and important questions which I cannot yet answer for certain. That it will take a long time before all this snow melts away, and advance becomes fairly practicable, is certain; at what time the ice may become slacker, and progress by means of the lanes possible, we cannot say; and up to this we have taken nothing, with the exception of two ivory gulls and a small fish. We did, indeed, see another fish swimming near the surface of the water, but it was no larger than the other. Where we are just now, there seems to be little prospect of capturing anything. I have not seen a single seal the last few days; though yesterday I saw the snowed-down track of a bear. Meanwhile we see ivory gulls continually; but they are still too small to be worth a cartridge; yesterday, however, I saw a large gull, probably *larus argentatus*.

"I determined to make one more attempt to get on by striking farther east, and this time I was successful in finding a passage across by way of a number of small floes. On the other side there was rather old compact ice, partially of formation a summer old, which seemed to have been near land, as it was irregular, and much intermixed with earthy matter. We have travelled over this ice-field ever since without coming on lanes; but it was uneven, and we came to grief several times. In other places again it was pretty good.

"We began our march at 8 o'clock on Wednesday afternoon, and halted here at 5 o'clock this morning.[92] Later on in the forenoon the wind went over to the north-east, and the temperature fell. The snow froze hard, and eventually the going became pretty good. The crust on the snow bore the dogs up, and also the sledges to a certain extent, and we looked forward to good going on the following day; but in this we were doomed to disappointment. No sooner had we got inside the tent than it began to snow, and kept briskly at it the whole day whilst we slept, and yesterday evening, when we turned out to get breakfast ready and start off, it was still snowing, and deep, loose snow covered everything; a state of things bad beyond description. There was no sense in going on, and we decided to wait and see how matters would turn out. Meanwhile we were hungry, but as we could not afford a full breakfast I prepared a small portion of fish soup, and we returned to the bag again: Johansen to sleep on, I to re-reckon all my observations from the time we left the *Fram*, and see if some error might not explain the mystery why no land was yet to be found. The sun had partially appeared, and I tried, though in vain, to take an observation. I stood waiting for more than an hour with the theodolite up, but the sun went in again and remained out of sight. I have calculated and calculated and thought and thought, but can find no mistake of any importance, and the whole thing is a riddle to me. I am beginning seriously to doubt that we may be too far west after all. I simply cannot conceive that we are too far east; for in such a case we cannot, at any rate, be more than 5° farther east than our observations[93] make us. Supposing, for instance, that our watches have gone too fast, 'Johansen'[94] cannot, at all events, have gained more than double its previous escapement. I have assumed an escapement of five seconds; but supposing that the escapement has been ten seconds this does not make more difference than 6' 40" in eighty days (the time from our departure from the *Fram* till the last observation) that is 1° 40' farther east than we ought to be. Assuming, too, that I have calculated our days' marches at too great length, in the days between April 8th and 13th, and that instead of 36 English geographical miles or rather more than 40 statute miles, we have only gone 24 English geographical miles, or 28 statute miles (less we cannot possibly have gone), we should then have been in 89° E. instead of in 86° E. on the 13th as we supposed. That is 3° farther east, or with the figures above, let us say together 5° farther east, i.e., we now instead of being in longitude 61° E. should be in 66° E.,[95] or about 70 miles from Cape Fligely. But it seems to me we ought to see land south of us just the same. Wilczek Land cannot be so low and slope suddenly so far to the south, when Cape Buda-Pest is said to lie in about 61° E. and 82° N., and should thus be not so much as 50 miles from us. No, this is inconceivable. On the other hand, it is not any easier to suppose ourselves west of it; we must have drifted very materially between April 8th and 13th, or my watch must have stopped for a time before April 2nd. The observations from April 2nd, 4th, and 8th seem, indeed, to indicate that we drifted considerably westwards. On the 2nd we appeared to be in 103° 6' E., on the 4th in 99° 59' E., and April 8th in 95° 7' E. Between these dates there were no marches of importance; between the observations on the 2nd and the 4th there was only a short half-day's march; and between the 4th and the 7th a couple, which amounted to nothing, and could only have carried us a little westwards. This is as much as to say that we must have drifted 8°, or let us reckon at any rate 7° westwards in the six days and nights. Assuming that the drift was the same during the five days and nights between the 8th and 13th, we then get 7° farther west than we suppose. We should consequently now be in 54° E., instead of in 61° E., and not more than 36 to 40 miles from Cape Fligely and close by Oscar's Land. We ought to see something of them, I think. Let us assume meanwhile that the drift westwards was strong in the period before April 2nd also, and grant the possibility that my watch did stop at that time (which I fear is not excluded), and we may then be any distance west for all we can tell. It is this possibility which I begin to think of more and more. Meanwhile, apparently there is nothing for it but to continue as we have done already — perhaps a little more south — and a solution must come.

"When, after having concluded my calculations, I had taken a nap and again turned out at midday to-day, the condition of the snow proved to be no better; in fact, rather worse. The new snow was wet and sticky and the going as heavy as it well could be. However, it was necessary to make an attempt to get on, there was nothing gained by waiting there, and progress is progress be it ever so little. I took a single altitude about midday, but it was not sharp."

"Saturday, June 15th. The middle of June and still no prospect of an end to this; things only became worse instead. So bad as yesterday, though, it has never been, and worse, happily, it can hardly be. The sledges ran terribly heavy in the loose, wet, newly-fallen snow, which was deep to boot, and sometimes when they stopped — and that was continually — they stuck as if glued to the spot. It was all we could do to move them when we pushed with all our might. Then to this was added the fact that one's snowshoes ran equally badly, and masses of snow collected underneath them the minute one stopped; one's feet kept twisting continually from this cause, and ice formed under them, so that one suddenly slid off the snowshoes and into the snow, till far above one's knees, when one tried to pull or help the sledges; but there was nothing for it but to scramble up and on to them again. To wade along in such snow without them is an impossibility, and, as I have said before, though fastening them on securely would have been a better plan, yet it would have been too troublesome, seeing that we had to take them off continually to get the

'Kaifas'.

sledges over ridges and lanes. In addition to all this, wherever one turns, the ice is uneven and full of mounds and old ridges, and it is only by wriggling along like an eel, so to speak, that one can get on at all. There are lanes, too, and they compel one to make long detours or go long distances over thin, small floes, ridges, and other abominations. We struggled along, however, a little way, working on our old plan of two turns, but a quick method it could not be called. The dogs are becoming more and more worn-out. 'Lilleraeven,' the last survivor of my team, can now hardly walk — there is no question of hauling — he staggers like a drunken man, and when he falls can hardly rise to his feet again. To-day he is going to be killed, I am thankful to say, and we shall be spared seeing him. 'Storraeven,' too, is getting very slack in the traces; the only one of mine which pulls at all is 'Kaifas,' and that is only as long as one of us is helping behind. To keep on longer in such circumstances is only wearing out men and dogs to no purpose, and is also using up more provender than is necessary. We therefore renounced dinner, and halted at about ten yesterday evening, after having begun the march at half-past four in the afternoon. I had, however, stopped to take an observation on the way. It is not easy to get hold of the sun nowadays, and one must make the most of him when he is to be seen through the driving clouds; clear he will never be. Yesterday afternoon, after an unconscionable wait, and after having put up the instrument in vain a couple of times, I finally got a wretched single altitude.

"Yesterday evening I calculated through these observations and find that, contrary to our expectations, we have drifted strongly westwards, having come from 61° 16′ E., which was our longitude on June 4th, right to about 57° 40′ E. But then we have also drifted a good way north again, up to 82° 26′ N., after being down in 82° 17.8′ on the same date, and we have been pushing southwards as hard as we could the whole time. However, we are glad to see that there is so much movement in the ice, for then there is hope of our drifting out eventually towards open water; for that we can get there by our own efforts alone over this shocking ice I am beginning to doubt. This country and this going are too bad, and my hope now is in lanes and slack ice. Happily, a north-east wind has sprung up. Yesterday there was a fresh breeze from the north-north-west (magnetic), and the same again today. Only let it blow on; if it has set us north-west it can also set us south-west, and eventually out towards our goal, towards Franz Josef Land or Spitzbergen. I doubt more than ever our being east of Cape Fligely after this observation, and I begin to believe more and more in the possibility that the first land we shall see — if we see any, and I hope we may — will be Spitzbergen. In that case we should not even get a glimpse of Franz Josef Land, the land of which I have dreamed golden dreams day and night. But still if it is not to be, then well and good. Spitzbergen is good enough, and if we are as far west as we seem to be, I have greater hope than before of finding slacker ice and open water; and then for Spitzbergen! But there is still a serious question to be faced, and that is to procure ourselves enough food for the journey.

"I have slept here some time on purpose, after having spent a good while on my calculations and speculations as to our drift and our future. We have nothing to hurry for in this state of the snow; it is hardly better to-day than it was yesterday, and then, on account of the mild temperature, it is better to travel by night than by day. The best thing to do is to spin out the time as long as possible without consuming more than absolutely necessary of the provisions; the summer cannot but improve matters, and we have still three months of it before us. The question is, can we procure ourselves food during that time? It would be strange, I think, if we could not. There are birds about continually; I saw another large gull yesterday, probably the herring or silver gull (*larus argentatus*) — but to support life for any length of time on such small fry we have not cartridges enough. On seal or bear all my hopes are fixed; just one before our provisions give out, and the evil hour is warded off for a long time to come."

"Sunday, June 16th. Yesterday was as bad as it well could be, the surface enough to make one desperate, and the ice rough. I very much doubted whether the wisest thing would not be to kill the dogs and keep them as food for ourselves, and try to make our way on as best we could without them. In that manner we should have provender for fifteen or perhaps twenty days longer, and should be able to make some progress at the same time. There does not seem much to be done in that line, however, and perhaps the right thing to do is to wait. But, on the other hand, perhaps, it is not far to land or open water, or, at any rate, to slack ice, and then every mile we can make southwards is of importance. I have, therefore, come to the conclusion that we must use the dogs to get on with as best we can — perhaps there will be a change before we expect it; if nothing else then, perhaps, some better ice, like that we had before. Meanwhile we were obliged to kill two dogs yesterday. 'Lilleraeven' could hardly go when we started; his legs seemed to be quite paralysed and he fell down and could not get up again. After I had dragged him and the sledge for a time and had tried in vain to make him go, I had to put him on the load, and when we came to some hummocks where there was shelter from the north wind, Johansen killed him, while I went forward to find a way. Meanwhile my other dog, 'Storraeven,' was in almost as bad a plight. Haul he could not, and the difficulty was to make him go on so that he was not dragged with the sledge. He went a little way, stumbling and falling, and being helped up repeatedly, but soon he was just as bad as 'Lilleraeven' had been, lagged behind, got the traces under the sledge runners, and was dragged with it. As I thought I had enough to do in hauling the sledge I let him go, in the hope that he would, at any rate, follow us. He did so for a little while, but then stopped behind, and Johansen was compelled to fetch him and put him on his load, and when we camped he was killed too.

"'Kaifas' is the only dog I have left to help me haul my sledge, and Johansen has 'Haren' and 'Suggen.' We have rations for them for ten days from the two slaughtered dogs, but how far we shall be able to get with them the gods alone know. Not very far, I am afraid. Meanwhile our hitherto somewhat primitive method of hauling had to be improved on. With two dog-harnesses we accordingly made ourselves proper hauling-gear,[96] and therewith all idea of using snowshoes not securely fastened on had to be abandoned. One's feet twisted and slipped and slid off the snowshoes and deep down into the bottomless snow, which in addition turned to ice under our feet, and with our smooth komager-soles was as slippery as eel-skin to stand on. Then we fastened them on, and where the ice was even, it really was possible to drag the sledge, even with only one dog beside one. I saw that given passable snow and passable country to work on, we could make some progress during the day, though as soon as there was the slightest irregularity in the ice the sledges stood perfectly still. It was necessary to strain at the harness all one knew and then perhaps fail to make the sledge budge an inch. Then back one had to go to it, and after exerting one's strength to the utmost, it would finally glide over the obstacle and on towards a new one, where exactly the same process had to be gone through. If it was wished to turn the sledge in the deep snow where it stood embedded, matters were no better; it was only by lifting it bodily that one could get it on at all. So we went on step by step until perhaps we came on a small extent of level ice where we could increase the pace. If, however, we came on lanes and ridges, things were worse than ever, one man cannot manage a sledge alone, but two must be put to each sledge. Then when we have followed up the track I have marked out beforehand, I have to start off again and find a way between the hummocks. To go direct, hauling the sledge, is not advisable where the ice is uneven, as it only means getting into difficulties and being constrained eventually to turn back. In this way we are grinding along, but it goes without saying that speed and long marches are not the order of the day. But still as it is we make a little way, and that is better than nothing; it is, besides, the only thing we can do, seeing that it is impossible to crawl into a lair and hibernate for a month or so till progress is possible again.

"To judge by the sky, there must be a number of lanes in the south and south-west. Perhaps our trying mode of advance is leading us to something better. We began at about ten yesterday evening, and stopped at six this morning. We have not had dinner the last few days in order to save a meal, as we do not think this ice and our progress generally is worth much food. With the same object, we this morning collected the blood of 'Storraeven' and converted it into a sort of porridge instead of the 'fiskegratin.' It was good, even if it was only dog's blood, and at any rate we have a portion of fish-flour to the good. Before we turned into the bag last night we inspected our cartridges, and found to our joy that we had 148 shot-gun cartridges, 181 rifle cartridges, and in addition 14 spherical shot cartridges. With so much ammunition, we should be able to increase our provisions for some time to come, if necessary, for if nothing else should fall to our guns there would always be birds, and 148 birds will go a long way. If we use half-charges, we can eke out our ammunition still further. We have, moreover, half a pound of gunpowder and some spherical shot for the rifles, also caps for reloading the cartridges. This discovery has put me in good spirits, for, truth to tell, I did not think our prospects were inordinately bright. We shall now, perhaps, be able to manage for three months, and within that time something must happen. In addition to what we can shoot, we can also catch gulls with a hook, and if the worst should come to the worst, and we set seriously to work, we can probably take some animalculae and the like with the net. It may happen that we shall not get to Spitzbergen in time to find a vessel, and must winter there, but it will be a life of luxury compared with this in the drift-ice, not knowing where we are nor whither drifting, and not seeing our goal, in spite of all our toil. I should not like to have this time over again. We have paid dearly for letting our watches run down that time. If there was no one waiting at home, a winter in Spitzbergen would be quite enticing. I lie here and dream of how comfortably and well we could manage there. Everything outside of this ice seems rosy, and out of it we shall be some time or other! We must comfort ourselves with the adage that night is darkest before the dawn. Of course it somewhat depends on *how* dark the night is to be, and considerably darker than it is now it might very well be. But our hopes are fixed on the summer. Yes, it *must* be better as summer gradually comes on."

So on we went forwards; and day after day we were going through exactly the same toil, in the same heavy snow, in which the sledges stuck fast ceaselessly. Dogs and men did their best, but with little effect, and in addition we began to be uneasy as to our means of subsistence. The dogs' rations were reduced to a minimum, to enable us to keep life going as long as possible. We were hungry and toil-worn from morning to night and from night to morning, all five of us. We determined to shoot whatever came in our way, even gulls and fulmars; but now, of course, none of this game ever came within range.

The lanes grew worse and worse, filled generally with slush and brash. We were often compelled to go long distances over nothing but small pieces, where one went through continually. On June 18th "a strong wind from the west (magnetic), sprang up, which tears and rattles at the tent. We are going back, I suppose, whence we came, only farther north perhaps. So we are buffeted by wind and current, and so it will go on, perhaps the whole summer through, without our being able to master it. A meridian altitude that day made us in 82° 19′ N., so we had come down again a little. I saw and shot a couple of fulmars and a Brünnich's guillemot (*uria brünnichii*), and these eked out our rations but, to our distress, I fired at a couple of seals in the lanes and missed my mark. How we wished we could get hold of such a prize! "Meanwhile there is a good deal of life here now," I write on June 20th. "Little auks fly backwards and forwards in numbers, and they sit and chatter and show themselves just outside the tent-door; it is quite a pleasure to see them, but a pity they are so small that they are not worth a shot. We have not seen them in flocks yet, but in couples as a rule. It is remarkable how bird-life has increased since the west wind set in the day before yesterday. It is particularly striking how the little auks have suddenly appeared in myriads; they whiz past the tent here with their cheery twitter, and it gives one the feeling of having come down to more hospitable regions. This sudden finding of Brünnich's guillemots seems also curious, but it does no good. Land is not to be descried, and the snow is in as wretched a condition as it can be. A proper thaw, so that the snow can disappear more quickly, does not come. Yesterday morning before breakfast I went for a walk southwards to see what were our chances of advance. The ice was flat and good for a little way, but lanes soon began which were worse than ever. Our only expedient now is to resort to strong measures and launch the kayaks, in spite of the fact that they leak; we must then travel as much as possible by way of the lanes, and with this resolution I turn back. The snow is still the same, very wet, so that one sank deep in between the hummocks, and there are plenty of them. We could not afford a proper breakfast, so we took 1 2/3 oz. bread and 1 2/3 oz. pemmican per man, and then set to work to mend the pumps and put the kayaks in order for ferrying, so that their contents should not be spoiled by water leaking in. Among other things, a hole had to be patched in mine which I had not seen before.

"We had a frugal supper, 2 ozs. aleuronate bread and 1 oz. butter per man, and crept into the bag to sleep as long as possible and kill the time without eating. The only thing to be done is to try and hold out till the snow has melted, and advance is more practicable. At one in the afternoon we turned out to a rather more abundant breakfast of 'fiskegratin,' but we do not dare to eat as much as we require any longer. We are looking forward to trying our new tactics, and instead of attempting to conquer nature, obeying her and taking advantage of the lanes. We must get some way, at any rate, by this means; and the farther south the more prospect of lanes and the greater chance of something falling to our guns.

"Otherwise it is a dull existence enough, no prospect for the moment of being able to get on, impassable packed ice in every direction, rapidly diminishing provisions, and now, too, nothing to be caught or shot. An attempt I made at fishing with the net failed entirely — a pteropod (*clio borealis*) and a few crustacea were the whole result. I lie awake at night by the hour racking my brain to find a way out of our difficulties. Well, well, there will be one eventually!

"Saturday, June 22nd. Half-past nine a.m., after a good breakfast of seal's-flesh, seal-liver, blubber, and soup.

"Here I lie dreaming dreams of brightness; life is all sunshine again. What a little incident is necessary to change the whole aspect of affairs! Yesterday and the last few days were dull and gloomy; everything seemed hopeless, the ice impassable, no game to be found; and then comes the incident of a seal rising near our kayaks and rolling about round us. Johansen has time to give it a ball just as it is disappearing, and it floats while I harpoon it — the first and only bearded seal we have yet seen — and we have abundance of food and fuel for upwards of a month. We need hurry no longer; we can settle down, adapt the kayaks and sledges better for ferrying over the lanes, capture seals if possible, and await a change in the state of the ice. We have eaten our fill both at supper and breakfast, after being ravenous for many days. The future seems bright and certain now, no clouds of darkness to be seen any longer.

"It was hardly with great expectations that we started off on Thursday evening. A hard crust which had formed on the top of the soft snow did not improve matters; the sledges often cut through this, and were not to be moved before one lifted them forward again and when it was a case of turning amid the uneven ice, they stuck fast in the crust. The ice was uneven and bad, and the snow loose and water-soaked, so that, even with snowshoes on, we sank deep into it ourselves. There were lanes besides and though tolerably easy to cross, as they were often packed together, they necessitated a winding route. We saw clearly that to continue in this way was impossible. The only resource was to disburden ourselves of everything which could in any way be dispensed with, and start afresh as quickly as we could, with only provisions, kayaks, guns, and the most necessary clothing, in order, at any rate, to reach land before our last crumb of food was eaten up. We went over the things to see what we could part with: the medicine-bag, the spare horizontal bars belonging to the sledges, reserve snowshoes and thick, rough socks, soiled shirts, and the tent. When it came to the sleeping-bag we heaved a deep sigh, but, wet and heavy as it always is now, that had to go, too. We had, moreover, to contrive wooden grips under the kayaks, so that we can without further trouble set the whole thing afloat when we have to cross a lane, and be able to drag the sledges up on the other side and go on at once. If it should then, as now, be impossible for us to launch the sledges, because sleeping-bag, clothes, sacks of provender, etc., are lying on them as soft dunnage for the kayaks, it will take too much time. At every lane we should be obliged to unlash the loads, lift the kayaks off the sledges and into the water, lash them together there, then place the sledges across them, and finally go through the same manoeuvres in inverse order on the other side. We should not get very far in the day in that manner.

"Firmly determined to make these alterations, the very next day we started off. We soon came to a long pool, which it was necessary to ferry over. The kayaks were soon launched and lying side by side on the water well stiffened with the snowshoes under the straps,[97] a thoroughly steady fleet. Then the sledges, with their loads, were run out to them, one forward, one astern. We had been concerned about the dogs and how we should get them to go with us, but they followed the sledges out on to the kayaks and lay down as if they had done nothing else all their lives. 'Kaifas' seated himself in the bow of my kayak, and the two others astern.

"A seal had come up near us while we were occupied with all this, but I thought to wait before shooting it till the kayaks were ready, and thus be certain of getting it before it sank. Of course it did not show itself again. These seals seem to be enchanted, and as if they were only sent to delay us. Twice that day before I had seen them and watched in vain for them to appear again. I had even achieved missing one, the third time I have missed my mark. It looks bad for the ammunition if I am going on like this, but I have discovered that I aimed too high for these short ranges, and had shot over them. So then we set off across the blue waves on our first long voyage. A highly remarkable convoy we must have been, laden as we were with sledges, sacks, guns, and dogs; a tribe of gipsies, Johansen said it was. If anyone had suddenly come upon us then, he would hardly have known what to make of the troupe, and certainly would not have taken us for Polar explorers. Paddling between the sledges and the snowshoes which projected far out on either side, was not easy work, but we managed to get along, and were soon of the opinion that we should think ourselves lucky could we go on like this the whole day, instead of hauling and wading through the snow. Our kayaks could hardly have been called water-tight, and we had recourse to the pumps several times, but we could easily have reconciled ourselves to that, and only wished we had more open water to travel over. At last we reached the end of the pool; I jumped ashore on the edge of the ice, to pull up the kayaks, and suddenly heard a great splash beside us. It was a seal which had been lying there. Soon afterwards I heard a similar splash on the other side, and then for the third time a huge head appeared, blowing and swimming backwards and forwards, but alas, only to dive deep under the edge of the ice before we had time to get the guns out. It was a fine, large blue or bearded seal.

"We were quite sure that it had disappeared for good, but no sooner had I got one of the sledges half-way up the side than the immense head came up again close beside the kayaks, blowing and repeating the same manoeuvres as before. I looked round for my gun, but could not reach it where it was lying on the kayak. 'Take the gun, Johansen, quick, and blaze away; but quick, fool: sharp, quick!' In a moment he had thrown the gun to his cheek, and just as the seal was on the point of disappearing under the edge I heard the report. The animal made a little turn, and then lay floating, the blood flowing from its head. I dropped the sledge, seized the harpoon, and quick as lightning threw it deep into the fat back of the seal, which lay quivering on the surface of the water. Then it began to move; there was still life in it; and, anxious lest the harpoon with its thin line should not hold if the huge animal began to quicken in earnest, I pulled my knife out of its sheath and stuck it into the seal's throat, whence a stream of blood came flowing out. The water was red with it for a long distance, and it made me quite sorry to see the wherewithal for a good meal being wasted like this. But there was nothing to be done; not on any account would I lose that animal, and for the sake of safety gave it another harpoon. Meanwhile the sledge, which had been half dragged up on to the ice, slid down again, and the kayaks, with Johansen and the dogs came adrift. He tried to pull the sledge up on to the kayak, but without success, and so it remained with one end in the water and one on the canoe. It heeled the whole fleet over, and Johansen's kayak canted till one side was in the water; it leaked, moreover, like a sieve, and the water rose in it with alarming rapidity. The cooker which was on the deck fell off, and drifted gaily away before the wind with all its valuable contents, borne high up in the water by the aluminium cap, which happily was water-tight. The snowshoes fell off and floated about, and the fleet sank yet deeper and deeper. Meanwhile I stood holding our precious prize, not daring to let go. The whole thing was a scene of the most complete dissolution. Johansen's kayak had by this time heeled over to such an extent that the water reached the open seam on the deck, and the craft filled immediately. I had no choice left but to let go the seal, and drag up the kayak before it sank. This done, heavy as it was and full of water, the seal's turn came next, and this was much worse. We had our work cut out to haul the immense animal hand over hand up on to the ice, but our rejoicing was loud when we at last succeeded, and we almost fell to dancing round it in the excess of our delight. A water-logged kayak and soaked effects we thought nothing of at such a supreme moment. Here was food and fuel for a long time.

"Then came the rescuing and drying of our things. First and foremost, of course, the ammunition; it was all our stock. But happily the cartridges were fairly watertight, and had not suffered much damage. Even the shot cartridges, the cases of which were of paper, had not lain long enough to become wholly permeated. Such, however, was not the case with a supply of powder, the small tin box in which we kept it was entirely full of water. The other things were not so important, though it was hardly a comforting discovery to find that the bread was soaked through with salt water.

"We found a camping-ground not far off. The tent was soon pitched, our catch cut up and placed in safety, and, I may say, seldom has the drift-ice housed beings so well satisfied as the two who sat that morning in the bag and feasted on seal's flesh blubber, and soup as long as they could find any room to stow it. We concurred in the opinion that a better meal we could not have had. Then down we crawled into the dear bag, which for the present there was no need to part with, and slept the sleep of the just in the knowledge that for the immediate future, at any rate, we need have no anxiety.

It is my opinion that for the time being we can do nothing better than remain where we are; live on our catch without encroaching on the sledge provisions, and thus await the time when the ice shall slacken more or the condition of the snow improve. Meanwhile we will rig up wooden grips on our sledges, and try to make the kayaks water-tight. Furthermore we will lighten our equipment as much as we possibly can. If we were to go on we should only be obliged to leave a great deal of our meat and blubber behind us, and this, in these circumstances, I think would be madness."

"Sunday, June 23rd. So this is St. John's Eve, and Sunday too. How merry and happy all the school-boys are to-day; how the folk at home are starting forth in crowds to the beautiful Norwegian woods and valleys... and here are we still in the drift-ice; cooking and frying with blubber, eating it and seal's-flesh until the train-oil drips off us, and, above all, not knowing when there will be an end to it all. Perhaps we still have a winter before us. I could hardly have conceived that we should be here now!

"It is a pleasing change, however, after having reduced our rations and fuel to a minimum to be able to launch out into excesses, and eat as much and as often as we like. It is a state of things hardly to be realised at present. The food is agreeable to the taste and we like it better and better. My own opinion is that blubber is excellent both raw and fried, and it can well take the place of butter. The meat, in our eyes, is as good as meat can be. We had it yesterday for breakfast in the shape of meat and soup served with raw blubber. For dinner I fried a highly-successful steak not to be surpassed by the 'Grand' [Hotel], though a good 'seidel' of bock beer would have been a welcome addition. For supper I made blood-pancakes fried in blubber instead of butter, and they were a success, inasmuch as Johansen pronounced them 'first-class,' to say nothing of my own sentiments. This frying, however, inside the tent over a train-oil lamp is a doubtful pleasure. If the lamp itself does not smoke the blubber does, causing the unfortunate cook the most excruciating pain in the eyes; he can hardly keep them open and they water copiously. But the consequences could be even worse. The train-oil lamp which I had contrived out of a sheet of German silver became over-heated one day, under the hot frying-pan, and at last the whole thing caught fire, both the lumps of blubber and the train-oil. The flame shot up into the air, while ! tried by every means in my power to put it out, but it only grew worse. The best thing would have been to convey the whole lamp outside, but there was no time for it. The tent began to fill with suffocating smoke and as a last resort I unfortunately seized a handful of snow and threw it on to the burning train-oil. It sputtered and crackled, boiling oil flew in all directions, and from the lamp itself rose a sea of flames which filled the whole tent and burned everything they came near. Half suffocated, we both threw ourselves against the closed door, bursting off the buttons, and dashed headlong into the open air; glad, indeed, to have escaped with our lives. With this explosion the lamp went out; but when we came to examine the tent we found an enormous hole burned in the silk wall above the place where the frying-pan had stood. One of our sledge-sails had to pay the penalty for that hole. We crept back into the tent again, congratulating ourselves, however, on having got off so easily, and, after a great deal of trouble, rekindled a fire so that I could fry the last pancake. We then ate it with sugar, in the best of spirits, and pronounced it the most delicious fare we had ever tasted. We had good reason, too, to be in spirits, for our observation for the day made us in 82° 4′ 3″ N. lat. and 57° 48′ E. long. In spite of westerly and, in a measure, south-westerly winds, we had come nearly 14′ south in three days and next to nothing east. A highly surprising and satisfactory discovery. Outside, the north wind was still blowing, and consequently we were drifting south towards more clement regions.

"Wednesday, June 26th. June 24th was naturally celebrated with great festivities. In the first place, it was that day two years since we started from home; secondly, it was a hundred days since we left the *Fram* (not really, it was two days on), and thirdly, it was Midsummer Day. It was, of course a holiday, and we passed it in dreaming of good times to come, in studying our charts, our future prospects, and in reading anything readable that was to be found, i.e., the almanack and navigation tables. Johansen took a walk along the lanes, and also managed to miss a ringed seal or 'snad' as we call it in Norwegian, in a pool here east of us. Then came supper rather late in the night — consisting of blood-pancakes with sugar, and unsurpassed in flavour. The frying over the oil lamp took a long time, and in order to have them hot we had to eat each one as it was fried, a mode of procedure which promoted a healthy appetite between each pancake. Thereafter we stewed some of our red whortleberries, and they tasted no less good, although they had been soaked in salt water in Johansen's kayak during the catastrophe of a couple of days ago; and after a glorious meal we turned into the bag at 8 o'clock yesterday morning.

"At midday, again, I got up and went out to take a meridian altitude. The weather was brilliant, and it was so long since we had had anything of the kind that I could hardly remember it. I sat up on the hummock waiting for the sun to come to the meridian; basking in its rays, and looking out over the stretches of ice where the snow glittered and sparkled on all sides; and at the pool in front of me lying shining and still as a mountain lake, and reflecting its icy banks in the clear water. Not a breath of wind stirred — so still, so still; and the sun baked, and I dreamed myself at home...

"Before going into the tent, I went to fetch some salt-water for the soup we were to have for breakfast; but just at that moment a seal came up by the side of the ice, and I ran back for my gun and kayak. Out on the water I discovered that it was leaking like a sieve from lying in the sun, and I had to paddle back faster than I came out, to avoid sinking. As I was emptying the kayak, up came the seal again in front of me, and this time my shot took effect; the animal lay floating on the water like a cork. It was not many minutes before I had the leaking craft on the water again, and my harpoon in the animal's neck. I towed it in while the kayak gradually filled, and my legs, or, rather, that part which follows closely above the legs when one is sitting in a canoe, became soaked with water, and my 'komager' gradually filled. After having dragged the seal up to the tent, 'flensed' it, collected all the blood which was to be had, and cut it up, I crept into the tent, put on some dry underclothes, and into the bag again, while the wet ones were drying outside in the sun. It is easy enough to keep oneself warm in the tent now. The heat was so great inside it last night that we could hardly sleep, although we lay on the bag instead of in it. When I came back with the seal, I discovered that Johansen's bare foot was sticking out of the tent at a place where the peg had given way; he was sleeping soundly, and had no idea of it. After having a small piece of chocolate to commemorate the happy capture, and, looking over my observations, we again settled down to rest.

"It appears, remarkably enough, from our latitude that we are still on the same spot without any further drift southwards, in spite of the northerly winds. Can the ice be landlocked? It is not impossible; far off land, at any rate, we cannot be."

Thursday, June 27th. The same monotonous life, the same wind, the same misty weather, and the same cogitations as to what the future will bring. There was a gale from the north last night with a fall of hard granular snow, which lashed against the tent walls so that one might think it to be good honest rain. It melted on the walls directly, and the water ran down them. It is cosy in here, however, and the wind does not reach us; we can lie in our warm bag, and listen to the flapping of the tent, and imagine that we are drifting rapidly westwards, although perhaps we are not moving from the spot. But if this wind does not move us, the only explanation is that the ice is land-locked, and that we cannot be far off shore. We must wait for an east wind, I suppose, to drive us farther west, and then afterwards south. My hope is that we shall drift into the channel between Franz Josef Land and Spitzbergen while we are lying here. The weather was raw and windy with snowfall, so that it was hardly suitable for out-door work, particularly as, unfortunately, there was no need to hurry.

"The lanes have changed very much of late; there is hardly anything left of the pool in front of us over which we paddled, and there has been pressure around us in all directions. I hope the ice will be well ground into pieces, as this enables it to slacken more quickly when the time comes; but that will not be before far on in July, and we ought to have the patience to wait for it perhaps.

"Yesterday we cut some of the seal's flesh into thin slices and hung them up to dry. We must increase our travelling store and prepare pemmican or dried meat; it will be the easiest way of carrying it with us. Johansen yesterday found a pond of fresh water close by, which is very convenient, and we need no longer melt ice; it is the first good water we have found for cooking purposes. If the seals are few and far between, there are birds still, I am thankful to say. Last night a couple of ivory gulls, *larus eburneus*, were bold enough to settle down on our seal-skin, close beside the tent wall, and pecked at the blubber. They were sent off once or twice but returned. If the meat fall short we must resort to catching birds."

Thus the days passed by, one exactly like the other; we waited and waited for the snow to melt and worked desultorily meanwhile at getting ourselves ready to proceed. This life reminded me of some Eskimos who journeyed up a fjord to collect grass for hay; but when they arrived at their destination found it quite short, and so settled down and waited till it was long enough to cut. A suitable condition of the snow was long in coming; on June 29th I write: "Will not the temperature rise sufficiently to make something like an effectual clearance of the snow. We try to pass the time as best we can in talking of how delightful it will be when we get home, and how we shall enjoy life and all its charms, and go through a calculation of chances as to how soon that may be; but sometimes, too, we talk of how well we will arrange for the winter in Spitzbergen, if we should not reach home this year. If it should come to that, we may not even get so far, but have to winter on some place ashore here — no, it can never come to that!"

"Sunday, June 30th. So this is the end of June, and we are about the same place as when we began the month. And the state of the snow? Well, better it certainly is not; but the day is fine. It is so warm that we are quite hot lying here inside the tent. Through the open door we can see out over the ice where the sun is glittering through white sailing cirrus clouds on the dazzling whiteness. And then there is a Sunday calm, with a faint breeze mostly from the south-east, I think. Ah me, it is lovely at home today, I am sure, with everything in bloom and the fjord quivering in the sunlight; and you are sitting out on the point with Liv, perhaps, or are on the water in your boat. And then my eye wanders out through the door again, and I am reminded there is many an ice-floe between now and then, before the time when I shall see it all once more.

"Here we lie far up in the north; two grim, black, soot-stained barbarians, stirring a mess of soup in a kettle and surrounded on all sides by ice; by ice and nothing else — shining and white, possessed of all the purity we ourselves lack. Alas, it is all too pure! One's eye searched to the very horizon for a dark spot to rest on, but in vain. When will it really come to pass? Now we have waited for it two months. All the birds seem to have disappeared to-day; not even a cheery little auk to be seen. They were here until yesterday and we have heard them flying north and south, probably to and from land, where they have gone, I suppose, now that there is so little water about in these parts. If only we could move as easily as they."

"Wednesday, July 3rd. Why write again? What have I to commit to these pages? Nothing but the same overpowering longing to be home and away from this monotony, One day just like the other, with the exception, perhaps, that before it was warm and quiet, while the last two days there has been a south wind blowing, and we are drifting northwards. Found from a meridian altitude yesterday that we have drifted back to 82° 8.4′ N., while the longitude is about the same. Both yesterday and the day before we had to a certain extent really brilliant sunshine, and this for us is a great rarity. The horizon in the south was fairly clear yesterday, which it has not been for a long time; but we searched it in vain for land. I do not understand it... We had a fall of snow last night, and it dripped in here so that the bag became wet. This constant snowfall, which will not turn to rain, is enough to make one despair. It generally takes the form of a thick layer of new snow on the top of the old, and this delays the thaw.

"This wind seems to have formed some lanes in the ice again, and there is a little more bird-life. We saw some little auks again yesterday; they came from the south, probably from land."

"Saturday, July 6th. +33.8° Fahr. (+1° C.). Rain. At last, after a fortnight, we seem to have got the weather we have been waiting for. It has rained the whole night and forenoon, and is still at it, real good rain; so now, perhaps, this everlasting snow will take itself off; it is as soft and loose as scum. If only this rain would go on for seven days! But before we have time to look round there will be a cold wind with snow, a crust will form and again we must wait. I am too used to disappointment to believe in anything. This is a school of patience; but nevertheless the rain has put us in good spirits.

"The days drag wearily on. We work in an intermittent way at the kayak-grips of wood for our sledges, and at caulking and painting our kayaks to make them water-tight. The painting, however, causes me a good deal of trouble. I burned bones here for many days till the whole place smelled like the bone-dust works at Lysaker; then came the toilsome process of pounding and grating them to make them perfectly fine and even. The bone-dust was thereupon mixed with train oil, and at last I got as far as a trial, but the paint proved uncompromisingly to be perfectly useless. So now I must mix it with soot, as I had first intended and add more oil. I am now occupied in smoking the place out in my attempts to make soot, but all my exertions, when it comes to collecting it, only result in a little pinch, although the smoke towered in the air, and they might have seen it in Spitzbergen. There is a great deal to do battle with when one has not a shop next door. What would I not give for a little bucket of oil-paint, only common lamp black! Well, well, we shall find a way out of the difficulty eventually; but meanwhile we are growing like sweeps.

"On Wednesday evening 'Haren' was killed; poor beast, he was not good for much latterly, but he had been a first-rate dog, and it was hard, I fancy, for Johansen to part with him; he looked sorrowfully at the animal before it went to the happy hunting-grounds, or wherever it may, be draught-dogs go to; perhaps to places where there are plains of level ice and no ridges and lanes. There are only two dogs left now — 'Suggen' and 'Kaifas' — and we must keep them alive as long as we can, and have use for them.

"The day before yesterday, in the evening, we suddenly discovered a black hillock to the east. We examined it through the glass and it looked absolutely like a black rock emerging from the snows. It also somewhat exceeded the neighbouring hummocks in height. I scrutinised it carefully from the highest ridge hereabouts, but could not make it out. I thought it too big to be only a piled-up hummock mixed with black ice or earthy matter, and I have never seen anything of the kind before.

That it is an island seems highly improbable; for although we are certainly drifting, it remains in the same position in relation to us. We saw it yesterday, and see it still to-day in the same quarter. I think the most reasonable supposition is that it is an ice-berg.

"No sooner does the horizon clear in the south than one of us may be seen taking his customary walk to the 'watch-tower' (a hummock beside the tent) to scan for land, sometimes with a glass, sometimes without it; but there is nothing to be seen but the same bare horizon.[98]

"Every day I take a turn round the ice in our neighbourhood to see if the snow has decreased, but it always seems to be about the same, and sometimes I have moments of doubt as to whether it will clear away at all this summer. If not, our prospects will be more than dark. The best we can hope for will then be a winter somewhere or other on Franz Josef Land. But now the rain has come. It is pouring down the tent walls and dripping on the ice. Everything looks hopeful again, and we are picturing the delights of the autumn and winter at home!"

"Wednesday, July 10th. It is a curious thing that now, when I really have something of a little more interest than usual to relate, I have less inclination to write than ever. Everything seems to become more and more indifferent. One longs only for one single thing, and still the ice is lying out there covered with impassable snow.

"But what was it I had to say? Oh, yes, that we made ourselves such a good bed yesterday with bearskins under the bag, that we slept the clock round without knowing it, and I thought it was six in the morning when I turned out. When I came out of the tent I thought there was something remarkable about the position of the sun, and pondered over it for a little while, until I came to the conclusion that it was six in the evening, and that we had slumbered for twenty-two hours. We have not slept much of late, as we have been broken on the wheel, so to speak, by the snowshoes we had to place under the bag, in order to keep it clear of the pools of water under us. The apologies for hair still existing here and there on the skin at the bottom of the bag do not afford much protection against the sharp edges of the snowshoes.

"This beneficent rain continued the whole day on Saturday, doing away with a fair amount of snow, and we rejoice to hear it. To celebrate the good weather we determined to have chocolate for supper; otherwise we live entirely on our catch. We had the chocolate accordingly, and served with raw blubber it tasted quite excellent. It was the cause of a great disappointment, however, for after having looked forward immoderately to this, now so rare, treat, I managed clumsily to upset my whole cup, so that all the precious contents ran out over the ice. While I was lying waiting for a second cup — it was boiling over the train-oil lamp — 'Kaifas' began to bark outside. Not doubting but that he had seen an animal, I jumped up to hurry off to the look-out hummock to scan the ice. Not a little surprised was I when I poked my head out of the tent-door to see a bear come jogging up to the dogs and begin sniffing at 'Kaifas.' I sprang to the gun, which stood ready in the snow beside the tent, and pulled off the case, the bear meanwhile standing astonished and glaring at me. I sent it a ball through the shoulder and chest, certain that it would drop on the spot. It half staggered over, and then turned round and made off, and before I could extract a new cartridge from my pocket, which was full of everything else, was away among the hummocks. I could not get a shot at it where it was, and set off in pursuit. I had not gone many steps before we saw (Johansen had followed me) two more heads appearing a little way farther on. They belonged to two cubs, which were standing on their hind-legs and looking at their mother, who came reeling towards them, with a trail of blood behind her. Then off they went, all three, over a lane, and a wild chase began over plains and ridges and lanes and every kind of obstacle, but it made no difference to their pace. A wonderful thing this love of sport; it is like setting fire to a fuse. Whereat other times it would be laborious work to get on at all, where one sinks to the knees in the snow, and where one would hesitate before choosing a way over the lane, let only the spark be kindled, and one clears every obstacle without thinking about it. The bear was severely wounded, and dragged her left fore-leg; she did not go fast, but always so fast that I had my work cut out to keep near her. The cubs ran round her in their solicitude, and generally a little way in front, as if to get her to come with them; they little knew what was the matter with her. Suddenly they all three looked back at me as I was crashing after them as fast as I could. I had been within range many times, but the bear had her hind-quarters towards me, and when I fired I meant to be sure of making an end of her, as I only had three cartridges with me, one for each of them. At last, on the top of a huge hummock, I got a sight of her broadside on, and there, too, she dropped. The cubs hurried anxiously up to her when she fell — it made one sorry to see them — they sniffed at and pushed her, and ran round and round, at a loss what to do in their despair. Meanwhile I had put another cartridge in the rifle, and picked off the other cub as it was standing on a projection. It fell over the declivity with a growl, and down on to its mother. Still more frightened than before, the other cub hastened to its succour; but, poor thing, what could it do? While its brother rolled over, growling, it stood there looking sorrowfully sometimes at it, sometimes at the mother who lay dying in a pool of blood. When I approached it turned its head away indifferently; what did it care about me now? All its kindred, everything it held dear, lay there mutilated and destroyed. It no longer knew whither to go, and did not move from the spot. I went right up to it, and, with a spherical ball through the breast, it fell dead beside its mother.

"Johansen soon came up. A lane had detained him, so that he had lost ground. We opened the animals, took out the entrails, and then went back to the tent to fetch the sledges and dogs and proper flaying-knives. Our second cup of chocolate in the tent tasted very good after this interruption. When we had skinned and cut up the two bears we left them in a heap, covered over with the skins to protect the meat from the gulls; the third one we took back with us. The next day we fetched the others, and now have more meat food than we shall be able to consume, I hope. It is a good thing, though, that we can give the dogs as much raw meat as they will eat; they certainly require it. 'Suggen,' poor thing, is in a very bad way, and it is a question whether we can get any more work out of him. When we took him with us after the bears the first day, he could not walk, and we had to place him on the sledge; but then he howled so terrifically, as much as to say it was beneath his dignity to be transported in this way, that Johansen had to take him home again. The dogs seem to be attacked with a paralysis of the legs: they fall down, and have the greatest difficulty in rising. It has been the same with all of them, from 'Gulen' downwards. 'Kaifas,' however, is as fresh and well as ever.

"It is remarkable how large these cubs were. I could hardly imagine that they were born this year, and should without hesitation have put them down as a year old if the she-bear had not been in milk, and it is hardly to be supposed that the cubs would suck for a year and a half. Those we shot by the *Fram* on November 4th last year were hardly half the size of these. It would seem as if the polar bear produces its young at different times of the year. In the paunches of the cubs were pieces of skin from a seal."

"Monday, July 15th. As we were working at the kayaks yesterday, a Ross's gull (*radostethia rosea*) came flying by. It was a full-grown bird, and made a turn when just over us, showing its pretty rose-coloured breast, and then disappeared again in the mist south-wards. On Thursday I saw another adult Ross's gull, with a black ring round its neck; it came from the north-east, and flew in a south-westerly direction. Otherwise it is remarkable how all the birds have disappeared from here. The little auk is no longer to be seen or heard; the only birds are an ivory gull now and then and occasionally a fulmar."

"Wednesday, July 17th. At last the time is drawing near when we can be off again and start homewards in earnest. The snow has decreased sufficiently to make advance fairly easy. We are doing our utmost to get ready. The grips on the sledges are nicely arranged and provided with cushions of bear-skin on Johansen's and of cloth on mine. This is in order to give the kayaks a firm and soft bed and prevent chafing. The kayaks are painted with soot and train-oil, and have been caulked with pastels (for drawing), crushed and also mixed with train-oil; that is to say, as far as these various ingredients would go. We are now using a mixture of stearine, pitch, and resin,[99] to finish up with. A thorough revision of our equipment will take place, and everything not absolutely invaluable will be left behind. We must say good-bye here to the sleeping-bag and tent.[100] Our days of comfort are past, and henceforth until we are on board the sloop we will live under the open sky.

"Meanwhile we have lain here — 'Longing Camp,' as we call it — and let the time slip by. We have eaten bear-meat morning, noon, and night, and, so far from being tired of it, have made the discovery that the breast of the cubs is quite a delicacy. It is remarkable that this exclusive meat and fat diet has not caused us the slightest discomfort in any way, and we have no craving for farinaceous food, although we might, perhaps, regard a large calve as the acme of happiness. Every now and then we cheer ourselves up with lime-juice grog, a blood-pancake, or some stewed whortleberries, and let our imaginations run riot over all the amenities of civilisation which we mean to enjoy to the full when we get home! Perhaps it will be many a long day before we get there, perhaps there will be many a hard trial to overcome. But no; I will believe the best. There are still two months of summer left, and in them something can be done."

"Friday, July 19th. Two full-grown Ross's gulls flew over here from the north-east and went west this morning. When far off they uttered cries which reminded me of that of the wryneck, and which I at first thought came from a little auk. They flew quite low, just over my head, and the rose-colour of their under-parts could be seen plainly. Another Ross's gull flew by here yesterday. It is strange that there should be so many of them. Where are we?"

"Tuesday, July 23rd. Yesterday forenoon we at last got clear of 'Longing Camp,' and now, I am thankful to say, we are again on the move. We have worked day and night to get off. First we thought it would be on the 19th, then the 20th, and then the 21st, but something always cropped up that had to be done before we could leave. The bread, which had been soaked in sea-water, had to be carefully dried in the frying-pan over the lamp, and this took several days; then the socks had to be patched, and the kayaks carefully looked over, etc. We were determined to start on our last journey home in good repair, and so we did. Everything goes like wild-fire.

The chances of progress are better than we expected, although the ice is anything but even: the sledges are lighter to draw now that everything that can be dispensed with is left behind, and the snow, too, has decreased considerably. On the last part of the journey yesterday we could even go without snowshoes, and, as a matter of course, progress among the ridges and irregularities, where they are difficult to manage, is quicker without them. Johansen performed a feat by crossing a lane alone in his kayak, with 'Suggen' lying on the fore-deck, while he himself knelt on the after-deck and balanced the craft as he paddled. I began to try the same with mine, but found it too cranky to risk the attempt and preferred to tow it over, with 'Kaifas' on the deck, while I went carefully alongside and jumped over on some pieces of ice.

"We have now the advantage of finding drinking-water everywhere. We are also eating our old provender again; but, curiously enough, neither Johansen nor I think the farinaceous food as good as one might suppose after a month of meat diet. It is good to be under way again, and not the least pleasant part about it is our lighter sledges; but then we certainly left a good deal behind at 'Longing Camp.' In addition to a respectable mound of meat and blubber, we left three fine bear-skins. Our friend the bag, too, is lying on the top of the bears, a quantity of wood consisting of the boards from under the sledges, the snowshoes and other things, more than half of Blessing's fine medicaments — plaster of Paris bandages, soft steam, sterilised gauze bandages, hygroscopic cotton wadding — to say nothing of a good aluminium glass horizon, rope, our combined frying-pan and melter, half an aluminium cap belonging to the cooker, sheets of German silver, a train-oil lamp of the same, bags, tools, sail-cloth, Finn shoes, our wolf-skin fingerless gloves, also woollen ones, a geological hammer, half a shirt, socks, and other sundries, all strewn about in chaotic confusion. Instead of all these we have an augmentation in the form of a sack of dried seal's and bear's flesh and the other half of the aluminium cap full of blubber. We are now thoroughly divested of all superfluous articles, and there is hardly so much as a bit of wood to be had if one should want a stick to slip through the end of the hauling rope."

Chapter 15

Land at Last

"WEDNESDAY, July 24th. At last the marvel has come to pass — land, land, and after we had almost given up our belief in it! After nearly two years, we again see something rising above that never-ending white line on the horizon yonder — a white line which for countless ages has stretched over this lonely sea, and which for millenniums to come shall stretch in the same way. We are leaving it, and leaving no trace behind us; for the track of our little caravan across the endless plains has long ago disappeared. A new life is beginning for us; for the ice it is ever the same.

"It has long haunted our dreams, this land, and now it comes like a vision, like fairy-land. Drift-white, it arches above the horizon like distant clouds, which one is afraid will disappear every minute. The most wonderful thing is that we have seen this land all the time without knowing it. I examined it several times with the telescope from 'Longing Camp' in the belief that it might be snowfields, but always came to the conclusion that it was only clouds, as I could never discover any dark point. Then, too, it seemed to change form, which, I suppose, must be attributed to the mist which always lay over it; but it always came back again at the same place with its remarkable regular curves. I now remember that dark crag we saw east of us at the camp, and which I took to be an iceberg. It must certainly have been a little islet[10] of some kind.

"The ice was worse and more broken than ever yesterday; it was, indeed, a labour to force one's way over pressure-ridges like veritable mountains, with valleys and clefts in between; but on we went in good spirits, and made some progress. At lanes where a crossing was difficult to find, we did not hesitate to launch kayaks and sledges, and were soon over in this manner. Sometimes after a very bad bit we would come across some flat ice for a short distance, and over this we would go like wildfire, splashing through ponds and puddles. While I was on ahead at one time yesterday morning, Johansen went up on to a hummock to look at the ice, and remarked a curious black stripe over the horizon; but he supposed it to be only a cloud, he said, and I thought no more about the matter. When, some while later, I also ascended a hummock to look at the ice, I became aware of the same black stripe; it ran obliquely from the horizon up into what I supposed to be a white bank of clouds. The longer I looked at this bank and stripe the more unusual I thought them, until I was constrained to fetch the glass. No sooner had I fixed it on the black part than it struck me at once that this must be land, and that not far off. There was a large snow-field out of which black rocks projected. It was not long before Johansen had the glass to his eye, and convinced himself that we really had land before us. We both of us naturally became highly elated. I then saw a similar white arching outline, a little farther east; but it was for the most part covered with white mist from which it could hardly be distinguished, and moreover was continually changing form. It soon, however, came out entirely, and was considerably larger and higher than the former, but there was not a black speck to be seen on it. So this was what land looked like now that we had come to it! I had imagined it in many forms, with high peaks and glittering glaciers, but never like this. There was nothing kindly about this, but it was indeed no less welcome, and on the whole we could not expect it to be otherwise than snow-covered, with all the snow which falls here.

"So then we pitched the tent and had a feast suited to the occasion; lobscouse made of potatoes (for the last time but one, we had saved them long for this occasion), pemmican, dried bear's and seal's-flesh and bear tongues chopped up together. After this was a second course consisting of bread crumbs fried in bear's grease, also vril-food and butter, and a piece of chocolate to wind up."

We thought this land so near that it could not possibly take long to reach it, certainly not longer than till next evening. Johansen was even certain that we should do it the same day, but nevertheless thirteen days were to elapse, occupied in the same monotonous drudgery over the drift-ice.

On July 25th I write: "When we stopped in the fog yesterday evening we had a feeling that we must have come well near land. This morning when we turned out, the first thing Johansen did when he went to fetch some water for me to cook with was, of course, to climb up on the nearest hummock and look at the land. There it lay, considerably nearer than before, and he is quite certain that we shall reach it before night." I also discovered a new land to our west (S. 60° W. magnetic) that day; a regular, shield-like, arched outline, similar to the other land; and it was low above the horizon, and appeared to be a long way off.[102]

We went on our way as fast as we could across lanes and rough ice, but did not get far in the day, and the land did not seem to be much nearer. In reality there was no difference to be seen, although we tried to imagine that it was steadily growing higher. On Saturday, July 27th. I seem to have a suspicion that in point of fact we were drifting away from land, I write: "The wind began to blow from the S.S.W. (magnetic), just as we were getting off yesterday, and increased as the day went on. It was easy to perceive by the atmosphere that the wind was driving the ice off the land and land-lanes formed particularly on the east side of it. When I was up on a hummock, yesterday evening, I observed a black stripe on the horizon under land; I examined it with the glass, and as I had surmised there was an ice-edge or glacier stretching far in a westerly direction; and there was plainly a broad lane in front of it, to judge by the dark bank of mist which lay there. It seems to me that land cannot be far off, and if the ice is tolerably passable we may reach it to-day. The wind continued last night, but it has quieted down now, and there is sunshine outside. We try by every means in our power to get a comfortable night's rest in our new bag of blankets. We have tried lying on the bare ice, on the snowshoes, and to-night on the bare ice again; but it must be confessed that it is hard and never will be very comfortable; a little chilly, too, when one is wet ? but we shall appreciate a good warm bed all the more when we get it."

"Tuesday, July 30th. We make incredibly slow progress; but we are pushing our way nearer land all the same. Every kind of hindrance seems to beset us: now I am suffering so much from my back (lumbago?) that yesterday it was only by exerting all my strength of will that I could drag myself along. In difficult places Johansen had to help me with my sledge. It began yesterday, and at the end of our march he had to go first and find the way. Yesterday I was much worse, and how I am to-day I do not know before I begin to walk but I ought to be thankful that I can drag myself along at all, though it is with endless pain. We had to halt and camp on account of rain yesterday morning at three, after only having gone nine hours. The rain succeeded in making us wet before we had found a suitable place for the tent. Here we have been a whole day while it has been pouring down, and we have hardly become drier. There are puddles under us and the bag is soaked on the underside. The wind has gone round to the west just now, and it has stopped raining, so we made some porridge for breakfast and think of going on again; but if it should begin to rain again we must stop, as it will not do to get wet through when we have no change of clothes. It is anything but pleasant as it is to lie with wet legs and feet that are like icicles, and not have a dry thread to put on. Full-grown Ross's gulls were seen singly four times to-day, and when Johansen was out to fetch water this morning he saw two. [103]

"Wednesday, July 31st. The ice is as disintegrated and impracticable as can well be conceived. The continual friction and packing of the floes against each other grinds up the ice so that the water is full of brash and small pieces; to ferry over this in the kayaks is impossible, and the search is long before we eventually find a hazardous crossing. Sometimes we have to form one by pushing small floes together, or must ferry the sledges over on a little floe. We spend much time and labour on each single lane, and progress becomes slow in this way. My back still painful, Johansen had to go ahead yesterday also; and evening and morning he is obliged to take off my boots and socks, for I am unable to do it myself. He is touchingly unselfish, and takes care of me as if I were a child; everything he thinks can ease me he does quietly, without my knowing it. Poor fellow, he has to work doubly hard now, and does not know how this will end. I feel very much better to-day, however, and it is to be hoped shall soon be all right."

"Thursday, August 1st. Ice with more obstacles than here — is it to be found, I wonder? But we are working slowly on, and that being the case we ought, perhaps, to be satisfied. We have also had a change — a brilliantly fine day; but it seems to me the south wind we have had, and which opened the lanes, has put us a good way farther off land again. We have also drifted a long distance to the east, and no longer see the most westerly land with the black rocks, which we remarked at first. It would seem as if the Ross's gulls keep to land here; we see them daily.

"One thing, however, I am rejoicing over; my back is almost well, so that I shall not delay our progress any more. I have some idea now what it would be like if one of us became seriously ill. Our fate would then be sealed, I think."

"Friday, August 2nd. It seems as if everything conspired to delay us, and that we shall never get away from this drift-ice. My back is well again now; the ice was more passable yesterday than before, so that we nearly made a good day's march; but in return wind and current set us from shore, and we are farther away again. Against these two enemies all fighting is in vain, I am afraid. We have drifted far off to the south-east, have got the north point of the land about due west of us, and we are now in about 81° 36' N. My only hope now is that this drift eastwards, away from land, may stop or alter its course, and thus bring us nearer land. It is unfortunate that the lanes are covered with young ice, which it would be disastrous to put the kayaks through. If this gets worse, things will look very bad. Meanwhile we have nothing to do but go on as fast as we can. If we are going to drift back into the ice again, then — then —."

"Saturday, August 3rd. Inconceivable toil. We never could go on with it were it not for the fact that we must. We have made wretchedly little progress even if we have made any at all. We have had no food for the dogs the last few days except the ivory gulls and fulmars we have been able to shoot, and that has been a couple a day. Yesterday the dogs only had a little bit of blubber each."

"Sunday, August 4th. These lanes are desperate work and tax one's strength. We often have to go several hundred yards on mere brash or from block to block, dragging the sledges after us, and in constant fear of their capsizing into the water. Johansen was very nearly in yesterday, but, as always hitherto, he managed to save himself. The dogs fall in and get a bath continually."

"Monday, August 5th. We have never had worse ice than yesterday, but we managed to force our way on a little, nevertheless, and two happy incidents marked the day: the first was that Johansen was not eaten up by a bear; and the second, that we saw open water under the glacier edge ashore.

"We set off about 7 o'clock yesterday morning and got on to ice as bad as it could be. It was as if some giant had hurled down enormous blocks pell-mell, and had strewn wet snow in between them with water underneath; and into this we sank above our knees. There were also numbers of deep pools in between the blocks. It was like toiling over hill and dale, up and down over block after block, and ridge after ridge, with deep clefts in between; not a clear space big enough to pitch a tent on even, and thus it went on the whole time. To put a coping-stone to our misery, there was such a mist that we could not see a hundred yards in front of us. After an exhausting march we at last reached a lane where we had to ferry over in the kayaks. After having cleared the side of the lane from young ice and brash, I drew my sledge to the edge of the ice, and was holding it to prevent it slipping in, when I heard a scuffle behind me, and Johansen, who had just turned round to pull his sledge flush with mine,[104] cried: 'Take the gun!' I turned round and saw an enormous bear throwing itself on him, and Johansen on his back. I tried to seize my gun, which was in its case on the fore-deck, but at the same moment the kayak slipped into the water. My first thought was to throw myself into the water over the kayak and fire from there, but I recognised how risky it would be. I began to pull the kayak, with its heavy cargo, on to the high edge of the ice again as quickly as I could, and was on my knees pulling and tugging to get at my gun. I had no time to look round and see what was going on behind me, when I heard Johansen quietly say: 'You must look sharp if you want to be in time.'

"Look sharp? I should think so! At last I got hold of the butt-end, dragged the gun out, turned round in a sitting posture, and cocked the shot-barrel. The bear was standing not two yards off, ready to make an end of my dog, 'Kaifas.' There was no time to lose in cocking the other barrel, so I gave it a charge of shot behind the ear, and it fell down dead between us.

"The bear must have followed our track like a cat, and, covered by the ice-blocks, have slunk up while we were clearing the ice from the lane and had our backs to him. We could see by the trail how it had crept over a small ridge just behind us under cover of a mound by Johansen's kayak. While the latter, without suspecting anything or looking round, went back and stooped down to pick up the hauling-rope, he suddenly caught sight of an animal crouched up at the end of the kayak, but thought it was 'Suggen'; and before he had time to realise that it was so big he received a cuff on the ear which made him see fireworks, and then, as I mentioned before, over he went on his back. He tried to defend himself as best he could with his fists. With one hand he seized the throat of the animal, and held fast, clenching it with all his might. It was just as the bear was about to bite Johansen in the head that he uttered the memorable words, 'Look sharp'! The bear kept glancing at me continually, speculating, no doubt, as to what I was going to do; but then caught sight of the dog and turned towards it. Johansen let go as quick as thought, and wriggled himself away, while the bear gave 'Suggen' a cuff which made him howl lustily, just as he does when we thrash him. Then 'Kaifas' got a slap on the nose. Meanwhile Johansen had struggled to his legs, and when I fired had got his gun, which was sticking out of the kayak hole. The only harm done was that the bear had scraped some grime off Johansen's right cheek, so that he has a white stripe on it, and had given him a slight wound in one hand; 'Kaifas' had also got a scratch on his nose.

"Hardly had the bear fallen before we saw two more peeping over a hummock a little way off ? cubs who, naturally, wanted to see the result of the maternal chase. They were two large cubs. I thought it was not worth while to sacrifice a cartridge on them, but Johansen expressed his opinion that young bear's flesh was much more delicate in flavour than old. He would only shoot one, he said, and started off. However, the cubs took to their heels, although they came back a little while later, and we could hear them at a long distance growling after their mother.

"Johansen sent one of them a ball, but the range was too long, and he only wounded it. With some terrific growls, it started off again, and Johansen after it; but he gave up the chase soon, as he saw it promised to be a long one. While we were cutting up the she-bear the cubs came back on the other side of the lane, and the whole time we were there we had them walking round us. When we had fed the dogs well, and had eaten some of the raw meat ourselves, and had furthermore stowed away in the kayaks the meat we had cut off the legs, we at last ferried over the lane and went on our way.

"The ice was not good; and, to make bad worse, we immediately came on some terrible lanes, full of nothing but tightly packed lumps of ice. In some places there were whole seas of it, and it was enough to make one despair. Among all this loose ice we came on an unusually thick old floe, with high mounds on it and pools in between. It was from one of these mounds that I observed through the glass the open water at the foot of the glacier, and now we cannot have far to go. But the ice looks very bad on ahead, and each piece when it is like this may take a long time to travel over.

"As we went along we heard the wounded bear lowing ceaselessly behind us; it filled the whole of this silent world of ice with its bitter plaint over the cruelty of man. It was miserable to hear it; and if we had had time, we should undoubtedly have gone back and sacrificed a cartridge on it. We saw the cubs go off to the place where the mother was lying, and thought to ourselves that we had got rid of them, but heard them soon afterwards, and even when we had camped they were not far off."

"Wednesday, August 7th. At last we are near land; at last the drift-ice lies behind us, and before us is open water, open, it is to be hoped, to the end. Yesterday was the day. When we came out of the tent the evening of the day before yesterday we both thought we must be nearer the edge of the glacier than ever, and with fresh courage, and in the faint hope of reaching land that day, we started on our journey. Yet we dared not think our life on the drift-ice was so nearly at an end. After wandering about on it for five months and suffering so many disappointments, we were only too well prepared for a new defeat. We thought, however, that the ice looked more promising farther on, though before we had gone far we came to broad lanes full of slush and foul, uneven ice, with hills and dales, and deep snow and water, into which we sank up to our thighs. After a couple of lanes of this kind, matters improved a little, and we got on to some flat ice. After having gone over this for a while, it became apparent how much nearer we were to the edge of the glacier. It could not possibly be far off now. We eagerly harnessed ourselves to the sledges again, put on a spurt, and away we went through snow and water, over mounds and ridges. We went as hard as we could, and what did we care if we sank into water till far above our fur leggings, so that both they and our 'komager' filled and gurgled like a pump? What did it matter to us now so long as we got on?

"We soon reached plains, and over them we went quicker and quicker. We waded through ponds where the spray flew up on all sides. Nearer and nearer we came, and by the dark water-sky before us, which continually rose higher, we could see how we were drawing near to open water. We did not even notice bears now. There seemed to be plenty about, tracks, both old and new, crossing and recrossing; one had even inspected the tent while we were asleep, and by the fresh trail we could see how it had come down wind in lee of us. We had no use for a bear now: we had food enough. We were soon able to see the open water under the wall of the glacier, and our steps lengthened even more. As I was striding along, I thought of the march of the Ten Thousand through Asia, when Xenophon's soldiers, after a year's war against superior forces, at last saw the sea from a mountain and cried, 'Thalatta! thalatta!' Maybe this sea was just as welcome to us after our months in the endless white drift-ice.

"At last, at last, I stood by the edge of the ice. Before me lay the dark surface of the sea, with floating white floes; far away the glacier wall rose abruptly from the water; over the whole lay a sombre, foggy light. Joy welled up in our hearts at this sight, and we could not give it expression in words. Behind us lay all our troubles, before us the waterway home. I waved my hat to Johansen, who was a little way behind, and he waved his in answer and shouted, 'Hurrah!' Such an event had to be celebrated in some way, and we did it by having a piece of chocolate each.

"While we were standing there looking at the water the large head of a seal came up, and then disappeared silently; but soon more appeared. It is very reassuring to know that we can procure food at any minute we like.

"Now came the rigging of the kayaks for the voyage. Of course, the better way would have been to paddle singly, but, with the long, big sledges on the deck, this was not easy, and leave them behind I dared not; we might have good use for them yet. For the time being, therefore, there was nothing else to be done but to lash the two kayaks together side by side in our usual manner, stiffen them out with snowshoes under the straps, and place the sledges athwart them, one before and one behind.

"It was sad to think we could not take our two last dogs with us, but we should probably have no further use for them, and it would not have done to take them with us on the decks of our kayaks. We were sorry to part with them; we had become very fond of these two survivors. Faithful and enduring, they had followed us the whole journey through; and, now that better times had come, they must say farewell to life. Destroy them in the same way as the others, we could not; we sacrificed a cartridge on each of them. I shot Johansen's, and he shot mine.

"So then we were ready to set off. It was a real pleasure to let the kayaks dance over the water and hear the little waves plashing against the sides. For two years we had not seen such a surface of water before us. We had not gone far before we found

Unusual stratification of the ice, 7 August 1895.

that the wind was so good that we ought to make use of it, and so we rigged up a sail on our fleet. We glided easily before the wind in towards the land we had so longed for all these many months. What a change after having forced one's way inch by inch and foot by foot on ice! The mist had hidden the land from us for a while, but now it parted, and we saw the glacier rising straight in front of us. At the same moment the sun burst forth, and a more beautiful morning I can hardly remember. We were soon underneath the glacier, and had to lower our sail and paddle westwards along the wall of ice, which was from 50 to 60 feet in height, and on which a landing was impossible. It seemed as if there must be little movement in this glacier; the water had eaten its way deep underneath it at the foot, and there was no noise of falling fragments or the cracking of crevasses to be heard, as there generally is with large glaciers. It was also quite even on the top, and no crevasses were to be seen. Up the entire height of the wall there was stratification, which was unusually marked. We soon discovered that a tidal current was running westwards along the wall of the glacier with great rapidity, and took advantage of it to make good progress. To find a camping-ground, however, was not easy, and at last we were reduced to taking up our abode on a drifting floe. It was glorious, though, to go to rest in the certainty that we should not wake to drudgery in the drift-ice.

"When we turned out to-day we found that the ice had packed around us, and I do not know yet how we shall get out of it, though there is open water not far off to our west."

"Thursday, August 8th. After hauling our impedimenta over some floes we got into open water yesterday without much difficulty. When we had reached the edge of the water, we made a paddle each from our snowshoe-staffs, to which we bound blades made of broken-off snowshoes. They were a great improvement on the somewhat clumsy paddles, with canvas blades lashed to bamboo sticks. I was very much inclined to chop off our sledges, so that they would only be half as long as before; by so doing we could carry them on the after-deck of the kayaks, and could thus each paddle alone, and our advance would be much quicker than by paddling the twin kayaks. However, I thought, perhaps, it was unadvisable. The water looked promising enough on ahead, but there was mist, and we could not see far; we knew nothing of the country or the coast we had come to, and might yet have good use for the sledges. We therefore set off in our double kayak, as before, with the sledges athwart the deck fore and aft.

"The mist soon rose a little; it was then a dead calm; the surface of the water lay like a great mirror before us, with bits of ice and an occasional floe drifting on it. It was a marvellously beautiful sight, and it was indeed glorious to sit there in our light vessels and glide over the surface without any exertion. Suddenly a seal rose in front of us, and over us flew continually ivory gulls and fulmars and kittiwakes. Little auks we also saw, and some Ross's gulls, and a couple of terns. There was no want of animal-life here, nor of food when we should require it.

"We found open water, broader and broader, as we paddled on our way beside the wall of ice; but it would not clear so that we could see something of our surroundings. The mist still hung obstinately over it,

"Our course, at first, lay west to north (magnetic); but the land always trended more and more to the west and south-west; the expanse of water grew greater and soon it widened out to a large sea, stretching in a south-westerly direction. A breeze sprang up from the north-north-east, and there was considerable motion which was not pleasant, as in our double craft the seas continually washed up between the two and wetted us. We put in towards evening and pitched the tent on the shore-ice, and just as we did so it began to rain, so that it was high time to be under a roof."

"Friday, August 9th. Yesterday morning we had again to drag the sledges with the kayaks over some ice which had drifted in front of our camping ground, and during this operation I managed to fall into the water and get wet. It was with difficulty we finally got through and out into open water. After a while we again found our way closed, and were obliged to take to hauling over some floes, but after this we had good open water the whole day. It was a north-easterly wind which had set the ice towards the land, and it was lucky we had got so far, as behind us, to judge by the atmosphere, the sea was much blocked. The mist hung over the land so that we saw little of it. According as we advanced we were able to hold a more southerly course, and the wind being nearly on the quarter we set sail about 1 o'clock, and continued sailing all day till we stopped yesterday evening. Our sail, however, was interrupted once when it was necessary to paddle round an ice point north of where we are now; the contrary current was so strong that it was as much as we could do to make way against it, and it was only after considerable exertion that we succeeded in doubling the point. We have seen little of the land we are skirting up to, this on account of the mist; but as far as I can make out it consists of islands. First there was a large island covered with an ice-sheet; then west of it a smaller one, on which are the two crags of rock which first made us aware of the vicinity of land; next came a long fjord or sound with massive shore-ice in it; and then a small, low headland, or rather an island, south of which we are now encamped. This shore-ice lying along the land is very remarkable. It is unusually massive and uneven; it seems to be composed of huge blocks welded together, which in a great measure, at any rate, must proceed from the ice-sheet. There has also, perhaps, been violent pressure against the land, which has heaved the sea-ice up together with pieces of ice from the calving of the glacier, and the whole has frozen together into a conglomerate mass. A medium-sized iceberg lay off the headland north of us, where the current was so strong. Where we are now lying, however, there is flat fjord-ice between the low island here and a larger one farther south.

"This land grows more of a problem, and I am more than ever at a loss to know where we are. It is very remarkable to me that the coast continually trends to the south instead of to the west. I could explain it all best by supposing ourselves to be on the west coast of the archipelago of Franz Josef Land, were it not that the variation, I think, is too great, and also for the number of Ross's gulls there still are. Not one has with certainty been seen in Spitzbergen, and if my supposition is right this should not be far off. Yesterday we saw a number of them again; they are quite as common here as the other species of gull."

"Saturday, August 10th. We went up on to the little islet we had camped by. It was covered by a glacier, which curved over it in the shape of a shield; there were slopes to all sides; but so slight was the gradient that our snowshoes would not even run of themselves on the crust of snow. From the ridge we had a fair view, and, as the mist lifted just then, we saw the land about us tolerably well. We now perceived plainly that what we had been skirting along was only islands. The first one was the biggest. The other land, with the two rocky crags, had, as we could see, a strip of bare land along the shore on the north-west side. Was it there, perhaps, the Ross's gulls congregated, and had their breeding-grounds? The island to our south also looked large; it appeared to be entirely covered by a glacier.[105] Between the islands, and as far as we could perceive south-east and east, the sea was covered by perfectly flat fjord-ice, but no land was to be discerned in that direction. There were no icebergs here, though we saw some later in the day on the south side of the island lying to the south of us.

"The glacier covering the little island on which we stood joined the fjord-ice almost imperceptibly, only a few small fissures along the shore indicated where it probably began. There could not be any great rise and fall in the ice here, consequent on the tide, as the fissures would then, as a matter of course, have been considerably larger. This seemed remarkable, as the tidal current ran swift as a river here. On the west side of the island there lay in front of the glacier a rampart of ice and snow, which was probably formed of pieces of glacier-ice and sea-ice welded together. It had the same character as the massive shore-ice which we had seen previously running along the land. This rampart went over imperceptibly with an even slope into the glacier within it.

"About three in the afternoon we finally set off in open water and sailed till eight or so in the evening; the water was then closed, and we were compelled to haul the fleet over flat ice to open water on the other side. But here, too, our progress seemed blocked, and as the current was against us we pitched the tent."

"On August 10th we were compelled partly to haul our sledges over the ice, partly to row in open water in a south-westerly direction. When we reached navigable waters again, we passed a flock of walruses lying on a floe. It was a pleasure to see so much food collected at one spot, but we did not take any notice of them as, for the time being, we had meat and blubber enough. After dinner we managed, in the mist, to wander down a long bay into the shore-ice where there was no outlet; we had to turn back, and this delayed us considerably. We now kept a more westerly course, following the often massive and uneven edge of the ice; but the current was dead against us, and in addition young ice had been forming all day as we rowed along; the weather had been cold and still, with falling snow, and this began to be so thick that we could not make way against it any longer. We therefore went ashore on the ice, and hauled until ten in the evening.

"Bear-tracks, old and new, in all directions, both the single ones of old bachelors and those of she-bears with cubs. It looks as if they had had a general rendezvous, or as if a flock of them had roamed backwards and forwards. I have never seen so many bear-tracks in one place in my life.

"We have certainly done 14 or 15 miles to-day; but still I think our progress is too slow if we are to reach Spitzbergen this year, and I am always wondering if we ought not to cut the ends off our sledges so that each can paddle his own kayak. This young ice, however, which grows steadily worse and the eleven degrees below freezing we now have make me hold my hand. Perhaps winter is upon us, and then the sledges may be very necessary.

"It is a curious sensation to paddle in the mist as we are doing without being able to see a mile in front of us. The land we found we have left behind us. We are always in hopes of clear weather in order to see where the land lies in front of us — for land there must be.

This flat unbroken ice must be attached to land of some kind; but clear weather we are not to have, it appears. Mist without ceasing; we must push on as it is."

After having hauled some distance farther over the ice, we came to open water again the following day (August 11th) and paddled for four or five hours. While I was on a hummock inspecting the waters ahead, a huge monster of a walrus came up quite near us. It lay puffing and glaring at us on the surface of the water, but we took no notice of it, got into our kayaks and went on. Suddenly it came up again by the side of us, raised itself high out of the water, snorted so that the air shook, and threatened to thrust its tusks into our frail craft. We seized our guns, but at the same moment it disappeared, and came up immediately afterwards on the other side, by Johansen's kayak, where it repeated the same manoeuvre. I said to him that if the animal showed signs of attacking us we must spend a cartridge on it. It came up several times and disappeared again; we could see it down in the water passing rapidly on its side under our vessels, and afraid lest it should make a hole in the bottom with its tusks, we thrust our paddles down into the water and frightened it away; but suddenly it came up again right by Johansen's kayak, and more savage than ever. He sent it a charge straight in the eyes, it uttered a terrific bellow, rolled over and disappeared, leaving a trail of blood on the water behind it. We paddled on as hard as we could, knowing that the shot might have dangerous consequences, but we were relieved when we heard the walrus come up far behind us at the place where it had disappeared.

We had paddled quietly on, and had long forgotten all about the walrus, when I suddenly saw Johansen jump into the air and felt his kayak receive a violent shock. I had no idea what it was, and looked round to see if some block of floating ice had capsized and struck the bottom of his kayak; but suddenly I saw another walrus rise up in the water beside us. I seized my gun, and as the animal would not turn its head so that I could aim at a spot behind the ear where it is more easily wounded, I was constrained to put a ball in the middle of its forehead; there was no time to be lost. Happily this was enough and it lay there dead and floating on the water. With great difficulty we managed to make a hole in the thick skin, and after cutting ourselves some strips of blubber and meat from the back we went on our way again.

At 7 in the evening the tidal current turned and the channel closed. There was no more water to be found. Instead of taking to hauling over the ice, we determined to wait for the opening of the channel when the tide should turn next day, and meanwhile to cut off the ends of our sledges, as I had so long been thinking of doing, and make ourselves some good double paddles so that we could put on greater pace, and, in our single kayaks, make the most of the channel during the time it was open. While we were occupied in doing this the mist cleared off at last, and there lay land stretched out in front of us, extending a long way south and west from S.E. right up to N.N.W. It appeared to be a chain of islands with sounds between them. They were chiefly covered with glaciers, only here and there were perpendicular black mountain-walls to be seen. It was a sight to make one rejoice to see so much land at one time. But where were we? This seemed a more difficult question to answer than ever. Could we, after all, have arrived at the east side of Franz Josef Land? It seemed very reasonable to suppose this to be the case. But then we must be very far east, and must expect a long voyage before we could reach Cape Fligely, on Crown-Prince Rudolf Land. Meanwhile we worked hard to get the sledges ready, but as the mist gradually lifted, and it became clearer and clearer, we could not help continually leaving them, to climb up on to the hummock beside us to look at the country, and speculate on this insoluble problem. We did not get to bed till seven in the morning of August 12th.

"Tuesday, August 13th. After having slept a few hours, we turned out of the bag again, for the current had turned, and there was a wide channel. In our single kayaks we made good headway, but after going about five miles the channel closed, and we had to clamber on to the ice. We thought it advisable to wait until the tidal current turned, and see if there were not a channel running farther. If not we must lash proper grips of wood to our curtailed sledges, and commence hauling towards a sound running through the land, which I see about W.N.W. (true), and which, according to Payer's Chart, I take to be Rawlinson's Sound."

But the crack did not open, and when it came to the point we had to continue on our way hauling.

"Wednesday, August 14th. We dragged our sledges and loads over a number of

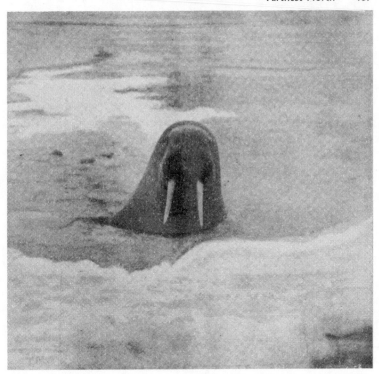

floes and ferried across lanes, arriving finally at a lane which ran westwards, in which we could paddle; but it soon packed together again, and we were stopped. The ivory gulls are very bold, and last night stole a piece of blubber lying close by the tent wall."

The following day we had to make our way as well as we could by paddling short distances in the lanes or hauling our loads over floes smaller or larger, as the case might be. The current, which was running like a mill race, ground them together in its career. Our progress with our short stumpy sledges was nothing very great, and of water suitable for paddling in we found less and less. We stopped several times and waited for the ice to open at the turn of the tide, but it did not do so, and on the morning of August 15th we gave it up, turned inwards and took to the shore ice for good. We set our course westwards towards the sound we had seen for several days now, and had struggled so to reach. The surface of the ice was tolerably even and we got over the ground well. On the way we passed a frozen-in iceberg, which was the highest we saw in these parts — some 50 to 60 feet, I should say.[106] I wished to go up it to get a better view of our environment, but it was too steep, and we did not get higher than a third part up the side.

"In the evening we at last reached the islands we had been steering for for the last few days, and for the first time for two years had bare land under foot — the delight of the feeling of being able to jump from block to block of granite[107] is indescribable, and the delight was not lessened when in a little sheltered corner among the stones we found moss and flowers, beautiful poppies (*papaver nudicaule*). Saxifraga nivalis, and a Stellaria (*sp.?*). It goes without saying that the Norwegian flag had to wave over this our first bare land, and a banquet was prepared. Our petroleum, meanwhile, had given out several days previously, and we had to contrive another lamp in which train-oil could be used. The smoking hot lobscouse, made of pemmican and the last of our potatoes, was delicious, and we sat inside the tent and kicked the bare grit under us to our hearts' content.

"Where we are is becoming more and more incomprehensible. There appears to be a broad sound west of us, but what is it? The island[108] we are now on, and where we have slept splendidly (this is written on the morning of August 16th) on dry land, with no melting of the ice in puddles underneath us, is a long moraine-like ridge running about north and south (magnetic), and consists almost exclusively of small and large — generally very large — blocks of stone, with, I should say, occasional stationary crags. The blocks are in a measure rounded off, but I have found no striation on them. The whole island barely rises above the snow-field in which it lies, and which slopes in a gradual decline down to the surrounding ice. On our west there is a bare island, somewhat higher, which we have seen for several days. Along the shore there is a decided strand-line (terrace). North of us are two small islets and a small rock or skerry.

"As I mentioned before (August 13th) I had at first supposed the sound on our west to be Rawlinson's Sound, but this now appeared impossible as there was nothing to be seen of Dove Glacier, by which it is bounded on one side. If this was now our position, we must have traversed the glacier and Wilczek Land without noticing any trace of either; for we had travelled westwards a good half degree south of Cape Buda-Pest. The possibility that we could be in this region we consequently now held to be finally excluded. We must have come to a new land in the western part of Franz Josef Land or Archipelago, and so far west that we had seen nothing of the countries discovered by Payer. But so far west that we had not even seen anything of Oscar's

The first camp on land (Houen's island), 16 August 1895.

Land, which ought to be situated in 82° N. and 52° E.? This was indeed incomprehensible; but was there any other explanation?

"Saturday, August 17th. Yesterday was a good day. We are in open water on the west coast of Franz Josef's Land, as far as I can make out, and may again hope to get home this year. About noon yesterday we walked across the ice from our moraine-islet to the higher island west of us. As I was ready before Johansen, I went on first to examine the island a little. As he was following me he caught sight of a bear on the level ice to leeward. It came jogging up against the wind straight towards him. He had his gun ready, but when a little nearer the bear stopped, reconsidered the situation, suddenly turned tail and was soon out of sight.

"This island[109] we came to seemed to me one of most lovely spots on the face of the earth. A beautiful flat beach, an old strand-line with shells strewn about, a narrow belt of clear water along the shore, where snails and sea-urchins (echinus) were visible at the bottom, and amphipoda were swimming about. In the cliffs overhead were hundreds of screaming little auks, and beside us the snow buntings fluttered from stone to stone with their cheerful twitter. Suddenly the sun burst forth through the light fleecy clouds, and the day seemed to be all sunshine. Here was life and bare land; we were no longer on the eternal drift ice! At the bottom of the sea just beyond the beach I could see whole forests of seaweed (laminaria and fucus). Under the cliffs here and there were drifts of beautiful rose-coloured snow.[110]

"On the north side of the island we found the breeding-place of numbers of Glaucus gulls; they were sitting with their young in ledges of the cliffs. Of course we had to climb up and secure a photograph of this unusual scene of family life, and as we stood there high up on the cliff's side we could see the drift-ice whence we had come. It lay beneath us like a white plain, and disappeared far away on the horizon. Beyond this lay what we had journeyed, and farther away still the Fram and our comrades were drifting.

"I had thought of going to the top of this island to get a better view, and perhaps come nearer solving the problem of our whereabouts. But when we were on the west side of it the mist came back and settled on the top ; we had to content ourselves with only going a little way up the slope to look at our future course west ward. Some way out we saw open water; it looked like the sea itself, but before one could get to it there was a good deal of ice. We came down again and started off. Along the land there was a channel running some distance farther, and we tried it, but it was covered everywhere with a thin layer of new ice which we did not dare to break through in our kayaks, and risk cutting a hole in them; so, finally, a little way farther south we put in to drag up the kayaks and take to the ice again. While we were doing this one huge bearded seal after another stuck its head up by the side of the ice and gazed wonderingly at us with its great eyes; then, with a violent header, and splashing the water in all directions, it would disappear, to come up again soon afterwards on the other side. They kept playing round us, blowing, diving, reappearing, and throwing themselves over so that the water foamed round them. It would have been easy enough to capture one had we required it.

Leaving behind [Torup's] island, 17 August 1895.

A breeding place of *Glaucus* gulls. Exploring [Torup's] island, 17 August 1895.

"At last, after a good deal of exertion, we stood at the margin of the ice ; the blue expanse of water lay before us as far as the eye could reach, and we thought that for the future we had to do with it alone. To the north[III] there was land, the steep, black, basalt cliffs of which fell perpendicularly into the sea. We saw headland after headland standing out northwards, and farthest off of all we could descry a bluish glacier. The interior was everywhere covered with an ice-sheet. Below the clouds, and over the land, was a strip of ruddy, night sky, which was reflected in the melancholy, rocking sea.

"So we paddled on along the side of the glacier which covered the whole country south of us. We became more and more excited as we approached the headland to the west. Would the coast trend south here, and was there no more land westward? It was this we expected to decide our fate: decide whether we should reach home that year or be compelled to winter somewhere on land. Nearer and nearer we came to it along the edge of the perpendicular wall of ice. At last we reached the headland, and our hearts bounded with joy to see so much water, only water, westwards, and the coast trending south-west. We also saw a bare mountain projecting from the ice-sheet a little way farther on; it was a curious high ridge, as sharp as a knife-blade. It was as steep and sharp as anything I have seen, it was all of dark, columnar basalt, and so jagged and peaked that it looked like a comb. In the middle of the mountain there was a gap or couloir, and there we crept up to inspect the sea-way southwards. The wall of rock was anything but broad there, and fell away on the south side in a perpendicular drop of several hundred feet. A cutting wind was blowing in the couloir. While we were lying there, I suddenly heard a noise behind me, and on looking round I saw two foxes fighting over a little auk which they had just caught. They clawed and tugged and bit as hard as they could on the very edge of the chasm; then they suddenly caught sight of us, not twenty feet away from them. They stopped fighting, looked up wonderingly, and began to run round and peep at us, first from one side, then from the other. Over us myriads of little auks flew backwards and forwards, screaming shrilly from the ledges in the mountain-side. So far as we could make out, there appeared to be open sea along the land to the westward. The wind was favourable, and, although we were tired, we decided to take advantage of the opportunity, have something to eat, rig up mast and sail on our canoes, and get afloat. We sailed till the morning, when the wind went down, and then we landed on the shore-ice again and camped.[112]

"I am as happy as a child in the thought that we are now at last really on the west coast of Franz Josef Land, with open water before us, and independent of ice and currents."

"Wednesday, August 24th. The vicissitudes of this life will never come to an end. When I wrote last I was full of hope and courage; and here we are stopped by stress of weather for four days and three nights, with the ice packed as tight as it can be against the coast. We see nothing but piled-up ridges, hummocks, and broken ice in all directions. Courage is still here, but hope, the hope of soon being home — that was relinquished a long time ago, and before us lies the certainty of a long, dark winter in these surroundings.

"It was at midnight between the 17th and 8th that we set off from our last camping-ground in splendid weather. Though it was cloudy and the sun invisible, there was along the horizon in the north the most glorious ruddy glow with golden sun-tipped clouds, and the sea lay shining and dreamy in the distance: a marvellous night... On the surface of the sea, smooth as a mirror, without a block of ice as far as the eye could reach, glided the kayaks, the water purling off the paddles at every

Campsite on the ice-shore (Cape Brögger), 18 August 1895.

silent stroke. It was like being in a gondola on the Canale Grande. But there was something almost uncanny about all this stillness, and the barometer had gone down rapidly. Meanwhile, we sped towards the headland in the south-south-west, which I thought was about 12 miles off. After some hours we espied ice ahead, but both of us thought that it was only a loose chain of pieces drifting with the current, and we paddled confidently on. But as we gradually drew nearer we saw that the ice was fairly compact, and extended a greater and greater distance; though from the low kayaks it was not easy to see the exact extent of the pack. We accordingly disembarked and climbed up on a hummock to find out our best route. The sight which met us was anything but encouraging. Off the headland we were steering for, were a number of islets and rocks, extending some distance out to sea; it was they that were locking the ice, which lay in every direction, between them and outside them. Near us it was slack, but farther off it looked much worse, so that further advance by sea was altogether out of the question. Our only expedient was to take to the edge of the shore-ice, and hope for the chance that a lane might run along it some way farther on. On the way in, we passed a seal lying on a floe, and as our larder was beginning to grow empty, I tried to get a shot at it, but it dived into the water before we came within range.

"As we were paddling along through some small bits of ice my kayak suddenly received a violent shock from underneath. I looked round in amazement as I had not noticed any large piece of ice hereabouts. There was nothing of the kind to be seen either, but worse enemies were about. No sooner had I glanced down than I saw a huge walrus cleaving through the water astern, and it suddenly came up, raised itself and stood on end just before Johansen, who was following in my wake. Afraid lest the animal should have its tusks through the deck of his craft the next minute, he backed as hard as he could and felt for his gun, which he had down in the kayak. I was not long either in pulling my gun out of its cover. The animal crashed snorting into the water again, however, dived under Johansen's kayak, and came up just behind him. Johansen, thinking he had had enough of such a neighbour, scrambled incontinently on to the floe nearest him. After having waited a while, with my gun ready for the walrus to come up close by me, I followed his example. I very nearly came in for the cold bath which the walrus had omitted to give me, for the edge of the ice gave way just as I set my foot on it, and the kayak drifted off with me standing upright in it, and trying to balance it as best I could, in order not to capsize. If the walrus had reappeared at that moment, I should certainly have received it in its own element. Finally, I succeeded in getting up on to the ice, and for a long time afterwards the walrus swam round and round our floe, where we made the best of the situation by having dinner. Sometimes it was near Johansen's kayak, sometimes near mine. We could see how it darted about in the water under the kayaks, and it had evidently the greatest desire to attack us again. We thought of giving it a ball to get rid of it, but had no great wish to part with a cartridge, and besides it only showed us its nose and forehead, which are not exactly the most vital spots to aim at when one's object is to kill with one shot. It was a great ox-walrus. There is something remarkably fantastic and pre-historic about these monsters. I could not help thinking of a merman, or something of the kind, as it lay there just under the surface of the water blowing and snorting for quite a long while at a time, and glaring at us with its round glassy eyes. After having continued in this way for some time, it disappeared just as tracklessly as it had come; and as we had finished our dinner, we were able to go on our way again, glad, a second time, not to have been upset, or destroyed by its tusks. The most curious thing about it was that it came so entirely without warning — suddenly rising up from the deep. Johansen had certainly heard a great splash behind him some time before, which he took to be a seal, but perhaps it may have been the walrus.

"The lane along the shore-ice gave us little satisfaction, as it was completely covered with young ice and we could make no way. In addition to this a wind from the S.S.W. sprang up, which drove the ice on to us, so there was nothing for it but to put in to the edge of the ice and wait until it should slacken again. We spread out the bag, folded the tent over us, and prepared for rest in the hope of soon being able to go on. But this was not to be, the wind freshened, the ice packed tighter and tighter, there was soon no open water to be seen in any direction and even the open sea, whence we had come, disappeared; all our hopes of getting home that year sank at one blow. After a while we realised that there was nothing to be done but to drag our loads further in on to the shore-ice and camp. To try and haul the canoes farther over this pack, which was worse than any ice we had come across since we began our voyage, we thought was useless. We should get very little distance in the day, and it might cost us dear with the kayaks on the short sledges, among all these ridges and hummocks; and so we lay there day and night waiting for the wind to go down or to change But it blew from the same quarter the whole time, and matters were not improved by a heavy fall of snow which made the ice absolutely impracticable.

Our situation was not an attractive one; in front of us massive broken sea-ice, close by land, and the gods alone know if it will open main this year; a good way behind us land which looked anything but inviting to spend the winter on; around us impassable ice, and our provender very much on the decline. The south coast of the country and Eira Harbour now appeared to our imagination a veritable land of Canaan, and we thought that if only we were there all our troubles would be over. We hoped to be able to find Leigh-Smith's hut there, or at any rate some remains of it, so that we should have something to live in, and we also hoped that where there no doubt was much open water it would be easy to find game. We regretted not having shot some seals while they were numerous; on the night when we left our last camping-place there were plenty of them about. As Johansen was standing on the edge of the ice doing something to his kayak, a seal came up just in front of him; he thought it was of a kind he had not seen before, and shouted to me. But at the same moment up came one black poll after another quiet and silent, from ten to twenty in number, all gazing at him with their great eyes. He was quite nonplussed, thought there was something uncanny about it, and then they disappeared just as noiselessly as they had come.

"I consoled him by telling him they really were of a kind we had not seen before on our journey; they were young harp, or saddleback seal (*phoca groenlandica*). We saw several schools of them again later in the day.

"Meanwhile we killed time as best we could: chiefly by sleeping. On the early morning of the 21st, just as I lay thinking what would become of us if the ice should not slacken and we had no opportunity of adding to our larder — the chances I thought did not seem very promising — I heard something pawing and moving outside. It might as usual be the packing of the ice, but still I thought it was more like something on four legs. I jumped up, saying to Johansen that it must be a bear, and then I suddenly heard it sniffing by the tent-wall. I peeped out through some holes in one side of it and saw nothing; then I went across to a big hole on the other side of the tent and there I saw an enormous bear just outside. It caught sight of me, too, at the same moment and slunk away, but then stopped again and looked at the tent. I snatched my gun down from the tent-pole, stuck it through the hole and sent the bear a ball in the middle of the chest. It fell forward; but raised itself again and struggled off, so I had to give it the contents of the other barrel in the side. It still staggered on, but fell down between some hummocks a little way off. An unusually large he-bear, and for the time all our troubles for food were ended. The wind however, continued steadily from the same quarter. As there was not much shelter where we were encamped, and furthermore, as we were uncomfortably near the ridge where the ice was continually packing, we removed and took up our abode farther in on the shore-ice, where we are still lying. Last night there was a bear about again, but not quite so near the tent.

"We went on an excursion inland[113] yesterday to see what our prospects might be if we should be forced to spend a winter here. I had hoped to find flatter ice farther in, but instead it grew worse and worse the nearer we went to land, and right in by the headland it was towering up, and almost impassable. The ice was piled against the very wall of the glacier. We went up on the glacier, and looked at the sound to the north of the headland. A little way in the ice appeared to be flatter, more like fjord-ice, but nowhere could we see lanes where there might be a chance of capturing seal. There was no place for a hut either about here; while, on the other hand, we found on the south side of the headland quite a smiling spot where the ground was fairly level, and where there was some herbage and an abundance of moss and stones for building purposes. But outside it, again, the ice towered up on the shore in chaotic confusion on all sides. It was a little more level in the direction of the fjord or sound which ran far inland to the south, and there it soon turned to flat fjord-ice; but there were no lanes there either where we could hope to capture seal. There did not seem much prospect of game, but we comforted ourselves with the reflection that there were tracks of bears in every direction, and bears would, in case of necessity, be our one resource for both food and clothes. In the cliffs above us crowds of little auks had their nests, as on all such places that we have passed by. We also saw a fox. The rock-formation was a coarse-grained basalt; but by the side of the glacier we discovered a mound of loose, half-crumbled argillaceous schist, in which, however, we did not find any fossils. Some blocks which we thought very much like granite were also strewn about.[114] Everywhere along the beach the glaciers were covered with red snow, which had a very beautiful effect in the sunshine.

"We were both agreed that it might be possible to winter here, but hoped it was the first and last time we should set foot on the spot. The way to it, too, was so bad that we hardly knew how we should get the sledges and kayaks there.

"To-day, at last, the change we have longed and waited for so long has come. Last night the south-west wind quieted down; the barometer, which I have been tapping daily in vain, has at last begun to rise a little, and the wind has gone round to the opposite quarter. The question now is whether, if it keep there, it will be able to drive the ice out again."

Here comes a great gap in my diary, and not till far on in the winter (Friday, December 6th) do I write: "I must at last try and patch the hole in my diary. There has been so much to see about that I have got no writing done; that excuse, however, is no longer available, as we sleep nearly the whole twenty-four hours."

After having written my journal for the 24th August, I went out to look for a better and more sheltered place, as the wind had changed, and now blew straight into the tent. I hoped, too, that this land-wind might open up the ice, and I therefore first set off to see whether any sign of slackening was to be discovered at the edge of the shore ice; but the floes lay packed together as solidly as ever. I found, however, a capital place for pitching the tent, and we were busy moving thither when we suddenly discovered that the ice had split off to the landward, and already there was a broad channel. We certainly wanted the ice to open up, but not on our landward side; and now it was a question of getting across on to the shore ice again at any price, so as not to drift out to sea with the pack. But the wind had risen to a stiff breeze, and it seemed more than doubtful whether we could manage to pull up against it, even for so short a distance as across the channel. This was rapidly growing broader and broader. We had, however, to make an attempt, and, therefore, set off along the edge towards a spot farther east, which we thought would give us a little more shelter for launching our kayaks. On arriving, however, we found that it would be no easy matter to launch them here either without getting them filled with water. It blew so that the spoondrift was driven over the sea, and the spray was dashed far in over the ice. There was little else to be done but to pitch our tent and wait for better times. We were now more than ever in need of shelter to keep the tent from being torn by the wind, but search and tramp up and down as we might we could find no permanent resting-place, and at last had to content ourselves with the scant shelter of a little elevation which we thought would do. We had not lain long before the gusts of wind made such onslaughts on the tent that we found it advisable to take it down, to avoid having it torn to pieces. We could now sleep securely in our bags beneath the prostrate tent, and let the wind rage above us. After a time I awoke, and noticed that the wind had subsided so much that we could once more raise our tent, and I crept out to look at the weather. I was less pleasantly surprised on discovering that we were already far out to sea; we must have drifted eight or ten miles from land, and between it and us lay open sea. The land now lay quite low, far off on the horizon. In the meantime, however, the weather had considerably improved, and we once more set out along the edge of the ice to try to get our kayaks launched. But it was no easy matter. It was still blowing hard, and the sea ran high. In addition to this, there were a number of loose floes beyond, and these were in constant motion, so that we had to be on the alert to prevent the kayaks from being crushed between them. After some futile attempts we at length got afloat, but only to discover that the wind and the waves were too strong: we should scarcely be able to make any progress against them. Our only resource, therefore, was to sail if this were practicable. We went alongside an ice promontory, lashed the kayaks together, raised the mast, and again put to sea. We soon had our single sail hoisted, and to our unspeakable satisfaction we now found that we got along capitally. At last we should be able to bid farewell to the ice, where we had been compelled to abandon our hope of reaching home that year. We now continued sailing hour after hour, and made good progress; but then the wind dropped too much for our single sail, and I ventured to set the whole double sail. Hardly had we done so, when the wind again sprang up, and we dashed foaming through the water. This soon, however, became a little too much; the sea washed over the lee kayak, the mast bent dangerously, and the situation did not look very pleasant; there was nothing for it but to lower the sail again as quickly as possible. The single sail was again hoisted, and we were cured for some time of wishing to try anything more.

We sailed steadily and well the whole day, and now at last had to pass the difficult cape; but it was evening before we left it behind; and now the wind dropped so much that the whole double sail had to be hoisted again, and even then progress was slow. We kept on, however, during the night, along the shore, determined to make as much use of the wind as possible. We passed a low promontory covered by a gently-sloping glacier;[115] around it lay a number of islands, which must, we thought, have held the ice fast. A little farther on we came under some high basaltic cliffs, and here the wind dropped completely. As it was also hazy, and we could discern land and islands both to right and left of us, so that we did not know in what direction to steer, we put in here, drew the kayaks up on shore, pitched the tent, and cooked ourselves a good meal of warm food, which we relished greatly, from the consciousness of having done a good day's work. Above our heads, all up the face of the cliff, the little auks kept up a continual hubbub, faithfully supported by the ivory gulls, kittiwakes, burgomasters, and skuas. We slept none the worse for that however. This was a beautiful mountain. It consisted of the finest columnar basalt one could wish to see, with its buttresses and niches up the face of the cliff, and its countless points and spires along every crest, reminding one of Milan Cathedral. From top to bottom it was only column upon column; at the base they were all lost in the talus.

When we turned out the following morning, the weather had so far cleared that we could better see the way we ought to take. It appeared as if a deep fjord, or sound ran in eastwards in front of us; and our way distinctly lay round a promontory which we had to the S.S.W. on the other side of the fjord. In that direction the water appeared to be open, while within the fjord lay solid ice, and out to sea drift-ice lay everywhere. Through the misty atmosphere we could also distinguish several islands.[16] Here, too, as we usually found in the morning, a great quantity of ice had drifted in in the course of the night — great, flat, and thin floes which had settled themselves in front of us — and it looked as if we should have hard work to get out into open water. Things went a little better than we expected, however, and we got through before it closed in entirely. In front of us now lay open water right past the promontory far ahead; the weather was good, and everything seemed to promise a successful day. As it began to blow a little from the fjord, and we hoped it might become a sailing wind, we put in beside a little rocky island, which looked just like a great stone[17] sticking up out of the sea, and there rigged up mast and sail. But the sailing wind came to nothing, and we were soon obliged to unrig, and take to paddling. We had not paddled far, when the wind went round to the opposite quarter, the south-west. It increased rapidly and soon the sea ran high, the sky became overcast in the south, and it looked as if the weather might become stormy. We were still several miles from the land on the other side of the fjord, and we might have many hours of hard paddling before we gained it. This land, too, looked far from inviting, as it lay there, entirely covered with glacier from the summit right to the shore; only in one place did a little rock emerge. To leeward we had the margin of the shore-ice, low and affording no protection. The waves broke right upon it, and it would not be a good place to seek refuge in, should such a proceeding become necessary; it would be best to get in under land and see how the weather would turn out. We did not like the prospect of once more being enclosed in the drift-ice; we had had enough of that by this time, so we made for some land which lay a little way behind us, and looked very inviting. Should matters turn out badly, a good place for wintering in might be found there.

Scarcely had I set foot on land, when I saw a bear a little way up the shore; and drew up our kayaks to go and shoot it. In the meantime it came shambling along the shore towards us, so we lay down quietly behind the kayaks and waited. When close up to us it caught sight of our footprints in the snow, and while it was snuffing at them Johansen sent a bullet behind its shoulder. The bear roared and tried to run, but the bullet had gone through the spine, and the hind part of its body was paralysed and refused to perform its functions. In perplexity the bear sat down, and bit and tore its hind paws until the blood flowed; it was as if it were chastising them to make them do their duty. Then it tried again to move away, but with the same result; the hind part of its body was no longer amenable to discipline, and dragged behind, so that it could only shuffle along on its fore-legs, going round in a ring. A ball through the skull put an end to its sufferings.

When we had skinned it, we made an excursion inland to inspect our new domain, and were now not a little surprised to see two walruses lying quietly on the ice close to the spot where I had first caught sight of the bear. This seemed to me to show how little heed walruses pay to bears, who will never attack them if they can help it. I had more decisive proofs of this subsequently. In the sea beyond we also saw a walrus, which kept putting up its head and breathing so hard that it could be heard a long way off. A little later, I saw him approach the edge of the ice and disappear, only to appear again in the tidal channel close to the shore, a good way from the edge of the ice. He struck his great tusks into the edge of the ice, while he lay breathing hard, just like an exhausted swimmer. Then he raised himself high up on his tusks, and looked across the ice towards the others lying there, and then dived down again. He soon reappeared with a great deal of noise farther in, and the same performance was gone through again. A walrus's head is not a beautiful object as it appears above the ice. With its huge tusks, its coarse whisker bristles, and clumsy shape, there is something wild and goblin-like about it which, I can easily understand, might inspire fear in more superstitious times, and give rise to the idea of fabulous monsters, with which in ancient days these seas were thought to swarm. At last the walrus came up in the hole beside which the others were lying, and raised himself a little way up on to the edge of the ice by his tusks; but upon this the bigger of the two, a huge old bull, suddenly awoke to life. He grunted menacingly, and moved about restlessly. The new-comer bowed his head respectfully down to the ice, but soon pulled himself cautiously up on to the floe, so as to get a hold with his fore-paddle, and then drew himself a little way in. Now the old bull was thoroughly roused. He turned round, bellowed, and floundered up to the new-comer in order to dig his enormous tusks into his back. The latter, who appeared to be the old bull's equal both as regards tusks and size, bowed humbly, and laid his head down upon

The last tent site (right) of 1895.

the ice just like a slave before his sultan. The old bull returned to his companion, and lay quietly down as before, but no sooner did the new-comer stir, after having lain for some time in this servile posture, than the old bull grunted and thrust at him, and he once more respectfully drew back. This was repeated several times. At length, after much manoeuvring backwards and forwards, the new-comer succeeded in drawing himself on to the floe, and finally up beside the others. I thought the tender passion must have something to do with these proceedings; but I discovered afterwards that all three were males. And it is in this friendly manner that walruses receive their guests. It appears to be a specially chosen member of the flock that has these hospitable duties to perform. I am inclined to think it is the leader, who is asserting his dignity, and wishes to impress upon every new-comer that he is to be obeyed. These animals must be exceedingly sociable, when, in spite of such treatment, they thus constantly seek one another's society, and always lie close together. When we returned a little later to look at them, another had arrived, and by the following morning six lay there side by side. It is not easy to believe that these lumps lying on the ice are living animals. With head drawn in and hind-legs flat beneath the body, they will lie motionless hour after hour, looking like enormous sausages. It is easy to see that these fellows lie there in security, and fearful of nothing in the world.

After having seen as much as we wanted of the walruses at close quarters, we went back, prepared a good meal from the newly slaughtered bear, and lay down to sleep. On the shore below the tent, the ivory gulls were making a fearful hubbub. They had gathered in scores from all quarters, and could not agree as to the fair division of the bear's entrails; they fought incessantly, filling the air with their angry cries. It is one of nature's unaccountable freaks to have made this bird so pretty, while giving it such an ugly voice. At a little distance the burgomasters sat solemnly looking on and uttering their somewhat more melodious notes. Out in the sea the walruses were blowing and bellowing incessantly, but everything passed unheeded by the two weary warriors in the tent; they slept soundly, with the bare ground for their couch. In the middle of the night we were awakened, however, by a peculiar sound; it was just like some one whimpering and crying, and making great ado. I started up, and looked out of the peep-hole. Two bears were standing down beside our bear's flesh, a she-bear and her young one, and both sniffing at the bloody marks in the snow, while the she-bear wailed as if mourning for a dear departed one. I lost no time in seizing my gun, and was just putting it cautiously out, when the she-bear caught sight of me at the peep-hole, and off they both set, the mother in front, and the young one trotting after as fast as it could. I just let them run — we had really no use for them — and then we turned over and went to sleep again.

Nothing came of the storm we had feared. The wind blew hard enough, however, to rend and tear our now well-worn tent, and there was no shelter where we lay. We hoped to go on during the following day, but found, to our disappointment, that the way was blocked; the wind had again driven the ice in. We must remain for the present where we were; but in that case we would make ourselves as comfortable as possible. The first thing to be done was to seek for a warm, well-sheltered place for the tent, but this was not to be found. There was nothing for it but to get something built up of stone. We quarried stone in the débris at the bottom of the cliff, and got together as much as we could. The only quarrying implement we had was a runner that had been cut off a hand-sledge; but our two hands were what we had to use most. We worked away during the night; what we had at first only intended to be a shelter from the wind grew little by little into four walls; and we now kept at it until we had finished a small hut. It was nothing very wonderful, Heaven knows, not long enough for a man of my height to lie straight inside — I had to stick my feet out at the door — and just broad enough to admit of our lying side by side, and leave room for the cooking apparatus. It was worst, however, with regard to the height. There was room to lie down, but to sit up decently straight was an impossibility for me. The roof was made of our thin and fragile silk tent, spread over snowshoes and bamboo rods. We closed the doorway with our coats, and the walls were so loosely put together that we could see daylight between the stones on all sides. We afterwards called it the den, and a dreadful den it was, too; but we were none the less proud of our handiwork. It would not blow down, at any rate, even though the wind did blow right through it. When we had got our bearskin in as a couch and lay warm and comfortable in our bag, while a good potful of meat bubbled over the train-oil lamp, we thought existence a pleasure; and the fact of there being so much smoke that our eyes became red and the tears streamed down our cheeks could not destroy our feeling of content.

As progress southwards was blocked also on the following day [August 28th], and as autumn was now drawing on, I at last resolved on remaining here for the winter. I thought that we still had more than 138 miles to travel in order to reach Eira Harbour or Leigh Smith's wintering-place;[118] it might take us a long time to get there, and then we were not sure of finding any hut; and when we did get there, it would be more than doubtful if, before the winter set in, there would be time to build a house, and also gather stores for the winter. It was undoubtedly the safest plan to begin at once to prepare for wintering, while there was still plenty of game to be bad; and this was a good spot to winter in. The first thing I should like to have done was to have shot the walruses that had been lying on the ice during the first day or two; but now, of course, they were gone. The sea, however, was swarming with them; they bellowed and blew night and day, and, in order to be ready for an encounter with them, we emptied our kayaks to make them more easy of manipulation in this somewhat dangerous chase. While thus engaged, Johansen caught sight of two bears — a she-bear and her cub — coming along the edge of the ice from the south. We lost no time in getting our guns and setting off towards them. By the time they reached the shore they were within range, and Johansen sent a bullet through the mother's chest. She roared, bit at the wound, staggered a few steps, and fell. The young one could not make out what was the matter with its mother, and ran round, snuffing at her. When we approached, it went off a little way up the slope, but soon came back again and took up a position over its mother, as if to defend her against us. A charge of small shot put an end to its life.

This was a good beginning to our winter store. As I was returning to the hut to fetch the seal-knives, I heard cries in the air above me. There were actually two geese flying south! With what longing I looked after them as they disappeared, only wishing that I could have followed them to the land towards which they were now wending their flight!

Next to food and fuel, the most important thing was to get a hut built. To build the walls of this was not difficult; there was plenty of stone and moss. The roof presented greater difficulty, and we had as yet no idea what to make it of. Fortunately, I found a sound drift-wood pine-log thrown up on to the shore not far from our den; this would make a capital ridge-piece for the roof of our future house. And if there was one, there might be others. One of our first acts, therefore, was to make an excursion up along the shore and search; but all we found was one short, rotten piece of wood, which was good for nothing, and some chips of another piece. I then began to think of using walrus-hides for the roof instead.

The following day [August 29th] we prepared to try our luck at walrus-hunting. We had no great desire to attack the animals in single kayaks, we had had enough of that, I thought, and the prospect of being upset or of having a tusk driven through the bottom of the kayak, or into one's thigh, was not altogether alluring. The kayaks were therefore lashed together, and, seated upon the ring, we put out towards a big bull, which lay and dived just outside. We were well equipped with guns and harpoons, and thought that it was all quite simple. Nor was it difficult to get within range, and we emptied our barrels into the animal's head. It lay stunned for a moment, and we rowed towards it, but suddenly it began to splash and whirl round in the water, completely beside itself. I shouted out that we must back, but it was too late: the walrus got under the kayaks, and we received several blows underneath in the violence of its contortions, before it finally dived. It soon came up again, and now the sound of its breathing resounded on all sides, while blood streamed from its mouth and nostrils, and dyed the surrounding water. We lost no time in rowing up to it, and pouring a fresh volley into its head. Again it dived, and we cautiously drew back, to avoid receiving an attack from below. It soon appeared again, and we once more rowed up to it. These manoeuvres were repeated, and each time it came to the surface it received at least one bullet in the head, and grew more and more exhausted; but, as it always faced us, it was difficult to give it a mortal wound behind the ear. The blood, however, now flowed in streams. During one of these manoeuvres, I was in the act of placing my gun hurriedly in its case on the deck, in order to row nearer, forgetting that it was cocked, when all at once it went off. I was rather alarmed, thinking the ball had gone through the bottom of the kayak, and I began feeling my legs. They were uninjured, however, and as I did not hear the water rushing in either, I was reassured. The ball had passed through the deck, and out through the side a little above the water-line. We had now had enough of this sport, however; the walrus only lay gasping for breath, and just as we rowed towards it it turned its head a little, and received two bullets just behind the ear. It lay still, and we rowed up to throw our harpoon; but before we got near enough, it sank and disappeared. It was a melancholy ending to the affair; in all nine cartridges had been expended to no purpose, and we silently rowed to shore, not a little crestfallen. We tried no more walrus-hunting from kayaks that day; but we now saw that a walrus had come up on to the shore ice a little way off. Perhaps we were to receive compensation there for the one we had just lost. It was not long before another came up beside the first. After having taken an observation and given them time to compose themselves, we set off. Having bellowed and made a horrible noise out there for some time, they now lay asleep and unsuspecting, and we stole cautiously up to them, I in front and Johansen close at my heels. I first went up to the head of the nearer one, which was lying with its back to us. As it had drawn its head well down, and it was difficult to get a shot at a vulnerable spot, I passed behind it, and up to the head of the other one. The animals still lay motionless, asleep in the sun. The second was in a better position for a shot, and, when I saw Johansen standing ready at the head of the first, I fired at the back of the neck. The animal turned over a little, and lay there dead. At the report the first started up, but at the same moment received Johansen's bullet. Half stunned, it turned its gigantic body round towards us; in a moment I had discharged the ball from my smooth-bore at it, but, like Johansen, I hit too far forward in the head. The blood streamed from its nostrils and mouth, and it breathed and coughed till the air vibrated. Supporting itself upon its enormous tusks, it now lay still, coughing blood like a consumptive person, and quite indifferent to us. In spite of its huge body and shapeless appearance, which called up to the imagination bogie, giant, and kraken, and other evil things, there was something so gently supplicating and helpless in its round eyes as it lay there, that its goblin exterior and one's own need were forgotten in pity for it. It almost seemed like murder. I put an end to its sufferings by a bullet behind the ear, but those eyes haunt me yet; it seemed as if in them lay the prayer for existence of the whole helpless walrus race. But it is lost; it has man as its pursuer. It cannot, however, be denied that we rejoiced at the thought of all the meat and blubber we had now brought down in one encounter; it made up for the cartridges expended upon the one that sank. But we had not got them on land yet, and it would be a long piece of work to get them skinned, and cut up, and brought home. The first thing we did was to go after sledges and knives. As there was a possibility, too, of the ice breaking off and being set adrift, I also thought it wise to take the kayaks on the sledges at the same time, for it had begun to blow a little from the fjord. But for this fortunate precaution, it is not easy to say what would have become of us. While we were engaged in skinning, the wind rose rapidly, and soon became a storm. To landward of us was the narrow channel or lane beside which the walruses had been lying. I feared that the ice might open here, and we drift away. While we worked, I, therefore, kept an eye on it to see if it grew broader. It remained unchanged, and we went on skinning as fast as we could. When the first walrus was half skinned, I happened to look landwards across the ice, and discovered that it had broken off a good way from us, and that the part on which we stood had already been drifting for some time; there was black water between us and the shore-ice, and the wind was blowing so that the spray flew fron the foaming waves. There was no time to be lost; it was more than doubtful whether we should be able to paddle any great distance against that wind and sea, but as yet the ice did not appear to have drifted a greater distance from the land than we could cross, if we made haste. We could not bring ourselves to give up entirely the huge animals we had brought down, and we hurriedly cut off as much flesh as we could get at, and flung it into the kayaks. We then cut off about a quarter of the skin, with the blubber on it, and threw it on the top, and then set off for the shore. We had scarcely abandoned our booty before the gulls bore down in scores upon the half-skinned carcass. Happy creatures! Wind and waves and drifting were nothing to them; they screamed and made a hubbub and thought what a feast they were having. As long as we could see the carcasses as they drifted out to sea, we saw the birds continually gathering in larger and larger flocks about them like clouds of snow. In the meantime we were doing our utmost to gain the ice, but it had developed cracks and channels in every direction. We managed to get some distance in the kayaks; but while I was crossing a wide channel on some loose floes I alighted on such poor ice that it sank under my weight, and I had to jump back quickly to escape a bath. We tried in several places, but everywhere it sank beneath us and our sledges, and there was nothing for it but to take to the water, keeping along the lee-side of the ice. But we had not rowed far before we perceived that it was of no use to have our kayaks lashed together in such a wind; we had to row singly, and sacrifice the walrus-hide and blubber, which it then became impossible to take with us. At present it was lying across the stern of both kayaks. While we were busy effecting these changes we were surrounded, before we were aware of it, by ice, and had to pull the kayaks up hastily to save them from being crushed. We now tried to get out at several places, but the ice was in constant motion; it ground round as in a whirlpool. If a channel opened, we had no sooner launched our kayaks than it once more closed violently, and we had to snatch them up in the greatest haste. Several times they were within a hair's-breadth of being smashed. Meanwhile the storm was steadily increasing, the spray dashed over us, and we drifted farther and farther out to sea.

At length, however, we got clear, and now discovered, to our joy, that by exerting our utmost strength we could just force the kayaks on against the wind. It was a hard pull, and our arms ached; but still we crept slowly on towards land. The sea was choppy and bad, but our kayaks were good sea-boats, and even mine, with the bullet-hole in it, did so well that I kept to some extent dry. The wind came now and then in such gusts, that we felt as if it might lift us out of the water and upset us; but gradually, as we drew nearer in under the high cliffs, it became quieter, and at last, after a long time, we reached the shore, and could take breath. We then rowed in smoother water along the shore up to our camping-place. It was with genuine satisfaction that we clambered on shore that night, and how unspeakably comfortable it was to be lying again snugly within four walls in our little den, wet though we were. A good potful of meat was prepared, and our appetite was ravenous. It was, indeed, with sorrow that we thought of the lost walruses now drifting out there in the storm; but we were glad that we were not still in their company.

I had not slept long, when I was awakened by Johansen, who said there was a bear outside. Even when only half awake, I heard a strange, low grunting just outside the doorway. I started up, seized my gun, and crept out. A she-bear, with two large cubs, was going up the shore; they had just passed close by our door. I aimed at the she-bear, but, in my haste, I missed her. She started and looked round; and as she turned her broad side to me I sent a bullet through her chest. She gave a fearful roar, and all three started off down the shore. There the mother dropped in a pool on the ice, but the young ones ran on, and rushed into the sea, dashing up the foam as they went, and began to swim out. I hastened down to the mother, who was striving and striving to get out of the pool, but in vain. To save ourselves the labour of dragging the heavy animal out, I waited until she had drawn herself up on to the edge, and then put an end to her existence. Meanwhile the young ones had reached a piece of ice. It was very close quarters for two, and only just large enough to hold them; but there they sat balancing and dipping up and down in the waves. Every now and then one of them fell off, but patiently clambered up again. They cried plaintively and incessantly, and kept looking towards land, unable to understand why their mother was so long in coming.

The wind was still high, and they drifted quickly out to sea before it with the current. We thought they would at last swim to land to look for their mother, and that we must wait; we, therefore, hid ourselves among the stones, so that they should not be afraid of coming on our account. We could still hear them complaining, but the sound became more and more distant, and they grew smaller and smaller out there on the blue waves, till at last it was all we could do to distinguish them as two white dots far out upon the dark plain. We had long been tired of this, and went to our kayaks. But here a sad sight met our eyes. All the walrus flesh which we had brought home with so much trouble lay scattered about on the shore, torn and mangled; and every bit of fat or blubber to be found on it had been devoured. The bears must have been rummaging finely here while we slept. One of the kayaks, in which the meat had been lying, was thrown half into the water, the other high up among the stones. The bears had been right into them, and dragged out the meat; but, fortunately, they were none the worse, so it was easy to forgive the bears, and we benefited by the exchange of bear's flesh for walrus flesh.

We then launched the kayaks, and put off to chase the young ones to land. As soon as ever they saw us on the water they became uneasy, and while we were still some way off one of them took to the water. The other hesitated for a while, as if afraid of the water, while the first waited impatiently; but at last they both went in. We made a wide circuit round them, and began to drive them towards the land, one of us on each side of them. It was easy to make them go in whatever direction we wanted, and Johansen could not say enough in praise of this simple method of getting bears from one place to another. We did not need to row hard to keep up with them; we went slowly and easily, but surely, towards land. We saw several walruses in the vicinity, but fortunately escaped being attacked by any of them. From the very first it was evident how much better the bear that first went into the water swam, although it was the smallest and thinnest. It waited, however, patiently for the other, and kept it company; but at last the pace of the latter became too slow for its companion, who struck out for the shore, the distance between the two growing greater and greater. They had kept incessantly turning their heads to look anxiously at us, and now the one that was left behind looked round even more helplessly than before. While I set off after the first bear, Johansen watched the second, and we drove them ashore by our den, and shot them there.

We had thus taken three bears on that day, and this was a good set-off against our walruses, which had drifted out to sea, and, what was no less fortunate, we found the sunken walrus from the day before floating just at the edge of the shore. We lost no time in towing it into a place of safety in a creek and making it fast. It made a difference to our winter store.

It was late before we turned in that night after having skinned the bears, laid them in a heap, and covered them with the skins to prevent the gulls from getting at them. We slept well, for we had to make up for two nights.

It was not until September 2nd that we could set to work on the skinning of our walrus, which still lay in the water. Close to our den there was an opening in the strand-ice,[119] connecting the inner channel between the strand-ice and the land with the outer sea. It was in this opening that we had made it fast, and we hoped to be able to draw it on land here; the glacier ice went with a gentle incline right out into the water, so that it seemed to promise well. We rounded off the edge of the ice, made a tackle by drawing the rope through a loop we cut in the skin of the head, used our broken-off runner of a sledge as a handspike at the end of the rope, and cut notches in the ice up the beach as a fulcrum for the handspike. But work and toil as we might it was all we could do to get the huge head up over the edge of the ice. In the midst of this Johansen cried: "I say, look there!" I turned. A large walrus was swimming straight up the channel towards us. It did not seem to be in any hurry, but only opened wide its round eyes, and gazed in astonishment at us and at what we were doing. I suppose that, seeing a comrade, it had come in to see what we were doing with him. Quietly, slowly, and with dignity, it came right up to the edge where we stood. Fortunately we had our guns with us, and when I approached with mine it only rose up in the water, and gazed long and searchingly at me. I waited patiently until it turned a little, and then sent a bullet into the back of its head. It was stunned for a time, but soon began to move, so that more shots were required. While Johansen ran for cartridges and a harpoon, I had to fight with it as I best could, and try to prevent it, with a stick, from splashing out of the channel again. At last Johansen returned, and I did for this walrus. We were delighted over our good fortune, but what the walrus wanted in that narrow channel we have always wondered. These animals must be uncommonly curious. While we were skinning the bears two days before, a walrus with its young one came close in to the edge of the ice and gazed at us; it dived several times, but always returned, and, at last, drew the whole of the fore part of its body up on to the ice, in order to see better. This it did several times, and my approaching to within a few yards of it did not drive it away; it was only when I went up close to it with my gun that it suddenly came to its senses, and threw itself backwards into the water again, and we could see it far below moving off with its young one by its side.

We now had two great walruses with enormous tusks, floating in our channel. We tried once more to drag one of them up, but the attempt was as unsuccessful as before. At last we saw that our only course was to skin them in the water, but this was neither an easy nor an agreeable task. When at last, late in the evening, we had got one side of one animal skinned, it was low water, the walrus lay on the bottom, and there was no possibility of turning it over, no matter how we toiled and pulled. We had to wait for high tide the following day, in order to get at the other side.

While we were busy with the walruses that day, we suddenly saw the whole fjord white with white whales, gambolling all round as far as the eye could see. There was an incredible number of them. In the course of an hour they had entirely disappeared. Where they came from and whither they went I was not able to discover.

During the succeeding days we toiled at our task of skinning and cutting up the walruses, and bringing all up into a safe place on the beach. It was disgusting work lying on the animals out in the water, and having to cut down as far as one could reach below the surface of the water. We could put up with getting wet, for one gets dry in time; but what was worse was that we could not avoid being saturated with blubber and oil and blood from head to foot, and our poor clothes that we should have to live in for another year before we could change, fared badly during those days. They so absorbed oil that it went right through to the skin. This walrus business was unquestionably the worst work of the whole expedition, and had it not been a sheer necessity, we should have let the animals lie where they were; but we needed fuel for the winter, even if we could have done without the meat. When at last the task was completed, and we had two great heaps of blubber and meat on shore, well covered by the thick walrus hides, we were not a little pleased.

During this time the gulls were living in luxury. There was abundance of refuse, blubber, entrails and other internal organs. They gathered in large flocks from all quarters, both ivory and glaucus gulls, and kept up a perpetual screaming and noise both night and day. When they had eaten as much as they could manage, they generally sat out on the ice-hummocks and chattered together. When we came down to skin, they withdrew only a very little way from the carcasses, and sat waiting patiently in long rows on the ice beside us, or, led on by a few bold officers, drew continually nearer. No sooner did a little scrap of blubber fall, than two or three ivory gulls would pounce upon it, often at our very feet, and fight over it until the feathers flew. Outside the fulmars were sailing in their silent, ghost-like flight to and fro over the surface of the water. Up and down the edge of the shore, flocks of kittiwakes moved incessantly, darting like an arrow, with a dull splash, towards the surface of the water, whenever a little crustacean appeared there. We were particularly fond of these birds, for they kept exclusively to the marine animals and left our blubber alone; and then they were so light and pretty. But up and down along the shore the skua (*stercorarius crepidata*) chased incessantly, and every now and again we were startled by a pitiful cry of distress above our heads; it was a kittiwake pursued by a skua. How often we followed with our eyes that wild chase up in the air, until at last the kittiwake had to drop its booty, and down shot the skua, catching it even before it touched the water! Happy creatures that can move with such freedom up there! Out in the water lay walruses, diving and bellowing, often whole herds of them; and high up in the air, to and fro, flew the little auks in swarms; you could hear the whirr of their wings far off. There were cries and life on all sides. But soon the sun will sink, the sea will close in, the birds will disappear one after another towards the south, the polar night will begin, and there will be profound, unbroken silence.

It was with pleasure that we, at last, on September 7th, set to work to build our hut. We had selected a good site in the neighbourhood, and from this time forward we might have been seen daily going out in the morning like other labourers, with a can of drinking-water in one hand and a gun in the other. We quarried stones up among the debris from the cliff, dragged them together, dug out the site, and built walls as well as we could. We had no tools worth mentioning; those we used most were our two hands. The cut-off sledge-runner again did duty as a pick, with which to loosen the fast-frozen stones, and when we could not manage to dig up the earth on our site with our hands we used a snowshoe staff with an iron ferrule. We made a spade out of the shoulder-blade of a walrus tied to a piece of a broken snowshoe-staff, and a mattock out of a walrus tusk tied to the cross-tree of a sledge. They were poor things to work with, but we managed it with patience, and little by little there arose solid walls of stone with moss and earth between. The weather was growing gradually colder, and hindered us not a little in our work. The soil we had to dig in hardened, and the stones that had to be quarried froze fast; and there came snow too. But great was our surprise when we crept out of our den on the morning of the 12th of September to find the most delightful thaw, with 4° C. of heat (39.2° Fahr.). This was almost the highest temperature we had experienced throughout the expedition. On every side streams were tumbling in foaming falls down from mountain and glacier, humming along merrily among the stones down to the sea. Water trickled and tinkled everywhere; as if by a stroke of magic, life had returned to frozen nature, and the hill looked green all over. One could fancy oneself far south, and forget that a long, long winter was drawing near. The day after, everything was changed again. The gentle gods of the south, who yesterday had put forth their last energies, had once more fled; the cold had returned, snow had fallen and covered every trace: it would not yield again. This little strip of bare ground, too, was in the power of the genii of the cold and darkness; they held sway now, right down to the sea. I stood looking out over it. How desolate and forsaken this spell-bound Nature looked! My eye fell upon the ground at my feet. Down there among the stones, the poppy still reared its beautiful blossoms above the snow; the last rays of the departing sun would once more kiss its yellow petals, and then it would creep beneath its covering to sleep through the long winter, and awake again to new life in the spring. Ah, to be able to do the same!

After a week's work, the walls of our hut were finished. They were not high, scarcely 3 feet above the ground; but we had dug down the same distance into the ground, so we reckoned that it would be high enough to stand up in. Now the thing was to get it roofed, but this was not so easy. The only materials we had towards it were, as before mentioned, the log we had found, and the walrus-hides. The log, which was quite 12 inches across, Johansen at last, after a day's work, succeeded in cutting in two with our little axe, and with no less labour, we rolled it up over the talus, and on to the level, and it was laid on the roof as the ridge-piece. Then there were the hides; but they were stiff and frozen fast to the meat and blubber heaps which they covered. With much difficulty he at length loosened them by using wedges of walrus tusks, stone, and wood. To transport these great skins over the long distance to our hut was a no less difficult matter. However, by rolling them, carrying them, and dragging them we accomplished this too; but to get the frozen skins stretched over the hut was the worst of all. We got on pretty well with three half-shins, just managing to bend them a little; but the fourth half was frozen quite stiff, and we had to find a hole in the ice, and sink it in the sea, to thaw it.

It was almost a cause for anxiety, I thought, that all this time we saw nothing of any bears. They were what we had to live upon all through the winter, and the six we had would not go far. I thought, however, that it might easily be accounted for, as the fjord-ice, to which the bear prefers to keep, had taken its departure on the day when we had nearly drifted out to sea with the walruses, and I thought that, when the ice now formed again, bears would appear once more. It was, therefore, a relief when one morning (September 23rd) I caught sight of a bear in front of me, just as I came round the promontory to look at the skin that we had in soak in the sea. It was standing on the shore close by the skin. It had not seen me, and I quickly drew back to let Johansen, who was following with his gun, pass me, while I ran back to fetch mine. When I returned, Johansen lay on the same spot behind a stone, and had not fired. There were two bears, one by the hut and one by the shore; and Johansen could not get up to the one without being seen by the other. When I had gone after my gun, the bear had turned its steps towards the hut; but just as it reached it, Johansen suddenly saw two bear's paws come quickly over the edge of

A herd of walruses.

the wall, and hit out at the first bear, and a head followed immediately after. This fellow was busy gnawing at our roof-hides, which he had torn down and bent, so that we had to put them into the sea too, to get them thawed. The first bear had to retreat to the shore once more, where we afterwards discovered it had drawn up our hide, and had been scraping the fat off it. Under cover of some hummocks we now ran towards it. It noticed us, and set off running, and I was only able to send a bullet through its body from behind. Shouting out to Johansen that he must look after the other bear, I set off running, and, after a couple of hours' pursuit up the fjord, I at last chased it up under the wall of a glacier, where it prepared to defend itself. I went right up to it, but it growled and hissed, and made one or two attacks on me from the elevation on which it stood, before I finally put an end to its existence. When I got back Johansen was busy skinning the other bear. It had been alarmed by us when we attacked the first, and had gone a long way out over the ice; it had then returned to look for its companion, and Johansen had shot it. Our winter store was increasing.

The next day (September 24th), as we were setting out to work at our hut, we saw a large herd of walruses lying out on the ice. We had both had more than enough of these animals, and had very little inclination for them. Johansen was of candid opinion that we had no need for them, and could let them lie in peace, but I thought it was rather improvident to have food and fuel lying at one's very door, and make no use of them, so we set off with our guns. To steal up to the animals, under cover of some elevations on the ice, was a matter of small difficulty, and we had soon come within 40 feet of them, and could lie there quietly and watch them. The point was to choose one's victim, and make good use of one's shot, so as not to waste cartridges. There were both old and young animals, and, having had more than enough of big ones, we decided to try for the two smallest that we could see; we thought we had no need of more than two. As we lay waiting for them to turn their heads, and give us the chance of a good shot, we had plenty of opportunity to watch them. They are strange animals. They lay incessantly poking one another in the back with their huge tusks, both the big old ones and the little young ones. If one of them turned over a little, so as to come near and disturb his neighbour, the latter immediately raised itself grunting and dug its tusks into the back of the first. It was by no means a gentle caress, and it is well for them that they have such a thick hide; but, as it was, the blood ran down the backs of several of them. The other would, perhaps, start up too, and return the little attention in the same manner. But it was when another guest came up from the sea that there was a stir in the camp; they all grunted in chorus, and one of the old bulls that lay nearest to the new arrival, gave him some well-meant blows. The newcomer, however, drew himself cautiously up, bowed respectfully, and little by little drew himself in among the others, who also then gave him as many blows as time and circumstances would permit, until they finally composed themselves again, and lay quiet until another interruption came. We waited in vain for the animals we had picked out to turn their heads enough to let us get a good shot; but as they were comparatively small, we thought that a bullet in the middle of the forehead might be enough for them, and at last we fired. They started up, however, and turned over half-stunned into the water. Then there was a commotion! The whole herd quickly raised their ugly heads, glared at us, and one by one plunged out over the edge of the ice. We had hastily loaded again, and as it was not difficult now to get a good shot, we fired, and there lay two animals, one young and one old. Most of the others dived, only one remaining quietly, lying and looking wonderingly, now at its two dead companions, and now at us as we came up to it. We did not quite know what to do; we thought that the two that were now lying there would give us more than enough to do, but nevertheless it was tempting to take this great monster as well, while we were about it. While Johansen was standing with his gun, considering whether he should fire or not, I took the opportunity of photographing both him and the walrus. It ended,

Johansen taking aim, 24 September.

however, in our letting it go unharmed; we did not think we could afford to sacrifice more cartridges upon it. Meantime the water beyond was seething with furious animals, as they broke up the ice round about and filled the air with their roaring. The big bull himself seemed especially anxious to get at us; he kept returning to the edge of the ice, getting half up on to it to grunt and bellow at us, and look long at his dead comrades, whom he evidently wished to take with him. But we would not waste more cartridges upon them, and he threw himself back, only to return again immediately. Gradually the whole herd departed, and we could hear the big bull's grunting becoming more and more distant; but suddenly his huge head appeared again at the edge of the ice, close to us, as he challenged us with a roar, and then disappeared again as quickly as he had come. This was repeated three or four times, after our having, in the intervals, heard him far out; but at last he disappeared entirely, and we continued our work of skinning in peace. We very quickly skinned the smaller of the walruses; it was easy to manipulate compared to those we were accustomed to. The other, however, was a great fellow that could not be easily turned over in the hollow in the snow where he lay; so we contented our-selves with skinning one side from head to tail, and then went home again with our blubber and skins. We now thought we should have blubber enough for winter fuel, and had also abundance of skins for covering the roof of our hut.

The walruses still kept near us for some time. Every now and then we would hear some violent blows on the ice from beneath, two or three in succession, and then a great head would burst up with a crash through the ice. It would remain there for a time panting and puffing so that it would be heard a long way off, and then vanish again. On September 25th, while we were pulling our roof-hides out of the water, at a hole near the shore, we heard the same crashing in the ice a little farther out, and a walrus came up and then dived again. "Look there! It won't be long before we have him in this hole." The words were scarcely spoken, when our hide in the water was pushed aside and a huge head, with bristles and two long tusks, popped up in front of us. It gazed fixedly and wickedly at us standing there, then there was a tremendous splash — and it was gone.

Our hides were now so far softened in the sea, that we could stretch them over the roof. They were so long that they reached from one side of the hut right over the ridge-piece down to the other side, and we stretched them by hanging large stones at both ends, attached by strips of hide, thus weighing them down over the edges of the wall, and we then piled stones upon them. By the aid of stones, moss, strips of hide, and snow to cover everything, we made the edges of the walls to some extent close-fitting. To make the hut habitable, we still had to construct benches of stone to lie upon inside it, and also a door. This consisted of an opening in one corner of the wall, which led into a short passage, dug out in the ground, and subsequently roofed over with blocks of ice on very much the same principle as the passage to an Eskimo's house. We had not dug this passage so long as we wished, before the ground was frozen too hard for our implements. It was so low that we had to creep through it in a squatting posture to get into the hut. The inner opening was covered with a bear-skin curtain, sewn firmly to the walrus-hide of the roof; the outer end was covered with a loose bear-skin laid over the opening. It began to grow cold now, as low as −20° C. (4° below zero Fahr.), and living in our low den, where we had not room to move, became more and more intolerable; the smoke, too, from the oil-lamp when we did any cooking, always affected our eyes. We grew daily more impatient to move into our new house, which now appeared to us the acme of comfort. Our ever-recurring remark while we were building was, how nice and snug it would be when we got in, and we depicted to one another the many pleasant hours we should spend there. We were, of course, anxious to discover all the bright points that we could in our existence. The hut was certainly not large; it was 10 feet long and 6 feet wide, and when you lay across it, you kicked the wall on one side, and butted it on the other. You could move in it a little, however, and even I could almost stand upright under the roof. This was a thought which especially appealed to us. Fancy having a place sheltered from the wind where you could stretch your limbs a little! We had not had that since last March on board the *Fram*. It was long, however, before everything was in order, and we would not move in until it was quite finished.

The day we had skinned our last walruses, I had taken several tendons from their backs, thinking they might be very useful when we made ourselves clothes for the winter, for we were entirely without thread for that purpose. Not until a few days afterwards (September 26th) did I recollect that these tendons had been left on the ice beside the carcasses. I went out there to look for them, but found to my sorrow that gulls and foxes had long since made away with them. It was some comfort, however, to find traces of a bear, which must have been at the carcasses during the night, and as I looked about I caught sight of Johansen running after me, making signs, and pointing out towards the sea. I turned that way and there was a large bear, walking to and fro, and looking at us. We had soon fetched our guns, and, while Johansen remained near the land to receive the bear if it came that way, I made a wide circuit round it on the ice to drive it landwards, if it should prove to be frightened. In the meantime, it had lain down out there beside some holes, I suppose to watch for seals. I stole up to it; it saw me and at first came nearer, but then thought better of it, and moved away again, slowly and majestically, out over the new ice. I had no great desire to follow it in that direction, and, though the range was long, I thought I must try it. First one shot it passed over. Then one more: that hit. The bear started, made several leaps, and then in anger struck the ice until it broke, and the bear fell through. There it lay splashing and splashing, and breaking the thin ice with its weight as it tried to get out again. I was soon beside it, but did not want to sacrifice another cartridge; I had faint hopes, too, that it would manage to get out of the water by itself, and thus save us the trouble of dragging such a heavy animal out. I called to Johansen to come with a rope, sledges, and knives, and in the meantime I walked up and down waiting and watching. The bear laboured hard, and made the opening in the ice larger and larger. It was wounded in one of its fore-legs, so that it could use only the other, and the two hind-legs. It kept on taking hold and pulling itself up. But no sooner had it got half up than the ice gave way, and it sank down again. By degrees its movements became more and more feeble, till at last it only lay still and panted. Then came a few spasms, its legs stiffened, its head sank down into the water, and all was still. While I was walking up and down I several times heard walruses round about, as they butted holes in the ice, and put their heads through; and I was thinking to myself that I should soon have them here too. At that moment the bear received a violent blow from beneath, pushing it to one side, and up came a huge head with great tusks; it snorted, looked contemptuously at the bear, then gazed for a while wonderingly at me, as I stood on the ice, and finally disappeared again. This had the effect of making me think the old solid ice, a little farther in, a pleasanter place of sojourn than the new ice. My suspicion that the walrus entertains no fear for the bear was more than ever strengthened. At last Johansen came with a rope. We slipped a running noose round the bear's neck, and tried to haul it out, but soon discovered that this was beyond our power; all we did was to break the ice under the animal, wherever we tried. It seemed hard to have to give it up; it was a big bear and seemed to be unusually fat; but to continue in this way until we had towed up to the edge of the thick ice would be a lengthy proceeding. By cutting quite a narrow crack in the new ice, only wide enough to draw the rope through, up to the edge of a large piece of ice which was quite near, we got pretty well out of the difficulty. It was now an easy matter to draw the bear thither under the ice, and after breaking a sufficiently large hole, we drew it out there. At last we had got it skinned and cut up, and, heavily laden with our booty, we turned our steps homewards, late in the evening, to our den. As we approached the beach where our kayaks were lying upon one of our heaps of walrus-blubber and meat, Johansen suddenly whispered to me: "I say, look there!" I looked up, and there stood three bears on the heaps, tearing at the blubber. They were a she-bear and two young ones. "Oh dear!" said I; "shall we have to set to at bears again." I was tired, and, to tell the truth, had far more desire for our sleeping-bag and a good potful of meat. In a trice we had got our guns out, and were approaching cautiously; but they had caught sight of us, and set off over the ice. It was with an undeniable feeling of gratitude that we watched their retreating forms. A little later, while I was standing cutting up the meat, and Johansen had gone to fetch water, I heard him whistle. I looked up, and he pointed out over the ice. There in the dusk were the three bears coming back; our blubber-heap had been too tempting for them. I crept with my gun behind some stones close to the heap. The bears came straight on, looking neither to right nor left, and as they passed me I took as good an aim at the she-bear as the darkness would allow, and fired. She roared, bit her side, and all three set off out over the ice. There the mother fell, and the young ones stood astonished and troubled beside her until we approached, when they fled, and it was impossible to get within range of them. They kept at a respectful distance, and watched us while we dragged the dead bear to land, and skinned it. When we went out next morning, they were standing sniffing at the skin and meat; but before we could get within range they saw us, and were off again. We now saw that they had been there all night, and had eaten up their own mother's stomach, which had contained some pieces of blubber. In the afternoon they returned once more; and again we attempted, but in vain, to get a shot at them. Next morning (Saturday, September 28th), when we crawled out, we caught sight of a large bear lying asleep on our blubber-heap. Johansen crept up close to it, under cover of some stones. The bear heard something moving, raised its head, and looked round. At the same instant Johansen fired, and the bullet went right through the bear's throat, just below the cranium. It got slowly up, looked contemptuously at Johansen, considered a little, and then walked quietly away with long measured steps as if nothing had happened. It soon had a couple of bullets from each of us in its body, and fell out on the thin ice. It was so full of food that, as it lay there, blubber and oil and water ran out of its mouth on to the ice, which began gradually to sink under its weight, until it lay in a large pool, and we hastily dragged it in to the shore, before the ice gave way beneath it. It was one of the largest bears I have ever seen, but also one of the leanest; for there was not a trace of fat upon it, neither underneath the skin, nor among the entrails. It must have been fasting for a long time, and been uncommonly hungry; for it had consumed an incredible quantity of our blubber. And how it had pulled it about! First it had thrown one kayak off, then it had scattered the blubber about in all directions, scraping off the best of the fat upon almost every single piece, then it had gathered the blubber together again in another place, and then, happy with the happiness of satiety, had lain down to sleep upon it, perhaps so as to have it handy when it woke up again. Previous to attacking the blubber-heap it had accomplished another piece of work, which we only discovered later on. It had killed both the young bears that had been visiting us; we found them not far off, with broken skulls, and frozen stiff. We could see by the foot-prints how it had run after them out over the new ice, first one and then the other, and had dragged them on land, and laid them down without touching them again. What pleasure it can have had in doing, this, I do not understand, but it must have regarded them as competitors in the struggle for food. Or was it, perhaps, a cross old gentleman, who did not like young people? "It is so nice and quiet here now," said the ogre, when he had cleared the country.

Our winter store now began quite to inspire confidence.

At length, on the evening of that day, we moved into our new hut; but our first night there was a cold one. Hitherto we had slept in one bag all the time, and even the one we had made by sewing together our two blankets had been fairly adequate. But now we thought it would not be necessary to sleep in one bag any longer, as we should make the hut so warm by burning train-oil lamps in it, that we could very well lie each in our own berth with a blanket over us, and so we had unpicked the bag. Lamps were made by turning up the corners of some sheets of German silver, filling them with crushed blubber, and laying in this, by way of a wick, some pieces of stuff from the bandages in the medicine-bag. They burned capitally, and gave such a good light, too, that we thought it looked very snug; but it neither was nor ever would be sufficient to warm our still rather permeable hut, and we lay and shivered with cold all night. We almost thought it was the coldest night we had had. Breakfast next morning tasted excellent, and the quantity of bear-broth we consumed in order to put a little warmth into our bodies is incredible. We at once decided to alter this by making along the back wall of the hut a sleeping-shelf broad enough for us to lie beside one another. The blankets were sewn together again, we spread bear-skins under us, and were as comfortable as we could be under the circumstances; and we made no further attempt to part company at night. It was impossible to make the substratum at all even, with the rough, angular stones which, now that everything was frozen, were all we had at our disposal, and therefore we lay tossing and twisting the whole winter to find something like a comfortable place among all the knobs. But it was hard, and remained so, and we always had some tender spots on our body, and even sores on our hips with lying. But for all that we slept. In one corner of the hut we made a little hearth to boil and roast upon. In the roof above we cut a round hole in the walrus-hide, and made a smoke-board up to it of bear-skin. We had not used this hearth long before we saw the necessity of building a chimney to prevent the wind from beating down, and so filling the hut with smoke, as to make it sometimes intolerable. The only materials we had for building this were ice and snow; but with these we erected a grand chimney on the roof, which served its purpose, and made a good draught. It was not quite permanent, however; the hole in it constantly widened with use, and it was not altogether guiltless of sometimes dripping down on to the hearth; but there was abundance of this building material, and it was not difficult to renew the chimney when it was in need of repair. This had to be done two or three times during the course of the winter. On more exposed spots we employed walrus-flesh, bone, and such-like materials to strengthen it.

Our cookery was as simple as possible. It consisted in boiling bear's flesh and soup (bouillon) in the morning, and frying steak in the evening. We consumed large quantities at every meal, and, strange to say, we never grew tired of this food, but always ate it with a ravenous appetite. We sometimes either ate blubber with it, or dipped the pieces of meat in a little oil. A long time might often pass when we ate almost nothing but meat, and scarcely tasted fat; but, when one of us felt inclined for it again, he would, perhaps, fish up some pieces of burnt blubber out of the lamps, or eat what was left of the blubber from which we had melted the lamp-oil. We called these cakes, and thought them uncommonly nice, and we were always talking of how delicious they would have been if we could have had a little sugar on them.

We still had some of the provisions we had brought from the *Fram*, but these we decided not to use during the winter. They were placed in a depot to be kept until the spring, when we should move on. The depot was well loaded with stones to prevent the foxes from running away with the bags. They were impudent enough already, and took all the movable property they could lay hold of. I discovered, for instance, on October 10th, that they had gone off with a quantity of odds and ends I had left in another depot during the erection of the hut; they had taken everything that they could possibly carry with them, such as pieces of bamboo, steel wire, harpoons and harpoon-lines, my collection of stones, mosses, etc., which were stored in small sail-cloth bags. Perhaps the worst of all was that they had gone off with a large ball of twine, which had been our hope and comfort when thinking of the time when we should want to make clothes, shoes, and sleeping-bags of bearskin for the winter; for we had reckoned on making thread out of the twine. It was fortunate that they had not gone off with the theodolite, and our other instruments which stood there; but these must have been too heavy for them. I was angry when I made this discovery, and what made it more aggravating, it happened on my birthday. And matters did not improve, when, while hunting about in the twilight on the beach above the place where the things had been lying, to see if I could at any rate discover tracks to show which way those demons had taken them, I met a fox that stopped at a distance of 20 feet from me, sat down, and uttered some exasperating howls so piercing and weird, that I had to stop my ears. It was evidently on its way to my things again, and was now provoked at being disturbed. I got hold of some large stones and flung them at it. It ran off a little way, but then seated itself upon the edge of the glacier and howled on, while I went home to the hut in a rage, lay down and speculated as to what we should do to be revenged on the obnoxious animals. We could not spare cartridges to shoot them with, but we might make a trap of stones. This we determined to do, but nothing ever came of it; there were always so many other things to occupy us at first, while we still had the opportunity, before the snow covered the talus, and while it was light enough to find suitable stones. Meanwhile the foxes continued to annoy us. One day they had taken our thermometer,[120] which we always kept outside the hut, and gone off with it. We searched for it in vain for a long time, until at last we found it buried in a heap of snow a little way off. From that time we were very careful to place a stone over it at night, but one morning found that the foxes had turned over the stone, and had gone off with the thermometer again. The only thing we found this time was the case, which they had thrown away a little way off. The thermometer itself we were never to see again; the snow had unfortunately drifted in the night, so that the tracks had disappeared. Goodness only knows what fox-hole it now adorns; but from that day we learned a lesson, and henceforward fastened our last thermometer securely.

Meanwhile time passed. The sun sank lower and lower, until on the 15th October we saw it for the last time above the ridge to the south; the days grew rapidly darker, and then began our third polar night.

We shot two more bears in the autumn, one on the 8th and one on the 21st October; but from that time we saw no more until the following spring. When I awoke on the morning of the 8th October, I heard the crunching of heavy steps in the snow outside, and then began a rummaging about among our meat and blubber up on the roof. I could hear it was a bear, and crept out with my gun, but when I came out of the passage, I could see nothing in the moonlight. The animal had noticed me, and had already disappeared. We did not altogether regret this, as we had no great desire to set to at the cold task of skinning now, in a wind, and with 39° (70.2° Fahr.) of frost.

There was not much variety in our life. It consisted in cooking and eating breakfast in the morning. Then, perhaps, came another nap, after which we would go out to get a little exercise. Of this, however, we took no more than was necessary, as our clothes, saturated as they were with fat, and worn and torn in many places, were not exactly adapted for remaining in the open air in winter. Our wind-clothes, which we should have had outside as a protection against the wind, were so worn and torn that we could not use them; and we had so little thread to patch them with, that I did not think we ought to use any of it until the spring, when we had to prepare for our start. I had counted on being able to make ourselves clothes of bear-skins, but it took time to cleanse them from all blubber and fat, and it was even a slower business getting them dried. The only way to do this was to spread them out under the roof of the hut, but there was room for only one at a time. When at last one was ready, we had first of all to use it on our bed, for we were lying on raw, greasy skins, which were gradually rotting. When our bed had been put in order with dried skins, we had to think about making a sleeping-bag, as, after a time, the blanket-bag that we had got rather cold to sleep in. About Christmas time, accordingly, we at last managed to make ourselves a bear-skin bag. In this way all the skins we could prepare were used up, and we continued to wear the clothes we had throughout the winter.

These walks, too, were a doubtful pleasure, because there is always a wind there, and it blew hard under the steep cliff. We felt it a wonderful relief when it occasionally happened to be almost calm. As a rule the wind howled above us, and lashed the snow along, so that everything was wrapped in mist. Many days would sometimes pass almost without our putting our heads out of the passage, and it was only bare necessity that drove us out to fetch ice for drinking-water, or a leg or carcass of a bear for food, or some blubber for fuel. As a rule we also brought in some sea-water ice, or, if there were an opening or a crack to be found, a little sea-water for our soup.

When we came in, and had mustered up appetite for another meal, we had to prepare supper, eat till we were satisfied, and then get into our bag and sleep as long as possible, to pass the time. On the whole we had quite a comfortable time in our hut. By means of our train-oil lamps we could keep the temperature in the middle of the room at about freezing point. Near the wall, however, it was considerably colder, and there the damp deposited itself in the shape of beautiful hoar-frost crystals, so that the stones were quite white, and in happy moments we could dream that we dwelt in marble halls. This splendour, however, had its disadvantages, for when the outside temperature rose, or when we heated up the hut a little, rivulets ran down the wall into our sleeping-bag. We took turns at being cook, and Tuesday, when one ended his cooking-week, and the other began, afforded on that account the one variation in our lives, and formed a boundary-mark by which we divided out our time. We always reckoned up how many cooking-weeks we had before we should break up our camp in the spring. I had hoped to get so much done this winter, work up my observations and notes, and write some of the account of our journey; but very little was done. It was not only the poor, flickering light of the oil-lamp which hindered me, nor yet the uncomfortable position, either lying on one's back, or sitting up and fidgeting about on the hard stones, while the part of the body thus exposed to pressure ached; but altogether these surroundings did not predispose one to work. The brain worked dully, and I never felt inclined to write anything. Perhaps, too, this was owing to the impossibility of keeping what you wrote upon clean; if you only took hold of a piece of paper your fingers left a dark brown, greasy mark, and if a corner of your clothes brushed across it, a dark streak appeared. Our journals of this period look dreadful. They are "black books" in the literal sense of the term. Ah! how we longed for the time when we should once more be able to write on clean white paper and with black ink. I often had difficulty in reading the pencil notes I had written the day before, and now, in writing this book, it is all I can do to find out what was once written on these dirty, dark brown pages. I expose them to all possible lights, I examine them with a magnifying glass; but notwithstanding, I often have to give it up.

The entries in my journal for this time are exceedingly meagre; there are sometimes weeks when there is nothing but the most necessary meteorological observations with remarks. The chief reason for this is that our life was so monotonous that there was nothing to write about. The same thoughts came and went day after day; there was no more variety in them than in our conversation. The very emptiness of the journal really gives the best representation of our life during the nine months we lived there.

"Wednesday, November 27th. −23° C. (9.4° below zero Fahr.). It is windy weather, the snow whirling about your ears, directly you put your head out of the passage. Everything is grey; the black stones can be made out in the snow a little way up the beach, and above you can just divine the presence of the dark cliff; but wherever else the gaze is turned, out to sea, or up the fjord, there is the same leaden darkness, one is shut out from the wide world, shut into oneself. The wind comes in sharp gusts, driving the snow before it; but up under the crest of the mountain it whistles and roars in the crevices and holes of the basaltic walls — the same never-ending song that it has sung through the thousands of years that are past, and will go on singing through thousands of years to come. And the snow whirls along in its age-old dance; it spreads itself in all the crevices and hollows, but it does not succeed in covering up the stones on the beach; black as ever, they project into the night. On the open space in front of the hut, two figures are running up and down like shadows in the winter darkness to keep themselves warm, and so they will run up and down on the path they have trampled out, day after day, till the spring comes."

"Sunday, December 1st. Wonderfully beautiful weather for the last few days; one can never weary of going up and down outside, while the moon transforms the whole of this ice world into a fairy-land. The hut is still in shadow under the mountain which hangs above it, dark and lowering; but the moonlight floats over ice and fjord, and is cast back glittering from every snowy ridge and hill. A weird beauty, without feeling, as though of a dead planet, built of shining white marble, just so must the mountains stand there, frozen and icy cold; just so must the lakes lie congealed beneath their snowy covering; and now as ever the moon sails silently and slowly on her endless course through the lifeless space. And everything so still, so awfully still, with the silence that shall one day reign, when the earth again becomes desolate and empty, when the fox will no more haunt these moraines, when the bear will no longer wander about on the ice out there, when even the wind will not rage — infinite silence! In the flaming aurora borealis, the spirit of space hovers over the frozen waters. The soul bows down before the majesty of night and death."

"Monday, December 2nd. Morning. To-day I can hear it blowing again outside, and we shall have an unpleasant walk. It is bitterly cold now in our worn, greasy clothes. It is not so bad when there is no wind; but even if there is only a little, it goes right through one. But what does it matter? Will not the spring one day come here, too? Yes; and over us arches the same heaven now as always, high and calm as ever; and as we walk up and down here shivering, we gaze into the boundless starry space, and all our privations and sorrows shrink into nothingness. Starlit night, thou art sublimely beautiful, but dost thou not lend our spirit too mighty wings, greater than we can control? Could'st thou but solve the riddle of existence! We feel ourselves the centre of the universe, and struggle for life, for immortality, one seeking it here, another hereafter; while thy silent splendour proclaims: at the command of the Eternal, you came into existence on a paltry planet, as diminutive links in the endless chain of transformations; at another command, you will be wiped out again. Who then, through an eternity of eternities, will remember that there once was an ephemeral being who could bind sound and light in chains, and who was purblind enough to spend years of his brief existence in drifting through frozen seas? Is, then, the whole thing but the meteor of a moment? Will the whole history of the world evaporate like a dark, gold-edged cloud in the glow of evening — achieving nothing, leaving no trace, passing like a caprice?

"Evening. That fox is playing us a great many tricks, whatever he can move he goes off with. He has once gnawed off the band with which the door-skin is fastened, and every now and then we hear him at it again, and have to go out and knock on the roof of the passage. To-day he went off with one of our sails, in which our salt-water ice was lying. We were not a little alarmed, when we went to fetch ice, and found sail and all gone. We had no doubt as to who had been there, but we could not under any circumstances afford to lose our precious sail on which we depended for our voyage to Spitzbergen in the spring, and we tramped about in the dark, up the beach, over the level, and down towards the sea. We looked everywhere, but nothing was to be seen of it. At last we had almost given it up, when Johansen, in going on to the ice to get more salt-water ice, found it at the edge of the shore. Our joy was great; but it was wonderful that the fox had been able to drag that great sail, full of ice too, so far. Down there, however, it had come unfolded, and then he could do nothing with it. But what does he want with things like this? Is it to lie upon in his winter den? One would almost think so. I only wish I could come upon that den, and find the thermometer again, and the ball of twine, and the harpoon line, and all the other precious things he has taken, the brute!"

"Thursday, December 5th. It seems as if it would never end. But patience a little longer, and spring will come, the fairest spring that earth can give us. There is furious weather outside, and snow, and it is pleasant to lie here in our warm hut, eating steak, and listening to the wind raging over us."

"Tuesday, December 10th. It has been a bad wind. Johansen discovered to-day that his kayak had disappeared. After some search he found it again several hundred feet off, up the beach; it was a good deal knocked about, too. The wind must first have lifted it right over my kayak, and then over one big stone after another. It begins to be too much of a good thing when even the kayaks take to flying about in the air. The atmosphere is dark out over the sea, so the wind has probably broken up the ice, and driven it out, and there is open water once more.[121]

"Last night it all at once grew wonderfully calm, and the air was surprisingly mild. It was delightful to be out, and it is long since we have had such a long walk on our beat. It does one good to stretch one's legs now and then, otherwise I suppose we should become quite stiff here in our winter lair. Fancy, only 12° (21½° F.) of frost in the middle of December! We might almost imagine ourselves at home — forget that we were in a land of snow to the north of the eighty-first parallel."

"Thursday, December 12th. Between 6 and 9 this morning there were a number of shooting stars, most of them in Serpentarius. Some came right from the Great Bear; afterwards they chiefly came from the Bull, or Aldebaran, or the Pleiades. Several of them were very bright, and some drew a streak of shining dust after them. Lovely weather. But night and day are now equally dark. We walk up and down, up and down, on the level, in the darkness. Heaven only knows how many steps we shall take on that level before the winter ends. Through the gloom we could see faintly only the black cliffs, and the rocky ridges, and the great stones on the beach, which the wind always sweeps clean. Above us the sky, clear and brilliant with stars, sheds its peace over the earth; far in the west falls shower after shower of stars, some faint, scarcely visible, others bright like Roman candles, all with a message from distant worlds. Low in the south lies a bank of clouds, now and again outlined by the gleam of the northern lights; but out over the sea the sky is dark; there is open water there. It is quite pleasant to look at it; one does not feel so shut in; it is like a connecting link with life that dark sea, the mighty artery of the world, which carries tidings from land to land, from people to people, on which civilisation is borne victorious through the earth; next summer it will carry us home."

Thursday, December 19th. —28.5° (19.3° below zero Fahr.). It has turned cold again, and is bitter weather to be out in. But what does it signify? We are comfortable and warm in here, and do not need to go out more than we like. All the out-of-door work we have is to bring in fresh and salt water ice two or three times a week, meat and blubber now and again, and very occasionally a skin to dry under the roof. And Christmas, the season of rejoicing, is drawing near. At home every one is busy now, scarcely knowing how to get time for everything; but here there is no bustle; all we want is to make the time pass. Ah, to sleep, sleep! The pot is simmering pleasantly over the hearth; I am sitting waiting for breakfast, and gazing into the flickering flames, while my thoughts travel far away. What is the strange power in fire and light that all created beings seek them, from the primary lump of protoplasm in the sea, to the roving child of man, who stops in his wanderings, makes up a fire in the wood, and sits down to dismiss all care, and revel in the crackling warmth. Involuntarily do these snake-like, fiery tongues arrest the eye; you gaze down into them as if you could read your fate there, and memories glide past in motley train. What, then, is privation? what the present? Forget it, forget yourself; you have the power to recall all that is beautiful, and then wait for the summer... By the light of the lamp she sits sewing in the winter evening. Beside her stands a little maiden with blue eyes and golden hair, playing with a doll. She looks tenderly at the child, and strokes her hair; but her eyes fill, and the big tears fall upon her work.

"Johansen is lying beside me asleep; he smiles in his sleep. Poor fellow! he must be dreaming he is at home at Christmas time with those he loves. But sleep on, sleep and dream, while the winter passes; for then comes spring — the spring of life."

"Sunday, December 22nd. Walked about outside for a long time yesterday evening, while Johansen was having a thorough cleaning in the hut, in preparation for Christmas. This consisted chiefly in scraping the ashes out of the hearth, gathering up the refuse of bone and meat, and throwing it away, and then breaking up the ice, which has frozen together with all kinds of rubbish and refuse, into a thick layer upon the floor, making the hut rather low in the roof.

"The northern lights were wonderful. However often we see this weird play of light, we never tire of gazing at it; it seems to cast a spell over both sight and sense till it is impossible to tear oneself away. It begins to dawn with a pale, yellow, spectral light behind the mountain in the east, like the reflection of a fire far away. It broadens, and soon the whole of the eastern sky is one glowing mass of fire. Now it fades again, and gathers in a brightly luminous belt of mist stretching towards the south-west, with only a few patches of luminous haze visible here and there. After a while, scattered rays suddenly shoot up from the fiery mist, almost reaching to the zenith;

then more; they play over the belt in a wild chase from east to west. They seem to be always darting nearer from a long, long way off. But suddenly a perfect veil of rays showers from the zenith out over the northern sky; they are so fine and bright, like the finest of glittering silver threads. Is it the fire-giant Surt himself, striking his mighty silver harp, so that the strings tremble and sparkle in the glow of the flames of Muspelheim? Yes, it is harp music, wildly storming in the darkness; it is the riotous war-dance of Surt's sons. And again, at times, it is like softly playing, gently-rocking, silvery waves, on which dreams travel into unknown worlds.

"The winter solstice has come, and the sun is at its lowest; but still, at midday we can just see a faint glimmer of it over the ridges in the south. Now it is again beginning to mount northwards; day by day it will grow lighter and lighter, and the time will pass rapidly. Oh, how well I can now understand our fore-fathers' old custom of holding an uproarious sacrificial banquet in the middle of winter, when the power of the winter darkness was broken. We would hold an uproarious feast here, if we had anything to feast with; but we have nothing. What need is there either? We shall hold our silent festival in the spirit, and think of the spring.

"In my walk I look at Jupiter over there above the crest of the mountain — Jupiter, the planet of the home; it seems to smile at us, and I recognise my good attendant spirit. Am I superstitious? This life and this scenery might well make one so; and, in fact, is not every one superstitious, each in his own way? Have not I a firm belief in my star, and that we shall meet again? It has scarcely forsaken me for a day. Death, I believe, can never approach before one's mission is accomplished, never comes without one feeling its proximity; and yet a cold fate may one day cut the thread without warning."

"Tuesday, December 24th. At 2 p.m. to-day −24° C. (11.2° below zero Fahr.). And this is Christmas Eve, cold and windy out of doors, and cold and draughty indoors. How desolate it is! Never before have we had such a Christmas Eve.

"At home the bells are now ringing Christmas in. I can hear their sound as it swings through the air from the church tower. How beautiful it is!

"Now the candles are being lighted on the Christmas-trees, the children are let in and dance round in joyous delight. I must have a Christmas party for children when I get home. This is the time of rejoicing, and there is feasting in every cottage at home. And we are keeping the festival in our little way. Johansen has turned his shirt, and put the outside shirt next to him; I have done the same, and then I have changed my drawers, and put on the others that I had wrung out in warm water. And I have washed myself, too, in a quarter of a cup of warm water, with the discarded drawers as sponge and towel. Now I feel quite another being; my clothes

The winter cabin, photographed in moonlight on New Year's Eve 1895.

do not stick to my body as much as they did. Then for supper we had 'fiskegratin,' made of powdered fish and maize-meal, with train-oil to it instead of butter, both fried and boiled (one as dry as the other), and for dessert we had bread fried in train-oil. To-morrow morning we are going to have chocolate and bread.[122]

"Wednesday, December 25th. We have got lovely Christmas weather, hardly any wind, and such bright, beautiful moonlight. It gives one quite a solemn feeling. It is the peace of thousands of years. In the afternoon the northern lights were exceptionally beautiful. When I came out at six o'clock there was a bright, pale yellow bow in the southern sky. It remained for a long time almost unchanged, and then began to grow much brighter at the upper margin of the bow behind the mountain crests in the east. It smouldered for some time, and then all at once light darted out westwards along the bow; streamers shot up all along it towards the zenith, and in an instant the whole of the southern sky from the arc to the zenith was aflame. It flickered and blazed, it whirled round like a whirlwind (moving with the sun), rays darted backwards and forwards, now red and reddish-violet, now yellow, green, and dazzling white; now the rays were red at the bottom, and yellow and green farther up, and then again this order was inverted. Higher and higher it rose; now it came on the north side of the zenith too, for a moment there was a splendid corona, and then it all became one whirling mass of fire up there; it was like a whirlpool of fire in red, yellow, and green, and the eye was dazzled with looking at it. It then drew across to the northern sky, where it remained a long time, but not in such brilliancy. The arc from which it had sprung in the south was still visible, but soon disappeared. The movement of the rays was chiefly from west to east, but sometimes the reverse. It afterwards flared up brightly several times in the northern sky; I counted as many as six parallel bands at one time, but they did not attain to the brightness of the former ones.

"And this is Christmas Day. There are family dinners going on at home. I can see the dignified old father standing smiling and happy in the doorway to welcome children and grandchildren. Out-of-doors the snow is falling softly and silently in big flakes, the young folk come rushing in fresh and rosy, stamp the snow off their feet in the passage, shake their things and hang them up, and then enter the drawing-room, where the fire is crackling comfortably and cosily in the stove; and they can see the snowflakes falling outside, and covering the Christmas corn-sheaf. A delicious smell of roasting comes from the kitchen, and in the dining-room the long table is laid for a good, old-fashioned dinner with good old wine. How nice and comfortable everything is! One might fall ill with longing to be home. But wait, wait, when summer comes...

"Oh, the road to the stars is both long and difficult."

"Tuesday, December 31st. And this year too is vanishing. It has been strange, but after all it has perhaps not been so bad.

"They are ringing out the old year now at home. Our church-bell is the icy wind howling over glacier and snowfield, howling fiercely as it whirls the drifting snow on high in cloud after cloud, and sweeps it down upon us from the crest of the mountain up yonder. Far in up the fjord you can see the clouds of snow chasing one another over the ice in front of the gusts of wind, and the snow-dust glittering in the moonlight. And the full moon sails silent and still out of one year into another. She shines alike upon the good and the evil, nor does she notice the wants and yearnings of the new year. Solitary, forsaken, hundreds of miles from all that one holds dear; but the thoughts flit restlessly to and fro on their silent paths. Once more a leaf is turned in the book of eternity, a new blank page is opened, and no one knows what will be written on it."

find an endurable position among the rough stones. However, time crawls on, and now little Liv's birthday has come. She is three years old to-day, and must be a big girl now. Poor little thing! You don't miss your father now; and next birthday I shall be with you, I hope. What good friends we shall be! You shall ride-a-cock-horse, and I will tell you stories from the north about bears, foxes, walruses, and all the strange animals up there in the ice. No, I can't bear to think of it."

"Saturday, February 1st. Here I am down with rheumatism. Outside it is growing gradually lighter day by day, the sky above the glaciers in the south grows redder, until at last one day the sun will rise above the crest, and our last winter night be past. Spring is coming! I have often thought spring sad. Was it because it vanished so quickly, because it carried promises that summer never fulfilled? But there is no sadness in this spring; its promises will be kept; it would be too cruel if they were not."

It was a strange existence, lying thus in a hut underground the whole winter through, without a thing to turn one's hand to. How we longed for a book! How delightful our life on board the *Fram* appeared, when we had the whole library to fall back upon. We would often tell each other how beautiful this sort of life would have been after all, if we had only had anything to read. Johansen always spoke with a sigh of Het'se's novels; he had specially liked those on board, and he had not been able to finish the last one he was reading. The little readable matter which was to be found in our navigation-table and almanack I had read so many times already that I knew it almost by heart — all about the Norwegian royal family, all about persons apparently drowned, and all about self-help for fishermen. Yet it as always a comfort to see these books; the sight of the printed letters gave one a feeling that there was after all a little bit of the civilised man left. All that we really had to talk about had long ago been thoroughly thrashed out, and, indeed, there were not many thoughts of common interest that we had not exchanged. The chief pleasure left to us was to picture to each other how we should make up next winter at home for everything we had missed during our sojourn here. We felt that we should have learnt for good and all to set store by all the good things of life, such as food, drink, clothes, shoes, house, home, good neighbours, and all the rest of it. Frequently we occupied ourselves, too, in calculating how far the *Fram* could have drifted, and whether there was any possibility of her getting home to Norway before us. It seemed a safe assumption that she might drift out into the sea between Spitzbergen and Greenland next summer or autumn, and probability seemed to point to her being in Norway in August or September. But there was just the possibility that she might arrive earlier in the summer; or, on the other hand, we might not reach home until later in the autumn. This was the great question to which we could give no certain answer, and we reflected with sorrow, that she might perhaps get home first. What would our friends then think about us? Scarcely anyone would have the least hope of seeing us again, not even our comrades on board the *Fram*. It seemed to us, however, that this could scarcely happen; we could not but reach home in July, and it was hardly to be expected that the *Fram* could be free from the ice so early in the summer.

But where were we? And how great was the distance we had to travel? Over and over again I calculated through our observations of the autumn and summer and spring, but the whole matter was a perpetual puzzle. It seemed clear, indeed, that we must be lying somewhere far to the west, perhaps off the west coast of Franz Josef Land, a little north of Cape Lofley, as I had conjectured in the autumn. But, if that were so, what could the lands be which we had seen to the northward? And what was the land to which we had first come? From the first group of islands, which I had called White Land (Hvidtenland), to where we now lie, we had passed about 7° of longitude — that our observations proved conclusively. But if we were now in the longitude of Cape Fligely, these islands must lie on a meridian so far east that it would fall between King Oscar's Land and Crown Prince Rudolf Land; and yet we had been much further east and had seen nothing of these lands. How was this to be explained? And furthermore, the land we saw had disappeared to the southward; and we saw no indication of islands further east. No, we could not have been near any known land; we must be upon some island lying further west, in the strait between Franz Josef Land and Spitzbergen; and we could not but think of the hitherto so enigmatic Gillies Land. But this, too, seemed difficult to explain; for it was hard to understand how, in this comparatively narrow strait, such an extensive mass of land as this could find room without coming so near the North-East Land of Spitzbergen that it could easily be seen from it. No other conclusion, however, seemed at all plausible. We had long ago given up the idea that our watches could be even approximately right; for in that case, as already mentioned, we must have come right across Payer's Wilczek Land and Dove Glacier without having noticed them. This theory was consequently excluded. There were other things, too, that greatly puzzled me. If we were on a new land, near Spitzbergen, why were the rose gulls never seen there, while we had found them in flocks here to the north? And then there was the great variation of the compass. Unfortunately I had no chart of the variations with me, and I could not remember where the zero meridian of variation lay — the boundary line between easterly and westerly variation. I thought, however, that it lay somewhere near the North-East Land; and here we had still a variation of about 20°. The whole thing was and remained an insoluble riddle.

As the daylight began to lengthen later in the spring, I made a discovery which had the effect of still more hopelessly bewildering us. At two points on the horizon about W.S.W., I fancied that I could see land looming in the air. The appearance recurred again and again, and at last I was quite certain that it really was land; but it must be very far away; at least 69 miles, I thought.[124] If it had been difficult to find room between Franz Josef Land and North-East Land for the islands we had hitherto seen, it was more difficult still to find room for these new ones. Could it be the North-East Land itself? This seemed scarcely credible. This land must lie in about 81° or so northward, while the North-East Land does not reach much north of 80°. But at least these islands must be pretty near North-East Land, and if we once reached them, we could not have much farther to go, and would perhaps find open water all the way to the Tromsö sloop, on which our fancy had now dwelt for over a year, and which was to take us home.

The thought of all the good things we should find on board that sloop was what comforted us whenever the time hung unendurably heavy on our hands. Our life was not, indeed, altogether luxurious. How we longed for a change in the uniformity of our diet. If only we could have had a little sugar and farinaceous food, in addition to all the excellent meat we had, we could have lived like princes. Our thoughts dwelt longingly on great platters full of cakes, not to mention bread and potatoes. How we would make up for lost time when we got back; and we would begin as soon as we got on board that Tromsö sloop. Would they have potatoes on board? Would they have fresh bread? At worst, even hard ship's bread would not be so bad, especially if we could get it fried in sugar and butter. But better even than food would be the clean clothes we could put on. And then books — only to think of books! The clothes we lived in were horrible! and when we wanted to enjoy a really delightful hour we would set to work imagining a great, bright, clean shop, where the walls were hung with nothing but new, clean, soft woollen clothes, from which we could pick out everything we wanted. Only to think of shirts, vests, drawers, soft and warm woollen trousers, deliciously comfortable jerseys, and then clean woollen stockings and warm felt slippers — could anything more delightful be imagined? And then a Turkish bath! We would sit up side by side in our sleeping-bag for hours at a time, and talk of all these things. They seemed almost unimaginable. Fancy being able to throw away all the heavy, oily rags we had to live in, glued as they were to our bodies. Our legs suffered most; for there our trousers stuck fast to our knees, so that when we moved they abraded and tore the skin inside our thighs till it was all raw and bleeding. I had the greatest difficulty in keeping these sores from becoming altogether too ingrained with fat and dirt, and had to be perpetually washing them with moss, or a rag from one of the bandages in our medicine-bag, and a little water, which I warmed in a cup over the lamp. I have never before understood what a magnificent invention soap really is. We made all sorts of attempts to wash the worst of the dirt away; but they were all equally unsuccessful. Water had no effect upon all this grease; it was better to scour oneself with moss and sand. We could find plenty of sand in the walls of the hut, when we hacked the ice off them. The best method, however, was to get our hands thoroughly lubricated with warm bears' blood and train-oil, and then scrub it off again with moss. They thus became as white and soft as the hands of the most delicate lady, and we could scarcely believe that they belonged to our own bodies. When there was none of this toilet preparation to be had, we found the next best plan was to scrape our skin with a knife.

If it was difficult to get our own bodies clean, it was a sheer impossibility as regards our clothes. We tried all possible ways; we washed them both in Eskimo fashion and in our own; but neither was of much avail. We boiled our shirts in the pot hour after hour, but took them out only to find them just as full of grease as when we put them in. Then we took to wringing the train-oil out of them. This was a little better; but the only thing that produced any real effect was to boil them, and then scrape them with a knife while they were still warm. By holding them in our teeth and our left hand and stretching them out, while we scraped them all over with the right hand, we managed to get amazing quantities of fat out of them; and we could almost have believed that they were quite clean when we put them on again after they were dry. The fat which we scraped off was, of course, a welcome addition to our fuel.

In the meanwhile our hair and beard grew entirely wild. It is true we had scissors and could have cut them; but as our supply of clothes was by no means too lavish, we thought it kept us a little warmer to have all this hair, which began to flow down over our shoulders. But it was coal-black like our faces, and we thought our teeth and the whites of our eyes shone with an uncanny whiteness now that we could see each other again in the daylight of the spring. On the whole, however, we were so accustomed to each other's appearance that we really found nothing remarkable about it, and not until we fell in with other people and found that they were not precisely of that opinion, did we begin to recognise that our outer man was, perhaps, open to criticism.

It was a strange life, and in many ways it put our patience to a severe test; but it was not so unendurable as one might suppose. We, at any rate, thought that, all things considered, we were fairly well off. Our spirits were good the whole time; we looked serenely towards the future, and rejoiced in the thought of all the delights it had in store for us. We did not even have recourse to quarrelling to while away the time. After our return, Johansen was once asked how we two had got on during the winter, and whether we had managed not to fall out with each other; for it is said to be a severe test for two men to live so long together in perfect isolation. "Oh, no," he answered, "we didn't quarrel; the only thing was that I have the bad habit of snoring in my sleep, and then Nansen used to kick me in the back." I cannot deny that this is the case; I gave him many a well-meant kick, but fortunately he only shook himself a little and slept calmly on.

Thus did our time pass. We did our best to sleep away as much as possible of it. We carried this art to a high pitch of perfection, and could sometimes put in as much as 20 hours' sleep in 24. If anyone still holds to the old superstition that scurvy is due to lack of exercise, he may look upon us as living evidences to the contrary; for all the time our health was excellent. As the light now began to return with the spring, however, we were more inclined to go out. Besides, it was not always so cold now, and we had to restrict our sleep a little. Then, too, the time for our departure was approaching, and we had plenty to occupy us in the way of preparation and so forth.

"Tuesday, February 25th. Lovely weather to be out in to-day; it is as though spring were beginning. We have seen the first birds, first a flock of half a score of little auks (*mergulus alle*), then a flock of four; they came from the south along the land, evidently through the sound in the south-east, and disappeared behind the mountain crest to the north-west of us. Once more we heard their cheerful twittering, and it roused a responsive echo in the soul. A little later we heard it again, and then it seemed as if they were perched on the mountain above us. It was the first greeting from life. Blessed birds, how welcome you are! "It was quite like a spring evening at home; the sun's red glow faded little by little into golden clouds, and the moon rose. I went up and down outside, and dreamt I was in Norway on a spring evening."

"Wednesday, February 26th. To-day we ought to have had the sun again, but the sky was cloudy."

"Friday, February 28th. I have discovered that it is possible to get twelve threads out of a bit of twine, and am as happy as a king. We have thread enough now, and our wind-clothes shall be whole once more. It is possible, too, to ravel out the canvas in the bags, and use it for thread."

"Saturday, February 29th. The sun high above the glacier to-day. We must begin to economise in train-oil in earnest now if we are to get away from here, or there will be too little blubber for the journey."

"Wednesday, March 4th. When Johansen went out this morning, the mountain above us was covered with little auks, which flew twittering from crest to crest, and sat all over the glacier. When we went out again later on, they were gone."

"Friday, March 6th. We are faring badly now. We have to sleep in the dark to save oil, and can only cook once a day."

"Sunday, March 8th. Shot a bear. Johansen saw ten flocks of little auks flying up the sound this morning.

"Tuesday, March 10th. That bear the day before yesterday came in the nick of time, and an amusing fellow he was too. We were very badly off both for blubber and meat, but most for blubber, and we were longing for a bear; we thought it must be about time for them to come again now. I had just spent Sunday morning in mending my wind-trousers and patching my 'komager' so as to be all ready if a bear should come. Johansen, whose cooking week it was, had been sewing a little too, and was just cleaning up the hut for Sunday, and taking out some bone and meat: he had taken it as far as the passage. But no sooner had he raised the skin over the opening out there, than I heard him come tumbling head foremost in again over the bone heap and say: 'There's a bear standing just outside the door.' He snatched his gun down from where it hung, under the roof, and again put his head into the passage, but drew it quickly back, saying, 'He is standing close by, and must be thinking about coming in.' He managed to draw aside a corner of the door-skin, just enough to give him elbow room to shoot, but it was not altogether easy. The passage was narrow enough before, and now, in addition, it was full of all the back-bones and scraps of meat. I saw him once lift the gun to his shoulder, as he lay crouched together, but take it down again; he had forgotten to cock it, and the bear had moved a little away, so that he only saw its muzzle and paws. But now it began scraping down in the passage with one paw, as if it wanted to come in, and Johansen thought he must fire, even if he could not see. He put out his gun, pointing the barrel at the upper edge of the opening; he thought the shot must go right into the bear's breast, and so he fired. I heard a dull growl, and the crunching of the snow under heavy foot-steps, which went up towards the talus. Johansen loaded again, and put his head out at the opening. He said he saw it going up there, and that it didn't seem up to much, and forthwith he rushed after it. I, meanwhile, was lying head foremost in the bag hunting for a sock which I could *not* find. At last, after a long search, I found it — on the floor, of course. Then I, too, was ready; and well equipped with gun, cartridges, knife, and file (to sharpen the seal-knife), I followed. I had my wind-trousers on, too; they had been hanging unused all through the winter's cold, for want of thread to mend them with, but now, when the temperature was only −2° C. (28.4° F.), they of course had to come out. I followed the tracks; they went westwards and northwards along the shore. After a little while I at last met Johansen, who said that the bear lay farther on; he had at last got up to it, and finished it with a shot in the back. While he returned to fetch the sledges, I went on to begin skinning. It was not to be done quite so quickly, however. As I approached the place where I thought it must be lying, I caught sight of the 'dead bear' far ahead, trotting pretty briskly along the shore. Now and then it stopped to look round at me. I ran out on to the ice, to get outside it, if possible, and drive it back, so that we should not have so far to drag it. When I had kept on at this for some time, and was about on a level with it, it began clambering up the glacier, and under some ragged rock. I had not reckoned on a 'dead bear' being able to do this, and the only thing was to stop it as soon as possible; but, just as I got within range, it disappeared over the crest. Soon I saw it again, a good deal higher up and far out of range. It was craning its neck to see if I were following. I went up some way after it, but, as it went on along the mountain more quickly than I could follow it in the deep snow, under which, moreover, there were crevices into which I kept falling up to my waist, I preferred to clamber down on to the fjord-ice again.

In a little while the bear emerged from beneath a perpendicular cliff with a precipitous bit of talus beneath it. Here it began to crawl carefully along at the very top of the talus. I was now afraid of its lying down in a place like this where we could not get at it, and even though the range was long I felt I must fire and see if I could not make it fall over. It did not look as if it had too firm a footing up there. It was blowing like anything here under the cliff, and I saw that the bear had to lie flat down and hold on with its claws when the worst gusts came, and then, too, it had only three paws to hold on with: the right fore-leg had been broken. I went up to a big stone at the lower edge of the talus, took good aim and fired. I saw the bullet strike the snow just beneath it, but whether it was hit or not, it started up and tried to jump over a drift, but slipped, and rolled over. It tried several times to stop itself, but went on, until at last it found its feet, and began to crawl slowly up again. Meanwhile I had loaded again, and the range was now shorter. I fired once more. It stood still a moment, then slipped farther and farther down the drift, at first slowly, then quicker and quicker, rolling over and over. I thought it was coming straight towards me, but comforted myself with the thought that the stone I was standing behind was a good solid one. I squatted down and quickly put a fresh cartridge into my gun. The bear had now arrived at the talus below the drift; it came tearing down, together with stones and lumps of snow, in a series of leaps, each longer than the last. It was a strange sight, this great white body flying through the air, and turning somersault after somersault, as if it had been a piece of wood. At last it took one tremendous leap, and landed against an enormous stone. There was a regular crash, and there it lay close beside me; a few spasms passed through it, and all was over. It was an uncommonly large he-bear, with a beautiful thick fur, which one might well wish to have at home; but the best thing of all was that it was very fat. It was so windy that the gusts were apt to blow you over, if you were not prepared for them; but with the air so mild as it was, wind did not matter much; it would not have been such bad work to skin it, had it not been that it was lying in a hollow, and was so big that one man could not stir it. After a time, however, Johansen came, and at last we had got it dismembered, and had dragged it down to the ice, and piled it on the sledge. We had not gone far, however, before we found that it would be too heavy for us to draw all at once against this wind, and for such a distance. We laid half of it in a heap on the ice, and spread the skin over it, intending to fetch it in a day or two; and even then we had difficulty enough in fighting on against the wind, in the dark, so that it was late at night before we got home. But it was long since we had so much enjoyed our homecoming, and being able to lie down in our bag, and sup off fresh meat and hot soup."

We lived on that bear for six weeks.

"When Johansen was out this morning at 6, he thought he saw little auks in millions flying up the sound. When we went out at 2 in the afternoon; there was an unceasing passage of flock after flock out to sea, and this continued until late in the afternoon. I saw two guillemots (*uria grylle*), too, fly over our heads. They are the first we have seen."[125]

"Wednesday, March 25th. There is the same dark water-sky behind the promontory in the south-west, stretching thence westwards almost to the extreme west. It has been there all through this mild weather with south-westerly wind, from the very beginning of the month. There seems to be always open water there, for no sooner is the sky overcast, than the reflection of water appears in that quarter."

"Thursday, April 2nd. As I awoke at about 8 this evening (our morning happened to fall in the evening to-day), we heard an animal rustling about outside, and gnawing at something. We did not take much notice of it, thinking it was a fox, busy as usual with some meat up on the roof; and if it did seem to be making rather more noise than we had of late been accustomed to hear from foxes, yet it was scarcely noise enough to come from a bear. We did not take into consideration that the snow was not so cold and crackling now as it had been earlier in the winter. When Johansen went out to read the thermometer, he saw that it was a bear that had been there. It had gone round the hut, but had evidently not liked all the bears' carcasses, and had not ventured past them up to the walrus blubber on the roof. At the opening of the passage and the chimney it had sniffed hard, doubtless enjoying the delicious scent of burnt blubber and live human flesh. Then it had dragged a walrus-hide, that was lying outside, a little way off, and scraped the blubber off it. It had come from the ice obliquely up the hill following the scent, had then followed our footsteps from the hut to the place where we get salt water, and had thence gone farther out over the ice until it had got scent of the walrus-carcasses out there, and was going towards them when Johansen caught sight of it. There it set to work to gnaw. As my gun was not fit to use at the moment, I took Johansen's and went alone. The bear was so busy gnawing and tearing pieces off the carcass that I could get close up to it from behind without troubling about cover. Wishing to try how near I could get, I went on, and it was not until I was so near that I could almost touch it with the muzzle of my gun that it heard my steps, so busy had it been. It started round, gazed defiantly and astonished at me, and I saluted it with a charge right in its face. It threw up its head, sneezed, and blew blood out over the snow, as it turned round again and galloped away. I was going to load again, but the cartridge jammed, and it was only by using my knife that I got it out. While I was doing this, the bear had bethought himself, stopped, turned towards me, and snorted angrily, as he made up his mind to set upon me. He then went up on to a piece of ice close by, placed himself in an attitude of defence, and stretched out his neck towards me, while the blood poured from his mouth and nostrils. The ball had gone right through his head, but without touching the brain. At last I had put another cartridge in, but had to give him five shots before I finally killed him. At each shot he fell, but got up again. I was not accustomed to the sights on Johansen's gun, and shot rather too high with it. At last I grew angry, rushed up to him, and finished him off."

We were beginning to be well supplied with blubber and meat for the journey south, and were now busy fitting ourselves out. And there was a great deal to be done. We had to begin to make ourselves new clothes out of our blankets; our wind-clothes had to be patched and mended; our "komager" had to be soled, and we had to make socks and gloves out of bear-skin. Then we had to make a light, good sleeping-bag of bear-skin. All this would take time; and from this time we worked industriously at our needle from early morning till late at night. Our hut was suddenly transformed into a busy tailor's and shoemaker's workroom, where we sat side by side in the sleeping-bag upon the stone-bed, and sewed and sewed and thought about the home-coming. We got thread by unravelling the cotton canvas of some provision bags. It need hardly be said that we were always talking about the prospects for our journey, and we found great comfort in the persistence of the dark sky in the south-west, which indicated much open water in that direction. I consequently thought we should have good use for our kayaks on the journey to Spitzbergen. I mention this open water several times in my journal. For instance, on April 12th: "open water from the promontory in the south-west, northwards as far as we can see." By this I mean, of course, that there was dark air over the whole horizon in this direction, showing clearly that there was open water there. This could not really surprise us; indeed, we ought to have been prepared for it, since Payer had found open water in the middle of April at a more northerly point on the west coast of Crown-Prince Rudolf Land; and this had been continually in my thoughts all through the winter.

Another thing which made us believe in the close vicinity of the sea, was that we were daily visited by ivory gulls and fulmars, sometimes skuas also. We saw the first ivory gulls on March 12th; throughout April they became more and more numerous, and soon we had plenty both of them and of the burgomasters (*larus glaucus*) sitting on our roof and round the hut, and drumming and pecking at the bones and remains of bears they found there. During the winter the continual gnawing of the foxes at the meat up there, had entertained us and reminded us that we were not quite forsaken by living things; when half asleep we could often imagine that we were in our beds at home, and heard the rats and mice holding their revels in the attic above us. With the coming of daylight, the foxes vanished. They now found plenty of little auks up in the clefts of the mountains and had no longer to depend on our stone-hard frozen bear-meat. But now we had the drumming of the gulls instead; but they did not call up the same illusions, and, when we had them on the roof just over our heads, were often very tiresome, and even disturbed our sleep, so that we had to knock on the roof, or go out and frighten them away, which, however, had the desired effect only for a few minutes.

On the 18th of April, while I was at work on some solar time observations, I happened to look up, and was surprised to see a bear standing just opposite to me down on the ice by the shore. It must have been standing there a long time, wondering what I was about. I ran to the hut for a gun; but when I returned it took to its heels, and I was not eager to follow it.

"Sunday, April 19th. I was awakened at 7 o'clock this morning by the heavy steps of a bear outside. I wakened Johansen, who struck a light, and I got on my trousers and 'komager' and crept out with loaded gun. During the night a great deal of snow had, as usual, drifted over the skin that covered the opening, and was difficult to break through. At last by kicking with all my might from below, I managed to knock the snow off, and put my head out into the daylight, which was quite dazzling after the darkness down in the hut. I saw nothing, but knew that the bear must be standing just behind the hut. Then I heard a snorting and blowing, and off went the brute in a clumsy bear's-gallop up the slope. I did not know whether to shoot or not, and to tell the truth I had little inclination for bear-skinning in this bitter weather; but half at random, I sent a shot after it, which of course missed, and I was not sorry. I did not shoot again; the one shot was enough to frighten it, and keep it from coming again for the present; we did not want it, if only it would leave our things in peace. At the cleft to the north it looked back, and then went on. As usual it had come against the wind, and must have scented us far west upon the ice. It had made several tacks to leeward to us, had been at the entrance of the hut, where it had left a visiting-card, and had then gone straight to a mound at the back of us, where there is some walrus blubber, surrounded on all sides by bears' carcasses. These had no terrors for it. The bear-skin which covered it, it had dragged a long way, but fortunately it had not succeeded in getting anything eaten before I came."

"Sunday, May 3rd. When Johansen came in this morning, he said he had seen a bear out on the ice; it was coming in. He went out a little later to look for it, but did not see it; it had probably gone into the bay to the north. We expected a visit from it, however, as the wind was that way; and as we sat later in the day, sewing as hard as we could sew, we heard heavy footsteps on the snow outside. They stopped, went backwards and forwards a little, and then something was drawn along, and all was quiet. Johansen crept cautiously out with his gun. When he put his head out of the hole, and his eyes had recovered from the first dazzling effects of the daylight, he saw the bear standing gnawing at a bear-skin. A bullet through the head killed it on the spot. It was a lean little animal, but worth taking, inasmuch as it saved us the trouble of thawing up carcasses, in order to cut provisions for our journey off them. Frozen stiff as they now are, we cannot cut them up outside in the cold, but have to bring them into the hut, and soften them in the warmth, before we can cut anything off them, and this takes time. Two bears were here on a visit last night, but they turned back again at the sledge, which is stuck up on end in the moraine to the west of us, to serve as a stand for our thermometer."

As we were breakfasting on May 9th, we again heard a bear's footstep outside, and being afraid that it was going to eat up our blubber, we had no other resource than to shoot it. We now had far more meat than we required, and did not care to use more cartridges on these animals for the present; but what grieved us most was the thought of all the beautiful bear-skins which we should leave behind us. The time was now drawing near when we should break up our camp, and we worked eagerly at our preparations. Our clothes were now ready. The entry for Tuesday May 12th, runs thus: "Took leave to-day of my old trousers. I was quite sad at the thought of the good service they had done; but they are now so heavy with oil and dirt that they must be several times their original weight, and, if they were squeezed, oil would ooze out of them." It was undeniably pleasant to put on the new, light, soft trousers of blanket, which were, to some extent, free from grease. As, however, this material was loose in texture, I was afraid it might wear out before we reached Spitzbergen, and we had therefore strengthened it both inside and outside with pieces of an old pair of drawers, and of a shirt, to protect it from wear.

While I was taking some observations outside the hut on Saturday, May 16th, I saw a bear with quite a small young one out on the ice. I had just taken a turn out there, and they were examining my tracks. The mother went first, going up on to all the hummocks I had been upon, turning round and snuffing, and looking at the tracks, and then descending again, and going on. The tiny young one trotted along behind, exactly repeating the movements of its mother. At last they grew tired of this, and turned their steps towards the shore, disappearing behind the promontory to the north of us. Shortly after Johansen came out, and I told him about it, and said: "I expect we shall soon see them in the cleft up there, as the wind is that way." I had scarcely said it, when, looking across, we saw them both standing, stretching their necks, snuffing and looking at us and the hut. We did not want to shoot them, as we had abundance of food; but we thought it would be amusing to go nearer and watch them, and then, if possible, frighten them sufficiently to keep them from visiting us in the night, so that we could sleep in peace. When we approached, the mother snorted angrily, turned several times as if to go, pushing the young one on first, but turned back again to observe us more closely. At last they jogged slowly off, continually hesitating and looking back. When they got down to the shore, they again went quite slowly among the hummocks, and I ran after them. The mother went first, the young one trotting after exactly in her footsteps. I was soon close to them, the mother saw me, started, and tried to get the young one to go with her; but I now discovered that it could run no faster than I could follow it. As soon as the mother saw this, she turned round, snorted and came storming right at me. I halted, and prepared to shoot, in case she should come too near, and in the meantime the little one tramped on as fast as it could. The mother halted at the distance of a few paces from me, snorted and hissed again, looked round at the young one, and when the latter had got a good way on, trotted after it. I ran on again, and overtook the young one, and again the mother went through the same manoeuvres; she seemed to have the greatest possible desire to strike me to the earth, but then the young one had again got ahead a little, and she did not wait to do it but trotted after. This was repeated several times, and then they began to clamber up the glacier, the mother in front, the young one after. But the latter did not get on very fast; it trudged along as well as it could in its mother's footsteps in the deep snow; it reminded me exactly of a child in trousers, as it clambered up and kept looking round, half frightened, half curious. It was touching to see how incessantly the mother turned round to hasten it on, now and then jogging it with her head, hissing and snorting all the while at me standing quietly below and looking on. When they reached the crest the mother stopped and hissed worse than ever, and when she had let the young one pass her, they both disappeared over the glacier, and I went back to continue my work.

For the last few weeks a feverish activity had reigned in our hut. We had become more and more impatient to make a start; but there was still a great deal to be done. We realised in bitter earnest that we had no longer the *Fram*'s stores to fall back upon. On board the *Fram* there might be one or two things lacking; but here we lacked practically everything. What would we not have given even for a single box of dog-biscuits — for ourselves — out of the *Fram*'s abundance? Where were we to find all that we needed? "For a sledge expedition, one must lay in light and nourishing provisions, which at the same time afford as much variety as possible; one must have light and warm clothing, strong and practical sledges," etc., etc. — we knew by heart all these maxims of the Arctic text-book. The journey that lay before us, indeed, was not a very great one; the thing was simply to reach Spitzbergen and get on board the sloop; but it was long enough after all to make it necessary for us to take certain measures of precaution.

When we dug up the stores which we had buried at the beginning of the winter, and opened the bags, we found that there were some miserable remains of a commissariat which had once, indeed, been good, but was now for the most part mouldy and spoilt by the damp of the previous autumn. Our flour, our precious flour, had got mildewed, and had to be thrown away. The chocolate had been dissolved by the damp, and no longer existed; and the pemmican — well — it had a strange appearance, and when we tasted it — ugh! It too had to be thrown away. There remained a certain quantity of fish-flour, some aleuronate flour, and some damp half-moulded bread, which we carefully boiled in train-oil, partly to dry it, as all damp was expelled by the boiling oil, partly to render it more nutritious by impregnating it with fat. We thought it tasted delightful, and preserved it carefully for festal occasions, and times when all other food failed us. Had we been able to dry bear's flesh, we should have managed very well; but the weather was too raw and cold, and the strips of flesh we hung up became only half dry. There was nothing for it but to lay in a store of as much cut-up raw flesh and blubber as we could carry with us. Then we filled the three tin boxes that had held our petroleum with train-oil, which we used as fuel. For cooking on the journey we would use the pot belonging to our cooking apparatus; and our lamp we used as a brazier in which to burn blubber and train-oil together. These provisions and this fuel did not constitute a particularly light equipment; but it had this advantage that we should probably be able to replace what we consumed of it by the way. It was to be hoped that we should find plenty of game.

Our short sledges were a greater trouble to us, for of course we could not get them lengthened now. If we failed to find open water all the way over to Spitzbergen, and were compelled to drag them over the uneven drift-ice, we could scarcely imagine how we should get on with the kayaks lying on these short sledges, without getting them knocked to pieces on hummocks and pressure-ridges; for the kayaks were supported only at the middle, while both ends projected far beyond the sledge, and at the slightest inequality these ends hacked against the ice, and scraped holes in the sail-cloth. We had to protect them well by lashing bear-skins under them; and then we had to make the best grips we could contrive out of the scanty wood we had, to fix on the sledges. This was no easy matter, for the great point was to make the grips high in order to raise the kayaks as much as possible, and keep them clear of the ice; and then they had to be well lashed in order to keep their places. But we had no cord to lash them with, and had to make it for ourselves of raw bear-skin or walrus-hide, which is not the best possible material for lashings. This difficulty, too, we overcame, and got our kayaks to lie steadily and well. We of course laid the heaviest part of their cargo as much as possible in the middle, so that the ends should not be broken down by the weight. Our own personal equipment was quite as difficult to get in order. I have mentioned that we made ourselves new clothes, and this took a long time with two such inexpert tailors; but practice made us gradually more skilful, and I think we had good reason to be proud of the results we finally achieved. When we at last put them on, the clothes had quite an imposing appearance — so we thought at any rate. We saved them up and kept them hanging as long as possible, in order that they might still be new when we started. Johansen, I believe, did not wear his new coat before we fell in with other people. He declared he must keep it fresh till we arrived in Norway; he could not go about like a pirate when he got among his countrymen again. The poor remains of underclothes that we possessed had of course to be thoroughly washed before we started, so that it should be possible to move in them without their rasping too many holes in our skin. The washing we accomplished as above described. Our foot-gear was in anything but a satisfactory condition. Socks, indeed, we could make of bear-skin; but the worst of it was that the soles of our "komager" were almost worn out. We managed, however, to make soles of a sort out of walrus hide, by scraping about half its thickness away, and then drying it over the lamp. With these soles we mended our "komager" after the fashion of the Finns; we had plenty of "senne" thread (sedge thread), and we managed to get our komagers pretty well watertight again. Thus in spite of everything we were tolerably well off for clothes, though it cannot be said that those we had were remarkable for their cleanliness. To protect us against wind and rain we had still our wind-clothes, which we had patched and stitched together as well as we could; but it took a terrible time, for the whole garments now consisted of scarcely anything else but patches and seams, and when you had sewn up a hole at one place, they split at another the next time you put them on. The sleeves were particularly bad, and at last I tore both sleeves off my jacket, so that I should not have the annoyance of seeing them perpetually stripped away.

It was very desirable, too, that we should have a tolerably light sleeping-bag. The one we had brought with us no longer existed, as we had made clothes out of the blankets; so the only thing was to try and make as light a bag as possible out of bearskin. By, picking out the thinnest skins we possessed, we managed to make one not so much heavier than the reindeer-skin bag which we had taken with us on leaving the *Fram*. A greater difficulty was to procure a practicable tent. The one we had had was out of the question. It had been worn and torn to pieces on our five months' journey of the year before, and what was left of it the foxes had made an end of, as we had had it lying spread over our meat and blubber heap in the autumn to protect it against the gulls. The foxes had gnawed and torn it in all directions, and had carried off great strips of it which we found scattered around. We speculated a great deal as to how we could make ourselves a new tent. The only thing we could think of was to put our sledges, with the kayaks upon them, parallel to each other at the distance of about a man's height, then pile snow around them at the sides until they were closed in, lay our snow-shoes and bamboo staffs across, and then spread our two sails, laced together, over the whole, so that they should reach the ground on both sides. In this way we managed to male ourselves a quite effective shelter, the kayaks forming the roof ridges, and the sails the side walls of the tent. It was not quite impervious to drifting snow, and we had usually a good deal of trouble in stopping up cracks and openings with our wind-clothes and things of that sort.

But the most important part of our equipment was, after all, our firearms, and these, fortunately, we had kept in tolerably good order. We cleaned the rifles thoroughly and rubbed them with train-oil. We had also a little vaseline and gun-oil left for the locks. On taking stock of our ammunition, we found to our joy that we still had about 100 rifle cartridges and 110 small shot cartridges. We had thus, enough, if necessary, for several more winters.

Chapter 17

The Journey Southwards

AT LAST, on Tuesday, May 19th, we were ready for the start. Our sledges stood loaded and lashed. The last thing we did was to photograph our hut both outside and inside, and to leave in it a short report of our journey. It ran thus:

"Tuesday, May 19th, 1896. We were frozen in north of Kotelnoi at about 78° 43' N. lat., September 22nd, 1893. Drifted north-westward during the following year, as we had expected to do. Johansen and I left the *Fram*, March 14th, 1895, at about 84° 4' N. lat. and 103° E. long.,[126] to push on northward. The command of the remainder of the expedition was transferred to Sverdrup. Found no land northwards. On April 6th, 1895, we had to turn back at 86° 14' N. lat., and about 95° E. long., the ice having become impassable. Shaped our course for Cape Fligely; but our watches having stopped, we did not know our longitude with certainty, and arrived on August 6th, 1895, at four glacier-covered islands to the north of this line of islands, at about 81° 30' N. lat., and about 7° E. of this place. Reached this place August 26th, 1895, and thought it safest to winter here. Lived on bears' flesh. Are starting to-day south-westward along the land, intending to cross over to Spitzbergen at the nearest point. We conjecture that we are on Gillies Land.

"FRIDTJOF NANSEN."

This earliest report of our journey was deposited in a brass tube which had formed the cylinder of the air-pump of our "Primus." The tube was closed with a plug of wood and hung by a wire to the roof-tree of the hut.

At length, on Tuesday, the 19th May, we were ready, and at 7 p.m. left our winter lair, and began our journey south. After having had so little exercise all the winter, we were not much disposed for walking, and thought our sledges with the loaded kayaks heavy to pull along. In order not to do too much at first, but make our joints supple before we began to exert ourselves seriously, we walked for only a few hours the first day, and then, well satisfied, pitched our camp. There was such a wonderfully happy feeling in knowing that we were, at last, on the move, and that we were actually going homewards.

The following day (Wednesday, May 20th) we also did only a short day's march. We were making for the promontory to the south-west of us that we had been looking at all the winter. Judging from the sky, it was on the further side of this headland that we should find open water. We were very eager to see how the land lay ahead of this point. If we were north of Cape Lofley, the land must begin to trend to the south-east. If, on the other hand, the trend of the coast was to the south-west, then this must be a new land further west, and near Gillies Land.

The next day (Thursday, May 21st) we reached this promontory, and pitched our camp there. All through the winter we had called it the Cape of Good Hope, as we expected to find different conditions there, which would facilitate our advance; and our hopes were not to be disappointed. From the crest of the mountain I saw open water not far off to the south, and also two new snow-lands, one large one in front (in the south, 40° W.), and one not much smaller in the west (S. 85° W.). It was completely covered with glacier, and looked like an evenly vaulted shield. I could not see clearly how the coast ran on account of a headland to the southward. But it did not seem to trend to the south-east, so that we could not be near Cape Lofley. We now hoped that we might be able to launch our kayaks the very next day, and that we should then make rapid progress in a south-westerly direction; but in this we were disappointed. The next day there was a snowstorm, and we had to stay where we were. As I lay in the bag in the morning, preparing breakfast, I all at once caught sight of a bear walking quietly past us at a distance of about twenty paces. It looked at us and our kayaks once or twice, but could not quite make out what we were, as the wind was in another direction and it could not get scent of us, so it continued its way. I let it go unharmed; we still had food enough.

On Saturday, May 23rd, the weather was still bad, but we went ahead a little way to examine our road onward. The point to be found out was whether we ought at once to make for the open water; that lay on the other side of an island to the west, or whether we ought to travel southwards upon the shore ice along the land. We came to a headland consisting of uncommonly marked columnar basalt, which on account of its peculiar form we called the "Castle." We here saw that the land stretched farther in a southerly direction, and that the open water went the same way, only separated from the land by a belt of shore ice. As the latter appeared to be full of cracks, we decided to go over to the island in the west, and put to sea as quickly as

Southwards, May 1896.

possible. We therefore returned and made all ready. Our preparations consisted first and foremost in carefully caulking the seams of our kayaks by melting stearine over them, and then re-stowing the cargo so as to leave room for us to sit in them. The following day (Sunday, May 24th) we moved on west-wards towards the island, and as the wind was easterly, and we were able to employ sails on the sledges, we got on pretty quickly across the flat ice. As we approached the island, however, a storm blew up from the south-west, and after the sledges had upset several times, we were obliged to take down our sails. The sky became overcast, the air grew misty, and we worked our way against the strong wind in towards the land. The thing was to get to land as quickly as possible, as we might evidently expect bad weather. But now the ice became treacherous. As we approached the land there were a number of cracks in every direction, and these were covered with a layer of snow so that it was difficult to see them. While Johansen was busy lashing the sail and mast securely to the deck of his kayak, so that the wind should not carry them away, I went on ahead as fast as I could to look for a camping-ground, but all of a sudden the ice sank beneath me, and I lay in the water in a broad crack which had been concealed by the snow. I tried to get out again, but with my snowshoes firmly fastened it was not possible to get them through all the rubble of snow and lumps of ice that had fallen into the water on the top of them. In addition to this I was fastened to the sledge by the harness so that I could not turn round. Fortunately, in the act of falling, I had dug my pike-staff into the ice on the opposite side of the crack, and holding myself up by its aid and the one arm that I had got above the edge of the ice, I lay waiting patiently for Johansen to come and pull me out. I was sure he must have seen me fall in, but could not turn enough to look back. When I thought a long time had passed, and I felt the staff giving way and the water creeping further and further up my body, I began to call out, but received no answer. I shouted louder for help, and at last heard a "Hullo!" far behind. After some little time, when the water was up to my chest, and it would not have been long before I was right under, Johansen came up, and I was pulled out. He had been so occupied with his sledge that he had not noticed that I was in the water until the last time I called. This experience had the effect of making me careful in the future not to go on such deceitful ice with my snowshoes firmly attached. By observing a little more caution, we at length reached the land, and found a camping-place where there was a certain amount of shelter. To our surprise we discovered a number of walruses lying along the shore here, herd upon herd, beside the cracks; but we took no notice of them either, for the present; we thought we still had a sufficient supply of food and blubber to draw upon.

During the succeeding days, the storm raged, and we could not move. The entry for Tuesday, May 26th, is as follows: "We have lain weatherbound yesterday and to-day beneath the glacier cliff on the north side of this island. The snow is so wet that it will be difficult to get anywhere; but it is to be hoped that the open channel outside is not far off, and we shall get on quickly there when once the storm abates. We shall then make up for this long delay." But our stay was to be longer than we thought. On Thursday, May 28th, the journal says: "We were up on the island yesterday, and saw open sea to the south, but are still lying weather-bound as before. I only moved our tent-place a little on account of the cracks; the ice threatened to open just beneath us. There are a great many walruses here. When we go out over the ice, the fellows follow us and come up in the cracks beside us. We can often hear them grunting as they go, and butting at the ice under our feet."

That day, however, the storm so far abated that we were able to move southwards along the east side of the island. On the way we passed a large open pool in the shore ice between this island and the land. It must have been shallow here, for there was a strong current, which was probably the cause of this pool being kept open. We passed two or three herds of walruses lying on the ice near it. Concerning these, I wrote that evening: "I went up to one herd of about nine to take photographs of the animals. I went close up to them behind a little mound, and they did not see me; but directly I rose up not more than 20 feet away from them a female with her young one plunged into the water through a hole close by. I could not get the others to stir, however much I shouted. Johansen now joined me, and, although he threw lumps of snow and ice at them, they would not move; they only struck their tusks into the lumps, and snuffed at them, while I kept on photographing them. When I went right up to them, most of them at last got up and floundered away towards the hole, and one plunged in; but the others stopped and composed themselves to sleep again. Soon, too, the one that had first disappeared came back and crept on to the ice. The two that lay nearest to me never stirred at all; they raised their heads a little once or twice, looked contemptuously at me as I stood three paces from them, laid their heads down and went to sleep again. They barely moved when I pricked them in the snout with my pike-staff, but I was able to get a pretty good photograph of them. I thought I now had enough, but before I went I gave the nearest one a parting poke in the snout with my pike-staff; it got right up, grunted discontentedly, looked in astonishment at me with its great round eyes, and then quietly began to scratch the back of its head, and I got another photograph, whereupon it again lay quietly down. When we went on, they all immediately settled themselves again, and were lying like immovable masses of flesh when we finally rounded the promontory, and lost sight of them."

Once more we had snow-storms, and now lay weather-bound on the south side of the island.

"Friday, May 29th. Lying weather-bound.

"Saturday, May 30th. Lying weather-bound, stopping up the tent against the driving snow, while the wind flits round us, attacking first one side and then another." It was all we could do to keep ourselves tolerably dry during this time, with the snow drifting in through the cracks on all sides, on us and our bag, melting and saturating everything.

"Monday, June 1st. Yesterday it at last grew a little calmer, and cleared up so that we had bright sunshine in the evening. We rejoiced in the thought of moving on, got our kayaks and everything ready to launch, and crept into our bag to turn out early this morning for a fine day, as we thought. The only thing that made it a little doubtful was, that the barometer had ceased rising, had fallen again 1 millim., in fact. In the night the storm came on again — the same driving snow, only with this difference, that now the wind is going round the compass with the sun, so there must soon be an end of it. This is beginning to be too much of a good thing; I am now seriously afraid that the *Fram* will get home before us. I went for a walk inland yesterday. There were flat clay and gravel stretches everywhere. I saw numerous traces of geese, and in one place some white egg-shell, undoubtedly belonging to a goose's egg." We therefore called the island Goose Island.[127]

"Tuesday, June 2nd. Still lay weather-bound last night, and to-day it has been windier than ever. But now, towards evening, it has begun to abate a little, with a brightening sky, and sunshine now and again, so we hope that there will really be a change for the better. Here we lie in a hollow in the snow, getting wetter and wetter, and thinking that it is June already, and everything looks beautiful at home, while we have got no farther than this. But it cannot be much longer before we are there. It is too much to think of! If only I could be sure about the *Fram*! If she arrives before us, what will those poor waiting ones do!"

At length on Wednesday, June 3rd, we went on, but now the west wind had driven the ice landwards, so that there was no longer open sea to travel south upon, and there was nothing for it but to go over the ice along the land. However the wind was from the north and we could put up a sail on our sledges, and thus get along pretty fast. We still saw several walruses on the ice, and there were also some in the water that were continually putting their heads up in the cracks and grunting after us. The ice we were crossing here was remarkably thin and bad, and as we got farther south it became even worse. It was so weighed down with the masses of snow that lay upon it, that there was water beneath the snow wherever we turned. We had to make towards land as quickly as possible, as it looked still worse farther south. By going on snow-shoes, however, we kept fairly well on the top of the snow, though often both sledge and snow-shoes sank down into the water below, and stuck fast; and no little trouble would be spent in getting everything safely on to firmer ice again. At last, however, we got in under a high, perpendicular basaltic cliff,[128] which swarmed with auks. This was the first time we had seen these birds in any great quantity; hitherto we had only seen one or two singly. We took it as a sign that we were approaching better known regions. Alongside of it, to the south-east, there was a small rocky knoll, where numbers of fulmar seemed to be breeding. Our supply of food was now getting very low, and we had been hoping for a visit from some bear or other; but now that we needed them, they of course kept away. We then determined to shoot birds, but the auks flew too high, and all we got was a couple of fulmars. As we just then passed a herd of walruses, we determined to take some of this despised food, and we shot one of them, killing it on the spot. At the report the others raised their heads a little, but only to let them fall again, and went on sleeping. To get our prize skinned with these brutes lying round us was not to be thought of, and we must drive them into the water in some way or other. This was no easy matter, however. We went up to them, shouted and hallooed, but they only looked at us lazily, and did not move. Then we hit them with snowshoe-staves; they became angry, and struck their tusks into the ice until the chips flew, but still would not move. At last, however, by continuing to poke and beat, we drove the whole herd into the water, but it was not quick work. In stately, dignified procession they drew back, and shambled slowly off, one after the other, to the water's edge. Here they again looked round at us, grunted discontentedly, and then plunged into the water one by one. But while we were cutting up their comrade, they kept coming up again in the crack beside us, grunting and creeping half up on to the ice, as if to demand an explanation of our conduct.

After having supplied ourselves with as much meat and blubber as we thought we needed for the moment, as well as a quantity of blood, we pitched our tent close by and boiled a good mess of blood-porridge, which consisted of a wonderful mixture of blood, powdered fish, Indian meal, and blubber. We still had a good wind, and sailed away merrily with our sledges all night. When we got to the promontory to the south of us, we came to open water, which here ran right up to the edge of the glacier-covered land; and all we had to do was to launch our kayaks, and set off along by the glacier cliff, in open sea for the first time this year. It was strange to be using paddles again, and to see the water swarming with birds, auks, and little auks and kittiwakes all round. The land was covered with glacier, the basaltic rock only projecting in one or two places. There were moraines, too, in several places on the glaciers. We were not a little surprised, after going some way, when we discovered a flock of eider-ducks on the water. A little later we saw two geese sitting on the shore, and felt as if we had come into quite civilised regions again. After a couple of hours' paddling our progress south was stopped by shore-ice, while the open water extended due west towards some land we had previously seen in that direction, but which was now covered by mist. We were very much in doubt as to which way to choose, whether to go on in the open water westwards — which must take us towards Spitzbergen — or to leave it and again take to our sledges over the smooth shore-ice to the south. Although the air was thick, and we could not see far, we felt convinced that by going over the ice, we should at last reach open water on the south side of these islands among which we were. Perhaps we might there find a shorter route to Spitzbergen. In the meantime morning was far advanced (June 5th), and we pitched our camp well-pleased at having got so far south.[129]

As it was still so hazy the following day (Saturday, June 6th) that we could not see any more of our surroundings than before, and as there was a strong north wind, which would be inconvenient in crossing the open sea westwards, we determined on going southwards over the shore-ice. We were once more able to use a sail on our sledges, and we got on better than ever. We often went along without any exertion; we could stand on our snow-shoes, each in front of our sledge, holding the steering-pole (a bamboo cane bound firmly to the stem of the kayaks), and letting the wind carry us along. In the gusts we often went along like feathers, at other times we had to pull a little ourselves. We made good progress, and kept on until far on into the night, as we wanted to make as much use of the wind as possible. We crossed right over the broad sound we had had in front of us, and did not stop until we were able to pitch our camp by an island on its southern side.

Next evening (Sunday, June 7th) we went on again still southwards before the same northerly wind, and we could sail well. We had hoped to be able to reach the land before we again pitched our camp, but it was further than we had thought, and at last when morning (Monday, June 8th) was far advanced, we had to stop in the middle of the ice in a furious storm. The numerous islands among which we now were, seemed more and more mysterious to us. I find in my journal for that day: "Are continually discovering new islands or lands to the south. There is one great land of snow beyond us in the west, and it seems to extend southwards a long way." This snow-land seemed to us extremely mysterious; we had not yet discovered a single dark patch upon it, only snow and ice everywhere. We had no clear idea of its extent, as we had only caught glimpses of it now and then, when the mist lifted a little. It seemed to be quite low, but we thought that it must be of a wider extent than any of the lands we had hitherto travelled along. To the east we found island upon island, and sounds and fjords the whole way along. We mapped it all as well as we could, but this did not help us to find out where we were; they seemed to be only a crowd of small islands, and, every now and then, a view of what we took to be the ocean to the east, opened up between them.

The ice over which we were now travelling was remarkably different from that which we had had farther north, near our winter-hut; it was considerably thinner, and covered, too, with very thick snow, so that it was not in a good condition for travelling over. When, therefore, the following day (Tuesday, June 9th) it also began to stick in lumps to our snowshoes and the sledge-runners, they both worked rather heavily; but the wind was still favourable, and we sailed along well notwithstanding. As we were sailing full speed, flying before the wind, and had almost reached the land, Johansen and his sledge suddenly sank down, and it was with difficulty that he managed to back himself and his things against the wind and on to the firmer ice. As I was rushing along, I saw that the snow in front of me had a suspiciously wet colour, and my snowshoes began to cut through; but fortunately I still had time to luff before any further misfortune occurred. We had to take down our sails, and make a long detour westwards, before we could continue our sail. Next day, also, the snow clogged, but the wind had freshened, and we sailed better than ever.

As the land to the east[130] now appeared to trend to the south-east, we steered for the southernmost point of a land to the south-west.[131] It began to be more and more exciting. We thought we must have covered about 14 miles that day, and reckoned that we must be in 80° 8′ N. lat., and we still had land in the south. If it continued far in that direction, it was certain that we could not be on Franz Josef Land (as I still thought might be the case); but we could not see far in this hazy atmosphere, and then it was remarkable that the coast on the east began to run in an easterly direction. I thought it might agree with Leigh Smith's map of Markham Sound. In that case we must have come south through a sound which neither he nor Payer could have seen, and we were therefore not so far out of our longitude after all. But no! in our journey southward we could not possibly have passed right across Payer's Dove Glacier and his various islands and lands without having seen them. There must still be a land farther west of this between Franz Josef Land and Spitzbergen; Payer's map could not be altogether wrong. I wanted to reach the land in the south-west, but had to stop on the ice; it was too far.

"Our provisions are getting low; we have a little meat for one more day, but there is no living thing to be seen, not a seal on the ice, and no open water anywhere. How long is this going on? If we do not soon reach open sea again, where there may be game to be had, things will not look very pleasant."

"Tuesday, June 16th. The last few days have been so eventful that there has been no time to write. I must try to make up for lost time this beautiful morning, while the sun is peeping in under the tent. The sea lies blue and shining outside, and one can lie and fancy oneself at home on a June morning."

On Friday, June 12th, we started again at 4 a.m. with sails on our sledges. There had been frost, so the snow was in much better condition again. It had been very windy in the night, too, so we hoped for a good day. On the preceding day it had cleared up so that we could at last see distinctly the lands around. We now discovered that we must steer in a more westerly direction than we had done during the preceding days, in order to reach the south point of the land to the west. The lands to the east disappeared eastwards, so we had said good-bye to them the day before. We now saw, too, that there was a broad sound in the land to the west,[132] and that it was one entire land, as we had taken it to be. The land north of this sound was now so far away, that I could only just see it. In the meantime the wind had dropped a good deal; the ice, too, became more and more uneven — it was evident that we had come to the drift-ice, and it was much harder work than we had expected. We could see by the air that there must be open water to the south, and as we went on, we heard, to our joy, the sound of breakers. At 6 a.m. we stopped to rest a little, and on going up on to a hummock to take a longitude observation I saw the water not far off. From a higher piece of glacier ice we could see it better. It extended towards the promontory to the south-west. Even though the wind had become a little westerly now, we still hoped to be able to sail along the edge of the ice, and determined to go to the water by the shortest way. We were quickly at the edge of the ice, and once more saw the blue water spread out before us. We soon had our kayaks lashed together, and the sail up, and put to sea. Nor were our hopes disappointed; we sailed well all day long. At times the wind was so strong that we cut through the water, and the waves washed unpleasantly over our kayaks; but we got on, and we had to put up with being a little wet. We soon passed the point we had been making for,[33] and here we saw that the land ran westwards, that the edge of the unbroken shore-ice extended in the same direction, and that we had water in front of us. In good spirits, we sailed westwards along the margin of the ice. So we were at last at the south of the land in which we had been wandering for so long, and where we had spent a long winter. It struck me more than ever that, in spite of everything, this south coast would agree well with Leigh Smith's map of Franz Josef Land and the country surrounding their winter quarters; but then I remembered Payer's map, and dismissed the thought.

In the evening we put in to the edge of the ice, so as to stretch our legs a little; they were stiff with sitting in the kayak all day, and we wanted to get a little view over the water to the west, by ascending a hummock. As we went ashore the question arose as to how we should moor our precious vessel. "Take one of the braces," said Johansen; he was standing on the ice. "But is it strong enough?" "Yes," he answered; "I have used it as a halyard on my sledge-sail all the time." "Oh, well, it doesn't require much to hold these light kayaks," said I, a little ashamed of having been so timid, and I moored them with the halyard, which was a strap cut from a raw walrus-hide. We had been on the ice a little while, moving up and down close to the kayaks. The wind had dropped considerably, and seemed to be more westerly, making it doubtful whether we could make use of it any longer, and we went up on to a hummock close by to ascertain this better. As we stood there, Johansen suddenly cried: "I say! the kayaks are adrift!" We ran down as hard as we could. They were already a little way out, and were drifting quickly off; the painter had given way. "Here, take my watch!" I said to Johansen, giving it to him; and as quickly as possible I threw off some clothing, so as to be able to swim more easily: I did not dare to take everything off, as I might so easily get cramp. I sprang into the water, but the wind was off the ice, and the light kayaks, with their high rigging, gave it a good hold. They were already well out, and were drifting rapidly. The water was icy cold, it was hard work swimming with clothes on, and the kayaks drifted farther and farther, often quicker than I could swim. It seemed more than doubtful whether I could manage it. But all our hope was drifting there; all we possessed was on board; we had not even a knife with us; and whether I got cramp and sank here, or turned back without the kayaks, it would come to pretty much the same thing; so I exerted myself to the utmost. When I got tired I turned over, and swam on my back, and then I could see Johansen walking restlessly up and down on the ice. Poor lad! He could not stand still, and thought it dreadful not to be able to do anything. He had not much hope that I could do it, but it would not improve matters in the least if he threw himself into the water too. He said afterwards that these were the worst moments he had ever lived through. But when I turned over again, and saw that I was nearer the kayaks, my courage rose, and I redoubled my exertions. I felt, however, that my limbs, were gradually stiffening and losing all feeling, and I knew that in a short time I should not be able to move them. But there was not far to go now; if I could only hold out a little longer, we should be saved — and I went on. The strokes became more and more feeble, but the distance became shorter and shorter, and I began to think I should reach the kayaks. At last I was able to stretch out my hand to the snowshoe, which lay across the sterns; I grasped it, pulled myself in to the edge of the kayak — and we were saved. I tried to pull myself up, but the whole of my body was so stiff with cold, that this was an impossibility. For a moment I thought that after all it was too late; I was to get so far, but not be able to get in. After a little, however, I managed to swing one leg up on to the edge of the sledge which lay on the deck, and in this way managed to tumble up. There I sat, but so stiff with cold, that I had difficulty in paddling. Nor was it easy to paddle in the double vessel, where I first had to take one or two strokes on one side, and then step into the other kayak to take a few strokes on the other side. If I had been able to separate them, and row in one while I towed the other, it would have been easy enough; but I could not undertake that piece of work, for I should have been stiff before it was done; the thing to be done was to keep warm by rowing as hard as I could. The cold had robbed my whole body of feeling, but when the gusts of wind came they seemed to go right through me as I stood there in my thin, wet woollen shirt. I shivered, my teeth chattered, and I was numb almost all over; but I could still use the paddle, and I should get warm when I got back on to the ice again. Two auks were lying close to the bow, and the thought of having auk for supper was too tempting; we were in want of food now. I got hold of my gun, and shot them with one discharge.

Johansen said afterwards that he started at the report thinking some accident had happened, and could not understand what I was about out there, but when he saw me paddle and pick up two birds he thought I had gone out of my mind. At last

I managed to reach the edge of the ice, but the current had driven me a long way from our landing-place. Johansen came along the edge of the ice, jumped into the kayak beside me, and we soon got back to our place. I was undeniably a good deal exhausted, and could barely manage to crawl on land. I could scarcely stand, and while I shook and trembled all over Johansen had to pull off the wet things I had on, put on the few dry ones I still had in reserve, and spread the sleeping-bag out upon the ice. I packed myself well into it, and he covered me with the sail and everything he could find to keep out the cold air. There I lay shivering for a long time, but gradually the warmth began to return to my body. For some time longer, however, my feet had no more feeling in them than icicles, for they had been partly naked in the water. While Johansen put up the tent and prepared supper, consisting of my two auks, I fell asleep. He let me sleep quietly, and when I awoke, supper had been ready for some time, and stood simmering over the fire. Auk and hot soup soon effaced the last traces of my swim. During the night my clothes were hung out to dry, and the next day were all nearly dry again.

As the tidal current was strong here, and there was no wind for sailing, we had to wait for the turn of the tide, so as not to have the current against us; and it was not until late the following evening that we went on again. We paddled and got on well until towards morning (June 14th), when we came to some great herds of walrus on the ice. Our supply of meat was exhausted but for some auks we had shot, and we had not many pieces of blubber left. We would rather have had a bear, but as we had seen none lately, it was perhaps best to supply ourselves here. We put in, and went up to one herd behind a hummock. We preferred young ones, as they were much easier to manipulate; and there were several here. I first shot one quite small, and then another. The full-grown animals started up at the first report, and looked round; and at the second shot the whole herd began to go into the water. The mothers, however, would not leave their dead young ones. One sniffed at its young one, and pushed it, evidently unable to make out what was the matter; it only saw the blood spurting from its head. It cried and wailed like a human being. At last, when the herd began to plunge in, the mother pushed her young one before her towards the water. I now feared that I should lose my booty, and ran forward to save it; but she was too, quick for me. She took the young one by one fore-leg, and disappeared with it like lightning into the depths.

The other mother did the same. I hardly knew how it had all happened, and remained standing at the edge looking down after them. I thought the young ones must rise to the surface again, but there was nothing to be seen; they had disappeared for good; the mothers must have taken them a long way. I then went towards another herd, where there were also young ones, and shot one of them; but, made wiser by experience, I shot the mother too. It was a touching sight to see her bend over her dead young one before she was shot, and even in death she lay holding it with one fore-leg. So now we had meat and blubber enough to last a long time, and meat, too, that was delicious, for the side of young walrus tastes like loin of mutton. To this we added a dozen auks, so our larder was now well furnished with good food; and if we needed more, the water was full of auks and other food, so there was no dearth.

The walruses here were innumerable. The herds that had been lying on the ice, and had now disappeared, were large; but there had been many more in the water outside. It seemed to seethe with them on every side, great and small; and when I estimate their number to have been at least 300, it is certainly not over the mark.

At 1.30 the next morning (Monday, June 15th) we proceeded on our way in beautifully calm weather. As walruses swarmed on all sides, we did not much like paddling singly, and for some distance lashed the kayaks together; for we knew how obtrusive these gentlemen could be. The day before they had come pretty near, popped up close beside my kayak, and several times followed us closely a long distance, but without doing us any harm. I was inclined to think it was curiosity, and that they were not really dangerous; but Johansen was not so sure of this. He thought we had had experience to the contrary, and urged that at any rate caution could do no harm. All day long we saw herds, that often followed us a long way, pressing in round the kayaks. We kept close to the edge of the ice; and if any came too near, we put in, if possible, on an ice-foot.[134] We also kept close together or beside one another. We paddled past one large herd on the ice, and could hear them a long way off lowing like cows.

We glided quickly on along the coast, but unfortunately a mist hung over it, so that it was often impossible to determine whether they were channels or glaciers between the dark patches which we could just distinguish upon it. I wanted very much to have seen a little more of this land. My suspicion that we were in the neighbourhood of the Leigh Smith winter quarters had become stronger than ever. Our latitude, as also the direction of the coast-line and the situation of the islands and sounds, seemed to agree far too well to admit of the possibility of imagining that another such group of islands could lie in the short distance between Franz Josef Land and Spitzbergen. Such a coincidence would be altogether too remarkable. Moreover, we caught glimpses of land in the far west which in that case could not lie far from North-East Land. But Payer's map of the land north of this? Johansen maintained with reason that Payer could not possibly have made such mistakes as we should in that case be obliged to assume.

"Towards morning we rowed for some time without seeing any walrus, and now felt more secure. Just then we saw a solitary rover pop up a little in front of us. Johansen, who was in front at the time, put in to a sunken ledge of ice; and although I really thought that this was caution carried to excess, I was on the point of following his example. I had not got so far, however, when suddenly the walrus shot up beside me, threw itself on to the edge of the kayak, took hold farther over the deck with one fore-flipper, and as it tried to upset me aimed a blow at the kayak with its tusks. I held on as tightly as possible, so as not to be upset into the water, and struck at the animal's head with the paddle as hard as I could. It took hold of the kayak once more, and tilted me up, so that the deck was almost under water, then let go, and raised itself right up. I seized my gun, but at the same moment it turned round and disappeared as quickly as it had come. The whole thing had happened in a moment, and I was just going to remark to Johansen that we were fortunate in escaping so easily from that adventure, when I noticed that my legs were wet. I listened, and now heard the water trickling into the kayak under me. To turn and run her in on to the sunken ledge of ice was the work of a moment, but I sank there. The thing was to get out and on to the ice, the kayak all the time getting fuller. The edge of the ice was high and loose, but I managed to get up; and Johansen, by tilting the sinking kayak over to starboard, so that the leak came above the water, managed to bring her to a place where the ice was low enough to admit of our drawing her up. All I possessed was floating about inside, soaked through. What I most regret is that the water has got into the photographic apparatus, and perhaps my precious photographs are ruined.

"So here we lie, with all our worldly goods spread out to dry and a kayak that must be mended before we can face the walrus again. It is a good big rent that he has made, at least six inches long; but it is fortunate that it was no worse. How easily he might have wounded me in the thigh with that tusk of his! And it would have fared ill with me if we had been farther out, and not just at such a convenient place by the edge of the ice, where there was a sunken ledge. The sleeping-bag was soaking wet; we wrung it out as well as we could, turned the hair outside, and have spent a capital night in it."

On the evening of the same day, I wrote: "To-day I have patched my kayak, and we have gone over all the seams in both kayaks with stearine; so now we hope we shall be able to go on in quite sound boats. In the meantime the walruses are lying outside, staring at us with their great, round eyes, grunting and blowing, and now and then clambering up on the edge of the ice, as though they wanted to drive us away.

"Tuesday, June 23rd. "'Do I sleep? do I dream? / Do I wonder and doubt? / Are things what they seem? / Or is visions about?'

What has happened? I can still scarcely grasp it. How incessant are the vicissitudes in this wandering life! A few days ago swimming in the water for dear life, attacked by walrus, living the savage life which I have lived for more than a year now, and sure of a long journey before us, over ice and sea, through unknown regions, before we should meet with other human beings — a journey full of the same ups and downs, the same disappointments, that we have become so accustomed to — and now living the life of a civilised European, surrounded by everything that civilisation can afford of luxury and good living, with abundance of water, soap, towels, clean, soft woollen clothes, books, and everything that we have been sighing for all these weary months.

"It was past midday on June 17th when I turned out to prepare breakfast. I had been down to the edge of the ice to fetch salt water, had made up the fire, cut up the meat, and put it in the pot, and had already taken off one boot preparatory to creeping into the bag again, when I saw that the mist over the land had risen a little since the preceding day. I thought it would be as well to take the opportunity of having a look round, so I put on my boot again, and went up on to a hummock near to look at the land beyond. A gentle breeze came from the land, bearing with it a confused noise of thousands of bird-voices from the mountain there. As I listened to these sounds of life and movement, watched flocks of auks flying to and fro above my head, and as my eye followed the line of coast, stopping at the dark, naked cliffs, glancing at the cold, icy plains and glaciers in a land which I believed to be unseen by any human eye and untrodden by any human foot, reposing in arctic majesty behind its mantle of mist — a sound suddenly reached my ear, so like the barking of a dog, that I started. It was only a couple of barks, but it could not be anything else. I strained my ears, but heard no more, only the same bubbling noise of thousands of birds. I must have been mistaken, after all; it was only birds I had heard; and again my eye passed from sound to island in the west. Then the barking came again, first single barks, then full cry; there was one deep bark, and one sharper; there was no longer any room for doubt. At that moment, I remembered having heard two reports the day before, which I thought sounded like shots, but I had explained them away as noises in the ice. I now shouted to Johansen that I heard dogs farther inland. Johansen started up from the bag where he lay sleeping, and tumbled out of the tent. 'Dogs?' He could not quite take it in, but had to get up and listen with his own ears, while I got breakfast ready. He very much doubted the possibility of such a thing, yet fancied once or twice that he heard something which might be taken for the barking of dogs;

but then it was drowned again in the bird-noises, and, everything considered, he thought that what I had heard was nothing more than that. I said he might believe what he liked, but I meant to set off as quickly as possible, and was impatient to get breakfast swallowed. I had emptied the last of the Indian meal into the soup, feeling sure that we should have farinaceous food enough by the evening. As we were eating we discussed who it could be, whether our countrymen or Englishmen. If it was the English expedition to Franz Josef Land which had been in contemplation when we started, what should we do? 'Oh, we'll just have to remain with them a day or two,' said Johansen, 'and then we'll have to go on to Spitzbergen, else it will be too long before we get home." We were quite agreed on this point; but we would take care to get some good provisions for the voyage out of them. While I went on, Johansen was to stay behind and mind the kayaks, so that we should run no risk of their drifting away with the ice. I got out my snowshoes, glass, and gun, and was ready. Before starting, I went up once more to listen, and look out a road across the uneven ice to the land. But there was not a sound like the barking of dogs, only noisy auks, harsh-toned little auks, and screaming kittiwakes. Was it these, after all, that I had heard? I set off in doubt. Then in front of me I saw the fresh tracks of an animal. They could hardly have been made by a fox, for if they were, the foxes here must be bigger than any I had ever seen. But dogs? Could a dog have been no more than a few hundred paces from us in the night without barking, or without our having heard it? It seemed scarcely probable; but whatever it was, it could never have been a fox. A wolf, then? I went on, my mind full of strange thoughts, hovering between certainty and doubt. Was all our toil, were all our troubles, privations, and sufferings, to end here? It seemed incredible, and yet — Out of the shadowland of doubt, certainty was at last beginning to dawn. Again the sound of a dog yelping reached my ear, more distinctly than ever; I saw more and more tracks which could be nothing but those of a dog. Among them were foxes' tracks and how small they looked! A long time passed, and nothing was to be heard but the noise of the birds. Again arose doubt as to whether it was all an illusion. Perhaps it was only a dream. But then I remembered the dogs' tracks; they, at any rate, were no delusion. But if there were people here, we could scarcely be on Gillies Land or a new land, as we had believed all the winter. We must after all be upon the south side of Franz Josef Land, and the suspicion I had had a few days ago was correct, namely, that we had come south through an unknown sound and out between Hooker Island and Northbrook Island, and were now off the latter, in spite of the impossibility of reconciling our position with Payer's map.

"It was with a strange mixture of feelings that I made my way in towards land among the numerous hummocks and inequalities. Suddenly I thought I heard a shout from a human voice, a strange voice, the first for three years. How my heart beat, and the blood rushed to my brain, as I ran up on to a hummock, and hallooed with all the strength of my lungs. Behind that one human voice in the midst of the icy desert, this one message from life, stood home and she who was waiting there; and I saw nothing else as I made my way between bergs and ice-ridges. Soon I heard another shout, and saw, too, from an ice-ridge, a dark form moving among the hummocks farther in. It was a dog; but farther off came another figure, and that was a man. Who was it? Was it Jackson or one of his companions, or was it perhaps a fellow-countryman? We approached one another quickly; I waved my hat: he did the same. I heard him speak to the dog, and I listened. It was English, and as I drew nearer I thought I recognised Mr. Jackson, whom I remembered once to have seen.

"I raised my hat; we extended a hand to one another, with a hearty 'How do you do?' Above us a roof of mist, shutting out the world around, beneath our feet the rugged, packed drift-ice, and in the background a glimpse of the land, all ice, glacier, and mist. On one side the civilised European in an English check suit and high rubber water-boots, well shaved, well groomed, bringing with him a perfume of scented soap, perceptible to the wild man's sharpened senses; on the other side the wild man, clad in dirty rags, black with oil and soot, with long, uncombed hair and shaggy beard, black with smoke, with a face in which the natural fair complexion could not possibly be discerned through the thick layer of fat and soot which a winter's endeavours with warm water, moss, rags, and at last a knife had sought in vain to remove. No one suspected who he was or whence he came.

"Jackson: 'I'm immensely glad to see you.'

"'Thank you, I am also.'

"'Have you a ship here?'

"'No; my ship is not here.'

"'How many are there of you?'

"'I have one companion at the ice-edge.'

"As we talked, we had begun to go in towards land. I took it for granted that he had recognised me, or at any rate understood who it was that was hidden behind this savage exterior, not thinking that a total stranger would be received so heartily. Suddenly he stopped, looked me full in the face, and said quickly:

"'Aren't you Nansen?' — 'Yes, I am.'

"'By Jove! I am glad to see you!'

"And he seized my hand and shook it again, while his whole face became one smile of welcome, and delight at the unexpected meeting beamed from his dark eyes.

"'Where have you come from now?' he asked.

"'I left the *Fram* in 84° N. lat., after having drifted for two years, and I reached the 86° 15' parallel, where we had to turn and make for Franz Josef Land. We were, however, obliged to stop for the winter somewhere north here, and are now on our route to Spitzbergen.'

"'I congratulate you most heartily. You have made a good trip of it, and I am awfully glad to be the first person to congratulate you on your return.'"

"Once more he seized my hand, and shook it heartily. I could not have been welcomed more warmly; that handshake was more than a mere form. In his hospitable English manner, he said at once that he had 'plenty of room' for us, and that he was expecting his ship every day. By 'plenty of room' I discovered afterwards that he meant that there were still a few square feet on the floor of their but that were not occupied at night by himself and his sleeping companions. But 'heart-room makes house-room,' and of the former there was no lack. As soon as I could get a word in, I asked how things were getting on at home, and he was able to give me the welcome intelligence that my wife and child had both been in the best of health when he left two years ago. Then came Norway's turn, and Norwegian politics; but he knew nothing about that, and I took it as a sign that they must be all right too. He now asked if we could not go out at once, and fetch Johansen and our belongings; but I thought that our kayaks would be too heavy for us to drag over this packed-up ice alone, and that if he had men enough it would certainly be better to send them out. If we only gave Johansen notice by a salute from our guns, he would wait patiently; so we each fired two shots. We soon met several men: Mr. Armitage, the second in command, Mr. Child, the photographer, and the doctor, Mr. Koetlitz. As they approached, Jackson gave them a sign, and let them understand who I was; and I was again welcomed heartily. We met yet others: the botanist, Mr. Fisher, Mr. Burgess, and the Finn Blomqvist (his real name was Melenius). Fisher has since told me that he at once thought it must be me when he saw a man out on the ice; but he quite gave up that idea when he met me, for he had seen me described as a fair man, and here was a dark man, with black hair and beard. When they were all there, Jackson said that I had reached 86° 15' N. lat., and from seven powerful lungs I was given a triple British cheer, that echoed among the hummocks. Jackson immediately sent his men off to fetch sledges and go out to Johansen, while we went on towards the house which I now thought I could see on the shore. Jackson now told me that he had letters for me from home, and that both last spring and this he had had them with him when he went north, on the chance of our meeting. We now found that in March he must have been at no great distance south of our winter-hut,[135] but had to turn there, as he was stopped by open water, the same open water over which we had seen the dark atmosphere all the

Meeting Jackson, Cape Flora, 17 June 1896.

winter. Only when we came up nearly to the houses did he inquire more particularly about the *Fram* and our drifting, and I briefly told him our story. He told me afterwards that from the time we met he had believed that the ship had been destroyed, and that we two were the only survivors of the expedition. He thought he had seen a sad expression in my face when he first asked about the ship, and was afraid of touching on the subject again. Indeed, he had even quietly warned his men not to ask. It was only through a chance remark of mine that he found out his mistake, and began to inquire more particularly about the *Fram* and the others.

"Then we arrived at the house, a low Russian timber hut, lying on a flat terrace, an old shore-line, beneath the mountain, and 50 feet above the sea. It was surrounded by a stable and four circular tent-houses, in which stores were kept. We entered a comfortable, warm nest in the midst of these desolate, wintry surroundings, the roof and walls covered with green cloth. On the walls hung photographs, etchings, photo-lithographs, and shelves everywhere, containing books and instruments; under the roof clothes and shoes hung drying, and from the little stove in the middle of the floor of this snug room the warm coal fire shone out a hospitable welcome. A strange feeling came over me as I seated myself in a comfortable chair in these unwonted surroundings. At one stroke of changing fate, all responsibility, all troubles, were swept away from a mind that had been oppressed by them during three long years; I was in a safe haven, in the midst of the ice, and the longings of three years were lulled in the golden sunshine of the dawning day. My duty was done: my task was ended; now I could rest, only rest and wait.

"A carefully soldered tin packet was handed to me; it contained letters from Norway. It was almost with a trembling hand and a beating heart that I opened it; and there were tidings, only good tidings, from home. A delightful feeling of peace settled upon the soul.

"Then dinner was served, and how nice it was to have bread butter, milk, sugar, coffee, and everything that a year had taught us to do without and yet to long for. But the height of comfort was reached when we were able to throw off our dirty rags, have a warm bath, and get rid of as much dirt as was possible in one bout; but we only succeeded in becoming anything like clean after several days and many attempts. Then clean, soft clothes from head to foot, hair cut, and the shaggy beard shaved off, and the transformation from savage to European was complete, and even more sudden than in the reverse direction. How delightfully comfortable it was to be able to put on one's clothes without being made greasy, but most of all to be able to move without feeling them stick to the body with every movement.

"It was not very long before Johansen and the others followed, with the kayaks and our things. Johansen related how these warm-hearted Englishmen had given him and the Norwegian flag a hearty cheer when they came up and saw it waving beside a dirty woollen shirt on a bamboo rod which he had put up by my orders, so that I could find my way back to him. On the way hither they had not allowed him to touch the sledges, he had only to walk beside them like a passenger, and he said that, of all the ways in which we had travelled over drift-ice, this was without comparison the most comfortable. His reception in the hut was scarcely less hospitable than mine, and he soon went through the same transformation that I had undergone. I no longer recognise my comrade of the long winter night, and search in vain for any trace of the tramp who wandered up and down that desolate shore, beneath the steep talus and the dark basalt cliff, outside the low underground hut. The black, sooty troglodyte has vanished, and in his place sits a well-favoured, healthy-looking European citizen in a comfortable chair, puffing away at a short pipe or a cigar, and with a book before him, doing his best to learn English. It seems to me that he gets fatter and fatter every day, with an almost alarming rapidity. It is indeed surprising that we have both gained considerably in weight since we left the *Fram*. When I came here, I myself weighed about 14½ stone, or nearly 22 lbs. more than I did when I left the *Fram*; while

Nansen in front of Jackson's hut.

Johansen weighs over 11 stone 11 lbs., having gained a little more than 13 lbs. This is the result of a winter's feeding on nothing but bear's meat and fat in an Arctic climate. It is not quite like the experiences of others in parallel circumstances; it must be our laziness that has done it. And here we are, living in peace and quietness, waiting for the ship from home and for what the future will bring us, while everything is being done for us to make us forget a winter's privations. We could not have fallen into better hands, and it is impossible to describe the unequalled hospitality and kindness we meet with on all hands, and the comfort we feel. Is it the year's privations and want of human society, is it common interests, that so draw us to these men in these desolate regions? I do not know; but we are never tired of talking, and it seems as if we had known one another for years, instead of having met for the first time a few days ago."

"Wednesday, June 23rd. It is now three years since we left home. As we sat at the dinner-table this evening, Hayward, the cook, came rushing in and said there was a bear outside. We went out, Jackson with his camera and I with my rifle. We saw the head of the bear above the edge of the shore; it was sniffing the air in the direction of the hut, while a couple of dogs stood at a respectful distance and barked. As we approached, it came right up over the edge to us, stopped, showed its teeth, and hissed, then turned round and went slowly back down towards the shore. To hinder it enough for Jackson to get near and photograph it, I sent a bullet into its hind-quarters as it disappeared over the edge. This helped, and a ball in the left shoulder still more. Surrounded by a few dogs, it now made a stand. The dogs grew bolder, and a couple of shots in the muzzle from Jackson's revolver made the bear quite furious. It sprang first at one dog, 'Misere,' caught hold of it by the back, and flung it a good way out over the ice, then sprang at the other, seizing it by one paw and tearing one toe badly. It then found an old tin box, bit it flat, and flung it far away. It was wild with fury, but a ball behind the ear ended its sufferings. It was a she-bear, with milk in the breast; but there was no sign of any embryo, and no young one was discovered in the neighbourhood."

"Sunday, July 15th. This evening, when Jackson and the doctor were up on the mountain shooting auks, the dogs began to make a tremendous row, especially the bear-dog 'Nimrod,' which is chained outside the door, and howled and whined in a suspicious manner. Armitage went out, coming back a little while after and asking if I cared to shoot a bear. I accompanied him, with my rifle and camera. The bear had taken flight to a little hummock out on the ice south of the house, and was lying at full length on the top of it, with 'Misere' and a couple of puppies round it, standing at a little distance and barking persistently. As we approached, it fled over the ice; the range was long, but, nevertheless, we sent a few shots after it, thinking we might perhaps retard its progress. With one of these I was fortunate enough to hit it in the hind-quarters, and it now fled to a new ice-hill. Here I was able to get nearer to it. It was evidently very much enraged; and when I came under the hummock where it stood, it showed its teeth, and hissed at me, and repeatedly gave signs of wanting to jump down on top of me. On these occasions I rapidly got ready my rifle instead of the camera. It scraped away the loose snow from under its feet to get a better footing for the leap which, however, it never took; and I re-exchanged my rifle for my camera. In the meantime, Jackson had arrived, with his camera, on the other side; and when we had taken all the photographs we wanted, we shot the bear. It was an unusually large she-bear."

One of the first things we did when we came to Mr. Jackson's station was of course to make a close comparison of our watches with his chronometer; and Mr. Armitage was also kind enough to take careful time observations for me. It now appears that we had not been so far out after all. We had put our watches about 26 minutes wrong, making a difference of about 6½° in longitude. A protracted comparison undertaken by Mr. Armitage also showed that the escapement of our watches was very nearly what we had assumed. With the help of this information, I was now enabled to work out our longitude observations pretty correctly; and one of the first tasks I here set about, now that we once more had access to paper, writing and drawing-materials, and all that we had longed for so much during the winter, was to prepare a sketch-map of Franz Josef Land, as our observations led me to conclude that it must actually be. Mr. Jackson very kindly allowed me to consult the map he had made of that part of the land which he had explored. This enabled me to dispense with the labour of reckoning out my own observations in these localities. Furthermore, I have to thank Mr. Jackson for aid in every possible way, with navigation-tables, Nautical Almanack,[136] scales, and all sorts of drawing material.

It is by a comparison of Payer's map, Jackson's map, and my own observations, that I have made out the sketch-map here reproduced. I have altered Payer's and Jackson's map only at places where my observations differ essentially from theirs. I make no pretence to give more than a provisional sketch; I had not even time to work out my own observations with absolute accuracy. When this has been done, and if I can gain access to all Payer's material, no doubt a considerably more trustworthy map can be produced. The only importance which I claim for the accompanying map is that it shows roughly how what we have hitherto called Franz Josef Land is cut up into innumerable small islands, without any continuous and extensive mass of land. Much of Payer's map I found to coincide well enough with our observations. But the enigma over which we had pondered the whole winter still remained unsolved. Where were Dove Glacier and the whole northern part of Wilczek Land? Where were the islands which Payer had named Braun Island, Hoffmann Island, and Freeden Island? The last might, no doubt, be identified with the southernmost island of Hvidtenland (White Land), but the others had completely disappeared. I pondered for a long time over the question how such a mistake could have crept into a map by such a man as Payer — an experienced topographer, whose maps, as a rule, bear the stamp of great accuracy and care, and a Polar traveller for whose ability I have always entertained a high respect. I examined his account of his voyage, and there I found that he expressly mentions that during the time he was coasting along this Dove Glacier he had a great deal of fog, which quite concealed the land ahead. But one day (it was April 7th, 1874) he says: "At this latitude (81° 23′) it seemed as if Wilczek Land suddenly terminated, but when the sun scattered the driving mists we saw the glittering ranges of its enormous glaciers — the Dove Glaciers — shining down on us. Towards the north-east we could trace land trending to a cape lying in the grey distance: Cape Buda-Pesth, as it was afterwards called. The prospect thus opened to us of a vast glacier land conflicted with the general impression we had formed of the resemblance between the newly discovered region and Spitzbergen; for glaciers of such extraordinary magnitude presuppose the existence of a country stretching far into the interior."

I have often thought over this description, and I cannot find in Payer's book any other information that throws light upon the mystery. Although, according to this, it would appear as if they had had clear weather that day, there must, nevertheless, have been fog-banks lying over Hvidtenland, uniting it with Wilczek Land to the south and stretching northwards towards Crown-Prince Rudolf Land. The sun shining on these fog-banks must have glittered so that they were taken for glaciers along a continuous coast. I can all the more easily understand this mistake as I was myself on the point of falling into it. As before related, if the weather had not cleared on the evening of June 11th, enabling us to discern the sound between Northbrook Island and Peter Head (Alexandra Land), we should have remained under the impression that we had here continuous land, and should have represented it as such in mapping this region.

Mr. Jackson and I frequently discussed the naming of the lands we had explored. I asked him whether he would object to my naming the land on which I had wintered "Frederick Jackson's Island," as a small token of our gratitude for the hospitality he had shown us. We had made the discovery that this island was separated by sounds from the land farther north, which Payer had named Karl Alexander Land. For the rest, I refrained from giving names to any of the places which Jackson had seen before I saw them.

The country around Cape Flora proved to be very interesting from a geological point of view, and as often as time permitted I investigated its structure, either alone, or more frequently in company with the doctor and geologist of the English expedition, Dr. Koetlitz. We made many an interesting excursion together up and down those steep moraines in search of fossils, which in certain places we found in great numbers. It appeared that from the sea-level up to a height of about 500 or 600 feet the land consisted of a soft clay mixed with lumps of a red-brown clay sandstone, in which lumps the fossils chiefly abounded. But the earth was so overstrewn with loose stones which had rolled down from the basalt walls above, that it was difficult to reach it. For a long time I maintained that all this clay was only a comparatively late strand formation; but the doctor was indefatigable in his efforts to convince me that it really was an old and very extensive formation, stretching right under the superimposed basalt. At last I had to yield, when we arrived at the topmost stratum of the clay, and I saw it actually going under the basalt, and found some shallower strata of basalt lower down in the clay. An examination of the fossils, which consisted for the most part of ammonites and belemnites, convinced me that the whole of this clay formation must date from the Jurassic period. At several places Dr. Koetlitz had found thin strata of coal in the clay. Petrified wood was also of common occurrence. But over the clay formation lay a mighty bed of basalt 600 or 700 feet in height, which was certainly not the least interesting feature of the country. It was distinguished by its coarse-grained structure from the majority of typical basalts, and seemed to be closely related to those which are found in Spitzbergen and North-East Land.[137] The basalt, however, seems to vary a good deal in appearance here in Franz Josef Land. That which we found further north — for example, at Cape M'Clintock and on Goose Island — was considerably more coarse-grained than that which we found here. The situation of the basalt here on Northbrook Island and the surrounding islands was also very different from that which we had observed farther north. It is here met with, as a rule, only at a height of 500 or 600 feet above the sea, while on the more northerly islands — from 81° northwards — it reached right to the shore. Thus it dropped in an almost perpendicular wall straight into the sea at Jackson's Cape Fisher, in 81°. It was the same at Cape M'Clintock, at our winter cabin, at the headland of columnar basalt where we passed the night of August 25th, 1895, at Cape Clements Markham, and at the sharp point of rock where we landed on the night between August 16th and 17th. The structure seemed to be similar, too, so far as we had seen, on the south side of Crown-Prince Rudolf's Land. Wherever we had been to the northward I had kept a sharp look-out for strata whose fossils could give us any information as to the geological age of this country. According to what I here found at Cape Flora, it appeared as if a great part, at least, of this basalt dated from the Jurassic period, as it lay immediately above, and was partly intermixed with, strata of this age. Moreover, on the top of the basalt, as will presently appear, vegetable fossils were found dating from the later part of the Jurassic period. It thus seems as though Franz Josef Land were of a comparatively old formation. All these horizontal strata of basalt, stretching over all the islands at about the same height, seem to indicate that there was once a continuous mass of land here, which in the course of time, being exposed to various disintegrating forces such as frost, damp, snow, glaciers, and the sea, has been split up and worn away, and has in part disappeared under the sea, so that now only scattered islands and rocks remain, separated from each other by fjords and sounds. As these formations bear a certain resemblance to what has been found in several places in Spitzbergen and North-East Land, we may plausibly assume that these two groups of islands originally belonged to the same mass of land. It would, therefore, be interesting to investigate the as yet unknown region which separates them, the region which we should have had to traverse had we not fallen in with Jackson and his expedition. There is doubtless much that is new, and especially many new islands, to be found in this strait — possibly a continuous series of islands, so that there may be some difficulty in determining where the one archipelago ends and the other begins. The investigation of this region is a problem of no small scientific importance, which we may hope that the Jackson-Harmsworth Expedition will succeed in solving.

How far the Franz Josef Land archipelago stretches towards the north cannot as yet be determined with certainty. According to our experience, indeed, it would seem improbable that there is land of any great extent in that direction. It is true that Payer, when he was upon Crown-Prince Rudolf's Land, saw Petermann's Land and Oscar's Land, the first to the north and the second to the west; but that Petermann's Land, at any rate, cannot be of any size, seems to be proved by our observations, since we saw no land at all as we came southwards a good way east of it, and the ice seemed to drift to the westward practically unimpeded when we were in its latitude. That King Oscar's Land also cannot be of any great extent seems to me evident from what we saw in the course of the winter and spring, as the wind swept the ice unhindered away from the land, so that there can scarcely be any extensive and continuous mass of land to the north or north-west to keep it back.

It is, perhaps, even more difficult to determine how far the Franz Josef Land archipelago stretches to the eastward. From all we saw, I should judge that Wilczek

Land cannot be of any great extent; but there may nevertheless be new islands further to the east. This seems probable, indeed, from the fact that in June and July, 1895, we remained almost motionless at about 82° 5′ N. lat., in spite of a long continuance of northerly winds; whence it seemed that there must be a stretch of land south of us obstructing, like a long wall, the further drift of the ice to the southward. But it is useless to discuss this question minutely here, as it, too, will doubtless be answered authoritatively by the English expedition.

Another feature of Northbrook Island which greatly interested me was the evidence it presented of changes in the level of the sea. I have already mentioned that Jackson's hut lay on an old strand-line or terrace about from 40 to 50 feet high, but there were also several other strand-lines, both lower and higher. Thus I found that Leigh Smith, who also had wintered on this headland, had built his hut upon an old strand-line 17 feet above the sea-level, while at other places I found strand-lines at a height of 80 feet. I had already noticed such strand-lines at different elevations when I first arrived in the previous autumn at the more northern part of this region (for example, on Torup's Island). Indeed we had lived all the winter on such a terrace.

Jackson had found whales' skeletons at several places about Cape Flora. Close to his hut, for instance, at a height of 50 feet, there laid the skull of a whale, a balaena, possibly a Greenland whale (*balaena mysticetus?*). At a point farther north there lay fragments of a whole skeleton, probably of the same species. The underjaw was 18 feet 3 inches long; but these bones lay at an elevation of not more than 9 feet above the present sea-level. I also found other indications that the sea must at a comparatively recent period have risen above these low strand-terraces. For instance, they were at many points strewn with mussel shells. This land, then, seems to have been subjected to changes of level analogous to those which have occurred in other northern countries, of which, as above mentioned, I had also seen indications on the north coast of Asia.

One day when Mr. Jackson and Dr. Koetlitz were out on an excursion together they found on a "nunatak," or spur of rock, projecting above a glacier on the north side of Cape Flora, two places which were strewn with vegetable fossils. This discovery, of course, aroused my keenest interest, and on July the 17th Dr. Koetlitz and I set out for the spot together. The spur of rock consisted entirely of basalt, at some points showing a marked columnar structure, and projected in the middle of the glacier, at a height which I estimated at 600 or 700 feet above the sea. Unfortunately there was no time to measure its elevation exactly. At two points on the surface of the basalt there was a layer consisting of innumerable fragments of sandstone. In almost every one of these impressions were to be found, for the most part of the needles and 21 leaves of pine-trees, but also of small fern-leaves. We picked up as many of these treasures as we could carry, and returned that evening heavily laden and in high contentment. On a snowshoe excursion, some days later, Johansen also chanced unwittingly upon the same place, and gathered fossils, which he brought to me. Since my return home, this collection of vegetable fossils has been examined by Professor Nathorst, and it appears that Mr. Jackson and Dr. Koetlitz have here made an extremely interesting find.

Professor Nathorst writes to me as follows: "In spite of their very fragmentary condition the vegetable fossils brought home by you are of great interest, as they give us our first insight into the plant world in regions north of the eightieth degree of latitude during the latter part of the Jurassic period. The most common are leaves of a fir-tree (pinus) which resembles the *pinus nordenskiöldi* (Heer) found in the Jurassic strata of Spitzbergen, East Siberia, and Japan, but which probably belongs to a different species. There occur also narrower leaves of another species, and furthermore male flowers and fragments of a pine cone[38] with several seeds (Figs. 1-3), one of which (Fig. 1) suggests the *pinus maakiana* (Heer) from the Jurassic strata of Siberia. Among traces of other pine-trees may be mentioned those of a broad-leaved taxites resembling *taxites gramineus* (Heer) specially found in the Jurassic strata of Spitzbergen and Siberia, which has leaves of about the same size as those of the *cephalotaxus fortunei*, at present existing in China and Japan. It is interesting, too, to find remains of the genus Feildenia (Figs. 4 and 5), which has as yet been found only in the Polar regions. It was first discovered by Nordenskiöld in the tertiary strata near Cape Staratschin on Spitzbergen, in 1868, and was described by Heer under the name of Torellia. It was subsequently found by Feilden in the tertiary strata at Discovery Bay, in Grinnell Land, during the English Polar Expedition of 1875-76; and Heer now changed the generic name to Feildenia, as Torellia had already been employed as the name of a mussel. This species has since been found by me in 1882 in the upper Jurassic strata of Spitzbergen. The leaves remind one of the leaves of the sub-species nageia of the existing genus podocarpus.

"The finest specimens of the whole collection are the leaves of a small gingko, of which one is complete (Fig. 6). This genus, with plum-like seeds and with leaves which, unlike those of other pine-trees, have a real leaf-blade, is found at present, in one single species only, in Japan, but existed in former times in numerous forms and in many regions. During the Jurassic period it flourished especially in East Siberia, and has also been found on Spitzbergen, in East Greenland (at Scoresby Sound), and at many places in Europe, etc. During the cretaceous and the tertiary periods it was still found on the west coast of Greenland at 70° N. lat. The leaf here reproduced belongs to a new species which might be called *ginkgo polaris,* and which is most closely related to the g. flabellata (Heer) from the Jurassic strata of Siberia. It bears a certain habitual resemblance to *ginkgo digitata* (Lindley and Hutton), particularly as found in the brown Jurassic strata of England and Spitzbergen; but its leaves are considerably smaller. Besides this species, one or two others may also occur in this collection, as well as fragments of the leaves of the genus czekanowskia, related to the ginkgo family, but with narrow leaf-blades resembling pine-needles.

"Ferns are very scantily represented. Such fragments as there are belong to four different types; but the species can scarcely be determined. One fragment belongs to the genus cladophlebis, common in jurassic strata; another suggests the thyrsopteris found in the jurassic strata of East Siberia and of England; a third suggests the onychiopsis characteristic of the upper jurassic strata. The fourth, again, seems to be closely related to the *asplenium (petruschinense),* which Heer has described, found in the Siberian jurassic strata. The specimen is remarkable from the fact that the epidermis cells of the leaf have left a clear impression on the rock.

"With its wealth of pine leaves, its poverty of ferns, and its lack of cycadeae, this Franz Josef Land flora has somewhat the same character as that of the upper jurassic flora of Spitzbergen, although the species are somewhat different. Like the Spitzbergen flora, it does not indicate a particularly genial climate, although doubtless enormously more so than that of the present day. The deposits must doubtless have occurred in the neighbourhood of a pine forest. So far as the specimens enable one to judge, the flora seems to belong rather to the upper (white) jurassic system than to the middle (brown) system."

It was undeniably a sudden transition to come straight from our long inert life in our winter lair, where one's scientific interests found little enough stimulus, right into the midst of this scientific oasis, where there was plenty of opportunity for work, where books and all necessary apparatus were at hand, and where one could employ one's leisure-moments in discussing with men of similar tastes all sorts of scientific questions connected with the Arctic zone. In the botanist of the expedition, Mr. Harry Fisher, I found a man full of the warmest interest in the fauna and flora of the Polar regions, and the exhaustive investigations which his residence here has enabled him to make into the plant-life and animal-life (especially the former) of the locality, both by sea and land, will certainly augment in a most valuable degree our knowledge of its biological conditions. I shall not easily forget the many pleasant talks in which he communicated to me his discoveries and observations. They were all eagerly absorbed by a mind long deprived of such sustenance. I felt like a piece of parched soil drinking in rain after a drought of a whole year.

But other diversions were also available. If my brain grew fatigued with unwonted labour, I could set off with Jackson for the top of the moraine to shoot auks, which swarmed under the basalt walls. They roosted in hundreds and hundreds on the shelves and ledges above us; at other places the kittiwakes brooded on their nests. It was a refreshing scene of life and activity. As we stood up there at a height of 500 feet, and could look far out over the sea, the auks flew in swarms backward and forwards over our heads, and every now and then we would knock over one or two as they passed. Every time a gun was fired, the report echoed through all the rocky clefts, and thousands of birds flew shrieking down from the ledges. It seemed as though a blast of wind had swept a great dust-cloud down from the crest above; but little by little they returned to their nests, many of them meanwhile falling to our guns. Jackson had here a capital larder, and he made ample use of it. Almost every day he was up under the rock shooting auks, which formed a daily dish at dinner. In the autumn great stores of them were laid in to last through the winter. At other times Jackson and Blomqvist would go up and gather eggs. They dragged a ladder up with them, and by its aid Jackson clambered up the perpendicular cliffs. This egg-hunting among the loose basalt cliffs where the stones were perpetually slipping away from under one, appeared to me such dare-devil work that I was chary of taking part in it. Far be it from me to deny, however, that the eggs made delicious eating, whether we had them soft-boiled for breakfast, or made into pancakes for dinner. It was remarkable how entirely I had got out of training for climbing in precipitous places. I well remember that the first time I went up the moraine with Jackson, I had to stop and take breath every hundred paces or so. This was, no doubt, due to our long inactivity; perhaps, too, I had become somewhat anaemic during the winter in our lair. But there was more than that in it; the very height and steepness made me uneasy, I was inclined to turn dizzy, and had great difficulty in coming down again, preferring, if possible, simply to sit down and slide. After a while this passed off a little, and I became more accustomed to the heights again. I also became less short-winded, and at last I could climb almost like a normal human being. In the meantime the days wore on, and still we saw nothing of the *Windward*. Johansen and I began to get a little impatient. We discussed the possibility that the ship might not make its way through the ice, and that we should have to winter here after all. This idea was not particularly attractive to us — to be so near home and yet not to reach home. We regretted that we had not at once pushed on for Spitzbergen; perhaps we should by this time have reached the much talked-of sloop. When we came to think of it, why on earth had we stopped here? That was easily explained. These people were so kind and hospitable to us that it would have been more than Spartan had we been able to resist their amiability. And then we had gone through a good deal before we arrived, and here was a warm cosy nest, where we had nothing to do but to sit down and wait. Waiting, however, is not always the easiest of work, and we began seriously to think of setting off again for Spitzbergen. But had we not delayed too long? It was the middle of July, and although we should probably get on quickly enough, we might meet with unexpected impediments, and it might take us a month or more to reach the waters in which we could hope to find a ship. That would bring us to the middle or perhaps to the end of August, by which time the sloops had begun to make for home. If we did not come across one at once, when we got into September it would be difficult enough to get hold of one, and then we should perhaps be in for another winter of it after all. No, it was best to remain here, for there was every chance that the ship would make its appearance. The best time for navigating these waters is August and the beginning of September, when there is generally the least ice. We must trust to that, and let the time pass as best it might. There were others than we who waited impatiently for the ship. Four members of the English expedition were also to go home in her, after two years' absence.

"Monday, July 10th. We begin to get more and more impatient for the arrival of the vessel, but the ice is still tolerably thick here. Jackson says that she should have been here by the middle of June, and thinks that there has, several times, been sufficiently open water for her to have got through; but I have my doubts about that. Though only a little scattered ice is to be seen here, even from a height of 500 feet, that does not mean much; there may be more ice farther south blocking the way. One day Jackson and the doctor were on the top of the mountain here, and from that point, too, there seemed to be very little ice in the south; but I am not convinced any the more. I think all experience goes to show that there must still be plenty of ice in the sea to the south. What Mr. Jackson says about the *Windward* having been able to get through as early as July last year without needing to touch the ice, adding that then, too, there was no ice to be seen from here, I do not find at all conclusive. During the last few days more ice has again come drifting in from the east. I long to get away. What if we are shut in here all the winter? Then we shall have done wrong in stopping here. Why did we not continue our journey to Spitzbergen? We should have been at home by now. The eye wanders out over the boundless white plain. Not one dark streak of water-ice, ice! ? shut out from the world, from the throbbing life, the life that we believed to be so near.

"Low down on the horizon there is a strip of blue-grey cloud. Far, far away beyond the ice there is open water, and perhaps there, rocked on long swelling billows from the great ocean, lies the vessel which is to bear us to the familiar shores; the vessel which brings tidings from home, and from those we love.

"Dream, dream of home and beauty! Stray bird, here among the ice and snow you will seek for them all in vain. Dream the golden dream of future re-union!"

"Tuesday, July 2lst. Have at last got a good wind from the north which is sending the ice out to sea. There is nothing but open sea to be seen this evening; now perhaps there is hope of soon seeing the vessel."

"Wednesday, July 22nd. Continual changes and continual disappointments. Yesterday hope was strong; today the wind has changed to the south-east, and driven the ice in again. We may still have to wait a long time."

"Sunday, July 26th. The vessel has come at last. I was awakened this morning by feeling some one pull my legs. It was Jackson, who, with beaming countenance, announced that the *Windward* had come. I jumped up and looked out of the window. There she was, just beyond the edge of the ice, steaming slowly in to find an anchorage. Wonderful to see a ship again! How high the rigging seemed, and the hull! It was like an island. There would be tidings on board from the great world far beyond."

There was a general stir. Every man was up, arrayed in the most wonderful costumes, to gaze out of the window. Jackson and Blomqvist rushed off as soon as they had got on their clothes. As I scarcely had anything to do on board at present I went to bed again, but it was not long before Blomqvist came panting back, sent by the thoughtful Jackson, to say that all was well at home, and that nothing had been heard of the *Fram*. This was the first thing Jackson had asked about. I felt my heart as light as a feather. He said, too, that when Jackson had told the men who had come to meet him on the ice about us and our journey, they had greeted the intelligence with three hearty cheers.

I had hardly slept two hours that night, and not much more the night before. I tried to sleep, but there was no rest to be had; I might just as well dress and go on board. As I drew near the vessel, I was greeted with ringing cheers by the whole crew gathered on the deck, where I was heartily received by the excellent Captain Brown, commander of the *Windward*, by Dr. Bruce and Mr. Wilton, who were both to winter with Jackson, and by the ship's company. We went below into the roomy, snug cabin, and all kinds of news were eagerly swallowed by listening ears, while an excellent breakfast with fresh potatoes and other delicacies glided down past a palate which needed less than that to satisfy it. There were remarkable pieces of news indeed. One of the first was that now they could photograph people through doors several inches thick. I confess I pricked up my ears at this information. That they could photograph a bullet buried in a person's body was wonderful too, but nothing to this. And then we heard that the Japanese had thrashed the Chinese, and a good deal more. Not least remarkable, we thought, was the interest which the whole world now seemed to take in the Arctic regions. Spitzbergen had become a tourist country; a Norwegian steamship company (the Vesteraalen) had started a regular passenger service to it,[139] a hotel had been built up there, and there was a post-office and a Spitzbergen stamp. And then we heard that Andree was there waiting for wind to go to the Pole in a balloon. If we had pursued our course to Spitzbergen, we should thus have dropped into the very middle of all this. We should have found a hotel and tourists, and should have been brought home in a comfortable modern steamboat, very different from the whaling sloop we had been talking of all the winter, and, indeed, all the previous year. People are apt to think that it would be amusing to see themselves, and I form no exception to this rule. I would have given a good deal to see us in our unwashed, unsophisticated condition, as we came out of our winter lair, plumping into the middle of a band of English tourists, male and female. I doubt whether there would then have been much embracing or shaking of hands, but I don't doubt that there would have been a great deal of peering through ventilators or any other loophole that could have been found.

The *Windward* had left London on June 9th, and Vardö on the 25th. They had brought four reindeer with them for Jackson, but no horses as he had expected.[140] One reindeer had died on the voyage.

Every one was now busily employed in unlading the *Windward*, and bringing to land the supplies of provisions, coal, reindeer-moss and other such things which it had brought for the expedition. Both the ship's crew and the members of the English expedition took part in this work, which proceeded rapidly, and had soon made a level road over the uneven ice, and now load after load was driven on sledges to land. In less than a week Captain Brown was ready to start for home, and only awaited Jackson's letters and telegrams. They took a few more days, and then everything was ready. In the meantime, however, a gale had sprung up, blowing on the shore, the *Windward's* moorings at the edge of the ice had given way, she was set adrift and obliged to seek a haven farther in, where, however, it was so shallow that there was only one or two feet of water beneath her keel. Meanwhile, the wind drove the ice in, the navigable water closed in all round it outside, and the floes were continually drawing nearer. For a time the situation looked anything but pleasant; but fortunately the ice did not reach the vessel, and she thus escaped being screwed out of the water. After a delay of a couple of days on this account the vessel got out again.

And now we were to bid adieu to this last station on our route where we had met with such a cordial and hospitable reception. A feverish energy came over the little colony. Those who were going home had to make themselves ready for the voyage, and those who were to remain had to bring their letters and other things on board. This, however, was sufficiently difficult. The vessel lay waiting impatiently and incessantly sounding her steam-whistle; and a quantity of loose ice had packed itself together outside the edge of the shore ice, so that it was not easy to move. At last, however, those who were to remain had gone on shore, and we who were going home were all on board — that is to say, Mr. Fisher, the botanist, Mr. Child, the chemist, Mr. Burgess, and the Finn, Blomqvist, of the English expedition, along with Johansen and myself. As the sun burst through the clouds above Cape Flora we waved our hats, and sent our last cheer as a farewell to the six men standing like a little dark spot on the floe in that great icy solitude; and under full sail and steam we set out on the 7th August, with a fair wind, over the undulating surface of the ocean, towards the south.

Fortune favoured us. On her northward voyage the *Windward* had much and difficult ice to combat with, before she at last broke through, and came in to land. Now, too, we met a quantity of ice, but it was slack and comparatively easy to get through. We were stopped in a few places, and had to break a way through with the engine; but the ship was in good hands. From his long experience as a whaler, Captain Brown knew well how to contend with greater odds than the thin ice we met with here — the only ice that is found in this sea. From morning till night he sat up in the crow's-nest as long as there was a bit of ice in the water. He gave himself little time for sleep; the point was, as he often said to me, to bring us home before the *Fram* arrived, for he understood well what a blow it would give to those near and dear to us if she got home before us.

Thanks to him, we had as short and pleasant a homeward voyage as few, if any, can have had from these inhospitable regions, where we had spent three years. From the moment we set foot on deck, he did everything to make us comfortable and at home on board, and we spent many a pleasant hour together, which will never be forgotten by either of us. But it was not only the captain who treated us in this way. Every man of the excellent crew showed us kindness and goodwill in every way. I cannot think of them — of the little steward for instance, when he popped his head into the cabin to ask what he could get for us, or wakened me in the morning with his cheery voice, or sang his songs for us — without a feeling of unspeakable well-being and happiness. Then, too, we were continually drawing nearer home; we could count the days and hours that must pass before we could reach a Norwegian port, and be once more in communication with the world.

From the experience he had had on the northward voyage, Captain Brown had

Eva Nansen on the *Otaria*.

come to the conclusion that he would find his way out of the ice most easily by first steering in a south-easterly direction towards Novaya Zemlya, which he thought would be the nearest way to the open sea. This proved also to be exactly the case. After having gone about 220 knots through the ice, we came into the open sea at the end of a long bay, which ran northwards into the ice. It was just at the right spot; had we been a little farther east or a little farther west, we might have spent as many weeks drifting about in the ice, as we now spent days in it. Once more we saw the blue ocean itself in front of us, and we shaped our course straight for Vardö. It was an indescribably delightful feeling once more to gaze over the blue expanse, as we paced up and down the deck, and were day by day carried nearer home. One morning, as we stood looking over the sea, our gaze was arrested by something; what could that be away on the horizon? We ran on to the bridge and looked through the glass. The first sail. Fancy being once more in waters where other people went to and fro! But it was far away; we could not go to it. Then we saw more, and later in the day four great monsters ahead. They were British men-of-war, probably on their way home after having been at Vadsö for the eclipse of the sun, which was to have taken place on August 9th. Later in the evening (August 12th) I saw something dark ahead, low down on the horizon. What was it? I saw it on the starboard bow, stretching low and even towards the south. I looked again and again. It was land, it was Norway! I stood as if turned to stone, and gazed and gazed out into the night at this same dark line, and a fear began to tremble in my breast. What were the tidings that awaited me there?

When I came on deck next morning we were close under the land. It was a bare and naked shore we had come up to, scarcely more inviting than the land we had left up in the mist of the Arctic Ocean — but it was Norway. The captain had mistaken the coast in the night and had come in too far north, and we were still to have some labour in beating down against wind and sea, before we could reach Vardö. We passed several vessels, and dipped our flag to them. We passed the revenue cutter; she came alongside, but they had nothing to do there, and no one came on board. Then came pilots, father and son. They greeted Brown, but were not prepared to meet a countryman on board an English vessel. They were a little surprised to hear me speak Norwegian, but did not pay much attention to it. But when Brown asked them if they knew who I was, the old man gazed at me again, and a gleam, as it were, of a possible recognition crept over his face. But when the name Nansen dropped from the lips of the warm-hearted Brown, as he took the old man by the shoulders and shook him in his delight at being able to give him such news, an expression came into the old pilot's weather-beaten face, a mixture of joy and petrified astonishment, which was indescribable. He seized my hand, and wished me welcome back to life; the people here at home had long ago laid me in my grave. And then came questions as to news from the expedition, and news from home. Nothing had yet been heard of the *Fram*, and a load was lifted from my breast, when I knew that those at home had been spared that anxiety.

Then, silently and unobserved, the *Windward* glided, with colours flying, into Vardö Haven. Before the anchor was dropped, I was in a boat with Johansen on our way to the telegraph station. We put in at the quay, but there was still so much of our former piratical appearance left that no one recognised us; they scarcely looked at us, and the only being that took any notice of the returned wanderers was an intelligent cow, which stopped in the middle of a narrow street, and stared at us in astonishment, as we tried to pass. That cow was so delightfully summery to look at that I felt inclined to go up and pat her; I felt now that I really was in Norway. When I got to the telegraph-station I laid a huge bundle down on the counter, and said that it consisted of telegrams that I should like to have sent as soon as possible. There were nearly a hundred of them; one or two rather long, of about a thousand words each.

The head of the telegraph office looked hard at me, and quietly took up the bundle; but as his eye fell upon the signature of the telegram that lay on the top, his face suddenly changed, he wheeled sharp round, and went over to the lady clerk who was sitting at the table. When he again turned and came towards me his face was radiant, and he bade me a hearty welcome. The telegrams should be despatched as quickly as possible, he said; but it would take several days and nights to get them all through. And then the instrument began to tick and tick, and to send through the country and the world the news that two members of the Norwegian Polar Expedition had returned safe and sound, and that I expected the *Fram* home in the course of the autumn. I pitied the four young ladies in the telegraph office at Vardö; they had hard work of it during the following days. Not only had all my telegrams to be despatched, but hundreds streamed in from the south — both to us and to people in the town, begging them to obtain information about us. Amongst the first were telegrams to my wife, to the King of Norway, and to the Norwegian Government. The last ran as follows:

"To His Excellency Secretary Hagerup

"I have the pleasure of announcing to you and to the Norwegian Government that the Expedition has carried out its plan, has traversed the unknown Polar Sea from north of the New Siberian Islands, and has explored the region north of Franz Josef Land as far as 86° 14′ N. lat. No land was seen north of 82°.

"Lieutenant Johansen and I left the *Fram* and the other members of the Expedition on March 14th, 1895, in 84° N. lat. and 102° 27′ E. long. We went northward to explore the sea north of the *Fram*'s course, and then came south to Franz Josef Land, whence the *Windward* has now brought us.

"I expect the *Fram* to return this year.

"FRIDTJOF NANSEN.

As I was leaving the telegraph-office, the manager told me that my friend Professor Mohn was in the town, staying, he understood, at the hotel. Strange that Mohn, a man so intimately connected with the expedition, should be the first friend I was to meet! Even while we were handing in our telegrams, the news of our arrival had begun to filter through the town, and people were gradually flocking together to see the two Polar bears who strode through the streets to the hotel. I rushed in and enquired for Mohn. He was in his room, number so and so, they told me; but he was taking his siesta. I had no respect for siestas at that moment; I thundered at the door and tore it open. There lay Mohn on the sofa, reading, with a long pipe in his mouth. He started up and stared fixedly, like a madman, at the long figure standing on the threshold; his pipe fell to the ground, his face twitched, and then he burst out: "Can it be true? Is it Fridtjof Nansen?" I believe he was alarmed about himself, thinking he had seen an apparition; but when he heard my well-known voice, the tears came to his eyes, and crying, "Thank God, you're still alive!" he rushed into my arms. Then came Johansen's turn. It was a moment of wild rejoicing, and numberless were the questions asked and answered on both sides. As one thing after another came into our heads, the questions rained around without coherence and almost without meaning. The whole thing seemed so incredible that a long time passed before we even collected ourselves sufficiently to sit down, and I could tell him in a somewhat more connected fashion what experiences we had gone through during these three years. But where was the *Fram*? Had we left her? Where were the others? Was anything amiss? These questions poured forth with breathless anxiety, and it was no doubt the hardest thing of all to understand that there was nothing amiss, and yet that we had left our splendid ship. But, little by little, even that became comprehensible; and then all was rejoicing, and champagne and cigars presently appeared on the scene. Another acquaintance from the south was also in the hotel; he came in to speak to Mohn; but seeing that he had visitors, was on the point of going again. Then he stopped, stared at us, discovered who the visitors were, and stood as though nailed to the spot; and then we all drank to the Expedition and to Norway. It was clear that we must stop there that evening, and we sat the whole afternoon talking and talking without a pause. But meanwhile the whole town had learnt the names of its newly-arrived guests, and when we looked out of the window the street was full of people, and from all the flagstaffs over the town, and from all the masts in the harbour, the Norwegian flag waved in the evening sunshine. And then came telegrams in torrents, all of them bringing good news. Now all our troubles were over. Only the arrival of the *Fram* was wanting to complete things; but we were quite at ease about her; she would soon turn up. The first thing we had to do, now that we were on Norwegian soil, and could look about us a little, was to replenish our wardrobe. But it was now no joke to make our way through the streets, and if we went into a shop, it was soon overflowing with people.

Thus we spent some never-to-be-forgotten days in Vardö, and the hospitality with which we met was lavish and cordial. After we had said good-bye to our hosts on board the *Windward* and thanked them for all the kindness they had shown us, Captain Brown weighed anchor on the morning of Sunday, the 16th, to go on to Hammerfest. He wanted to pay his respects to my wife, who was to meet us there. On August 21st Johansen and I arrived at Hammerfest. Everywhere on the way people had greeted us with flowers and flags, and now, as we sailed into its harbour, the northernmost town in Norway was in festal array from the sea to the highest hill-top, and thousands of people were afoot. To my surprise, I also met here my old friend, Sir George Baden-Powell, whose fine yacht, the *Otaria*, was in the harbour. He had just returned from a very successful scientific expedition to Novaya Zemlya, where he had been with several English astronomers to observe the solar eclipse of August 9th. With true English hospitality, he placed his yacht entirely at my disposal, and I willingly accepted his generous invitation.

Sir George Baden-Powell was one of the last people I had seen in England. When we parted — it was in the autumn of 1892 — he asked me where we ought to be looked for if we were too long away. I answered that it would be of little use to look for us — it would be like searching for a needle in a hay-stack. He told me I must not think that people would be content to sit still and do nothing. In England, at any rate, he was sure that something would be done and where ought they to go? "Well," I replied, "I can scarcely think of any other place than Franz Josef Land; for if the *Fram* goes to the bottom, or we are obliged to abandon her, we must come out that way. If the *Fram* does not go to the bottom, and the drift is as I believe it to be, we shall reach the open sea between Spitzbergen and Greenland." Sir George now thought that the time had come to look for us, and since he could not do more for the present, it was his intention, after having carried out his expedition to Novaya Zemlya, to skirt along the edge of the ice, and see if he could not pick up any news of us. Then, just at the right moment, we made our appearance at Hammerfest. In the evening, my wife arrived, and my secretary, Christofersen; and after having attended a brilliant fête given that night by the town of Hammerfest in our honour, we took up our quarters on board the *Otaria*, where the days now glided past so smoothly that we scarcely noticed the lapse of time. Telegrams of congratulation, and testimonies of goodwill and hearty rejoicing, arrived in an unbroken stream from all quarters of the world.

But the *Fram*? I had telegraphed confidently that I expected her home this year; but why had she not already arrived? I began more and more to think over this, and the more I calculated all chances and possibilities, the more firmly was I convinced that she ought to be out of the ice by this time, if nothing had gone amiss. It was strange that she was not already here, and I thought with horror that if the autumn should pass without news of her, the coming winter and summer would be anything but pleasant.

Just as I had turned out on the morning of August 20th, Sir George knocked at my door and said there was a man there who insisted on speaking to me. I answered that I wasn't dressed yet, but that I would come immediately. "Oh, that doesn't matter," said he, "come as you are." I was a little surprised at all this urgency, and asked what it was all about. He said he did not know, but it was evidently something pressing. I nevertheless put on my clothes, and then went out into the saloon. There stood a gentleman with a telegram in his hand, who introduced himself as the head of the telegraph office, and said that he had a telegram to deliver to me which he thought would interest me, so he had come with it himself. Something that would interest me? There was only one thing left in the world that could really interest me. With trembling hands I tore open the telegram:

"Fridtjof Nansen: *Fram* arrived in good condition. All well on board. Shall start at once for Tromsö. Welcome home. "OTTO SVERDRUP."

I felt as if I should have choked, and all I could say was, "The *Fram* has arrived!" Sir George, who was standing by, gave a great leap of joy; Johansen's face was radiant; Christofersen was quite overcome with gladness; and there in the midst of us stood the head of the telegraph office, enjoying the effect he had produced. In an instant I dashed into my cabin to shout to my wife that the *Fram* had arrived; she was dressed and out in double quick time. But I could scarcely believe it — it seemed like a fairy tale. I read the telegram again and again before I could assure myself that it was not all a dream; and then there came a strange, serene happiness over my mind such as I had never known before.

There was jubilation on board and over all the harbour and town. From the *Windward*, which was just weighing anchor to precede us to Tromsö, we heard ringing cheers for the *Fram* and the Norwegian flag. We had intended to start for Tromsö that afternoon, but now we agreed to get under weigh as quickly as possible, so as to try to overtake the *Fram* at Skjaervö, which lay just on our route. I attempted to stop her by a telegram to Sverdrup, but it arrived too late.

It was a lively breakfast we had that morning. Johansen and I spoke of how incredible it seemed that we should soon press our comrades' hands again. Sir George was almost beside himself with joy; every now and then he would spring up from his chair, thump the table, and cry: "The *Fram* has arrived! The *Fram* has really arrived!" Lady Baden-Powell was quietly happy; she enjoyed our joy.

The next day we entered Tromsö harbour, and there lay the *Fram*, strong and broad and weather-beaten. It was strange to see again that high rigging and the hull we knew so well. When last we saw her she was half buried in the ice; now she floated freely and proudly on the blue sea, in Norwegian waters. We glided alongside of her. The crew of the *Otaria* greeted the gallant ship with three times three English cheers, and the *Fram* replied with a nine-fold Norwegian hurrah. We dropped our anchor, and the next moment the *Otaria* was boarded by the *Fram*'s sturdy crew.

The meeting which followed I shall not attempt to describe. I don't think any of us knew anything clearly, except that we were all together again — we were in Norway — and the expedition had fulfilled its task.

Then we set off together southward along the Norwegian coast. First came the tug *Haalogaland*, chartered by the Government, then the *Fram*, heavy and slow, but so much the surer, and last the elegant *Oataria*, with my wife and me on board, which was to take us to Trondhjem. What a blessed sensation it was to sit in peace at last, and see others take the lead and pick out the way.

Wherever we passed, the heart of the Norwegian people went out to us, from the steamers crowded with holiday-making townsfolk, and from the poorest fishing-boat that lay alone among the skerries. It seemed as if old Mother Norway were proud of us, as if she pressed us in a close and warm embrace, and thanked us for what we had done. And what was it, after all? We had only done our duty, we had simply accomplished the task we had undertaken, and it was we who owed her thanks for the right to sail under her flag. I remember one morning in particular. It was in Brönösund — the morning was still grey and chill when I was called up — there were so many people who wanted to greet us. I was half asleep when I came on deck. The whole sound was crowded with boats. We had been going slowly through them, but now the *Haalogaland* in front put on more speed, and we too went a little quicker. A fisherman in his boat toiled at the oars to keep up with us; it was no easy work. Then he shouted up to me:

"You don't want to buy any fish, do you?"

"No, I don't think we do."

"Suppose you can't tell me where Nansen is? Is he on board the *Fram*?"

"No, I believe he's on board this ship," was the reply.

"Oh, I wonder if I couldn't get on board? I'm so desperately anxious to see him."

"It can hardly be done, I'm afraid; they haven't time to stop now."

"That's a pity. I want to see the man himself."

He went on rowing. It became harder and harder to keep up, but he stared fixedly at me as I leant on the rail smiling, while Christofersen stood laughing at my side.

"Since you're so anxious to see the man himself, I may tell you that you see him now," said I.

"Is it you! Is it you! Didn't I guess as much Welcome home again!"

And thereupon the fisherman dropped his oars, stood up in his boat, and took off his cap. As we went on through the splendour of the morning and I sat on the deck of the luxurious English yacht, and saw the beautiful barren coast stretching ahead in the sunshine, I realised to the full for the first time how near this land and this people lay to my heart. If we had sent a single gleam of sunlight over their lives, these three years had not been wasted.

> This Norway, this Norway...
> It is dear to us, so dear,
> And no people has a fairer land than this our homeland here.

> Oh, the shepherding in spring,
> When the birds begin to sing,
> When the mountain-peak glitters and green grows the lea,
> And the turbulent river sweeps brown to the sea
> Whoso knows Norway must well understand
> How her sons can suffer for such a land.

One felt all the vitality and vigour throbbing in this people, and saw as in a vision its great and rich future, when all its shackled forces shall be unfettered and set free.

Now one had returned to life, and it stretched before one full of light and hope. Then came the evenings when the sun sank far out behind the blue sea, and the clear melancholy of autumn lay over the face of the waters. It was too beautiful to believe in. A feeling of dread came over one; but the silhouette of a woman's form, standing out against the glow of the evening sky, gave peace and security.

So we passed from town to town, from fête to fête, along the coast of Norway. It was on September 9th that the *Fram* steamed up Christiania Fjord and met with a reception such as a prince might have envied. The stout old men-of-war, *Nordstjernen* and *Elida*, the new and elegant *Valkyrie*, and the nimble little torpedo-boats, led the way for us. Steamboats swarmed around all black with people. There were flags high and low, salutes, hurrahs, waving of handkerchiefs and hats, radiant faces everywhere, the whole fjord one multitudinous welcome. There lay home, and the well-known strand before it, glittering and smiling in the sunshine. Then steamers on steamers again, shouts after shouts; and we all stood hat in hand bowing as they cheered.

The whole of Peppervik was one mass of boats and people and flags and waving pennants. Then the men-of-war saluted with thirteen guns apiece, and the old fort of Akershus followed with its thirteen peals of thunder, that echoed from the hills around.

In the evening I stood on the strand out by the fjord. The echoes had died away, and the pine woods stood silent and dark around. On the headland the last embers of a bonfire of welcome still smouldered and smoked, and the sea rippling at my feet seemed to whisper: "Now you are at home." The deep peace of the autumn evening sank beneficently over the weary spirit.

I could not but recall that rainy morning in June when I last set foot on this strand. More than three years had passed; we had toiled and we had sown, and now the harvest had come. In my heart I sobbed and wept for joy and thankfulness.

The ice and the long moonlit polar nights, with all their yearning, seemed like a far-off dream from another world — a dream that had come and passed away. But what would life be worth without its dreams?

The *Windward* leaving Tromsö.

Conclusion

WHAT, then, are the results of the Norwegian Polar Expedition? This is a question which the reader might fairly expect to find answered here; but the scientific observations brought back are so varied and voluminous that it will be some time yet before they can be dealt with by specialists and before any general estimate of their significance can be formed. It will, therefore, be necessary to publish these results in separate scientific publications; and if I now attempted to give an idea of them, it would necessarily be imperfect, and might easily prove misleading. I shall, therefore, confine myself to pointing out a few of their more important features.

In the first place, we have demonstrated that the sea in the immediate neighborhood of the Pole, and in which, in my opinion, the Pole itself in all probability lies, is a deep basin, not a shallow one, containing many expanses of land and islands, as people were formerly inclined to assume. It is certainly a continuation of the deep channel which extends from the Atlantic Ocean northward between Spitzbergen and Greenland. The extent of this deep sea is a question which it is not at present easy to answer; but we at least know that it extends a long way north of Franz Josef Land, and eastward right to the New Siberian Islands. I believe that it extends still farther east, as, I think, may be inferred from the fact that the more the *Jeannette* expedition drifted north, the greater depth of sea did they find. For various reasons, I am led to believe that in a northerly direction also this deep sea is of considerable extent. In the first place, nothing was observed, either during the drift of the *Fram* or during our sledge expedition to the north, that would point to the proximity of any considerable expanse of land; the ice seemed to drift unimpeded, particularly in a northerly direction. The way in which the drift set straight to the north as soon as there was a southerly wind was most striking. It was with the greatest difficulty that the wind could head the drift back towards the southeast. Had there been any considerable expanse of land within reasonable distance to the north of us, it would have blocked the free movement of the ice in that direction.

Besides, the large quantity of drift-ice, which drifts southward with great rapidity along the east coast of Greenland all the way down to Cape Farewell and beyond it, seems to point in the same direction. Such extensive ice-fields must have a still larger breadth of sea to come from than that through which we drifted. Had the *Fram* continued her drift instead of breaking loose to the north of Spitzbergen, she would certainly have come down along the coast of Greenland; but probably she would not have got close in to that coast, but would have had a certain quantity of ice between her and it; and that ice must come from a sea lying north of our route. On the other hand, it is quite probable that land may exist to a considerable extent on the other side of the Pole between the Pole and the North American archipelago. It appears to me only reasonable to assume that this multitude of islands must extend farther towards the north.

As a result of our expedition, I think we can now form a fairly clear idea of the way in which the drift-ice is continually moving from one side of the polar basin north of Bering Strait and the coast of Siberia, and across the regions around the Pole, and out towards the Atlantic Ocean. Where geographers at one time were disposed to locate a solid, immovable, and massive ice-mantle, covering the northern extremity of our globe, we now find a continually breaking and shifting expanse of drift-ice. The evidence which even before our expedition had induced me to believe most strongly in this theory is supplied by the Siberian drift-wood that is continually being carried to Greenland, as well as the mud found on the ice, as it could scarcely be of other than Siberian origin. We found several indications of this kind during our expedition, even when we were as far north as 86°, furnishing valuable indications as to the movement of the ice.

The force which sets this ice in motion is certainly for the most part supplied by the winds; and as in the sea north of Siberia the prevailing winds are southeasterly or easterly, whereas north of Spitzbergen they are northeasterly, they must carry the ice in the direction in which we found the drift. From the numerous observations I made I established the existence of a slow current in the water under the ice, travelling in the same direction. But it will be some time before the results of these investigations can be calculated and checked.

The hydrographic observations made during the expedition furnished some surprising data. Thus, for instance, it was customary to look upon the polar basin as being filled with cold water, the temperature of which stood somewhere about −1.5° C. Consequently our observations showing that under the cold surface there was warmer water, sometimes at a temperature as high as +1° C., were surprising. Again, this water was more briny than the water of the polar basin has been assumed to be. This warmer and more strongly saline water must clearly originate from the warmer current of the Atlantic Ocean (the Gulf Stream), flowing in a north and northeasterly direction off

Novaya Zemlya and along the west coast of Spitzbergen, and then diving under the colder, but lighter and less briny, water of the Polar Sea, and filling up the depths of the polar basin. As I have stated in the course of my narrative, this more briny water was, as a rule, warmest at a depth of from 200 to 250 fathoms, beyond which it would decrease in temperature, though not uniformly, as the depth increased. Near the bottom the temperature rose again, though only slightly. These hydrographic observations appear to modify to a not inconsiderable extent the theories hitherto entertained as to the direction of the currents in the northern seas; but it is a difficult matter to deal with, as there is a great mass of material, and its further treatment will demand both time and patience. It must therefore be left to subsequent scientific publications.

Still less do I contemplate attempting to enter here into a discussion on the numerous magnetic, astronomical, and meteorological observations taken.

On the whole, it may probably be said that, although the expedition has left many problems for the future to solve in connection with the polar area, it has, nevertheless, gone far to lift the veil of mystery which has hitherto shrouded those regions, and we have been put in a position to form a tolerably clear and reasonable idea of a portion of our globe that formerly lay in darkness, which only the imagination could penetrate. And should we in the near future get a bird's-eye view of the regions around the Pole as seen from a balloon, all the most material features will be familiar to us.

But there still remains a great deal to be investigated, and this can only be done by years of observation, to which end a new drift, like that of the Fram, would be invaluable. Guided by our experience, explorers will be in a position to equip themselves still better; but a more convenient method for the scientific investigation of unknown regions cannot easily be imagined. On board a vessel of this kind explorers may settle themselves quite as comfortably as in a fixed scientific station. They can carry their laboratories with them, and the most delicate experiments of all kinds can be carried out. I hope that such an expedition may be undertaken ere long, and if it goes through Bering Strait and thence northward, or perhaps slightly to the north-east, I shall be very much surprised if observations are not taken which will prove of far greater scope and importance than those made by us. But it will require patience: the drift will be more protracted than ours, and the explorers must be well equipped.

There is also another lesson which I think our expedition has taught-namely, that a good deal can be achieved with small resources. Even if explorers have to live in Eskimo fashion and content themselves with the barest necessaries, they may, provided they are suitably equipped, make good headway and cover considerable distances in regions which have hitherto been regarded as almost inaccessible.

Endnotes

1   See *The First Crossing of Greenland* by Fridtjof Nansen.

2   Mr. Lytzen, of Julianehaab, afterwards contributed an article to the *Geografisk Tidsskrift* (8th Vol., 1885-86, pp. 49-51, Copenhagen), in which he expressed himself, so far at least as I understand him, in the same sense, and remarkably enough, suggested that this circumstance might possibly be found to have an important bearing on Arctic exploration. He says: "It will therefore be seen that Polar explorers who seek to advance towards the Pole from the Siberian Sea will probably at one place or another be hemmed in by the ice, but these masses of ice will be carried by the current along the Greenland coast. It is not, therefore, altogether impossible that, if the ship of such an expedition is able to survive the pressure of the masses of ice for any length of time, it will arrive safely at South Greenland; but in that case it must be prepared to spend several years on the way."

3   See on this point Dr. Y. Nielsen in *Forhandlinger i Videnskabssel skabet i Christiania.* Meeting held June 11th, 1886.

4   Since writing the above I have tried to make such a calculation, and have come to the conclusion that the aggregate rainfall is not so large as I had at first supposed. See my paper in *The Norwegian Geographical Society's Annual,* III, 1891-92, p. 95; and *The Geographical Journal,* London, 1893, p. 5.

5   The discovery during our expedition of a great depth in the polar basin renders it highly probable that this assumption is correct.

6   The experience of our expedition however does not point to any such eastward-flowing current along the Siberian coast.

7   I first thought of choosing the route through Bering Strait, because I imagined that I could reach the New Siberian Islands safer and earlier in the year from that side. On further investigation I found that this was doubtful, and I decided on the shorter route through the Kara Sea and north of Cape Chelyuskin.

8   As subsequently stated in my lecture in London (*Geographical Society's Journal,* p. 18), I purposed to go north along the west coast of the New Siberian Islands, as I thought that the warm water coming from the Iena would keep the sea open here.

9   See the Society's Annual, III, 1892, p. 9 r.

10   Both my lecture and the discussion are printed in *The Geographical Journal, London,* vol, I, 1893, pp. 1-32.

11   After our return home, Admiral Nares, in the most chivalrous fashion, sent me a letter of congratulation, in which he said that the *Fram's* remarkable voyage over the Polar Sea proved that my theory was correct, and his scepticism unfounded.

12   With reference to his statement that Leigh-Smith had observed such icebergs on the north-west coast of Franz Josef's Land, it may be remarked that no human being has ever been there.

13   This oil, by means of a specially constructed steam-jet apparatus, was injected into the furnaces

in the form of a fine spray, where it burned in a very economical and saving manner, giving forth a great amount of heat. The apparatus was one which has been applied to locomotives in England, whence it was procured. It appeared, however, that it tended to overheat the boiler at one particular point, where it made a dent, so that we soon abandoned this method of firing.

14 I had thought of procuring dogs from the Eskimo of Greenland and Hudson Bay, but there proved to be insuperable difficulties in the way of getting them conveyed from there.

15 These depôts were arranged most carefully and every precaution so well taken that we certainly should not have suffered from famine had we gone there. In the northernmost depot at Stan Durnova on the west coast of Kotelnoi, at 75° 37′ N.L., we should have found provisions for a week; with these we could easily have made our way 65 miles southwards along the coast to the second depot at Urassalach, where, in a house built by Baron Von Toll in 1886, we should have found provisions for a whole month. Lastly, a third depot in a house on the south side of Little Liakhoff Island, with provisions for two months, would have enabled us to reach the mainland with ease.

16 Both Hovland, who piloted us from Christiania to Bergen, and Johan Hågensen who took us from Bergen to Vardö, were most kindly placed at the disposal of the expedition by the Nordenfjeldske Steamship Company of Trondhjem.

17 English in the original.!

18 Ditto.

19 The ordinary male dog is liable to get inflammation of the scrotum from the friction of the trace.

20 There is a white reflection from white ice, so that the sky above fields of ice has a light or whitish appearance; wherever there is open water it is blue or dark. In this way the Arctic navigator can judge by the appearance of the sky what is the state of the sea at a considerable distance.

21 It is true that in his account of the voyage he expressly states that the continued very thick fog "prevented us from doing more than mapping out most vaguely the islands among and past which the *Vega* sought her way."

22 Later, when I had investigated the state of matters outside Nordenskiöld's Taimur Island, it seemed to me that the same remark applied here with even better reason, as no sledge expedition could go round the coast of this island, without seeing Almquist's Islands, which lie so near, for instance, to Cape Lapteff, that they ought to be seen even in very thick weather. It would be less excusable to omit marking these islands, which are much larger, than to omit the small ones lying off the coast of the large island (or as I now consider it, group of large islands) we were at present skirting.

23 In his account of his voyage Nordenskiöld writes as follows of the condition of this channel: "We were met by only small quantities of that sort of ice which has a layer of fresh-water ice on the top of the salt, and we noticed that it was all melting fjord or river ice. I hardly think that we came all day on a single piece of ice big enough to have cut up a seal upon."

24 Peter Henriksen.

25 This silk bag-net is intended to be dragged after a boat or ship to catch the living animals or plant organisms at various depths. We used them constantly during our drifting, sinking them to different depths under the ice, and they often brought up rich spoils.

26 This phosphorescence is principally due to small luminous crustacea (kopepodae).

27 Markham's account gives us to understand that on the north side of Grinnell Land he came across hummocks which measured 43 feet. I do not feel at all certain that these were not in reality icebergs; but it is no doubt possible that such hummocks might be formed by violent pressure against land or something resembling it. After our experience, however, I cannot believe in the possibility of their occurring in open sea.

28 On a later occasion, they bored down 30 feet without reaching the lower surface of the ice.

29 When we had fire in the stoves later, especially during the following winter, there was not a sign of damp anywhere — neither in the saloon nor small cabins. It was, if anything, rather too dry, for the panels of the walls and roof dried and shrank considerably.

30 Apparently modelled on the title of the well-known magazine, *Kringsjaa* which means "A Look Around" or "Survey." *Framsjaa* might be translated "The *Fram's* Look-Out."

31 The name Peter Henriksen generally went by on board.

32 Refers to the fact that Amundsen hated card-playing more than anything else in the world. He called cards "the devil's playbooks."

33 Nickname of our meteorologist, Johansen, Professor Mohn being a distinguished Norwegian meteorologist.

34 This signature proved to be forged, and gave rise to a lawsuit so long and intricate that space does not permit an account of it to be given.

35 He says "ei borsja" for "a gun" instead of "en bosse".

36 The nickname of the starboard four-berth cabin.

37 A Norwegian newspaper.

38 In spite of this bending of the strata, the surface of the ice and snow remained even.

39 Our name for light trousers of thin close cotton, which we used as a protection against the wind and snow.

40 This gull is often called by this name, after its first discoverer. It has acquired its other name, "rose gull," from its pink colour.

41 Up to now they had their kennels on deck.

42 The anniversary of the Norwegian Constitution.

43 "Normal Arbeidsdage" = normal working day.

44 Our nickname for the cooking range in the galley.

45 Up to this day I am not quite clear as to what these emblems were intended to signify. That the doctor, from want of practice, would have been glad of a normal day's work ("Normal Arbeidsdag") can readily be explained, but why the meteorologists should cry out for universal suffrage passes my comprehension. Did they want to overthrow despotism?

46 With reference to the resolution of the Storthing on June 9th, 1880.

47 It was seal, walrus, and bear's flesh from last autumn, which was used for the dogs. During the winter it had been hung up in the ship, and was still quite fresh. But henceforth it was stored on the ice until, before autumn set in, it was consumed. It is remarkable how well meat keeps in these regions. On June 28th we had reindeer-steak for dinner that we had killed on the Siberian coast in September of the previous year.

48 The same kind of dust that I found on the ice on the east coast of Greenland, which is mentioned in the Introduction to this book.

49 This dust, which is to be seen in summer on the upper surface of almost all polar ice of any age, is, no doubt, for the most part, dust that hovers in the earth's atmosphere. It probably descends with the falling snow, and gradually accumulates into a surface layer as the snow melts during the summer. Larger quantities of mud, however, are also often to be found on the ice, which strongly resemble this dust in colour, but are doubtless more directly connected with land, heir, formed on floes that have originally lain in close proximity to it. (Compare *Wissensch. Ergebnisse von Dr. F. Nansens durchquerung von Grönland. Erganzungsheft* No. 105, *zu Petermanns Mitteilungen.*)

50 I have not yet had the time to examine them closely.

51 We always had a line, with a net at the end, hanging out, in order to see the direction we were drifting in, or to ascertain whether there was any perceptible current in the water.

52 See note 44.

53 It was two years later to a day that the *Fram* put in at Skiervö, on the coast of Norway.

54 During the summer we had made a kitchen of the chart-room on deck, because of the good daylight there; and besides the galley proper was to be cleaned and painted.

55 Pettersen had been advanced from smith to cook, and he and Juell took turns of a fortnight each in the galley.

56 See *Geographical Journal*, London, 1893. See also the map in *Naturen*, 1890, and the *Norwegian Geographical Society's Year Book*, I, 1890.

57 These were the puppies born on December 13th, 1893; only four of them were now alive.

[58] We had no covering over the ship the first winter, as we thought it would make it too dark, and make it difficult to find one's way about on deck. But when we put in one the second winter, we found that it was an improvement.

[59] This luminous veil, which was always spread over the sky, was less distinct on the firmament immediately overhead, but became more and more conspicuous near the horizon, though it never actually reached down to it; indeed, in the north and south it generally terminated in a low, faintly outlined arch over a kind of dark segment. The luminosity of this veil was so strong that through it I could never with any certainty distinguish the Milky Way.

[60] Used in hoisting up the lead-line.

[61] There must he an error here, as the distance to Cape Fligely from the point proposed, 83° N. lat. and 110° E. long., is quite 460 miles; I had probably taken the longitude as 100° instead of 110°.

[62] During the actual expedition the dogs had to be content with a much smaller daily ration, on an average scarcely more than 9 or 10 ozs.

[63] He did not return after all.

[64] We had for this purpose used our pure grape-spirit.

[65] The word svalkelem, which has throughout been translated "gang-way," means rather a sort of port-hole. As the svalkelem, however, was the means of exit from and entrance to the ship, "gangway" seemed the most convenient expression for it.

[66] The cross-bars on the sledge that connect the perpendicular supports of the runners with each other.

[67] The sledge runners were connected in front by a bow, consisting of three or four pieces of rattan cane lashed together; it is to this bow the hauling lines are fastened.

[68] This odometer had been made on board, shortly before starting, out of the works of an old anemometer. The odometer was fastened behind the last sledge, and indicated fairly correctly the distance covered by us.

[69] They were 12 feet long, 1 foot 9½ inches broad, and rode about 5 inches above the snow.

[70] Compare my description of "finsko" (Finn shoes) in *The First Crossing of Greenland*.

[71] I had also had prepared a large quantity of pemmican, consisting of equal parts of meat-powder and vegetable fat (from the cocoa-nut). This pemmican, however, proved to be rather an unfortunate invention; even the dogs would not eat it after they lead tasted it once or twice. Perhaps this is accounted for by the fact that vegetable fat is heavily digested, and contains acids which irritate the mucous membranes of the stomach and throat.

[72] It was not advisable for many reasons to cross the lanes in the kayaks, now that the temperature was so low. Even if the water in the lanes had not nearly always been covered with a more or less thick layer of ice, the kayaks would have become much heavier from the immediate freezing of the water which would have entered them, for they proved to be not absolutely impervious; and this ice we had then no means of dislodging.

[73] Used by the Lapps to their dogs.

[74] Whereas eating snow may increase the above-mentioned feeling of thirst, and have disagreeable consequences in other ways, sucking a piece of ice, which will soon quench it, may safely be resorted to, particularly if it be held in the hand a little while before putting it in the mouth. Many travellers have, no doubt, had the same experience.

[75] We always kept a supply of our various provisions in small bags inside the "kayaks," so that we could get out whatever we wanted for our daily consumption without undoing the big sacks, which were sewn up or securely fastened in other ways.

[76] When I left the ship I had purposed to travel northwards for 50 days, for which time we had taken provender for the dogs.

[77] This was the latitude I got by a rough estimation, but on further calculation it proved to be 86° 13.6′ N.; the longitude was about 95° E.

[78] I felt convinced we could not have reached such a westerly longitude, but assumed this for the sake of certainty, as I would rather come down on the east side of Franz Josef Land than on

the west side. Should we reach the latitude of Petermann's Land or Prince Rudolf Land without seeing them, I should in the former case be certain that we had them on our west, and could then look for them in that direction, whereas, in the event of our not finding land and being uncertain whether we were too far east or too far west, we should not then know in what direction we ought to look for it.

79   We saw no real ice-mountains at any period of our journey before we got under land; everything was sea-ice. The same was the case during the drift of the *Fram*.

80   In point of fact it was nearly three months (till July 24th) before this marvel happened.

81   As on the previous day, the ice on the north side of the lane was moving westwards, in comparison with that on the south side. The same thing was the case, or could be seen to have been so, with the lanes we met with later in the day. We naturally conceived this to mean that there was a strong westerly drift in the ice northward, while that southward was retained by land.

82   The lanes form most frequently in windy weather, as the ice is then set in motion.

83   In point of fact we were then about 6° farther east than we thought. I had on April 14th, it will be remembered (compare my notes for that day), surmised that the longitude I then set down (86° E.) was more westerly than that we were actually in.

84   For melting water in the cooker it is better to use ice than snow, particularly if the latter be not old and granular. Newly fallen snow gives little water, and requires considerably more heat to warm it. That part of salt-water ice which is above the surface of the sea, and, in particular, prominent pieces which have been exposed to the rays of the sun during a summer and are thus freed from the greater part of their salt, furnish excellent drinking-water. Some expeditions have harboured the superstition that drinking-water from ice in which there was the least salt was injurious. This is a mistake which cost, for instance, the members of the *Jeannette* expedition much unnecessary trouble, as they thought it imperative to distil the water before they could drink it without incurring the risk of scurvy.

85   As will be understood by our later discoveries, my surmises were not quite correct. We really were at that time north or north-east of Wilczek's Land, which seems to be only a little island. Meanwhile there must have been extensive open water the previous autumn where this ice was formed. But when it is shown later how much open water we saw on the north-west coast of Franz Josef Land even in winter, this can easily be imagined.

86   Whereas Finn shoes are made of reindeer-skin with the hair on, "komager" are made of under-tanned hide without hair, generally from the ox or bearded seal (*phoca barbata*), with tops of reindeer-skin. They are strong and waterproof (see description of equipment).

87   It was undoubtedly from seals, which often utter a sound like a protracted "ho."

88   It was from about 82° 52' N. South to 82° 19' N. that we travelled over young ice of this description; that is to say, there must have been open water over a distance of fully 32 English geographical miles (33' of latitude). We also found ice of this kind farther south for a long distance, and the open sea must have been considerably greater.

89   It was the first diary I used on the sledge-journey.

90   Until this day we had eaten what we required without weighing out rations. It proved that after all we did not eat more than I had originally allowed per day, i.e., 2 kg of dried food. We now reduced these day's rations considerably.

91   It was probably pressure of the floes against each other which caused this movement. We noticed the same motion several times later.

92   We found water on the ice here, suitable for cooking, for the first time. It was, however, somewhat salt, so that the "fiskegratin" was too well seasoned.

93   As it proved later, we were, in reality, about 6' farther east than we thought.

94   I called my watch thus after Johannsen, the watchmaker in London, who supplied it.

95   In reality we were somewhat near the point I here assume (we were in 67° E., approximately). The reason why we did not see the land here mentioned was because it does not exist; as was proved later.

96   A proper hauling harness is an important item, and in the long run is much less trying than

the ordinary hauling strap or rope crosswise over the chest and one shoulder. The form of harness I use consists of two straps, which are passed over both shoulders, like the straps of a knapsack, and are fastened crosswise over the back to a leather belt, where the hauling-rope from the sledge is also attached. It is thus in one's power during the work of hauling to distribute the strain equally between both shoulders and the belt (i.e., the thighs and abdomen). The hauling "centre of gravity" is in this manner lower in the body, just above the legs, which do the work, and the hauling-rope does not, as is usually the case, press only on the upper part of the body.

97 Certain straps which are fixed on the "kayak," just in front of the occupant, and through which the paddle is passed when shooting, etc. The blade thus lying laterally on the water very much increases the steadiness of the occupants.

98 Compare, however, what I say on this subject later, i.e., July 24th.

99 This was taken in case it might be wanted for soldering the cooking apparatus or the German silver plates under the sledge-runners.

100 We eventually decided to retain this, however.

101 This supposition is extremely doubtful.

102 It proved later that this must be Crown Prince Rudolf Land.

103 We saw more and more of these remarkable birds the farther we went.

104 As a rule, we crossed the lanes in this manner: we placed the sledges, with the kayaks on, side by side, lashed them together, stiffened them by running the snowshoes across under the straps, which also steadied them, and then launched them as they were, with the sledges lashed underneath. When across we had only to haul them up on the other side.

105 The first island I called "Eva's Island," the second "Liv's Island," and the little one we were then on "Adelaide's Island." The fourth island south of us had, perhaps, already been seen by Payer, and named by him "Freeden Island." The whole group of islands I named "Hvidtenland" (White Land).

106 Icebergs of considerable size have been described as haling been seen off Franz Josef Land, but I can only say with reference to this that during the whole of our voyage through this archipelago we saw nothing of we kind. The one mentioned here was the biggest of all those we came across, and they were, compared with the Greenland icebergs, quite insignificant masses of glacier-ice.

107 I have called it granite in my diary, but it was in reality a very coarse-grained basalt. The specimens I took have unfortunately been lost.

108 Houen's Island.

109 Torup's Island.

110 It owes its colour to a beautiful minute red alga which grows on the snow (generally *spaerella nivalis*). There were also some yellowish-green patches which must be attributable to another species.

111 It proved later to be Crown Prince Rudolf Land.

112 Off Brögger's Foreland.

113 On Helland's Foreland.

114 I took specimens of the different rock-formations, lichens, etc., that we came across: but in the course of the winter the collection was stolen by the foxes, and I thus brought little home from the tracts north of our winter hut.

115 As this promontory is probably the land Jackson saw farthest north in the spring of 1895, it has no name upon my map. It is otherwise with the islands outside, which he did not notice. They are only indicated approximately (as Geelmuyden Island and Alexander's Island), as I am not certain of either their number or their exact situation.

116 These three islands, whose bearings we were subsequently enabled to take, and which we could see from our winter hut, are probably the land which Jackson saw and took to be "King Oscar Land." In consequence of his having seen them from only one point (his Cape Fisher), due south, in 81°, he has placed them 40' too far north (in 82°), having over-estimated their distance. (See his map in the *Geographical Journal*, Vol. VII, No. 6, December, 1896, London.)

117 Called 'Steinen' on the map.

118   I now thought I could safely conclude that we were on the west coast of Franz Josef Land, and were at this moment a little north of Leigh Smith's most north-westerly point, Cape Lofley, which should lie a little south of 81° N. lat., while our observation that day made us about 81° 19′ N. lat.

119   Ice which is frozen fast to the bottom, and is therefore often left lying like an icy base along the shore, even after the sea is free from ice. On account of the warm water which comes from the land, an open channel is often formed between this ice-base and the shore.

120   It was a registering thermometer, which was also used as a sling-thermometer.

121   It often blew, very fresh there under the mountain. Another time, one of my snowshoes, which was stuck into the snowdrift beside the hut, was broken short off by the wind. It was a strong piece of maple.

122   Christmas Eve and New Year's Eve were the only occasions on which we allowed ourselves to take any of the provisions which we were keeping for our journey southwards.

123   These rumblings in the glacier are due to rifts which are formed in the mass of ice when the cold causes it to contract. New rifts seemed to be formed only when the temperature sank lower than it had previously been in the course of that winter; at least it was only then that we heard the rumblings.

124   It proved afterwards that the distance was about 56 miles.

125   We had now, as the spring advanced, a good opportunity of seeing how the little auk in great flocks and the black guillemots in smaller numbers, invariably set forth from land at certain times of the day towards the open sea, and then at other times returned in unbroken lines up the ice-bound fjords to their nest-rocks again.

126   A slip of the pen; it ought to be 102° E. long.

127   Jackson, who saw it in the spring of 1893, called it Mary Elizabeth Island.

128   Jackson's "Cape Fisher".

129   This was on the south side of Jackson's "Cape Richthofen," the most northerly point which Jackson had reached earlier the same spring.

130   It proved afterwards to be "Hooker Island."

131   It proved to be "Northbrook Island."

132   The sound between Northbrook Island and Bruce Island on the one side and Peter Head on Alexandra Land on the other side.

133   Cape Barents.

134   The ice-foot is the part of a floe which often projects into the water under the surface. It is formed through the thawing of the upper part of the ice in the summer-time by the warmer surface layer of the sea.

135   He had reached Cape Richthofen, about 35 miles to the south of us.

136   We did not have any Nautical Almanack for 1896, and had hitherto used the almamck for the previous year.

137   Where they are generally called diabases.

138   Leigh-Smith had already brought back from Spitzbergen a fossil cone, which Carruthers classified as a pinus; but he regarded it as belonging to the upper part of the cretaceous system.

139   I did not dream that Sverdrup a year after would be in command of this steamer.

140   Jackson had brought with him several Russian horses, which he had used along with dogs on his sledge expeditions. Only one of these horses was alive at the time of our arrival.

List of the Sledging Equipment

Kayak (Nansen's); Pump (for pumping kayaks in case of leakage); Sail; Axe and geological hammer; Gun and case; Two small wooden rods belonging to cooker; Theodolite and case ; Three reserve cross-pieces for sledges; Some pieces of wood; Harpoon line; Cooker, with two mugs, ladle, and two spoons; Petroleum lamp (Primus); Pocket-flask; Bag, with sundry articles of clothing ; Blanket ; Jersey; Finn-shoes filled with grass; Cap for fitting over opening in kayak; One pair "komager"; Two pair kayak gloves and one harpoon and line; One waterproof sealskin kayak overcoat ; Tool-bag; Bag of sewing materials, including sail-; maker's palm, sail needles, and other sundries.; Three Norwegian flags; Medicines, &c; Photographic camera; One cassette and one tin box of films; One wooden cup; One rope (for lashing kayak to sledge) ; Pieces of reindeer-skin to prevent kayaks from chafing; Wooden shovel; Snowshoe-staff with disc at bottom; One bamboo staff; Two oak staffs; Seven reserve dog harnesses and two reserve hauling ropes; One coil of rope; Four bamboo poles, for masts and for steering sledges; One bag of bread 2.7kg, whey-powder 1.5kg, sugar 1kg, albuminous flour 0.8kg, lime juice-tablets 0.73kg, Frame-food stamina tablets 1.1kg; As boat's grips, upon the sledges, were: Three sacks of pemmican (together) 108.2; One sack "leverpostei" or "paté," made of calf's liver 42.7kg;

Albuminous flour 6.8kg, ; Wheat flour 7kg; Whey powder 7kg, ; Cornflour 4kg; Sugar 3.2kg; Vril food 14.2kg; Austrian pemmican 5.9kg; Chocolate 5.8kg; Oatmeal 5kg; Dried red whortleberries 0.4kg; Two sacks of white bread (together) 31.5kg; One sack of aleuronate bread 21.2kg; Two sacks of white bread 21.2kg; "Special

food" (mixture of pea-flour, meat-powder, fat etc.) 29kg; Butter 39kg; Fish-flour 15.5kg; Dried-potatoes 6.9kg; One reindeer-skin sleeping bag 9kg; Two steel-wire ropes, with couples for 28 dogs ; One pair of hickory snow-shoes;

Kayak (Johansen's); Two pieces of reindeer-skin, to prevent chafing; A supply of dog shoes; One Eskimo shooting-sledge with sail (intended for possible seal-shooting on the ice); Two sledge sails; Pump ; Oar-blades (made of canvas stretched on frames, and intended to be lashed to the snowshoe-staffs); Gun; Flask; Net (for catching crustacea in the sea) ; One pair "komager "; Waterproof kayak overcoat of sealskin ; Fur-gaiters; Two reserve pieces of wood; Two tins of petroleum (about 5 gallons) ; Several reserve snow-shoe fastenings ; Lantern for changing-plates, &c. ; Artificial glass horizon; Bag with cords and Nautical Almanack Pocket sextant; Two packets of matches; One reserve sheet of German silver (for repaving plates under sledge-runners) ; Pitch; Two minimum thermometers in cases ; Three quicksilver thermometers in cases; One compass ; One aluminium compass; telescope; "Sennegraes" or sedge for Finn-shoes; Bag with cartridges ; Leather pouch with reserve shooting requisites, parts for gun-locks, reserve cocks, balls, powder, &c.; Leather pouch with glass bottle, one spoon, ; and five pencils; Bag with navigation tables, Nautical ; Almanack, cards, &c.; Tin box with diaries, letters, photographs, ; observation-journals, &c.; One cap for covering hole in deck of ; " kayak; One sack of meat-chocolate 8kg; One bag of soups 3kg, cocoa 3.35kg, fish-flour 1.7 kg, wheat-flour 9 kg, chocolate 2kg, oatmeal 2kg, vril-food 2kg; As grips upon the sledge were: One sack of oatmeal 13.2kg, pemmican 52.3kg, liver "paté" 50.8kg